THE
CHAMPAGNE
GUIDE

 2016—2017

For Alison Glover

Published in 2015 by Hardie Grant Books

Hardie Grant Books (Australia)
Ground Floor, Building 1
658 Church Street
Richmond, Victoria 3121
www.hardiegrant.com.au

Hardie Grant Books (UK)
5th & 6th Floors
52–54 Southwark Street
London SE1 1UN
www.hardiegrant.co.uk

A Cataloguing-in-Publication entry is available from the catalogue of the
National Library of Australia at www.nla.gov.au
The Champagne Guide 2016–2017
ISBN 978 1 74379 008 3

Publishing Director: Fran Berry
Project Editor: Rachel Day
Editor: Katri Hilden
Design Manager: Mark Campbell
Designer: Susanne Geppert
Cover Designer: Andy Warren
Photographer: Tyson Stelzer
Production Manager: Todd Rechner

Colour reproduction by Splitting Image Colour Studio
Printed and bound in China by 1010 Printing International Limited

THE
CHAMPAGNE
GUIDE

2016—2017

THE DEFINITIVE GUIDE
TO CHAMPAGNE

TYSON STELZER

INTERNATIONAL WINE & SPIRIT
COMMUNICATOR OF THE YEAR 2015

hardie grant books

CONTENTS

The joy of the harvest 7
Bienvenue! 11
Using this guide 12
On the house 13
Champagne vintages 19
Down to earth 24

The chef in the cellar 25
Chalk it up 27
Fizzers 28
House rules 30
Just a spoonful of sugar 31
Awash with bubbles 32

Epilogue 347
Index 348
Glossary 356
Author thanks 360

Agrapart & Fils............34
Alfred Gratien............38
André Clouet............41
André Jacquart............45
AR Lenoble............47
Armand de Brignac............51
Ayala............52
Barons de Rothschild......55
Benoît Lahaye............57
Bérêche & Fils............60
Billecart-Salmon............65
Boizel............72
Bollinger............75
Bonnaire............81
Bruno Paillard............83
Camille Savès............85
Cattier............88
Charles Heidsieck............91
Charpentier............95
Claude Carré & Fils......97
Couche Père & Fils......98
Cuvée Carbon............99
De Sousa & Fils............100
Delamotte............104

Deutz............106
Devaux............111
Diebolt-Vallois............114
Dom Pérignon............117
Dosnon & Lepage......124
Dumangin J. Fils......126
Duval-Leroy............130
Egly-Ouriet............134
Emmanuel Brochet......137
Eric Rodez............140
Fleury Père & Fils......145
Francis Boulard & Fille 149
Franck Bonville............152
G.H. Mumm............153
Gaston Chiquet............157
Gatinois............160
Geoffroy............163
Georges Laval............168
Godmé Père et Fils......171
Gosset............174
Guy Charlemagne......178
H. Billiot Fils............180
Henri Giraud............181
Henri Goutorbe............183

Henriot............184
Huré Frères............187
J. Lassalle............188
Jacquart............191
Jacques Picard............193
Jacques Selosse............196
Jacquesson............200
Jacquinot & Fils............206
Jérôme Prévost............207
Joseph Perrier............210
Krug............211
Laherte Frères............218
Lallier............222
Lanson............223
Larmandier-Bernier......227
Laurent-Perrier............233
Le Brun-Servenay......236
Le Mesnil............239
Lombard & Cie............240
Louis Roederer............243
Mailly Grand Cru......251
Marc Hébrart............255
Marguet Père & Fils......256
Moët & Chandon......258

Nicolas Feuillatte........265
Palmer & Co............267
Pascal Doquet............269
Paul Bara............273
Paul Clouet............274
Paul Déthune............275
Paul Goerg............277
Perrier-Jouët............279
Philipponnat............282
Pierre Gimonnet & Fils 286
Pierre Péters............293
Piper-Heidsieck............298
Pol Roger............302
Roger Coulon............308
Ruinart............309
Salon............312
Taittinger............314
Tarlant............320
Ulysse Collin............325
Vazart-Coquart & Fils. 326
Veuve Clicquot............329
Veuve Fourny & Fils......337
Vilmart & Cie............343

OPPOSITE, CLOCKWISE FROM TOP LEFT: All the colour of vintage 2014 in grand cru pinot noir, ripe for harvest in Aÿ in the Vallée de la Marne; picking grand cru chardonnay in Cramant on the Côtes des Blancs; the library wines cellar of Charles Heidsieck in a Roman crayère dug under Reims in the 2nd century AD; pinot noir ready to be pressed at Lanson in Verzenay on the Montagne de Reims; dawn in Hautvillers at the end of harvest; on the Route Touristique du Champagne in Mareuil-sur-Aÿ.

The joy of the harvest
La joie de vivre de la vendange

The first glow of early autumn dawn announces the most anticipated day of the year in an ancient northern village. Silky, softly filtered light awakens dew-kissed grand cru chalk soil, rousing its fragile, salty fragrance, untainted by the frenetic activity of the hours to come. Stirring in expectation, the forest exhales its enchantingly vulgar perfume of dank undergrowth, as the first leaves of fall are liberated by majestic oaks standing sentinel atop the Montagne de Reims. From their privileged outlook on the celebrated south-facing slope of the fabled French hamlet of Bouzy, the vines stand attentive to it all, inscribing the detail of every scent of the season in the record of their fruits.

The stony austerity of a grey winter morning, the golden, honeyed radiance of high noon in spring, the dusty breath of a late afternoon midsummer north wind: all are remembered. Today, the pale autumn sun illuminates a pastel panorama in lines of vines immaculately hedged into perfectly furrowed rows, each transitioning, in its own time, to ochre, auburn and russet. It's the vine's announcement that its record of the year is complete. Champagne is ready for harvest.

And so they come. From Spain and Portugal, from Eastern Europe and Asia, and most of all from the nearby villages of Champagne. They come with baskets, buckets and razor-sharp snips to comb the rows like ants, scavenging every last bunch. Picking crates, stacked high at the ends of the rows, quickly brim with the verdant, luminescent green of just-ripe chardonnay and the regal, deep velvet blue of pinot noir and meunier.

Within hours, bronzed biceps are hurling crate after crate with robotic precision, quickly filling every press in the village. And then the aromas erupt. Not pungent or exuberant, but elegantly subtle, delicately fresh and euphorically pure, the essence of the graceful innocence that is champagne. The narrow streets of the village come to life with the perfume of vintage: the yeast-filled fragrance of vibrant ferments wafting from one doorway, the unmistakable toasty aromas of

A picker heaves a harvesting crate up the celebrated grand cru slope of Bouzy during vintage 2014.

oak barrels from another. Even the roads themselves join the olfactory soirée, as sweet juice dripping from picking crates caramelises on hot exhausts. 'It's like driving on marmalade!' says Olivier Krug, the director of Krug, whose nose is attuned to every nuance on the streets of Bouzy.

And then everyone stops for lunch. Trestle tables are lined up anywhere space can be made in wineries, press centres or gardens, lavishly laden with hearty fare of beef, pork, potatoes and pasta, topped off with mandatory cheese and dessert courses. This is no quick worker's snack, but a jovial two-hour affair. No surprise that many of Champagne's harvest workers are professionals on vacation, some returning every harvest for decades. They come because they love the atmosphere. They set up campervans and pitch tents on any vacant patch between vineyards and light bonfires every night. This is the one week of the year when the region's sleepy little villages buzz with life and every Michelin-starred restaurant is booked out. No wonder they call it *la joie de vivre de la vendange* — the joy of the harvest.

But vintage in Champagne is no casual stroll in the vines. 'We work very hard for the whole year to produce good grapes, and we cannot afford to compromise the picking, because in one day you can destroy an entire year of work!' exclaims Veuve Clicquot chef de cave Dominique Demarville. As far as Champagne appellation law is concerned, machine harvesting does not exist. Every one of more than three billion bunches of grapes must be harvested by hand, all in less than a few short weeks, and in some villages it's all over in just a few days. The logistics of pulling this off are nothing short of staggering. It takes 120,000 pickers to harvest Champagne. As soon as the grapes are off, everything is done in grandiose proportions. Narrow streets of quaint villages become bottlenecks as every vehicle that can carry pickers or grapes is on duty: oversized 4WD tractors, trucks, panel vans, buses, trailers the size of buses, even horse floats. Front-end loaders of mine-site proportions load pallets stacked high with picking bins. Tankers ferrying a quarter of a million Euros' worth of juice between wineries in each load. The sheer scale and precision of this operation is astonishing. And in September 2014, I experienced it all for myself for the very first time.

Immersing myself in Champagne for the entire duration of harvest, I was privileged to long days shadowing 25 chef de caves, from the smallest growers to the two largest houses of all: a full day with chef de caves Benoît Gouez and Richard Geoffroy at Moët & Chandon, and multiple visits with Dominique Demarville at Veuve Clicquot. No stage of production was off limits, and no conversation was off the record. Delving deeper into the rabbit hole of Champagne than ever before, I was as excited as a kid with a golden ticket, and more than a little nervous. The 2014 harvest gave me more reason to be uneasy than ever. And not only because of the manic pressure of this compacted vintage.

It was in July that it first came. A wall of gunmetal grey, forked with lightning, tumbling down the Vallée de la Marne. It rains all the time in Champagne. But not like this. Not for two months. Never in recorded history has it rained like this in August. The coolest summer in 20 years does not bode well for ripening grapes in the most northerly winegrowing region

in France, and vines have long memories. A sodden summer brings the dreadful threat of rot that could obliterate an entire harvest.

It was not so much the prospect of another bad-tempered season and dashed harvest hopes that had me nervous. My fear was of something even more sinister. Much has been said of Champagne's struggles to care for the health of its vines, to deal with significant overcropping, to cope with the tribulations of recent economic unrest, not to mention inherent complications at every stage of the most complex wine production process of all. And it all comes to a head during harvest. Going behind the curtain, fully behind the curtain, of the most guarded and secretive wine culture on earth, just what would I smell out?

After countless visits to vineyards, growers, press houses, wineries and cellars, I discovered a Champagne of immense complexity beyond what I had ever conceived. And, at complete odds to my expectations, I came away more optimistic about the present and future of this place than I ever imagined.

There's a big picture at play. The global economic crisis, followed by year after year of economic doom across Europe (with no sign of recovering anytime soon), has burnt Champagne, and it could not have come at a better time. The crisis hit precisely when Champagne was staring down the barrel of record demand, and in anticipation it was brazenly bolstering its already inflated yields, while scurrying to extend its borders to enlarge the appellation. While no one would ever admit as much, this was the shake-up that Champagne had to have to temper spiralling yields and better consider its growth plan. And weak European markets have forced the region to be more proactive than ever in engaging its smaller export markets, which can only help to shore up the long-term stability of its sales channels.

The most astute houses and growers have been listening to what their markets want, and never have the guarded Champenois been more open to sharing the wonderful truth behind their cuvées. Labels have been refreshed and websites revamped to provide more informative detail. When Krug launched its innovative ID code to unlock the full story of each of its cuvées, every house and grower was watching. Louis Roederer was the first to follow, equipping its website to decode bottling codes. Veuve Clicquot was next, with QR codes on some cuvées, and plans to roll out across its full range. The CIVC, guardian of Champagne's regulatory requirements, is even contemplating mandating disgorgement dates on back labels. Bring it on!

Chardonnay harvest 2014 on the golden south-east facing slopes of Cramant, the mightiest grand cru of the Côte des Blancs.

A late-harvest mist shrouds the village of Avize, which ranks alongside its neighbour Cramant as the first grand cru of the Côte des Blancs.

Champagne's wildly fluctuating vintage conditions make the communication of such detail all the more pertinent. The region struggles to cope with one of the wine world's most tumultuous climates, and this has only been exacerbated in the wake of global warming. Louis Roederer chef de cave Jean-Baptiste Lécaillon suggests climate change has been to blame for a more dramatic contrast between wet and dry periods in Champagne, exemplified by the wet summer of 2014. A positive spin-off has been dry Septembers, a godsend in the month that seals the fate of the vintage.

Champagne has been dealt no shortage of challenging seasons in recent years, and yet the Champenois continue to produce remarkable wines, not in spite of this struggle, but because of it. 'To have a good vintage, the grapes must suffer,' explains celebrated grower Didier Gimonnet, citing three of the great vintages of recent decades. He recalls, '2012 was difficult, with lots of disease in the vineyards, because the climate was very harsh — but it was because of this that we had great quality. The 1996 was not produced under good climatic conditions, and nor was 2008.'

All is not perfect in Champagne. I saw some rot in the 2014 harvest, particularly in the thin-skinned meunier and pinot noir. And not everyone sorts to select the best grapes. In most press houses I saw just as much rotten fruit as I witnessed in the vineyards.

There will always be rotten grapes in this region perpetually gripped by climatic, political and economic unrest. And yet it is this very tension that has shaped a people who have held their ground on the front line of wars for millennia, and who have the resilience and sheer genius, under the most harrowing of circumstances, to create the most celebrated wine in the world.

Champagne's most diligent growers and houses are working frenetically to increasingly refine the finer details of viticulture and vinification with each passing vintage. With natural and economic climates stacked against them, they have only intensified their resolve to improve quality, first in the vines, and second in the wineries. 'I really believe the key to the future of champagne is in the vineyards, not in the cellars,' says Lécaillon, whose viticultural initiative is unparalleled in all of Champagne.

Relationships with growers are changing as even the biggest houses engage more closely, taking an active interest in soils and viticultural practices, tasting grapes more often throughout the ripening season, and vinifying small parcels separately. 'I have been working on the relationship between growers and champagne houses for 20 years, and something is changing now,' says Dominique Demarville, whose engagement and support has fostered loyal growers. Last year, he established a new association to support Veuve Clicquot's young growers.

A new generation of talented young people is rising through the ranks in Champagne, and not only the trendy young growers on everyone's lips in hip wine bars. A new generation of energy and enthusiasm is blossoming in Champagne, in young growers taking over from their parents and striving for a quality imperative never seen before, and in super-intelligent and energetic young minds afforded increasing influence in the larger houses, upholding a respect for heritage and house style, while setting a dynamic precedent for improvement and innovation.

The number of enthusiastic young people working at every level, even at Moët & Chandon, is inspirational. 'Ten years ago, there was a strong "small is beautiful" focus, and all the journalists were writing about the alternative producers, but today the big companies are young and innovative, too,' reveals small Bouzy grower Jean-François Clouet.

The future of Champagne is in capable hands. And the opportunities are unprecedented. Globally, sparkling wine sales are increasing at double the rate of still wines and, with careful strategic planning and a little prudence, Champagne could emerge from the current crisis stronger than it has ever been.

If it is to do so, the region will need to be sensitive in managing its changing balance. The depression of the French market has eroded sales of grower champagnes every year for the past six years, even though the number of growers bottling their own champagnes has risen.

'Every year, we are losing sales to the big houses,' reveals Dizy grower-producer Nicolas Chiquet. Demarville believes the balance in Champagne will change, and more and more small growers will stop bottling. 'And so we are creating a new generation of growers who don't necessarily want to sell bottles, but who want to be top growers and sell their fruit to the leading houses,' he says. This need not be a catastrophe for Champagne, and Demarville predicts that the top growers will increase, while poor growers sell their fruit. 'In the next 10 years, 35% of growers will retire, and most will lease or sell their vines to other growers.'

It's another dramatic chapter in the evolution of a region that Lécaillon describes as a 'permanent innovation'. In the village of Bouzy, this is a history that has played out over 2000 harvests, since the Romans first planted vines on these distinguished slopes.

Tonight, as twilight closes in on the final day of harvest, there are smiles in Bouzy. It's been a high-pressure, compacted vintage of split-second timing, ultimately saved by an idyllic September. A gentle breeze ushers in a low, dense fog along the Vallée de la Marne, enshrouding the village, signalling the change of seasons. The vines have done their duty for another year, and have put on their final display of pastel colour before bedding down for another bitterly cold winter.

Pickers bundle their baskets and snips into panel vans and cars, honking at other teams in celebration as they roll down the hill to the village. An impromptu procession erupts in the streets of Bouzy, with cars adorned with vines, hazard lights pulsating and horns blaring. The sounds of the cochelets — lavish feasts to end the harvest — echo through the streets long into the night, with rousing sing-alongs fuelled by champagne and ratafia.

'I love the atmosphere at this time of year!' says Olivier Krug. 'The days are long and tiring, but it is relaxing for me to drive through the vineyards.' He pauses in the crystalline air of the Bouzy twilight. 'I love coming in the evening and being alone in the sea of vines. I am as relaxed as when I am fishing.'

He breathes deeply and inhales the last, fleeting aromas of harvest. But they are not lost, preserved immortally in a bottle of champagne. *La joie de vivre de la vendange.*

Pinot noir ripe for harvest in September 2014 on the grand cru slopes above the village of Bouzy, where vines have thrived for 2000 years.

Bienvenue!
Welcome to the most up-to-date Champagne Guide

There's a dazzling world of champagne to be discovered. Never has a greater variety of styles, wider diversity of brands or more exquisite quality emerged from the source of the finest fizz on earth. Champagne offers more options than ever to add sparkle to your occasion, your cuisine, your mood and your taste. It's a thrilling chase to find just the right bottle, but it can be a daunting task, too. This book dares to get under the surface of this vast and complex place to uncover the character of every champagne and take the guesswork out of your next bottle of bubbles.

The intricate personality of a bottle of champagne is shaped by its house style, vintages, grape varieties, reserve wines, winemaking techniques, chef de cave preferences, maturation time, dosage, time since disgorgement and, of course, the terroir of the vineyards themselves.

In the following pages, you'll discover not just what these things mean but, most importantly, how they smell, taste and feel in 685 champagnes from 120 houses, all of which have been tasted recently, providing an up-to-date snapshot of champagnes just as you'll find them this year.

UP-TO-THE-MOMENT GUIDE
Champagne is a fast-moving target, and an up-to-the-minute guide to the champagnes to drink this year is just as critical as it is for any other wine. This is why this book is very different to every other champagne guide. Time is everything in the development of champagne, and the landscape of the wines on the shelves is changing rapidly.

Since my last edition, new vintages have landed and non-vintages have rolled on to new blends. On occasions when last year's vintage is still current, I've retasted the wine and written an all-new review. I'm amazed how quickly some have blossomed, and others have wilted.

Champagne is the most intricately complex of all wines to craft, and hence to assess. Every bottle is different, according to how long it has relied upon the sustaining presence of lees prior to disgorgement, how long it has evolved post-disgorgement, the composition

of the blend and the dosage for that disgorgement, not to mention how it has travelled. Even non-vintage blends change every vintage as an ever more temperamental mother nature foils even the most skilful blenders. This presents a dilemma in communicating meaningful guidance on each cuvée, and I have again earnestly sought to retaste as many wines outside Champagne as possible, in some cases in as many as five different places.

This has all led me to a bold step which I believe to be unprecedented in champagne publishing — inclusion not only of disgorgement date, base vintage and location of tasting, but also of different scores for the same cuvée when these details change. A complex undertaking, but I'm convinced there's no other way to fairly interpret champagne for its markets across the globe.

To guarantee that you're up to speed with the very latest in Champagne, I've added a new chapter on Champagne vintages, dating from 2014 to 1995 (see pages 19–23), updated all 95 champagne producers, dropped a few lesser estates and added 23 important players. There simply aren't enough pages to include everything, so 25 houses and scores for 95 cuvées that didn't make the cut are featured in the index.

To stay fully up-to-date on everything champagne, tune in to podcasts and stories at my new site, ChampagneHQ.com.

A new era in champagne has arrived, and there has never been a better time to raise a glass to discover the intricate personality of the most celebrated beverage on earth. Get ready to sparkle.

Using this guide

Chasing the best fizz that money can buy? Bienvenue! *Your glass is about to froth over. You'll be astounded at what Champagne has to offer if you know what to look for this year, and the following pages will guarantee you don't miss a thing. Even in the lowest price bracket, I've found seven champagnes worthy of a gold medal in a wine show.*

What do my scores mean?

Points are a quick way to highlight the best champagnes in each category. There has been much controversy surrounding wine scores in recent years. It is of course a travesty to reduce the grand complexities of champagne to a single number, but I persist in doing so because many readers find this useful. As always, my descriptions are infinitely more informative than scores, and more detailed than ever this year.

I persevere with the international 100 point system, not because I endorse it, but simply because it is universally understood. Broadly, anything less than 85 is faulty, less than 90 is sound but unexciting, and 91 is where all the real fun begins. A 94 point champagne has impeccable purity and immaculate balance — a gold medal in a wine show. Beyond, it's not greater concentration of flavour, more obvious fruit or more clever winemaking tricks that set it apart. True greatness is declared by something more profound: the inimitable stamp of place — 'terroir' to the French, articulated most eloquently in length of finish and palate texture. Persistence of aftertaste and depth of mineral character distinguish the very finest champagnes.

100 The pinnacle of character, balance and persistence. This year, just 0.5% of champagnes tasted scored 100 points. Sadly, they're all ear-splittingly expensive back vintages.

99 Almost perfection (20 on the 20 point scale). Less than 1% of champagnes tasted. Look out for one $$$ cuvée in the stratosphere this year.

98 An exceedingly rare calibre of world-class distinction. Less than 3% of champagnes tasted. The prestige cuvées of the top houses tend to rule this territory.

97 More than exceptional. Less than 4% of champagnes tasted. Look out for three $$$ cuvées.

96 Exceptional. Top gold or trophy standard in a wine show (19/20); 10% of champagnes tasted. There's something for everyone here this year, including 14 $$ cuvées.

95 Offering an edge that pushes beyond excellent; 13% of champagnes tasted. Look out for three $ cuvées.

94 Excellent champagne that I love. Gold medal in a wine show (18.5/20). Less than 14% of champagnes tasted. Look out for six $ cuvées.

93 Almost excellent; 15% of champagnes tasted.

92 A very good wine that characterises its place and variety; 10% of champagnes tasted.

91 Better than good, offering an edge of distinction. Silver medal (17/20); 9% of champagnes tasted. With more than 540 champagnes at 91 or above this year, why drink anything less?

90 A good wine that I like; 5% of champagnes tasted. Only buy if it's cheap.

89 Better than sound and almost good; 6% of champagnes tasted.

88 Sound. Worth buying if it's cheap. Bronze medal standard (15.5/20); 2% of champagnes tasted.

87 Almost sound; 3% of champagnes tasted.

86 Simple and ordinary; 2% of champagnes tasted.

85 Ordinary and boring, though without notable faults (14/20); 1% of champagnes tasted.

84 Borderline faulty. Less than 1% of champagnes tasted.

83 Faulty. Caution!

82 Distinctly faulty (12/20).

81 Exceedingly faulty. Stand well clear.

80 Horrid. You've been warned.

See page 348 for a full list of wines by score.

PRICE

Whether you're on the hunt for a bargain or a decadent splurge, this guide will help you find the right bottle in no time. Each cuvée is price-coded to indicate what you can expect to pay in an average retail store. Champagne is one of the most readily discounted wines on the shelves, so shop around and you're sure to find the big brands on special. Back-vintage champagnes not currently available are listed without indication of price, featured throughout the guide to provide an insight into the potential of the most age-worthy cuvées.

	Euros (France)	Great British Pounds	US Dollars	Australian Dollars	Hong Kong Dollars	Singapore Dollars
$	‹€25	‹£30	‹$50	‹$60	‹$400	‹$80
$$	€25–50	£30–50	$50–80	$60–100	$400–550	$80–140
$$$	€51–65	£51–65	$81–100	$101–150	$551–650	$141–160
$$$$	€66–140	£66–130	$101–200	$151–300	$651–1100	$161–250
$$$$$	›€140	›£130	›$200	›$300	›$1100	›$250

ON THE HOUSE

The Best Champagnes of the Year lists on the following pages highlight the most important wines in this book. These are the finest fizzes that money can buy this year, the most reliable bargains, the most pristine big blends, the most sought-after growers, the most sublime rosés, the most brilliant blanc de blancs, the most balanced low-dosage champagnes, and the upper reaches of the stratosphere of prestige.

The Champagne Guide 2016–2017 Hall of Honour acknowledges the finest houses of the year. A house is only as worthy as its current cuvées, so its rating is based exclusively on the quality of its wines in the market this year, not on past performance or museum wines. History and reputation count for nothing if the wines you can buy don't live up to expectation.

I have made a small exception to this, in compensating for the difficult 2011 and 2010 base vintages where these have let down non-vintage cuvées. Underperforming houses do not deserve your attention nor mine, so unless a house scores at least 5 out of 10, it does not score at all.

Roughly, to rate 10 out of 10, the entry non-vintage cuvée of the house would typically score 95/100, vintage cuvées around 96, and prestige cuvées 97. To attain 5 out of 10, these drop to 91, 93 and 94 respectively.

There is a prudent saying in Champagne that if you make a good brut NV, you are a good house. The entry-level cuvées that comprise the majority of the house's production bear a strong weighting in its rating.

These ratings are by their nature highly controversial. As Champagne house styles increasingly diversify, it is ever more challenging to reduce their grand complexities to a single number. I encourage you to use these only as a guide to quickly home in on the very best houses.

HALL OF HONOUR

The Champagne Guide

• 2016—2017 •

10/10

BOLLINGER	75
EGLY-OURIET	134
KRUG	211
SALON	312

9/10

BILLECART-SALMON	65
DE SOUSA & FILS	100
DOM PÉRIGNON	117
JACQUESSON	200
LOUIS ROEDERER	243
POL ROGER	302

8/10

ANDRÉ CLOUET	41
DEUTZ	106
GOSSET	174
LARMANDIER-BERNIER	227
PAUL BARA	273
PIERRE GIMONNET & FILS	286
PIERRE PÉTERS	293
TAITTINGER	314

7/10

AGRAPART & FILS	34
AR LENOBLE	47
BENOÎT LAHAYE	57
BÉRÊCHE ET FILS	60
BRUNO PAILLARD	83
CHARLES HEIDSIECK	91
EMMANUEL BROCHET	137
ERIC RODEZ	140
GATINOIS	160
HENRIOT	184
JACQUES SELOSSE	196
JÉRÔME PRÉVOST	207
LE BRUN-SERVENAY	236
PASCAL DOQUET	269
PAUL DÉTHUNE	275
RUINART	309
VEUVE CLICQUOT	329
VEUVE FOURNY & FILS	337
VILMART & CIE	343

6/10

ALFRED GRATIEN	38
ANDRÉ JACQUART	45
BONNAIRE	81
CAMILLE SAVÈS	85
DELAMOTTE	104
DEVAUX	111
DIEBOLT-VALLOIS	114
DOSNON & LEPAGE	124
DUMANGIN J. FILS	126
DUVAL-LEROY	130
FLEURY PÈRE & FILS	145
GASTON CHIQUET	157
GEOFFROY	163
GODMÉ PÈRE ET FILS	171
GUY CHARLEMAGNE	178
HURÉ FRÈRES	187
J. LASSALLE	188
LANSON	223
LAURENT-PERRIER	233
MARC HÉBRART	255
PHILIPPONNAT	282
PIPER-HEIDSIECK	298
TARLANT	320
ULYSSE COLLIN	325
VAZART COQUART ET FILS	326

5/10

AYALA	52
BARONS DE ROTHSCHILD	55
CHARPENTIER	95
CLAUDE CARRÉ ET FILS	97
COUCHE PÈRE ET FILS	98
H. BILLIOT FILS	180
HENRI GIRAUD	181
HENRI GOUTORBE	183
JACQUES PICARD	193
JACQUINOT & FILS	206
JOSEPH PERRIER	210
LE MESNIL	239
MAILLY GRAND CRU	251
PALMER & CO	267
PERRIER-JOUËT	279
ROGER COULON	308

The Best Champagnes of the Year

❧ Under $ ❧

Agrapart & Fils Terroirs Blanc de Blancs Grand Cru Extra Brut NV
$ • 95 POINTS • PAGE 35

Diebolt-Vallois Blanc de Blancs NV
$ • 95 POINTS • PAGE 115

Franck Bonville Grand Cru Avize Blanc de Blancs Brut Millésime 2008
$ • 95 POINTS • PAGE 152

Bonnaire Blanc de Blancs Grand Cru NV
$ • 94 POINTS • PAGE 81

Dumangin J. Fils Le Rosé Brut NV
$ • 94 POINTS • PAGE 128

Guy Charlemagne Grand Cru Reserve Blanc de Blancs Brut NV
$ • 94 POINTS • PAGE 178

Tarlant Zero Brut Nature NV
$ • 94 POINTS • PAGE 322

Agrapart & Fils 7 Crus Brut NV
$ • 93 POINTS • PAGE 35

AR Lenoble Cuvée Intense Brut NV
$ • 93 POINTS • PAGE 48

Bonnaire Grand Cru Blanc de Blancs Millésime 2005
$ • 93 POINTS • PAGE 82

Charpentier Rosé Brut NV
$ • 93 POINTS • PAGE 96

Dumangin J. Fils L'Extra-Brut 1er Cru NV
$ • 93 POINTS • PAGE 129

Henri Goutorbe Brut Tradition NV
$ • 93 POINTS • PAGE 183

Palmer & Co Brut Réserve NV
$ • 93 POINTS • PAGE 267

Pierre Gimonnet & Fils Cuis Premier Cru Brut Blanc de Blancs NV
$ • 93 POINTS • PAGE 288

Tarlant Brut Reserve NV
$ • 93 POINTS • PAGE 322

Tarlant Rosé Zero Brut Nature NV
$ • 93 POINTS • PAGE 323

❧ Under $$ ❧

André Clouet 1911 NV
$$ • 96 POINTS • PAGE 44

André Clouet Brut Millesime 2002
$$ • 96 POINTS • PAGE 43

André Clouet Brut Millesime 2008
$$ • 96 POINTS • PAGE 43

Camille Savès Cuvée Anais Jolicoeur 2008
$$ • 96 POINTS • PAGE 87

Camille Savès Cuvee Prestige Brut NV
$$ • 96 POINTS • PAGE 87

Gatinois Aÿ Grand Cru Brut Millésime 2008
$$ • 96 POINTS • PAGE 162

J. Lassalle Cuvée Angéline Premier Cru Brut Millésime 2008
$$ • 96 POINTS • PAGE 190

Pascal Doquet Vertus Premier Cru Coeur de Terroir 2004
$$ • 96 POINTS • PAGE 271

André Clouet Grande Réserve Blanc de Noirs Brut NV
$$ • 95 POINTS • PAGE 42

Bollinger Special Cuvee Brut NV
$$ • 95 POINTS • PAGE 78

Camille Savès Carte d'Or NV
$$ • 95 POINTS • PAGE 86

Camille Savès Millésime 2008
$$ • 95 POINTS • PAGE 86

Pascal Doquet Vertus Coeur de Terroir 2002
$$ • 95 POINTS • PAGE 272

Philipponnat Blanc de Noirs Brut 2008
$$ • 95 POINTS • PAGE 284

❧ Under $$$ ❧

Deutz Brut Millésimé 2008
$$$ • 96 POINTS • PAGE 107

Egly-Ouriet Grand Cru Brut Tradition NV
$$$ • 96 POINTS • PAGE 135

Gosset Grand Millésime 2004
$$$ • 96 POINTS • PAGE 176

Le Brun-Servenay Exhilarante Vieilles Vignes Millesime 2006
$$$ • 96 POINTS • PAGE 238

Louis Roederer Brut Vintage 2008
$$$ • 96 POINTS • PAGE 246

Pol Roger Brut Vintage 2004
$$$ • 96 POINTS • PAGE 305

Taittinger Cuvée Prélude Grand Crus Brut NV
$$$ • 96 POINTS • PAGE 317

Veuve Clicquot Vintage Brut 2008
$$$ • 96 POINTS • PAGE 332

J. Lassalle Special Club 2006
$$$ • 95 POINTS • PAGE 190

Lanson Extra Age Brut NV
$$$ • 95 POINTS • PAGE 226

Louis Roederer Brut Vintage 2007
$$$ • 95 POINTS • PAGE 246

Mailly Grand Cru Blanc de Noirs NV
$$$ • 95 POINTS • PAGE 253

Paul Déthune Cuvée Prestige Princesse des Thunes Brut NV
$$$ • 95 POINTS • PAGE 276

Paul Goerg Cuvée Lady 2002
$$$ • 95 POINTS • PAGE 278

Vazart-Coquart & Fils Special Club 2006
$$$ • 95 POINTS • PAGE 328

Veuve Clicquot Vintage Brut 2004
$$$ • 95 POINTS • PAGE 333

Vilmart & Cie Grand Cellier d'Or Brut Premier Cru 2009
$$$ • 95 POINTS • PAGE 345

❧ *Under $$$$* ❧

Billecart-Salmon Cuvée Nicolas François Billecart 2002
$$$$ • 99 POINTS • PAGE 70

Billecart-Salmon Cuvée Nicolas François Billecart 2000
$$$$ • 98 POINTS • PAGE 71

Gosset Cuvée Celebris Rosé Brut 1998
$$$$ • 98 POINTS • PAGE 177

Veuve Clicquot La Grande Dame Brut 2004
$$$$ • 98 POINTS • PAGE 334

Billecart-Salmon Blanc de Blancs Brut 2004
$$$$ • 97 POINTS • PAGE 70

Deutz Cuvée William Deutz Brut Millésimé 2002
$$$$ • 97 POINTS • PAGE 109

Duval-Leroy Femme de Champagne 2000
$$$$ • 97 POINTS • PAGE 133

Egly-Ouriet Grand Cru Blanc De Noirs Vieilles Vignes NV
$$$$ • 97 POINTS • PAGE 136

Gosset Cuvée Celebris Rosé Extra Brut 2007
$$$$ • 97 POINTS • PAGE 177

Gosset Cuvée Celebris Vintage Extra Brut 2002
$$$$ • 97 POINTS • PAGE 177

Krug Grande Cuvée NV
$$$$ • 97 POINTS • PAGE 215

Agrapart & Fils Venus Blanc de Blancs Grand Cru Brut Nature 2008
$$$$ • 96 POINTS • PAGE 37

Duval-Leroy Femme de Champagne 2004
$$$$ • 96 POINTS • PAGE 133

Eric Rodez Empriente de Terroir Pinot Noir 2002
$$$$ • 96 POINTS • PAGE 142

Jacques Selosse Initiale Blanc de Blancs Brut NV
$$$$ • 96 POINTS • PAGE 197

Lanson Noble Cuvée Brut Millésimé 2000
$$$$ • 96 POINTS • PAGE 226

Mailly Grand Cru L'Intemporelle Millésimé Brut 2008
$$$$ • 96 POINTS • PAGE 254

Mailly Grand Cru L'Intemporelle Rosé Brut 2008
$$$$ • 96 POINTS • PAGE 254

Paul Bara Comtesse Marie de France Blanc de Noirs 2002
$$$$ • 96 POINTS • PAGE 273

Piper-Heidsieck Rare Millesime 2002
$$$$ • 96 POINTS • PAGE 301

Veuve Clicquot La Grande Dame Brut 2006
$$$$ • 96 POINTS • PAGE 334

Vilmart & Cie Coeur de Cuvée Premier Cru 2006
$$$$ • 96 POINTS • PAGE 346

❧ *Under $$$$$* ❧

Dom Pérignon Oenotheque 1996
$$$$$ • 100 POINTS • PAGE 123

Krug Collection 1982
$$$$$ • 100 POINTS • PAGE 217

Pol Roger Cuvée Sir Winston Churchill 1996
$$$$$ • 99 POINTS • PAGE 307

Pol Roger Cuvée Sir Winston Churchill 2002
$$$$$ • 99 POINTS • PAGE 307

Charles Heidsieck Blanc de Millénaires 1995
$$$$$ • 98 POINTS • PAGE 94

Dom Pérignon P2 1998
$$$$$ • 98 POINTS • PAGE 123

Dom Pérignon P2 Rosé 1995
$$$$$ • 98 POINTS • PAGE 122

Krug Rosé Brut NV
$$$$$ • 98 POINTS • PAGE 214

Krug Vintage 2000
$$$$$ • 98 POINTS • PAGE 216

Louis Roederer Cristal 1995
$$$$$ • 98 POINTS • PAGE 250

Pol Roger Cuvée Sir Winston Churchill 2004
$$$$$ • 98 POINTS • PAGE 306

Veuve Clicquot Cave Privée Rosé Brut 1979
$$$$$ • 98 POINTS • PAGE 336

Veuve Clicquot Cave Privée Rosé Brut 1990
$$$$$ • 98 POINTS • PAGE 336

Bollinger R.D. Extra Brut 2002
$$$$$ • 97 POINTS • PAGE 79

Deutz Amour de Deutz Rosé Brut 2006
$$$$$ • 97 POINTS • PAGE 110

Dom Pérignon 2004
$$$$$ • 97 POINTS • PAGE 120

Henriot Cuve 38 La Réserve Perpétuelle Blanc de Blancs NV
$$$$$ • 97 POINTS • PAGE 186

Jacques Selosse Millésime Blanc de Blancs Brut 2002
$$$$$ • 97 POINTS • PAGE 199

Jacquesson Avize Champ Caïn Récolte Extra Brut 2005
$$$$$ • 97 POINTS • PAGE 204

Jacquesson Dégorgement Tardif Extra Brut Millésime 1995
$$$$$ • 97 POINTS • PAGE 205

Krug Clos du Mesnil 2003
$$$$$ • 97 POINTS • PAGE 217

Laurent-Perrier Grande Siècle NV
$$$$$ • 97 POINTS • PAGE 235

Piper-Heidsieck Rare Millesime 1998
$$$$$ • 97 POINTS • PAGE 301

Pol Roger Cuvée Sir Winston Churchill 2000
$$$$$ • 97 POINTS • PAGE 307

Salon Cuvée S Blanc de Blancs 1997
$$$$$ • 97 POINTS • PAGE 313

Salon Cuvée S Blanc de Blancs 2002
$$$$$ • 97 POINTS • PAGE 313

Taittinger Comtes de Champagne Blanc de Blancs 2006
$$$$$ • 97 POINTS • PAGE 318

Veuve Clicquot Cave Privée Rosé Brut 1989
$$$$$ • 97 POINTS • PAGE 336

The Best Blanc de Blancs Champagnes of the Year $$-$$$

PIERRE PÉTERS CUVÉE SPÉCIALE
BLANC DE BLANCS LES CHÉTILLONS
2008
$$$ • 99 POINTS • PAGE 297

PASCAL DOQUET LE MESNIL-SUR-
OGER GRAND CRU COEUR DE
TERROIR BLANC DE BLANCS BRUT
2002
$$$ • 97 POINTS • PAGE 272

PIERRE GIMONNET & FILS SPECIAL
CLUB MILLESIME DE COLLECTION
BLANC DE BLANCS 2008
$$$ • 97 POINTS • PAGE 292

PIERRE PÉTERS CUVÉE SPÉCIALE
BLANC DE BLANCS LES CHÉTILLONS
2007
$$$ • 97 POINTS • PAGE 297

PIERRE PÉTERS CUVÉE LA RÉSERVE
OUBLIÉE BLANC DE BLANCS BRUT
NV
$$ • 96 POINTS • PAGE 296

VAZART-COQUART & FILS BRUT
GRAND BOUQUET BLANC DE BLANCS
2008
$$ • 96 POINTS • PAGE 328

DE SOUSA & FILS CUVÉE DES
CAUDALIES BLANC DE BLANCS
GRAND CRU BRUT NV
$$$ • 96 POINTS • PAGE 103

DEUTZ BLANC DE BLANCS BRUT
2008
$$$ • 96 POINTS • PAGE 108

LOUIS ROEDERER BLANC DE BLANCS
2008
$$$ • 96 POINTS • PAGE 247

PASCAL DOQUET LE MESNIL-SUR-
OGER GRAND CRU COEUR DE
TERROIR BLANC DE BLANCS BRUT
2004
$$$ • 96 POINTS • PAGE 272

PIERRE GIMONNET & FILS SPECIAL
CLUB GRANDS TERROIRS DE
CHARDONNAY 2006
$$$ • 96 POINTS • PAGE 292

PIERRE PÉTERS CUVÉE SPÉCIALE
BLANC DE BLANCS LES CHÉTILLONS
2009
$$$ • 96 POINTS • PAGE 297

POL ROGER BLANC DE BLANCS BRUT
2004
$$$ • 96 POINTS • PAGE 305

POL ROGER BLANC DE BLANCS BRUT
2008
$$$ • 96 POINTS • PAGE 304

AR LENOBLE GRAND CRU BLANC DE
BLANCS CHOUILLY BRUT 2008
$$ • 95 POINTS • PAGE 49

DE SOUSA & FILS GRAND CRU
RÉSERVE BLANC DE BLANCS BRUT
NV
$$ • 95 POINTS • PAGE 102

DELAMOTTE BLANC DE BLANCS NV
$$ • 95 POINTS • PAGE 105

HENRI GIRAUD ESPRIT DE GIRAUD
BLANC DE BLANCS NV
$$ • 95 POINTS • PAGE 182

LE BRUN-SERVENAY CUVÉE
CHARDONNAY BRUT MILLÉSIME
VIEILLES VIGNES 2005
$$ • 95 POINTS • PAGE 238

PIERRE GIMONNET & FILS CUVEE
GASTRONOME 1er CRU BLANC DE
BLANCS CUVÉE BRUT 2008
$$ • 95 POINTS • PAGE 290

ANDRÉ JACQUART EXPERIENCE
MILLÉSIMÉ LE MESNIL-SUR-OGER
BLANC DE BLANCS GRAND CRU
2006
$$$ • 95 POINTS • PAGE 46

AR LENOBLE COLLECTION RARE
GRAND CRU BLANC DE BLANCS 2002
$$$ • 95 POINTS • PAGE 50

AR LENOBLE CUVÉE GENTILHOMME
GRAND CRU BLANC DE BLANCS
MILLÉSIME BRUT 2006
$$$ • 95 POINTS • PAGE 50

BILLECART-SALMON BLANC DE
BLANCS GRAND CRU BRUT NV
$$$ • 95 POINTS • PAGE 68

BRUNO PAILLARD BLANC DE BLANCS
2004
$$$ • 95 POINTS • PAGE 84

BRUNO PAILLARD BLANC DE BLANCS
RESERVE PRIVÉE BRUT NV
$$$ • 95 POINTS • PAGE 84

DELAMOTTE BLANC DE BLANCS 2007
$$$ • 95 POINTS • PAGE 104

DEUTZ BLANC DE BLANCS 2007
$$$ • 95 POINTS • PAGE 109

GOSSET GRAND BLANC DE BLANCS
BRUT NV
$$$ • 95 POINTS • PAGE 176

LOUIS ROEDERER BLANC DE BLANCS
2009
$$$ • 95 POINTS • PAGE 247

PIERRE GIMONNET & FILS SPECIAL
CLUB BLANC DE BLANCS 2009
$$$ • 95 POINTS • PAGE 291

POL ROGER BLANC DE BLANCS BRUT
2006
$$$ • 95 POINTS • PAGE 305

Chardonnay vines at the end of harvest 2014 in Avize, source of some of the most precise, mineral and age-worthy grand cru blanc de blancs.

The Best Rosé Champagnes of the Year $$-$$$

Bollinger Rosé Brut NV
$$ • 96 points • page 78

Henriot Rosé Millésime 2008
$$ • 96 points • page 185

Charles Heidsieck Rosé Millésime 2006
$$$ • 96 points • page 93

De Sousa & Fils Cuvée des Caudalies Brut Rosé NV
$$$ • 96 points • page 103

Deutz Brut Rosé 2009
$$$ • 96 points • page 109

Egly-Ouriet Grand Cru Brut Rosé NV
$$$ • 96 points • page 136

Gosset Grand Rosé Brut NV
$$$ • 96 points • page 176

Louis Roederer Rosé 2008
$$$ • 96 points • page 248

Veuve Clicquot Vintage Rosé 2008
$$$ • 96 points • page 333

Alfred Gratien Cuvée Brut Classique Rosé NV
$$ • 95 points • page 39

Charpentier Terre d'Emotion Rosé NV
$$ • 95 points • page 96

De Sousa & Fils Brut Rosé NV
$$ • 95 points • page 102

Le Brun-Servenay Cuvée Brut Rosé NV
$$ • 95 points • page 237

Billecart-Salmon Brut Rosé NV
$$$ • 95 points • page 69

Jacquesson Dizy Terres Rouges Rosé Récolte Extra Brut 2008
$$$ • 95 points • page 204

Larmandier-Bernier Rosé de Saignée Premier Cru Extra Brut NV
$$$ • 95 points • page 230

Louis Roederer Rosé 2009
$$$ • 95 points • page 247

Pol Roger Brut Rosé 2004
$$$ • 95 points • page 306

Pol Roger Brut Rosé 2006
$$$ • 95 points • page 306

Veuve Clicquot Vintage Rosé 2004
$$$ • 95 points • page 333

The Best Low-Dosage Champagnes of the Year $$-$$$

Benoît Lahaye Extra Brut 2008
$$ • 96 points • page 59

Eric Rodez Cuvée Zéro Dosage NV
$$ • 96 points • page 143

Agrapart & Fils Minéral Blanc De Blancs Grand Cru Extra Brut 2008
$$$ • 96 points • page 36

Benoît Lahaye Blanc de Noirs Extra Brut NV
$$ • 95 points • page 58

Benoît Lahaye Rosé de Macération Extra Brut NV
$$ • 95 points • page 59

Guy Charlemagne Mesnillésime Extra Brut 2004
$$ • 95 points • page 179

Jacquesson Cuvée No 737 Extra Brut NV
$$ • 95 points • page 203

Pierre Gimonnet & Fils Extra Brut Cuvée Oenophile 1er Cru Blanc de Blancs Non Dosé 2008
$$ • 95 points • page 291

Tarlant Cuvée Louis Hommage à Louis Tarlant Vin de Rivière Extra Brut NV
$$ • 95 points • page 324

Veuve Fourny & Fils Cuvée Blanc de Blancs Vertus Premier Cru Vintage Extra Brut 2006
$$ • 95 points • page 341

Veuve Fourny & Fils Cuvée Blanc de Blancs Vertus Premier Cru Vintage Extra Brut 2008
$$ • 95 points • page 341

Agrapart & Fils Minéral Blanc De Blancs Grand Cru Extra Brut 2007
$$$ • 95 points • page 36

Duval-Leroy Blanc de Blancs Brut Nature Millésime 2002
$$$ • 95 points • page 132

Emmanuel Brochet Les Hauts Meuniers Extra Brut 2008
$$$ • 95 points • page 139

Jérôme Prévost La Closerie Les Béguines
$$$ • 95 points • page 209

Le Brun-Servenay Blanc de Blancs X.B. Extra Brut 2.5 NV
$$$ • 95 points • page 238

Tarlant La Vigne d'Antan Non Greffée Chardonnay Brut Nature 2002
$$$ • 95 points • page 324

CHAMPAGNE VINTAGES

The vast complexity and diversity of Champagne and the varied micro-climates of its 320 villages have long driven me to resist writing generic vintage reports. But the more I taste champagne, the more I see distinctive moods of each season underscoring the voice of each terroir and house style. 'The magic of champagne belongs to the climate, not the soil,' says Louis Roederer chef de cave Jean-Baptiste Lécaillon. 'The climate is stronger, and the wines tell the story of the rain and the sun.'

This is particularly pronounced in the wines released this year. The last edition of this guide caught many new vintage releases from the great 2002 and 2004 seasons, and a great deal of non-vintage wines based on the brilliant 2008 harvest. This year, most vintage releases have shifted to the trickier 2005 and 2006 harvests, while the harrowing 2011 and 2010 seasons have marked many non-vintages.

The tumultuous climate of Champagne makes the stamp of the season more dramatic than in any other wine region, so an insight into the personality of every harvest is more pertinent in your search for great champagne this year than ever.

There's a disconcerting trend in Champagne to release vintage wines more often. While some chef de caves argue that a progressive warming of the climate has rendered more seasons capable of standing alone, I am increasingly unconvinced of the merits of warm seasons like 2001, 2003 and 2005. Many houses and growers were ambitious in releasing vintage wines from 2003 and 2005. We have now entered an era in which greater consumer discernment is necessary in selecting vintages. There are notable exceptions highlighted throughout this guide, but the general rule for the first decade of the new millennium is to stick with the even years.

I've introduced a little twist to traditional historic vintage reports. Each of the following assessments is written according to how this vintage is looking today, and the cuvées I've singled out have all been tasted recently. In cool, stable, dark conditions, the enduring vintages of 1996, 2002, 2004, 2008 and 2012 are capable of maturing magnificently for decades, and I hope you might be enticed to lay down a bottle or two.

So, by popular demand, here it is: my first ever guide to the last 20 vintages in Champagne.

2014

An exceptional season on the Montagne de Reims and Côte des Bar, excellent in the Côte des Blancs, though the Vallée de la Marne suffered from rot and lacked maturity. The vivacity of a cold summer contrasts the rounded fleshiness of a warm harvest. The wettest August on record and the coldest summer in 20 years were followed by an idyllic September. Those who spent the harvest in Champagne recall a compacted vintage saved by the warm autumn sun. There was no rescuing meunier after twice the usual summer rainfall in the Vallée de la Marne, though diligent viticulture helped in the Côte des Blancs, producing chardonnay charged with excellent acidity and ripeness, leading Veuve Fourny chef de cave Emmanuel Fourny to dub this *l'année du vigneron*, the year of the vine grower. The Montagne de Reims received only 10% more summer rainfall than usual, and Louis Roederer chef de cave Jean-Baptiste Lécaillon reported 'some of the best fruit we have produced'. When I visited Eric Rodez in Ambonnay just after he'd emptied his last press load, he was excited like a boy at Christmas, declaring, 'This may be the harvest of my career!' Houses sourcing predominantly from the northern Montagne de Reims and Côte des Blancs declared vintage cuvées.

2013

A late, cool, elongated harvest of high acidity. The early-ripening villages of the Côte des Blancs, southern Montagne de Reims and eastern Vallée de la Marne suffered poor flowering, which proved to be a blessing, tempering yields in an otherwise higher-yielding vintage, advancing ripeness, with good results. For Moët & Chandon chef de cave Benoît Gouez, 'on paper, 2013 was as good as 2012 for chardonnay and pinot noir in the grand and premier crus'. Later-ripening villages were delayed by high yields, afflicted by rain in September and a cold, windy October. It was not until well into that month that ripeness was achieved, with stringent selection required to avoid rot. This proved a particularly challenging year in the western Marne and Côte des Bar. Such were the acidities that Louis Roederer put a record number of parcels through malolactic fermentation. Severe July hailstorms battered some 3000 hectares, with more than 300 hectares completely destroyed, particularly around Épernay and the Côte des Blancs, where 10–20% of the grand cru crop was lost.

2012

A stark reminder that blanket generalisations are grossly inadequate in Champagne's grand diversity. I visited and tasted the vins clairs in early 2013 and was amazed at their scintillating acidity, expressive concentration, entrancing purity and classic refinement, yet surprised by the polarising reports about the vintage.

Superlatives rolled: 'The vintage of my career' (Dumangin), 'amazing' (Veuve Clicquot), 'very, very good' (Jacquesson), 'perfect balance' (Mumm), 'spectacular, one of the three classic vintages so far this century' (Louis Roederer), 'very similar to 2002' (Taittinger), 'better than 2002 or 2008' (Pierre Gimonnet), 'better than 1996' (Vilmart), 'challenging yet beautiful' (Devaux), 'just fantastic, wow!' (Billecart-Salmon).

Then this: 'One of the toughest seasons I can recall in 25 years' (Larmandier-Bernier), 'challenging' (Dom Pérignon), 'very difficult' (Piper Heidsieck), 'tough' (Pierre Péters). 'For a good vintage in Champagne, we do not want a good summer,' clarifies Didier Gimonnet. 'The grapes must suffer!'

Record rainfall between March and July made diligence in controlling rot paramount, a nightmare for some organic and biodynamic growers. While a few of the most fanatical growers reported bumper yields, most lost one-third of their crop. A cool summer upheld dizzying acidity, while perfect conditions from mid-August produced generous sugar ripeness, so much so that some growers saw no need to chaptalise.

Those who waited and picked ripe were rewarded, and there will be many spectacularly concentrated, acid-driven, long-lived vintage cuvées made this season, though there are notable exceptions: Salon did not make a 2012, Ruinart did not see the stamina in chardonnay to produce a Dom Ruinart, and Krug will not release a vintage cuvée, instead keeping its small crop in reserve.

2011 · 2/10

A dismal vintage marked by underripeness, dilution and widespread rot. I visited at the height of summer in mid-July, and for two weeks there was not one day of sunshine to ripen the harvest. Misty mornings made way for sullen, grey days, frequently sodden with downpours. Summer was otherwise hot, furnishing a short growing cycle and grapes devoid of complexity and character. In spite of a lack of ripeness, the threat of rot during a rain-interrupted harvest prompted the CIVC to announce some of the earliest harvest dates in history. For all the inconsistencies of 2011, Veuve Clicquot chef de cave Dominique Demarville upholds the season as evidence Champagne is still capable of producing strong acidity. Very few vintage wines were produced. The 2011 is the predominant base of non-vintage champagnes on the shelves this year, marked by dusty, dry, mushroomy rot. Its impact is exacerbated by the weakness of 2010, hampering any hopes of resurrecting non-vintage cuvées with generous reserves.

2010 · 3/10

A challenging season, with ripe fruit marred by dilution, low acidity and rampant rot. A hot, dry summer ended abruptly in a mid-August deluge, prompting a devastating outburst of botrytis across the Marne. 'There was such a fog of dry rot in the air I couldn't see the guys throwing the grapes into the press!' one Montagne de Reims grower revealed. Sorting was paramount, and some houses elected to keep less than their appellation allowance. This proved to put a timely damper on production after the global financial crisis significantly dented champagne sales in 2009.

2009 · 6/10

Dry, hot continental weather produced a sunny, ripe vintage of rounded exuberance, clean and appealing right away, without the acidity to age, making 2009 the antithesis of the tense, enduring 2008. While this vintage will forever lurk in the shadow of its predecessor, it is a season with some surprises. 'An excellent vintage!' found Jacquesson's Jean-Hervé Chiquet, and for Didier Gimonnet of Pierre Gimonnet, one of the best of the decade after 2002. The greatest 2009 vintage champagnes today are Deutz Brut Rosé, Pierre Péters Cuvée Spéciale Blanc de Blancs Les Chétillons, with more yet to be released, though very few vintage wines were made, perhaps as much in response to the global financial crisis as the pedigree of the season.

2008 · 10/10

A vintage of classic finesse, crystalline purity, tightly clenched acidity and monumental longevity, 2008 is the essence of champagne. It will be decades before the full distinction of this transcendental season becomes truly apparent, but I have ever-rising confidence that it will eclipse even 1996 and every season since. There is no more exquisite recipe for champagne than a wet spring, a cool, not particularly sunny, yet dry, summer, followed by idyllic, bright days and cool nights, lingering gloriously for the entire duration of harvest. The result was textbook ripeness of 9.6–9.8 degrees potential, and heightened acidities of 8.5–8.6g/L. To Vazart-Coquart chef de cave Jean-Pierre Vazart, 2008 is 1996 with balance. Even many lesser growers and houses produced admirable results in this near-perfect vintage, while the flagship cuvées of the top houses will endure for half a century. The greatest 2008 vintage champagnes today are Pierre Gimonnet & Fils Special Club Millésime de Collection Blanc de Blancs, and Pierre Péters Cuvée Spéciale Blanc de Blancs Les Chétillons, with many, many more stunners yet to be released.

2007 · 7/10

A vintage of delicacy and finesse, with endurance, if not concentration, terroir expression or distinctive character. A warm winter made for an early season, retarded by a wet, cold and rot-inducing summer. Harvest was saved by a north wind and sunny days from mid-August, furnishing adequate maturity while upholding good acid levels. This proved to be a highly variable vintage from one village to the next, largely dependent upon picking date, vineyard care and sorting regime. Following the warm, sunny style of 2006, the elegance of 2007 is sometimes compared to that of 1997 following 1996. To Dom Pérignon chef de cave Richard Geoffroy, '2007 was slight — it never happened!' Those who harvested later were rewarded with better expression and character. The greatest 2007 vintage champagnes today are Gosset Cuvée Celebris Rosé Extra Brut, and Pierre Péters Cuvée Spéciale Blanc de Blancs Les Chétillons, with more yet to be released.

2006 · 6/10

A soft, fruity, approachable vintage, without particularly distinct structure, already at its peak at less than a decade of age. A warm June, record hot July, cold, rainy August and sunny September produced ripe, clean fruit of 10.2% average degrees potential and low acidity of just 7g/L. Moët & Chandon chef de cave Benoît Gouez says 2006 is about 'amplitude, volume and expansive mouthfeel', likening it to 1999. To Didier Gimonnet, it has the structure and 'clumsy richness' of 2005 and the minerality of 2004. The greatest 2006 vintage champagnes today are Deutz Amour de Deutz Rosé Brut, Emmanuel Brochet Extra Brut Premier Cru Millésime, Louis Roederer Cristal, Paul Bara Special Club Rosé, Pierre Péters Cuvée Spéciale Blanc de Blancs Les Chétillons and Taittinger Comtes de Champagne Blanc de Blancs, with more yet to be released.

2005 · 5/10

A hot, tricky season of overripe character and dry phenolic grip, lacking freshness and elegance, with most cuvées already at their peak at a decade of age. Extremes of heat spikes alternating with heavy rainfall triggered mildew attacks in July, though a cool August and mild September prompted an elongated harvest. Ultimately, a mature vintage of 9.8% degrees potential, with some pinot noir and meunier afflicted by botrytis. The greatest 2005 vintage champagnes today are Jacquesson Avize Champ Caïn Récolte Extra Brut, Jacquesson Aÿ Vauzelle Terme Récolte Extra Brut, Jacquesson Dizy Corne Bautray Récolte Extra Brut, Pierre Gimonnet & Fils Millésime de Collection Blanc de Blancs, Pierre Gimonnet & Fils Special Club Blanc de Blancs, Pierre Péters Cuvée Spéciale Blanc de Blancs Les Chétillons, Taittinger Comtes de Champagne Rosé, and more yet to be released.

2004 · 8/10

A magnificent vintage of fine aromatic profile, lightness, finesse, energy, mineral definition and terroir expression. Record high yields took everyone by surprise in producing champagnes of beauty and stamina. With energy in the vines in reserve after the tiny 2003 season, the enormous 2004 harvest was evidence that you can make great champagne from high yields, provided the vines are in balance. A warm, sunny July was followed by a cool, wet August, but the crucial first three weeks of September were idyllically sunny and dry, producing properly ripe fruit of well-structured acidity. 'One would expect that high yields would mean less minerality, but in 2004 we had both, testimony to the extraordinary terroir of Champagne!' exclaims Didier Gimonnet. The greatest 2004 vintage champagnes today are Billecart-Salmon Blanc de Blancs Brut, De Sousa Cuvée des Caudalies Grand Cru Millésime Brut, Dom Pérignon, Louis Roederer Cristal Rosé, Pierre

Péters Cuvée Spéciale Blanc de Blancs Les Chétillons, Pol Roger Cuvée Sir Winston Churchill, Taittinger Comtes de Champagne Blanc de Blancs, Veuve Clicquot La Grande Dame Brut, Veuve Clicquot La Grande Dame Rosé, and more yet to be released.

2003 · 2/10

A calamitous vintage of pronounced concentration, overripe flavour profile, low acidity and hard phenolic bitterness that leaves most cuvées finishing astringent, coarse, dry and short. The most devastating April frosts in 70 years decimated 43% of the crop, hitting Côte des Blancs chardonnay hardest, wiping out 90% of Avize and Le Mesnil-sur-Oger; in early June, violent hailstorms battered the Montagne de Reims and Vallée de la Marne. Summer was the hottest to ever hit Champagne, with a sweltering August averaging 10°C above the norm, shrivelling grapes like raisins, prompting the earliest start to harvest since 1822. Of what little fruit remained in the Marne, opulent, overripe pinot noir and meunier boasted high sugar levels and low acidity. 'The perfect description of a nightmare,' in the words of Charles Heidsieck chef de cave Cyril Brun. Dom Pérignon registered the lowest acidity it has ever recorded. Says Richard Geoffroy, '2003 is border territory for Champagne, as border as it can be'. This is not a vintage for the cellar, and most are now well past their prime. Krug is the grand exception that proves the rule, testimony to stringent selection and tiny production. The greatest 2003 vintage champagnes today are Gosset Cuvée Celebris Rosé Extra Brut, Krug Clos du Mesnil, Krug Vintage and Le Brun-Servenay Cuvée Chardonnay Brut Millésime Vielles Vignes.

2002 · 9/10

A benchmark harvest that balances finesse, power and structure like no other in Champagne's recent history. The best wines possess decades of potential. A well-mannered season of continental climatic influence, with perfect harvest conditions from 10 September of dry, sunny days fostering ripe fruit intensity, and cool nights maintaining acidities a fraction below average. 'The 2002 was revenge for the challenging 2001, with nature giving everything that it withheld!' exclaims Piper-Heidsieck chef de cave Régis Camus. Didier Gimonnet considers it the greatest vintage since 1990, 'exemplifying the ultimate balance between elegance, concentration and freshness, nearly the best wine we could obtain in this domain'. It's impossible to list all the greatest 2002 vintage champagnes, but the very

best today are Billecart-Salmon Cuvée Elisabeth Salmon Brut Rosé, Billecart-Salmon Cuvée Nicolas François Billecart, Dom Pérignon, Jacquesson Aÿ Vauzelle Terme Recolte Brut, Pol Roger Cuvée Sir Winston Churchill, Taittinger Comtes de Champagne Blanc de Blancs, with more yet to come.

2001 · 1/10

Olivier Krug rates 2001 as Champagne's worst vintage in two decades. A dire season of incessant rain from early in the season all the way through to harvest, with particularly violent rain and hail from the latter part of July destroying 800 hectares across 55 communes. A cold September was accompanied by torrential rain and less sun than Champagne had seen in 45 years, cementing the fate of the season, diluting the wines and producing low ripeness of just 8.5% degrees potential. Virtually no vintage wines were produced.

2000 · 7/10

A warm, voluptuously ripe year of deep colour and rich fruit well suited to early drinking, with many cuvées now a deep yellow hue and quickly coming to the end of their peak. Dubbed *gourmandise orageuse* — stormy indulgence — by Krug, 2000 was a tumultuous season delivering some of the most destructive hailstorms ever to lash Champagne, with 2900 hectares completely devastated across 114 communes. Warm, dry conditions arrived in August, after a hot June and cold July, and held out throughout harvest, producing abundant, large grapes, blessed with above-average levels of sugar (9.8% degrees potential), slightly lower than average acidities, and very little disease. The greatest 2000 vintage champagnes today are Billecart-Salmon Cuvée Nicolas François Billecart, Billecart-Salmon Cuvée Elisabeth Salmon Brut Rosé, Bollinger La Grande Année, Dom Pérignon Rosé, Duval-Leroy Femme de Champagne, Krug Clos du Mesnil, Krug Vintage, Pierre Péters Cuvée Spéciale Blanc de Blancs Les Chétillons, Pol Roger Cuvée Sir Winston Churchill, and Taittinger Comtes de Champagne Blanc de Blancs.

1999 · 6/10

A fruity, soft season lacking acid drive, with most cuvées now past their prime; a warm vintage of continental climatic influence, recording Champagne's hottest summer since 1959 (though 2003 trumped it), and higher than usual rainfall. Harvest started optimistically, but hopes were diluted by heavy, persistent rain.

The Champagne Guide

The result was a vintage of high maturity and low malic acidity (just 6.5g/L total acidity), likened to 1989 by Jean-Baptiste Lécaillon. The greatest 1999 vintage champagnes today are Billecart-Salmon Blanc de Blancs Brut, Billecart-Salmon Le Clos Sainte-Hilaire, Bollinger La Grande Année Rosé, Larmandier-Bernier Special Club, Pol Roger Cuvée Sir Winston Churchill, Salon Cuvée S Blanc de Blancs, and Taittinger Comtes de Champagne Blanc de Blancs.

1998 · 7/10

The most enduring cuvées of 1998 retain elegant freshness amidst the expressive presence of the season, though lesser cuvées are now tired and heavy. Evidence that it is ultimately the weather at harvest that bears the strongest influence on the calibre of the vintage, 1998 followed a dismal progression of a wet, rot-inducing July, debilitating August heatwave, and rain storms in early September. It was not until mid-September that the weather finally delivered warm, dry conditions for harvest. Balanced ripeness of 9.8% degrees potential and strong acid levels of 9.8g/L came as the first surprise; the unwavering stamina of the best cuvées of the season the second. The greatest 1998 vintage champagnes today are Billecart-Salmon Cuvée Nicolas François Billecart, Billecart-Salmon Grande Cuvée, Billecart-Salmon Le Clos Saint-Hilaire, Dom Pérignon P2, Gosset Cuvée Celebris Extra Brut Vintage, Gosset Cuvée Celebris Rosé Brut, Krug Clos du Mesnil, Krug Clos d'Ambonnay, Krug Vintage, Piper-Heidsieck Rare Millesime, Pol Roger Cuvée Sir Winston Churchill, Taittinger Comtes de Champagne Blanc de Blancs, and Veuve Clicquot La Grande Dame Brut.

1997 · 4/10

The least vintage of the latter years of that century, 1997 was a ripe, rounded, accessible season, forever lost between the memory of 1996 and 1998. A tough lead-up to harvest saw 1997 plagued by frost, hail, uneven set and rot, producing the lowest yields since 1985. A hot July and very warm August were finally rescued by a bone-dry harvest, producing a high 10.2% degrees potential, and surprisingly good acidities for such ripeness. Salon registered acidity on equal par with 1996, infusing freshness and brightness. Few vintage wines were released; most are now well past their peak. The most notable exceptions are Jacquesson Avize Dégorgement Tardif Extra Brut, Salon Cuvée S Blanc de Blancs, and Pierre Péters Cuvée Spéciale Blanc de Blancs Les Chétillons.

1996 · 10/10

One of Champagne's most enduring, spectacular and lauded vintages, with both acidity and ripeness in extreme proportions, rendering its wines unbalanced in their youth. They are only beginning to find their poise after two decades, and the best will effortlessly endure for a lifetime. This vintage has gone down in history as the perfect 10/10 season of 10° potential alcohol and 10g/L acidity — to this day the highest acidity ever recorded for Dom Pérignon. A less than ideal summer alternating between rain and intense heat was followed by rain until 20 September, then clear, sunny days, cool nights, and a strong north wind. This wind proved the key to the vintage, not only evaporating the threat of rot but, crucially, dehydrating the grapes and concentrating sugar and acidity to levels not seen since 1928. Quickly hailed among the greatest vintages of all time, some have since raised reservations, as some cuvées matured in flavour before their intense acidities softened. No such fear for the finest cuvées, the best of which are only now coming into their own, with glorious years of potential stretching ahead. The greatest 1996 vintage champagnes today are Billecart-Salmon Grande Cuvée, Bollinger R.D. Extra Brut, Dom Pérignon Oenothèque, Duval-Leroy Femme de Champagne, René Geoffroy Cuvée Autrefois, Henriot La Cuvée des Enchanteleurs, Krug Vintage, Larmandier-Bernier Special Club, Louis Roederer Brut Rosé, Pierre Péters Cuvée Spéciale Blanc de Blancs Les Chétillons, Pol Roger Cuvée Sir Winston Churchill, Salon Cuvée S Blanc de Blancs, and Taittinger Comtes de Champagne Rosé.

1995 · 8/10

A vintage of elegant opulence, refined power and classic endurance, marvellously evidenced in a set of cuvées that have attained a lofty magnificence at 20 years of age, with a bright future stretching before them. Long forgotten in the shadow of 1996, 1995 is more classic and arguably more consistent, if less showy. This was Champagne's finest season since 1990, with a hot, dry summer accelerating maturity, and a sunny, late harvest furnishing good ripeness of 9.2% degrees potential and normal acidity levels. In 2014 Didier Gimonnet hosted a tasting with the French press to ascertain the best vintage of the 1990s. After 1990 was deemed too rich and 1996 too acidic, the winner was 1995. The greatest 1995 vintage champagnes today are Charles Heidsieck Blanc des Millénaires, Dom Pérignon P2 Rosé, Jacquesson Dégorgement Tardif Extra Brut Millésime, Louis Roederer Cristal, and Salon Cuvée S Blanc de Blancs.

DOWN TO EARTH

On a small range of hills rising less than impressively from a chalk plain 145 kilometres north-east of Paris lies the patchwork of 33,700 hectares of vineyards that is Champagne. Too exposed to wind and rain and not sufficiently blessed by the sun, there is no chance of ripening grapes on the flatter land here. And yet this land sends a shiver down my spine every time I come close. By some miracle, its drab hillsides produce fruits that thousands of winegrowers around the globe strive desperately to emulate, yet none have equalled.

Austere and impoverished soft white chalk is Champagne's secret, a remnant of an ancient seabed. Cool, damp cellars are easily hewn from it, and the score marks of their Roman creators are still visible 17 centuries later. Its true blessing is espoused in the vineyards, bestowing its fruits with crystalline minerality, reflecting and storing heat and retaining moisture — a perfectly regulated vine humidifier.

Champagne comprises five districts.

THE MONTAGNE DE REIMS

The Montagne de Reims is no mountain — more a wooded hillock, rising to an unimpressive 180 metres above the surrounding plains and just 275 metres above sea level. Yet even this elevation is sufficient to orientate some of Champagne's mightiest vineyards. The vines of the Montagne de Reims follow the slope of a hillside topped with dense forest, in a backward 'C' formation from Villers-Allerand on the northern slopes, reaching a crescendo in the thundering grand crus of Bouzy and Ambonnay in the south. These stand alongside Verzenay as the Montagne de Reims' finest villages. Pinot noir is king of these chalky sites, and nowhere in Champagne produces its equal. There are also substantial plantings of meunier, and chardonnay is on the rise.

The 'Petite Montagne' is a north-western extension of the Montagne de Reims, extending north of Reims itself, nurturing Champagne's most northerly vineyards on soils of sand and clay, well suited to meunier.

CÔTE DES BLANCS

Chardonnay is left largely to the Côte des Blancs, 96% of which is planted to the variety, the remainder largely pinot noir in the commune of Vertus in the south.

This region has again put forward a large proportion of highlights in this year's guide. With dramatic slopes, warmer days and thinner topsoils making chalk more accessible than anywhere else in the region, the Côte des Blancs produces Champagne's most regular fruit, and its most reliable, exhilarating and mineral-infused wines. This is why many are sold unblended as blanc de blancs. These are among the most searingly structured and long-lived wines of Champagne. There is perhaps no village in Champagne capable of standing alone as confidently as Le Mesnil-sur-Oger, though Cramant, Avize, Oger and the premier cru of Vertus command great respect.

VALLÉE DE LA MARNE

More than half of the Vallée de la Marne is planted to meunier, although pinot noir plantings are on the increase. The south-facing sites of Aÿ and Mareuil-sur-Aÿ towards its eastern end rival the great grand crus of the Montagne de Reims. Its cooler western reaches of clay soils are exclusively the territory of meunier, easier to grow and ripen than pinot noir and chardonnay.

CÔTE DE SÉZANNE

The Côte de Sézanne is a little way south of the Côte des Blancs and shares the same south-east orientation and dominance of chardonnay. Its soils are heavier and its wines more rustic.

CÔTE DES BAR

More than 100 kilometres south-east of the Côte des Blancs, the outpost of the Aube (Côte des Bar) is closer to Burgundy than to Reims. Pinot noir is the principal grape here, comprising four-fifths of the region's plantings, producing vigorous and more rustic wines. Planted largely during the late 1980s, vine maturity is now in step with the rest of the region, and the Aube has enjoyed significant increases in quality in recent years. Its finest villages are Celles-sur-Ource, Les Riceys and Urville.

The chef in the cellar
How champagne is made

Champagne must be the most successfully processed creation in all of agricultural history, through a convoluted, painstaking method designed expressly to transform an insipidly austere and undrinkably acidic juice into the most celebrated beverage in the world. Every element of the champagne process is geared towards making its searing acidity less challenging — bubbles, yeast, chaptalisation, dosage, blending and ageing. The genius of champagne production calls on more tricks than any other wine style to create flavour, complexity and balance. The traditional method by which this is achieved is known as Méthode Traditionnelle.

Pressing

How can white wine be made from the dark-skinned grapes of pinot noir and meunier? The secret is careful, selective harvesting and immediate, gentle pressing, to avoid staining the clear juice. All grapes in Champagne are handpicked and gently pressed nearby as whole bunches in four-tonne lots. By law, only the first 2550 litres of juice from every four tonnes of grapes may be used. On current yields, this equates to an average production of 10,000 bottles per hectare.

The *coeur de la cuvée*, the 'heart of the cuvée', is the middle of the pressing, yielding the purest juice.

The tailles — coarser, inferior juice that flows last from the press — is used in varying levels according to the house style, and rarely at all in the finest cuvées.

Settling

Débourbage is the settling of solids and impurities from the must (pressed grape juice), allowing clear juice to be drawn off from the top.

This process is taken to another level by the houses of Billecart-Salmon and Pol Roger, who perform a second settling of the must at cold temperature, producing particularly exquisite and fresh champagnes.

First fermentation

The 'alcoholic' fermentation of champagne takes place in stainless steel tanks. Traditional oak barrels are coming back into vogue for fermentation and/or maturation, to increase suppleness, texture, power and complexity. The 'degrees potential' ripeness at which grapes are picked roughly equates to the potential alcohol of the finished wine. Most champagne producers 'chaptalise' prior to fermentation by adding sugar or concentrated grape juice to increase the alcoholic strength. Some makers 'inoculate' the ferment with cultured yeasts, while others rely on wild yeasts.

Malolactic fermentation

Malolactic fermentation converts tart 'malic' (green apple) acid into softer 'lactic' (dairy) acid. This process is practised by most houses to soften their wines. Notable exceptions include Gosset, Lanson and Salon.

With the advent of warmer vintages, an increasing number of houses are experimenting with blocking malolactic fermentation.

Assemblage

Skilful blending is Champagne's answer to its erratic seasons. Challenging vintages are handled by blending wines from different vineyards, different vintages (reserve wines) and different grapes.

Champagne is usually a blend of chardonnay (for structure, elegance and finesse), pinot noir (for perfume, body and richness) and meunier (for plump fruitiness). Blanc de blancs ('white wine from white grapes') is usually chardonnay, and blanc de noirs ('white wine from red grapes') usually pinot noir/meunier.

The key distinguishing factor between champagne houses lies in the cuvée — the blend created in assembling different wines. There is no skill in the winemaking world that I envy more than that of the chef de cave in blending a fine champagne, uniting different ingredients according to each harvest in a blend today that must be consistent with the house style when it emerges from the cellar in years to come.

RESERVE WINES (FOR NV BLENDS)

Non-vintage wines are deepened by a portion of older vintage 'reserve' wines stored in tank, barrel or bottle. These are crucial for maintaining consistency in Champagne's wildly fluctuating seasons.

TIRAGE

Prior to bottling, a *liqueur de tirage* of sugar and wine is added (see 'Second fermentation', further down).

BOTTLING

Wines are bottled and sealed under crown seal, or occasionally cork. They may be filtered and cold stabilised at this time to remove any solids.

SECOND FERMENTATION

The sugar added to champagne prior to bottling induces a secondary fermentation in the bottle known as the *prise de mousse*. Under the pressure of a sealed bottle, the carbon dioxide produced dissolves in the wine, creating sparkling wine. The finer the still wine and the cooler the cellar in which this fermentation occurs, the smaller the bubbles. Larger bottles ferment more slowly — one reason why magnums are superior and half bottles are inferior to standard bottles. A finer bead is an indicator of quality.

MATURATION

Acidity is the key to champagne, but its astringency makes these wines unapproachable in their youth. The mellowing, softening effect of age is crucial to the champagne style. Dead yeast cells ('lees') from the second fermentation remain in the bottle and contribute subtly to champagne's complexity. The longer this process of 'autolysis' persists the better, improving mouthfeel and longevity, and adding biscuity, bready nuances to the flavour profile.

The mandatory minimum in champagne is 15 months for non-vintage and three years for vintage wines, but reputable producers always far exceed these minima, typically ageing non-vintage cuvées 3–4 years, vintage cuvées 7–8 years, and prestige cuvées sometimes 10 years or more.

RIDDLING (*REMUAGE*)

In the early 19th century, Antoine Müller, cellar master of the widow Clicquot (Veuve Clicquot), invented a method of cleaning the wine of the sediment created when it ferments in bottle, without losing its bubbles. A wooden desk (*pupitre*) pierced with holes holds the mature bottles sideways. Each bottle is given a quarter-rotation every day, and slowly tilted from horizontal to upside down. The lees sediment collects in the neck of the bottle. This process of 'remuage' is performed by a 'riddler', who can turn 50,000–60,000 bottles every day!

In modern times, the riddling process has been taken over by gyropalettes in most champagne houses. These giant robotic arms slowly rotate large cages of bottles. The effect is the same, perhaps even more consistent, albeit without the romance.

A gyro can riddle a cage of bottles in as little as three days, but many estates use a longer cycle of a week or more.

DISGORGEMENT (*DÉGORGEMENT*)

After riddling, the sediment is settled on the inside of the cork or crown cap. The neck of the bottle is then frozen, the cap released, and the plug of sediment shot out (*dégorgement* in French), leaving perfectly clear wine behind.

DOSAGE (THE FINAL ADDITION)

To replace the volume lost through disgorgement, the bottle is topped up with sweetened wine (*liqueur d'expédition*) and a new cork is inserted.

'Zero dosage' champagnes are topped up with dry wine. See page 31 for dosage trends.

MAKING ROSÉ CHAMPAGNE

About 10% of champagne production is rosé, made in the same manner as white champagne, with a subtle difference. Colour is achieved in one of three ways.

Most commonly, a 'blending method' (*rosé d'assemblage*) is used, in which a tiny quantity of pinot noir or meunier (made as a table wine) is added — often only 5–10%, but sometimes as much as 20%. A rapid increase in demand for rosé has recently put pressure on supplies of quality red wine for blending in Champagne.

The *saignée* method adds free-run juice from just-crushed red grapes, producing the finest, palest wines. A 'limited maceration' method produces darker, heavier wines through a quick soak on red grape skins.

Rosé production is tricky, not only in marrying champagne's acidity with red wine tannin, but in determining the desired depth of colour long before it is set. Yeast is a highly effective fining agent, leaching colour during both primary and secondary fermentations.

CHALK IT UP
Minerality

*M*inerality is a strong candidate for the most elusive concept in wine tasting. Misconceptions abound. It's regarded by some to be an intangible character in wine, by others as an absence of fruit, an attempt to describe any element that isn't fruity, or even as the kerosene notes of mature riesling or other aromatic whites.

Minerality is categorically none of these things. Minerality is the texture and mouthfeel of a wine derived from its soil. It is every bit as tangible as acidity or tannin, albeit more elusive to measure and define.

The signature of minerality is articulated in champagne more eloquently than in any other wine. Minerality lifts a champagne off the two-dimensional page of aroma and flavour, inflating it into a three-dimensional, life-sized form of texture and feeling.

In the village of Avize, Pascal Agrapart describes the minerality of one of his most distinctive vineyards as reminiscent of blackboard chalk dust from his school days. Champagne is very much more than fruit and acid, sugar and bubbles. Minerality adds a structural intensity and a textural perspective, fine-grained in the Côte des Blancs, and more coarse in the Côte des Bar.

And it has another dimension, one of mineral personality. There are terroirs of Champagne of savoury minerality, of spicy minerality, of salty liquorice mineral texture in Vertus, of neutral minerality in the Montagne de Reims and, most pronounced of all, terroirs of the Côte des Blancs of salty minerality that heave and froth with the very waves of the sea that deposited its chalk subsoils millennia ago. Not with the fresh coastal seaspray hints of Bordeaux or Jerez but here, more than 200 kilometres from any sea, resonating with an ocean that receded 55 million years prior. Drinking champagne is not only a modern history lesson in recent vintages, villages and family backgrounds, but an ancient historical encounter with the very geology of the continent itself. Could a wine capture anything more profound?

The French put it better than we do. *L'eau de roche ou le sel de la terre* — 'the water of the rock (crystal) or the salt of the earth' — says fanatical terroirist Anselme Selosse of Jacques Selosse, whose roots are embedded firmly in the bedrock of Avize. 'In its purity, its trans-parency, its specificity, a great wine of terroir can only be of *l'eau de roche*,' he says. In nearby Le Mesnil-sur-Oger, grower Rodolphe Péters speaks of minerality of 'ocean flavours, oyster shells and sea salt'. His Le Mesnil vineyard Les Chétillons embodies this as dramatically as any in Champagne, with minerality that remains transfixed even after three decades of bottle age. 'It is a stake, it remains for a very long time,' he declares.

Minerality is the timeless fingerprint of the land. Acidity and sugar give voice to the vagaries of sun and sky, fruit derives its identity from the grape variety, but minerality speaks of a much more ancient origin, the soil itself, snapped into sharp focus in a cold climate. When we speak of terroir in its highest order we speak of cool places: the patchwork of Burgundy, riesling slopes of Germany, chalk of Sancerre, grand crus of Alsace, rolling hills of Barolo. Its expression in the fields of the southern Rhône, Provence, even the noble plains of Bordeaux, shares nothing of the same precision. The icy touch of Champagne, the coldest of all, awakens the soil and gives birth in its fruits.

The deeply chalk mineral slopes of Oger and Le Mesnil-sur-Oger.

Fizzers

Corked, oxidised and lightstruck

The inconsistent condition in which champagne reaches its markets is the single most significant factor impeding its quality today. I've had countless conversations and written a great deal on corked, oxidised and lightstruck champagnes over the past five years and, for the first time ever, I am delighted and relieved to report that dramatic change is at hand.

CORKED

Across my champagne tastings over many years, I've encountered 5–7% of bottles destroyed by cork taint. Imparted randomly by natural corks, cork taint gives a mouldy, 'wet cardboard' or 'wet dog' character to champagne. It suppresses fruit and shortens the length of finish. In its most subtle form, it may simply have a slight dulling effect on the bouquet and palate.

Of well over 1200 bottles that I tasted recently for this edition, just four were cork tainted: two Dom Pérignons, one Geoffroy and one old Moët & Chandon. This equates to well under 0.5%, a remarkable turnaround. Did I just happen to get lucky, or is it possible that Champagne is finally on track to solving its cork taint crisis?

Houses that have made a serious commitment to eradicating cork taint have demonstrated that it is indeed possible to eradicate this sinister threat. One in six champagnes is now sealed with Mytik DIAM, a micro-agglomerate closure moulded from granulated fragments of cork which have been treated to extract cork taint and some 150 other molecules that might produce 'off' characters. I have never seen cork taint in any DIAM-sealed wine.

There is hope even for those houses that uphold an attachment to natural corks. 'Cork suppliers are well aware of batches afflicted with higher levels of taint and mix these through good batches to maintain acceptable averages,' I was informed by a former head of the CIVC Research & Development unit, and long-standing chef de cave for several significant houses. 'Most houses use 1.5% cork taint as the threshold for rejecting a batch of corks, but the lower the rate demanded, the better the corks supplied.'

Louis Roederer tests 460 corks in every batch of 100,000. This is repeated for 200 batches every year, and sometimes a batch is tested twice. If a single tainted cork is found, the entire batch is rejected. The company rejects one batch in three. No doubt this is why, in all my years of tasting, I've only ever found one cork-tainted bottle of Roederer. If only every house were so stringent in its cork testing.

If you encounter a cork-tainted bottle, always take it back and request a replacement.

OXIDISED

Champagne is the most fragile of all wine styles, and particularly susceptible to degradation in contact with oxygen. Oxidation shows itself in champagne as premature development, flattening fruit expression, contributing characters of burnt orange or vinegar, and drying out the finish. It can occur before a champagne is bottled, at disgorgement, or after it is shipped, losing freshness from sealing faults, poor transportation, bad storage conditions or simply sitting on the shelf too long.

Oxidation is the biggest threat to the consistency of champagne today. In my tastings for this guide, significant degradation from oxidation afflicted 45 in 685 cuvées, more than 6.5%. I have only counted seriously oxidised cuvées, not those simply stale and fruit-flat. Champagne's oxidation problem outranks its cork taint issue by an order of magnitude. Of these 45 cuvées, almost one-third represented random oxidation (the next bottle opened was pristine), most likely due to an inconsistent cork or, occasionally, DIAM. Just four of the 45 could be put down to old age (greater than 15 years of age), though the vast majority (30 cuvées in all) were non-vintage.

Long barrel ageing and a low-sulphur regime make wines in the cellar of Jacques Selosse particularly susceptible to oxidation.

Champagne's oxidation predicament is aggravated on two fronts. Winemakers use sulphur dioxide as a preservative to protect wine from oxidation, and there is an alarming trend among some Champagne growers to reduce or even eliminate its use. At the same time, increasing use of oak barrels provides more opportunity for oxygen contact during base wine ageing. Long barrel ageing with a low sulphur regime is the most dangerous mix, exemplified most dramatically this year by Jacques Selosse (four oxidised cuvées) and Georges Laval (three oxidised).

Oxidation is appropriately a hot topic in champagne commentary right now, but we do well to exercise a level of moderation. In December 2013, British wine writer Tom Stevenson singled out Bollinger and Gosset among the 'most overrated champagne producers' for 'serious oxidation problems'. I have investigated both houses meticulously, poring over the technical specifications of their wines (including independent lab results), visiting both houses to observe their processes during harvest and, most importantly, tasting every cuvée over and over in different markets, even leaving opened bottles for days and weeks to examine their deterioration. With the exception of a single aberrant bottle of Bollinger

R.D. 2002, I am convinced that neither Bollinger nor Gosset suffers from oxidation. To the contrary, both houses are currently at the top of their games.

LIGHTSTRUCK

There is another factor that plagues champagne freshness. Did you know that if you leave a bottle in the light it might taste like onions, garlic or cabbage?

'Lightstruck' is the menacing effect of degradation of wine exposed to ultraviolet light from fluorescent lamps and, worse, sunlight. There is no wine more susceptible to lightstruck than champagne in clear glass bottles, diminishing citrus aromas and producing reductive characters such as sulphur, corn, gherkin, bacon, gunsmoke or burnt rubber.

Lightstruck can even deteriorate champagne in your glass. One afternoon in the middle of a recent Brisbane winter, Moët & Chandon chef de cave Benoît Gouez poured me a glass of his 2006 Vintage on a sunny upstairs balcony. In just five minutes it was lightstruck and he immediately summonsed a repour.

Keep your bottles in the dark, and if they come in a box, cellophane or bag, keep them covered until they're opened. As always, return any bottle that's out of condition.

HOUSE RULES
The 'grower versus house' fallacy

The stark distinction drawn around the world between Champagne négociant houses, cooperatives and grower producers is perplexing. Champagne drinkers who pop only the household names of the big brands miss an important dimension of the great diversity of Champagne's finest offerings. Those who hunt fanatically for nothing but small growers miss an equally exciting experience. The very notion of imposing such a division undermines the complex and diverse relationships between champagne brands and the vineyards from which they are sourced. In Champagne itself, there is no such segregation, and its very suggestion is vigorously dismissed by both sides.

'We need to change this stupid, simplistic view of the market!' exclaims chef de cave Jean-Baptiste Lécaillon, who blends Louis Roederer's vintage cuvées exclusively from estate sources. 'There are some champagne growers who are more négociants than growers, and some négociants who are more growers than négociants.' The lines are blurring as négociants increasingly purchase vineyards, growers source from many villages rather than just their own, and cooperatives focus increasingly on selling their own brands.

Many houses are following the lead of growers in launching single-vineyard and zero-dosage cuvées; the first new Louis Roederer cuvée in 40 years achieves both at once. 'We hear so much about the growers being able to make no dosage because they have the grapes, and the négociants can't do it because they need to use dosage to hide a lack of quality,' explains Lécaillon. 'So we wanted to make this cuvée to show that we can do it. It's not that growers make their wines in the vineyard and négociants make their wines in the cellar.'

When celebrated Vertus growers Pierre and Sophie Larmandier established their 'Trait d'Union' group of like-minded growers to promote their brands together, they invited the house of Jacquesson to join them. 'It's very easy to have an "us and them" approach — but this is not in the spirit of Champagne,' says Pierre. 'We wanted Jacquesson to be part of our group as they share many philosophies of growers.'

Jacquesson's Jean-Hervé Chiquet protested when Paris wine merchant Cave Augé positioned his house with the négociants and excluded his cuvées from its grower tastings. 'Twenty years ago, the growers and négociants occupied two totally different worlds, even socially — a hangover from the 20th century, when the big, rich négociants bought fruit from poor, little growers,' he explains. 'But now the gap is closing fast. For years it was the houses making the best wines and promoting the category, but now this separation does not exist — it is a completely different approach.'

Deep friendships and respect exist between even the largest houses and smallest growers. 'It's my view that we are not competitors, we are in the same boat, with different philosophies and styles, and it is important that Champagne maintains its diversity,' emphasises Veuve Clicquot chef de cave Dominique Demarville. 'It is not a question of good wine or not.'

Any qualitative attempt to distinguish between estate-grown and purchased fruit is tenuous at best. 'When we blend Comtes de Champagne, we forget the origin of the vats,' explains Taittinger deputy general manager, Damien Le Sueur. 'We have vats from our own vineyards, vats from growers which we vinify, and vats vinified by others, and we taste them anonymously. The blend we choose often happens to be about half from our own vineyards and half from others.'

Even among the smallest producers, the récoltant-manipulant label is not as highly prized as might be imagined. The acclaimed little 9.5 hectare estate of Bérêche et Fils recently relinquished its récoltant title in favour of négociant status, to open up the flexibility to purchase more vineyards and buy from other growers.

This book makes no attempt to segregate champagne producers into intrinsically simplistic and prejudiced categories of houses, cooperatives and grower producers.

Just a spoonful of sugar

The searing levels of acidity inherent in grapes grown in Champagne's bitterly cold climate scream out for a little sweetness to temper their impact. In the final stage of the champagne process, the bottle is topped up with 'dosage' — usually a mixture of wine and sugar syrup. Over the centuries, dosage levels have gradually lowered, and in recent years the catchcry seems to have become 'how low can you go?' Is progressively lower dosage really the most delightful way for champagne?

Two hundred years ago, champagne was as sweet as dessert wine today, sometimes with as much as 330g/L of sugar, more than twice the sweetness of Coca-Cola!

'The most brilliant idea of the centuries has been to make champagne an apéritif instead of a dessert wine — a genius idea!' exclaims Veuve Clicquot chef de cave, Dominique Demarville. 'If we were still a dessert wine, we would be nothing.'

Until recently, to qualify as 'brut', champagne required less than 15g/L of sweetness — a little less than a teaspoon of sugar in a cup of coffee. This has now been lowered to a maximum of 12g/L. 'Extra brut' requires less than 6g/L, and 'brut nature' or 'brut zero' less than 3g/L, since even wines of zero dosage usually have a touch of sweetness remaining from fermentation.

Antoine Roland-Billecart of Billecart-Salmon likens dosage to make-up. 'If there are no problems and you want to show the real character of the wine, you don't need a high dosage,' he says. 'The significant decrease in dosage over the past decade has been very important in allowing the fruit to show to its full capacity.'

We should all raise a glass to celebrate Champagne's low-sugar diet, and to many of the region's most fanatical houses and growers who have progressively refined their wines with lower dosage. Sweetness can mask many evils, and for too long Champagne has notoriously bolstered inferior fruit with excessive sugar.

Champagne's sweet dreams may be a thing of the past, but has it all gone too far? 'Zero dosage' is all the rage, and the intent of the 'Coke Zero' movement of the wine world is certainly noble, but too many champagne brands have joined the parade simply because it's the thing to do. Dogmatically slashing dosage to zero purely for the sake of branding is self-defeating.

'We're going to see more wines with lower dosage, but dosage is crucial for balance,' points out Demar-ville. 'Many are simply releasing their brut NV without dosage, but to make it well it must be a special blend.'

A carefully tweaked low dosage is not designed to make a wine taste sweet. The effect of just 5g/L (a spoonful of sugar in an entire bottle) can be astounding. Floral aromas are lifted, the palate is softened and more harmonious, the fruit is more expressive and, in the most delightful way, it doesn't taste sweet. Sugar also builds longevity, reacting with amino acids to give roasted, honeyed characters.

Champagne's most progressive makers carefully tweak the dosage of every cuvée, every year, to create a precise balance. Sometimes zero dosage is the right answer, but let's not become so caught up in the fanfare that we miss the many excellent brut and extra brut wines on the shelves. The majority of Champagne's most refined wines this year have a dosage of 4–8g/L.

Some houses have made the mistake of simply releasing their standard cuvée without any dosage, usually with thin, insipid results. Only the most fanatical houses can pull this off successfully. When François Domi blended Billecart-Salmon's Extra Brut, he started with the Brut Réserve and experimented with dosages of 0–8g/L, settling on zero for 'the best expression of delicacy, finesse and elegance'.

More often, the most balanced zero-dosage wines are custom-built from the ground up. When Pol Roger blends its Pure Brut it avoids components with high acidity, favouring those with more floral aromas.

Has the 'no added sugar' campaign of Champagne run its full course? Suggestions are emerging that the market has been put off by harsh acidity, and the zero-dosage trend is beginning to wane.

With warmer vintages to contend with, will chaptalisation by the addition of sugar prior to fermentation be the next thing to go?

AWASH WITH BUBBLES
How to serve champagne

CHAMPAGNE GLASSES

Using decent glassware is essential for fully appreciating wine, and all the more for champagne.

How important? 'We worked with wine glass company Riedel for more than a year to develop a glass which was ideal for Krug Grande Cuvée,' Olivier Krug told me. 'They proposed 26 glasses and I would take them home to try with my wife until very late at night!'

The more I visit and taste with the Champenois, the more I appreciate the way a large glass draws a champagne out of itself. Champagne holds its bead longest in an elongated glass, but don't select one so narrow that you can't get your nose in to appreciate the bouquet. 'It's not just about the bubbles. Champagne is a wine, not just scenery!' says Duval-Leroy Sales Manager Michel Brismontier, who serves champagne in normal wine glasses rather than flutes.

The Champenois prefer slightly wider glasses than typical champagne flutes, to allow their finest cuvées sufficient space to open out. Think halfway between a flute and a fine white wine glass. All good glasses curve in slightly at the top. The finer the glass, the better they

The 11°C and 95% humidity cellars of Deutz under Aÿ.

look at the table, and the less the champagne will warm up when you pour it. Cut, engraved or coloured glasses make it harder to appreciate the wine's appearance.

The glass I use most often is the Riedel Vinum XL Champagne. This is the largest glass I've found, with a bowl of white wine glass proportions that draws down into the stem sufficiently to produce a focused stream of bubbles. Moët & Chandon use these as their tasting glass and tell me they were designed in the 1960s. They'll set you back as much as a bottle of non-vintage champagne (each!), making for an expensive but worthwhile investment in champagne enjoyment.

My second-favourite glass is one-fifth of the price. The Luigi Bormioli Magnifico Flute is very nearly as large as the Riedel and just a little heavier. If you can't find these, grab a medium-sized white wine glass over a champagne flute for any serious bottle of fizz.

The traditional flat champagne 'coupe' glasses are now practically unheard of in Champagne, except in historical ceremony. They are inferior because the large surface area evaporates both bead and aroma rapidly. The wide, flanged rim means that the wine is spilled to the sides of the tongue, where sensitivity to acidity is heightened.

It's paramount that there is not the slightest residue of detergent in the glass, as this will instantly destroy the mousse (bubbles) and the taste. Riedel recommends washing under warm water without detergent, and polishing with microfibre towels. Never dry a glass by holding the base and twisting the bowl, as this may snap the stem.

SERVING TEMPERATURE

'The temperature of service is very important,' emphasises Oliver Krug, who admits to being obsessed with the quality of service. 'We may work for 10 or 20 years to create Grande Cuvée, ship it in the best refrigerated container, and then you might be served the first Krug of your life in a stupid flute as cold as ice, and you miss 99% of the pleasure and the message!'

Antoine Roland-Billecart of Billecart-Salmon says wine is like a human being in the cold. 'Put yourself out in the snow and you won't show anything either, you'll be all covered up!' he says. 'Three degrees breaks everything in champagne. It should be served at cellar temperature, and never below 8°C.' Cellar temperature for the Champenois means 10°C.

Champagne is often served much too cold. Poured at fridge temperature, it will taste flavourless and acidic. The only exceptions are particularly sweet styles, which are best toned down with a stern chill. In general, the finer the wine, the warmer I tend to serve it. The Champenois suggest 8–10°C for non-vintage and rosé styles, and 10–12°C for vintage and prestige wines.

If you're pulling a bottle out of a climate-controlled cellar, it will need to be cooled a little further, so pop it in the fridge for half an hour. If it's at room temperature to start with, 3–4 hours in the fridge or 15 minutes in an ice bucket might be in order. On a warm day, serve champagne a touch cooler, as it will soon warm up.

Always hold a champagne glass by its base or stem, to avoid warming the wine in your hand. This will also reduce the likelihood of any aromas on your hands interfering with its delicate bouquet.

AGE AND CELLARING

Twenty-year-old champagne is one of my favourite indulgences, and a top vintage wine or prestige cuvée will comfortably go the distance. Generally, aim to drink vintage champagnes between eight and 15 years after vintage, and non-vintage wines within five years. Most entry-level NVs have little to gain from bottle ageing, but exceptions are noted throughout this guide. Late-disgorged vintages are held on lees in the cellar and can improve over many decades.

Late-disgorged champagne is generally best consumed within a few years of disgorgement, as it doesn't tend to cellar confidently post-disgorgement. 'Disgorgement is a shock for a wine, like a human going into surgery,' explains Antoine Roland-Billecart. 'When you're young, you recover much better. When an old champagne is disgorged, it may oxidise.' This is why Billecart disgorges its museum stock at the same time as its standard releases. Different houses have different philosophies, and there are always exceptions. I've tasted very old late-disgorged bottles that have held up magnificently five years after disgorgement.

Champagne spends the first years of its life in a dark, humid, chalk cellar under Champagne at a constant temperature of 8–10°C, so it will get a rude shock if it's thrust into a warmer environment. Champagne is highly fussy when it comes to proper cellaring conditions and, unless you live somewhere particularly cold, if you don't have a climate-controlled cellar, err on the side of caution and drink it within a few years.

Champagne in clear glass bottles is remarkably light sensitive, so keep it in the dark at all times. If it comes in a box, bag or cellophane wrap, keep it covered until you serve it. See page 29 for more on the effects of light on champagne.

HOW TO OPEN A BOTTLE OF BUBBLY

Opening a champagne bottle is pretty easy, but some people make such a fuss about it that they end up stuffing it up altogether. There are a few basic points to grasp before spraying your friends with fizz.

First, ensure that nobody has shaken the bottle before you get hold of it (not funny!). Always have a target glass nearby to pour the first gush into, but not too close (I once inadvertently shot the bowl clean off one of those expensive Riedels with a stray cork!). Check the firing range for chandeliers and unsuspecting passers-by and re-aim if necessary.

Remove the capsule using the pull-tab, if it has one. Hold the bottle at 45 degrees and remove the cage with six half-turns of the wire, keeping your thumb firmly over the end of the cork, in case it attempts to fire out of the bottle. I prefer to loosen the cage and leave it on the cork, which can assist with grip.

Twist the bottle (not the cork) slowly and ease the cork out gently. If you encounter a stubborn, young cork, use a clean tea towel to improve your grip. When the cork is almost out, tilt it sideways to release the gas slowly. It should make a gentle hiss, not an ostentatious pop. This is important, as it maintains the maximum bead (bubbles) in the wine and reduces the risk of a dramatic gush.

HOW TO POUR CHAMPAGNE

Check that the wine tastes right, then pour half a glass for each drinker, topping them up after the 'mousse' has subsided. You can choose to tilt the glass to minimise frothing — I do. Sparkling wine is the only style where you can break the rule of never more than half-filling a glass, but do leave sufficient room for your nose so you can appreciate the bouquet!

The Champenois sometimes recommend decanting champagne. This does offer some advantages in encouraging older or more robust champagnes to open up, but I have never been successful without losing most of the bubbles.

AGRAPART & FILS

(A-gra-pah e Feess)

7/10

57 Avenue Jean Jaurès 51190 Avize

www.champagne-agrapart.com

'If we have good grapes we have good wines,' is Pascal Agrapart's refreshing philosophy. While many others rigidly pursue regimes in the vineyard and winery because that's the way it's always been done, or is the latest fad, the ethos and practice of Agrapart are quite the antithesis. This fanatical Avize grower upholds practices not far from organics or biodynamics, yet has never sought certification under either, preferring to maintain the freedom to listen sensitively to the rhythm of the seasons and respond to the benefit of his vines. His restless pursuit of a detailed expression of place is articulated in the purity and crystalline mineral expression of his wines.

In Champagne it is a rare claim to be the fourth generation to produce champagne from one's own vineyards. Yet Pascal and brother Fabrice Agrapart do so not with a staid reliance on the ways of their forebears, but with a progressive and at times courageous sense of spontaneity.

Inspired by Burgundy to make wines of character true to their place, Agrapart upholds terroir as being more important than variety. Chardonnay comprises 95% of almost 10 hectares of enviable estate plantings, mainly in the grand crus of Avize, Oger, Cramant and Oiry, divided across 62 plots of vines of an impressive average age of 40 years — some more than 65 years.

Every effort is focused on encouraging the roots of these old vines into the mother rock to draw out the mineral character of each site. Vineyard management is painstakingly eco-friendly, with no chemical pesticides or herbicides used. Vineyards are ploughed to break up surface roots, aerate the soil and maintain microbial life, while organic fertilisers, compost and manure are adapted according to soil analyses.

Pascal Agrapart upholds that '25% of the wine is made by the soil and 25% by the weather', and points out that the micro-climates are very different in each of his parcels. This poses a greater challenge to an organic regime than would a single site.

'I don't want to have certification because I want to be able to plough the soil when I can, and use chemicals when I need to,' he says. The disease threat of the wet 2012 vintage necessitated chemical treatments.

Agrapart works his 1959 vines in his 'La Fosse' vineyard in Avize only by hand and horse, and he's more down-to-earth about this than anyone else I've met in Champagne. 'There is no compacting of the soil, and perhaps there is more oxygen and microbial life, and perhaps the roots go deeper, and perhaps there is more minerality in the wine. Perhaps, perhaps! Perhaps it is better — and perhaps it's just sentimental!'

Each winemaking element is designed to preserve the detail of the vineyard. Sensitive, intelligent use of large, old oak for vinification, and ageing of finer parcels for vintage wines and non-vintage reserves are not for woody flavour, but oxidation — for Agrapart, 'oxidation is not the enemy of wine'. He buys five-year-old barrels from Burgundy and the Loire and maintains them until they're very old. Larger 600-litre puncheons are favoured, for a higher ratio of wine to wood.

Wild yeasts from the vineyards further draw out the character of each site. Full malolactic fermentation is encouraged, for stability, balance and evolution of the wine, which he suggests removes the need for sterile filtration and high levels of sulphur dioxide preservative. The results are usually clean and precise.

The energy of Agrapart's grand cru chardonnay vineyards and the endurance injected through barrel fermentation make these very long-lived cuvées that appreciate extended lees ageing prior to release. Ageing a minimum of three years for non-vintage and seven for vintage cuvées necessitates a stock of 360,000 bottles to sustain an annual production of 90,000. This is a significant production for hand-riddling, but the hands-on approach of the estate is maintained.

Most of Agrapart's seven cuvées are blanc de blancs, with a little pinot in his entry wine, and a single-field blend of six grape varieties. Low dosages are used throughout, which he suggests reduces the importance of ageing the wine between disgorgement and release. While disgorgement dates aren't printed on back labels, they're easy to decode from the cork. The number is the year of disgorgement, and the letter is the month (A for January, B for February, and so on).

Agrapart's wines are characterful, deeply mineral expressions of their terroirs, given articulate voice through diligent attention to detail. A recent tasting of Minéral from the difficult 1984 season (97 points) was resounding evidence of the endurance of this exceptional grower and his remarkable terroirs.

AGRAPART & FILS 7 CRUS BRUT NV $

93 points • TASTED IN AVIZE

A blend of equal parts of 2011 from young vines aged 20-40 years in lesser sites, and 2010 from good parcels; 25% of 2010 components matured in barrels; 90% chardonnay and an increasing percentage of pinot noir (10%) from Avize, Oger, Oiry, Cramant, Avenay Val d'Or, Bergères-lès-Vertus and Mardeuil; full malolactic fermentation; aged 3 years on lees; 7g/L dosage

Agrapart's precision and attention to detail is proclaimed from the very first cuvée, though without quite the incisive freshness of last year's blend. There's more body and more spice here, layered with the complexity of blood orange, mixed spice and ginger, lingering long on the finish. It's textural, mouth-filling, soft and creamy, proclaiming a well-crafted blend.

AGRAPART & FILS TERROIRS BLANC DE BLANCS GRAND CRU EXTRA BRUT NV $

95 points • 2010 AND 2009 BLEND • TASTED IN AVIZE
94 points • 2009 AND 2008 BLEND • TASTED IN SYDNEY & MELBOURNE

A classification of better parcels than 7 Crus; 20-40-year-old vines in Avize, Oger, Cramant and Oiry; equal portions of 2010 and 2009; 50% of 2009 component matured in barrels; full malolactic fermentation; aged 4 years on lees; low dosage of 5g/L

A seamlessly crafted blanc de blancs of enticing purity and approachability, the 2010 and 2009 blend even more magnificent in its mineral expression, freshness and vivacity than the excellent 2009 and 2008, which has evolved into an intense and generous style of peach and roast nuts, while upholding its tense, mineral mouthfeel. The 2010 and 2009 blend sings with the freshness of lemon and grapefruit, tangy grapefruit zest definition and notes of fresh almonds. Deeply embedded in grand cru chalk soils, it's soft, salty and frothy, creamy in texture and lingering with great length and poise. A beautifully crafted and terroir-infused cuvée.

AGRAPART & FILS COMPLANTÉE GRAND CRU EXTRA BRUT NV $$

91 points • TASTED IN AVIZE

A blend of 2011 and 2010 of co-planted pinot noir, meunier, pinot blanc, arbane, petit meslier and chardonnay from young vines planted in 2002; vinified in oak barrels; full malolactic fermentation; aged on lees under cork; unfiltered; low dosage of 5g/L; just 1300 bottles produced

Still the least of Agrapart's cuvées: such young vines cannot capture the persistence, harmony or mineral depth of his old vines. Yet there is grip, structure, finesse and focus here, and the presence of fine, salty minerality is unmistakable. It showcases the full sweep of its six varieties, spanning everything from fresh pear and apple fruit accented to grapefruit zest, pepper and bitter almond skin. Accurate acid line keeps everything in focus. Try it with oysters.

AGRAPART & FILS MINÉRAL BLANC DE BLANCS GRAND CRU EXTRA BRUT 2008 $$$

96 points • TASTED IN AVIZE

A 50/50 blend of 40-year-old vines from nearby parcels in Avize and Cramant; Avize vinified in tank, Cramant in old oak barrels; full malolactic fermentation; no filtration; 5 years on yeast lees; low dosage of 3-4g/L

Mineral, indeed, boring deep into the hard white chalk very close to the surface of these two vineyards, charged with the high notes and pronounced acidity of 2008. The 2006 reflected the softness of early morning light filtered through fine mist and the 2008 glistens with bright, stark midday sunlight at the height of summer. It's taut and high tensile, with pristine youthful definition of primary lemon fruit, crunchy pear and apple. Chalk mineral texture is magnificently pronounced, reverberating with a seasalt definition characteristic of the great sites of the Côte des Blancs. Barrel fermentation has brought a little creaminess to the texture and a touch of roast almond complexity, but the theme remains resolutely that of youthful purity and well-scaffolded structure, demanding long ageing. It will live effortlessly for decades.

AGRAPART & FILS MINÉRAL BLANC DE BLANCS GRAND CRU EXTRA BRUT 2007 $$$

95 points • TASTED IN SYDNEY & MELBOURNE

Recipe as above

There is a riper mood to 2007 in comparison with the vintages before and after, expressed in the character and focus of peach, pear and apple fruit, evolving into preserved lemon, toasted brioche and roast nuts. Its fruit presence and toasty complexity is juxtaposed with the mineral tension of these vineyards, which shines brilliantly amidst a ripe acid line on a very long finish.

The Champagne Guide

Agrapart & Fils l'Avizoise Blanc de Blancs Grand Cru Extra Brut 2008 $$$$

94 points • Tasted in Avize

From 55-year-old vines in two parcels on the best slopes of Avize; made exclusively in old oak barrels; full malolactic fermentation; aged on lees under natural cork for 5 years; unfiltered; low dosage of 3g/L

Just 600–800 metres from the parcels that comprise Minéral, here the soils are clay over chalk, expressing a very different personality of frothy, salty chalk texture that contrasts the creamy mouthfeel of full barrel fermentation. The hazelnut, roasted coffee bean and spice notes of barrel complexity counterpoint a core of sour grapefruit and lemon pith, and the bracing tension and endurance of 2008 acidity. The accord is a little disjointed at this age, but charged with enduring potential.

Agrapart & Fils Vénus Blanc de Blancs Grand Cru Brut Nature 2008 $$$$

96 points • Tasted in Avize

'La Fosse', a single 1959 planting of just one-third of 1 hectare on chalk in Avize; tended only by hand and horse; made exclusively in old oak barrels; full malolactic fermentation; unfiltered; aged on lees under natural cork for 5 years; zero dosage

Pascal Agrapart describes the minerality of Vénus as reminiscent of the chalk dust from the blackboard when he was at school. Breathe deep: the intensity of the chalk minerality of this cuvée is something to behold. The high-tensile acid line of 2008 is heightened by zero dosage, defining a searing champagne that screams for at least two decades in the cellar to settle. One hundred percent barrel fermentation brings notes of toasted almonds and somehow elevates the salt mineral texture of the village, like the high notes of the strings of an orchestra are propelled by rumbling depths of percussion and horns. A cuvée of textural precision and grand mineral persistence, this is an intellectual style, a philharmonic experience rather than a mosh pit encounter. Everything is in the right place for a magnificent future.

Agrapart & Fils Expérience Blanc de Blancs Grand Cru Brut Nature NV $$$$

94 points • Tasted in Avize

Blend of equal parts of the parcels that comprise l'Avizoise and Minéral; 2007 and 2008 vintages; no chaptalisation; wild yeast for both first and second fermentations; vinified in barrel; aged on cork; full malolactic fermentation; zero dosage

Two years can work wonders, and this cuvée has miraculously blossomed into a freshness, definition and potential completely invisible two years ago. Tight, fresh grapefruit and lemon zest are massaged with the textural mouthfeel and roast nut and charcuterie hints of barrel fermentation, underscored by a taut acid line of vibrant lemon juice and the prominent salt minerality of the village. Primary citrus fruit, acid tension and accurate line remain the focus on a long and well-defined finish. This is evidently a difficult cuvée to predict, but my hunch is that it's only going to get better in the coming years.

ALFRED GRATIEN

(Al-fre Gra-shah)

6/10

30 RUE MAURICE CERVEAUX 51201 EPERNAY

www.alfredgratien.com

A lfred Gratien is a small house, producing 300,000 bottles annually, with a long history of making wines of complexity. Its champagnes are made in a rigorously classical way, with the first fermentation and at least six months of ageing taking place exclusively in 1000 small 228-litre neutral barriques, of 12-years average age, previously used three times in Chablis. Reserve wines are stored in large oak barrels. Malolactic fermentation is systematically avoided, to ensure that the champagne retains its original character, maintaining freshness as it ages and preserving the aroma of the grapes and the land from which they came.

Alfred Gratien was acquired by the Henkell & Co group in 2004, retaining its own small holdings of just four hectares of vineyards and 65 growers from which grapes are sourced. The house considers its barrels a key to its relationship with its growers, allowing it to keep every plot separate. Every barrel is labelled with the name of the village and the grower, and each grower is invited to come to taste their own wines every second year.

Henkell & Co invested considerably in the house, building a new cuverie for blending of the young wines. At just 9°C, its cellars are some of the coldest in Champagne. This is too cold for the second fermentation to kick off, so bottles are first held in the barrel hall for two weeks. It then takes 70–80 days to complete the second fermentation in the cellar below. The house maintains a considerable stock of 1.5 million bottles, since long ageing is important for softening malic acidity.

Since 2007, the new owners have wisely left the house in the hands of young Nicolas Jaeger, the fourth generation of the Jaeger family to serve as chef de cave of the house. Production has doubled in the past 14 years, and the target is to reach the capacity of the facility of 400,000–450,000 bottles by 2020.

Gratien's non-vintage cuvées are deeply complex wines that retain a zingy freshness, thanks to lively malic acidity, softened gently by a minimum of three years bottle ageing. Its vintage cuvées are a real step up, always a majority of chardonnay, and typically from the Côte des Blancs' greatest grand crus. Vintage wines are aged under natural cork, which Jaeger claims assists in preventing oxidation and enhancing tertiary aromas, complexity and firmness. He tastes every bottle as it is disgorged and rejects 1% to cork taint and 2% to leakage or other variation. With full barrel vinification and no malolactic fermentation, these are long-ageing champagnes of fine, creamy bead, lively acid line and well-managed, barrel-matured complexity. It's a style particularly flattering to rosé.

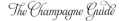

Alfred Gratien Brut Nature NV $$

91 points • Tasted in Épernay

46% chardonnay, 29% pinot noir, 26% meunier; based on the warm and less acidic vintage of 2007, with 15% reserves from 2006; zero dosage

Alfred Gratien's first ever Brut Nature was made in response to market demand. It leads out focused, fine and pure, charged with taut malic acid line and layered complexity of gingernut biscuits and brioche, but then falters on a firm, dry, chewy, short close. It would benefit from dosage to elongate and even out the finish.

Alfred Gratien Cuvée Brut Classique Rosé NV $$

95 points • Disgorged June 2014 • Tasted in Épernay & Brisbane

46% chardonnay, 29% meunier, 25% pinot noir; 2009 base vintage with 15% reserves from 2008; the Brut Classique with 10-12% red wine from a contract maker in Bouzy; no malolactic fermentation; 9g/L dosage

The Gratien house style is more flattering to rosé than it is even to white sparkling, expressing precise red cherry, raspberry and strawberry fruit of greater elegance and delicacy than its medium crimson hue might predict. It's creamy and silky, drawn out by finely integrated acidity, balanced dosage and gentle chalk mineral texture. The bottle tasted in Brisbane lacked the brightness, fruit definition and precision of that tasted in Champagne, and instead developed into a realm of red apple and roast nuts.

Alfred Gratien Cuvée Brut Classique NV $$

93 points • 2009 base vintage with 15% reserves from 2008 • Disgorged June 2014
• 46% chardonnay, 29% pinot noir, 25% meunier • Tasted in Brisbane & Melbourne
94 points • 2008 base vintage • 41% chardonnay, 32% pinot noir, 27% meunier
• Tasted in Épernay

Fermented in oak barriques; aged at least 4 years; no malolactic fermentation; dosage 9g/L

Barrel maturation and long bottle ageing are reflected in a medium to full straw hue. There's an acute contrast here between the taut twang of malic acidity, heightened in 2008, and a complex backdrop of barrel fermentation character, creamy texture and fine chalk mineral focus. It handles this accord confidently, evenly harmonising body, drive and cut. Excellent bright lemon juice, citrus zest and fresh red berry focus meets all the character of nougat, brioche, mixed spice, gingernut biscuits and dried nectarine, before becoming green coffee bean in time.

Sunset during vintage 2014 over Moët's Mont Aigu Lodge in Chouilly, the northernmost grand cru of the Côte des Blancs.

ALFRED GRATIEN GRAND CRU BLANC DE BLANCS BRUT 2007 $$

92 points • Tasted in Épernay

A roughly even mix of the grand crus of Cramant, Le Mesnil-sur-Oger, Oger, Avize and Chouilly; 6g/L dosage

A cuvée of full straw hue and notes of fresh lemon zest, the barrel and bottle-derived character of brioche and a hint of fennel. The clash of malic acidity with wood lends a sappy note, making for a rustic and chewy style. It finishes with good acid drive, harmony and fine mineral texture.

ALFRED GRATIEN BRUT MILLÉSIME 2000 $$

94 points • Tasted in Épernay, Brisbane & Melbourne

64% chardonnay, 25% pinot noir, 11% meunier; aged 12 years on lees under cork; 15,000–20,000 bottles; no malolactic fermentation; 6g/L dosage

This is classic 2000 vintage, in all of its supple, rounded, glowing yellow mirabelle plum, grilled pineapple, white peach and lemon glory, sustained marvellously by vibrant and well-integrated malic acidity. A marathon of 12 years on lees has coaxed out rising notes of toasty complexity, silky butteriness and mixed spice, without interrupting the gliding flow of subtle chalk minerality. Bottles tasted in Australia were much more developed, showing tertiary notes of green olives and wood smoke, well into the twilight of their life.

ALFRED GRATIEN CUVÉE PARADIS BRUT 2006 $$$$

94 points • Disgorged June 2014 • Tasted in Épernay & Brisbane

65% chardonnay, 35% pinot noir; a blend of the best barrels from the cellar; 6g/L dosage

A touch of extra development from bottles tasted more recently in Brisbane proved to be flattering for this cuvée, toning its firm malic acidity and enriching the roundness of barrel complexity and fine, creamy bead. The focus of lemon, grapefruit and red berries is evolving into brioche, dried fruits, orange rind and roast nuts, and in the most recent bottles even nougat, marzipan and gingernut biscuits. Well-defined acidity and persistence are upheld seamlessly.

ALFRED GRATIEN CUVÉE PARADIS ROSÉ NV $$$$

95 points • Tasted in Épernay

Approximately 12% red wine from Bouzy pinot noir, added to Cuvée Paradis of 2007 base; 55% chardonnay, 45% pinot noir

A medium crimson copper hue does little to anticipate lovely pure aromas of plum and red cherry fruit. The palate returns to the savoury and complex style expected from a barrel-fermented cuvée, with notes of grilled tomato, gentle red berry fruits and lingering, focused acidity. A rosé of fine mineral mouthfeel, fine, creamy bead and elegant persistence.

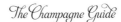
The Champagne Guide

ANDRÉ CLOUET

(An-dray Cloo-ay)

(8/10)

8 RUE GAMBETTA 51150 BOUZY

Bouzy and Ambonnay are the epicentre of pinot noir in Champagne, and the Clouet family is the privileged custodian of eight hectares of estate vines in the best middle slopes of both villages. These are rich and concentrated expressions of pinot noir, wines of deep complexity, multifaceted interest and engaging character, yet with remarkable restraint and sense of control. Tasting after tasting confirm my impression that this small and relatively unknown grower ranks high among Champagne's finest practitioners of pinot noir — and represents one of the best value of all.

Young chef de cave Jean-François Clouet is deeply passionate about the remarkable sweep of history that has played out in this place over two millennia, and every time I visit he speaks more of this than he does of vines, winery, cellar or tastings. He shows me original documents of his village of Bouzy in his archive and takes me to another part of town to recount another branch of history: Attila the Hun, the Catalonic Field Battle, the birth of the monarchy, the crusades, the Templars, Marie Antoinette. 'To understand Champagne you need to understand its political history,' he says.

For Clouet's family, that history began here in 1492, and his family still resides in the house his ancestors built in Bouzy in 1741. 'My family was making wine in Champagne at the same time Dom Pérignon was starring!' he exclaims. This history lives on, not only in the spectacular labels designed by Jean-François' great-grandfather in 1911 (harking back to the family's printer heritage, making books for the king since 1491), but in a traditional approach in the vineyards. 'I like the idea of the work of human hands in pruning, performing the same actions as my grandfather and even the Romans, who planted vines here 2000 years ago.'

The flamboyant Jean-François is one of the upcoming rockstars of Champagne. He is inherently talented as a winemaker, keenly insightful, at once deeply rooted in his family's history and yet daringly creative, with a distinctly modern twist to his approach. It is his goal that some day none of his champagnes will have any dosage at all, an ideal that he rightly describes as revolutionary.

'Not to be snobby or arrogant, but I have a real sense that a zero-dosage wine from a single village can really showcase the pedigree of the village,' he suggests. 'You have to be an extremely good winemaker to make zero-dosage champagne.' And if anyone can do it anywhere, Jean-François can in Bouzy and Ambonnay. To this end, for some years he has experimented with using Sauternes barriques from Château Doisy Daëne for alcoholic fermentation. 'It gives the illusion of the wine being sweet, when it is not sweet at all!' he claims. The result, to my astonishment, is quite magnificent.

When Clouet began working on the estate 10 years ago, he took note of those embarking on organic and biodynamic regimes. 'Biodynamics and organics look good on paper,' he says, 'but my idea is that it is simply important to take care of the ground by hand without the use of herbicides.' Stringent sorting during harvest maintains freshness and purity in his cuvées.

Clouet's focus remains resolutely on pinot noir, which comprises 100% of every cuvée except his Millésime, a 50/50 blend of pinot noir and chardonnay. 'I am frustrated with the idea of blending from everywhere!' he exclaims. 'I love pure pinot noir! No make-up and no compromise!'

Clouet is fascinated by the geological history of his soils, and makes it his goal to express the minerality of pure chalk in his wines. 'Fantastic minerality and low dosage are important for good pinot noir,' he claims. His cuvées receive low dosages of 6g/L.

In 2011 Clouet embarked on a significant project he dubs 'Clouet world', a substantial logistics facility for disgorgement, remuage and bottling on land he inherited just outside the village.

As seriously as he takes his responsibilities, Clouet doesn't take himself too seriously. 'Champagne is always for flirting!' he grins. And he likens his wines to independent films. 'I love Hollywood movies, but sometimes I want to watch something independent. Winemaking in Champagne is the same,' he says. 'One is not better than the other. Dom Pérignon and Pol Roger are fantastic, with all the action of James Bond in *Skyfall*, but sometimes I have a taste for something else.'

His champagnes offer that something else, without the Hollywood budget, yet with pyrotechnics all of their own.

ANDRÉ CLOUET SILVER BRUT NATURE NV $$

94 points • TASTED IN BOUZY

100% Bouzy and Ambonnay pinot noir from 2012 and 2011; Grande Réserve with zero dosage; 30% fermented in Sauternes barriques from Doisy Daëne

Jean-François Clouet's zero-dosage ideal is manifested with magnificent clarity, showcasing pinot noir of such depth and richness that it has absolutely no need for dosage. The great 2012 season brings tension and precision, with the primary freshness of lemon and white cherry fruit all but trumping any flavours of barrel fermentation. Pronounced chalk mineral acidity provides seasalt definition, with a creamy, frothy texture heightened in barrels. A zero dosage of persistence, tension and confidence.

ANDRÉ CLOUET GRANDE RÉSERVE BLANC DE NOIRS BRUT NV $$

95 points • TASTED IN BOUZY, SYDNEY & MELBOURNE

100% Bouzy and Ambonnay pinot noir; 2012 base vintage; 6g/L dosage

As magnificent as I have seen Clouet's entry cuvée, a captivating interplay of the luscious, succulent, rich red cherry and plum fruits of Bouzy, the brightness and tension of well-defined acid line and the expressive definition of chalk minerality. It's pure, impeccably poised and very long. Classic Bouzy of the finest order. Bottles tasted in Australia, suspected to be based on the 2009 harvest, show much more pronounced toffee and gingernut biscuit development.

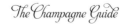

The Champagne Guide

André Clouet Rosé No 3 Brut NV $$

94 points • Disgorged November 2014 • Tasted in Bouzy, Sydney, Melbourne & Brisbane

100% Bouzy and Ambonnay pinot noir; 2012 base vintage

Jean-François' 'Clouet No 3' was inspired by Coco Chanel, the number introduced for the first time this year to denote the style, recognising that the colour is different each year, and with the number 3 representing a light, elegant apéritif style. Elegance and freshness are his goals for rosé, avoiding what he describes as the 'full, rustic and heavy' styles of the past.

Clouet's rosé epitomises elegance and focus, while flamboyantly celebrating the generous red cherry, strawberry, watermelon and pink pepper fruit of Bouzy. It encapsulates that wonderful talent of pinot noir to build and rise on the finish, all the while retaining graceful precision as delicate as rose petal perfume. Structure is fine and elegant, driven both by the chalk minerality of the village and a very finely executed tannin presence. It finishes with great length and poise of exquisite red cherry fruit. A pristine and enticingly priced rosé. Older disgorgements have taken on savoury suggestions of tamarillo, while upholding their primary integrity.

André Clouet Brut Millésime 2008 $$

96 points • Tasted in Bouzy

A little more than 50% chardonnay, the remainder pinot noir from Bouzy and Ambonnay; 6g/L dosage

On its release two years ago, I adored this expression of an exceptional vintage from this top grower, and its freeze-frame slow-motion evolution since has only exemplified its potential. Its impeccable, backward, primary focus on Bouzy's red cherry and strawberry fruits is breathtaking, charged with the tension and precision of a backbone of electric 2008 acidity. Finesse and poise are framed in deep-set concentration, the signature of its villages, painted in the vivid colours of 2008. Subtle mixed spice complexity is beginning to peek out, but it remains very fresh and impeccably pure, carrying with unrelenting fruit depth, persistence and an ever-present undercurrent that froths with well-defined, finely chalky minerality. Wow.

André Clouet Brut Millésime 2009 $$

94 points • Tasted in Bouzy

50% pinot noir and 50% chardonnay; disgorged on the day I tasted it in early 2015; zero dosage

Impressively reserved, tense, strict and backward in this just disgorged guise, this is a focused vintage of crunchy lemon and pink grapefruit, yet the generosity of Clouet manifests itself in nuances of blood orange and white cherry. Salt minerality is prominent, expressive and persistent, and the acid line is bracingly youthful, promising great things in years to come. Another excellent Clouet.

André Clouet Brut Millésime 2002 $$

96 points • Tasted in Melbourne

A remarkable expression of an exceptional season, rich and inviting in its warm generosity of honey biscuits, grilled pineapple and brioche. It's simultaneously rich and taut, with layers of ripe, succulent fruit underlined by fine, chalky minerality and taut, fine acid structure, all of which linger very long and mineral-fine, upholding great poise and balance. Evidence of the calibre of Clouet in achieving grand longevity within a style of enticing generosity.

André Clouet 1911 NV $$

96 points • Tasted in Bouzy

A magnificent recipe: 100% pinot noir from Clouet's 10 best plots, dubbed by Jean-François 'the golden square of Bouzy'; 50% 2002 fermented in Doisy Daëne Sauternes barriques; 50% solera of reserve wines; full malolactic fermentation; a symbolic production of just 1911 bottles; 6g/L dosage

Clouet's flagship is a radiant, golden silk-satin ballgown of ravishing complexity and breathtaking grace, a delicate high-heeled balancing act of refreshing poise in the midst of profound concentration. Its richness ventures to champagne's outer limits of succulent white fruits of all kinds, baked white peach, grilled pineapple and fig. Celebrating a generous 50% reserve from solera, its rumbling maturity is proclaimed in hints of golden fruit cake, mixed spice and butter, yet upholds impeccable freshness and poise for such magnificent depth of complexity, lingering with outstanding persistence of silky acid line, gentle minerality and beautifully creamy bead. It has not diminished one iota since I first encountered it two years ago, holding its posture of tall, slender magnificence for minutes without ever dropping its determined gaze. It's achieved its magnificent peak, and will hold it confidently for some years yet.

André Clouet Le Clos 2008 $$$$$

95 points • Tasted in Bouzy

Single vineyard; only released in magnums; zero dosage

The Clouet Clos between the house and the cuverie on the lower edge of Bouzy is not the family's finest terroir, without the characteristic chalk mineral definition of their hillside sites, and it takes an exceptional season to infuse it with the confidence to stand alone. However, 2008 delivered that season, with a captivating tension and introverted reticence containing grand complexity waiting to burst out. Layers of gingernut biscuits, anise, glacé orange, fig, mixed spice, baked white peach, golden fruit cake and roast almonds define a multi-layered allure compressed into a coiled core of lemon and white cherry fruit. In time, notes of plum liqueur and black cherry emerge to declare the depth and impact of Bouzy, rising to the rhythm of an exceptional season, which coaxes out a pronounced chalk mineral texture of crystalline definition, glittering through a long finish. Wait at least five years, and preferably ten.

André Clouet Le Clos 2006 $$$$$

91 points • Tasted in Bouzy

Magnum

I was the first journalist to taste the first vintage of Clouet's new flagship. Since that first encounter, it has lifted and begun to flesh out, which helps this young, tight and firm style. It's a textural and full wine of bruised apple, pear and lemon fruit, ginger cake and spice, driven more by gentle phenolic grip than by acidity or minerality. It finishes short and shows some notes of development that work against its purity and freshness. Wait for the magnificent 2008 instead.

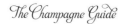

The Champagne Guide

ANDRÉ JACQUART

(An-dray Zhah-khah)

6/10

63 AVE DE BAMMENTAL 51130 VERTUS
www.a-jacquart-fils.com

ANDRÉ JACQUART

Merging the family estates of fifth-generation growers, brother and sister Marie and Benoît Doyard, in 2004, blessed André Jacquart with enviable vineyard holdings of 16 hectares of chardonnay in the great Côte des Blancs terroirs of Le Mesnil-sur-Oger and Vertus, three hectares of pinot noir in the Aube and four in the Aisne. A move from Le Mesnil to Vertus, the purchase of two new presses and 200 barrels in the same year, and the estate was reborn. In a laudable and unusual move for Champagne, production has been reduced by almost one-third since then, in pursuit of quality.

Marie and Benoît, grandchildren of André Jacquart, use just half of the family's holdings for their own wines, exclusively from vines with an average age of more than 40 years in their best sites in Le Mesnil-sur-Oger and Vertus.

Vineyards are managed sustainably, with a focus on organic viticulture and the use of biodegradable inputs. Yields are restricted by de-budding to around two-thirds of the permitted levels, and several pickings are performed in each site to select only ripe grapes.

This level of ripeness allows malolactic fermentation to be blocked across all cuvées, which in turn calls for softening through barrel fermentation and long ageing. Fermentation takes place in both stainless steel tanks and barrels aged 2–6 years. Wines in barrel are fermented by natural yeasts and aged in barrel for 5–8 months. Non-vintage cuvées are aged a minimum of four years on lees, and vintage cuvées at least five years. Both are aged a further 12 months post-disgorgement, prior to release — significantly longer than most in Champagne.

André Jacquart's champagnes are wines of impressively accurate fruit, well-defined terroir expression, and vivid mineral personality. Even barrel work and long ageing are insufficient to tame the bold combination of 100% Le Mesnil and Vertus chardonnay, full malic acidity and low dosage of typically just 3–4g/L, making these quite edgy and assertive wines.

These are not crowd-pleasing champagnes, but styles that will stretch and delight the well-seasoned champagne enthusiast, charged with the sustaining endurance of malic acidity.

ANDRÉ JACQUART BRUT EXPÉRIENCE BLANC DE BLANCS PREMIER CRU NV $$

93 points • TASTED IN MELBOURNE

2007 vintage with reserves of 2006 and 2005; 60% Vertus, 40% Le Mesnil-sur-Oger; 40% barrel fermented in 4-year-old Burgundy barrels; low dosage of 4g/L

Rigorous attention to low yields and ripe fruit is announced from the outset, with grand terroirs defining a style very much consistent with last year's blend. The tension of Vertus chardonnay is contrasted with the depth and power of Le Mesnil-sur-Oger, creating a blanc de blancs that is at once fresh and tangy with grapefruit crunch, and succulent and fleshy with the gorgeous richness of juicy white summer fruits and mixed spice intrigue. Barrel fermentation builds texture, suppleness and subtle toasted almond notes, while elegantly integrated dosage frames lively malic acidity as the highlight of a long finish.

ANDRÉ JACQUART EXPERIENCE MILLÉSIMÉ LE MESNIL-SUR-OGER BLANC DE BLANCS GRAND CRU 2006 $$$

95 points • TASTED IN MELBOURNE

50+-year-old vines in the best southern lieux-dits of Le Mesnil-sur-Oger; 100% barrel fermented in third-use oak, aged on lees for more than 60 months; low dosage of 3g/L

The passage of time proves the endurance of Le Mesnil-sur-Oger and the sustaining power of malic acidity. Two years after release, this intricately and intelligently assembled cuvée continues to blossom and expand, evolving from a place of vibrant grapefruit and lemon zest to all the intensity and richness of baked apples and mixed spice. Barrel fermentation character is now well integrated, a backdrop of inimitable Le Mesnil salty chalk mineral structure remains resolute and its malic acidity retains liveliness yet integration and effortlessness.

Early morning pinot noir harvest 2014 on the edge of the forest of the Montagne de Reims at the top of the grand cru slopes of Bouzy.

AR Lenoble

(A.R. Ler-nob-ler)

(7/10)

www.champagne-lenoble.com

'*The two important things for making great champagne are the quality of your grapes and the size of your stock,' declares Antoine Malassagne, who is richly blessed with both. With his sister Anne, he is the fourth generation to manage the family cellars and vineyards of the Graser-Malassagne family. The 18 hectares of the small house of Lenoble transcend its position in the centre of the village of Damery, in the middle of the Vallée de la Marne, thanks to a majority of holdings in the core of the Côte des Blancs grand cru of Chouilly. The chardonnay from these vines defines Lenoble's finest cuvées, supplemented with chardonnay and pinot noir from estate vineyards in Bisseuil and Damery. The remainder of its needs, including all meunier, is sourced from Damery growers. For an annual production of 400,000 bottles, Lenoble's cellar stock of 1.5 million is sizeable, furnishing long ageing of 3–4 years for non-vintage cuvées, and six or more for vintage wines. True to its name, a noble approach in the vines and the cellar produces well-composed and tantalisingly affordable cuvées that showcase the strength, structure, definition and opulence of Chouilly.*

Lenoble was established in 18th century cellars in Damery almost a century ago. When Antoine Malassagne returned to the family company in 1996, he was unimpressed with traditional techniques and set about improving practices in the vineyards and winery in 1998. 'I am starting to see the results of our efforts in the past three or four vintages,' he told me recently.

A natural approach in the vineyards has seen the elimination of herbicides and pesticides, ploughing to control weeds and aerate the soil, use of organic manure, and cultivation of grasses in the mid-rows of some vineyards to moderate yields and increase ripeness. 'I am nearly organic but not quite, as I am concerned

about using copper sulphate to combat mildew,' says Malassagne, a qualified chemical engineer. For these initiatives, Lenoble was the second in Champagne after Bollinger to receive High Environmental Value certification.

Malassagne's philosophy of making champagne is to vinify it like still wine. The winery was rebuilt in 2008 and maintains three wooden presses between 30 and 45 years of age. All parcels are vinified separately, with the best parcels from the finest seasons fermented in small Burgundy barrels for oxidative character. 'Champagne is a very delicate wine, and the barrel needs to support the wine rather than dominating,' he emphasises. His cuvées reflect an increasingly sensitive use of oak, with no more than one-third of any blend vinified in barrels.

'I like buying new barrels, as you know what you're getting.' To reduce new oak character, the first year's fermentation is sold for distillation — a costly and time-consuming process. Brand new 5000-litre foudres have been recently acquired for ageing reserves for 4–5 months post-fermentation. 'I buy more and more big barrels, because they impart less oaky flavour than small barrels and produce clear, clean wines of finesse and complexity.'

Lenoble adapts vinification to suit the harvest, with malolactic fermentation used selectively, according to the season and the parcel, and not at all in reserve wines. 'It's difficult to find a balance between finesse and intensity,' Malassagne admits. Dosage is very low, no more than 5g/L.

Driven by a scientific mind, Malassagne is constantly experimenting to refine the details and improve his wines, rather than following trends. He has trialled wild yeasts, bâtonnage and Hungarian oak, though is not convinced of any. He doesn't produce the same non-vintage wines each vintage. 'I try to improve and make the best wines I can every year,' he explains. 'Generation after generation, we try to improve vinification and practices in the vines.'

AR Lenoble Cuvée Intense Brut NV $

93 points • 2011 base vintage • Disgorged October 2014 • Tasted in Brisbane & Sydney

30% Chouilly chardonnay, 35% Bisseuil pinot noir, 35% Damery meunier; 25% reserves from 2010 and 2009; 18% vinified in oak; fermentation 30-40% of reserves without malolactic fermentation; 5g/L dosage

An impeccably crafted wine from noble fruit sources, offering sensational value for money. A compelling harmony between fruit intensity of grapefruit, red cherry, golden delicious apple and white peach, the biscuity, honeyed appeal of bottle age and a touch of oak, and a well-focused malic acid line. Low dosage sits comfortably in the midst of impeccably ripe fruit. A cuvée of class that transcends its difficult base vintage and its refreshingly affordable price, declaring integrity in accurate palate line and impressive persistence.

AR Lenoble Grand Cru Blanc de Blancs Chouilly Brut NV $$

94 points • 2010 base vintage • Disgorged November 2014 • Tasted in Brisbane

35% reserves from 2009 and 2008; 22% vinified in oak; 5g/L dosage

Classic Chouilly, a showcase for the rounded, buttery presence and glowing locut, yellow mirabelle plum and golden delicious apple opulence of the village, accurately controlled by well-defined acid line (thanks to strategic retention of some malic acidity), soft, rounded chalk minerality and the subtle, creamy texture of barrel vinification. There are hints of anise, cherry kernel and nutmeg along the way. It's expertly crafted, showing sensitive use of oak to heighten the personality of the terroir, culminating in a finish of ripe fruit and invisibly integrated dosage.

The Champagne Guide

AR Lenoble Grand Cru Blanc de Blancs Chouilly Brut 2008 $$

95 points • Disgorged October 2014 • Tasted in Brisbane & Damery

10% vinified in oak; 4g/L dosage

The tension and definition of the energetic 2008 vintage is endearing in the opulent village of Chouilly, and Malassagne has sensitively matched the elegance of the vintage with a subtle 10% oak vinification and a very light dosage. Youthful lemon, pear and apple fruit of impressive poise and proportion is propelled by a wonderful line of glistening 2008 acidity and frothing salt mineral texture, elongating a finish of magnificent line and persistence. Oak lends an appealing, almost invisible note of vanilla and almond. A masterful and age-worthy contrast between the rounded intensity of Chouilly and the vivacious drive of a terrific season.

AR Lenoble Blanc de Noirs Bisseuil Premier Cru Brut 2009 $$

93 points • Disgorged November 2014 • Tasted in Brisbane

100% Bisseuil pinot noir; 28% vinified in small oak barrels and aged in large oak foudres; no malolactic fermentation; 3–4g/L dosage

Malassagne's goal here is distinctiveness, richness and opulence, and so there's a little more oak here than in his blanc de blancs cuvées. However, Bisseuil is not a particularly powerful cru for pinot noir, and its elegant and gentle red cherry and strawberry fruits jostle a little at first with the coffee beans, dark chocolate and vanilla of oak. He suggests that it just needs time, and he's right. It's evolving commendably with time in bottle, with tight malic acidity beginning to soften, and it settles into a comfortable balance even as it warms in the glass, admirably evading oak structure to give voice to soft chalk minerality. A cuvée to cellar for a couple of years, then serve a little warmer, with plenty of swirling in a large glass.

AR Lenoble Rosé Terroirs Brut NV $$

92 points • 2011 base vintage • Disgorged June 2014 • Tasted in Brisbane

88% Chouilly chardonnay, 12% Bisseuil pinot noir; 15% reserves from 2010; 15% vinified in oak

Lenoble's pinot noir and meunier is too rich to stand alone as a rosé, so the house tactically calls upon the structure and fresh acid drive of its Chouilly chardonnay. In colour, tannin structure and oak presence, there's a more toned demeanour to this cuvée at the moment. It's a precocious thing, with a momentary fanfare of tangelo, candied strawberry and musk that proclaims the opulence of Chouilly, then immediately vanishes. The citrus fruits of Chouilly are heightened by a touch of Bisseuil pinot noir, and the discreetly handled texture of a touch of oak. It concludes elegant and fine.

AR Lenoble Cuvée Gentilhomme Grand Cru Blanc de Blancs Millésime Brut 2006 $$$

95 points • Disgorged April 2014 • Tasted in Brisbane

100% Chouilly chardonnay; 30% vinified in oak; 3g/L dosage

Lenoble's 'Gentleman' is an affable fellow of considerable depth and concentration, upholding every bit of the marvellous character of his first outing two years ago, now more heightened in toasty maturity. This is a champagne fully up to roast-chicken combat on the table, packed with fleshy white summer fruits, honey, nougat, roast nuts, even the full potency of fruit-mince spice. It holds impressive energy within rich proportions, with biceps structured with the fibrous muscle of Chouilly, now immaculately presented in a silk jacket of soft, harmonious acidity and threads of fine chalk minerality. True to the generous and early-maturing 2006 vintage, it's now attained its handsome finest, with concentration that does not break for minutes on the finish.

AR Lenoble Cuvée Les Aventures Grand Cru Blanc de Blancs Brut NV $$$

93 points • 2006 base vintage • Disgorged September 2014 • Tasted in Brisbane

100% Chouilly chardonnay from a single half-hectare plot; 40% reserves from 2002; 34% vinified in oak; aged on cork; 3g/L dosage; just 2000 bottles released each year

Blended only from seasons released as vintages in their own right, the philosophy of 'The Adventures of Lenoble' is to showcase what a small terroir in Chouilly can produce in top years. Quite a quest it is, engineered and structured with a scaffold of Chouilly tension, amplified by barrel fermentation. It's softened and toned a little since its release, exemplified by another couple of years on tirage under cork, its tense, coiled acidity still well defined, though now calm and integrated, and the classic yellow fruits of Chouilly now further progressed on their journey towards toast, roast nuts, green olives and coffee beans. Wood work is the most pronounced of any Lenoble cuvée, in notes of savoury, spicy charcuterie complexity and a creamy texture of gentle phenolic grip, yet it upholds its poise and characterful definition. This is a powerful and formidable experience for the adventurous, yet never heavy or broad, promising that the journey will continue for some years yet. It's main-course ready, and deserves to be served a little warmer, in large glasses.

Lenoble Collection Rare Grand Cru Blanc de Blancs 2002 $$$

95 points • Disgorged August 2014 • Tasted in Damery

100% Chouilly chardonnay; full malolactic fermentation; 2g/L dosage

A re-release that shouts the full, lavish grandeur of mature Chouilly in fig jam, ripe yellow mirabelle plums, then butter, honey, gingernut biscuits, toasted baguette, ultimately evolving into coffee beans in time. Long lees age has polished a fine, creamy bead and mouth-filling texture, while fine chalk minerality and well-defined 2002 acidity keep the finish neatly honed.

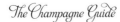
The Champagne Guide

Armand de Brignac

(Ah-mon de Brin-yak)

6 rue Dom Pérignon 51500 Chigny-les-Roses

www.armanddebrignac.com

ARMAND DE BRIGNAC
CHAMPAGNE

*W*hen the house of Cattier set out to make the most expensive champagne in the world in 2000, they could not have dreamed of the exposure it would receive. In what Cattier describes as 'a great miracle', US hip-hop sensation Shawn Carter (Jay Z) discovered the wine in his local wine shop in New York shortly after its release in 2006. To the 'great surprise' and delight of Cattier, Jay Z immediately featured the champagne in his new video clip. On the day of the release of the clip, the US distributor of Armand de Brignac received more than 700 requests for the champagne. Less than a decade later, more than 100,000 bottles are sold in 110 countries annually.

The striking gold, silver and emerald-clad livery and glam Ace of Spades branding are among Champagne's most lux designs of recent times. But is the wine inside worth the hype and not inconsiderable price?

The focus of Armand de Brignac is said to be pinot noir and meunier, though the current blend comprises 40% of each pinot noir and chardonnay. Sourcing is from the most 'emblematic' villages of Champagne, mostly premier crus and grand crus on the Montagne de Reims and Côte des Blancs, but unclassified villages comprise about 10% of the mix. There are three cuvées, with Brut Gold representing 85% of production, Rosé 10% and Blanc de Blancs 5%. A Demi-Sec will be introduced soon.

Each cuvée is a young non-vintage blend, in a fruity style, to contrast with Cattier's older Clos du Moulin. Dosage is aged in oak barrels for one year. The recipe is sound, though on paper there's nothing to distinguish it from the entry NV blends of many houses. Like them, the current release is based on the 2011 vintage.

Armand de Brignac Brut Gold NV $$$$$

93 points • Disgorged mid-2014 • Tasted in Chigny-les-Roses

40% pinot noir, 40% chardonnay, 20% meunier; 2011, 2009 and 2008, bottled in 2012; less than 9g/L dosage

Despite multiple visits to Cattier and many requests, I've been granted only one taste of Armand de Brignac, and that from a bottle opened a week prior, with an acknowledged loss of freshness and mousse. Nonetheless, it retains the vibrancy of lemon citrus, balanced acidity, impressive presence of chalk mineral mouthfeel, fine bead, integrated dosage and persistent finish. It's evenly balanced and well made, albeit very young and straightforward for its price.

AYALA

(Eye-yah-lah)

5/10

2 BLVD DU NORD BP36 51160 AŸ

www.champagne-ayala.fr

*B*ig changes are at hand at Ayala, and its wines are beginning to shine. A youthful enthusiasm is breathing through its grand, historic premises of Château d'Aÿ. The house that had been left sleeping until it was purchased by Bollinger in 2005 is now wide awake, and its elegant, chardonnay-charged cuvées are showing promise.

In 2011, Ayala assistant chef de cave and former Bollinger quality manager Caroline Latrive was appointed chef de cave at the age of 36. A year later, former Bollinger chief administrative officer, Hadrien Mouflard, was appointed managing director of Ayala at the age of 32. In the same year, the production facilities of the house were modernised with the purchase of new, small 25–100hL temperature-controlled vats.

'For me, it is a big change,' Mouflard explained when I visited recently. 'We need to capitalise on 150 years of great heritage and history of the house and to translate this into a contemporary style and feel, with the energy and the freedom to innovate.' This means reinventing the house with new packaging and a wine style to differentiate it from Bollinger and other houses.

Labels have been recently changed to stately black, the style of the house a century ago, but the big changes at Ayala go much deeper, boring to the core of the house style. In an attempt to emphasise freshness, elegance and balance, average dosage levels have been lowered from 11g/L of sweetness to just 7g/L. To distinguish it from the pinot-dominant style of Bollinger, the percentage of chardonnay in the key wine of the house,

Ayala Brut Majeur, has been raised from 25–30% to more than 40%. And, again in contrast to its stablemate, every cuvée is vinified in stainless steel tanks, in a quest for minerality, purity and freshness.

Ayala sources from some 50 growers and 75 hectares, laying claim to less than five hectares of its own vineyards, but this is somewhat misleading as it continues to access fruit from the original 40 hectares retained by its previous owners. It is also in the fortunate position of sharing vineyard sources with Bollinger — a very easy share, thanks to Ayala's strong reliance on chardonnay.

Ayala is a medium-sized house with an annual production of 700,000 bottles, up from 400,000 a decade ago, with a medium-term aspiration to increase to 1 million, equal to its production a century ago. There are currently 3 million bottles in its 2.5 kilometres of cellars, 25 metres under Aÿ, where non-vintage wines spend 30 months on lees, vintage wines six years, and prestige wines up to ten. Perle d'Ayala wines are aged under natural cork, said to produce a wine more resilient to the effects of oxygen during ageing. As with Bollinger, this necessitates hand disgorgement, and

The Champagne Guide

every bottle must be checked for taint. All wines undergo full malolactic fermentation.

Ayala's long history with dry wines began in 1870, just a decade after the house was founded, with the release of a champagne of 22g/L residual (in a market of typically 100–150g/L). The house claims to have produced the first zero-dosage champagne (in contention with Perrier-Jouët). However, Ayala's success with this style is uncontested, with its Brut Nature Zero Dosage finding tremendous popularity by the glass in London.

Ayala's noble practice of printing the disgorgement date on the back of each bottle gives consumers a chance to identify a fresh disgorgement — an opportunity precious few champagne houses deliver.

AYALA BRUT MAJEUR NV $$

86 points • DISGORGED MAY 2014 • TASTED IN BRISBANE
90 points • 2010 BASE VINTAGE WITH 25% RESERVES FROM 2009 AND 2008 • DISGORGED DECEMBER 2013 • TASTED IN AŸ
92 points • 2008 BASE VINTAGE WITH RESERVES FROM 2007 • DISGORGED OCTOBER 2011 • TASTED IN MELBOURNE

40% chardonnay, 40% pinot noir, 20% meunier; sourced from 25 villages; aged more than 3 years on lees; 7g/L dosage; 80% of production of the house

To this day, no Brut Majeur is more pristine and refined than the October 2011 disgorgement, thanks to the brilliant 2008 base vintage. There is still some kicking around, and with disgorgement dates printed on back labels, you might be able to find it. The vagaries of Champagne vintages make the 2010 base more coarse and dry, with steely structure and considerable grip. Its chardonnay lead is reflected in distinctive fruit focus of grapefruit, apple and pear. I can only assume that the current May 2014 disgorgement suffers from the challenging 2011 season, which would explain its disappointingly dry, dusty style, dominated by mushroom notes. A disgorgement to avoid.

AYALA BRUT NATURE NV $$

92 points • DISGORGED APRIL 2014 • TASTED IN AŸ

Brut Majeur, sans dosage; aged for another year (4 years in total); 40% chardonnay, 40% pinot noir, 20% meunier; 2009 base with 2008 reserves; 30,000-40,000 bottles per year; zero dosage

I've always preferred the low dosage Brut Majeur to the no-dosage incarnation, which is often less fresh, but the effect of the base vintage is pronounced in the Ayala house style, and the strength of 2009 and 2008 shine in this pure and vivacious release. Lively lemon, grapefruit and crunchy red apple are underlined by accurate, steely acid drive, prominent chalk mineral structure, good length and balance. It's perfect for oyster action.

AYALA ROSÉ MAJEUR NV $$

86 points • DISGORGED FEBRUARY 2014 • TASTED IN AŸ

51% chardonnay, 40% pinot noir, 9% meunier; 2010 base with 2009 reserves; 6% red wine from Aÿ made by Bollinger; aged more than 3 years on lees; 7g/L dosage

The tricky 2010 vintage rears its head in this savoury, dry rosé of dusty, pencilly character and coarse phenolic grip. There are some tomato and red berry fruits, but the theme remains drying astringency with a short finish.

Ayala Blanc de Blancs Brut 2007 $$$

94 points • Disgorged December 2013 • Tasted in Aÿ & Brisbane

25% Le Mesnil-sur-Oger, 25% Chouilly, 25% Cramant, 25% Cuis, Avize and Vertus; aged on lees more than 6 years; 6g/L dosage; 30,000-40,000 bottles

Managing director Hadrien Mouflard considers this the flagship of the new Ayala, and in sheer quality terms he's probably on the money. It's a wonderful celebration of the chardonnay personality of Ayala, in all its lively, vibrant, energetic and crystalline mineral style. It has upheld its pretty elegance while building complexity of nougat, grilled bread and dried pear during eight years in bottle. Dosage and acidity have found a comfortable balance in the six months since its release, drawn out by a magnificent undercurrent of firm, fine chalk mineral grip. It will age confidently for the medium-term, but be sure to keep this clear bottle in absolute darkness.

Ayala Blanc de Blancs Grand Cru 2004 $$$

94 points • Tasted in Melbourne

50% Le Mesnil-sur-Oger, 20% Cramant, 25% Chouilly; 6 years on lees, 7g/L dosage

First released in 2011, it took until 2013 for this cuvée to really come into its own, and my goodness it's only getting better. Beautifully refined and focused, it's upholding wonderful freshness of primary lemon zest, energised by focused mineral structure and fine acid grip. Subtle brioche maturity is somehow even less pronounced than it was two years ago, finishing with excellent length, well-integrated dosage and mineral carry.

Ayala Cuvée Perle d'Ayala Millésimé Brut 2005 $$$$

94 points • Tasted in Aÿ

80% chardonnay from Le Mesnil-sur-Oger, Chouilly and Cramant; 20% pinot noir from Aÿ; aged 8 years on lees under natural cork; 6g/L dosage; 10,000 bottles

Confirming the ascension of the house in recent years, Ayala's flagship is more admirable in the coarse 2005 season than the outstanding 2002 vintage. The phenolic grip of the year is evident in biscuity dustiness, and the ripeness of the year in boiled sweets notes, yet a fruity presence of ripe golden delicious apple, grapefruit and star fruit goes a long way towards refining it. The result is a refreshingly elegant take on the season, true to the style of the house, finishing with the excellent persistence, focus and mineral definition of grand cru Côte des Blancs chardonnay.

Ayala Perle d'Ayala Millésimé Brut Nature 2002 $$$$

91 points • Tasted in Aÿ

The same composition as the Blanc de Blancs (50% Le Mesnil-sur-Oger, 20% Cramant, 25% Chouilly) plus 20% Aÿ pinot noir; aged on natural cork; 6g/L dosage

Perle 2002 has been kicking around for about four years now, and it was at its best two years ago. It's now toasty and more reductive than I've seen it, with notes of gunflint and fennel supporting its primary grapefruit zest. The palate is tense and firm, having lost the silky succulence that endeared it, and is instead a little shaky on the finish.

The Champagne Guide

Barons de Rothschild

(Bah-roh de Roths-shield)

5/10

2 RUE CAMILLE LENOIR 51100 REIMS

www.champagne-bdr.com

CHAMPAGNE
BARONS DE ROTHSCHILD
PRODUCE OF FRANCE

The biggest challenge facing the launch of a new champagne brand lies in securing premium grapes. It takes a family as well connected as the Rothschilds to build a champagne house around chardonnay from the grand crus and premier crus of the Côte des Blancs. 'It's a war to buy grapes in Champagne, and especially in the Côte des Blancs,' says CEO and managing director Frédéric Mairesse. Within a decade, their well-crafted suite of young, fruity wines have set a precedent for what can be achieved from a standing start, even in this highly competitive region.

When the Rothschilds of the fabled Bordeaux Château Lafite, Château Mouton and Château Clarke united to establish their own champagne house, it was the first time the three competing branches of the family had worked together in 160 years. They began scoping out fruit sources in 2003, and by 2005 had secured an impressive portfolio of long-term contracts with growers, giving access to 20 hectares of vineyards, largely in Le Mesnil-sur-Oger, Oger and Cramant.

This has since quadrupled to 82 hectares from more than 45 growers managing more than 90% premier cru and grand cru vineyards. This is more than the 60 hectares required for the production of the house, permitting a selection of the best, and sale of the rest. About 500,000 bottles are produced each year, and in 2014 sales reached 270,000 across 60 countries.

BdR has ascribed its deep, rapid infiltration of the Côte des Blancs to its network of relationships through the Rothschild family and the strategic placement of its winery in Vertus. A princely €10 million was invested in Caves de Vertus, retaining the underground cellar and rebuilding the winery. Jean-Philippe Moulin was employed as winemaker in 2007, bringing a wealth of experience with chardonnay from his years at Ruinart.

The families remain closely involved and visit often, but Moulin was granted the freedom to make the wines as he saw best and to age them as long as he deemed necessary. His focus rests resolutely on cool fermentation exclusively in small stainless steel tanks, although there has been some experimentation with barrel fermentation for a yet-to-be-released 2006 grand cru blanc de blancs prestige cuvée. A high proportion of chardonnay across all cuvées calls for long ageing, with whites resting on their lees for four years, and rosés for three. The house had 2 million bottles in the cellar before it released its first bottle, and now has 2.7 million.

Small amounts of meunier have been removed from the blends to emphasise the longer-ageing chardonnay and pinot noir. Dosage has been lowered from 7–8g/L on first release in 2009 to 5–6g/L today.

Barons de Rothschild Brut NV $$

92 points • Tasted in Vertus, Sydney & Melbourne

60% chardonnay, 40% pinot noir and meunier; 2008 base; two-thirds of the production of the house; 6g/L dosage

Pretty yellow mirabelle plums and lemon freshness are layered with the brioche and vanilla of long bottle ageing, laced together with a creamy mouthfeel and soft chalk mineral structure. It's fresher than its age suggests, energised by the poise and excellent acidity of 2008, finishing with enticing length and balance. Bottles tasted in Australia showed more red cherry and red apple fruit and more pronounced development in characters of toast, honey, ginger and mixed spice. This cuvée remains the key focus of the house. Lovers of champagne, the family remains the biggest client. Every dinner for each brand in the portfolio begins and ends with champagne.

Barons de Rothschild Extra Brut NV $$

91 points • Tasted in Vertus

Same base as the brut; 50% chardonnay from Le Mesnil-sur-Oger, Oger, Avize, Cramant and Vertus; 50% pinot noir from Verzenay, Bouzy, Ambonnay, Avenay and Ludes; 2007 base vintage with 40% reserves from 2005 and 2006; 2g/L dosage

A tense and closed extra brut of tight lemon juice acidity, pear and golden delicious apple fruit. A dry finish of grapefruit pith texture looks a little taut.

Barons de Rothschild Blanc de Blancs Brut NV $$$

94 points • Disgorged July 2014 • Tasted in Vertus, Sydney & Melbourne

2008 base with 40% reserves from 2007 and 2006; Le Mesnil-sur-Oger, Oger, Avize, Cramant and a little Vertus; 7g/L dosage

Barons de Rothschild's impressive sourcing in the top villages of the Côte des Blancs makes its Blanc de Blancs its top cuvée, confidently meeting its brief of elegance and purity in the great 2008 vintage. It's fresh, tangy and charged with grapefruit, lemon, a long-lingering acid line and fine chalk mineral structure. The freshness and drive of 2008 provides vivacity and energy, while long lees ageing builds finesse and creaminess to its structure and subtle almond meal notes to a long finish. Bottles tasted in Australia showed more pronounced bottle age characters of toast and honey, while upholding lemon-accented poise and chalk mineral finesse.

Barons de Rothschild Rosé NV $$$

92 points • Disgorged July 2014 • Tasted in Vertus, Brisbane, Sydney & Melbourne

Same base as the blanc de blancs, with 15% pinot noir vinified as red wine from Vertus and Verzenay in a purpose-built winery using the same sorting table and small tanks as Lafite and Mouton; 2009 base vintage; 6g/L dosage

The elegance of Vertus and Verzenay pinot noir lends but a pale salmon copper hue to create a refined, apéritif style that the house dubs 'pink chardonnay'. More than four years on lees makes this typically quite a developed cuvée, with subtle red berry, pink grapefruit and rose hip notes evolving into a secondary, savoury and spicy demeanour of biscuits, toast, roast nuts and orange. The minerality of the Côte des Blancs defines a textural and chalk-bright palate with balanced dosage and a short finish.

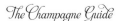
The Champagne Guide

BENOÎT LAHAYE

(Bur-nwah La-ay)

33 RUE JEANNE D'ARC 51150 BOUZY

A BOUZY

BENOÎT LAHAYE
CHAMPAGNE
GRAND CRU

*O*nly the most daring and fastidious growers practise a certified biodynamic regime in a climate as erratic as Champagne's. Benoît Lahaye is among the more thoughtful of these, an advocate of natural winegrowing from the beginning. His champagnes are a testimony to ripe fruit and intuitive practice in the vineyard and cuverie: powerful, exuberant and characterful wines of creamy mouthfeel, yet never heavy.

After taking responsibility for the family estate in 1993, Benoît ceased systematic herbicides the very next year and progressively introduced cover crops to encourage competition and prevent erosion. He achieved full organic certification in 2007, and biodynamic in 2010, but didn't stop there, attempting to reduce soil compaction by introducing his Burgundy horse, named Tamise, to work the vines. He thanks such techniques for higher ripeness and natural acid retention.

In the heart of the pinot noir epicentre of Bouzy, Lahaye's 4.8-hectare estate is planted to 88% pinot noir: three hectares in Bouzy, one next door in Ambonnay, and tiny parcels in Tauxières-Mutry and Vertus. Vine age is impressive, infusing a fantastic mineral expression in his cuvées, even as young vins clairs. A ripe style produced by full maturity in the vineyard is his aspiration, and he notes that everyone in Vertus except Pierre Larmandier and Pascal Doquet finishes harvest before he begins. It has only been since 1996 that Lahaye has bottled his own champagnes, today producing just 50,000 bottles annually.

Lahaye's natural, minimalist, intuitive approach extends to the cellar. Since 2012, all base wines have been fermented in 205-litre barriques of between new and 15 years of age, though he emphasises that his is not an oxidative style, preferring to leave oxidative development to occur in the bottle. This year he purchased new small tanks — two 300-litre Tuscan amphorae — and has ordered a few more to enhance fruit and mineral expression in his rosé. He's also testing two 200-litre egg fermenters for red wines.

Natural yeasts are used for every ferment, with malolactic fermentation blocked or allowed, according to the parcel and the season. Vintage wines are aged under cork or crown seal, with corks favoured for more structured seasons, and capsules for more expansive vintages. Lahaye has progressively decreased dosage, with Brut NV released as both brut and brut nature.

'I prefer to work in the vineyard, so I am automating the cellar as much as I can, to make more time to work in the vines,' he told me when I visited recently. This hasn't always been smooth: he had just lost 500 bottles, almost one-third of the production, of an old-vine cuvée, when the basket was dropped by his new gyro-palette. He built a new cellar for barrels in 2013, with an air pump for natural cooling, and has a new automatic disgorgement machine arriving shortly.

Lahaye has used full malolactic fermentation since 2008 to enhance complexity and permit the reduction of sulphur as a preservative. Some parcels are made without sulphur in the right seasons. His attention to detail extends to his labels, with disgorgement date, dosage and assemblage on the back of every cuvée.

BENOÎT LAHAYE BRUT NATURE NV $$

94 points • DISGORGED NOVEMBER 2014 • TASTED IN BOUZY

90% pinot noir, 10% chardonnay; 80% Bouzy, 20% Ambonnay; average vine age 35 years; harvested at 10.3-11 degrees potential alcohol; 2012 base vintage with 2011 and 2010 reserves; fermented in oak barrels; zero dosage; 6000 bottles

The ripe style of Lahaye works seamlessly without dosage, showcasing the excellent red cherry and strawberry fruit depth of Bouzy and Ambonnay. This conspires with barrel fermentation to infuse a full straw hue with a copper tint, yet retains excellent freshness of lemon zest notes and impressive acid line. It's all set off with complex notes of anise and nutmeg, lingering on a long finish of softly mineral texture.

BENOÎT LAHAYE BLANC DE NOIRS EXTRA BRUT NV $$

95 points • DISGORGED NOVEMBER 2014 • TASTED IN BOUZY

100% pinot noir, 80% Bouzy and 20% Tauxières-Mutry for mineral strictness; harvested at 10.8 degrees potential; fermented in oak barrels; 24 months on lees; 4g/L dosage; 8000 bottles

Lahaye's aspiration here is richness and minerality, and the wine delivers on both fronts emphatically. The power of red fruits here is monumental, oozing with red cherries, red berry compote and fruit cake, accented with nutmeg and hints of cocoa. Such fleshy exuberance commands structural support, which it offers abundantly in textured minerality, vibrant acid line and excellent length. This is a distinctive, characterful and beautifully crafted blanc de noirs that proclaims the exuberance of Bouzy without the heaviness that this village can sometimes exude.

BENOÎT LAHAYE VIOLAINE NV $$$$

94 points • DISGORGED JULY 2014 • TASTED IN BOUZY

100% 2010 and first released at 3 years of age, with successive releases to be labelled as vintage wines; 50% chardonnay and 50% pinot noir from Bouzy and Tauxières-Mutry planted 1989 and 1990; wild fermented in oak barrels; no sulphur; zero dosage; 2800 bottles and only 1000 released to date

A cuvée of excellent fleshy peach and ripe red berry fruits, with all the complexity of barrel fermentation expressed as brioche, mixed spice and a hint of crème brûlée. Barrel work and lees age conspire to create a very creamy mouthfeel, while well-defined acidity keeps it lively and fresh, culminating in fine, soft, salty mineral structure and excellent length.

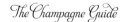

Benoît Lahaye Rosé de Macération Extra Brut NV $$

95 points • Disgorged January 2015 • Tasted in Bouzy

100% 2012 pinot noir from a single, low-yielding 1973 Bouzy parcel, but released too young to label as a vintage; 10% crushed berries and 90% whole berries macerated on skins for 24 hours, then pressed like a white wine for finesse; fermented in stainless steel tanks; 3g/L dosage; 2700 bottles

The colour is a pretty pale salmon, though Lahaye says it's not colour that he's aiming for in this characterful and textural rosé. The freshness and gentle spiciness of pinot noir are upheld in allusions of pink pepper, watermelon, pomegranate and strawberry hull, even hints of licorice and white pepper. Soft, chalk minerality and very fine, well-managed tannins build a captivatingly textural and creamy structure of impeccable length and line.

Benoît Lahaye Extra Brut 2008 $$

96 points • Disgorged October 2014 • Tasted in Bouzy

70% Bouzy pinot noir planted in 1966 and 30% Bouzy chardonnay planted in 1960; picked ripe at 11.2 degrees potential; wild fermented in oak barrels; 4g/L dosage

The energising effect of the scintillating 2008 season on ripe fruit in grand terroirs is like the breath of a cool sea breeze in a soft midsummer twilight. The delicious purity of ripe red cherries, the exotics of raspberries, the crunch of pink pepper and the delicate air of rose petals rise in unison in a style at once fleshy, succulent, creamy and silky and at the same time gorgeously focused, crystalline, tangy and energetic. Lahaye describes the minerality of his parcels meeting the minerality of 2008. The result is brilliant and superfine like quartz powder, with seamless line, magnificent acidity and incredible length.

Benoît Lahaye Le Jardin de la Grosse Pierre 2010 $$$$

93 points • Tasted in Bouzy

Benoît's late grandfather loved these two parcels in Bouzy and their history, planted in 1923 and 1952, and he worked them until he was 81. Benoît says 20 years of biodynamics have given them a new life, and he works these older vines with his horse. A blend of pinot noir, meunier, chardonnay, pinot blanc, chardonnay, arbane, petit meslier and others, co-harvested at 11.2 degrees potential and co-fermented in oak barrels with bâtonnage; zero dosage; 1680 bottles

A well-crafted and exuberant wine that achieves surprising coherence and seamlessness for such a recipe. Its complexity is a given, spanning the full exotic sweep of star fruit, kiwi fruit, pink grapefruit, lemon zest, spice, brioche, butter and nuts. Lively acidity is well contrasted by a creamy mouthfeel.

BÉRÊCHE & FILS

(Bair-aysh e Feess)

7/10

LE CRAON DE LUDES 51500 LUDES

www.champagne-bereche-et-fils.com

GRAND VIN DE CHAMPAGNE

Bérêche & Fils

PROPRIÉTAIRES DE VIGNES

Young brothers Raphaël and Vincent Bérêche exemplify an enthusiastic and talented new generation that is transforming some of Champagne's smaller, longstanding estates. Working alongside their father, Jean-Pierre, the brothers represent the fifth generation of the family to grow and make champagnes with a very real sense of purity and craftsmanship. They are rightly celebrated among the leading minds of Champagne's young generation, and their extensive range of current cuvées is proof of their talent. Theirs are intelligent and perceptive minds, not afraid to change and adapt, reflected resoundingly in an ever more refined house style.

While many would uphold organic or biodynamic certification as the holy grail of viticulture, Champagne's tumultuous climate makes such ideals in many sites infeasible at best. After several visits to Bérêche's cellars on the edge of the forest above Craon de Ludes, I was left with the overwhelming impression that any philosophy in force in the vines and wines of Bérêche is one of intuitive sensitivity, agile adaptability and good sense.

'We take a bit of this and a bit of that,' Raphaël declares unassumingly. 'We work in an organic way, but if there is too much rain in July and disease breaks out, we use a systemic chemical and then continue with our organic approach.' He's the first to admit Champagne is a difficult place to attempt to control everything, particularly in an estate as far-flung as this.

Since 1950, Bérêche's holdings have grown from just 2.5 hectares in Ludes to a total of 9.5 hectares, centred around Ludes and neighbouring Chigny-les-Roses, and extending as far as Trépail in the eastern Montagne de

Reims, Ormes west of Reims, and Mareuil-le-Port and Festigny in the Vallée de la Marne.

Raphaël emphasises the importance of managing all the vines themselves, to control yields. A modest production of 85,000 bottles from 9.5 hectares of mature vines averaging 38 years of age reflects particularly low yields. 'One problem of Champagne is that the yields are sometimes too high,' he admits. His brother Vincent has managed the vineyards since 2008, achieving balanced vines and fully mature fruit by maintaining yields of just 60–65hL/hectare — less than two-thirds the regional average. 'If we have higher yields, we need to put more products on the vines and there is a greater risk of disease,' Raphaël explains. 'It's like me: if I ate at [nearby restaurant] Le Grand Cerf every day I would die in two weeks!'

Bérêche encourages balance in his vines through spontaneous grass grown in the mid-rows. Herbicide use has been eliminated since Raphaël began in 2004. He believes this is the most important treatment to avoid, for the sake of the pH and acidity of the finished wines.

Biodynamics has been trialled since 2007 on a three-hectare plot in front of the house, as a test for the whole estate, but Raphaël admits that it's easier to manage nearby than 40 kilometres away in Festigny. 'We are just nine people and 9.5 hectares, so it's very important that we don't lose our crop!' he says.

Bérêche's simple and natural approach in the vineyard carries into the cellar, where labour-intensive, traditional techniques are favoured, from pressing and first fermentation to disgorgement. The brothers visit the vineyards three or four times to choose the right moment to harvest, and pickers are paid by the hour, not by the kilogram, to encourage stringent selection. Everything is pressed at the estate in Craon de Ludes. When I visited one Sunday morning two-thirds of the way through vintage 2014, I found Raphaël had been working until 2am and was at the press again by 7.30. He is hard-working, reflective and intuitive in responding to the seasons. While long, slow, natural primary fermentations are the goal, if the ferments run too long, they are energised with commercial yeasts. He likes the idea of yeasts from the domaine and the grape, but admits they're really derived from the cellar and barrels.

Fermentation is equally divided between oak barrels and old enamel-lined concrete tanks. 'Enamelled tanks are not as aesthetic in the cellar as stainless steel, but they're better for the wine,' he affirms, pointing out that stainless steel creates more reductive wines and requires chemicals to clean. Slightly larger and older 300-litre Burgundy barrels are preferred to Champagne's traditional 205-litre barrels, as their more subtle influence on the wine maintains fruit precision.

Wines are matured for extended periods in both barrels and tanks prior to bottling. Ageing on lees with a little bâtonnage allows the wines to become slightly reductive, providing protection from oxidation, even with only very small additions of sulphur dioxide. A low-sulphur regime is a priority, with small additions to maintain freshness only on the press and after fermentation, and none at bottling or disgorgement. Bérêche prizes low pH, dissolved carbon dioxide gas and sugar in the dosage ahead of sulphur dioxide for preserving freshness. This seems to work most of the time, although I have occasionally noted funky barrel notes in some cuvées. To his credit, Raphaël has recognised when sulphur levels are too low and corrected in subsequent releases.

Even with such low sulphur levels, Bérêche has no trouble fully blocking malolactic fermentation, thanks to very cold (8°C) cellars at the top of Craon de Ludes. 'Historically, Champagne did not have malolactic

Raphaël Bérêche draws a sample of red wine, a particularly compelling Coteaux Champenois of the northern Montagne.

fermentation,' Raphaël points out. 'This was only introduced in the 1980s, to make it easier to drink, and to reduce the time in the cellar.'

Bérêche is working to increase the time each cuvée is aged, with a new cellar under the house to increase capacity for reserve wines. With the exception of the entry Brut NV and Extra Brut NV, all cuvées are aged on cork instead of crown seal, to increase oxygen interaction and produce a more creamy bead and a more open, characterful and complex wine, with a more logical coherence of nose and palate.

Cork ageing necessitates hand disgorgement, and it takes two people to taste and disgorge 1200 bottles a day. A traditional *liqueur d'expédition* is used in place of grape concentrate, at very low levels of dosage, so as to faithfully preserve tension and minerality in the wines. Raphaël highlights that even 2–3g/L of dosage is important for ageing, and does not regard his Extra Brut NV as a style to age for more than five years. Back labels of all cuvées are impressively informative, disclosing dosage, disgorgement date and base vintage.

Bérêche recently relinquished its RM status in favour of NM, so as to have the flexibility to purchase more vineyards and buy from growers. 'We wanted to buy a 0.3 hectare plot in Mailly-Champagne, but the authorities only permitted us to buy half because they said we were too big,' Raphaël explains. Their NM status has opened up the opportunity to selectively purchase tiny quantities of mature champagnes from top terroirs to sell under their Raphaël et Vincent Bérêche label. Next year the brothers will release a Le Mesnil 1999 magnum, an Oger 2001 and a Mailly-Champagne 2006.

The wines of Bérêche are vinous champagnes of dry complexity. Even as young vins clairs, these are wines generously expressive of both ripe fruit intensity and the mineral signature of their sites. Raphaël and Vincent have succeeded in progressively toning the assertive temperament of malic acidity, barrel ferment-ation and low dosage, making for champagnes that will confidently keep fanatics enthralled.

BÉRÊCHE & FILS CAMPANIA REMENSIS NV $$$

93 points • DISGORGED OCTOBER 2012 • TASTED IN CRAON DE LUDES

2009 base vintage; no malolactic fermentation; 3g/L dosage

A brand new cuvée that I've never seen anywhere but Bérêche's cellar, this is a very restrained rosé of lovely texture and structure. Raphaël is critical of saignée rosé for its heaviness, instead crafting this as a blend with a very small addition of red wine. Its colour is medium crimson, surprisingly deep for a rosé as elegant and refreshing as this, and a credit to his method of blending in black glasses to judge the addition of red wine on nose and palate rather than colour. It's fresh and taut, with gorgeous notes of red apple, red cherry and strawberry hull. Tight malic acidity and low dosage accentuate chalky mineral texture, while lingering red cherry pinot character is apparently reinforced by ageing under cork.

BÉRÊCHE & FILS CAMPANIA REMENSIS EXTRA BRUT ROSÉ 2010 $$$

94 points • DISGORGED JUNE 2014 • TASTED IN CRAON DE LUDES

70% pinot noir and 30% chardonnay; a core of fruit from Ormes with 5% red wine; just one barrel

This is the second release of Bérêche's rosé, the first deemed too rich so the red wine was sensitively wound back here to produce a pretty medium salmon hue and a savoury and softly textural style of well-defined presence and elegant persistence. Red apple and gentle red berry focus are accented by savoury, charcuterie barrel ferment notes. A seamless balance is achieved in uniting a creamy, silky texture with focused malic acid drive.

BÉRÊCHE & FILS LES BEAUX REGARDS CHARDONNAY BRUT NATURE 2010 $$$

93 points • DISGORGED JANUARY 2014 • TASTED IN CRAON DE LUDES

Single plot Ludes; 2g/L dosage

A jousting contest between the focused white fruits, grapefruit and lemon of ripe chardonnay, impaled by the structure of firm, high-tensile acidity, fine tannin grip and pronounced salty chalk minerality. Subtle charcuterie and boiled sausage notes of barrel fermentation quickly dissipate to allow the fruit to play its part. A wine of excellent line, length, confidence and drive, demanding a decade in the cellar to settle itself down.

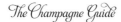

BÉRÊCHE & FILS VALLÉE DE LA MARNE RIVE GAUCHE PINOT MEUNIER EXTRA BRUT 2010 $$$

92 points • DISGORGED DECEMBER 2013 • TASTED IN CRAON DE LUDES

Single plot from the family's best parcel of old meunier vines planted in 1969 on the left bank of Mareuil-le-Port in the Vallée de la Marne; vinified in 350–600L barrels; aged on lees in barrel for 8 months and under cork at least 30 months; no malolactic fermentation; 3g/L dosage

Raphaël confesses that it took lots of sorting of botrytis to extract this wine from the difficult 2010 season. The result is a deep hue of full straw with a copper tint and a characterful expression of meunier akin to blood orange, red apple and Christmas spice, emphasised by barrel fermentation. For all this, it upholds lemon definition, good acid line and softly textured structure, making for a bright and cheerful meunier style.

BÉRÊCHE & FILS BRUT RÉSERVE NV $$

89 points • 2011 BASE • DISGORGED FEBRUARY 2014 • TASTED IN CRAON DE LUDES
94 points • 2012 BASE • DISGORGED JULY 2014 • TASTED IN CRAON DE LUDES

35% pinot noir, 35% chardonnay, 30% meunier; 20% fermented in old barrels, the remainder in enamel-lined tanks; aged at least 24 months; no malolactic fermentation on the base wine, perhaps on the reserves; 7g/L dosage; 30% reserves from a perpetual reserve commenced in 1985, with two-thirds of each demi-muid removed as the reserve each year, providing a depth of complexity while maintaining chalky freshness in the reserves

Bérêche admits that this is his most difficult wine to make, with an aspiration of richness, finesse, chalk minerality, creamy texture and a clean, bright finish. He achieved this with impeccable precision with the 2012 base, in lovely focus of pear, apple and grapefruit, energised with well-defined malic acid tension and finely textured mineral mouthfeel. Barrique fermentation overlays subtle nutty, spicy complexity and gentle richness, which provide a calming influence of internal harmony, while sustaining the potential to age. The challenging 2011 season produces a savoury, hard wine of tense acid grip.

BÉRÊCHE & FILS LE CRAN LUDES PREMIER CRU 2007 $$$$

95 points • DISGORGED MAY 2014 • TASTED IN CRAON DE LUDES

From two plots near the house at the top of the hill in Ludes; 55% chardonnay, 40% pinot noir, 5% meunier; 100% barrel fermented in 205L, 228L and 500L barrels; aged on lees for 8 months and under cork a minimum of 60 months; no malolactic fermentation; 2g/L dosage

Bérêche releases a vintage every year and is frank in admitting that it was in 2007 that he started to understand what he wanted to do, describing 2006 as too natural (too little sulphur), 2005 too rich and 2004 too oaky. The 2007 is his best yet, an excellent expression of the village and the vintage, a captivating contrast between the ripeness of grilled pineapple and the tension of grapefruit and malic acidity, brushed with the charcuterie complexity of barrel fermentation and the roast almonds and brioche of maturity. The combination is harmonious and seamless, with excellent concentration and persistence.

BÉRÊCHE & FILS REFLET D'ANTAN BRUT NV $$$

93 points • DISGORGED JUNE 2014 • TASTED IN CRAON DE LUDES

The reserve wine for the Brut NV from perpetual solera reserve (see above); one-third of each of the three varieties from Ludes and Chigny-les-Roses; no malolactic fermentation; aged on cork a minimum of 3 years; 2009 vintage base; 6g/L dosage

Bérêche's reserve is finding a harmony between the succulence of juicy yellow summer fruits of pineapple exuberance and the savoury charcuterie, vanilla, mixed spice and anise of barrel work. Its fruit triumphs on a long and full finish of well-toned malic acidity, expressive, fine, salt chalk mineral texture. It's powerful, yet never heavy or imposing, a champagne of expression and character before comfortable appeal.

RAPHAËL ET VINCENT BÉRÊCHE COTE PREMIER CRU EXTRA BRUT NV $$

90 points • DISGORGED DECEMBER 2013 • TASTED IN CRAON DE LUDES

80% Avize, 20% Gueux; 2007 base vintage with 5% reserves; aged 70 months on lees; 3g/L dosage

A rich and mature blend from Bérêche's négociant sourcing, with a full straw hue and excellent complexity of pineapple, yellow fruits, dried fruits and roast nuts. Dryness on the aftertaste reflects premature development. A powerful style that sadly topples over on the finish.

RAPHAËL ET VINCENT BÉRÊCHE VALLÉE DE LA MARNE GRAND CRU EXTRA BRUT 2002 $$$$

94 points • DISGORGED DECEMBER 2013 • TASTED IN CRAON DE LUDES

60% pinot noir and 40% chardonnay from the top of the hill in Aÿ; 2g/L dosage; 1680 bottles

Sourced from a deceased négociant, this is a lovely, voluptuous Aÿ style of ripe yellow summer fruits, layered with fig, dried peach and roast nuts. The persistence and fine chalk mineral texture of the village shine. It's just beginning to dry out on the finish, though confidently holding its own for now.

BÉRÊCHE & FILS COTEAUX CHAMPENOIS ORMES ROUGE 2012 $$

92 points • TASTED IN CRAON DE LUDES

1965 vines of pinot noir and meunier; fermented with 75% stems; 540 bottles

Raphaël makes one of the best white Coteaux Champenois I've tasted (2013 Ludes, from barrel), and loves the challenge of red winemaking in Champagne. His 2012 is a great example, vibrant purple in hue, with a tightly focused and fragrant demeanour of violets, black cherries, blackberries and pepper. A finely textured backbone of silky tannin grip, lively acid profile and great persistence demand at least a decade in the cellar.

BILLECART-SALMON

(Bill-khah Sal-moh)

9/10

40 RUE CARNOT BP8 51160 MAREUIL-SUR-AŸ

www.champagne-billecart.fr

The art of crafting elegant, graceful champagne requires the most exacting skill. Sweetness, richness and breadth cover all manner of sins in champagne, but a wine in its unadorned, raw nakedness reveals even the slightest blemish for all to see. The mark of Billecart is made not by the heavy footfall of concentration, power and presence, but rather by the fairy touch of delicacy and crystal-clear fidelity. Every one of its dozen cuvées articulately speaks the house philosophy of 'respecting the integrity of the fruit, freshness and acidity'.

On the surface, there appears little to distinguish the fruit sources of this medium-sized house in Mareuil-sur-Aÿ. Vineyard holdings are small, servicing a 2 million bottle annual production with just 20 hectares of estate vines and more than 300 hectares of purchased fruit managed by 185 growers. How does Billecart maintain such transcendental standards in each of its cuvées?

Antoine Roland-Billecart, who manages the house with his brother François, answers this question with a refreshingly frank honesty. 'We are not very focused on marketing,' he begins in impeccable English. 'Vinification is the key for us, and all the rest is bullshit.'

Its elegant delicacy places Billecart dizzyingly high among Champagne's finest houses, but also infuses its cuvées with an inherent fragility, rendering them particularly vulnerable to imperfections in closure, transportation or storage. Without disgorgement dates indicated on bottles, it's difficult to ascertain the age of non-vintage cuvées, but be sure to ask for fresh stock that hasn't lingered on retail shelves.

Billecart's vintage wines can be coiled up tight in their youth and appreciate plenty of time to open up in a large glass.

Over many hours of visits and intensive tastings with Antoine and cellar master François Domi, an enlightening picture emerges, illuminating some 11 spheres that account for the astounding performance of Billecart-Salmon.

LONGSTANDING FAMILY MANAGEMENT

Although not exclusively owned by the family, Billecart has been under family management since it was founded in 1818. The family still lives on site, and there is a long-visioned continuity at play. The eighth generation of the family, Nicolas Roland-Billecart, came on board alongside his father François, uncle Antoine and grandfather Jean in 2010.

'We are very lucky that my father still joins us for every tasting,' Antoine reflects. 'He began working in

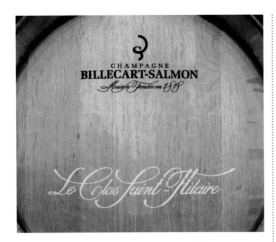

Billecart has increased use of oak more than 10-fold in 18 years.

wine when he was 16 and has over 70 harvests in his memory. His experience of terroir is so great that he can comment on the effect of every parcel in a blend and challenge us to consider what a wine will be like in 20 years. "This sample won't last, and in 15 years you're going to cry!" he tells us. He has such experience that he can feel a vintage by smelling and tasting the musts, building the blend in his mind before we even taste it.'

HANDS-ON VINEYARD MANAGEMENT

'It's easy to work for a company that is searching for quality as the goal across the whole process,' François Domi says. Starting with the fruit. 'The best grapes on the best terroirs are expensive, but this is our priority.'

Billecart's production has trebled in the past 20 years, and since that time they have set about acquiring vineyards centred around Mareuil-sur-Aÿ. In 2004, the family sold a 45% share in the firm, and in so doing secured access to an additional 80 hectares of grand cru fruit.

Today, the company also manages 65 hectares under lease arrangement, taking full control, from pruning to harvest. 'This is very important,' explains Antoine, 'because it enables us to conduct the vineyard the way we want, yielding 70hL/hectare rather than 85–90, ensuring consistent ripeness and balanced concentration and acidity.' A team of 40 local pickers is paid by the hour to be particularly selective in the most sensitive vineyards.

In vineyards under company control, there has been a return to a more natural way of growing vines and promoting soil health through an absence of pesticides and herbicides. Clos Saint-Hilaire has been worked biodynamically for 12 years, and other estate vineyards

are working towards the same regime. All growers are encouraged to grow grasses in the mid-rows to limit yields. A generational approach to farming, rather than a full biodynamic regime, is the aspiration.

PARCEL SELECTION

Even at a modest 70hL/hectare, Billecart's output is tiny for an estate sourcing from 320 hectares. Antoine considers the flexibility of sourcing grapes from 185 growers to be strategic, permitting vinification of 140% of production every year, with lesser parcels sold as still wines, or declassified to Billecart's second label, Charles Le Bel.

'It's great to own your own vineyards, but the opportunity to be selective is something fantastic!' Antoine exclaims. The decision was made recently to cap production at the current level of 2 million bottles.

METICULOUS PRODUCTION REGIME

The precision of Billecart is proclaimed in a squeaky-clean winery, even during my visit at the height of vintage 2014. Each element of its meticulous production is geared towards capturing every nuance in the fruit. Billecart presses half the fruit it purchases and uses a pneumatic press for larger parcels, because it's more gentle than the traditional press. One hundred 40hL tanks and some 450 barrels maintain individual control over every one of 280 parcels.

'We have to be very precise, increasing quality by being overly selective, keeping what we want and getting rid of what we don't want to keep,' explains Antoine. A massive new blending tank was commissioned in 2009 to lower the risk of oxidation and increase the consistency of the blends.

COLD SETTLING AND COOL FERMENTS

Perhaps Billecart's most revolutionary technique is its practice of double débourbage. After the standard clarification process to settle out solids, the juice is settled a second time at 4°C for at least 48 hours without use of enzymes. The house pioneered this technique in 1952, inspired by the brothers' maternal grandfather's experience in brewing beer. At this temperature, the coarser lees are removed without risk of oxidation, delivering pristine juice for fermentation. The process is expensive and time-consuming. 'Most of our colleagues thought we were crazy!' admits Antoine.

The juice is then brought up to just 13°C — never more than 14°C — for the primary fermentation. Antoine has growers and houses tell him it's impossible for yeast to work at this temperature. At 13°C, cultured yeasts from the natural yeasts of nearby villages take 3–4 weeks to complete fermentation. Such cool, long ferments are crucial for retaining greater freshness and delicacy than a standard champagne ferment of one week at 20°C. Parcels then stay on lees in tank for six months, crucial for development of personality, structure and aroma.

All parcels for non-vintage blends pass through malolactic fermentation, but for vintage wines this is dependent upon the season. For Antoine, 'respecting the style of the vintage is more important than anything else', and winemaking is adapted each year to suit.

INCREASING USE OF OAK

When Antoine comes to work every day he asks himself what can be done to improve vinification within the house style. As a devotee of Krug Clos du Mesnil — he openly volunteers the inaugural vintage as his favourite blanc de blancs of all time — it's no surprise Billecart has increased the use of oak barrels for fermentation since 1996. Fifty barrels in that year became 80 in 1997. A new barrel room now houses 500 barrels and two new large oak foudres, ranking Billecart fourth for barrels in Champagne, after Krug, Bollinger and Alfred Gratien. The plan is to replicate this room to add 25 80hL oak foudres.

Old barrels, having seen six or seven vintages in Burgundy, are used for the fermentation of all grand cru fruit, and bâtonnage is conducted weekly, according to taste. Barrels currently range from five to 15 years of age. The goal at Billecart, as always, is to encourage subtle complexity rather than overt character. 'Just to add some spice,' as Antoine puts it.

Antoine Roland-Billecart inspects chardonnay grapes with a grower.

LOW DOSAGE

Antoine considers a decrease in dosage over the past decade as crucial in allowing the fruit to show its full character. 'It is like make-up,' he proposes. 'You don't need it if there is no problem, and you want to show the real character of the wines.' Dosage levels are low: typically 8g/L in non-vintage wines, and around just 4g/L in vintage wines ('Extra Brut'). Any more sweetness might play havoc with such delicate styles.

DIFFERENT LIQUEUR FOR EVERY DOSAGE

The final nuance comes at disgorgement: every cuvée has a different liqueur at Billecart. Domi conducts many tastings with different dosages, from wines aged in barrel and those in tank, to determine which best suits each wine. A different liqueur is used for every disgorgement, so completely different liqueurs can be chosen for the start, the middle and the end of a cuvée.

LONG AGEING

Billecart's non-vintage wines are aged for 3–4 years, and its millésime collection a minimum 8–10 years (the 2002 Cuvée Nicolas François Billecart was released in 2013). Slow sales in 2012 permitted the Brut Réserve NV to be released after 36 months in the cellar, rather than the 24 months of recent years. Billecart holds a deep collection of reserves, with at least one-third of every harvest kept in reserve.

SUPERIOR CLOSURE

Finally, and crucially, all non-vintage wines except blanc de blancs have been sealed with DIAM cork since 2006. DIAM is not perfect, but it is demonstrably superior to natural cork. Billecart's Australian agent reported an immediate drop in returned bottles as soon as DIAM was introduced. Billecart is currently seven years into a 10-year trial of ageing of vintage wines under DIAM. I look forward to the day when Billecart's top wines are entrusted to a reliable closure.

THE GENIUS OF FRANÇOIS DOMI

Alongside the enthusiastic energy of Antoine Roland-Billecart, François Domi is the quietly spoken and reflective genius. He started in the lab at Billecart as an oenologist almost 30 years ago and describes himself today as part of the furniture. His unassuming manner means his name is never listed among Champagne's rockstars, but his greatest hits of the past two decades surely place him at the top of the charts.

BILLECART-SALMON BRUT RÉSERVE NV $$

93 points • 2011 BASE • DISGORGED FEBRUARY 2014 AND OCTOBER 2014 • TASTED IN MAREUIL-SUR-AŸ & RILLY-LA-MONTAGNE
92 points • 2010 BASE • TASTED IN SYDNEY, PERTH & MELBOURNE

44% reserves; 49% meunier, 32% chardonnay, 19% pinot noir; 8g/L dosage; DIAM closure; around 1.2 million bottles annually

Billecart's enchanting Brut Réserve upholds its aspiration of impressive freshness and elegance even in the difficult 2011 season, a credit to impressive levels of reserve wines, up from 35% to comprise a generous 44% of this blend. The blend has been tweaked, too, with more meunier and chardonnay this year.

Brut Réserve is a captivating contradiction, dressing one of Champagne's higher representations of meunier in one of the most delicate and graceful of attires. It glides onto the stage and sings with the pristine signature of the house, energising the red apple and red berry fruits of meunier with a breathtakingly refined melody of pure lemon zest, in a dazzling display of elegant, soft, crystalline chalk minerality and understated, fragrant elegance. There is only the slightest suggestion of the dryness of 2011 here, finishing with well-integrated dosage and good persistence.

The 2010 and 2008 base vintage blends retain freshness, bright acidity and mineral drive, though the 2009 base is now lacking freshness.

BILLECART-SALMON EXTRA BRUT NV $$

94 points • 2009 BASE • TASTED IN SYDNEY & MELBOURNE
94 points • 2007 BASE • TASTED IN MELBOURNE

40% meunier, 35% pinot noir, 25% chardonnay; 1–2g/L dosage; DIAM closure

One of the most refined almost zero-dosage champagnes, built on the same base as Brut Réserve — but crucially, not simply a zero-dosage version of the same. It's older, with an extra year on lees — 'not so it has more fat', explains Antoine, 'but so it is more rounded, with less angles'. The liqueur in the dosage is different, too, with 5mL of reserve wines contributing volume, structure and persistence. The 2009 base proclaims Billecart's refreshing clarity in a brittle shell of bone-shaking purity and citrus minerality, contrasting excellent focus, drive and integrity of vibrant lemon, grapefruit and crunchy pear with subtle brioche development.

BILLECART-SALMON BLANC DE BLANCS GRAND CRU BRUT NV $$$

95 points • 2009 BASE VINTAGE • DISGORGED MARCH 2014 • TASTED IN MAREUIL-SUR-AŸ, RILLY-LA-MONTAGNE, SYDNEY & MELBOURNE

Blend of 50% Avize for structure, Cramant for florals, Le Mesnil-sur-Oger for definition and Chouilly for depth; 25% reserves; a little bâtonnage in tanks for texture; 6g/L dosage; DIAM closure

'In your dreams,' responded Jean Roland-Billecart when his son Antoine proposed a non-vintage blanc de blancs. 'We don't have sufficient quantity of chardonnay, but if you find the grapes to produce it, go ahead.' And find them he did. Not just anywhere, but in the five grand crus of the Côte des Blancs, and in 1997 Billecart made its first non-vintage blanc de blancs.

The 2009 base is an impeccable follow-on to the arresting 2008. A magnificent accord of white citrus and white stone fruits meets the gentle patisserie, butter and nougat character of five years of maturity, creating an enticing style at once focused, honed and refreshing and at the same time creamy, soft and textural, energised by tense, energetic acidity and a softly rumbling undercurrent of grand cru minerality.

The Champagne Guide

BILLECART-SALMON BRUT ROSÉ NV $$$

95 points • 2010 BASE • TASTED IN SYDNEY, PERTH, YARRA VALLEY & MELBOURNE

40% chardonnay, 30% pinot noir, 30% meunier; just 7-8% pinot noir red wine from Mareuil-sur-Aÿ, more for aromatic effect than colour; partial malolactic fermentation; 9g/L dosage; DIAM closure

Some 20% of Billecart's production is rosé (400,000 bottles), claimed to be the biggest proportion of rosé in Champagne. The utter restraint of the house places delicate rosés very close to its heart, dubbed internally 'champagne rosé' rather than 'rosé champagne'. Antoine recounts a tasting in which he poured the wine into black glasses for sommeliers. Not one identified it as a rosé. 'When my grandfather began producing rosés in the early 1960s, most thought it a fanciful, artificial wine that lacked purity,' he recalls. 'He persevered, convinced it would have its place. Those sceptics are now making their own!'

    Epic refinement of pale salmon hue and gorgeously restrained red cherry, strawberry and rose petal nuances. Delightfully understated, eminently fresh and elegantly persistent, it carries with grace and poise amidst fine chalk mineral texture, taut acid focus and impeccably pure persistence. Enjoy it in its ravishing youth.

BILLECART-SALMON CUVÉE SOUS BOIS BRUT NV $$$

93 points • TASTED IN SYDNEY & MELBOURNE

One-third of each champagne variety; one-third reserve wines from the previous two harvests, which Antoine describes as 'the fourth third so it doesn't fit in the bottle!'; fully oak-fermented below 16°C; aged on lees in barrel with bâtonnage for 6 months; 7g/L dosage; DIAM closure

Sous bois is as distinctive for Billecart as its bold, modern label. 'With the diversity of Champagne's regions and the rise of growers, it's increasingly important for us to produce more interesting, small-production wines,' points out Antoine. Sous bois is literally 'under wood', inspired by oak-fermented parcels destined for Billecart's top cuvées. Its aspiration is to uphold the mandate of Billecart in freshness, tightness and elegance. This release is driven by lively acidity, toned lemon zest freshness and well-focused minerality, underscored by impressive magnitude and richness, with flamboyant swirls of caramel, roast nuts and honey. It sings with classic Billecart precision, while basking in the richness of barrel fermentation, silky and alluring, confronting and commanding, all at once. Don't serve it too cold, and give it lots of air in a large glass.

BILLECART-SALMON EXTRA BRUT VINTAGE 2006 $$$

92 points • DISGORGED DECEMBER 2013 • TASTED IN MAREUIL-SUR-AŸ
      & RILLY-LA-MONTAGNE

75% pinot noir, 25% chardonnay; a little less than 20% pinot barrel fermented; 3g/L dosage

Billecart is aiming for more personality in its wines, and this release reveals the character and dry structure of a ripe season, showcasing the diversity of the house in bridging its elegant cuvées and its richer sous bois style. The ripe yellow fruits of the season are united with the spice, brioche and preserved lemon of maturity, and notes of grilled toast and gunpowder reduction. Firm, dry phenolic structure is driven by grapefruit pith grip, accented by partial barrel fermentation. This is purposely a food champagne and is true to a lesser vintage, though it finishes with good length and well-integrated dosage.

BILLECART-SALMON BLANC DE BLANCS BRUT 2004 $$$$

97 points • DISGORGED IN 2013 • TASTED IN MAREUIL-SUR-AŸ

A blend of Le Mesnil-sur-Oger, Cramant, Avize and Chouilly; 15% fermented in barrels; 5g/L dosage

BdB 2004 makes a monumental declaration: from Billecart's proud position in the heart of pinot territory, this shows its command of the fabled chalk terroirs of the Côte des Blancs' A-list. From its introverted and stately magnificent stance two years ago it has intensified into a brilliantly luminous beacon that will continue to dazzle for decades. A wine of graceful allure, euphoric freshness and profound poise, it's breathtakingly elegant yet innately intense. Crystalline poise of fine-ground chalk minerality, faintly flinty nuance and pronounced acid line open into an expansive presence of white citrus and white stone fruits, in time disclosing in brioche, butter and subtle spice the magnificent hallmarks of more than a decade of maturity. Profound persistence and enticing interplay between primary citrus and long-aged complexity.

BILLECART-SALMON CUVÉE NICOLAS FRANÇOIS BILLECART 2002 $$$$

99 points • DISGORGED IN 2012 • TASTED IN MAREUIL-SUR-AŸ, SYDNEY, MELBOURNE & BRISBANE

60% Montagne de Reims pinot noir, 40% Côte des Blancs chardonnay; 18% barrel-fermented in old oak casks; partial malolactic fermentation; 4g/L dosage; 50,000 bottles

Some champagnes volunteer their life story within seconds of first introductions, like overworked movie trailers that leave you fully convinced you've seen the film. Others churn in your consciousness for days, slowly unravelling their story long after the credits have rolled. NFB 2002 has played out a captivating script since my first dramatic encounter in mid-2013, beginning to open magnificently to display remarkable complexity, yet at every moment clinging to impeccable elegance, coiled focus of malic acid tension and exhilarating chalk mineral texture. Even at 13 years of age it upholds brilliant primary definition of icy lemon citrus, with only subtle, graceful evolution of nougat and butter, promising decades of potential yet. As always, the greatness of Billecart is proclaimed not by impact or power, but by slowly rising complexity and profound chalk mineral presence. Its cascade of minerality is very fine, to the point of silkiness, yet simultaneously poised and confident.

Delightful poise and intricate craftsmanship proclaim one of the great Billecarts of the modern era, a champagne with many characters and subplots to reveal, to be enjoyed slowly in the presence of the most intimate company — and ideally not for at least another decade. It's every bit worthy of its price rise this year.

BILLECART-SALMON CUVÉE NICOLAS FRANÇOIS BILLECART 1988

98 points • TASTED IN RILLY-LA-MONTAGNE

Evidence of the sheer endurance of NFB, this is a magnificent bottle in impeccable condition. A medium yellow-gold hue introduces a palate with marmalade and exotic spice, tumbling with layers of fig, glacé peach and burnt butter. Sensational persistence and undeviating line, intricately interwoven with fine mineral mouthfeel. I have a good feeling that the 2002 is headed in this direction. We have a long time to wait!

The Champagne Guide

Billecart-Salmon Cuvée Nicolas François Billecart 2000 $$$$

98 points • Tasted in Sydney & Melbourne

60% Montagne de Reims pinot noir, 40% Côte des Blancs chardonnay; partially vinified in old oak casks; no malolactic fermentation; 4g/L dosage

This is still developing much slower than anyone, including its maker, François Domi, anticipated of the harrowing 2000 vintage. Such is the endurance of this cuvée that it has still not diminished one iota in the seven years since I first reviewed it in 2008 and named it Wine of the Year in the inaugural edition of *The Champagne Guide*.

A wine of wonderful volume and epic focus and liveliness, it sits within a frame of restrained mineral expression and pinpoint clarity. The pinot's authority is controlled by the chardonnay's tone. Malic acidity cracks the controlling whip, energising fresh, youthful notes of white citrus, flowing seamlessly into those warm, yellow late-summer fruits, becoming bees wax and butter. A whiff of grilled toast reduction adds another dimension, finishing with great power of chalk mineral texture. One of the greatest 2000s, holding its head high with sensational poise, magnificent acid drive and outstanding persistence. It continues to drink majestically, and who knows for how long? Two bottles I tasted in Australia were slightly lacking in freshness.

Billecart-Salmon Le Clos Sainte-Hilaire 1999 $$$$$

96 points • Disgorged July 2014 • Tasted in Mareuil-sur-Aÿ (twice)

1 hectare clos in Mareuil-sur-Aÿ; planted exclusively to pinot noir since 1964 and managed biodynamically since 2003; yielding a minuscule 40-45hL/hectare, less than one bottle per vine; harvested in two passes at full ripeness; two cuvées vinified in situ; fully fermented in oak; no malolactic fermentation; zero dosage; around 5000 bottles, only in top vintages

Le Clos Saint-Hilaire has no right to its profound echelon. It is but a premier cru, although this is more a reflection on the inadequacies of an oversimplified cru system. More significantly, in soil — deeper and less chalky than, for instance, the Clos des Goisses at the other end of the village — and in aspect (due east, far from the sought-after south-facing orientation), it has no claims to greatness. It is but a flat expanse beside the press house in the village. The genius of François Domi and the painstaking attention to detail of Billecart play a dramatic role. I could not name another wine at this level, anywhere in the world, of which the same could be said.

Alongside Krug Clos d'Ambonnay, Billecart Le Clos Saint-Hilaire is the king of blanc de noirs. It was conceived as Antoine and François Roland-Billecart stood on the wall of the clos late one night during harvest in 1995. With plenty of red wine in stock for rosé, they decided they could afford to put this pinot noir in the cellar for a decade to see how it looked on its own.

Le Clos Saint-Hilaire's fourth release is not the towering masterpiece of its predecessor, with its impeccable freshness and profound mineral clarity. François Domi describes it as opposite in personality to the 1998. I was the first outside the house to taste it, and on pouring he exclaimed, 'Le rosé de Saint-Hilaire!' It's deep in colour, a full yellow-gold hue, true to its power and depth in encapsulating a warm season at 16 years of age. Its concentration and ripeness embody an inky black spectrum of black plum and black cherry fruit, licorice, dark fruit cake, fig, blood orange, toffee, mocha and mixed spice, with a hint of warm hearth just beginning to emerge. This maelstrom is well contained and focused by malic acidity and the structural grip of mouth-embracing chalk mineral texture, though this warm season is structured more by drying grip than by acid tension. Nonetheless, it retains freshness, poise and profound persistence. A Clos Saint-Hilaire to drink in the next few years.

BOIZEL

(Bwah-zel)

46 AVENUE DE CHAMPAGNE 51200 EPERNAY

www.boizel.com

CHAMPAGNE

BOIZEL

MAISON FONDÉE EN 1834

Evelyne Roques-Boizel is the fifth generation to head Boizel. Seven hectares of estate vineyards are complemented with long-term contracts with growers in about 50 villages, boosted in 1994 after an injection of funds from the Lanson-BCC group. Boizel's clean, fruity style is achieved through fermentation in stainless steel vats at 18°C, full malolactic fermentation, and long ageing of non-vintage cuvées of at least three years. Vintage wines are aged five to seven years, after a small proportion of vinification in barrel. Back labels declare the blend and disgorgement date.

BOIZEL BRUT RÉSERVE NV $$

89 points • 2010 BASE VINTAGE • DISGORGED JUNE 2014 • TASTED IN BRISBANE
91 points • 2008 BASE VINTAGE • TASTED IN MELBOURNE

55% pinot noir from Mailly-Champagne, Venteuil and Pierry, 30% chardonnay from Vertus, Chouilly, Cuis and Nogent-l'Abbesse, 15% meunier from Vandiéres, Châtillon-sur-Marne and Mont-Saint-Père; 8g/L dosage

Boizel's entry wine is a citrusy and fruity style that contrasts lemon zest crunch with the toasty, honeyed notes of three years on lees. Low dosage keeps the acid tension in focus through a finish of line and length. There's character and fruit intensity here, albeit in a somewhat coarse and simplistic style.

BOIZEL BRUT ROSÉ NV $$

85 points • 2011 BASE VINTAGE • DISGORGED OCTOBER 2014 • TASTED IN BRISBANE
89 points • 2007 BASE VINTAGE • TASTED IN MELBOURNE

50% pinot noir, including 8% red wine, from Pierry, Cumières and Les Riceys, 30% meunier from Ferebrianges, Troissy and Châtillon-sur-Marne, 20% chardonnay from Vertus, Chouilly and Nogent-l'Abbesse; 2011 base vintage; 8g/L dosage

Delicacy of pomegranate and watermelon fruit is quashed by the coarse, dusty, mushroomy hardness of the rot inherent in the challenging 2011 season, rendering the finish astringent and callow.

Boizel Blanc de Blancs NV $

87 points • 2010 BASE VINTAGE • DISGORGED MARCH 2014 • TASTED IN BRISBANE

Cramant, Le Mesnil-sur-Oger, Vertus and Chouilly; 8g/L dosage

An elegant and restrained style of lemon zest, pear and golden delicious apple fruit, leading out gracefully, but collapsing on a dusty, coarse and phenolic finish.

Boizel Blanc de Noirs NV $

90 points • 2010 BASE VINTAGE • DISGORGED MARCH 2014 • TASTED IN BRISBANE

100% pinot noir from Les Riceys, Cumières and Mailly-Champagne; 8g/L dosage

The flattering personality of pinot noir from strong terroirs shines in red cherry and red berry fruits, crunchy red apples and the tang of pink grapefruit. It's fruit-focused, zesty and creamy all at the same time. A little phenolic grip braces the finish, but it has the fruit presence, line and length to handle it.

Boizel Ultime Extra-Brut NV $$$

91 points • 2006 BASE VINTAGE • DISGORGED MARCH 2014 • TASTED IN BRISBANE

50% pinot noir from Mailly-Champagne, Pierry and Chavot, 37% chardonnay from Avize, Oger and Le Mesnil-sur-Oger, 13% meunier from Passy-Grigny, Vandières and Cumières; zero dosage

A full straw hue reflects its considerable maturity of seven years on lees, which is regrettably not proclaimed anywhere on the label. There's no mistaking it in the glass, in rich and powerful aromas and flavours of butterscotch, toffee, toast, dried pear and preserved lemon. Such smooth, buttery silkiness and creamy bead contracts with a dry, grippy finish of bitter grapefruit zest that begs for a touch of dosage to bring integration and completeness. So close to greatness!

Boizel Grand Vintage 2007 $$$

88 points • DISGORGED OCTOBER 2014 • TASTED IN BRISBANE

50% pinot noir from Mailly-Champagne, Cumières and Les Riceys, 40% chardonnay from Cuis, Chouilly and Vertus, 10% meunier from Vandières and Verneuil; 3% oak; 8g/L dosage

Restrained red apple, pear and lemon zest fruit is underlined by the subtle brioche and honey notes of lees age. It has balance and poise but lacks fruit character and style, with a finish driven more by phenolic grip than acid line or mineral presence.

Boizel Joyau de France Brut Millésime 2000 $$$$

93 points • Disgorged March 2014 • Tasted in Brisbane

65% pinot noir from Mailly-Champagne, Pierry, Vertus and Cumières, 35% chardonnay from
Le Mesnil-sur-Oger, Avize, Oger and Vertus; 10% oak; 7g/L dosage

A glowing, full straw yellow hue characterises the 2000 harvest and betrays its maturity. It has
attained that place of tertiary complexity of coffee bean, cocoa, gingernut biscuits and dried
plums, having reached the end of its life, but doing so with confidence and grace, upholding its
joy in a finish of integrity and persistence, only now just beginning to dry out. Acidity, dosage
and texture are beautifully entwined.

Boizel Joyau de France Millésime 1996 $$$$

88 points • Tasted in Melbourne

60% pinot noir, 40% chardonnay

A vintage of ripe fruit with some raisined notes, beginning to develop toasty and honeyed maturity, though
clinging to the acid energy of 1996. It had been in Australia for three years before it reached me, and it was
no longer at its prime.

Boizel Joyau de France Brut Rosé 2004 $$$$

89 points • Disgorged October 2014 • Tasted in Brisbane

64% pinot noir, including 10% red wine from Mailly-Champagne, Vertus, Cumières and Les Riceys,
36% chardonnay from Oger, Avize and Vertus; 5g/L dosage

With a medium salmon orange hue, this is a dry and secondary style of developed red berry fruits and red apple,
having lost its primary vivacity without replacing it with any particular character of maturity. The result is firm,
dry and hollow, suggesting that it would likely have been better released some years ago.

Boizel Cuvée Sous Bois Brut 2000 $$$$$

92 points • Disgorged July 2014 • Tasted in Brisbane

50% pinot noir from Aÿ, Mailly-Champagne and Mareuil-sur-Aÿ; 40% chardonnay from Chouilly,
Vertus and Cramant; 10% meunier from Chigny-les-Roses; fully vinified in oak; 5g/L dosage

A full straw yellow hue celebrates vintage, maturity and oak. After 15 years, the toasty,
sappy notes of oak remain prominent, without disguising the signature, lush yellow fruits
of the generous 2000 vintage. The accord has certainly appreciated a long time in bottle to
harmonise and to build in silky butteriness, though a little dry extract lends a bitter grip
to a finish that is beginning to tire. Nonetheless, a persistent and confident cuvée, ready
to take on main-course fare.

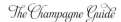
The Champagne Guide

BOLLINGER

(Boh-lahn-zhay)

www.champagne-bollinger.com

CHAMPAGNE
BOLLINGER
MAISON FONDÉE EN 1829

It's another world at Bollinger. Take everything you know about large champagne houses, the way champagne tastes, the way it's fermented, the way it's aged, even the ownership of the vineyards and the companies, and brace yourself for a very different story at Bollinger. I've met with the good Bollinger folk numerous times in recent years in Australia and in their illustrious maison in Aÿ, and on every occasion I have been astounded by the pace of change. If Bollinger wasn't your style five years ago, come hither! There's never been a better time to bask in the glory of this legendary house. These are ravishing champagnes that now rank high among the very best of the region. James Bond, you've finally got it right.

In early 2013 Mathieu Kauffmann announced his surprise resignation as chef de cave of Bollinger. The house appointed Gilles Descôtes as his replacement. After almost a decade of experience on Bollinger's tasting panel, overseeing the estate vineyards, managing grower relations and taking charge of production in 2012, he was a natural choice.

The Bollinger house style has long been a love-it-or-hate-it champagne, oft maligned for the aldehydes that can develop as a result of oxidation during barrel ageing (see 'Fizzers', page 28). Oxidation during fermentation is positive, but prior to fermentation it suppresses fruit, and post-fermentation it dulls the wine. The priority now is to suppress oxidation, creating fresher and less aldehydic wines, a priority that the house balances delicately with its priority of using as little sulphur dioxide preservative as possible. Exacting attention to the finer details has transformed Bollinger over the past decade, lifting its wines to the cleanest, most precise, least aldehydic it has ever made.

There are 10 facets that set Bollinger apart among champagne houses, beginning in the vineyards.

ESTATE VINEYARDS
Bollinger is a champagne of cathedral proportions: massive, impacting and magnificent. Its weight derives foremost from estate-grown pinot noir. 'We have pinot noir in our blood,' says Descôtes. 'We are nicknamed "The Burgundy house"!' Every cuvée has a minimum of 60% pinot noir, and an impressive 60% of the grapes come from estate vineyards. (The only other house boasting such proportions is Louis Roederer.) Centred around Aÿ, Champagne's pinot noir epicentre, Bollinger's mighty 164 hectares comprise 85% grand cru and premier cru vineyards. 'We liken ourselves more with champagne growers than houses, since our vineyards are such an important part of our house,' Descôtes declares.

The policy of the house is to only buy grapes that it can assess visually. It thus only sources from the

Marne, and favours Aÿ and the nearby villages of Louvois, Mareuil-sur-Aÿ, Verzy and Verzenay, though the great Côte des Blancs crus of Le Mesnil-sur-Oger, Cramant, Avize, Oger and Cuis are also important. Aÿ and Verzenay are at the core of every Bollinger blend. Grape maturity is pushed a little further at Bollinger through careful choice of harvest date, a blessing the house attributes to vineyard ownership. When I visited on the second-last day of harvest 2014, Bollinger's red wines for rosé had only just started fermenting, while most at Veuve Clicquot had already finished. Bollinger's balance of fruit is sourced from winegrowers who have worked with the house for many generations (every one of 120 parcels is vinified separately at Bollinger; there is no purchase of *vins sur lattes*). This accounts for the consistency, depth and complexity in Bollinger's wines.

The house is experimenting with organics in a few of its plots, though doesn't aspire to seeking certification.

NEW PRESS HOUSE

To reduce pre-ferment oxidation, a new press centre was constructed in neighbouring Mareuil-sur-Aÿ, within line of sight of the maison in Aÿ, in time for the 2003 vintage. Almost all the grapes of estate vineyards are transported by truck or tractor to Mareuil, where eight-tonne pneumatic presses are worked 24/7 to press 200 tonnes every day. Every grape variety, every cru and sometimes even individual growers are kept separate. To facilitate long ageing, no tailles is used in Bollinger's cuvées.

In 2013, Bollinger doubled its red wine processing capacity in response to increasing demand for rosé. Since 2005, the house has produced all of its own red wine from tiny yields of just 30hL/hectare. When I visited during harvest 2014, I was impressed by a stringent team of eight, fanatically working the sorting table as tiny grapes for red wines arrived at the press centre.

BARREL FERMENTATION

Bollinger uses only the cuvée (the first and best pressing) and ferments under temperature control in both stainless steel tanks and oak barrels. Use of barrels for fermentation and ageing is a key element in reinforcing Bollinger's house style, and Descôtes goes to great lengths to retain freshness and fruit purity through diligent barrel cleaning and cellar hygiene. Every barrel is tasted post-fermentation and again before blending.

The magnitude of this task becomes apparent after witnessing more than 3000 champagne barrels of 225-litre capacity stacked long and high, row after

A stringent team of eight works Bollinger's red wine sorting table.

row, plus 208 barrels of 400-litre capacity, made by Bollinger in 1903. To increase consistency, old barrels of at least three years of age are purchased annually from Bollinger-owned Burgundy négociant Chanson and maintained until they are 20–30 years old, by what Bollinger claims to be the last in-house cooper in Champagne. Bollinger's vintage wines are 100% barrel fermented, as are all of its reserve wines, and any other parcels with sufficient acidity to handle 6–7 months in barrel.

Comparing vins clairs (fermented still base wines) fermented in stainless steel and oak is enlightening, the barrel-fermented samples in no way woody (thanks to the age of Bollinger's barrels) but better integrated, more textured, more complex and better balanced. Bollinger considers barrels an insurance policy for the wine, providing controlled oxidation, and drawing out the longevity of Grande Année to 20 years and beyond.

FAMILY OWNERSHIP

With an annual production of a little more than 2.5 million bottles, Bollinger is the largest independent champagne house after Louis Roederer, owned and run completely by members of the Bollinger family. This provides the freedom to uphold practices, such as longer ageing under cork, that might be considered infeasible under a large owner.

LONGER AGEING

Bollinger keeps its cuvées on lees for long periods: a minimum of three years for non-vintages (until recently two and a half years), and eight years or longer for Grande Année (previously six). This is considered crucial for producing small bubbles and very fine, velvety textures.

More than 12 million bottles are held in storage in Bollinger's six kilometres of cellars over four levels under Aÿ, including 750,000 magnums of grand crus and premier crus fermented in barrels, bottled with natural corks and kept for between five and 15 years, or longer. There is a desire to increase production, but only at the very slow rate of 5000 bottles per year, so as to uphold quality. To sell one more bottle in five years' time, the house needs to put five more bottles in the cellar now.

Infused with the resilience of barrel maturation, Bollinger's white cuvées are rock-solid, and I rarely encounter bottle variation whenever and wherever in the world I taste them. They also possess propensity for great longevity (but its rosés are best drunk as youthful as possible). Her Majesty the Queen of England cellars her Special Cuvée for 10 years, and reportedly did not pop the 2001 disgorgement until 2010!

AGEING UNDER CORK

Bollinger upholds that ageing its reserve wines in magnum on natural cork rather than crown seal affords more complexity, a practice followed by a small number of growers and small houses, but no other sizeable house. Six grams of sugar is added for a *prise de mousse* (carbonic fermentation) to produce a light sparkle to retain fresh flavour and aroma in these reserve magnums, dubbed 'aromatic bombs' by the house.

It's not hard to see why very few houses age reserve wines under cork: it necessitates riddling and disgorgement by hand, not to mention wastage to cork taint. It takes a team of six people three weeks to open 80,000 reserve magnums by hand for the Special Cuvée and Rosé. It's a tedious and expensive process to check every bottle for cork taint by nose. Workers are instructed not to wear perfume on disgorgement days, and not to front up at all if they have a cold. The house reports a rejection rate to cork taint of less than half of 1%, but admits that even this is too much. The benefits of DIAM corks in eliminating cork taint are acknowledged, but they are considered aesthetically inferior, and the preference is for contact with natural, unglued cork.

It's not only Special Cuvée that's produced using a labour-intensive process at Bollinger. Vintage wines are hand disgorged, with every bottle tasted at disgorgement, and non-vintage rosé is hand riddled.

Asked about the practice of ageing under cork, Christian Pol Roger allegedly replied: 'It's a great idea, but we are not as crazy as you are at Bollinger!'

MALOLACTIC FERMENTATION

In the past, malolactic fermentation occurred haphazardly, only in those barrels and tanks that happened to progress naturally. In pursuit of greater consistency, malolactic bacteria are now introduced to ensure systematic completion of malolactic fermentation.

ONE BLEND

All 2 million bottles of Bollinger's Special Cuvée are triaged at once in a single blend in February, to maintain the consistency of each blend. To further promote freshness, Bollinger disgorges three times a year, with each disgorgement from the same original blend, yet subtly different due to a different length of time on lees.

Annoyingly, disgorgement dates are not stamped on non-vintage bottles (they are on the vintage wines). Labelling occurs shortly after disgorgement, so the labelling date provides a good indication. The first two digits of the labelling code on the neck of Special Cuvée and Rosé are the year and the next three digits are the number of the day of that year, so L1405002 means the 50th day of 2014.

The letter on the cork is the month of disgorgement and the number is the year, so 4A is January 2014.

MODERN FACILITIES

To further reduce post-ferment oxidation, in 2012 Bollinger installed one of Champagne's most modern disgorgement lines. A computerised system checks for defects in the seal of cork-sealed bottles, and rejects 3–4%. (If only it could detect cork taint, too!) When I visited, a cart was stacked 10 high with rejects destined to be used as liquor for dosage.

Since 2013, Bollinger has introduced a system of 'jetting' at disgorgement. A tiny droplet of water is sprayed to foam the wine and push out oxygen. Internal trials have revealed this process to greatly diminish oxidation during disgorgement. Bottling facilities were updated in 2005, 2008 and again in 2012, this time in preparation for a new bottle.

NEW BOTTLE

In 2012, Bollinger launched its gloriously refined '1846' bottle with a wider base, narrower neck and elegant curves. It is based on an original champagne bottle found in the Bollinger cellars dated 1846. The benefits are more than just aesthetic. With a neck three millimetres narrower, the new bottle has a neck cross-sectional area 20% smaller than the last, which slows the oxygen exchange, better for ageing. This neck is also said to take up 40–50% less oxygen during disgorgement.

For a champagne of breadth, depth and grandeur, and one that is readily available and affordable, Bollinger is in a world of its own. It's no surprise the house cannot keep up with demand and imposes allocations in every market.

Bollinger Special Cuvée Brut NV $$

95 points • Disgorged January 2014 and mid-2014 • Tasted in Aÿ, Brisbane, Melbourne & Perth

The complexity and richness of Special Cuvée is unparalleled among the entry-level non-vintage blends of every champagne house, short of ascending to the mesosphere of Krug. Its grand recipe explains why. The current release is a blend of 60% pinot noir, 25% chardonnay and 15% meunier, 50% from 2009, 45% from 2008 and 5% from the late 1990s, vinified in oak barrels and aged in magnum under cork. The small percentage of older reserves are considered crucial for maintaining consistency. In all, this equates to a mind-boggling 400 wines and a massive 50% of reserve wine — astonishing numbers unrivalled by other houses. Further intensity is derived from 30–40% of the blend in oak barrels, and a very high proportion of grand cru and premier cru fruit sources (more than 85%). Post-blending, the wine matures for between three and four years on lees in the cellar before it is disgorged and a light dosage of 8g/L is added. This cuvée represents 90% of the production of the house — more than 2 million bottles annually.

Benchmark Bollinger, fresh and vivacious, yet wonderfully resonant with all the depth and triumphant complexity that set Special Cuvée apart. A universe of complexity spans light years of white and black cherries, plums, fresh lemon zest, even the richness of ripe peach and pineapple. Deep reserves reverberate with Bollinger's signature notes of ginger, dried nectarine, mixed spice, toast, brioche, honey and roast nuts. For all this, it upholds achingly pristine citrus zest freshness throughout, riding on a tense acid line, culminating in a masterful crescendo of fine, frothing, salt-infused minerality. A worthy successor to the brilliant 2008/2007 blend.

Bollinger Rosé Brut NV $$

96 points • 2009 base vintage • Disgorged late 2013 • Tasted in Aÿ, Sydney, Melbourne, Perth & Brisbane

Bollinger Rosé NV has doubled in volume since its much-celebrated introduction in 2008, though it still represents just 200,000 bottles, merely one-tenth of Special Cuvée. The blend is now slightly different to Special Cuvée, here 62% pinot noir, 24% chardonnay and 14% meunier. Pinot noir red wine from the grand cru villages of Verzenay (predominantly) and Aÿ is given long pre-ferment maceration and matured in barrel for 12 months. The house prides itself on its red wine, and such is its strength, concentration, depth of colour and robust tannin structure that a tiny 5–6% is all that is required. Like Special Cuvée, it is matured 3–4 years on lees. The blend is more than 85% grand crus and premier crus, with a light dosage of 8g/L.

This is breathtaking rosé, full-bodied in every way, with magnificent body, spellbinding purity and impeccable poise. Greater elegance is the mandate, and it meets the brief with effortless grace, a medium salmon hue and vibrant liveliness in the midst of profound depth. Characterful intensity of coffee bean and dark chocolate celebrates its toasty, secondary side, seamlessly matched to a tangy core of pink grapefruit, wild strawberry and fig. It's all intricately laced together with fine-tuned acidity, a creamy bead and subtle tannin texture that reinforces soft chalk mineral texture, lingering long on a refined finish.

BOLLINGER LA GRANDE ANNÉE 2005 $$$$

95 points • DISGORGED OCTOBER 2014 • TASTED IN BRISBANE

70% pinot, 30% chardonnay; 13 crus, 95% Grand Crus (Aÿ and Verzenay for pinot, and Avize, Chouilly and Le Mesnil-sur-Oger for chardonnay); fermented and matured entirely in oak barrels; aged under natural cork 8.5 years; 6g/L dosage

Landing with all guns blazing ahead of a new James Bond release, this is a vintage that captures the full Spectre of grand Bollinger exuberance, with a fruit integrity rarely seen in 2005 at a decade of age. It glows with grilled pineapple, oozes with ripe peach and resonates with the depth of black cherries, before launching into a universe of Bollinger complexity in golden fruit cake, biscuits and roast nuts. The depth and body of Bollinger confidently steps up to the firm structure, dry astringency and grapefruit-like grip of the season, built more on phenolic presence than acid line, yet with the flesh, drive and persistence to carry it, culminating in a crescendo of seamless persistence. An earlier-drinking Bollinger and a great take on 2005.

BOLLINGER LA GRANDE ANNÉE ROSÉ 2005 $$$$$

95 points • DISGORGED SEPTEMBER 2014 • TASTED IN BRISBANE

72% pinot noir, 28% chardonnay; a blend of 13 crus, mainly Aÿ and Verzenay for pinot noir, and Avize, Chouilly and Le Mesnil-sur-Oger for chardonnay; 95% grand crus and 5% premier crus; 5% still red wine from La Côte Aux Enfants; fermented and matured entirely in oak barrels; aged under natural cork 8.5 years; 7g/L dosage

LGA Rosé is La Grande Année with a tiny inclusion of red wine from the same vintage. Bollinger's new rosé beckons from its radiant, full salmon copper gown with exuberant, extroverted and flamboyant appeal. Even a tiny dose of just 5% red wine heightens its purity and depth of gorgeous cherry fruits, cherry kernel and anise, hovering above a grand expanse of fruit mince spice, golden fruit cake, grilled pineapple, juicy peach and cherry liqueur. It intricately laces beautifully fine tannin structure with the grip and depth of the warm 2005 season, lingering very long with red cherry purity. It's attained its full magnificence already, a vintage to drink early.

BOLLINGER R.D. EXTRA BRUT 2002 $$$$$

97 points • DISGORGED SEPTEMBER 2013 • TASTED IN AŸ & BRISBANE

R.D. is Bollinger's 'Récemment Dégorgé', which confusingly is not necessarily 'recently disgorged', but a vintage of La Grande Année that has aged longer on its lees. The blend is 60% pinot noir and 40% chardonnay from 16 grand crus and seven premier crus, with less dosage than the LGA rendition: just 3–4g/L. The 2002 was an exhilarating La Grande Année of driving energy and a razor edge of structure that barely evolved across the years of its release cycle. It naturally makes for a brilliant and enduring R.D. — though double the price is a lot to pay for three more years on lees (11 all up), particularly when the LGA was still lingering on retail shelves when R.D. first landed. This is particularly exemplified in a vintage as long-lived as 2002, which will effortlessly take another decade or two in its stride. Smart collectors cellar LGA instead. The 2002 represents a magnificent R.D. of honed focus, youthful dynamism and wonderfully vibrant acid line, underscored by very fine chalk minerality. The enticing exuberance of pinot noir's red cherry and plum fruits strikes a wonderful interplay with the mixed spice of barrel fermentation and the integration of 13 years of age, creating creamy depth amidst tightly honed focus. It's loaded with all the gingernut biscuits, Christmas pudding, nougat, brioche, dried pear and honey you'd expect from Bollinger. Every bottle I have tasted has been beautifully fresh bar one, which was horridly oxidised, tasting of vinegar and onions.

BOLLINGER R.D. EXTRA BRUT 1996

100 points • DISGORGED OCTOBER 2013 • TASTED IN AŸ

The enduring 1996 vintage is but halfway through its life at almost 20 years of age, and R.D. embodies the mood of the season with exacting clarity: powerful, luscious and awe-inspiring in its complexity, pierced by sensational shards of acidity as bright as daylight streaming through gaping windows. It's breathtakingly youthful, clenching a tight core of tangy lemon fruit energised by magnificent chalk mineral drive. Only 1996 can deliver such concentration of structure and flavour simultaneously, loaded with butterscotch, spice, toast and dried fruits of monumental proportions. A grand paradox, both larger and lighter than life, a towering masterpiece with such an awesome future stretching out for decades before it: who can say what surprises may yet be in store?

BOLLINGER R.D. EXTRA BRUT 1988

99 points • DISGORGED OCTOBER 2013 • TASTED IN AŸ

This is where the great vintages of Bollinger are destined, a mesmerising place where wonderful complexity makes way for magnificent tertiary character, though never losing touch with its confidence and precision. A blend of 72% pinot noir and 28% chardonnay declares Bollinger depth and intensity in secondary white peach fruit becoming dried fruits, marzipan, nougat, vanilla and pipe smoke. Crunchy preserved lemon notes are well defined on an assured and very finely textured finish of pronounced chalk mineral presence. An undeviatingly persistent, seductive, silky and magnificent old Bollinger.

BOLLINGER EXTRA 1914

100 points • DISGORGED BETWEEN THE 1930S AND 1960S WITH ~6G/L DOSAGE • TASTED IN AŸ

Served blind direct from the private cellar of the family, I was put on the spot and asked to guess the vintage. It was clearly older than the 1988 prior, darker, with magnificent tertiary complexity of truffles, mushrooms, curry and warm hearth, yet sustaining a wonderful secondary core of preserved lemon, grapefruit and dried pear and a very fine, subtle yet present bead. It sustained such integrity, incredible length, breathtaking complexity and a very soft, lingering chalk mineral persistence. I deliberated for a moment and naively verbalised that the question for me was whether it was 1960s or 1970s and I would have to conclude that it was too fresh for 1960s. Bollinger president Jérôme Philipon leant over with a warm smile and said, 'It is a bit older than that,' and handed me the cork, clearly marked '1914'. It was the last day of vintage 2014, a century almost to the day from that excellent harvest at the beginning of World War I. Perhaps most remarkable of all, it showed no hint of fading even an hour later. Such is the timelessness of champagne.

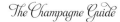

BONNAIRE

(Bohn-aire)

6/10

120 Rue d'Épernay 51530 Cramant

www.champagne-bonnaire.com

*B*onnaire is privileged to 13.5 hectares of well-situated vines in Cramant and 8.5 hectares in the Vallée de la Marne. Jean-Louis Bonnaire is the third generation to manage the house, which was founded by his maternal grandfather, Fernand Bouquemont, in 1932. Married to Marie-Thérèse Clouet, he also vinifies her Paul Clouet champagnes of Bouzy and sources a little Bouzy pinot noir for his own rosé. With the exception of Bonnaire Variance, all cuvées are vinified in stainless steel. The Bonnaire style is a creamy expression, led by Cramant chardonnay, with malolactic fermentation carried to completion. They represent good value for money.

BONNAIRE BLANC DE BLANCS GRAND CRU NV $

94 points • TASTED IN BOUZY

2010 base vintage with 15% reserves from 2009; chardonnay from Cramant and Bouzy; aged 3 years on lees; 8g/L dosage

A blanc de blancs that reflects great sites, particularly in Cramant, with fine precision, purity and great concentration. Pretty lemon zest and apple fruit is accented by the subtle brioche notes of three years on lees, underscored by a core of fine chalk mineral texture, well-defined acid line, nicely integrated dosage and excellent length.

Bonnaire Grand Cru Blanc de Blancs Millésime 2005 $

93 points • Tasted in Bouzy

Aged 6 years on lees; 8g/L dosage

An impressive expression of the difficult 2005 vintage, this is a blanc de blancs that celebrates the depth and concentration of privileged sites in Cramant. The primary characters of red apple, grapefruit and fig are still prominent after a decade, sustained by a core of focused acidity on a very long finish. With just a hint of honey on toast beginning to increase, it's ready to drink now.

Bonnaire Ver Sacrum Blanc de Blancs Brut NV $

92 points • Tasted in Bouzy

2006 base; a blend of Cramant and Bergères-les-Vertus; aged on natural cork for more than 6 years; 6g/L dosage

The crunchy pear and lemon zest of chardonnay are united with notes of mixed spice and roast hazelnuts from bottle development. This is a slightly oxidative style, which contracts the finish a little, though maintains expressive acidity, fine, mineral mouthfeel and plenty of character.

Bonnaire Variance Blanc de Blancs Brut NV $$

87 points • Tasted in Bouzy

2010 base vintage with 2009 reserves; a blend of Cramant and Bergères-les-Vertus; vinified and aged in barriques; matured at least 5 years on lees; 7g/L dosage

It is uncertain whether oxidation occurred during barrel fermentation or maturation on lees under cork, but the result is a developed colour of medium to full straw yellow hue, prematurely developed fruit and a slightly maderised, dried-out finish. It's complex, nutty and toasty, with grapefruit and orange zest character masking good structure and persistence.

Vintage 2014 under the windmill in the grand cru of Verzenay on the northern slopes of the Montagne de Reims.

BRUNO PAILLARD

(Broo-no Peye-yard)

AVENUE DE CHAMPAGNE 51100 REIMS

www.champagnebrunopaillard.com

Champagne

BRUNO PAILLARD

Reims-France

When former Lanson BCC director and CIVC communications director Bruno Paillard set out to establish his own champagne brand in 1981, he sold his Jaguar to finance the operation. 'It takes three generations to create a house,' he says. 'But there are some advantages starting three centuries after everyone else!' Three decades on, his finely crafted cuvées are evidence of what can be achieved with sufficient connections and determination.

It's no simple thing to establish a champagne house, and when Paillard set out he had no land, no stock, no vineyards and no right to even purchase fruit. What he did have was a great network and considerable knowledge. Then, a regulation banned any upstart from purchasing fruit, so, instead, he sourced wines from earlier vintages to establish his brand and gain purchasing rights.

A generation later, Paillard crafts 400,000–500,000 bottles annually — 'small enough to hand craft, but large enough to make the hard decisions and to be selective!' he says. The freedom to be selective is fundamental for Paillard, and he sets the rare precedent of selling half the fruit he presses, all of his second pressings, and anything else that doesn't meet the standard for his blends.

Sourcing spans 35 villages, with 32 hectares of estate vines supplying more than 50% of requirements. Vineyards are ploughed and worked with no herbicides, calling for a vineyard worker for every two hectares, rather than the average three hectares. Paillard says it takes 5–8 years to get the results he wants. 'A lot of people thought we were crazy to work this way!' he admits.

Paillard has been progressive from the outset, leading the way in using a gyropalette in Champagne, and was the first in the region to publish the disgorgement date on every bottle — more than controversial when he set out in 1983.

He built his winemaking facility next door to Piper-Heidsieck in Bezannes on the outskirts of Reims in 1990 and expanded its capacity in 2000. Every parcel is vinified separately in 100 tanks and 400 old oak barrels purchased after three vintages and kept for eight or nine. One-fifth of all base wines are fermented and matured in barrels and a Special Cuvée is entirely barrel fermented. All cuvées are aged long, with Brut NV and Rosé enjoying three years on lees, Blanc de Blancs four, Vintage eight and Special Cuvée 11–12.

Bruno devotes 10–20% of his time to responsibilities to support the region, and is currently chair of the Appellation Committee of the CIVC, overseeing the monumental task of updating the region's boundaries. He is ably assisted by his daughter, Alice, who takes responsibility for sales and marketing of the house.

Bruno Paillard Premiere Cuvée Brut NV $$

94 points • 2009 base vintage • Disgorged November 2012, April 2013 & November 2013 • Tasted in Sydney, Melbourne & Reims

45% pinot noir from the Montagne de Reims and Les Riceys, 33% chardonnay from the northern Côte des Blancs, 22% meunier from the Vallée de la Marne; 40% reserves; 20% ferment in old barrels; sourced from 35 villages; 6-7g/L dosage; 3-4 years on lees; 60% of the production of the house

Pinot noir leads this accurate, well-crafted apéritif style of elegant finesse and persistence. A primary red cherry, wild strawberry and lemon fruit focus is underlined by taut acidity and expressive chalk mineral depth. Nuances of honey, anise and ginger are building as it gains maturity. It's clean and taut, a low dosage keeping the finish fresh and lively.

Bruno Paillard Blanc de Blancs Reserve Privée Brut NV $$$

95 points • Disgorged June 2010 • Tasted in Sydney

4.5 atmospheres of pressure; 6g/L dosage; aged 4 years on lees; a blend of the grand crus of Oger, Le Mesnil-sur-Oger and Chouilly; no oak

Capturing finely crafted poise while proclaiming richness, depth and intensity is a virtue only of the finest grand crus of the Côte des Blancs. This is a delightfully mineral-driven blanc de blancs, chalky, fine and deep-set, showcasing noble fruit sources. Layers of white peach and apple linger long and even, accented with the spice and brioche of four years on lees. A tight close of taut grand cru acidity and understated dosage promises some years of potential yet.

Bruno Paillard Premiere Cuvée Brut Rosé NV $$$

93 points • 2009 base vintage • Disgorged March 2012 & January 2014 • Tasted in Sydney, Melbourne & Reims

70% pinot noir from Mailly, Verzenay, Bouzy, Verzy and Les Riceys, including 12-15% red wine, 30% chardonnay from Avize and Cramant; 3.5 years on lees; 6-7g/L dosage; 22-24% of the production of the house

A pretty, restrained rosé of pale salmon hue and pomegranate and watermelon flavours, underlined by excellent mineral expression, well interlaced with fine tannins. Enticing depth of plum, black cherry and strawberry fruit celebrates its pinot noir lead, while chardonnay builds tight acid structure and focus. A fine-boned style of mineral texture, elegant dosage and fine persistence. In a clear bottle without cellophane or box, be sure to keep it in the dark.

Bruno Paillard Blanc de Blancs 2004 $$$

95 points • Disgorged April 2013 • Tasted in Sydney & Melbourne

100% Côte des Blancs with 40% Le Mesnil and 40% Oger; 4.5 atmospheres of pressure; 8 years on lees; 5g/L dosage

Testimony to the heights of Bruno Paillard's fruit sources and long ageing, this is a backward blanc de blancs of allure, finesse, elegance and grand persistence. It's impressively poised and youthful, with a lemon, apple and pear lead, brushed with subtle toasted brioche development, underlined by fine, mineral mouthfeel and fine acid line.

CAMILLE SAVÈS

(Cah-mill Sah-ves)

6/10

4 RUE DE CONDÉ BP 22 51150 BOUZY

www.champagne-saves.com

Eugène Savès began estate-bottling champagne in Bouzy in 1910 and his 1880 press still stands proudly in front of the press house. Today, fourth-generation grower Hervé Savès riddles bottles for an hour every morning before carefully tending 10 hectares of family vineyards across 25 plots on the famed Montagne de Reims terroirs of Bouzy, Ambonnay, Tours-sur-Marne and Tauxières-Mutry.

When I visited Savès in 2014 I was impressed by the spotless order of his facilities, which are climate-controlled to 10–12°C. 'The precision of the vinification and cleanliness of the cellar are important for sustaining the minerality of our terroirs,' he explains. For the same reason, Savès has fully blocked malolactic fermentation in all of his cuvées since 1982. 'This respects the wine and you can feel the terroir and minerality.'

He points out that many other good growers in Bouzy are now also blocking malolactic, prompted by warmer vintages due to global warming. 'I would like to conserve the acidity and freshness,' he says.

Mature pinot noir (85%) and chardonnay (15%) vines are managed naturally with respect for the soil and crop-thinned to emphasise site character. Savès cultivates the soil and propagates grasses in the mid-rows. No insecticides or herbicides are used, but a synthetic fungicide prohibits a fully organic approach.

Wines are fermented and aged cool in climate-controlled small enamel-lined stainless steel tanks and oak barrels. In tasting reserves with Savès, I was impressed with the freshness, liveliness and fruit presence of his wines and at the very elegant influence even of new oak barrels. Savès is impressed with the effect of oak vinification and plans to buy more barrels and foudres. Wines spend at least four years on lees. An annual production of about 85,000 bottles includes a still pinot noir from old Bouzy vines. Red wine is a specialty for Savès and he makes the rouge for Alfred Gratien Cuvée Paradis.

Savès' attention to detail is exacting, right down to laser etching disgorgement dates on every bottle. His precise approach and mineral attentiveness is well matched with his bold terroirs, producing champagnes of confident, intense, pinot-led character, which are impeccably crafted, honed by malic acidity, and excellent value for money.

Camille Savès Carte Blanche NV $

92 points • Disgorged November 2013 • Tasted in Bouzy, Sydney, Melbourne & Brisbane

75% pinot noir and 25% chardonnay from Ambonnay, Bouzy, Tours-sur-Marne, Tauxières-Mutry; 2009 base with 2008 reserves; 9-10g/L dosage

Hervé Savès calls Bouzy 'the Chambertin of Champagne', and to temper its strength and dominance he adds a touch of chardonnay to his entry blend. The result is a beautifully pure and focused expression of some of Champagne's most powerful villages. Pretty lemon, red berry and red cherry fruits are accented with a note of wild tomato, culminating in a crescendo of pronounced, fine chalk minerality and tightly defined malic acidity.

Camille Savès Extra Brut NV $$

93 points • Disgorged November 2012 • Tasted in Bouzy

75% pinot noir and 25% chardonnay from Bouzy; 2008 base vintage with 2007 reserves; almost the same as Carte d'Or, with a lower dosage of 4g/L dosage

The precision of Savès, malic acidity, low dosage and energy of the 2008 season unite to create a Bouzy cuvée of unusually taut restraint and magnificent focus. A fresh emphasis on red cherries and lemons is brushed with brioche notes of three and a half years of lees maturity, underlined by refined texture, eminently chalk-focused minerality, a fine bead and persistent finish.

Camille Savès Carte d'Or NV $$

95 points • Disgorged September 2013 • Tasted in Bouzy

75% pinot noir, 25% chardonnay from Bouzy; 2008 base vintage with 2007 reserves; 8g/L dosage

This wine proclaims the grand presence of Bouzy and the focus of 2008, with delightful precision and line of lemon, red cherry and strawberry fruit. Malic acidity rings out in clear peals like church bells across fields of fine, chalk minerality. At once impeccably pristine and structured, yet with all the richness and magnificent presence of one of Champagne's most exuberant villages. Outstanding value.

Camille Savès Millésime 2008 $$

95 points • Disgorged December 2013 • Tasted in Bouzy

80% pinot noir and 20% chardonnay from old vines in the middle of the slope of Bouzy; 7g/L dosage; 12,000 bottles

Brilliant acidity pierces the gentle calm of deep yet floatingly airy mineral structure, like pinpoint starlight illuminating a soft landscape. Red fruits and lemon zest of pronounced definition are softened by the biscuity brioche effect of four and a half years of lees age. The result is effortless yet intense, well balanced yet incisive, engaging yet demanding at least five years and preferably 10 to come down to earth.

The Champagne Guide

Camille Savès Millésime 2000 $$

93 points • Disgorged in 2006 • Tasted in Bouzy

80% pinot noir and 20% chardonnay from Bouzy; 7g/L dosage

An old vintage still available, it's now evolved into a medium straw yellow hue and a jovial, full and rich accumulation of patisserie, brioche, crème brûlée, even notes of pineapple. It's just beginning to dry out a little on the finish, but confidently holds wonderful mineral definition.

Camille Savès Cuvée Anais Jolicoeur 2008 $$

96 points • Tasted in Bouzy

90% pinot noir and 10% chardonnay from Bouzy; fermented and matured 6-8 months in barrel; 7g/L dosage

Barrel fermentation and maturation to tone the high-tensile malic acidity of 2008 would seem a natural fit for pinot noir of the concentration of Bouzy, but the balance is a delicate one and a result as impeccably crafted as this is testimony to the talent and sensitivity of Hervé Savès. Immaculate lemon and red cherry fruit is seamlessly entwined with brioche, uniting the taut focus of malic acidity with the creamy silkiness of barrel fermentation. Freshness and purity are sustained at every moment of a long, focused finish, propelled by the fine texture and deep-set mineral presence of the village. It will live, though it's already irresistible. Named after Hervé's great-grandmother, wife of the founder, Camille Savès. She would be proud.

Camille Savès Cuvée Prestige Brut NV $$

96 points • Tasted in Bouzy

65% chardonnay and 35% pinot noir from Bouzy; 2008 base vintage and 2007 reserves; chardonnay fermented and matured in barrels; 8g/L dosage

Evidence that there's more to Bouzy than just pinot noir, this is a cuvée led by grand cru chardonnay of very distinct character to the Côte des Blancs. It's magnificently mineral, chalky, salty and fine, though a little more grainy and full here. It's an engaging amalgamation of delicacy and concentration, with exact mirabelle yellow plums and yellow fruits of all kinds meeting strawberry hull aromas and notes of brioche and mixed spice. It opens breathtakingly into an air of rose petal and lemon that permeates long through the palate. Outstanding structure, definition and a streamlined tail of persistence will sustain and build it long in the cellar. Wait at least five years, and preferably 10.

Camille Savès Cuvée Rosé NV $$

94 points • Disgorged November 2013 • Tasted in Bouzy

60% chardonnay, 28% pinot noir white wine from Bouzy; 12% Bouzy rouge; 2009 base; 2008 reserves; 8g/L dosage

The definition of malic acidity and Savès' restraint makes Bouzy rosé a naturally elegant hit, surprisingly but intelligently led by chardonnay. Savès' deeply coloured red wine infuses a full salmon hue and generosity, fruit presence and body, without disrupting the focus or restraint of rose petal, pink pepper and red cherry notes, a beautiful acid line, very fine chalk mineral texture, finely orchestrated tannin structure and lingering persistence.

CATTIER

(Ca-tiay)

6 RUE DOM PÉRIGNON 51500 CHIGNY-LES-ROSES

www.cattier.com

Every summer, roses burst into colour along the streets and premier cru vineyards of the romantic village of Chigny-les-Roses, on the northern slopes of the Montagne de Reims. The family-owned house of Cattier is the most famous in the village, a small négociant house with an annual production of a million bottles and no fewer than 19 cuvées, which just might be the most extensive portfolio in all of Champagne.

The Cattier family has long had its roots in the vines, owning vineyards in Chigny-les-Roses since at least 1763, and probably earlier, and selling its own wines since 1918. It now tends 33 hectares of mainly premier cru vineyards, mostly in Chigny-les-Roses and nearby Ludes, Rilly-la-Montagne and Taissy, half planted to pinot noir, and the remainder equally to chardonnay and meunier. Vineyards are managed with an environmentally sustainable philosophy, supplying around one-third of the needs of the house, and supplemented with grapes from across Champagne, particularly from the Montagne and chardonnay from the Côte des Blancs.

Head of the house and winemaker, Jean-Jacques Cattier, handed over responsibility to his son Alexandre in 2011, though still remains actively involved in the tastings, which he describes as the nicest part of the job. Alexandre takes responsibility for winemaking. Their cuvées are matured in some of the region's deepest cellars and are disgorged with dosages around 9–10g/L.

Cattier's profile was boosted when it launched the Armand de Brignac brand in 2006, but recent expansion of the ranges in both brands begs the question of whether Cattier is over-stretching its resources. Its top three cuvées exemplify the northern Montagne's elegant character.

CATTIER BRUT PREMIER CRU NV $

87 points • TASTED IN SYDNEY & MELBOURNE
90 points • 2011 BASE VINTAGE • TASTED IN CHIGNY-LES-ROSES

Three-vintage blend of 45% meunier, 30% pinot noir, 25% chardonnay; aged 2.5 years on lees; 10g/L dosage

The 2011 base is a crunchy and fruit-focused style of lemon zest and red apple fruit. It's short, simple and a touch candied, with dosage rounding out a fine, mineral mouthfeel. Nonetheless good value. Sales have been slow in Australia, and bottles tasted here look to be an old disgorgement, dusty, earthy and oxidised.

Cattier Brut Absolu NV $

89 points • Tasted in Chigny-les-Roses

Cattier's 'Cuvées Fascination' range is intended to break with tradition. In its elegantly streamlined missile-head-shaped bottle, this is a 2009 base vintage blend of 70% pinot noir and 30% chardonnay of just 10,000 bottles, in theory made specifically to handle zero dosage. It's a dry, neutral, firm and savoury style of grapefruit zest and apple, with a slightly coarse structure that would benefit from dosage, gentle salt minerality and a short finish.

Cattier Blanc de Blancs Brut NV $

89 points • Tasted in Chigny-les-Roses

Montagne de Reims; the house would like to be known for its blanc de blancs, intentionally a different style to the Côte des Blancs; 50,000 bottles

A little firmer and more rustic than Côte des Blancs chardonnay, this is a white peach and lemon fruited style of subtle mineral presence and a short finish.

Cattier Brut Vinothèque 2007 $$

88 points • Tasted in Chigny-les-Roses

One-third each of pinot noir, meunier and chardonnay; 80,000 bottles

I questioned the freshness of this bottle, which was not freshly opened, and the house did not volunteer another. It looks forward and toasty, with honeyed, roast nut development and firm phenolic grip disjoint to its vibrant acidity and lemon zest freshness.

Cattier Blanc de Noirs Brut NV $$

87 points • Tasted in Chigny-les-Roses

70% pinot noir and 30% meunier; 2008 base vintage; fewer than 10,000 bottles

The bottle had been open for some time and seemed slightly oxidised, but the house said that is the style, though I am sure a freshly opened bottle would show better. This one is toasty and rich, with good length, a powerful back palate and creamy bead.

Cattier Brut Rosé NV $$

89 points • Tasted in Chigny-les-Roses

50% pinot noir, 40% meunier and 10% chardonnay, including 10% Chigny-les-roses red wine from pinot noir and meunier; 9g/L dosage; 100,000 bottles

As global rosé demand rises, this cuvée has ascended to the second-largest selling of the house. It achieves its aspiration of a pale salmon hue and a light, refreshing, clean, crisp style. Red apple, watermelon and pink pepper notes are underwritten by fine mineral presence and soft, gentle tannin structure, finishing short and understated.

Cattier Cuvée Renaissance 2006 $$

93 points • Tasted in Chigny-les-Roses

40% pinot noir, 40% chardonnay and 20% meunier from across the Montagne de Reims, Côte des Blancs chardonnay and a little Vallée de la Marne

There's real character here. Definition and structure, too. There is depth of black fruits focus, licorice and coffee bean amidst apple and pear fruit. A soft acid structure is supported by fine, salty chalk mineral texture. It upholds the elegance and depth of the northern Montagne, energised with the vibrancy and chalk mineral structure of the Côte des Blancs, finished admirably with a soft, creamy bead.

Cattier Clos du Moulin Brut Premier Cru NV $$$

93 points • Tasted in Chigny-les-Roses

Clos du Moulin remains the most famous and most engaging cuvée of Cattier. From a single 2.2 hectare site on a gentle, windy ridge at the bottom of the village of Ludes, owned by the house since 1951, this is always a blend of three vintages, here 2007 (60%), 2006 and 2005. The clos is planted to roughly equal proportions of pinot noir and chardonnay, and this blend follows, with a dosage of 8g/L and a production of 17,208 bottles. A soft, fine and creamy style of white nectarine and fig fruit, has been massaged by 7 years of age into notes of brioche and subtle exotic spice. The mouthfeel is chalky and grainy, even a little rustic, with good acid focus and integrated dosage.

Cattier Clos du Moulin Rosé NV $$$$

95 points • Disgorged late 2014 • Tasted in Chigny-les-Roses

A new concept launched for Christmas 2013, here a blend of 2006 (60%), 2005 and 2004 of roughly 60% pinot noir and 40% chardonnay, including 10% pinot noir red wine; just 4284 bottles

This is the finest Cattier cuvée I have tasted, elevated by soft, salty and fresh minerality, impressively accented for this part of the world, thanks to the chalk under this special site in Ludes. It's a lovely, elegant northern Montagne style of restraint and persistence, with impressive definition of bright red cherry, raspberry and cherry kernel, surprisingly vibrant for its age. Extended lees ageing has slowly built notes of toasted bread and an enticingly creamy mouthfeel which lingers with persistence.

CHARLES HEIDSIECK

(Shahl E-dseek)

7/10

12 ALLÉE VIGNOBLE 51000 REIMS

www.charlesheidsieck.com

CHAMPAGNE
**CHARLES
HEIDSIECK**

Maison fondée à Reims en 1851

There are three champagne houses named Heidsieck, all from families once related, and Charles is the smallest and the best of them. With an annual production of just half a million bottles, Charles Heidsieck is made alongside the larger Piper-Heidsieck. The two houses admirably uphold distinctly unique styles, thanks to their insightful and talented chef de cave, Régis Camus, who has focused the vision of both houses for 22 years.

Camus distinguishes Charles by likening its mood to late summer and early autumn, describing its floral spectrum in tones of aromatic flowers, dried flowers and leaves. 'Charles is more about generosity and fleshy expression of late summer fruits, like biting into a peach and having the juice run down your face,' he alludes. 'It evokes dates, cream and a toasty register of warm brioche just out of the oven, or a crusty Parisian baguette.' This is a contemplative, mature, darker champagne style for cooler weather. The current releases confidently handle a broad sweep of 10.5–11g/L dosage across the range.

The late Daniel Thibault was the mastermind behind Charles Heidsieck's visionary 'mis en cave' concept, a non-vintage wine labelled with the year in which it was first bottled (an invaluable guide for the astute consumer, as 60% of the blend was from the preceding vintage). The idea was ingenious, the wine impressive, and Camus successfully fought to maintain the principle, in spite of marketing forces that boringly renamed it 'Brut Réserve'.

In addition to sporting smart new front labels, its back labels are now some of the most informative among champagne houses, detailing bottling and disgorgement dates, base vintage, proportion of reserve wines and number of crus in the blend. From the next release, all other Charles Heidsieck cuvées will follow suit.

With the relaunch of Charles Heidsieck in 2012, Thierry Roset was appointed chef de cave under Camus, after 25 years with the house. He had already refined the style by honing its sourcing from 120 villages to the 60 finest crus, with a particular focus on Ambonnay for pinot noir, Oger for chardonnay and Verneuil for meunier, simultaneously increasing the average age of reserve wines from an already considerable eight years to an incredible 10 years — impressive figures for a blend comprising 40% reserves.

The dynamic and sharp Stephen Leroux, who was brought on as director of Charles Heidsieck in early 2013, describes the effect of Roset's vision. 'When I joined Charles, I expected this to produce an even more powerful cuvée,' he admits. 'But the longer ageing of reserves gives more complexity and more depth, and honing the selection of crus makes the wines cleaner, fresher and more precise. The intensity of the old Charles was enormous, but the wines could be a bit weighty. The new Charles is powerful but not heavy.'

Roset passed away tragically and suddenly at the end of harvest 2014. During my visit in February 2015, the house announced the talented, insightful and articulate Cyril Brun as his successor. With 15 years overseeing wine development and communication at Veuve Clicquot, Brun is well qualified to define the next chapter of Heidsieck.

The global financial crisis hit Piper and Charles Heidsieck hard, throwing the company into some €240 million of debt, and forcing it to lay off a quarter of its staff. Owner Rémy Cointreau sold the brand to French fashion-led luxury company Société Européenne de Participations Industrielles (EPI) in early 2011. President Christopher Descours named Régis Camus as one of the key reasons the company committed to the purchase. 'We are recuperating after many years in which Rémy Cointreau were not focusing at all on Charles Heidsieck, so we disappeared from many markets,' admits Leroux.

Charles Heidsieck has a vision to grow its production slowly, bottling a little more than the half a million bottles it currently sells each year. Leroux's mantra is to rebuild its markets. 'If we do our job well, we might grow to 1.5 million bottles in 10 or 15 years' time,' he suggests. This is still a long way from where

Riddling racks in Charles Heidsieck's 2nd century crayères.

the house was 35 years ago, when its production of 4 million bottles was equal to that of Veuve Clicquot.

'Within the supply of the two houses, we have room to manoeuvre to achieve this growth in Charles,' Leroux explains. Just 5% of production is currently sourced from a total of 60 hectares across both houses, with the balance provided by some 400 growers. 'We are always looking for new vignerons, and our president, Christopher Descours, is looking to acquire some more land.'

With Brun's appointment completing a talented, dedicated team, I am quietly excited to see where Charles Heidsieck is headed. Its current cuvées are its finest yet.

CHARLES HEIDSIECK BRUT RÉSERVE NV $$

94 points • 2007 BASE VINTAGE • DISGORGED VARIOUSLY 2012, 2013 & 2014
• TASTED IN REIMS, SYDNEY, MELBOURNE & BRISBANE

Base wine one-third each of pinot noir, chardonnay and meunier from 60 villages, first Avize, then Vertus, Aÿ, Ambonnay, Verneuil and Oger; between 4.5 and 6.5 years on lees; 40% reserve wines of 50% pinot noir and 50% chardonnay aged an average of 10 years in tanks; full malolactic fermentation; 11.2g/L dosage

This is signature Charles Heidsieck, a generous wintertime cuvée of full straw hue that splendidly upholds its position among Champagne's richer NVs. The 2007 base has been current for a couple of years, confidently upholding its vivacious freshness of lemon zest and floral notes, thanks to regular disgorgement of new batches. The theme here is generous, mellow autumn leaf character of contemplative appeal. It's waxy, creamy and fleshy, brimming with juicy stone fruits, fig, pear and crunchy red apples, declaring its grand maturity in hints of coffee, cocoa and nougat. Fine chalk mineral mouthfeel juxtaposes a rounded, honeyed finish, ripe for drinking now.

The Champagne Guide

CHARLES HEIDSIECK ROSÉ RÉSERVE NV $$$

93 points • BASE VINTAGE 2007 • DISGORGED JANUARY 2014 • TASTED IN MELBOURNE & BRISBANE
95 points • BASE VINTAGE 2007 • DISGORGED JANUARY 2014 • TASTED IN REIMS

Aiming for a fresher style, one-third of each of the varieties, using 60-75% of the base wines of the brut with 20% reserve wines of 50% chardonnay and 50% pinot noir and 5-6% of pinot noir red wine from a solera system up to 5 years old, from Les Riceys, Bouzy, Ambonnay, Verzy, Verzenay and Aÿ; 11g/L dosage

The rounded autumn-leaf mood of this cuvée is at its best young and fresh. I've tasted the best bottles at the house, showcasing pretty white cherry and wild strawberry fruit and heightened tension between chalk mineral texture and very fine, skilfully handled tannins. Elsewhere, a toasty, spicy, savoury demeanour and medium copper hue are more pronounced, with characters of roast chestnuts, wood spice, baked apples, anise, pipe smoke and freshly baked patisserie.

CHARLES HEIDSIECK MILLÉSIME BRUT 2005 $$$

92 points • DISGORGED MAY 2014 • TASTED IN REIMS & BRISBANE

First release since 2000, with 2001 and 2003 write-offs and the more elegant 2002 and 2004 reserved for Piper-Heidsieck; 60% pinot noir, 40% chardonnay from just 11 villages, with a strong base of Ambonnay, then Verzy, Verzenay, Bouzy, Avize, Oger, Cramant, Vertus, Mailly and Vindey; 10.8g/L dosage

My first tasting of this cuvée was its first showing following its release in late 2014. After a five-year hiatus, 2005 is a bold vintage to choose for this cuvée, and it's not shy on muscle, nor the wood spice notes, almond-skin grip, drying phenolic texture and firm, chewy structure that defines the season. Still, Heidsieck has conjured a flattering take on this season, cunningly using creaminess, layers of ripe yellow summer fruits and honeyed dosage to counter this drying mouthfeel. The volume of the season and its pinot noir lead is well expressed in emerging notes of black cherry, notes of spice and hints of pepper, with a decade of maturity defining the aged complexity of roast chestnuts, mushrooms, wood smoke and the classic autumn-leaf character of the house.

CHARLES HEIDSIECK ROSE MILLÉSIME 2006 $$$

96 points • TASTED IN REIMS

63% pinot noir and 37% chardonnay, including 8% pinot noir red wine; a blend from 15 villages including Oger, Le Mesnil-sur-Oger, Cramant and Vertus for chardonnay, Avenay, Louvois, Tauxières, Ambonnay and Aÿ for pinot noir and Bouzy, Ambonnay, Les Riceys, Verzenay and Hautvillers for pinot noir red wine

My sneak preview was the first showing of this new vintage prior to its release in early 2015, and I was captivated by a delicacy that surprised me for both the house and the vintage. It's medium salmon copper in hue, with elegant wild strawberries and cherries melting seamlessly into a vortex of brioche, pink pepper and ginger, effortlessly capturing a complex array of diverse rosé personalities with seamless finesse, at once vivacious, contemplative and complex. Texture is marvellous, creamy and vibrant, all the while upholding chalk minerality as the defining theme. A champagne for long conversations on cool nights.

CHARLES HEIDSIECK ROSÉ MILLÉSIME 1999 $$$

94 points • TASTED IN REIMS

60% pinot noir, 40% chardonnay, plus 8% pinot noir red wine from Verzy and Verzenay; 15-17 crus, particularly Ambonnay, Verzy, Verzenay, Villers-Marmery, Chigny-les-Roses, Aÿ, Bouzy and Les Riceys for pinot noir and Oger for chardonnay; aged 12 years on lees; 10.5-11g/L dosage

For such a hot, low-acid vintage in Champagne, this wine holds quite incredible musk, rose petal and cherry aromas at 16 years of age. Its maturity is declared in a full salmon copper hue and layers of savoury spice and autumn leaves, opening out and evolving beautifully to cocoa powder in time. Its texture melds chalk minerality with fine tannin structure, beginning to dry a little on the finish, suggesting that it has now reached the twilight of its life.

CHARLES HEIDSIECK BLANC DE MILLÉNAIRES 1995 $$$$

98 points • DISGORGED JANUARY 2014 • TASTED IN REIMS, BRISBANE & YARRA VALLEY

20% each of Cramant, Avize, Oger, Le Mesnil-sur-Oger and Vertus; stored in Charles Heidsieck's crayères at 11°C and disgorged successively for release; 10.5g/L dosage, though lab analysis reveals 14g/L of total sugars

The only question that begs to be asked of the oldest currently available champagne in the last two editions of this guide is why, having been first released in 2007, it will still be on the shelves through 2016. 'They made shitloads of it and they weren't selling it!' answers Stephen Leroux, with frank sincerity. Remarkably, my score continues to climb — again. I was amazed at the plane of silken magnificence to which it transcended at 18 years of age, and the dizzying vivacity that it declares at a glorious two decades is nothing short of mindblowing. Before he passed away in 2014, Thierry Roset declared that he would probably never again be able to make another wine like this. It's an enigma, a grand testimony to the eternal Peter Pan endurance of the greatest crus of the Côte des Blancs, and it will live for decades yet. Its colour is shot with a brightness that eludes its age, and there's still yellow fruit crunch and freshness here, rumbling in tones of impeccable, soft chalk minerality, backed by succulent depth of grilled pineapple and butter. Its voice has deepened as it's emerged from adolescence, taking on the understated, magical allure of grand maturity in bees wax, sweet pipe smoke, coffee bean, green olive and warm hearth. Who knows what might yet be in store in the decades to come? Sit back and enjoy the enthralling spectacle with the one you love, in the largest glasses you can procure. At this age, there is invariably bottle variation, and I've encountered two oxidised bottles out of six that I've tasted recently.

CHARLES HEIDSIECK CHAMPAGNE CHARLIE 1985

98 points • TASTED IN REIMS

55% chardonnay, 45% pinot noir

This was the final Champagne Charlie cuvée, though there are plans afoot to revive this label. Of two bottles I've tasted on different occasions, one was past its best and beginning to deteriorate into a place of cellar mushroom, a little shaky on the finish (93 points). The other was in magnificent condition, heralding a wonderfully fresh core of preserved lemon, overlaid with all the smoky, tertiary fascination of 30 years in the bowels of the earth, finishing with seamless line and grand persistence.

The Champagne Guide

CHARPENTIER

(Shar-pon-tiay)

5/10

www.champagne-charpentier.com

The village of Charly-sur-Marne is situated halfway between Reims and Paris, 15 kilometres west of Château-Thierry. In this notably cool and wet part of Champagne, planting is dominated by meunier — 90% of the total — making the Charpentier family unique and unusual as its 72 parcels spread across 23 hectares, well-situated on the mid-slopes of several nearby crus, comprise 50% chardonnay. The family has sold its own wines since 1855 (still wines at the time) and Jean-Marc Charpentier is now the eighth generation of his family to manage the estate. In 1989 he married the daughter of a fifth-generation champagne grower in Charly-sur-Marne, providing the family with an impressively expanded resource of mature vines. Jean-Marc has been a pioneer of sustainable viticulture in Champagne since 1988, and some plots are now managed organically. The result is lower yields and increased resilience to disease, crucial in ripening chardonnay in this part of Champagne. Charpentier's cuvées are well crafted, long aged, sealed with DIAM closures and reflective of the softly textured character of the western Marne. They're also refreshingly affordable.

CHARPENTIER RÉSERVE BRUT NV $

90 points • TASTED IN MELBOURNE.

70% meunier, 20% chardonnay, 10% pinot noir; 25% reserve wines; aged 4 years on lees

A step up in depth and intensity from Charpentier's entry Brut Tradition NV, showcases the fleshy demeanour of meunier and the bready and honeyed development of four years of age.

CHARPENTIER ROSÉ BRUT NV $

93 points • 2009 BASE VINTAGE • TASTED IN MELBOURNE

52% meunier, 35% chardonnay, 13% red wine from meunier; aged 3 years on lees

An elegant style of medium salmon hue with the depth of pinot red fruits in pomegranate and strawberry, contrasting with lovely crunchy elegance. It's softly textured, with good acid balance and persistence.

CHARPENTIER BRUT MILLÉSIME 2008 $

92 points • TASTED IN MELBOURNE

8g/L dosage

Juxtaposing the energy and vivacity of 2008 with the fruity presence of meunier, this is a well balanced cuvée of taut acid profile and good persistence.

CHARPENTIER TERRE D'EMOTION BLANC DE NOIRS BRUT NV $$

93 points • TASTED IN MELBOURNE & HAUTVILLERS

2008 base with a little 2007 reserve from oak barrels

Charpentier's long-aged Terre d'Emotion carries attractive biscuity, brioche, honey and ginger notes of maturity, set against a classic meunier backdrop of rich, fleshy fruit presence of stone fruits, red apples, strawberries and mixed spice. It's enticing and complex, toasty and generous, with soft acidity, well-balanced dosage, a creamy bead and fine, soft mineral structure.

CHARPENTIER TERRE D'EMOTION ROSÉ NV $$

95 points • 2008 BASE VINTAGE • TASTED IN MELBOURNE

88% chardonnay and 12% meunier red wine from vines at least 65 years of age

An engaging and vibrant style of lively salmon hue, capturing the energy of 2008 in pretty red cherry and strawberry fruits of considerable character and presence, well set off by a honed finish of taut acidity and soft chalk mineral structure. A wine of excellent length, fruit focus and persistence, setting the bar for what can be achieved with chardonnay in the western Marne.

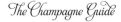

Claude Carré et Fils

(Clawd Cah-ray e Feess)

5/10

42 RUE VAUDEMANGE 51380 TRÉPAIL

*N*ext door to Ambonnay, the premier cru village of Trépail is one of Champagne's highest villages, and unique in the Montagne de Reims as better suited to chardonnay than pinot noir. Growers here for four generations, the Carré family produce 140,000 bottles of appealingly juicy, fruit-focused champagnes exclusively from their 13 hectares in the village. Their blanc de blancs cuvées are the highlights, led by the vintage Cuvée Passion.

Claude Carré et Fils Blanc de Blancs Premier Cru Brut NV $$

93 points • TASTED IN SYDNEY & MELBOURNE

DIAM closure

A succulent, fruity blanc de blancs that unashamedly proclaims the generosity and character of Trépail chardonnay, this year with more freshness, purity and vivacity than ever. Crunchy grapefruit meshes seamlessly with red apple and subtle cinnamon and brioche, structured with excellent acid line that sustains fine mineral texture, finishing with persistence, verve and well-integrated dosage. It's generous and nicely composed, with appealing fruit focus, perfect for big parties, certain to keep any crowd entertained.

Claude Carré et Fils Cuvée Passion Brut Millésime 2002 $$

94 points • TASTED IN SYDNEY & MELBOURNE

100% chardonnay; DIAM closure

A generous, enticing and silky blanc de blancs, a celebration of 13 years of maturity in tantalising brioche, ginger, glacé fruit and the crunchy outside shell of toasted marshmallows. It was at its prime two years ago and has upheld itself with consummate class, retaining just the right level of vibrant 2002 fruit energy in notes of lemon drops and lingering lemon zest freshness, contrasting neatly with fruit sweetness and biscuity development.

COUCHE PÈRE ET FILS

(Coosh Pear e Feess)

5/10

29 GRANDE RUE, 10110 BUXEUIL
www.champagne-couche.fr

CHAMPAGNE

Vincent
Couche

L'excellence par nature

V incent Couche produces organic wines from 10 hectares of primarily pinot noir in Buxeuil in the Aube and three hectares of chardonnay on chalk soil in Montgueux near Troyes. He has been undergoing biodynamic certification since 2008 and the first of his wines are now certified. Steep south- and west-facing slopes along the Seine River, together with high density of planting, produce grapes of maturity and flavour. Primary fermentations are conducted with wild yeasts and vinification occurs with little or no sulphur dioxide. Back labels are particularly informative, detailing vintages, dosage and disgorgement dates.

COUCHE PÈRE ET FILS PERLE DE NACRE BLANC DE BLANCS EXTRA BRUT NV $$

94 points • DISGORGED IN JANUARY 2012 • TASTED IN MELBOURNE • A BLEND OF 2004, 2003 & 2002

4g/L dosage

For its considerable maturity, this is a surprisingly tight, focused and youthful blanc de blancs of excellent fruit expression. The development of toasty complexity is subtle, promising a long future. Finely poised acidity of considerable energy, great persistence and impressively textural, mineral mouthfeel are testimony to the chalk presence and shallow soils (just 40 centimetres deep) of the far-flung Champagne outpost of Montgueux near Troyes. I've never visited, but this cuvée alone has inspired me to get there as soon as I can.

CUVÉE CARBON

(Coo-vay Cah-bon)

---

43 RUE PASTEUR 51160 CHAMPILLON-FRANCE

www.cuveecarbon.com

*C*uvée Carbon is the prestige cuvée of the grower Bertrand Devavry, created by Alexandre Mea-Devavry, who spent three years researching and developing its distinctive black carbon fibre bottle. It's released as a vintage champagne, vintage rosé and blanc de blancs, each sourced from Devavry's nine hectares of estate vineyards. The price is high and the concept is more compelling than its execution.

CUVÉE CARBON VINTAGE 2006 $$$$$

92 points • TASTED IN SYDNEY & MELBOURNE

80% chardonnay from Avize, Chouilly and Oger; 20% Aÿ pinot noir; no malolactic fermentation; aged 5 years on lees

The fruity immediacy of 2006 is on display in crunchy red apple and grapefruit flavours, with notes of ginger rising as it matures in bottle. This is a textural style of skinsy grip akin to apple or pear skin, culminating in a finish of balanced acidity and dosage.

As is mandated in all Champagne villages, Avize chardonnay is hand harvested as whole bunches and gently loaded into the press.

De Sousa & Fils

(De Soo-za e Feess)

9/10

12 Place Léon Bourgeois 51190 Avize

www.champagnedesousa.com

CHAMPAGNE

De Sousa

à Avize

Un Champagne de Précision

If you could write the perfect recipe for the greatest champagnes it might read something like this: a tiny grower based in Avize in the exact centre of the grand crus of the Côte des Blancs, sourcing chardonnay from estate vineyards on the finest slopes of the grand crus of Avize, Oger, Cramant and Le Mesnil-sur-Oger, and pinot noir and meunier from the grand crus of Aÿ and Ambonnay. Vines would be very old and painstakingly tended biodynamically by an experienced artisan, fanatical about drawing every detail of character and minerality from every site. Crop levels and dosage would be low, oak would be used generously when the fruit called for it and sparingly when it did not, blending would be performed from a deep pool of reserve wines, cuvées would mature long on their lees in cold cellars, and disgorgement dates and dosages would be printed on every bottle. Welcome to the wonderful world of De Sousa.

On paper, this might be the finest recipe in all of Champagne. But do the wines live up to it?

I first met third-generation head of the house Erick de Sousa over the gigantic French oak table in his tasting room in the heart of Avize. 'My job is to maximise the minerality in the vines,' he commenced, and everything from this point served to demonstrate his vision — every cuvée opened, every vineyard technique expounded, every cellar procedure demonstrated.

Over almost 30 years, Erick has refined the best of traditional thinking and progressive new methods to revitalise, transform and grow the estate to become one of the finest on the Côte des Blancs. Production

has increased to 100,000 bottles annually and vineyard holdings have grown to 42 plots spanning 9.5 hectares, including 2.5 hectares of coveted old vines in Avize, Cramant and Oger. With the exception of his entry Brut Tradition, every vineyard source is grand cru, with 70% of vines over 40 years of age and a significant percentage 50–60 years old. Some planted by his grandfather are more than 80 years old. 'I must give my wine the minerality that can only come from old vines,' he emphasises.

The roots of these old vines plunge deep into the soil, even as far as 35–40 metres into the chalk, he suggests. Here they extract the salts and trace elements that are fundamental to the structure of these wines. 'Minerality comes from the chalk,' he says.

Old vines have a natural moderating effect on yields, which generally average just 60hL/hectare from 8000 vines, 25–30% less than the average of the appellation. Such yields provide greater concentration and permit him to harvest only when the grapes have attained full ripeness. 'I want to maintain the maturity in the sugar level at harvest, but not too high, so as to keep a balance of acidity and minerality,' he explains. 'High maturity at harvest provides opulence, while minerality maintains freshness.' When I visited towards the end of harvest 2014, I was impressed with the cleanliness and purity of the juices, displaying intensity of flavour and great acid balance.

In his own words, Erick De Sousa 'lives in the rhythm of the vines' and regards his work in the vineyards as the key to the quality of the grapes. Respect for the vine and the earth is paramount, and he has spent a decade converting the domaine to biodynamic viticulture, with full certification granted in 2010. Biodynamics for him is about equipping his old vines to capture minerality, 'to encourage the vine to draw deeply the trace elements specific to each terroir and provide different characteristics to each cuvée'. The soil is ploughed for ventilation and to restore microbial life, with a horse in some vineyards.

To increase production, de Sousa purchased new cellars on the opposite side of the village square in 2004 for his négociant label, Zoémie de Sousa. With walls at least half a metre thick, the stable temperature is ideal for ageing wines. When he showed me through, I was surprised by the small scale of production. His enamelled tanks are tiny; he owns one foudre for ageing red wine, a small wooden vat for red wine fermentation, and little 225-litre barrels made from oak harvested in Avize and from a cooper friend in Burgundy.

Fruit from vines older than 50 years is fermented in small oak barrels, with regular bâtonnage to enhance depth and breadth. He has used about 15% new barrels for his top cuvées, but increased the proportion slightly in 2004. Chaptalisation is performed when necessary, the first fermentation is initiated with natural yeasts, and all wines pass through malolactic fermentation. Sulphur dioxide is used sparingly.

Narrow and atmospheric, the 200-year-old cellars under the house run 800 metres directly beneath the square in the middle of the village. A stable temperature of 10°C is ideal for long ageing. Here, the old method of poignettage is practised, in which autolytic flavours are enhanced by shaking the bottles by hand to stir up the lees. Bottles are also riddled by hand. De Sousa's

profound prestige Cuvée des Caudalies' claim to uniqueness is not so much that it is a prestige cuvée of non-vintage blend, but just how this blend is assembled. Sourced from chardonnay vines exceeding 50 years of age in Avize, Oger, Le Mesnil-sur-Oger and Cramant, and vinified in small barrels with no chaptalisation, it is blended as a solera of reserve wines that currently spans the 11 harvests from 1995 to 2005. Cuvée des Caudalies is also released as an ultra-complex vintage wine and a mesmerising rosé.

In addition to disgorgement dates, back labels now disclose the bottling date, which is a useful insight as the base vintage of NV cuvées is always the year prior.

De Sousa has risen to a rightful place among Champagne's greatest producers under Erick's visionary guidance over the past quarter century, now ably assisted by his three children, Charlotte, Julie and Valentin, all of whom have completed degrees at the local wine school. Theirs are masterfully grown and crafted wines, every one of which is brilliantly mineral, profoundly exact and beautifully fresh. At the end of a long tasting and vigorous conversation over that massive oak table, I tell Erick as much.

'It's all about mature vines with roots that go deep into the soil,' he replies with unassuming humility.

And it must also have a little to do with what is indeed the finest recipe in Champagne.

De Sousa ferments in small barrels for depth and breadth.

De Sousa & Fils Grand Cru Réserve Blanc de Blancs Brut NV $$

95 points • Disgorged February and October 2014 • Tasted in Avize & Brisbane

2010 base vintage with 20% reserves from 2009; Cramant, Avize, Oger and Le Mesnil-sur-Oger; vinified in tanks; 7g/L dosage

A blend of vineyards 25–30 years old, young by De Sousa standards, though an organic regime has encouraged deep root penetration and mineral pick-up. As ever, the minerality of this cuvée is a revelation, frothing with salty sea-surf chalk of impeccable definition. The 2010 base contrasts the mood of the breathtakingly refined delicacy of the 2008 two years ago. There's impressive depth and intensity here, fleshy and muscular, a grand expression of ripe fruit from strong grand crus, reflected in layers of anise, plum and even black cherry fruits rarely seen in chardonnay. It upholds its brilliance, finesse and purity, bursting with pristine definition of grapefruit, lemon, crunchy pear and red apple, charged with ever-present chalk minerality.

De Sousa & Fils Brut Rosé NV $$

95 points • Disgorged August 2014 • Tasted in Brisbane

92% chardonnay, 8% pinot noir red wine vinified in oak casks; 2012 base vintage; 7g/L dosage

Freshness and fruitiness are the aspirations of this young blend. Yet in the midst of its delicate and seductive nuances of rose petals, pink pepper and freshly picked strawberries and white cherries, the magnificent, salty chalk minerality of Avize makes a grand statement, uniting seamlessly with masterfully orchestrated, superfine tannins to create a delightful mouthfeel. A beguilingly graceful De Sousa Rosé that ranks among the finest yet.

Zoémie De Sousa Cuvée Umami Grand Cru Extra Brut Vintage 2009 $$$$$

95 points • Disgorged August 2013 • Tasted in Avize & Brisbane

70% chardonnay from Avize, and a little from Oger and Le Mesnil-sur-Oger; 30% pinot noir from Aÿ and Ambonnay; vines more than 50 years of age; vinified in new and old barrels; 3g/L dosage; 8000 bottles

De Sousa associates the Japanese concept of umami with the mouthfeel of salinity and sappiness derived from the chalk soils of the Côte des Blancs, drawn out by biodynamic viticulture. Coming from anyone else, I would dismiss such umami aspirations as a trite, contrived marketing line, but the texture and frothing seasalt minerality of this first release are an irrefutable testimony to the successful execution of an ambitious brief. Few estates in the world have the terroirs and the expertise to embody umami as emphatically as this. The 2009 was chosen for this first release for its strength and power, with a ripe fruit body of fleshy white peach and pear, nuances of ginger and roast almond barrel toastiness, all encased in a brittle mineral shell. A cuvée of breathtaking line and length, presenting a captivating alternative to the De Sousa style.

The Champagne Guide

De Sousa & Fils Cuvée des Caudalies Blanc de Blancs Grand Cru Brut NV $$$

96 points • Disgorged November 2013 • Tasted in Avize & Brisbane

2008 base with 50% reserves from a solera of every vintage from 1995 to 2007; 100% Avize chardonnay from vines aged over 50 years; fermented entirely in small oak barrels; 7g/L dosage

I tasted the Caudalies solera for the first time during the 2014 harvest and was stunned at its complexity. In this bottle — a blend of 14 vintages, all oak fermented — it might appear that its recipe could play havoc with purity and focus. To the contrary, and to the credit of the genius of Erick de Sousa and the all-conquering presence of Avize chalk, this is a wine of remarkable purity. Its minerality is an epiphany, frothing with sea surf, mouth-filling and all-encompassing; one of the most profoundly deep-set, salty chalk signatures in all of Champagne. The pristine energy of 2008 charges grapefruit and white fruits of all kinds, while a full 20 years of maturity brings a walk through an autumnal landscape in spicy complexity of golden leaves, fig, anise, almond, cherry kernel, dried pear and butter on toast. In the midst of such complexity, it maintains utter control and poise through an undeviating finish of grand persistence. A prestige cuvée in every regard except price.

De Sousa & Fils Cuvée des Caudalies Brut Rosé NV $$$

96 points • Disgorged September 2013 • Tasted in Brisbane

2008 base with 50% reserves from a solera of every vintage from 1995 to 2007; 90% Avize chardonnay from vines aged over 50 years; fermented entirely in small oak barrels; 10% Aÿ pinot noir vinified as red wine and matured in oak casks for 1 year; matured 4 years on lees

Such is the powerful colour, pure fruit and delicate structure of De Sousa's red wine that a 10% dose transforms a pristine blanc de blancs into one of Champagne's most spectacular rosés. Drinking Cuvée des Caudalies Rosé is nothing less than a deeply moving emotional experience, such is the relentless beauty of haunting red cherry and wild strawberry fruits that hover in suspension long through the finish. A maelstrom of complexity erupts in a riveting spectacle of understated power, framed in Avize tension and monumental mineral presence. A frothing wave of seasalt minerality lifts the wine in a towering spray, like a big ocean swell crashing against rocks, so pronounced that it lends a captivating, chewy sensation to the palate. The layered spice of a deep solera and barrel work are intricately entwined and perfectly integrated, concluding gracefully refined, with pencil-lead definition.

De Sousa & Fils Cuvée 3A Extra Brut NV $$

89 points • Disgorged March 2014 • Tasted in Brisbane

A blend of the 3 'A' grand crus of 50% Avize chardonnay, 25% Aÿ pinot noir and 25% Ambonnay pinot noir, blended prior to fermentation to increase harmony; 50% vinified in old oak barrels

This is a disappointingly toasty, nutty 3A, with oxidative development that produces a dried-out, dusty finish and astringent acidity, leaving it looking rustic and robust, lacking the distinguished refinement of the 2009 base. It had me immediately reaching for a back-up bottle — which was identical. Nonetheless, it upholds heightened chalk mineral expression and excellent persistence.

DELAMOTTE

(Deh-la-mot)

5-7 RUE DE LA BRÈCHE D'OGER 51190 LE MESNIL-SUR-OGER

www.salondelamotte.com

CHAMPAGNE

DELAMOTTE

Le Mesnil sur Oger depuis 1760

Delamotte is effectively the second label of Salon (page 312), though the house prefers to call them 'sister houses'. It has been Salon's neighbour for over a century, and celebrated its 250th birthday recently. The two joined forces in 1988, and the following year were bought by Laurent-Perrier, which handles the winemaking for both brands.

Delamotte produces 700,000 bottles annually from 35 hectares of its own vineyards, largely in Le Mesnil-sur-Oger, and a similar volume of purchased fruit. Chardonnay is sourced principally from the grand crus of Le Mesnil-sur-Oger, Oger, Avize and Cramant, and pinot noir for its Brut NV and Rosé primarily from Bouzy, Ambonnay and Tours-sur-Marne.

Delamotte also receives all the leftovers from Salon, and in years when Salon doesn't declare (two in five, to date), the entire Salon harvest is dedicated to Delamotte. All the fruit of the Jardin de Salon currently goes to Delamotte, and will for another vintage or two, since the vines are only 14 years of age. For other parcels, the ultimate destiny of each tank (there are no barrels here) is quickly determined post-fermentation, since Delamotte undergoes malolactic fermentation while Salon does not.

Delamotte has been riding a steep growth curve for the past couple of decades, almost quadrupling its output from 250,000 bottles, with a target of 1 million in the next three to four years, spurred by strong demand across Asia. The vision of Salon Delamotte president Didier Depond is to make Delamotte the reference house for blanc de blancs.

Since Salon is blanc de blancs, it's no surprise that Delamotte's blanc de blancs cuvées are its soaring highlights, and today represent close to 50% of production.

DELAMOTTE BLANC DE BLANCS 2007 $$$

95 points • TASTED IN BRISBANE

Roughly equal proportions of Le Mesnil-sur-Oger, Oger, Avize and Cramant

2007 immediately declares its magnificence, its pale straw hue and introverted demeanour promise a bright future. It's energetic in its fresh grand cru chalk mineral drive and focused line and length, yet calm and relaxed, with great purity flowing in the union of white citrus, white stone fruit and subtle almond and brioche of eight years' maturity.

Delamotte Brut NV $$

91 points • Base vintage 2008 • Disgorged 2012 • Tasted in Le Mesnil-sur-Oger
91 points • Base vintage 2009 • Tasted in Sydney & Melbourne
84 points • Base vintage 2010 • Disgorged June 2014 • Tasted in Brisbane

55% grand cru chardonnay, 35% grand cru pinot noir, 10% meunier; a blend of Oger, Avize, Cramant, Tours-sur-Marne, Ambonnay, Reuil and Fleury la Rivière; aged 3 years on lees; 7g/L dosage

The 2008 base is now a nutty, spicy, preserved lemon and red berry style, showing reductive complexity in toasted bread notes; 2009 is fresher and more lively, with crisp, clean fruit focus; 2010 is challenged by a tricky vintage, coarse, bitter and phenolic, with dry, dusty extract and mushroomy notes rendering it austere. Candied dosage is apparent in all three.

Delamotte Blanc de Blancs NV $$

95 points • 2008 base vintage • Tasted in Le Mesnil-sur-Oger, Sydney, Melbourne, Brisbane & Yarra Valley

Roughly equal proportions of Le Mesnil-sur-Oger for focus and attention, Oger for body and flesh, Avize for aromaticity and Cramant for harmony; 10% reserve wines; aged 4 years on lees; 7g/L dosage (lab analysis shows 11g/L total sugars)

The sublime 2008 base vintage sings with energetic, pristine vibrancy that eludes four years' lees age. Focused lemon zest, apple blossom, lime essence and lemon meringue of driving persistence are underscored by fresh chalk mineral structure. Subtle struck flint and grilled bread reduction is characteristic of the style, while age has built subtle, biscuity, candied almond, honeyed complexity, finishing with rounded sweetness and poised acid line. Outstanding.

Delamotte Rosé NV $$$

93 points • 2009 base • Tasted in Sydney & Melbourne

80% pinot noir from Bouzy, Ambonnay and Tours-sur-Marne, co-fermented with 20% Le Mesnil-sur-Oger chardonnay; similar saignée process as Laurent-Perrier; aged 3-4 years on lees; 8g/L dosage

This cuvée has never possessed resilience post-disgorgement, the freshest examples showing pretty restraint, radiating with a pale salmon hue and clean notes of rose petal, strawberry hull, red cherry and pink pepper. Elegant, graceful and finely textured, with chalk mineral mouthfeel. A year later, it's oxidised to a full crimson orange hue, flavours of orange fruit and a chewy, softly bitter phenolic grip, devoid of finesse and grace (89 points). Buy if you can trust your retailer for fresh stock.

Delamotte Blanc de Blancs 2004

94 points • Tasted in Le Mesnil-sur-Oger, Sydney & Melbourne

Roughly equal proportions of Le Mesnil-sur-Oger, Oger, Avize and Cramant

The purity and restraint of 2004 has endured more than a decade of maturity, upholding a pale straw hue and exacting freshness of lemon blossom, tense grapefruit and crunchy pear, becoming roast nuts and ginger, sustained by the inimitable, honed chalk mineral structure of the Côte des Blancs' finest grand crus. Pronounced reductive character of grilled toast appreciates a little time in glass to subside and let its purity of fruit emerge.

DEUTZ

(Derts)

8/10

6 RUE JEANSON 51160 AŸ

www.champagne-deutz.com

FONDÉ EN 1838

Champagne

DEUTZ

AY- FRANCE

*D*eutz is growing like a mad thing, tripling sales and production from 600,000 bottles in the late 1990s to more than 2 million every year from 2004 to 2008, dipping only slightly in response to the global economy and returning to 2 million in 2012. For such a breathtaking pace of expansion, the standards it has maintained are not only admirable, they're downright remarkable. The rough 2011 vintage aside, there isn't one wine out of place in this line of crisp, pure champagnes, impeccably crafted in a style of elegant finesse.

Deutz is still setting a cracking pace. The main press house in Aÿ was razed in 2010 and two new layers of cellars dug underneath. A completely new press house was erected just in time for vintage 2011, with new four- and eight-tonne presses, a new bottling line and increased capacity for reserve wines. These extensions increased cellar capacity from 8 million to 11.5 million bottles, and Deutz is now bottling its annual production target of 2.5 million bottles and it has secured the grape supply to sustain it.

Owned by Louis Roederer, the house lays claims to just 42 of the total 200 hectares from which it sources fruit, all in grand and premier cru villages in the Marne. Chardonnay and pinot noir are the focus for Deutz, with meunier comprising just 5% of its fruit. Most of the supply increase in recent years has come from purchased fruit. 'We are looking for vineyards to buy, but the availability of good vineyards is not high,' explains president Fabrice Rosset, the powerhouse

behind Deutz for almost 20 years. To reward quality, growers are paid based not only on the standard of their terroir, but the quality of grapes delivered. Growers are hearing of Deutz's reputation and calling the company to offer their grapes. 'This is the highest compliment we could be paid!' exclaims Rosset.

Can the house continue to maintain quality while following such a steep trajectory of growth? 'It is crucial that we maintain the same quality of supplies,' chef de cave Michel Davesne emphasises. The intention is to maintain the same suppliers, continuing to source from within 35 kilometres of Aÿ and using only the first pressings. He is confident the investments in the new winery and cellars will only aid the pursuit of quality.

Assuming the house can maintain reliable supply channels, Deutz will be well equipped to continue to achieve its target. Recently modernised disgorgement and warehousing facilities are already in operation, and 8 million bottles wait in anticipation in three kilometres of cellars extending into the hill, up to 65 metres deep beneath the vineyard behind Aÿ.

With sustainable agriculture a priority, Deutz is trialling organics and even biodynamics in the plot immediately above the winery. Chemical pesticides have been abandoned, and grasses cultivated in the mid-rows of some plots to avoid the use of herbicides and reduce yields. Pruning techniques and green harvests have also been adopted to reduce yields to slightly below the average.

Even in its young vins clairs, the clean, crisp, fresh, pristine focus of the house is abundantly clear. Deutz preserves the purity of its fruit through fermentation plot by plot in 350 stainless steel tanks (no barrels), temperature controlled to 16–17°C. Malolactic fermentation is encouraged systematically. Non-vintage wines are aged for two and a half years on lees, and are rested in the cellar for a further six months post-disgorgement. Dosages of around 9g/L are well balanced to the graceful style of the house.

'The key to Deutz is elegance,' expounds Rosset. 'The Deutz style is made on refinement and harmony – this is the quintessence of champagne.' Then he checks himself and grins warmly. 'I am exaggerating!'

But he's right. In its classic, eloquently labelled bottles, Deutz has upheld its air of consistently refreshing, pure lemon sunshine.

A candle illuminates the cellar under Deutz, a house whose cuvées shine with luminous, pinpoint clarity.

Deutz Brut Millésimé 2008 $$$

96 points • Disgorged October 2014 • Tasted in Brisbane

11g/L dosage

Only in the great 2008 vintage can supermodel curves, ballerina daintiness, gymnastic muscle and Olympian energy all coexist in one desperately precise body. Fairy-footed grace of rose petal and lemon blossom fragrance find a breathtaking tension with exceptional fruit depth, epic persistence and breathtakingly chalk-fine, frothing salt minerality. Another thrilling performance from the most enduring vintage since 1996.

Deutz Brut Millésimé 2007 $$$

95 points • Tasted in Aÿ

65% pinot noir, 30% chardonnay, 5% meunier

A very impressive vintage, with a pinot noir lead reflected in a full straw hue and magnificent depth of enticing yellow mirabelle plums and rich figs. Its maturity is declared in a panoply of burnt butter, toast, honey, brioche, butterscotch and mixed spice, drawn out effortlessly by lively acidity, a creamy bead and fine chalk mineral structure.

Deutz Brut Classic NV $$

94 points • Disgorged November 2013 • Tasted in Aÿ, Brisbane, Sydney
& Melbourne

2010 base vintage with 35% reserves; one-third of each of chardonnay, pinot noir and meunier;
a blend from 20-30 villages across the Marne, with a focus on Aÿ and Mareuil-sur-Aÿ; aged 3 years
in the cellar; 9g/L dosage; around 1.6 million bottles annually

Brut Classic is the barometer of Deutz, representing 80% of the volume of the house, and
the house gives it first priority. But if any cracks develop in the wake of increasing production,
they will surely appear here, and certainly in a season as shaky as 2010. To the contrary, quite
remarkably, this is as good as I have seen this refreshing apéritif. It presents an engaging contrast
between the racy tension of lemon and grapefruit, the presence and volume of red apple, pear
and white peach, and the elegant complexity of bottle age nuances of nougat, anise, brioche and
mixed spice. The vivacity and subtlety that define the signature of Deutz are upheld within a
style of cream bead, well-integrated dosage and expressive, long-lingering chalk mineral texture.

Deutz Rosé Brut NV $$

90 points • 2011 base • Disgorged October 2014 • Tasted in Aÿ & Brisbane
94 points • 2010 base vintage • Tasted in Sydney & Melbourne

90% pinot noir, including 8% red wine from Aÿ; 10% chardonnay; 30% reserves from the previous
two vintages; aged 3 years on lees; 9g/L dosage

The pure, fresh style of Deutz is perfectly suited to elegant and restrained rosé, and the
house is unusual in producing the style at three different levels. Fabrice Rosset admits that
the challenge is to maintain a consistent style every year. 'In vintages like 2001 and 2011, the
climatic conditions made it a real challenge to uphold the consistency of our non-vintage wines.'
It leaves its stamp here in a dry, dusty mouthfeel and notes of tamarillo. Nonetheless, some
subtle red cherry, pomegranate and pink pepper do manage to poke through amidst a creamy
bead, good acid line, well-integrated dosage and lingering persistence. The 2010 base vintage is
much more representative of a house accomplished in crafting pristine rosé right from its entry
cuvée. It's fine and elegant, with pristine red cherry and rose petal lift, excellent integration of
finely structured acidity, subtle dosage and refined, soft chalk mineral structure.

Deutz Blanc de Blancs Brut 2008 $$$

96 points • Disgorged February 2014 • Tasted in Aÿ & Brisbane

51% Avize, 41% Le Mesnil-sur-Oger and 8% Villers-Marmery; 11g/L dosage

The sublime 2008 season plays precisely to Deutz's brief of precision and minerality. Embedded
deeply in the two most confident chardonnay grand crus, this is a cuvée that encapsulates the
ultra-elegance and coiled-up power and intensity that define this vintage. Its chalk minerality
is breathtaking, surging and frothing with the seaspray of its terroirs. Freshness shines as pure
and stark as high-noon daylight in lemon, crunchy pear and yellow mirabelle plum, with all the
accumulated knowledge of seven years of age proclaimed in fresh almonds, brioche and nougat.
It's at once energetic and tense, yet intricately balanced and gentle, concluding in a crescendo of
astonishing persistence. Ready to go now, it will deepen with unrelenting resolve for decades.

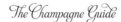
The Champagne Guide

Deutz Blanc de Blancs 2007　$$$

95 points • Tasted in Sydney & Melbourne

One of the first and most memorable 2007s that I ever tasted, from the day of its release this has been a wine of delicacy juxtaposed with power. Two years on, its focus and tension are unwavering, sustained by excellent, fine chalk mineral definition. Notes of struck-flint reduction waft over a precise palate of white pepper, crisp pear, crunchy golden delicious apple and subtle, simmering mixed spice.

Deutz Brut Vintage 2006　$$$

94 points • Tasted in Sydney & Melbourne

60% pinot noir from Aÿ, Mareuil-sur-Aÿ, Bouzy, Ambonnay and Verzenay; 30% chardonnay from Avize and Le Mesnil-sur-Oger; 10% meunier from the Vallée de la Marne; 10g/L dosage

Current for at least four years now, this vintage is every bit as engaging as it was on day one. Refined and effortless, it sustains an excellent core of primary citrus zest, slowly evolving into soft peach, toast and honey, drawn out through a long, even finish.

Deutz Brut Rosé 2009　$$$

96 points • Disgorged November 2013 • Tasted in Aÿ & Brisbane

80% pinot noir from Aÿ, Mareuil-sur-Aÿ, Bouzy and Verzenay, including 8% pinot noir red wine from Aÿ, Mareuil-sur-Aÿ, Cumaine and Charmont; 20% chardonnay; 9g/L dosage

I was completely besotted when Deutz's ultra-sensual 2008 Rosé walked onto the scene, and I never expected to fall for the 2009 in quite the same way but, gosh, it's silky, long-legged and downright gorgeous. This is grace in a salmon-crimson silk ballgown; a ravishing celebration of pinot noir in all its red cherry and strawberry succulence, trailing a smooth acid train and friendly chalk mineral texture. There's a seamlessness to this vintage that beckons you to dance all night, albeit without the fast moves and stiletto tension of 2008.

Deutz Cuvée William Deutz Brut Millésimé 2002　$$$$

97 points • Disgorged February 2014 • Tasted in Aÿ & Brisbane

62% pinot noir from Aÿ, Mareuil-sur-Aÿ, Bouzy, Louvois and Ambonnay; 27% chardonnay from Avize, Le Mesnil-sur-Oger, and a little from the Montagne de Reims; 11% meunier from Pierry and Chatillon-sur-Marne; 10g/L dosage

There is both a depth and a breadth to 2002, encapsulated in an incredible display of the freshness of Deutz, amplified by the intensity of pinot noir, elevated and energised by ultra-fine, chalk-rich minerality and set resolutely in a mature mould. This is a wine of contrasts and contradictions, but, profoundly, it maintains seamless persistence and breathtaking lightness. Youthful endurance is declared in vibrant lemon zest and young summer-fruit freshness, while the grand maturity of a dozen years in the cellar is articulated quietly in depth of brioche, gingernut biscuits, vanilla nougat, toast and honey. Prominent, silky chalk structure is the highlight of a mesmerising finish. It's ready to drink now, and anytime in the next decade.

Deutz Cuvée William Deutz 1999 $$$$

94 points • Tasted in Sydney & Melbourne

One of the rare cuvées to appear in all three editions of *The Champagne Guide* to date, and here it is for one final showing. It peaked two years ago, and is now coming towards the end of its prime, complex, full and long, with an impressive core of peach fruit and citrus zest becoming toasty, honeyed, spicy and buttery. Still great, but eclipsed in every way by the 2002.

Deutz Amour de Deutz Blanc de Blanc Brut Millésimé 2005 $$$$

93 points • Disgorged June 2014 • Tasted in Aÿ, Brisbane, Sydney & Melbourne

60% Avize, 35% Le Mesnil-sur-Oger, 5% Villers-Marmery; 10g/L dosage

I admire Fabrice Rosset for many reasons, not least his brutal honesty: '2005 is not my cup of tea, a vintage characterised by a vegetal character.' This cuvée is a triumph of this difficult season and it's been evolving into itself confidently since its release. True to the style of the house, there is a zesty vibrancy, an energetic freshness and an effortless grace here that's rarely expressed by this vintage. Crunchy pear, apple and grapefruit are evolving into nougat, vanilla custard, toast and spice. It concludes in a dry, brittle, almond skin-like phenolic texture, characteristic of 2005, yet diminishing with time post-disgorgement, thanks to a creamy body, expressive chalk mineral texture, substance, complexity and succulence that go some way towards softening and elongating the finish.

Deutz Amour de Deutz Rosé Brut 2006 $$$$$

97 points • Disgorged July and September 2014 • Tasted in Aÿ & Brisbane

55% pinot noir, mostly from Aÿ, Verzenay and Bouzy, including 8% red wine from three sites in Aÿ and Mareuil-sur-Aÿ, 45% chardonnay from Avize, Chouilly and Villers-Marmery; 10g/L dosage

A new king has ascended in the great kingdom of Deutz rosé, a brand new release, replacing William Deutz Rosé with an intentionally more elegant style and inadvertently offering a profound insight into the motivation of this house and its president. A few weeks before I visited in late 2014, Fabrice Rosset made the tough and costly decision never to release the entire 14,768 bottle production of Amour de Deutz Rosé 2005. He poured me an exclusive tasting of that never-to-be-released cuvée (94 points). Goodness, many reputable houses would release (and have) lesser prestige cuvées. I have long respected Deutz, and at that moment it won an all-new respect.

It takes all the wizardry and resources of Deutz to create a new rosé of such thrilling, towering magnificence. It is at once ethereal in its elegance, precise in its definition and fairy-light on its feet, yet there is grand presence and depth of fruit power driving it long and full on the finish. Capturing such a definitive platform of chalk mineral texture within a style of breathtakingly graceful elegance elevates it to another spiritual plane. Exquisite purity of red cherries, wild strawberries, rose hip, pink pepper and pomegranate define an impeccably crafted shape of exuberant yet immaculate refinement, and mesmerising persistence. A triumph, and an instant addition to Champagne's top rosé tier — and who else can claim that with a new cuvée?

DEVAUX

(Deh-voh)

6/10

DOMAINE DE VILLENEUVE, 10110 BAR-SUR-SEINE
www.champagne-devaux.fr

*C*hampagne Devaux is the label of the large Union Auboise cooperative based in Bar-sur-Seine in the heart of the Champagne outpost of Côte des Bar. Owned by more than 800 growers, with some 1400 hectares under vine, the cooperative is the largest grower in the region and sells a substantial quantity of juice to other houses. Its headquarters are located in the country, on the banks of the Seine, where the soil is too moist for subterranean storage, so air-conditioned, industrial warehousing is employed. This hardly reads like an endorsement, but the cooperative is innovative and progressive, and its value-for-money champagnes are well made, showcasing the fruit power and definition of the Côte des Bar.

The Union Auboise dedicates just 100 hectares to the production of Devaux, and even this is more than 1.5 times the requirement for producing 650,000 bottles each year. Chef de cave Michel Parisot visits every vineyard prior to harvest to decide which will be rejected.

Twenty-three years at Devaux have blessed Parisot with a keen insight into the diversity of terroirs across the many valleys of the large region of the Aube. He compares some with the soils of Chablis, and others with those of Burgundy — which comes as no surprise, with many of his vineyards closer to both than the Côte des Blancs.

'We are not about comparing the Côte des Bar with the Côte des Blancs,' he emphasises. 'We have vineyards in both, and we focus on the diversity of Champagne in its villages, landscapes and finished products.'

Pinot noir rules in the Côte des Bar, and leads most of Parisot's cuvées, but chardonnay is increasing in the region, showing particular promise in Urville, and finding representation in the wines accordingly. Since 1987, Devaux has turned its attention more resolutely towards the Aube, focusing on pinot noir and chardonnay, removing meunier from its cuvées.

Parisot works closely with his many growers, though a team of six full-time liaison officers is required to help them better manage their vineyards. 'We decided some years ago that we want to have a large representation of organic vines, and we tell our growers that this is how they should manage their vineyards,' Parisot reports. Devaux performs extensive experimental work, investigating different techniques in its vineyards.

Growers are paid a premium for fruit destined for the premium D de Devaux range, which currently represents 30% of the brand. There is an aspiration to increase this to 50%, and to slowly grow production by 5% every year, a conservative target given the vineyard resources at Devaux's disposal.

The house is equally progressive in vinification, creating a vast array of different parcels from every vintage. Parisot compares his philosophy to that of a perfumer, creating different flavours to assemble a blend of great complexity. 'The first work is in the vineyard; the second is to create many different possibilities for fermentation and vinification, so as to produce a large palette of flavours,' he says.

This defines an interesting and unusual house style that encompasses a bit of everything — tank fermentation, barrel fermentation, large barrels and small, bâtonnage, full malolactic, no malolactic. With 500 tanks and barrels of all sizes at his disposal, the permutations for Parisot's experimentation are vast, and in the rare and privileged position of selling an enormous 95% of every harvest to other houses, he is afforded the luxury to keep only those ferments that suit his blends.

Malolactic fermentation is completed for the Devaux range, and carried out or blocked for D de Devaux, according to the parcel and the year. Parisot likes the complexity of blending with the two so much that he will sometimes split parcels and allow part to go through malolactic fermentation.

The D de Devaux wines are fermented in oak barrels, and large stocks of reserve wines are kept in large oak tuns of 3000–7000-litre capacity for up to three years. This allows the opportunity for slow, natural oxidation. 'I don't like oxidative wines, I like well-developed wines,' Parisot emphasises. 'A good champagne should have just the beginning of oxidation flavours, but always maintain its freshness.'

A small percentage of reserves are fermented in small barrels and matured on lees with weekly bâtonnage for four months. After extensive trials, Parisot was surprised to discover that 300-litre barrels produce finer and more elegant wines than 600-litre demi-muids.

Parisot's latest pursuit has been in pioneering the use of local oak from the Côte des Bar, motivated by an imperative to improve the company's carbon footprint. He is working with the University of France to compare oak from the Côte des Bar, Montagne de Reims and Argonne, but it's still early days and he admits he is yet to identify any differences in flavour. 'We would like to determine whether a certain forest suits a particular parcel of pinot noir or chardonnay, but it will take us many years, and maybe we will find that the place of origin doesn't matter!' he admits.

A focus on raising quality since 1987 has seen a trend towards increasing use of reserve wines, an impressive increase in bottle age of non-vintage cuvées from two years to between three and five, and a progressive decrease in dosage to under 10g/L. Each of three or four different disgorgements for each cuvée receives a different dosage, generally 7–9g/L.

A number of cuvées are sealed under DIAM closures and Parisot is delighted. 'We have only had two complaints in four years regarding the look of these closures,' he says. Unfortunately, the D de Devaux range is still consigned to natural cork, but Parisot believes he's close to convincing the company's president to move the entire range across to DIAM.

Parisot's innovative and progressive spirit continues to drive advancement at Devaux. 'It is always possible to improve,' he maintains. 'We can't sit on our reputation. We must always look for ways to improve.'

DEVAUX GRANDE RÉSERVE BRUT NV $$

92 points • TASTED IN SYDNEY & MELBOURNE

2009 base with 20-25% reserves; a small portion of reserves aged in large oak tuns; 70% pinot noir, 30% chardonnay; full malolactic fermentation; aged at least 3 years; 9g/L dosage; DIAM closure

An impeccably assembled blend, showcasing the enticing generosity and definition of the Côte des Bar at an affordable price. The theme here is the richness of pinot noir's rounded peach personality, and this bottle had already been in Australia for a year before I tasted it, heightening its complexity of honey and lingering mixed spice, yet still impeccably enlivened with a vibrant acid backbone and soft minerality, bringing balance and focus to the finish.

The Champagne Guide

Devaux Blanc de Noirs NV $$

92 points • Tasted in Sydney & Melbourne

100% Côte des Bar pinot noir; full malolactic fermentation; aged at least 3 years; 9g/L dosage; DIAM closure

An unashamed celebration of the voluptuous fruit and impressive magnitude of Côte des Bar pinot noir. Blackberry and red apple fruit and spice of great intensity are massaged into a supple, buttery softness that lingers long. Well-balanced acidity keeps its considerable proportions in check.

Devaux Cuvée Rosée Brut NV $$

90 points • Tasted in Sydney & Melbourne

20% reserve wines, partially aged in barrel; 80% pinot noir and 20% chardonnay; 12-14% red wine; full malolactic fermentation; aged at least 3 years; 9g/L dosage; DIAM closure

The aim here is for an easy-drinking, fruity rosé, with a medium crimson hue infused by the addition of both red wine and maceration skin-contact rosé from Les Riceys. The result meets the brief in a pale salmon style of soft strawberry and red cherry fruit, layered with mixed spice. This bottle appears a little developed, finishing savoury and flat.

D de Devaux La Cuvée Brut NV $$

91 points • Tasted in Sydney & Melbourne

40% reserve wine from a perpetual solera; 60% pinot noir, 40% chardonnay; 80-85% malolactic fermentation; aged at least 5 years; 8g/L dosage

Michel Parisot has maintained a reserve solera in large oak tuns since 2002, and a sample including every vintage to 2011 showcased the complexity of maturity that can be built in a solera, while upholding wonderful purity, freshness and finesse. The bottle I tasted was more developed than I have seen this cuvée before — more toasty, spicy and honeyed, though upholding rounded balance and good persistence. Its dosage shows more prominently than it has in the past.

D de Devaux Ultra Extra Brut NV $$

91 points • Tasted in Sydney & Melbourne

Identical to D de Devaux La Cuvée Brut, with 2g/L dosage

Devaux purposely avoids a zero-dosage cuvée, favouring a dosage of 2g/L to provide better balance and persistence to the finish. The result is more taut, metallic and coiled than the equivalent La Cuvée, accenting lemon zest and chalk mineral structure on a firmer and more tense finish. A searing, ultra-dry champagne for the brave.

DIEBOLT-VALLOIS

(Dee-boh Val-wah)

6/10

84 RUE NEUVE 51530 CRAMANT

www.diebolt-vallois.com

In the grand tapestry of Champagne vineyards, the great crus are well celebrated, but prime placement within the village is perhaps the most important yet under-recognised privilege. In this the Diebolt-Vallois family is particularly blessed. The marriage of Jacques Diebolt and Nadia Vallois in 1960 marked the union of his old family vineyards, largely on the prized, steep, east-south-east facing slopes in the southern part of Cramant, with significant holdings that her family had cultivated since the 1400s, very close to Cramant in Cuis. Smaller holdings are located in Chouilly, Le Mesnil-sur-Oger, Épernay (in a plot just 20 metres from Chouilly), Marfaux in the Vallée de la Marne and in the Aube. Blanc de blancs are the showpiece of the terroirs of the northern Côte des Blancs, and the Diebolt family is masterful in uniting the radiant presence of Cramant with the pinpoint clarity of Cuis.

When Pol Roger managing director Laurent d'Harcourt graciously welcomed me to shadow him for a day at the height of vintage 2014, our first visit was to the Diebolt family in Cramant, such is the importance of this grower to Pol Roger. 'Monsieur Diebolt is a king of ageing blanc de blancs!' d'Harcourt exclaimed. The winery is pristine, and that day I saw some of the cleanest fruit I've seen going into any press in Champagne.

The family astutely manages its 14 hectares of vineyards, using grasses in the mid-rows and minimal treatments. Jacques and Nadia's daughter, Isabelle, spent the whole day of my visit with the pickers, continually checking quality and ensuring they were cutting out any rot.

A similar attentiveness is applied in the winery, where Isabelle and her brother Arnaud assist their father. 'We control everything from the land through the whole process, pressing and vinifying every parcel ourselves,' Isabelle told me. 'We focus on the terroirs of our vineyards, so we use small tanks, barrels (purchased from Burgundy after 3–4 vintages) and large oak vats to keep every parcel separate.' Fermentation temperature is carefully controlled at a cool 17.5°C. Wood is reserved for vintage cuvées, with the exception of some reserves for non-vintage blends, which are stored in 40hL casks of around 10 years of age to mature slowly in a deep, cool cellar 14 metres underground. The purity of the house is elegantly set off by low dosages of around 6–8g/L.

The house has increased its vineyard holdings in the hotly contested grand crus of Cramant, Chouilly and Le Mesnil-sur-Oger, hoping to increase production of their top cuvées. Their precise and enduring blanc de blancs are on restricted allocation globally.

The Champagne Guide

Diebolt-Vallois Brut Tradition NV $

91 points • Tasted in Cramant

2010 base vintage with 2009 reserves; 45% pinot noir, 40% chardonnay, 15% meunier; 7g/L dosage; 20,000 bottles

A lively, crunchy and pretty cuvée, led by the apple notes of pinot noir and the lemon purity of chardonnay. The palate is dry and savoury, structured with a good line of lemon juice acidity and let down by some phenolic firmness on the finish.

Diebolt-Vallois Blanc de Blancs NV $

95 points • Tasted in Cramant

2010 base vintage with 2009 reserves; Cuis, Chouilly and Épernay; vinified in tanks; 7g/L dosage; 60,000 bottles

An apéritif style by design, and a wonderfully pure and elegant expression of Diebolt-Vallois' well-positioned chardonnay vines in the northern Côte des Blancs. Deeply structured bath-salts minerality erupts from chalk soils in a shower of tight grapefruit, focused lemon and crunchy pink lady apple. Its energy is consummately controlled in a style of creamy softness, with impeccably integrated dosage, finishing very long, seamless and classy.

Diebolt-Vallois Brut Rosé NV $$

93 points • Tasted in Cramant

2010 base vintage with 2009 reserves; 63% pinot noir, 27% chardonnay, 10% meunier; largely from Épernay; Diebolt-Vallois purchases 1000L of old vine pinot noir red wine from a grower in Bouzy; 7g/L dosage; just 10,000 bottles

True to the elegant mood of the house, this pale salmon-tinted rosé is alive with the definition and youthful precociousness of rose hip, pink grapefruit, red apple, red cherry and strawberry. A fine, chalk mineral mouthfeel sets off a style of finesse.

Diebolt-Vallois Prestige Brut Blanc de Blancs NV $$

94 points • Tasted in Cramant

2011 base, with 2010 and 2009 reserves; 50% of reserves fermented in tanks and matured in large 8600L oak foudres for 1-2 years; almost equal parts Cramant and Chouilly, with a little Le Mesnil-sur-Oger; 7g/L

The aspiration here is a creamy take on grand cru chardonnay that unites the richness of oak maturation with the mineral definition sustained in tank. It meets the brief in body, structure and persistence, freshened by finely honed acidity. Tightly focused crunchy pear, taut grapefruit, tangy lemon and golden delicious apple are coaxed by layers of barrel-derived texture, offering subtle firmness to deep-set salt mineral presence.

DIEBOLT-VALLOIS BLANC DE BLANCS VINTAGE 2007 $$

93 points • TASTED IN CRAMANT

Chouilly and Cuis; vinified in tanks; just 10,000 bottles

Chouilly takes the lead in its floral, lemon blossom notes, squarely backed by the acid drive of Cuis. Lively lemon and crunchy apple fruit make way for lovely back palate richness of white peaches. This is a fleshy-bodied and well-textured wine that retains its focus through a finish accentuated by a line of well-integrated acidity and some gentle phenolic firmness, supporting fine chalk mineral structure.

DIEBOLT-VALLOIS FLEUR DE PASSION BLANC DE BLANCS 2006 $$$$

95 points • TASTED IN CRAMANT

Diebolt-Vallois' best selection of Cramant, from seven plots of very old vines of 50-65 years of age; fermented and matured for 6 months in small oak barrels between 8 and 22 years old; no malolactic fermentation, since these old vines do not produce as much acidity as other terroirs; built to age for 10 years; 6g/L dosage; tiny production of 8000 bottles

A paradox of rich, ripe fruit and honed energy, capturing the spirit of the great terroirs of Cramant. The freshness of lemon zest and crunchy apple and pear fruit contrasts the richness of fleshy white peach, fig, honey and ginger. Barrel fermentation brings brioche, spice and biscuity complexity to the party, upholding excellent body on a persistent finish of subtle grapefruit bitterness, focused acid tang and fine chalk minerality.

DIEBOLT-VALLOIS FLEUR DE PASSION BLANC DE BLANCS 2005 $$$$

92 points • TASTED IN CRAMANT

As above, with 5g/L dosage

A bold and full vintage of body and depth, exalting in a rich back palate with all the character of ginger, preserved lemon, biscuits and spice. Savoury, barrel-aged complexity unites with the grippy, chewy mouthfeel of 2005 phenolic presence and bitter grapefruit notes, supported by salt mineral texture and holding out with grand persistence. An authentic take on a difficult season.

DIEBOLT-VALLOIS CRAMANT BLANC DE BLANCS 1989

95 points • TASTED IN CRAMANT

This was the predecessor of Fleur de Passion, chardonnay from a single plot, vinified in barriques with no malolactic fermentation. At a full quarter-century of age, it's resounding evidence of the enduring longevity of Diebolt-Vallois, even in a warm season. Notes of grilled toast reduction and a green olive character representative of grand old Côte des Blancs chardonnay quickly make way for the ripe fruit personality of fig, white nectarine and glacé pineapple. Cramant declares its true grandeur in a finish of remarkable focus and freshness.

DOM PÉRIGNON

(Dom Pe-ri-ngon)

9/10

20 AVENUE DE CHAMPAGNE 51200 ÉPERNAY

www.domPérignon.com

www.creatingdomPérignon.com

Dom Pérignon

*D*om Pérignon is the prestige cuvée of Moët & Chandon, but so distinct are the production, style and sheer class of the wines that the two brands are best considered completely autonomous. The two are made in the same premises in Épernay, and some facilities are shared, but the winemaking teams are distinct. Of Moët's colossal resource of 1180 hectares of estate vineyards, some are designated as Moët, others Dom Pérignon, and the rest are vinified by Dom Pérignon and allocated at the time of blending. 'The Dom' is a wine of tension, power and long-ageing endurance, the king of the most readily available and perpetually discounted prestige cuvées.

Dom Pérignon is the vision of the talented and insightful Richard Geoffroy, dedicated to this cuvée since 1990, and who today also oversees the entire production of Moët & Chandon ('piloting the cruise liner!'). The man who deserves much of the credit for the rise of one of Champagne's most famous and celebrated brands of the modern age carries his responsibility with unassuming humility. When I congratulated him on his 25th year in early 2015, he praised the positive energy of his team and the extensive resources at his disposal. 'I must be the most privileged winemaker in the world!' he grinned.

Geoffroy works painstakingly to draw out the best wines he can in each season, while juggling the politics of big business and a frenetic travel schedule to introduce his wines to the world. While deeply embedded in the history and tradition of Champagne, he steers this sizeable house with a courageous sense of daring (more on this later), and there is no doubt he is one of the great minds of modern Champagne.

Alongside Louis Roederer Cristal, Dom Pérignon was the very first of champagne's prestige cuvées, introduced in the mid-1930s with the 1921 vintage. There are only two wines: a vintage and a vintage rosé, traditionally produced less than one year in two, released after a minimum of seven years' bottle ageing on lees, and again selectively in later life recently renamed, less than romantically, Dom Pérignon P2 and P3 (formerly 'Oenothèque'). There are no non-vintage wines. Every vintage is harvested and vinified, and the decision is made at the blending table as to whether the wine will be made and released, or the entire vintage sold off.

Dom Pérignon's production is a closely guarded secret and rumours abound in Champagne, with some putting annual sales at 3.5 million bottles, and others suggesting as many as 8 million each vintage. The company maintains it is very much less than this, divulging only that it's more than Krug's 600,000 bottles. There is a desire to increase production, but opportunities to

Dom Pérignon owns more of every grand cru than anyone else.

increase estate holdings are extremely limited. 'I would love to have more grand cru vineyards!' Geoffroy exclaims. 'We're already making as much as we can.'

VAST VINEYARD RESOURCES

Dom Pérignon is based on a core of five grand cru villages of pinot noir: Aÿ, Ambonnay, Bouzy, Verzenay and Mailly-Champagne; and four of chardonnay: Le Mesnil-sur-Oger, Avize, Cramant and Chouilly, in which the company owns 'huge' resources. In all, there are about 20 villages in the blend, including the premier crus of Hautvillers and Vertus. Estate vineyards in 14 of Champagne's 17 grand crus are called upon, and fruit is sometimes purchased from two of the others, but over the past decade more than 98% has come from estate sources, including the oldest vines of the premier cru of Hautvillers, the historical and spiritual home of Dom Pérignon.

The key to Dom Pérignon's sourcing is the vast diversity of vineyards at its disposal. Historically, particular sites have been dedicated to each Moët Hennessy house, and Dom Pérignon has had first choice. 'There are core grand crus for Dom Pérignon and we have a privilege to access the fruit sources of the other houses as we desire,' Geoffroy divulges. He is afforded 'tremendous latitude' to change the plots and take the very best that a given year has to offer. Blending is fundamental to Dom Pérignon, and Geoffroy upholds that this is more important than ever in vintage champagne. 'If there is one house able to make vineyard-specific wine styles, surely it is Dom Pérignon — we own more vineyards than anyone else in every grand cru,' he points out. 'If anyone is capable of making Le Mesnil, it is Dom Pérignon! But I want to use Le Mesnil in the blend.'

The Dom Pérignon house style is about a tension between chardonnay and pinot noir, in a blend of roughly 50/50, though it can drift to 60/40 in either direction, according to the season. Chardonnay is the limiting ingredient in production, and in the current time of short supply, Geoffroy is pleased to have the

security of a majority of estate vineyards and a single contract with a 'top cooperative'.

The precise moment of harvest is given the utmost attention, and the grapes are tasted twice every day. The window of picking is short — 'in 2008 it was vegetal on Monday and too ripe on Tuesday!' Geoffroy uses pH over acid, flavour and sugar as the most important indicator of properly ripe fruit. Waiting for sugar ripeness doesn't work in the wildly fluctuating vintages of current times. 'Ten degrees of sugar ripeness in 2003 was not like 10 degrees in 2004!' he points out.

Work is underway to redefine vineyard plots using observation tools such as aerial surveying, and to separately vinify each plot to further hone the detail of each parcel. Trials have also been conducted into an acceptable distance for fruit to be trucked between vineyard and press house, finding that a distance exceeding 15–20 kilometres can be problematic. Dom Pérignon is not afraid of some oxidation prior to fermentation in order to reduce phenolics in the juice, but this needs to be carefully controlled, according to the maturity of the grapes and their phenolic content.

REDUCTIVE WINEMAKING

'We are very dedicated to the fruit and the vineyards, but fermentation is just as important,' Geoffroy declares. Wines are fermented exclusively in stainless steel tanks, using a cultured house yeast strain, with sulphite added at the press to kill off indigenous wild yeasts. 'I love the idea of the yeast emptying into the wine to bring an added dimension; the organic meeting the mineral,' says Geoffroy. The wine is judiciously protected from oxidation post-fermentation. 'Our vision is to age our wine in a reductive way, as too much oxidation kills champagne's complexity, making it fat and heavy.'

Malolactic fermentation is run to completion using a culture co-inoculated with the primary fermentation, upheld as a key to achieving freshness as the wines build complexity and texture through long ageing. If vintages continue to warm, malolactic may be blocked in some parcels to maintain balance.

There is no rule for the dosage level in Dom Pérignon, which is determined through trials of different reserve wines and varying levels of sugar and sulphur dioxide six months prior to release. The dosage sweetness has diminished from 10g/L in 1996 to less than 7g/L today. 'Perhaps the maturity of the grapes is higher, or perhaps we're doing different things in the making?' postulates Geoffroy's offsider, Vincent Chaperon.

The decision to release a wine is made at the point of blending. 'Even in the lousiest years we go to the final blend with no preconceived ideas,' Geoffroy says. 'Since

Dom Pérignon has been Dom Pérignon we have always harvested a vintage every year.'

First released in 1959, Dom Pérignon Rosé represents just a few per cent of the blanc volume, and typically sells for close to twice the price. Only made in vintages in which phenolics are in balance, there is an attempt to make rosé in every vintage, but it's typically released every second year. It displays a riper fruit profile than the blanc, since the pinot noir for the red wine for blending is picked riper, with more aromatics and more jammy character. 'The challenge is to balance this to maintain delicacy in the wine,' Chaperon explains. 'It's a highly bodied wine that needs to maintain an equilibrium between authority and seduction.' Since 2000, the mandate has been to make a more substantial rosé style. 'Burgundy is all the rage and the market is looking for a more substantial style,' Geoffroy explains.

The key to Dom Pérignon lies in blending to achieve 'a state of completeness', a perfect balance of white and black grapes. 'Harmony is so intense,' is Geoffroy's line. 'It's like playing tennis. If you're not experienced you try to make it up with power, but if you have the right swing, it's effortless. You can forget about power and deliver intensity. When you hit it right, you hear it because the sound of the ball is different. You hear the pop! That's my quest. Dom Pérignon is about the pop.'

The new Dom Pérignon

Prior to 1990, Dom Pérignon released 29 vintages in 70 years — one release every two and a half years. Since Geoffroy commenced in 1990, the frequency has almost doubled, to 11 vintages in 15 seasons. This has recently increased further still. Since 1997, so far only 2001 has not been released. This is the first time in its almost century-long history that Dom Pérignon has released six out of seven vintages. 'My dream is to make Dom Pérignon every year,' Geoffroy reveals. 'I am a physician, my commitment is to bring vintages to life.'

Conspiracy theories abound, but he thanks an improvement in Champagne vintages for this trend. 'I have often been asked about global warming, and I am embarrassed to say that so far it has been for the better in Champagne!' he exclaims. 'Good crop sizes, more consistent yields, good consistency of quality, good levels of ripeness, lower acids and more rounded wines, which I'm very excited about.'

He admits he is not yet able to make Dom Pérignon every year. 'But if you cross global warming with smart viticulture and more precision in the winemaking, the only question is the volume of the blend.' In the difficult 2005 vintage, he released a smaller volume and suggested that in the most challenging years, a release might represent one-quarter or even one-eighth of a large vintage such as 2004.

It is bewildering that Dom Pérignon released a full production volume of the controversial 2003 vintage, a difficult and atypical season, when the hottest summer to ever hit Champagne was recorded. Geoffroy discloses that '2003 is high in phenolics, it's the key to the vintage'. The hard bitterness that this brings is my biggest concern with this vintage. He reveals it had the lowest acidity he's ever recorded, and then makes an unexpected announcement: 'I take it as it is. It's not about the style of Dom Pérignon, it's about the vintage. I am sick of the word "style". There is no style. Dom Pérignon is pushing the idea of vintage more than anything else.'

There's something noble and inherently authentic in this statement, something perhaps more Burgundian than it is Champenois: a wholesome celebration of the voice of the elements over the force of the hand of man. Yet in a climate as tumultuous and increasingly erratic as Champagne's, there is something deeply disturbing in this statement, too. It changes the game for Dom Pérignon.

The Dom Pérignon that we know and love has never been all about the vintage. Chaperon explained to me two years ago that 'Dom Pérignon is about creating a balance between the style of the vintage and the style of the house, and we are able to drive the vintage in the direction of our style by selecting the finest sites in each season. Whether we release a vintage is more a question of style than of quality.'

'Style' hasn't always been a dirty word for Dom Pérignon. Until recently, if the style of the vintage hadn't met the style of Dom Pérignon, it was never released. And there will always be Champagne vintages unworthy of standing alone. But it seems something changed in 2003. Geoffroy admits that '2003 is border territory for Champagne, as border as it can be. We took the risk, a technical risk. Frankly, we never lacked confidence, but we had to push harder.'

Is 2003 a one-off? Geoffroy alludes to a fundamental shift in the philosophy of the house. 'Some future vintages will be more than you might expect from Dom Pérignon,' he warns. 'In the past, Dom Pérignon has been very gentle and very accessible. But the decade of the 2000s is more about pushing the style. We are pushing the factor of vintage, covering a much broader span of scope than anything in the past, making wine in the character of the vintage by playing with the ripeness. We are not playing on the safe side as much as we used to, and as much as other champagne makers are, which implies that there is an element of risk. This is doing very good things for the brand, and I will keep taking the risks becasue it is the only way to keep the brand alive.'

Are we entering an era in which the consumer must exercise greater discretion in selecting vintages of Dom Pérignon? If 2003 suggested that we are, 2005 confirms it, and there are more vintages to come which are 'very much on the ripe side'.

THE PLENITUDES P1, P2 AND P3

Geoffroy speaks of three ages of peak maturity in Dom Pérignon's life, the first after 7–9 years (the standard release, formerly released at seven years of age and now nine or 10, the 'first plenitude,' dubbed P1), a second at 12–20 years (now P2, formerly 'Oenothèque') and a third at 35–40 years (P3, the 'plenitude of complexity').

Dom Pérignon makes these mature vintages available through an extremely limited library of releases, representing just 1–2% of only the most age-worthy vintages, and typically at double the price of the first release.

P1 and P2 are each disgorged as a single batch, and surprisingly not necessarily soon before release (1998 P2 was disgorged five years before release), but P3 tends to be disgorged progressively according to demand. P2 is released in vintage order and P3 in any order, as each vintage is ready. P2 and P3 are a testament to the remarkable battery pack of energy and vitality contained within the lees in a bottle of champagne, capable of sustaining a bottle for a lifetime. If a vintage is not deemed worthy of a P2 and P3 release, it is never released, even as P1. If it then didn't develop satisfactorily for P2 and P3, the theory is that they would not be re-released, though it hasn't happened yet.

P2 and P3 are based on the same wine as the standard release, sealed from the outset with a cork and cellared on lees for an extended time. Bottles are kept upside down so the lees settle inside the cork and impede oxygen ingress. Surprisingly, trials have found crown caps less reliable than corks beyond 10 years, perhaps due to phenolics and antioxidants leaching from the cork. 'After 10 years a cork is so superior to crown cap,' Geoffroy believes. 'There is a wonderful chemistry, which would be very difficult to reproduce with a different closure.'

The cork seal necessitates manual disgorgement of P1 and P2 releases, and each bottle is checked for cork taint as it is disgorged. 'On tirage you have an added effect from the first and second cork,' he explains. 'You may not detect any problem from the first cork, but after you insert the second cork it may become noticeable.' Further, as in any wine style, long-ageing under natural corks creates bottle variation, and no two P2 and P3s are alike, adding an element of risk to a significant outlay. The house reports more variation due to oxidation and reduction than to cork taint.

Dom Pérignon's best buy is always its standard blanc, and frequently discounted.

DREADED CORKS

The level of cork taint I've encountered in Dom Pérignon is alarming, though this year there were only two bottles in 26 (8%), much better than 4 bottles in 10 last year, though still among the worst in the region. An embarrassment in any wine, especially one of this reputation and price. As always, be sure to have any suspect bottle replaced.

DOM PÉRIGNON 2004 $$$$$

97 points • TASTED IN HAUTVILLERS, PERTH, MELBOURNE, SYDNEY & BRISBANE

52% pinot noir, 48% chardonnay

I've long been captivated by the aura of understated intensity and dramatic, high-voltage tension that radiates from Dom Pérignon 2004 and, one cork-tainted and one cork-flavoured bottle aside, all eight recent tastings have reaffirmed the marvellous endurance of this vintage. At more than a decade of age, it seems to transcend the very passage of time itself, projecting breathtaking lemon blossom and grapefruit zest freshness amidst classic Dom gunflint and grilled toast reduction. The freshest bottles are defined by coiled, backward restraint and electric acid drive. Towards the end of its release window, it's evolved to expansive generosity of yellow summer fruits, nougat and almonds, expressing spectacular depth of pinot noir, yet honed and precise, cut with the definition and energy of chardonnay. Subtle phenolic texture builds grip and structure, though never bitter, relying more on youthful and vibrant acid drive to sustain it. A heightened, brittle core of chalk mineral texture defines a finish of persistence, precision and grace. It is as confident and enduring as it was on day one, and it's only going to get better. Buy now and drink in five years, around when P2 2004 is scheduled to land.

Dom Pérignon 2005 $$$$$

94 points • Disgorged November 2013 • Tasted in Hautvillers

60-62% chardonnay, perhaps the highest ever; 38-40% pinot noir; a quarter of the production of 2004

Geoffroy says 2005 was the ripest vintage he has seen, as ripe as Burgundy or Bordeaux: '2005 is on the edge. It was not an easy vintage.' Acidity was low, and botrytis called for rigorous sorting. With a full 9.5 years of age, this is the oldest first release of Dom Pérignon yet, and the tricky 2005 season has benefited, coming into its own in the past six months. Tightly coiled grapefruit, apple and lemon zest have opened up to exotic, ripe fig, star fruit, pear and fennel, with subtle elements of gunflint reduction, in time showing hints of roasted chestnuts. The dry, structural grip and chewy mouthfeel of firm phenolics are characteristic of 2005, having softened thanks to long lees age. The 2005 is a vintage of power, sun and expansive presence, held in poise by the tang of lemon and grapefruit and the fine mineral presence of grand cru chalk. It finishes with energy and endurance, an impressive result for the season, though it will always be a lesser Dom.

Dom Pérignon 2003

92 points • The original disgorgement of late 2011 • Tasted in Hautvillers

60% pinot noir, 40% chardonnay

Dom Pérignon 2003 wears the battle scars of its challenging season, parading the exuberance of pinot noir that survived the hottest summer to ever hit Champagne, producing a hard phenolic bitterness that has always troubled me. To its credit, the voluptuous exuberance of this vintage has risen with another couple of years in bottle, particularly in the past six months, upholding its golden pineapple generosity and packing on layers of gingernut biscuits, toast and honey. The result is a more creamy mouthfeel, beginning to soften its chewy structure and subsume its bitterness, building persistence, though it still has some way to go. While 2003 remains one of the lesser Dom Pérignons, it's more forgiving now that it was on release, and that I never expected.

Dom Pérignon 2002

98 points • The original disgorgement of late 2010 • Tasted in Hautvillers

2002 represents a particularly ripe vintage for Dom Pérignon, yet recent performances have demonstrated its remarkably slow evolution. A lightning bolt of acidity strikes a dynamic core of fine, frothing chalk mineral structure, bursting with lemon sherbet freshness. Signature struck-flint reduction is subtle, and the gentle warmth of maturity is beginning to glow in notes of ginger, brioche, toast and butterscotch, with building intensity and creaminess. A benchmark Dom, magnificent now, with decades stretching marvellously before it.

Dom Pérignon Rosé 2000

95 points • Tasted in Hautvillers

An epic release for DP Rosé, but true to the generosity of the season, it's now attained the warm glow of the twilight of its life. A full copper crimson hue heralds a palate grounded on great presence and character of red and black cherries, with rising tertiary development of pipe smoke, Christmas spice and a savoury edge of layered intrigue. Deep strata of soft chalk mineral texture are suspended neatly between soft tannins and a fine, creamy bead.

Dom Pérignon Rosé 2004 $$$$$

96 points • Disgorged early 2012 • Tasted in Hautvillers

40% chardonnay; 30% pinot noir white wine and 30% pinot noir red wine, from Bouzy, Aÿ and Hautvillers

At 30%, this represents one of the highest doses of pinot noir red wine in a blended champagne rosé, up from 17–20% in the past, in line with Geoffroy's mandate to create a more substantial style. This makes for textural grip and structure, though a surprisingly pale crimson copper hue. Impressive freshness belies a full decade of maturity, in prevailing characters of freshly picked strawberries and raspberries, pomegranate and pink pepper. It finishes with profound length and a fine chalk mineral texture, which even its pinot tannins cannot smother.

Dom Pérignon Rosé 2003 $$$$$

92 points • Tasted in Hautvillers & Melbourne

20% pinot noir red wine from Aÿ, Bouzy and Hautvillers

To Geoffroy, this is a vintage of gravitas and depth, and there's no denying either. A full crimson copper in hue, it's loaded with wild complexity of blood oranges, wild strawberries, even cardamom and wood spice. Massive glasses (Geoffroy serves it in Riedel Oregon Pinot Noir glasses) accentuate pretty red cherry aromas. Its fruit integrity after more than a decade is laudable on the front, but falters through the mid-palate and finish, quickly vaporising into a callow, vacuous hole overwhelmed by robust phenolic grip. One bottle was obliterated by cork taint.

Dom Pérignon Rosé 2002

96 points • Tasted in Hautvillers

There is classically a luxurious decadence to Dom Pérignon rosé, exuding a warm amplitude built around ripe pinot noir red wine. The 2002 delivers a cunning twist to this recipe, an enchantingly refreshing take on savoury, charged with the confidence of high-strung acidity. Geoffroy describes 2002 pinot noir as intriguingly taking on some of the attributes one would expect of chardonnay. It was breathtakingly youthful at 11 years of age, and still retains an elegance of structure, focused control, persistent finish and fine chalk mineral mouthfeel. Presence and intensity are on the rise, with characterful, expressive layers of cherry, plum and red berries uniting with complex hints of honey and caramel.

Dom Pérignon P2 Rosé 1995 $$$$$

98 points • Disgorged late 2012 • Tasted in Hautvillers

Richard Geoffroy hails 1995 as the saviour vintage of his early days at Dom Pérignon, following four tough seasons, though forever lost in the shadow of 1996. Releases like this might just change that. At nigh-on two decades of age, with a medium salmon copper hue, the only suggestion of its grand maturity is its texture, captivatingly mouth-filling, at once soft and creamy from aeons on lees, and simultaneously structured, confident and definitively chalk mineral. A breathtakingly effortless gracefulness is driven by structure, yet in no way dry or old, projecting an integrity and a confidence that effuse from a core of elegant inner balance. Nuances of rose petals and primary red fruits possess a surprising freshness that belies its years, while subtle notes of game play just a delicate support role.

Dom Pérignon P2 1998 $$$$$

98 points • Disgorged in 2009 • Tasted in Melbourne & Hautvillers

First release 9g/L dosage, P2 6.5g/L

A core of energy and primary focus amidst enticing tertiary complexity and pronounced chalk mineral texture is utterly transfixing. The pace of evolution here is freeze-frame slow motion, effortlessly sustaining youthful lemon zest and lively white fruits on a tightly clenched acid line, contrasting the complexity of gunflint reduction and the billowing maturity of Parisienne baguette, toasted brioche, glacé peach, dried fig and roasted hazelnuts. More recent tastings have revealed suggestions of tertiary, smoky, iodine nuances. It's creamy, tense and tangy all at once, having attained an incredible plateau in its evolution, yet with plenty of life to ascend higher still.

Dom Pérignon Oenothèque 1996 $$$$$

100 points • Disgorged in 2008 • Tasted in Melbourne

50% pinot noir, 50% chardonnay; first release 10g/L dosage, Oenothèque 6g/L

Dom Pérignon Oenothèque 1996 is one of the greatest Doms of all, ranking among the top few champagnes on the shelves again this year. At this age, every bottle is different, and the most vivacious and energetic have not evolved one iota from the perfect bottle I tasted in 2013; the rest are but one point behind. Oenothèque 1996 is almost completely devoid of time evolution. Never have I tasted a champagne of this age of such energy, drive and acid tension, still achingly fragrant, floral and focused at 19 years of age. Its mineral texture is an epiphany, dancing with fairy lightness on a stage of solid chalk, slowly becoming ever more creamy as lees-derived texture inflates. Nuances of dried nectarine are emerging, yet never toasty or tertiary, even as 1998 is already. Dom Pérignon absolutely, finally and resoundingly silences the question on the lips of critics and connoisseurs for the past 19 years: will this bizarre and inimitable season of dehydrated concentration and low ripeness ever find balance between its intoxicating power and its searing acidity? It will and, my goodness, it has. And it will live for a lifetime.

Dom Pérignon Oenothèque 1990

100 points • Tasted in Hautvillers

Geoffroy describes his first vintage as 'defining everything about Dom Pérignon: the harmony, the integration, the opulence, the …' And then he runs out of words and waves his arms like he is about to take to flight. 'And all the more so with extra age.' Even a subtle hint of cork wood does not diminish this bottle. After almost a quarter century, it still sings with primary lemon zest, grapefruit and peach, amidst epic layers of pineapple, fig, butterscotch, gingernut biscuits and pipe smoke. It's a paradox of mouthfeel — creamy and silky, yet structured, mineral and focused. Length and line are haunting, undiminished for minutes.

DOSNON & LEPAGE

(Do-noh e Ler-pahg)

6/10

4 BIS RUE DU BAS DE LINGEY 10340 AVIREY-LINGEY

www.champagne-dosnon.com

The small cellar run by the young Davy Dosnon and Simon-Charles Lepage in Avirey-Lingey in the south-western reaches of the Côte des Bar is on the rise. A small annual production of just 50,000 bottles reflects an ever-more comfortable disposition of integration of low dosage and old oak. There is refinement, skill and craftsmanship on display in every cuvée, and the best represent great value for money.

Less than 50 kilometres north-east of Chablis, a little over a half-hour drive, Avirey-Lingey perhaps has more in common with the northern end of Burgundy than it does with other parts of Champagne, a comparison well familiar to the Gevrey-Chambertin-trained Simon-Charles. The local clay-limestone soils make for particularly rich fruit, and pinot noir takes a confident lead, as it does across the region, though this estate also takes pride in showcasing the rising credentials of Côte des Bar chardonnay in flying solo.

Complexity and fullness are the goals here. Fruit is sourced from two hectares of 25-year-old estate pinot noir vines (and a little chardonnay) and seven hectares of growers, farmed using sustainable viticulture. Harmony is the buzz word for Dosnon & Lepage and vines are essentially worked organically, while maintaining the flexibility to apply treatments in adverse seasons. Grasses are grown in the mid-rows, soils are tilled for aeration, no chemical treatments are used, and yields are controlled.

Minimal intervention is the philosophy in the winery, too, and fermentation and ageing take place exclusively in oak (minimum barrel age five years).

Indigenous yeasts are increasingly employed for primary fermentation, to build character and complexity. An intuitive philosophy sees malolactic fermentation allowed or blocked and bâtonnage performed or not, according to the character of the wine. A high 40% of reserve wine is used, and bottle maturation is never less than two years.

These are cuvées to enjoy young and fresh, as bottle age tends to induce oxidation. Ultra-modern labels appropriately set off the progressive approach of this boutique négociant.

Dosnon & Lepage Recolte Blanche Blanc de Blancs NV $$

90 points • 2009 BASE • TASTED IN SYDNEY

100% Côte des Bar chardonnay; vinified and aged in barrel

Côte des Bar chardonnay is richer than that of the Côte des Blancs, yet this is a particularly tight release for Dosnon & Lepage, defined by taut white fruits and reductive complexity, making for a complex, savoury and flinty style. It shows good mineral expression and persistence.

Dosnon & Lepage Recolte Blanc de Noire NV $$

92 points • DISGORGED FEBRUARY 2014 • TASTED IN SYDNEY & MELBOURNE

100% Côte des Bar pinot noir; vinified and aged in barrel; 7g/L dosage

This expressive blanc de noirs could confidently stand in for rosé at the table, with the fleshy depth of pinot noir characterised in red cherry and red apple fruits. It finishes long and taut, with fine mineral structure and a note of wet wood savouriness from barrel fermentation. One bottle tasted was oxidised.

Dosnon & Lepage Recolte Rosé NV $$

93 points • TASTED IN SYDNEY & MELBOURNE

100% pinot noir; same base as Recolte Blanc de Noire

A fresh and lively aperitif rosé of pale straw hue and elegant, focused, pretty strawberry and watermelon fruit, underlined by vibrant, tangy acidity. Excellent expression of chalk mineral texture is unexpected for the Aube. One bottle tasted was oxidised.

The premier cru of Trépail is one of the highest villages on the Montagne de Reims.

DUMANGIN J. FILS

(Dew-mohn-zhan J. Feess)

6/10

3 RUE DE RILLY 51500 CHIGNY-LES-ROSES

www.champagne-dumangin.com

CHAMPAGNE
DUMANGIN
J. Fils

'The secret to making great wine is attention to the fine details at every stage,' is the mantra of Gilles Dumangin. The fifth-generation chef de cave must be the hardest worker in Chigny-les-Roses. When I visited late one Sunday afternoon in July, he'd been at the bottling machine since 4am, as he had been every morning for the previous two weeks. The week before, his air-conditioner had died, then his brine chiller, then his labelling machine. He fixed all three himself. A self-confessed control freak, Gilles works 20–22 hours every day during harvest. And he loves it.

Such fanaticism defines every stage of production at Dumangin J. Fils. 'My wife spent one harvest with me and declared, "You are in love with your presses! You do not leave them for a moment!"' Gilles recounts. And he doesn't disagree. His old Coquards are 'the Rolls Royce' of champagne presses. 'The week and a half of harvest is a lovely time. I listen to my presses the whole time. I know them so well that if anything sounds different, I know something is wrong. If you can't press well, you can't make good champagne.'

I spent a day shadowing Gilles in the middle of harvest 2014 and I have not seen more focused attention to detail anywhere in Champagne. There was a subtle change in the sound of the press and he stopped mid-sentence and jumped to its attention.

These are handmade champagnes, and a production of just 150,000 bottles permits every step in the process to be performed manually by Gilles and his father Jacky, including riddling (by transfer between pallets). Every

parcel is kept separate, thanks to tiny tanks, some not much larger than a bar fridge. 'A house this size would normally have 20 tanks,' Gilles points out. 'I have 80.'

Based in the romantic little village of Chigny-les-Roses, on the northern slopes of the Montagne de Reims, in the old school building that Gilles' grandfather converted, the estate sources from 15 hectares in this and the surrounding villages. Gilles owns a little more than three hectares of his own vines; he purchases from his parents' two hectares of vineyards and a further nine hectares from growers with long-term contracts.

Irrespective of ownership, Gilles' principles for the management of the vines are consistent across all of his sources. 'I work mostly organically when I can, but I will save my harvest when I have to.' He interacts with each of the vineyards in the same way, monitoring the vines during the year, going into the vines to determine the optimal time for harvest, and supporting his own managers throughout the year in the same manner as he supports his growers. He is therefore technically a négociant-manipulant, but very much with the approach of a dedicated récoltant-manipulant. 'Would I produce better wines if I grew all the grapes myself?' he asks. 'No. I'd do everything the same way.'

This is pinot country, and both pinot and meunier feature heavily in the Dumangin style. Chardonnay finds its place, too, and the local quality is impressive, as his expressive single-vineyard, single-vintage blanc de blancs attests. Meunier is more important here than it is in most champagne houses. 'This is the grape that makes champagne what it is, providing its fruit and its easy-drinking style,' says Gilles, whose entry Grande Réserve NV contains an impressive 50% of the variety.

Gilles is obsessive about preserving fruit in optimal condition. In 2008 he terminated some contracts with growers of inferior vineyards, and signed up other vineyards to bring all of his sources to within seven kilometres of his beloved old Coquard PAM presses. 'They're so gentle,' he says, 'that the pips stay on the skins and the seeds remain inside!' The second press cut is used only in Brut 17 and Grande Réserve.

Gilles pioneered 18-kilogram picking crates rather than the usual 50-kilogram crates, so as not to crush the fruit at the bottom. When fruit arrives it never spends more than five minutes in the sun before he brings it into his air-conditioned press room. He personally presses every grape. 'I don't believe you can make very good wine if you don't press your own grapes,' he explains.

Non-vintage cuvées rely on deep stocks of reserve wines, with a full year's production volume in reserve, and the Grande Réserve and Extra Brut cuvées each boasting a whopping 60%. In every vintage 40% is kept in reserve. Rosé production is on the rise, now Dumangin's key cuvée, representing 50% of production. Since Rosé doesn't call for large reserves, an ever-increasing proportion of reserves are available for Brut 17, now 43%. All cuvées have traditionally undergone full malolactic fermentation, but such was the acid and sugar balance of his 2012 fruit that he blocked malolactic fermentation in some parcels for the first time and has continued in this practice since, necessitating rigorous cleaning and sanitisation in the winery. He also started trialling barrel fermentation in 2012.

For the past 15 years, Gilles has invested all his income back into his stocks, and now boasts an impressive 4.5–5 years' supply in storage.

To preserve the elegance of the terroirs of the northern Montagne, Gilles disgorges every shipment

Harvest 2014 on the elegant slopes of Chigny-les-Roses, on the northern edge of the Montagne de Reims.

of non-vintage wine to order, and seals every bottle with a DIAM cork. 'In my trials, the wines keep fresher under DIAM.' The dosage of every shipment is tweaked from its usual 10g/L sugar to suit. Dosages have been progressively lowered across the range over the past few years. 'From my tests, the wines stay fresher if they're disgorged just prior to shipment,' Gilles says. It's different for the vintage wines, which he finds hold their freshness best if disgorged 3–4 years after bottling.

For champagnes disgorged to order, back labels are impressively informative, disclosing disgorgement date, blend and dosage. Each disgorgement now receives a unique QR code to provide a great depth of information, including disgorgement date, blend, reserve wines, vineyards, food matches, reviews and importer's details.

Gilles' painstaking attention to detail shines in every bottle. I have been following his champagnes for almost a decade now, and they are cleaner, fresher, more precise and more focused than ever. As a result they effortlessly handle lower dosage than before, and all but the Brut 17 and Rosé are Extra Brut. These rank high among the best-value small-producer champagnes.

Dumangin J. Fils La Cuvée 17 Brut NV $

89 points • 2011 base vintage • Disgorged July 2014 & January 2015
• 8.8g/L dosage • Tasted in Chigny-les-Roses
93 points • 2010 base vintage • Disgorged November 2013 • 8g/L dosage
• Tasted in Chigny-les-Roses, Sydney & Melbourne

One-third each of pinot noir, meunier and chardonnay; 43% reserves

Brut 17 took a step up in refinement and purity with the 2009 base, after changing contracts to improve fruit sources, and 2010 follows impeccably, a beautifully refined apéritif style that captures the elegant, pinot-driven mood of the northern Montagne in pristine, pretty red cherry, red berry and pink grapefruit, with a clean lemon focus, fine mineral texture and well-integrated dosage. A cracking entry champagne. The 2011 base is dusty and dry, reflecting its harrowing season, but retains crisp freshness and reasonable persistence.

Dumangin J. Fils Le Rosé Brut NV $

94 points • 2009 base vintage • Disgorged variously between August 2013 & January 2015 • Tasted in Chigny-les-Roses, Sydney & Melbourne

47% chardonnay, 37% pinot noir, 16% pinot noir red wine from 2008, the highest proportion of red wine yet, reflecting the pale colour in 2008; reserves from 2008; 8.8g/L dosage; 50% of production

Gilles' rosé is a reflection of his precision, one of Champagne's most finely crafted and elegant rosés at a refreshingly affordable price. His elegant pinot noir is well suited to this style, neatly supported by the finesse of chardonnay. An air of rose petal fragrance and pink pepper spice dances over pretty strawberry hull, red cherry, watermelon and raspberry notes. Subtle, fine mineral texture embraces a soft, creamy bead, completing a rosé of graceful poise. This was the single rosé that I chose to serve at my 40th birthday party in 2015 (2008 base, from magnum).

Dumangin J. Fils Le Vintage Extra Brut Premier Cru 2004 $$

94 points • Disgorged July and December 2014 • Tasted in Chigny-les-Roses, Sydney & Melbourne

54% chardonnay, 46% pinot noir; liqueur aged in oak barrels 1-2 years; 4.4 g/L dosage; 15,000 bottles

Dumangin's vintage is blessed with 11 years of maturity, and its most recent showings have been the finest, testimony to Gilles' precision and the stamina of 2004. Such was the yield in this vintage that he produced three times the usual volume of this cuvée. Elegance, vivacity and backward, primary fruit freshness are the themes here, alive with lemon blossom, lemon sherbet, red apple and crisp pear, backed by the red cherry fruits of the northern Montagne. Time has ushered in toasty, honeyed ginger and mixed spice notes, concluding with great acid drive and soft chalk mineral presence.

The Champagne Guide

Dumangin J. Fils L'Extra-Brut Premier Cru NV $

93 points • 2009 base vintage • Disgorged August 2013 & July 2014 • Tasted in Chigny-les-Roses, Sydney & Melbourne

50% meunier, 25% chardonnay, 25% pinot noir; 2g/L dosage

Dumangin's Extra Brut is precise, clean and classy, with all the tension you'd expect from a dry take on northern Montagne finesse, yet sufficient generosity to hold its balance. Impressive definition of lemon juice, lemon zest, pear and red apple fruit is accented with the subtle spice of bottle development. Lingering, finely focused acid drive keeps the finish crisp and energetic. Try it with oysters.

Dumangin J. Fils Premium Single Vineyard Blanc de Blancs Dessus le Mont Extra Brut 2006 $$

91 points • Disgorged October 2014 • Tasted in Chigny-les-Roses

Harvested ripe and unchaptalised, so only made in years of sufficient ripeness; from a low vineyard on clay soils; 5g/L dosage

There's concentration here, and a medium to full straw hue, true to the ripeness of fruit targeted for this cuvée. It's spicy and peppery, with notes of flinty reduction, finishing long. Ripeness equates to gentle acidity, clay soils make for a soft mouthfeel, and phenolic ripeness translates into bitter texture akin to grapefruit pith.

Dumangin J. Fils Premium Single Vineyard Blanc de Blancs Dessus le Mont Brut 2005 $$

91 points • Disgorged January and June 2014 • Tasted in Chigny-les-Roses

5.3g/L dosage

Admirable freshness for 2005 at a decade of age, with grapefruit and lemon contrasting the richness, concentration and body of peach fruit, reflecting the ripeness of the style. Some reductive savoury notes last year have dissipated in more recent tastings. Age has coaxed out suggestions of almond meal, vanilla, anise and white chocolate, heightening a softly chewy mouthfeel.

Dumangin J. Fils Premium Single Vineyard Blanc de Blancs Extra Brut 2000 $$$$

92 points • Disgorged January 2015 • Tasted in Chigny-les-Roses

2g/L dosage

The first vintage of this label, re-released in 2015, having accumulated enticing layers of crème brûlée, vanilla, butterscotch, toffee, anise and mixed spice during a decade and a half in the cellar. It's a showcase for the depth of this ripe style, basking in the golden sunlight of the 2000 vintage, finishing long, chewy and soft.

DUVAL-LEROY

(Dew-val-Lair-wah)

6/10

69 AVE DE BAMMENTAL BP 37 51130 VERTUS

www.duval-leroy.com

The scale of Duval-Leroy's modern winery is a physical statement of the rapid progress at this family-owned company. Recently celebrating its 150th birthday, it now ranks in the top 15 champagne houses, thanks to its dynamic, visionary leader, Carol Duval-Leroy, who has grown the estate during the past two decades. Chardonnay takes the lead in these graceful and elegant wines, reflecting the bright fruit purity of the village of Vertus.

The imposing Duval-Leroy building looks more at home in Silicon Valley than a small village in Champagne. The entire façade is covered by 250 square metres of solar panels, sufficient for the electrical needs of the barrel room, tasting room and reception area. It makes a bold, immediate statement that Duval-Leroy has sunk a serious investment into its modernisation and growth. And that's just the beginning.

Step inside the largest facility in Vertus and you're greeted by lines of gleaming new tanks, all temperature controlled to between 16°C and 20°C to preserve delicacy during fermentation. Five gentle eight-tonne pneumatic presses are cleverly positioned above 30 settling tanks, delivering the must by gravity. Dug deep underground, this facility operates on multiple levels. Operations were modernised in 2009 when the facility was extended to integrate the entire production under one roof to improve efficiency and quality. A new barrel room was also added for fermentation of grand cru parcels.

Estate holdings comprise 60% chardonnay. The house controls 200 hectares in the Côte des Blancs

(including an impressive 150 hectares in Vertus, and holdings in every grand cru), Montagne de Reims and Côte de Sézanne, providing a generous one-third of all fruit required to produce 5–5.5 million bottles annually. It is serviced by five press centres, and 18 million bottles stored 30 kilometres away in Châlons-en-Champagne.

Duval-Leroy manages a sustainability regime that's more than just a solar panel façade. A 10-page document on its website details a diverse list of initiatives. Herbicide use has more than halved in the past decade, and all estate vineyards are cultivated organically or biodynamically — quite a feat for a house of this size. Fruit purchased from a number of organically certified growers finds its way into two organic champagnes.

It is apparently possible to ascertain the disgorgement date from the bottling code, but the house keeps this a closely guarded secret, for reasons I fail to understand.

Duval-Leroy achieves a lofty pinnacle in the towering magnificence of its prestige cuvée, Femme de Champagne.

Duval-Leroy Brut NV $$

88 points • Tasted in Sydney & Melbourne

70% pinot noir, 20% meunier, 10% chardonnay from 20 villages; aged a minimum of 30 months; 8g/L dosage

Duval-Leroy's two entry cuvées together total more than 4 million bottles annually, making up 80% of the production of the house. A very strong pinot noir lead in this cuvée creates a style of red apple fruit and crunchy grapefruit zest. Chardonnay is the star of Duval-Leroy and this cuvée, well, isn't. Some earthy notes and a little phenolic grip on the finish make for a much simpler and less polished cuvée than the Fleur de Champagne Premier Cru Brut.

Duval-Leroy Fleur de Champagne Premier Cru Brut NV $$

93 points • Tasted in Sydney & Melbourne

2011 base vintage with 10% reserve wines; 75% chardonnay, 25% pinot noir; 100% estate vines on 15 premier and grand crus in the Côte des Blancs and Montagne de Reims; 8g/L dosage

Duval-Leroy's signature NV is confidently led by estate-grown chardonnay, giving it a decisive edge over the pinot-dominated Brut NV. I was told this bottle was based on the 2011 vintage, but if it was, it was a miracle of focus and freshness in this harrowing season, singing with lemon and red apple fruit. The finish is drawn out by the excellent mineral focus and acid finesse of Vertus, finished with well-integrated dosage.

Duval-Leroy Rosé Prestige Brut NV $$

88 points • Tasted in Sydney & Melbourne

66% pinot noir saignée, 34% chardonnay from grand cru villages; aged 24 months on lees; 9g/L dosage

With a medium salmon copper hue, this is a rich and spicy rosé of red berry fruits, red apple and mixed spice, good acid line and balanced dosage. There are notes of biscuity development, but, like last year, it ultimately lacks freshness and carry.

Duval-Leroy Cuvée des Meilleurs Ouvriers de France Sommeliers Brut NV $$

91 points • Tasted in Brisbane

2008 base vintage; 60% chardonnay and 40% pinot noir from premier and grand crus; new cuvée in 2013, made in conjunction with the Meilleurs Ouvriers de France Sommeliers; low dosage of 3.5g/L

A delightfully complex non-vintage blend that embodies layers of character and energy. Quince, wood spice, locut and wild honey unite on a palate of firmly structured, dry grip and tight 2008 acid line. The tension in this interplay is heightened by very low dosage. It begs for food. A sommelier's wine, certainly.

DUVAL-LEROY BLANC DE BLANCS GRAND CRU MILLÉSIME 2006 $$

90 points • TASTED IN BRISBANE

Silky yellow fruits of nectarine and white peach contrast with bottle age layers of wood spice, honey and roast hazelnut bitterness, lingering long on a finish of even acid line, texture and grip. It's beginning to dry out and already appears to be at the end of its life.

DUVAL-LEROY BLANC DE BLANCS BRUT NATURE MILLÉSIME 2002 $$$

95 points • TASTED IN BRISBANE, SYDNEY & MELBOURNE

100% chardonnay from Avize, Cramant, Chouilly, Oger, Le Mesnil-sur-Oger and Vertus; 2.5g/L dosage

The great grand crus of the Côte des Blancs deliver their strength and generosity, intricately offset by the crisp freshness of Vertus. The result is a triumph of deep-chalk mineral presence and tremendous persistence, capturing the tension of 2002 and contrasting the bountiful richness of this great season with tightly clenched acid structure. It has evolved wonderfully from its stance of a few years ago, supporting preserved lemon and red apple fruit, set against a rising backdrop of mature characters of toast, wild honey, marmalade and a whiff of exotic pipe smoke. It's intelligently topped off with the lightest touch of dosage. The best bottles have years before them yet.

DUVAL-LEROY CLOS DES BOUVERIES BRUT 2005 $$$$

89 points • TASTED IN BRISBANE

100% chardonnay from a single clos in the heart of Vertus, belonging to the company for more than a century; partially aged in oak barrels; 4g/L dosage; 31,853 bottles

The concept of releasing a single-variety, single-vineyard wine in every single vintage in a climate as fickle as that of Champagne's is more than a little disconcerting. It's released altogether too young for a wine with significant oak treatment, and four years after release my hope was that age might have diminished that wall of oak and allowed the voice of the fruit and the site to emerge. Alas, the opposite has occurred, with fruit fading to subtle preserved lemon and golden delicious apple, while the toasty flavour and firm tannin grip of oak has risen, rendering the wine austere and coarse.

The Champagne Guide

DUVAL-LEROY FEMME DE CHAMPAGNE 2004 $$$$

96 points • TASTED IN VINAY

87% chardonnay from Avize, Chouilly and Le Mesnil-sur-Oger; 13% pinot noir from Ambonnay; 13% vinified and matured in old oak barrels; released exclusively in half bottles for reasons even the house could not explain; 5g/L dosage

Even in a half bottle, this cuvée has blossomed at a full decade of age, albeit still a little short of the lofty heights that Femme has attained in recent vintages (a consequence of the wine or of half-bottle maturation, we will never know). Generous fruit ripeness on release has now evolved to a delightfully complex realm of burnt butter, fig, gingernut biscuits, honey and dried peach. For such a marvellously mature place, it has admirably upheld vitality and freshness, in a refined chalk mineral mouthfeel and focused, lemon-tinged acidity that carries the finish with elegant drive and taut persistence.

DUVAL-LEROY FEMME DE CHAMPAGNE 2000 $$$$

97 points • TASTED IN BRISBANE

95% chardonnay from Avize, Chouilly, Oger and Le Mesnil-sur-Oger; 5% Bouzy pinot noir; 25% vinified and matured in oak barrels; 6g/L dosage

This release has always set a benchmark for slow evolution of the 2000 vintage, but such was the exceptional freshness of this bottle that I could hardly believe that it was indeed the 2000. A medium straw hue is magnificently pale and bright for its age and, particularly, for the deeply coloured 2000 vintage. The restraint, energy and focus of chardonnay is on grand parade here, with a definition and determination rare in this vintage at 15 years of age. White citrus and pear fruit is seamlessly and slowly evolving to build subtle nuances of roasted nuts and buttered toast. It's softening and harmonising impeccably, still flaunting the beautiful, rounded curves of 2000, yet retaining wonderful energy in its focused acid line, charging the finish with unexpected endurance. The deep-set mineral presence of grand cru chardonnay stands undeviated by the passage of time, with wonderful salty, sea-foam mineral texture churning, frothing and gliding very long on the finish. If you're a child of 2000, this is your 21st birthday extravagance.

DUVAL-LEROY FEMME DE CHAMPAGNE ROSÉ DE SAIGNÉE 2007 $$$$$

95 points • TASTED IN BRISBANE

100% grand cru pinot noir

A rosé of engaging character, from its full, bright crimson hue to its lively red cherry and strawberry fruit, to savoury notes of tomato and pronounced white pepper. It finishes with shades of red cherry liqueur and a hint of toasted coconut, structured by the grippy, fine tannins of pinot noir saignée, melding seamlessly with bright, salty chalk mineral presence. It's lively, characterful, primary and intricately crafted, though lacks a little in coherence and presence on the finish.

EGLY-OURIET

(Eglee-Ou-ree-yair)

10/10

15 RUE TRÉPAIL 51150 AMBONNAY

Egly-Ouriet enjoys a cult status shared by no other grower on the Montagne de Reims. This tiny, pristine operation in Ambonnay deserves its acclaim, capturing the profound complexity, intensity and grandeur of the Montagnes' finest terroirs, without sacrificing the precision that underlies the most revered champagnes. These are ravishingly vinous sparkling wines, consistently among the most exactingly balanced of Champagne's power set, handcrafted by a creative, thoughtful artisan who painstakingly tends his vines naturally to low yields and full maturity. On the basis of this year's cuvées, Egly-Ouriet is the finest grower in Champagne right now and the first I have ever rated 10/10.

Egly-Ouriet owns just under 12 hectares of grand cru vineyards planted to 70% pinot noir and 30% chardonnay, primarily in Ambonnay, 1.4 hectares in Verzenay, a few rows in Bouzy, and a two-hectare plot of very old meunier vines in Vrigny that produce a single-vineyard premier cru. Francis Egly, fourth-generation head of the estate, has bottled the entire harvest of 100,000 bottles since he took over in 1982. Previously, his father, Michel, bottled a small proportion since the 1970s, and his grandfather, Charles, bottled tiny quantities for family and friends since the 1950s.

'Champagne is like Burgundy,' Egly upholds. 'You go one kilometre and it is different. Ambonnay is completely different to Bouzy, where the soils are deeper. Ambonnay is a very "solaire" village, south-orientated, which is very important for maturity. The soil is very poor, generally only 20 centimetres deep, so you can smell the minerality of the chalk.' Egly works intuitively to preserve the detail of his grapes and their terroirs.

His approach in the vineyards is as natural as possible, without aspiring to organic or biodynamic certification. 'It is too complicated to practise specific regimes,' he maintains. An eco-friendly approach has seen a radical reduction in the use of fertilisers and chemical pesticides. The soil is manured, ploughed for aeration, and green harvests reduce crop levels by up to 50% for red wine for rosé and Coteaux Champenois. Otherwise, his yields are at the full level of 10 tonnes per hectare.

From vines averaging more than 45 years of age, Egly harvests at full maturity, typically at 12 or 13 degrees of potential alcohol, extremely ripe for Champagne, and never chaptalises. His goal is to harvest grapes as ripe as possible, and cites the best vintages as those of high maturity, naming under-maturity as Champagne's biggest problem. His aspiration is 'elegance and strength, but never heaviness'. He says champagne is like a bird; 'it has to stay aromatic and light'. Grapes are pressed slowly and fermented almost entirely in barriques, the balance in enamelled tanks (not stainless steel), using only natural yeasts. Egly maintains more than 200 barrels, in which his entire production is fermented (apart from 20% of Brut Tradition), not only for structure and longevity, but to facilitate vinification of different parcels separately to draw out more character of the terroir. Used barrels are purchased from his friend Dominique Laurent in Nuits-Saint-Georges.

Malolactic fermentation is allowed or barred depending on the vintage. Very low dosages are used — typically just 1–3g/L. 'I prefer to use a little sugar rather than following the fashion of no dosage,' he says. Long ageing on lees in barrel for 8–10 months and in bottle for at least 3–4 years furnishes considerable longevity.

A 2006 cellar expansion brought all winemaking operations together in the same building, with pressing, vinification and storage on successive levels, tempera-ture controlled at every stage. In 2008, Egly acquired two new presses, which he says have improved quality.

The back labels are among Champagne's most informative, declaring disgorgement dates, terroirs and number of months on lees. Wines are bottled in July following harvest, so it's easy to determine the base vintage. Important details appear on every bottle, alongside the philosophy of the house: 'This champagne is the expression of a "family" style that comes first and foremost from perfectly tended vineyards. The quality of grapes, the precision of blending and long *élevage* in the cellar allows us to offer you non-filtered champagnes in the purest champagne style.' A breath of fresh air in a region saturated with marketing froth.

I finally had the privilege of meeting Francis Egly in 2015, a man of generous warmth and careful precision, just like his champagnes.

EGLY-OURIET GRAND CRU BRUT TRADITION NV $$$

96 points • 2009 BASE VINTAGE • DISGORGED JANUARY & JULY 2014 • TASTED IN SYDNEY & MELBOURNE

70% pinot noir, 30% chardonnay; 80% vinified in barrel; aged 54 months on lees; 3–4g/L dosage

From the very first cuvée, Egly-Ouriet is distinguished for its ability to preserve exacting precision and outstanding chalk mineral focus in the midst of magnificent generosity. This is a vinous wine of calm authority, carrying the full grandeur and complexity of carefully tended, old-vine pinot noir on some of Champagne's most revered grand crus. It juxtaposes freshness and depth, a marvel of red cherries, plums, dried fruits and mixed spice of rippling intensity, showcasing four and a half years on lees, yet at every moment impeccably focused with scintillating acidity and mineral-infused poise. A paradox of luxurious generosity and crystalline purity.

EGLY-OURIET LES VIGNES DE VRIGNY PREMIER CRU BRUT NV $$$

93 points • 2010 BASE VINTAGE • DISGORGED SEPT 2014 • TASTED IN REIMS
95 points • 2008 BASE VINTAGE • DISGORGED JULY 2012 • TASTED IN YARRA VALLEY

Aged 36–38 months on lees; full malolactic fermentation; 5g/L total sugars (by lab analysis)

Egly-Ouriet crafts one of Champagne's most flattering single-vineyard meuniers, faithfully translating every detail of the succulent depth of this grape's enticing full golden yellow hue and its fleshy mirabelle plum, red cherry, dried pear and grapefruit character. The 2008 base vintage upholds the focused acidity and wonderfully heightened minerality of the season, while the 2010 base is evolving more quickly into hazelnut, mixed spice and butterscotch, though the freshness and focus of Egly prevails. A skilfully crafted meunier of refined, expressive chalk minerality, seamlessly dovetailing expansive generosity with tightly focused definition, finishing impeccably dry, gloriously persistent and exactingly honed.

EGLY-OURIET GRAND CRU BRUT ROSÉ NV $$$

96 points • 2009 BASE VINTAGE • DISGORGED SEPTEMBER 2014
• TASTED IN SYDNEY

Similar composition to Brut Tradition, with 8% red wine from Ambonnay; 2g/L dosage

Rumbling power with delicate finesse, this is a rosé of medium salmon hue, bursting with the exuberance and beguiling transparency of Ambonnay pinot noir. Fragrant rosebuds and wild strawberries open into glorious depth of black cherry fruits of exacting ripeness, cherry kernel, fig and mixed spice. Very fresh and focused for its age, with a universe of complexity lingering very long, precise and lively amidst fine chalk mineral texture.

EGLY-OURIET GRAND CRU BLANC DE NOIRS VIEILLES VIGNES NV $$$$

97 points • TASTED IN SYDNEY

2008 base vintage with 40% 2007 reserves; 100% pinot noir; 2g/L dosage

From a single lieu-dit, 'Les Crayères', planted in shallow soils in 1946, this warm amphitheatre high up the Ambonnay slope epitomises the golden sunlight, glowing warmth and magnificent mineral expression of Egly-Ouriet. A full golden straw hue anticipates tantalising layers of patisserie and butterscotch, opening into exact red cherry fruit and characterful morello cherry tang. With barely a foot of topsoil before the chalk, the mineral character of the site speaks articulately in softly salty tones that will stir the depths of your soul.

Of all the grand crus on the Montagne de Reims, none delivers a balance of concentration, structure and elegance like Ambonnay.

The Champagne Guide

EMMANUEL BROCHET

(Eman-yoo-el Bro-sheh)

(7/10)

7 IMPASSE BROCHET 51500 VILLERS-AUX-NOEUDS

Champagne

EMMANUEL
BROCHET

In the turning wheel of Champagne succession, it is virtually unheard of for a young grower-producer to be the first in his family to tend vines. All the more daring in the little-known premier cru village of Villers-aux-Noeuds, in which no one has made champagne for generations. Emmanuel Brochet defines a bold new frontier, bringing an old terroir to life with an intuition derived not from local knowledge, family history or personal experience, but from the sheer courage to respond to each plot, each season and each ferment individually. Most remarkable of all is the beautiful fruit character and pronounced terroir expression he has drawn from this place in a very short time. I know of no one in Champagne today who has achieved so much from so little so quickly as Emmanuel Brochet.

In the plains between the slopes of the Montagne de Reims and the sprawling southern suburbs of Reims, Villers-aux-Noeuds was once the proud custodian of 250 hectares of vines. The quaint little village is now home to just 27 hectares, planted on its best south-east slopes, spanning a wide diversity of soils, with chalk just 30 centimetres below the surface.

Emmanuel Brochet's family has owned vines here for generations, leasing them to others to tend until Emmanuel commenced in 1997. His mother's 2.5 hectare single vineyard 'Le Mont Benoit' is one of the better sites in the village, with a thin layer of 40 centimetres topsoil directly over chalk, and just 25 centimetres at the top of the slope. The vineyard is visible from the motorway, under the power lines, adjacent to the toll station near Champfleury. Planted to 37% meunier, 30% chardonnay and 23% pinot noir dating from 1962, half the block was replanted in 1986 after devastating frosts.

Emmanuel manages the site for his mother, paying her a rent of 0.6 hectares of fruit, leaving 1.9 hectares for his modest production of 10,000 bottles.

Without the constraints of family and village history, Brochet is blessed with the freedom to forge a brave path with a spontaneity rarely possible in this staid region. 'As the first winemaker of the family, I am lucky I do not have my family telling me what to do!' he grins. 'I do things because I want to, not because I have to.' This affords full licence to pursue his elegantly simple philosophy: 'A wine is good because the grapes are good. If there is good balance in the soils and in the vine, there is good balance in the wine. Every year is different, and we work it according to the season, not because we did it that way last year,' he says, admitting he's never written down anything he's done each vintage. 'I practise biodynamics, but this is not the most important thing, no more important than the soil, the vines or my state of mind.'

To achieve a good balance of acidity and sugar, Brochet harvests his fruit ripe; many of his neighbours have finished picking before he even starts. In respect for the soil, he commenced biodynamic certification in 2008 and completely abandoned use of chemicals in 2009, though he has no intention of mentioning biodynamics on his labels once certification is granted. 'It is important that my wines have no residues of pesticides, but many other elements are equally important,' he explains. 'If I put biodynamic certification on my labels, then I should also include my press, the house, the grapes, the soil, the place and my state of mind!'

Brochet has found the period of transition to organic certification difficult, selling all his reserve wines prior to 2010 to a négociant, as they were not organic. An annual production of 10,000 bottles is little over half of what 1.9 hectares would normally produce in Champagne, even with some vins clairs sold to négocians for cash flow. Biodynamics has reduced Brochet's yields to a tiny 35hL/hectare. He does not perform a green harvest and upholds that balanced fruit relies upon yields that are neither too large nor too small. 'Perhaps it's not that we produce too little yield, but that conventional viticulture produces too much?' he pointedly suggests. The equilibrium he has achieved in his vines produces a balance of sugar and acidity sufficient that he has no need to chaptalise, unusual in Champagne, and virtually unheard of in a lesser premier cru village.

MINIMALIST WINEMAKING

With no winery to inherit, Brochet sold his grapes until 2002 to finance the purchase of his equipment. He found a traditional 1960s two-tonne Coquard press in 2006, half the size of a traditional champagne press, and restored it 'like an old car'. He admits he prefers driving a tractor to driving a horse. 'I am a boy and I love machines!' says this off-road rally driver. Grapes are pressed on the day they are harvested and settled overnight before fermentation with wild yeasts entirely in barrels, in which the wine remains for 11 months.

The soil and the vines are Brochet's first priority, and he says that with good fruit he has little to do in the winery. 'My winemaking is very simple: an oxidative vinification and ageing on lees, which consume the oxygen, creating a balance between oxidation and reduction.' Adamant champagne should not have a woody taste, he buys old barrels as well as new, and keeps wines in barrel on their lees for an extended period of 11 months to reduce pick-up of oak flavours. Brochet likens winemaking in barrels to biodynamics: 'It's easier than in tanks, and the wines are more natural.' There is no bâtonnage, no filtration and no cold stabilisation.

Brochet is continually experimenting and refining his style. 'I tried putting my reserve wines in barrel, but without lees they became tired and woody, so for the past three years I've kept reserve wines in tank.' Generally he blocks malolactic fermentation in his vintage wines, but in 2012 he allowed it to proceed. 'With our warming weather, some people are saying that we should stop malo so as to retain acidity, but if you don't have a lot of acidity it's very hard to stop malo,' he explains. 'I would have to use a lot of preservative, and I don't want to do that.'

Brochet uses very small levels of preservative, and an extra brut dosage of around 4g/L in his cuvées, and trialled a zero-dosage wine from the same blend as his Le Mont Benoit NV last year, but found the acidity too pronounced at low temperatures. 'Sugar is a mediator, and a little is a technical support if you drink champagne too cold!' he says. The blend of this cuvée changes each year. 'The *cépage* is not important,' he upholds, 'and we can achieve great consistency each year even with different proportions of each variety. The wines taste of the vineyard and the soil, and that's the important thing. The soil is more important than the varieties.'

He maintains the flexibility to release wines 'when they are good to drink, not because I need the money', a rare opportunity in any young business. His wines are aged long, NVs generally 2–3 years and vintages 5–8 years. He has also broken with Champagne tradition in releasing vintage and even non-vintage blends non-sequentially, releasing 2009 before 2007 and 2008. He tastes vintages blind with his friends and releases those that are ready. Back labels are informative, specifying vintages, varieties and vinification details.

Brochet's wines showcase the unique mineral expression of his vineyard in a savoury chalk mouthfeel, a little coarser-grained in texture than that of the Côte des Blancs. I ask if this is unique to the village, or particular to the accessible chalk in his vineyard, and he says he has no idea. 'There is just one producer who makes wine in this village and it is me!' he exclaims. 'Everyone else sells their grapes to the cooperatives and négociants. Old wine growers always said they could make very good wines in this village. Two generations ago they kept the grapes separate and made very good wines.'

To Brochet, state of mind is an important ingredient of terroir. 'There is no stress here during harvest,' he says, having employed his two best friends to assist. 'It's very important to enjoy your work and I like working in the vineyard on the tractor. When I was young I played with toys and now I like to have fun playing with bigger toys in the vineyard and the winery!' A refreshing mindset for one who has achieved so much so quickly.

EMMANUEL BROCHET LE MONT BENOIT EXTRA BRUT NV $$

93 points • DISGORGED NOVEMBER 2014 • TASTED IN VILLERS-AUX-NOEUDS

~ 40% chardonnay, 40% meunier and 20% pinot noir, according to the production of the vineyard; 100% 2011 as the reserves were sold off since they were not organic; aged 11 months in barrel and 3 years in bottle; 4g/L dosage; ~6500 bottles

From a single vineyard and a single traumatic season, with no reserves, this should be a downright disaster. To the credit of Brochet and his site, it's a more than admirable result, a champagne of tension and persistence, contrasting a tight lemon and grapefruit core with the yellow summer fruits of Brochet's ripe style. Long barrel and bottle age have drawn out complexing notes of charcuterie, toast and wood spice, producing a creamy, soft texture and strong autolytic character. The minerality of the accessible chalk of the village is prominent, soft, supple and deeply salty. A wine of well-defined acid line, impressive length and seamless coherence.

EMMANUEL BROCHET LES HAUTS CHARDONNAY EXTRA BRUT 2009 $$$

92 points • DISGORGED FEBRUARY 2015 • TASTED IN VILLERS-AUX-NOEUDS

1962 vines from the top of the vineyard; aged in half new and half old barrels for 11 months; a selection of the best barrels of the heart of the cuvée; 3g/L dosage; tiny production of 1205 bottles

Brochet reserves his best old vine parcels for his vintage cuvées. Disgorged a day before I tasted it, with no dosage, it is predictably extreme in its youthful austerity, and will appreciate time and sugar to soften. With 50% new oak, its wood work is prominent, but Brochet's ripe fruit concentration has the stature to handle it. Notes of smoky almonds waft over a core of crunchy, lively grapefruit and lemon. The creamy texture of Brochet's long barrel aged style makes for a beautiful mouthfeel, calm persistence and velvety appeal. Its display of chalk minerality is pronounced, frothing with sea-surf salt, the signature of Villers-aux-Noeuds and of Brochet.

EMMANUEL BROCHET LES HAUTS MEUNIERS EXTRA BRUT 2008 $$$

95 points • DISGORGED FEBRUARY 2015 • TASTED IN VILLERS-AUX-NOEUDS

100% meunier from the old vines at the top of the vineyard; 30hL/hectare; aged on lees in barrel for 16 months; tiny production of 916 bottles; final releases to have 3g/L dosage; May 2015 release

Disgorged a day before I tasted it, with zero dosage, the poise and balance on display here are captivating from day one. This is Brochet's favourite cuvée, which he variously describes as 'extraterrestrial' and the 'soul music' of his range. It is as if meunier rises to Brochet's touch in the ethereal 2008 season, heightening its signature red cherry, red berry and red apple fruit and accenting its complexity of cherry kernel, golden fruit cake, fruit mince spice and pepper. Toasty oak is present, yet less prominent than in his chardonnay, with long barrel and bottle age drawing out the classic creamy, silky Brochet texture. Coherence, line and length are outstanding, culminating in fine, salty mineral persistence.

Eric Rodez

(E-ri Roh-day)

7/10

Rue de Isse 51150 Ambonnay

www.champagne-rodez.fr

Eric Rodez
Champagne

*O*rganic viticulture has become something of a catchcry in the modern wine world, but never have I seen a more profound statement of its impact than in Eric Rodez's magnificently positioned vineyard of 6.5 hectares on the glorious mid-slopes of Ambonnay. Standing on the edge of his rows of vines, he showed me tiny, sparse bunches. In the very next row, not more than a metre away, his neighbour's vines were loaded with full-sized bunches. The fanatical approach of this eighth-generation winegrower permeates every detail of his work, which embraces vinification in barriques, light dosages and a colossal resource of reserve wines spanning 20 years. The aspiration is to let the salty minerality and generous expression of one of Champagne's greatest grand crus sing through every cuvée. And sing they do.

When I first met Eric Rodez, who moonlights as mayor of Ambonnay, he immediately admitted his English is very limited and, my French being far worse, he proposed, 'Nous pourrons parler la langue des bulles!' — 'We can speak in the language of the bubbles!' As I soon discovered, where his bubbles are concerned, a particularly fine language it is.

Rodez makes eight wines, which he thinks of as eight 'melodies'. He likens them to a concert, where every tune evokes a different emotion. 'There is not enough emotion in champagne today!' he exclaims. 'I will not be the Coca-Cola of champagne — I will make emotional wine!' He thinks of his 35 parcels as 35 notes of music, each expressing five emotions, in their grape variety, vintage, vineyard location, method of fermentation, and malolactic fermentation ('forte') or not ('allegro').

The Rodez family have grown grapes in Ambonnay since 1757, and have made their own champagnes since the time of Eric's grandparents, but things changed when Eric began in 1984. 'That was not a good vintage,'

he recalls, and it prompted him to do things differently in the vineyard, initiating a methodology that he prefers to call 'integrated' rather than 'ecological'.

He borrows practices of organics and biodynamics, without seeking certification under either. 'Every year it is a new logic,' he explains. 'I do not have only one vision or one consistent process. My philosophy is to be free. Real life is not about following a recipe.' Use of chemicals is limited, grasses are cultivated in the mid-rows and yields are restricted to a tiny 30–40% of the permitted levels. 'To achieve music in the wine you need music in the grapes to begin with, and to achieve this you cannot have too high a yield,' he maintains. He is working hard to reduce the use of copper sulphate as a fungicide, just six kilograms per hectare in 2014, and ultimately aiming for four kilograms per hectare.

'To my colleagues, I am a little crazy!' he exclaims. 'But I am very happy. When you want to see the soil in the glass, you need to get the vine roots to go into the chalk,' he says. In his vineyards, the chalk is just

40 centimetres below the surface, but this is still deeper than in many parts of the Côte des Blancs, and it took 10 years from when he commenced biodynamics in 1989 before the roots tapped deep into the minerality of the chalk.

His philosophy now translates accurately into his profoundly salty mineral champagnes. He showed me a stunning barrel sample of 2010 pinot noir that displayed none of the botrytis problems that dogged this wet vintage. 'Thanks to low vegetation in the canopy, we had good ventilation and no botrytis in the vineyard,' he explains.

Expression of terroir is everything to Rodez, and he cheerfully admits that he doesn't aspire to make consistent wine each year. 'Every year is different and I will adapt my processes in the vineyards and in the cellar to suit. It is very important to me to make a wine of terroir, where you can taste the emotion.'

Exclusively in the heart of Ambonnay's mid-slope, his vineyards are planted to 60% pinot noir and 40% chardonnay, with an average vine age exceeding 30 years. As we left his vineyard and passed Krug's Clos d'Ambonnay on the lower slopes, he commented, 'There is more complexity in the mid-slopes and more minerality lower on the slopes.' I asked which was better and he paused for a long time, smiled knowingly and responded, 'Both are very important for blending!'

There are few small growers who understand blending more intricately than Rodez. His annual production of 45,000 bottles comprises a very large range of 11 cuvées, including six non-vintage blends, benefiting from a deep stock of reserve wines, currently extending as far back as 20 years.

His 35 plots of two varieties are vinified separately to produce 60 different wines, 80% of which are fermented and matured in small Burgundian barrels, mostly aged between three and 20 years. Three vintages in Burgundy and one at Krug taught him how to use barrels 'for sensuality, not oak flavour', maintaining that new barrels are not good for the equilibrium and personality of champagne. He is currently increasing old barrel vinification, finding that it offers greater persistence and complexity.

His reserve stocks presently comprise barrels of every vintage since 2000 except the dreaded 2001 and 2003. He showed me a 2006 chardonnay with power and length resembling a great white Burgundy. 'It's too big for champagne,' he says, 'but five or seven per cent is very important for the blend.'

Rodez tactically utilises the generosity of Ambonnay and the complexity of barrel fermentation, then enlivens his cuvées with selective use of malolactic fermentation, according to the parcel and the season, and low dosage. Grape juice rather than sugar is used to sweeten liqueurs, and all his wines currently contain no more than 5g/L dosage, allowing the character and minerality of these distinguished vineyards to sing with clarity and harmony. I visited Rodez during and after the 2014 harvest, and the expression of salt minerality in his vins clairs was exceptional. For all they represent, the wines of Eric Rodez are largely undiscovered, and offer incredible value for money.

Eric Rodez ferments 60 different batches, largely in small, aged Burgundian barrels for complexity and persistence of flavour.

ERIC RODEZ CUVÉE DES CRAYÈRES NV $$

93 points • 2010 BASE VINTAGE • TASTED IN AMBONNAY

2010 base (38%) with 25% 2009, 12% 2008, 8% 2007, 12% 2006 and 5% 2005; 60% pinot noir, 40% chardonnay; average vine age 29 years; 42% vinified in barrels; 38% of reserve wines without malolactic fermentation; aged 3 years on lees; 5g/L dosage

93 points • 2009 BASE VINTAGE • TASTED IN AMBONNAY

2009 base (42%) with 26% 2008, 11% 2007, 9% 2006, 10% 2005 and 4% 2002; 58% pinot noir, 42% chardonnay; average vine age 29 years; 35% vinified in barrels; 35% of reserve wines without malolactic fermentation; aged 3 years on lees; 5g/L dosage

Eric Rodez captures the personality of Ambonnay from his very first cuvée, in depth, complexity and structure. Such is the weight of reserve wines (more than 60%: remarkable in an entry cuvée) that the 2010 base has not been marked by this tricky year, but captures the expression of fleshy white nectarine, white peach and spice, and the structure of very fine, soft bath-salts minerality. Subtle savoury boiled-sausage barrel ferment character quickly dissipates from the 2009 base to reveal a core of excellent red berry and red apple fruit depth of impressive poise and elegance.

ERIC RODEZ CUVÉE BLANC DE NOIRS NV $$

94 points • 2008 BASE VINTAGE • TASTED IN AMBONNAY

40% 2008, 25% 2007, 18% 2006, 9% 2005, 5% 2004 and 3% 2002; average vine age 33 years; 75% vinified in barrel; 30% malolactic fermentation; 4g/L dosage

Eric Rodez crafts one of the best value blanc de noirs anywhere in Champagne. The enticing purity of Ambonnay pinot noir on show is something to behold, encapsulating the personality of the village in gorgeous intensity of black cherries and yellow mirabelle plums, with the crunchy vivacity of pink grapefruit. Small barrel maturation and deep reserves leave their mark in wood spice and vanilla, finding an even harmony with its fruit. The energy of 2008 makes for a blanc de noirs of freshness and tension, with well-defined malic acidity cleverly deployed to sketch out a firm, dry finish that froths with the inimitable chalk minerality of Ambonnay.

ERIC RODEZ EMPRIENTE DE TERROIR PINOT NOIR 2002 $$$$

96 points • TASTED IN AMBONNAY

100% pinot noir; average vine age 42 years; vinified entirely in oak barrels; no malolactic fermentation; 3g/L dosage

In total contrast to Rodez's blends, his 'imprint of terroir' is a single variety (pinot noir in some years, chardonnay in others) of a single year. The concentration on parade here is mesmerising, true to the body and depth of 2002, to the tune of Rodez's Ambonnay intensity. Sweet fruit of black cherries, yellow mirabelle plums and figs of considerable breadth are backed with all the fanfare of 13 years of age, layered with mocha, toast, honey biscuits, brioche and freshly baked golden fruit cake. Just when it seems the volume might get out of hand, it swoops into an impeccably focused finish, honed by malic acid definition and beautifully expressive bath-salts chalk minerality. It's right in the zone to drink now, creamy, silky and very, very long.

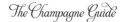

Eric Rodez Cuvée Zéro Dosage NV $$

96 points • 2006 BASE VINTAGE • TASTED IN AMBONNAY

70% pinot noir and 30% chardonnay; 59% 2006, 25% 2005, 12% 2004 and 4% 2002; average vine age 33 years; 82% vinified in barrels; 28% malolactic fermentation; zero dosage

Rodez admits that it's very difficult to create a good equilibrium in zero-dosage champagne every year. Testimony to his intuitive flexibility, last year this riveting cuvée was pure blanc de blancs and now it upholds its full magnificence with 70% pinot noir. What remains unchanged is that this is one of Champagne's richer zero-dosage offerings, and one of the most delicately balanced. While others create bone-dry champagne from taut, young fruit vinified in stainless steel and softened with malolactic, Rodez turns the entire concept on its head and ingeniously blends a tremendous depth of old wines vinified and aged in barrel from his wonderfully opulent Ambonnay fruit and kisses it with the lightest touch of malolactic. Already a magnificent nine years average age on release, the purity he achieves is game-changing, utilising the lively energy and vibrant lemon fruit of Ambonnay, tactically deploying the biscuity, toasty, ginger-accented complexity of barrel vinification and a deep stock of reserves to create internal harmony without any need for dosage. It finishes dry and structured, with beautiful flow, poise, profound persistence and the inimitable signature of Ambonnay salty minerality.

Eric Rodez Cuvée Les Beurys Pinot Noir 2010 $$$$

92 points • TASTED IN AMBONNAY

100% pinot noir; single plot Les Beurys; average vine age 35 years; vinified entirely in oak barrels; no malolactic fermentation; 3g/L dosage

This is a very young vintage champagne that screams out for more time in bottle to mature and allow its prominent oak and malic acidity to soften and integrate. In this youthful guise, its plum liqueur, black cherry and ginger personality is quashed by dominant wood spice and coarse tannin structure. But the oak settles even with time in glass. It has the length and acid structure to go the distance. Patience.

Eric Rodez Cuvée Les Genettes Pinot Noir 2010 $$$$

94 points • TASTED IN AMBONNAY

100% pinot noir; single plot Les Genettes; average vine age 41 years; vinified entirely in oak barrels; no malolactic fermentation; 3g/L dosage

Like Les Beurys, there is a youthful vivacity here that promises great things in time. There is delicacy and beauty, too, with pretty red cherry and strawberry hull characters of restraint and poise. The oak is subdued on the nose and appears gently on the back palate, but will still appreciate time for oak to integrate and structure to settle. It has great length, accurate line and a fine, chewy, mineral mouthfeel.

ERIC RODEZ CUVÉE DES GRANDS VINTAGES BRUT NV $$$

94 points • 2006 BASE VINTAGE • TASTED IN AMBONNAY

2006 base vintage (30%) with 17% 2005, 18% 2004, 14% 2002, 9% 2000, 7% 1999 and 4% 1998;
70% pinot noir; 30% chardonnay; no malolactic fermentation

95 points • 2005 BASE VINTAGE • TASTED IN AMBONNAY

2005 base vintage (35%) with 17% 2004, 16% 2002, 19% 2000, 6% 1999 and 7% 1998;
70% pinot noir; 30% chardonnay; no malolactic fermentation

97 points • 1999 BASE VINTAGE • TASTED IN AMBONNAY

1999 base vintage (40%) with 19% 1998, 15% 1996, 10% 1995, 8% 1993, 5% 1992 and 3% 1990;
60% pinot noir, 40% chardonnay; just 6% malolactic fermentation; fully vinified in barrels; reserves
kept in enamelled tanks; 3g/L dosage

An assemblage of the fruits of the first pressings of the best parcels across many years. The roll-call of vintages is
mind-blowing, not only in that it averages 12 years of age on release, but that it plunders the greatest seasons of
two decades, a line-up that must be unparalleled in Champagne, except perhaps in Krug itself, at three times the
price. Its deep, layered complexity matches the recipe, countering the grand intensity of Ambonnay pinot noir with
the finesse of chardonnay and the tension of malic acidity, upholding the churning salt minerality of the village on
a long, dry finish. The 2005 base is evolving to a place of coffee and mocha, proclaiming its grand maturity amidst
bold, chewy structure and sheer persistence that beg for another decade in the cellar. The 1999 base is evidence of
where it is headed, a wonderful place of secondary complexity of fantastic depth, sustained by lively acidity and
chalk mineral freshness. The harmony on show in this melody is a masterpiece of Rodez's talent as a composer.

ERIC RODEZ CUVÉE BLANC DE BLANCS NV $$

90 points • 2008 BASE • TASTED IN AMBONNAY

43% 2008, 15% 2007, 20% 2006, 16% 2005, 4% 2004 and 2% 2003; average vine age 33 years;
70% vinified in barrels; 30% malolactic fermentation; 4g/L dosage

Eric Rodez describes his blanc de blancs as more masculine and his blanc de noirs as more
feminine. Strength here is derived more from the vanillin and wood spice of oak than it is from
the lovely white peach and fig notes of Ambonnay chardonnay. Pinot noir may be the star of this
village, but chardonnay can certainly perform here, too, upholding persistence and expression of
salty mineral structure, but oak asserts itself more here than it has in recent years.

ERIC RODEZ EMPRIENTE DE TERROIR CHARDONNAY GRAND CRU 1998

96 points • TASTED IN AMBONNAY

100% chardonnay; no malolactic fermentation

A magnificent expression of the voluptuous tension of Ambonnay chardonnay. A full straw yellow hue anticipates
amazing depth and body of grilled pineapple, fig and brioche, countered by the energy and vivacity of chalk
mineral texture and malic acid cut. Enticing bitter grapefruit notes contrast succulent white peach, with rising
layers of bottle-derived almond complexity, lingering on a seamless and persistent finish.

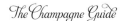

Fleury Père & Fils

(Floo-ree Pear e Feess)

6/10

43 Grande rue 10250 Courteron

www.champagne-fleury.fr

CHAMPAGNE

FLEURY

Jean-Pierre Fleury pioneered biodynamic viticulture in Champagne, tending his vines organically since 1970 and biodynamically since 1989. His family have been growers in the village of Couteron in the south of the Côte des Bar since 1895, and his grandfather was selling his own champagnes as early as the 1930s. Since 2004, the estate has been under the keen eye of Jean-Pierre's son, Jean-Sébastien, a trail-blazer who brings a sense of flair and daring no less courageous than his father's, constantly trialling new and at times brave techniques in the vineyard and winery. His wines encapsulate the character and expression of Côte des Bar fruit with carefully balanced oak, limited dosage and malolactic fermentation tweaked to draw out the personality of each cuvée. These value-for-money champagnes rightfully rank among the most respected in the Aube.

PIONEERING BIODYNAMICS

Jean-Pierre Fleury was regarded by some as a 'crazy hippie' when he started composting and tilling in 1970. 'When my father first talked about biodynamics, it was like something from a different planet!' Jean-Sébastien recalls.

Jean-Pierre's first trial in 1976 was a catastrophe, producing no grapes at all, due to excessive silicon sprays supposed to control mildew. It was not until 1989 that he trialled biodynamics again, and the whole estate was converted in 1992.

Within three years, two other growers in the village followed. Fleury now sources from 15 hectares of its own vines across 10 different parcels and eight hectares from these two neighbours, all biodynamically certified. Characteristic of the area, the estate is planted to a vast majority of pinot noir and a little chardonnay, pinot blanc and pinot gris.

'Our philosophy is to have healthy grapes,' emphasises Jean-Sébastien. With 22 years of hindsight, they have found biodynamics delivers more consistent crops. 'In seasons when others have low yields, we have higher volumes, and when they have high volumes, ours are medium.' Aiming for lower yields is not Fleury's philosophy.

'We try to take what the vines can bring,' Jean-Sébastien explains, adding that every vineyard brings something different each year, and he needs to be very careful to manage each parcel individually to maintain balance. In 22 years of biodynamics, Fleury was able to reach the yield set for the appellation in every year but three (2003, 2007 and 2012).

A biodynamic approach in Champagne's wild climate can be a nail-biting affair, and it's not getting any easier. The year 2012 was 'a good year for us to learn some new things, and we hope we won't have another year like it!' Jean-Sébastien bemoans. Winter brought frosts of -15°C for two weeks straight, followed by two spring frosts, rain disrupting flowering, and outbreaks of mildew, followed by two singeing summer days of 38°C and 41°C. 'The worst conditions for a good harvest,' he says.

Fleury continues to learn more from its biodynamic approach. Recent comparisons between organic, biodynamic and traditional viticulture in the Côte des Bar have found Fleury to achieve 1g more acidity at harvest in regular years, and 2.5g more in hot years. 'Acidity is very important to us,' Jean-Sébastien emphasises. 'Before we embarked on biodynamics, our malolactic fermentation was inconsistent, but high acidities now make it more consistent.' Fleury employs malolactic fermentation strategically, according to the acidity of each parcel.

Fleury has discovered that the roots of its vines have plunged deeper into the chalk following biodynamic conversion. With topsoil depths of between 40 centimetres and 1.5 metres, such deep roots are important for tapping into the mineral expression of each site. Prior to full conversion, comparisons were made between biodynamic and traditional viticulture and Jean-Sébastien recalls many tasters enquiring as to the percentage of chardonnay in blanc de noirs, such was the mineral expression of biodynamic parcels.

Fleury's inquisitive approach remains strong. 'We are always experimenting!' Jean-Sébastien announces, with wide eyes. Fleury is part of a group of biodynamic producers trialling alternatives to spraying copper sulphate as a fungicide, including essential oils and lower doses of new copper sprays. Others are trialling preparations based on local plant concoctions, harvesting on certain days of the biodynamic calendar, even playing different music to the vines.

Fleury's own trials are somewhat less far-fetched, employing a horse to cultivate the soil to determine whether or not there is a reduction in soil compaction, replanting using a massal selection of a variety of clones from biodynamic producers, and testing different grafting techniques.

BIODYNAMIC WINEMAKING

In the winery, Fleury has sought ways to introduce the principles of biodynamics in vinification. Its small, gravity-fed winery is intelligently constructed to follow the slope of the hill, with the press house at the top,

cuverie directly underneath, and barrels suspended on high frames on the lowest level. Jean-Sébastien's aim is to use no pumps, but admits that this is complicated. Two vertical presses were installed in 1990 and an automatic Coquard press in 2004. 'The pressing makes 50% of the quality,' claims Jean-Sébastien, who loves the delicacy of the new press for reducing colour pick-up and oxidation.

Reducing oxidation is a key priority for the house, which hasn't added sulphur as a preservative since 2008. 'In 2011 we made a half press with sulphur and half without and found that adding sulphur removed purity and expression of flavour,' Jean-Sébastien explains. 'We only adjust sulphur levels at disgorgement, because this is crucial for the wine to travel. I hope, touch wood, that we will not have a bad experience!' So far, so good. His no-sulphur Sonate No 9 cuvée showed pristine freshness in Australia nine months after disgorgement.

Fleury vinifies all parcels separately and, since 1997, 10% of production has been fermented and aged in oak barrels, mostly destined for vintage and reserve wines. To downplay oak flavour, barrels are purchased after three or four uses and maintained for 10–15 years. Reserve wines are stored in an impressive line of 6000-litre foudres. Jean-Sébastien is keen to trial different fermentation vessels, and hopes to buy egg fermenters and concrete tanks this year to assess their effect.

Jean-Pierre Fleury retired recently, leaving the estate in the capable hands of Jean-Sébastien, assisted by his artistic sister and viticulture-trained brother. Their imperative is to uphold the style of Fleury's existing cuvées, while actively pursuing the introduction of new labels, including a 100% oak-fermented pinot blanc, a low-sulphur, zero-dosage pinot noir and a distinctive extra brut pinot noir. The estate has doubled production to a total of 200,000 bottles in recent years, and is working to increase its export markets.

While disgorgement dates are printed on every bottle, they're not always easy to read. Labelling dates are printed much more clearly. Labelling generally occurs one to six months after disgorgement.

'Biodynamics explains how we can make our wines unique, but ultimately it's about the wine,' Jean-Sébastien emphasises. 'We'd like to be considered not only because our wines are organic or biodynamic, but because we have good grapes and make good wines.'

The champagnes of Fleury certainly live up to this aspiration and are worth discovering for their noble philosophy and, more importantly, for the character they bring at an affordable price.

The Champagne Guide

Fleury Père & Fils Blanc de Noirs Brut NV $$

94 points • Disgorged November 2014 • Tasted in Brisbane

Base vintage 2010 with reserves from 2009; 100% pinot noir; vinified in enamelled tanks; part of the blend kept as next year's reserve and aged in 60hL foudres; 8.6g/L dosage

Fleury's is a thrilling blanc de noirs that consistently captures the tension between the generous succulence and the poised energy of pinot noir. Pretty red cherry, red apple and strawberry fruits are energised by a refreshing backbone of tangy lemon and morello cherry acidity and fine, soft, Aube chalk mineral texture. It glides effortlessly through fields of crunchy strawberries and orchards of tangy red cherries on a long, even and refreshing finish. Don't discount the Aube — this cuvée walks all over many Marne blanc de noirs this year.

Fleury Père & Fils Fleur de l'Europe Brut Nature NV $$

92 points • Disgorged November 2014 • Tasted in Brisbane

2007 base vintage with 2006 reserves; 79% pinot noir, 21% chardonnay; 28% vinified in oak barrels; partial malolactic fermentation; 1.8g/L dosage

Fleur de l'Europe is purposely a more mature style, to contrast with Fleury's Blanc de Noirs. A cuvée of character and complexity, generous in its exuberant expression of Aube pinot noir and glamorous in its fresh pineapple, grilled banana, wild honey and toasted brioche complexity. An unmistakable dose of malic acidity assertively pulls this party into line on a tense and taut finish, underlined by slatey mineral texture and heightened by low dosage. This is not a style for the uninitiated, but it offers much to enthral the seasoned champagne fanatic, and it will age a good few years yet.

Fleury Père & Fils Notes Blanches Brut Nature NV $$

91 points • Disgorged October 2014 • Tasted in Brisbane

100% pinot blanc; 100% 2010, though not labelled as a vintage even though it's disgorged sufficiently late that it could be; 100% oak fermented; second release; 3g/L residual sugar; zero dosage

The Fleury family has cultivated pinot blanc since the time of great-grandfather Emile and his son Robert. A worthy follow-on to the inaugural release of Fleury's 'White Notes', yet even more honed, precise and tense, this is a true and compelling expression of sparkling pinot blanc to drink young and fresh. Texturally, pinot blanc behaves quite differently to chardonnay, making this a blanc de blancs of taut structure and fine-grained phenolic grip. Its tense structure has been well massaged by barrel fermentation and bottle age, creating creaminess amidst assertive acidity. Spice, pear, star fruit and a grapefruit bite, finishing with soft, salty minerality.

FLEURY PÈRE & FILS SONATE NO 9 OPUS 10 EXTRA BRUT NV $$$

93 points • DISGORGED JUNE 2014 • TASTED IN BRISBANE

Second release; 100% 2010; 76% pinot noir, 24% chardonnay; zero sulphur; 1.3g/L dosage; 7000 bottles

The inaugural Sonate No 9 was 100% 2009. Confusingly, its successor is still Sonate No 9, with 'Opus 10' added to denote 2010. Still, any declaration of base vintage on a non-vintage champagne is to be applauded. It leads out with impressive purity and expression of florals, vibrant citrus and red apples, with a little chardonnay introduced this year to provide definition to Aube pinot noir. Zero sulphur is always disconcerting, but to its credit it shows no deterioration in Australia nine months after disgorgement. It leads out generous and finishes very tense, suggesting that it needs time to soften and build depth, but will it hold its freshness without preservative? Taut, focused acidity suggests some malic acidity remains, driving the palate through layers of spice and even a note of wood spice, though there is no oak here. Fine, mineral texture lingers on a refreshing finish. An expressive and skilfully crafted cuvée.

FLEURY PÈRE & FILS ROSÉ DE SAIGNÉE BRUT NV $$

94 points • DISGORGED OCTOBER 2014 • TASTED IN BRISBANE

100% 2009; 100% pinot noir; macerated for 24 hours before pressing; no malolactic fermentation; 10.7g/L dosage

Rosé de Saignée is the pinnacle of Fleury, with different lengths of maceration making for a different colour every year, and the 2009 retains a particularly full, bright crimson hue, landing at the deeper end of the champagne rosé pool. From the same base vintage, this bottle was disgorged almost exactly two years after the bottle I tasted for the previous edition of this guide two years ago, and I love it even more now, which just might be a first for a six-year-old rosé. It's swimming with fresh rosewater, strawberries, raspberries and cherries, evolving to a more savoury and secondary dimension of cherry kernel, tomato, pomegranate and pink pepper, while retaining a red cherry tang. The sustaining presence of malic acidity is all-encompassing, defining a long, fresh and tangy finish. Its finely structured texture is even more engaging now than it was on release, its bead creamier and persistence every bit as magnificent. Kudos to Fleury.

FLEURY PÈRE & FILS EXTRA BRUT 2002 $$$

88 points • DISGORGED NOVEMBER 2014 • TASTED IN BRISBANE

77% pinot noir, 23% chardonnay; 43% of pinot noir fermented in 200L oak barrels; 3.3g/L dosage

Fleury has come a long way in the past decade, and this cuvée is still a hangover from the past. It's a bold and overt style that unites robust, rustic pineapple, locut and apple fruit with firm wood presence and a note of mushroom. It needs every bit of its 13 years of age, and then some, with phenolic grip and tense acid still quite assertive, with no suggestion it will relax anytime soon. It lacks the precision and refinement of Fleury's more recent cuvées.

FRANCIS BOULARD & FILLE

(Fron-sees Boo-lar e Fee)

ROUTE NATIONALE RD 944 51220 CAUROY-LES-HERMONVILLE
www.francis-boulard.com

Champagne
Francis Boulard

In Champagne's turning wheel of succession, estates are passed down through the generations and in 2010, one-third of Champagne Raymond Boulard became Francis Boulard. Fifth-generation winemaker Francis and his daughter Delphine manage their three-hectare domaine in out-of-the-way Massif de Saint-Thierry north of Reims with a focus on natural procedures in the vineyard and the winery.

Boulard's family had just two hectares of vineyards when he started working with his brother and sister in 1980. Over the next three decades, they grew the family estate to 12 hectares. 'We planted it ourselves, by hand,' he recalls. 'My life is to work in the vineyards and this is what I enjoy. I have only travelled on a plane once in my life.

'We started to work biodynamically in 2001 and my family disagreed, so we divorced ourselves from the family in 2009,' Boulard explains. His focus is on biodynamic practices, with all of their vineyards completing organic certification in 2015. 'I work organically, not only for the birds and the butterflies, but because it builds more complexity and body in the wines,' he says. He may one day seek biodynamic certification, not because he needs it to sell his wines, but for the collaboration with other biodynamic growers.

Planted to 30% chardonnay, 30% pinot noir and 40% meunier, Boulard's vines average 35 years of age and are mostly in Cormicy in the Saint-Thierry hills, planted largely to chardonnay, with 1.5 hectares of meunier in the Vallée de la Marne and a small pinot noir holding

in Mailly-Champagne. Boulard admits that it's tricky to maintain an organic regime in the Vallée de la Marne as 50 kilometres is a long way to travel along small roads to maintain a spray program. A green harvest is conducted when necessary, and grapes are harvested late for optimal maturity, with a target of 10% natural potential, reducing the need for chaptalisation.

Delicate pressing is achieved by means of a membrane press and wild yeast fermentation takes place in small wooden barrels and 20hL foudres, all old (average age 12 years). 'We don't do winemaking!' Boulard quips. 'We put the wine in the barrel, it ferments and then we bottle it.' He doesn't use chemicals, 'because as soon as you do something to the must or the wine, you lose part of the expression of the wine'. This can be a blessing and a curse. These are rustic and characterful wines of tension and at times hardness, too often reflecting the funky imprecision of old barrels.

Wines are vinified on fine lees with bâtonnage every 10–12 days, and malolactic fermentation is encouraged or blocked according to the cuvée. Dosages are very low;

some cuvées are offered as both brut nature and extra brut. Cuvées are disgorged every month, and back labels declare the blend, percentages of vintages, bottling and disgorgement dates and dosage. Annual production is 20,000–25,000 bottles, according to the season. When he divorced from the family, he purchased 60% of their stocks, providing him with a stock of pre-2009 vintages.

Some bottles Boulard poured for me were oxidised, having been open for up to two weeks. I have only included reviews of freshly opened bottles here.

FRANCIS BOULARD BLANC DE BLANCS BRUT NATURE NV $$

93 points • TASTED IN CAUROY-LES-HERMONVILLE

2011 base vintage; 35% reserves from 2010 and 2009; 100% chardonnay from Massif de Saint-Thierry and Mailly-Champagne; wild fermented in large foudres; zero dosage

Boulard's wines never lack personality, and this blanc de blancs unites layers of charcuterie, marmalade, orange and fig in a finely textured mouthfeel of chalk mineral definition, creamy bead and excellent line and length. It's a fantastic result for the challenging 2011 season.

FRANCIS BOULARD MILLÉSIME EXTRA BRUT 2006 $$

92 points • TASTED IN CAUROY-LES-HERMONVILLE

50% pinot noir, 50% chardonnay; wild fermented in large 20hL foudre; 3g/L dosage

A complex and distinctive wine from the Boulard family collection, packed with impressive complexity of roasted chestnuts, golden fruit cake, orange zest, coffee bean and dark chocolate. The mouthfeel is fine and textural, with large barrel complexity, a little structural grip and very good length.

FRANCIS BOULARD LES MURGIERS BLANC DE NOIRS BRUT NATURE NV $$

92 points • TASTED IN CAUROY-LES-HERMONVILLE

100% 2007; same wine as above, with zero dosage

Nutty barrel fermentation offers complexity, while retaining a resolute focus on fresh grapefruit, stone fruits, ginger and mixed spice. A wine of energy and length, with expressive salt minerality. Tense acidity leaves the finish taut, dry and a little hard. It looks better with a little dosage.

FRANCIS BOULARD LES MURGIERS BLANC DE NOIRS EXTRA BRUT NV $$

94 points • DISGORGED APRIL 2012 • TASTED IN CAUROY-LES-HERMONVILLE & MELBOURNE

70% meunier and 30% pinot noir from the Vallée de la Marne; wild fermented in old small oak barrels, large casks and half hogsheads; full malolactic fermentation; 3g/L dosage

Generous, fleshy, taut and focused, all at the same time, propelling crunchy lemon zest, red apple and white cherry fruit. A lovely fresh and textural style of chalk mineral structure and well-gauged low dosage accenting prominent acid line. A bottle tasted in Cauroy-les-Hermonville (100% 2007) was mushroomy and developed.

FRANCIS BOULARD LES RACHAIS BLANC DE BLANCS BRUT NATURE MILLÉSIME 2007 $$$

90 points • DISGORGED APRIL 2013 • TASTED IN MELBOURNE

100% chardonnay; single plot in the Massif de Saint-Thierry of average vine age 43 years; wild fermented and aged in small oak barrels with bâtonnage; full malolactic fermentation; zero dosage

A wine of impressive frame, drawn out with good length and taut, fine structure. The contrast between racy, razor-sharp acidity and funky old barrel notes is not for the timid.

FRANCIS BOULARD GRAND CRU GRANDE MONTAGNE EXTRA BRUT NV $$

86 points • TASTED IN CAUROY-LES-HERMONVILLE

2010 base vintage with 40% reserves from 2009 and 2008; 60% pinot noir, 40% chardonnay from Mailly-Champagne; wild fermented and aged in small oak barrels and half hogsheads; full malolactic fermentation

A champagne of character and taut chalk mineral expression. Charcuterie and boiled-sausage notes of old barrel maturation compete with tense, raw lemon juice acidity. It's young, hard and lacking in cleanliness and precision.

FRANCIS BOULARD BLANC DE BLANCS LES VIEILLES VIGNES EXTRA BRUT NV $$

91 points • TASTED IN CAUROY-LES-HERMONVILLE

100% 2011; 100% chardonnay; single plot of 35-year-old vines in the Massif de Saint-Thierry; wild fermented in small oak barrels and large foudres; full malolactic fermentation; 3.5g/L dosage

A characterful and textural blanc de blancs of well-defined primary lemon fruit, taut acidity and the fine, salt mineral texture of the Massif de Saint-Thierry. Time in barrel has instilled a layered pipe-smoke complexity.

FRANCK BONVILLE

(Fronk Bon-vee)

9 RUE PASTEUR 51190 AVIZE

www.champagne-franck-bonville.com

A s demand for the greatest Côtes des Blancs grand crus continues to spiral, the privilege of substantial, well-placed holdings cannot be overstated. Gilles and Ingrid Bonville and their son Olivier are in command of 20 hectares of prime grand cru turf, 15 in Avize, a little in Cramant, and old vines on the slope of Oger. The family have been growing grapes here for more than a century, and bottling their own champagnes since 1947. Olivier Bonville is the third generation of his family to make champagnes in Avize. Chardonnay is, of course, the theme of these tense, powerful champagnes, with red grapes for rosé sourced from the great estate of Paul Déthune in Ambonnay.

FRANCK BONVILLE GRAND CRU BLANC DE BLANCS NV $

89 points • DISGORGED JUNE 2013 • TASTED IN BRISBANE

2011 base; 30% 2010, 20% 2009; 70% Avize, 30% Oger; entire 2011 prestige production (Belles Voyes, Vintage & Prestige) declassified into this cuvée and the rosé; 5% vinified in oak; aged 2-2.5 years on lees; 6.7g/L dosage

Led by the intensity and power of impressive grand cru chardonnay, though even this is insufficient to completely foil the dry finish and phenolic grip of the difficult 2011 season. Nonetheless, excellent acid line, well-integrated dosage and fine mineral presence. Value.

FRANCK BONVILLE GRAND CRU AVIZE BLANC DE BLANCS BRUT MILLÉSIME 2008 $

95 points • DISGORGED APRIL 2013 • TASTED IN BRISBANE

Estate vineyards in Avize; aged on lees 4-5 years; 7.5g/L dosage

The tension of 2008 plays to the structure and definition of Avize to create a cuvée of vertical linearity, high-tensile frame and elongated longevity. The primary vivacity of grapefruit flesh and lemon zest is presented with grand cru volume and presence, underscored by a pronounced textural mouthfeel of signature Avize bath-salts chalk minerality, frothing and foaming on a very long finish. Outstanding now, and it will only get better over the coming decades.

G.H. MUMM

(G.H. Moom)

29 RUE DU CHAMPS DE MARS 51199 REIMS

www.mumm.com

*A*n annual production of 8 million bottles ranks Mumm number four by volume in Champagne after Moët, Clicquot and Feuillatte. Despite a turbulent history of acquisitions over the past century, Mumm has retained almost 218 hectares of vines, mostly planted to pinot noir, meeting 25% of its needs. The house has come a long way since my first visit during the snowfalls of Christmas 2001, recovering from its dark days of the 1980s and 1990s, due in part to the appointment of the 31-year-old Dominique Demarville as chef de cave in 1998 and his 35-year-old successor, Didier Mariotti, in 2006. Mumm now enjoys a higher percentage of chardonnay in its 'Cordon Rouge' house blend, as well as more reserve wine, longer maturation times and lower dosages. And there is more at hand.

In 1995, Mumm launched a 12-year plan to resurrect Cordon Rouge, encompassing harvesting, pressing and vinification, with a focus on building reserve wines since the late 1990s, but it was not until Pernod Ricard purchased the company in 2005 that sufficient funds were injected to fully realise this vision. 'The quality of Cordon Rouge was so bad 10–15 years ago, because of insufficient reserve wines, short ageing in the cellar and inconsistent blends for each vintage,' Mariotti admits.

A gleaming new winery was constructed in Reims in 2008 and extended in 2010 to house row after row of sparkling new stainless steel tanks, new disgorgement and bottling lines, and space for greater stocks of reserve wines. 'With a new winery and smaller vats we are able to home in on the terroir more accurately by producing smaller parcels for the blends,' Mariotti explains. New press centres were constructed in Mailly-Champagne and Verzy in 2010 to address concerns with fruit waiting for up to 10 hours to be pressed.

Grapes can now be moved just a few kilometres between press houses to avoid these delays.

Cordon Rouge is moving from 20% to an impressive 30% reserve wines, spanning four vintages, which Mariotti upholds as crucial for maintaining the consistency of the blend. It spends a minimum two and a half years on lees in the cellar, and Mariotti has worked to lower the dosage from 10g/L to 8g/L. 'I am very proud of this dosage, one of the lowest of any of the houses,' he claims.

The magnitude of his new winery is sufficient that all 8 million bottles of Cordon Rouge are now the same blend each year, a remarkable feat of logistical engineering. An identical blend is made once a week for 15–20 weeks. An extra 30% is produced, and kept in tank as the reserve for the following year.

Enthusiastic about raising quality, Didier Mariotti brings acute attention to detail to every part of the process from vineyard to market. He spends 70% of his time during harvest visiting growers, building relationships, seeing the quality of the fruit and gaining insight into the vintage. At the other end of the process, he tastes every wine from each warehouse in most export markets every six months, and checks the disgorgement date of cuvées in every restaurant he visits. He binned a couple of pallets of Rosé NV from the warehouse in Australia last year and reserved some de Cramant 2006 for internal use only because they were too old.

'It is important to be sure that the quality is maintained at every step,' he emphasises. 'You can work hard on the blend, ageing and disgorgement, but if you don't focus on the supply chain you can destroy everything.' Mumm now prints bottling and disgorgement dates on the back labels of its de Cramant, Blanc de Blancs and Blanc de Noirs, as well as its Brut Selection for the French market, as Mariotti believes it is always best to disclose the disgorgement date.

In a region where change comes slowly, Mariotti is eager to embrace innovation, even appointing a new winemaker dedicated to this purpose last year, with a focus on testing stoppers, lightstruck damage, matching champagne glasses to particular cuvées, as well as driving all manner of experiments in the winery.

'If you are not trialling, you are not moving,' declares Mariotti. 'Global warming, the markets and other things are changing, so we need to be asking questions about winemaking all the time.' This philosophy has inspired small trials of bâtonnage, malolactic fermentation, barrel ageing of liqueurs, even barrels of different coopers and varying levels of toast. All Mumm cuvées currently undergo full malolactic fermentation, though parcels with no malolactic are trialled each vintage. 'We need to be prepared for global warming,' Mariotti reveals, 'but so far our only response has been to harvest earlier.'

Mumm's windmill overlooks its historic stronghold of Verzenay.

Mariotti has a vision to bring more structure and complexity to non-vintage cuvées, by increasing ageing on lees, facilitated by maintaining 25 million bottles maturing at any time, and through greater proportions of reserve wines. 'With five years of wines in reserve I'm able to think about which reserves I use for each blend,' he explains. Barrel ageing with bâtonnage may in future be the third step, though Mariotti admits that 'in some of our experimentation with barrels, the results have been very, very bad! But it's good for the kids to play!'

Mumm has bottled half bottles of Cordon Rouge under DIAM closures for two years and is hoping to do the same for full bottles for export markets. Mariotti is convinced of DIAM's superiority. 'If we can guarantee no more cork problems, I don't know why we are waiting!' he exclaims. (This can't come too soon, as I've seen some cork effect in this cuvée.)

'It takes a long time to turn things around in Champagne!' he adds. This is especially true in a house the size of Mumm. Its non-vintage cuvées are on a slow ascent, with hope for further gains in years to come.

G.H. MUMM CORDON ROUGE BRUT NV $$

85 points • 2011 BASE VINTAGE • DISGORGED MAY 2014 • TASTED IN REIMS & BRISBANE
88 points • 2010 BASE VINTAGE • TASTED IN SYDNEY & MELBOURNE

45% pinot noir, 30% chardonnay, 25% meunier; 30% reserves spanning four vintages; 15-20% of the final blend is kept as reserve; 8g/L dosage; 8 million bottles

Cordon Rouge is a massive blend of between 300 and 450 tanks from more than 100 villages, representing more than 85% of Mumm's production. It's currently suffering a dip in the wake of a couple of weak vintages. The 2011 base shows some raw almond and bready notes, challenged by the mushroomy, earthy, dusty character of imperfect grapes. Honeyed dosage and lemony acidity sit disjoint amidst a coarse structure. The 2010 base shows more of the youthful, primary red apple and citrus fruit character and the subtle biscuit complexity typical of this cuvée.

The Champagne Guide

G.H. Mumm Le Rosé Brut NV $$

84 points • 2011 base vintage • Tasted in Reims
90 points • 2010 base vintage • Tasted in Sydney, Melbourne & Brisbane

55% pinot noir, 30% meunier, 15% chardonnay; 25% reserves; 14% red wine from meunier and pinot noir, purchased as finished wine; 6g/L dosage; 300,000-600,000 bottles

The 2011 base is a medium salmon pink rosé of musk, Turkish delight and hazelnut character, destroyed by the dry, dusty and coarse character of the vintage, rendering the finish awkwardly hard and phenolic. The 2010 base is the best I have ever seen this cuvée, a pale salmon celebration of fresh strawberries, crunchy red apples, tangy morello cherries, grapefruit and pink pepper. It's primary, fresh, fruit-focused, clean and lively, with impressive acid line and well-balanced dosage. A little tannin presence provides appropriate grip to a short finish.

G.H. Mumm Brut Millésime 2009 $$

91 points • Disgorged August 2014 • Tasted in Reims

68% pinot noir, 32% chardonnay; majority of Aÿ pinot noir and Avize chardonnay, with 8 other villages; 6g/L dosage

Mariotti has intelligently released the 2009 before the 2008, which is not yet ready. Due for launch in late 2015, my tasting in early 2015 revealed a young and reserved vintage that will appreciate more time in bottle to build character. Pear, lemon and grapefruit are becoming secondary, building notes of almond meal and freshly churned butter. It's a textural and chewy style with lees-derived mouthfeel and good persistence.

G.H. Mumm Brut Millésime 2006 $$

90 points • Tasted in Reims, Sydney, Melbourne & Brisbane

64% pinot nor, 36% chardonnay; majority of pinot noir from Verzenay and chardonnay from Oger; 6g/L dosage; DIAM closure

A relatively simple vintage for early drinking, already soft, rounded and immediate. Secondary complexity is building quickly in characters of honey biscuits, ginger, toasted coconut and a whiff of smoke, while succulent peach, fig and grapefruit are fading. It holds good length and integrity amidst a chewy, leesy mouthfeel and a little more honeyed dosage than this smooth vintage calls for.

G.H. Mumm Brut Selection Grand Cru NV $$

94 points • Disgorged June 2014 • Tasted in Reims

2005 base vintage with reserves from 2004, 2002, 1999 and 1998; pinot noir from Aÿ, Bouzy and Verzenay; chardonnay from Avize and Cramant; aged 8 years on lees; 6g/L dosage

Three more years on lees since release has worked wonders for this cuvée, enlivening its fruit, elongating its finish and downplaying the structure of 2005. It's an elegantly fruit-focused style of pale hue and gentle, primary red apple and pear fruits, with soft, slowly rising bready complexity. Vibrant acid structure and soft mineral tension are well contrasted with seamlessly balanced dosage. Impressive expression of five of the greatest grand crus.

G.H. Mumm Blanc de Noirs de Verzenay NV $$$

89 points • Disgorged October 2013 • Tasted in Reims

100% Verzenay pinot noir; base vintage 2002

I held great expectations for this new Mumm cuvée, built on the historic stronghold of the house in Verzenay in the great 2002 vintage, but I suspect the only bottle I had the opportunity to taste was prematurely developed. Vinegary sweet and sour notes detract from an otherwise elegant, mineral and graceful blanc de noirs.

G.H. Mumm de Cramant Blanc de Blancs Brut $$$$

93 points • 2007 base vintage • Disgorged May 2013 • Tasted in Reims, Sydney & Melbourne
92 points • 2010 base vintage • Tasted in Brisbane

100% Cramant chardonnay; DIAM closure; 50,000-100,000 bottles

In philosophy and pedigree, de Cramant is an altogether different tier in the world of Mumm, and it's their only cuvée that I buy. A rather young release, it's bottled at 4.5 atmospheres of pressure rather than the usual 6, to soften the impression of acidity. It's always been one variety (chardonnay), one village (Cramant) and one vintage, though never labelled as a vintage as it's sometimes released too young. To great relief, it's now labelled with bottling and disgorgement dates (the base vintage is the year prior to bottling). To maintain consistency, Mumm plays with selection of plots, fermentation temperature, addition of lees, blocking of malolactic fermentation and, unique in Champagne, even micro-oxygenation on some tanks. The 2007 is a big step up from the lifeless 2006, an elegant, restrained and focused vintage of youthful verve; a tribute to Cramant in its grapefruit, lemon, pear, white peach and granny smith characters. Gunflint reduction offers complexity, while maturity builds notes of almond and vanilla. There is a silky elegance, while upholding zesty, focused acidity. The finish is long, textural and dry, defined as much by lees age as the chalk minerality of Cramant. The 2010 upholds similar struck flint and charcuterie reductive character, on a peppery, drying palate that carries lemon zest of considerable persistence through a firm, dusty finish. A good result for a tricky season. Give it time.

G.H. Mumm Cuvée R. Lalou Brut 2002 $$$$$

94 points • Disgorged late 2013 • Tasted in Reims & Brisbane

Always a blend of 50% chardonnay and 50% pinot noir; 6g/L dosage; DIAM closure

Lalou was the prestige wine of the house between 1969 and 1985, but the bottle mould and recipe were lost in the wild ride of ownership changes, revived by Demarville in 1998. Only at the point of blending is the decision made as to which of 12 potential parcels of estate grand cru vineyards will win the golden ticket (as few as two, if the vintage is deemed worthy at all). The 2002 is a blend of eight parcels of vines more than 30 years of age in Mailly-Champagne, Bouzy, Verzenay, Verzy and Ambonnay for pinot noir, and Cramant and Avize for chardonnay. A liqueur of Cramant and Bouzy is aged in new and used barrels to build sufficiently to meet the power of the wine. Lalou is unashamedly built as a strong wine, and 2002 is a wonderfully complex rendition, seamlessly marrying the primary, secondary and tertiary phases of development. Yellow mirabelle plums and citrus are evolving into dried peach, mixed spice and brioche of silky, buttery smoothness, while nuances of old age begin in coffee, butterscotch, dark chocolate and subtle smouldering hearth. Thirteen years of maturity have built a full straw yellow hue and a creamy mouthfeel, while retaining brightness and integrity of acid line, promising a few more years of potential.

GASTON CHIQUET

(Gas-toh Shi-khe)

6/10

912 Ave du Général Leclerc 51530 Dizy

www.gastonchiquet.com

CHAMPAGNE
Gaston Chiquet
PROPRIÉTAIRE - RÉCOLTANT

'The point is to make "vin de terroir",' emphasises the young, eighth-generation Dizy grower Nicolas Chiquet. 'We are lucky to have some very nice vineyard locations, so our goal is to preserve the character of the fruit.' His assessment of the family's 23 hectares is politely modest. These are well-established vineyards on the privileged mid-slopes of Dizy, Hautvillers, Aÿ (including an impressive five hectares of chardonnay), Mareuil-sur-Aÿ, as well as in the Valley of the Ardre, close to Reims. With careful attention to sustainable viticulture, meticulous fruit handling and sensitive vinification, Nicolas and his brother Antoine's 'vin de terroir' ambition is brought to life in champagnes of fruit purity and fine, chalky minerality that represent impressive value for money.

The Chiquets have tended vines since 1746 and were among Champagne's first growers to make their own wines in 1919. The property in Dizy was purchased by the brothers' grandfather, Gaston, in 1935, with a deep and extensive cellar, more than sufficient for the current production of 220,000 bottles annually.

In villages famed for pinot noir, Gaston Chiquet is unusual in its 40% holdings of each of meunier and chardonnay. 'We speak well of the quality of meunier, even though it does not have the finesse to age like chardonnay or pinot noir. It provides roundness in the mouth for our non-vintage wines,' Nicolas Chiquet explains.

'Terroir is the most important thing and we have to be very humble in our approach,' adds Chiquet, who continuously adapts his vinification in response to the season. 'We want to work more on our vineyards than our wine, making "vin de terroir" rather than adding

oxygen through vinification in oak.' He compares this process to cooking.

'When you have good produce you have very little to do and it is perfect! This is why we have very natural winemaking processes. We do not want to change our fruit. We are very careful to adapt our vinification to keep the freshness in the juice, as we have a lot of power in our fruit.'

Vinification begins with one of the most sophisticated presses in Champagne, extracting the purest juice, though the old press is still used sometimes. 'The new press has had little influence, but how it's controlled is the key,' Chiquet says. Each of 35 different parcels is vinified separately in small stainless steel tanks, not oak barrels. 'Our terroirs can tend towards oxidation, so we phased out barrels since the 1940s,' Chiquet explains. To further protect against oxidation, wines are not aged long in tank, with bottle ageing preferred. Malolactic fermentation is carried out on all parcels and low dosages of typically 8g/L are used.

To preserve fruit character and reduce oxidation, DIAM closures have been used on every cuvée since 2009. 'The crown caps we use in the cellars are the best closures, but we can't sell our wines with them,' he says. 'DIAMs are very reliable, with a consistent level of oxygen ingress and no cork taint.' Every bottle is labelled

with its disgorgement date. 'This is very important to us. We have educated our customers and they know not to open a bottle soon after it has been disgorged.'

In 2014, Antoine's daughter, Marion, was employed as chef de cave. 'She's well travelled and it's excellent to have the involvement of the wider family,' says Nicolas.

Along with their cousins just around the corner at Jacquesson, the Chiquets make the finest champagnes of Dizy. True 'vin de terroir'.

GASTON CHIQUET INSOLENT BRUT NV $

87 points • 2012 BASE VINTAGE • DISGORGED MARCH 2014 • TASTED IN DIZY

60% meunier; sourced largely from Dizy and Hautvillers; average vine age 25 years; 60% first- and 40% second-press juice; tank fermented; full malolactic fermentation; 8g/L dosage; DIAM closure

A soft, light, young, meunier-led champagne for summer parties, more about drinkability than terroir expression, blended from any estate fruit of insufficient character or ageability for the house's other cuvées. It's by definition the least of the range, a short, simple champagne with some grip and firmness from second-press juice. It lacks distinction and character, but upholds pretty good expression of apple and pear fruit for a 'leftovers' cuvée. Drink as soon as possible.

GASTON CHIQUET BRUT TRADITION PREMIER CRU NV $$

89 points • 2010 BASE VINTAGE • DISGORGED MAY 2014 • TASTED IN DIZY

40% meunier, 35% chardonnay, 25% pinot noir; reserves from 2004 (14%) and 2009 (7%); 95% first press; 8g/L dosage

The same blend since the brothers' grandfather created the brand, hence the name. The tricky 2010 season has made for a lesser Tradition, with hints of mushroom and tilled earth. It's a citrusy style of grapefruit, mandarin and subtle lees complexity, with an even, persistent acid line and soft chalk minerality.

GASTON CHIQUET BLANC DE BLANCS D'AŸ GRAND CRU NV $$

94 points • 100% 2010 • DISGORGED MAY 2014 • TASTED IN DIZY

8g/L dosage

In 1935, Gaston Chiquet was among the first to plant chardonnay in Aÿ, and today claims five hectares of chardonnay and the only blanc de blancs in the village, a blend made by Nicolas' father and grandfather since 1955. It's always a vintage wine, yet released as an NV because the aspiration is to showcase the character of chardonnay in Aÿ, highlighting the terroir rather than the year. They like it when it's young and when it's 8–10 years of age, and not in between. To make 30,000 bottles, they harvest sufficient chardonnay to make double this capacity and then select the best parcels to suit this cuvée. The 2010 vintage plays to the philosophy of this cuvée, less floral, less fruity and more structured, with a wonderfully airy, mineral, chalk-infused texture that celebrates the earth of Aÿ. Fruit is subtle, in an exotic quince and red apple spectrum, with hints of grilled bread and gunpowder reduction, underlined by refined acidity which lingers on an impressively persistent finish.

GASTON CHIQUET CUVÉE DE RÉSERVE PREMIER CRU BRUT NV $$

91 points • 2005 BASE VINTAGE • DISGORGED OCTOBER 2012 • TASTED IN DIZY

Brut Tradition aged 5 years on lees; 45% meunier, 35% chardonnay, 20% pinot noir; average vine age 27 years; 8g/L dosage; DIAM closure

A release which looked marvellous two years ago is now showing subtle notes of burnt-orange oxidation, suggesting that it's edged past its peak. It's secondary, buttery, honeyed and spicy, with hints of rich dried peach, brioche and crème brûlée. It upholds integrity of structure in creamy lees texture and good persistence.

GASTON CHIQUET ROSÉ BRUT PREMIER CRU NV $$

90 points • 2010 BASE VINTAGE • DISGORGED MAY 2014 • TASTED IN DIZY

Brut Tradition without reserves; 12% red wine, half 2009 and half 2008 from the best plots of Dizy and Hautvillers; 9.2g/L dosage; ~22,000 bottles

Like the 2010 base Brut Tradition on which it is built, this is a lesser release for Chiquet Rosé. Medium salmon copper in hue, it's a savoury and rustic style of tomato and roast nuts, set against a gentle backdrop of strawberry fruit. A bright, persistent acid line and finely textured tannin structure make for a balanced and even style.

GASTON CHIQUET CUVÉE OR BRUT MILLÉSIMÉ 2005 $$

91 points • DISGORGED MARCH 2014 • TASTED IN DIZY

60% pinot noir from Dizy and Hautvillers, 40% chardonnay from Aÿ; 8g/L dosage

Parcels for vintage wines are chosen on their power and ability to age for 10 years without sensitivity to oxygen. This is an accurate reflection of the richness and power of both its terroirs and its vintage, yet retains a well-balanced acid line and freshness of lemon fruit. Bitter grapefruit pith mouthfeel reflects the phenolic structure inherent in the 2005 harvest. Age has brought notes of patisserie and the creamy texture of long lees maturity.

GASTON CHIQUET SPECIAL CLUB BRUT MILLÉSIMÉ 2007 $$

94 points • DISGORGED SEPTEMBER 2013 • TASTED IN DIZY

59% Dizy chardonnay, 11% Aÿ chardonnay, 30% Dizy pinot noir; 8g/L dosage; less than 20,000 bottles

This is an elegant vintage for Chiquet, sporting a refined new label to match. The more elegant parcels are selected for Special Club, providing an enticing contrast to the richness of Chiquet's other cuvées. At eight years of age, it's still a pale straw hue and refreshingly lively, capturing its graceful season in primary lemon fruit, underscored by the toasted brioche complexity of bottle age. A vibrant, linear acid line, soft, finely structured chalk minerality and well-integrated dosage define an alluring finish.

GATINOIS

(Ga-tin-wah)

7/10

7 RUE MARCEL MAILLY 51160 AŸ

www.champagne-gatinois.com

In the elegant reception room of Gatinois in the back streets of Aÿ, alongside a magnificent wine press still standing where it was constructed five generations ago, the Gatinois family tree is proudly displayed, tracing their history in the village back to 1696. Young Louis Cheval-Gatinois is the 12th successive generation to farm seven hectares of the family vineyards, enviably positioned on the majestic slopes of Aÿ. His family has made champagne here since probably the mid-1800s, which must place Gatinois among Champagne's oldest grower producers. Gatinois' generously coloured champagnes are among the finest in this revered village, resonating with the history of the house and the thundering power of its grand cru slopes, at every moment retaining exceptional definition and freshness.

In the convoluted history of Champagne succession and inheritance, the vineyards of the ancient village of Aÿ have been divided into ever-smaller plots, creating what Louis Cheval-Gatinois describes as 'a mosaic on the hillside'.

Gatinois has been privileged to retain seven hectares that have scarcely changed since the inception of the house, divided into 27 parcels of exclusively south-facing vines. Old vines provide depth and structure, blended with young vines for freshness and vivacity. A wide spread of sites across the full breadth of the village creates complexity. 'Some respond better in particular seasons, so we can pick what we want in each vintage,' explains Cheval-Gatinois, who knows his vineyards so well that he can recognise each plot purely on the appearance of the grapes when they arrive at the press house.

Pinot noir comprises some 90% of plantings, with a little less than one hectare of chardonnay to add fresh-ness and endurance to pinot's fleshy structure and aromatic intensity. Fruit is green harvested if appropriate to give low harvests of 65hL/hectare, yielding an annual production of just 50,000 bottles. Less than 10% of the harvest is sold to a few houses, including Bollinger. Low yields enable Gatinois to pick at high maturity, bringing colour and intensity to its champagnes.

The house employs its own team of pickers, who are instructed to be very selective and, importantly, are paid by the hour and not by the kilogram. Every bad grape is sorted from each basket that is brought to the press.

'The quality of the grapes is the thing that makes our champagnes,' Cheval-Gatinois declares. 'The secret to the colour and style of our champagnes is what we put in our press. My father taught me to be proud of what is in the press before we close it, to be able to pick any grape and have the very best quality.'

Vinification is meticulously hands-on, shared between just three workers in the vineyards and cellars. The house still maintains its manual press. 'People are surprised to see me working with a traditional press, but this is important to ensure that we do not lose any quality,' he explains. 'We have a very humble vinification as we do not want to have too much impact on the taste.' Vinification takes place entirely in stainless steel tanks, to preserve purity of grape aromas. 'I produce wines more in an oxidative than a reductive style as I like generous champagnes, but with the freshness imparted by the acidity of Aÿ.' The only barrels in the house are for red wines, and these are very old, so as to produce gentle oxidation without imparting wood characters.

For Gatinois, debourbage (settling of juice prior to fermentation) is important for purity and elegance. All cuvées undergo full malolactic fermentation and receive low dosages of around 6g/L. Zero-dosage champagne is not the aim here, as 'dosage is important to produce smoothness and openness in the mouth without feeling the sweetness'. Blending is conducted slowly and carefully in May following the harvest, achieving very clear base wines by allowing plenty of time for natural settling prior to bottling. Bottles are matured in Gatinois' cellars under Aÿ, and all 50,000 are painstakingly hand disgorged on site every year. 'If it weren't for the history of the estate I wouldn't hand disgorge, but I watched my father and my grandfather do it, so I do the same!'

Since taking charge five years ago, Louis has no desire to change the style. 'With such rich history behind me, I have a great opportunity to continue the philosophy of the house.' Skilfully capturing the exact character and great concentration of Aÿ, this tiny estate remains in capable hands. Eleven generations would be proud.

GATINOIS AŸ GRAND CRU BRUT TRADITION NV $$

92 points • 2010 BASE VINTAGE WITH 30% RESERVES FROM 2009 & 2008
• DISGORGED OCTOBER 2013 • TASTED IN AŸ & BRISBANE
89 points • 2009 BASE VINTAGE • TASTED IN SYDNEY & MELBOURNE
94 points • 2008 BASE VINTAGE • TASTED IN MELBOURNE

80% pinot noir, 20% chardonnay; part of the finished blend kept as reserve for the next year; full malolactic fermentation; 6g/L dosage

Full straw hue with a blush tint, expressing the magnificent depth of character and concentration of Aÿ pinot noir. The 2010 base vintage presents excellent tension between the definition and the volume of Aÿ, with tight lemon and grapefruit zest contrasting the presence of white cherry and strawberry hull, energised by racy acidity and underlined by prominent, fine, salty chalk mineral texture. Woodspice note, a dry firmness and bitter phenolic grip to the finish reflect a lesser season, yet it upholds good persistence and fruit presence. The 2009 base has dipped from its high point on release, looking a little oxidised after a couple of years in the market. The 2008, by comparison, still retains all the energy of this brilliant season.

The majestic, south-facing slopes of Aÿ in the historic centre of Champagne produce pinot noir of intensity and mineral definition.

GATINOIS AŸ GRAND CRU BRUT RÉSERVE NV $$

93 points • 2009 BASE VINTAGE • TASTED IN AŸ

20-30% reserves from 2007 and 2008

Made in the same manner and from similar parcels as Brut Tradition, and aged on lees for another year, this is purposely a more generous style that Cheval-Gatinois describes as more textural, more velvety and a more comfortable winter cuvée. It trumpets the magnificence of Aŷ in a deep hue of full straw with a blush tint, and expressive red cherry and strawberry fruit, charged with lively acidity and excellent, fine, salty chalk mineral texture. Some savoury dryness grips the finish but it maintains good length and well-integrated dosage.

GATINOIS AŸ GRAND CRU BRUT ROSÉ NV $$

94 points • 2010 BASE VINTAGE WITH 2009 RED WINE • TASTED IN AŸ
92 points • 2009 BASE VINTAGE • TASTED IN SYDNEY & MELBOURNE

Rosé is Cheval-Gatinois' favourite cuvée and he describes the aroma in the skins of the red wine of 2009 as if it was made from half cherries and half grapes. Rosé is well at home in the tension between the elegant style of Gatinois and the authority of Aŷ and even the difficult 2010 season has done nothing to thwart its harmony and poise. Pretty cherry, strawberry and tamarillo fruit is backed by beautifully fine, firm chalk mineral structure and a long, taut and dry finish of lingering fruit purity. The 2009 base has dipped a fraction from its high point after two years in the market, now a medium salmon copper hue, with spicy and biscuity complexity underscoring its red cherry and strawberry fruit, upholding poise and mineral definition.

GATINOIS AŸ GRAND CRU BRUT MILLÉSIMÉ 2008 $$

96 points • TASTED IN AŸ

85% pinot noir, 15% chardonnay; aged 4 years on lees

Cheval-Gatinois' aspiration is to produce champagnes particular to Aŷ and to the season, blending parcels from the middle of the slope that best encapsulate this balance for the vintage. He asserts 2008 is 'definitively an Aŷ vintage, perhaps the best example of what I aspire to produce: wine which is elegant, precise and very long, with every note well defined.' All the radiant splendour of Aŷ is delivered with the vigour of this classic season, a wine of exacting purity and precision. Delicate white cherry fruit glitters with the brilliance of ultra-fine Aŷ chalk mineral texture; a cuvée of unerring purity, bursting with energy and tension, yet impeccably silky in its seamless harmony. It will not be until at least 2018 that it really comes into its own, and it will then hold for at least another decade.

GATINOIS AŸ GRAND CRU BRUT MILLÉSIME 2006 $$

93 points • TASTED IN SYDNEY & MELBOURNE

85% pinot noir, 15% chardonnay; aged on lees a little under 5 years; 6g/L dosage; 5000 bottles

The generous yet focused 2006 has only recently begun to shed its full magnificence, still proclaiming its plethora of red cherry, red apple and strawberry fruit layers, slowly subsumed by the toasty gingernut biscuit complexity of maturity. A fine chalk mineral backbone sustains a long and intense finish.

GEOFFROY

(Zhof-wah)

6/10

4 RUE JEANSON 51160 AŸ

www.champagne-geoffroy.com

CHAMPAGNE
GEOFFROY

'*I am a winegrower,' says young, fifth-generation vigneron Jean-Baptiste Geoffroy. 'I need to be in the vineyard, this is my passion.' There is a well-considered sensibility about Geoffroy, and every detail of his work in the vineyard and winery follows a stringent regime, while maintaining practical common sense. With 11 glorious hectares in Cumières, and one in each of the nearby villages of Damery, Hautvillers and two in Fleury-la-Rivière, he is well placed to capture the fruit purity, poise and deep mineral fingerprint of some of the finer premier crus of the Vallée de la Marne. The sustaining presence of malic acidity makes his champagnes particularly long-lived.*

The finest grower in Cumières is no longer in Cumières. With winemaking facilities and cellars shared between his grandmother's house, his father's house and a neighbour, when the opportunity came to consolidate in 2008, Jean-Baptiste Geoffroy moved the whole operation 20 minutes (by tractor) down the road to a proud and spacious facility in Aÿ.

'Nothing has changed in the vineyards,' asserts Jean-Baptiste. 'I want to create a champagne of terroir, to achieve the best expression of the soil in the grapes.' To this end, his highest goal in the winery is to maintain freshness in every cuvée. This proved to be a challenge, working from three sites in Cumières, necessitating regular pumping and moving of bottles.

Now he can guarantee that his grapes are on the press less than an hour after they are harvested, in a facility ingeniously designed to do away with pumping altogether. Taking advantage of the hill behind, the harvest is delivered to the press on the third level of the building, and the juice flows by gravity to settling

tanks immediately below the press on the second level, then to fermentation on the first level, and finally to two levels of deep maturation cellars below. In 2012 he purchased a further 500 square metres of storage space in the village, not to increase production, but to relocate bottles to provide space to move his barrels deeper into the cellar, where the temperature is more stable.

Every step of production is geared towards maintaining freshness and vineyard character, which Geoffroy achieves with admirable consistency, even with low use of sulphur dioxide as a preservative. A traditional press is employed, which he admits is difficult to operate by hand, but worth every effort for quality. Each of 45 different parcels is pressed and vinified separately, and the tailles of each pressing separated and vinified independently.

Fermentation is conducted variously in the best vessels to facilitate controlled oxidation, generally small tanks for non-vintage wines, and small barrels and large foudres for vintage wines and the best pinot noir parcels, and Geoffroy has recently shown a preference for 350-litre barrels. Previously using only older barrels, he has recently introduced a turnover of younger barrels, purchased from Colin-Morey in Chassagne-Montrachet, though oak flavours and tannins can at times conflict with the elegance of his fruit.

Ferments rely on wild yeast, but are inoculated if they don't start naturally. To further preserve freshness, malolactic fermentation is avoided (but will occasionally start spontaneously). Only concentrated grape juice is used for dosage, because he says he couldn't find a good balance using sugar. 'This emphasises the taste of the grapes and the character of the soil,' he says.

Geoffroy generally uses extra brut dosages of less than 5g/L. As he puts it, 'A champagne must always be very fine, elegant and fresh. If you have good ripeness and good practice in the winery you don't need dosage.'

Ripeness is achieved through painstaking attention to every detail in the vineyard. Geoffroy's annual production of 130,000 bottles is sourced exclusively from his own vines, apart from 5% permitted under récoltant-manipulant registration. Pinot rules in this part of the world, and his holdings comprise 40% pinot noir and 40% meunier and 20% chardonnay.

EARTH-FRIENDLY APPROACH

His eco-friendly approach is close to organic, but falls purposely short of the constraints of certification. 'I like to say I am biological, without being biodynamic,' he says. To best express the soil in the grapes, vineyards are ploughed to discourage surface roots and drive the vines deeper into the subsoils. To the same end, several species of natural grasses are cultivated in the mid-rows to provide surface competition. He is currently introducing a horse to plough one vineyard in an attempt to reduce tractor compaction. Organic fertilisers encour-

Jean-Baptiste Geoffroy pumps over a red wine ferment.

age soil health, and herbicides are avoided. Sulphur and copper sulphate sprays are used where possible, but here he sometimes deviates from a strict organic regime, calling on other chemicals as required.

Geoffroy knows each of his 45 plots intimately, and treats each separately, regarding them variously as grand cru, premier cru or unclassified. The blanket classification of Cumières as premier cru makes no sense to him. 'On the poor soil and sand at the top of the hill near the forest, it is inferior to Damery, which is unclassified,' he clarifies. 'The early-ripening middle slope of the south-facing amphitheatre of Cumières north of the city is of grand cru quality, and to the west it is premier cru.' He points out each on a satellite photo, and his designations correspond precisely with green patches that betray the most vigorous vines. There is a natural regulation of vigour in Geoffroy's vines, with old vines and mid-row grasses limiting yields, ensuring earlier ripeness.

COTEAUX CHAMPENOIS RED WINES

This approach allows him to produce one of the most celebrated Coteaux Champenois still red wines, a passion he inherited from his father and grandfather. 'I make a red wine from the best grapes of my terroir, from the oldest vines and the lowest yields,' he says.

After experimenting extensively with red wine production in Beaujolais and Burgundy, Geoffroy produces red wine only in warmer vintages from Cumières pinot noir (meunier for the first time in 2008), releasing it as both a non-vintage and a vintage cuvée. The wines undergo malolactic fermentation and mature in 600-litre demi-muids for at least 12 months. These are long-ageing wines, with the potential to live for decades, and are only released when he deems them ready. Production is small and sporadic. 'It's good to make Coteaux Champenois when you don't need to!' he says. 'You can't make it to demand or in every vintage.'

In 2012, Geoffroy simplified the name of the estate from 'René Geoffroy' to 'Geoffroy' and introduced a new label, depicting the gate of the house in Aÿ to represent his new identity. 'It is not my philosophy to put my first name on the label, as I hope to one day pass the estate on to my children. There is no point changing the name with every generation,' he says.

Vintages, varieties, dosage and date of disgorgement are now displayed on the back of every label, a laudable commitment for a small grower who disgorges every 2–3 months and tweaks the dosage for each disgorgement.

With undeviating attention to well-situated vineyards, an enviable production facility larger than his needs — and no intention to grow production — Cumières' finest grower is as fine as ever.

The Champagne Guide

GEOFFROY EXPRESSION BRUT PREMIER CRU NV $$

93 points • 2010 BASE VINTAGE WITH 2009 RESERVES • DISGORGED MAY 2014
• TASTED IN AŸ

50% meunier, 40% pinot noir, 10% chardonnay from Cumières and a little from Hautvillers; tank fermented; no malolactic fermentation; 5g/L dosage; 50% of production volume, ~65,000 bottles

Even in the difficult 2010 season, this cuvée confidently meets its brief of easy drinking freshness. The rich fig and red apple fruits of Cumières meunier create a compelling contrast with crisp malic acidity and tight grapefruit and lemon zest notes. Three years on lees makes for generous maturity for an entry cuvée, reinforcing honey and fruit cake spice and a creamy texture.

GEOFFROY PURETÉ BRUT NATURE NV $$

91 points • 2009 BASE VINTAGE WITH 2008 RESERVES • DISGORGED JUNE 2014
• TASTED IN AŸ

50% meunier, 40% pinot noir, 10% chardonnay from Cumières and a little from Hautvillers; no dosage

Pureté is Expression with another year on lees and no dosage. Full malic acidity and no added sugar makes for a tense and steely champagne with accentuated salt minerality. Clean, precise, taut, young and high-strung, this is an oyster-ready style driven by crunchy acidity and lemon zest that will appreciate some years to soften and relax. In the meantime, it's strictly for champagne diehards.

GEOFFROY EMPREINTE BRUT PREMIER CRU 2008 $$

94 points • DISGORGED JUNE 2014 • TASTED IN AŸ

78% pinot noir, 16% meunier, 6% chardonnay; 76% fermented in tanks, 24% in large oak foudres; 6g/L dosage

Geoffroy is refining his style with each vintage, and responded to the elegant 2008 season sensitively with less oak and less dosage. The result captures his aspiration to portray the best expression of Cumières pinot noir, with pretty red berry and red apple fruits becoming subtle butterscotch, gingernut biscuits, brioche and spice. A crunchy, focused finish celebrates the vivacity and tension of malic acidity. Minerality is soft but supportive, true to Cumières, finishing generous and lively, promising medium-term potential.

GEOFFROY BRUT PREMIER CRU VOLUPTÉ 2007 $$$

92 points • DISGORGED DECEMBER 2013 • TASTED IN AŸ

80% Cumières chardonnay, 10% pinot noir, 10% meunier; 45% vinified in barrels and vats; 2g/L dosage

Low dosage and a full serve of malic acidity in a chardonnay-focused style make for a tense and steely champagne of impressive stature, which should be reserved for champagne aficionados. A high-strung lemon zest core is filled out with impressive complexity of fig, mixed spice and ginger cake, finishing long and dry, with firm minerality and prominent acidity. It's beautifully focused and just needs time to soften and calm down.

GEOFFROY ROSÉ DE SAIGNÉE PREMIER CRU BRUT NV $$

94 points • 2009 BASE VINTAGE • DISGORGED JUNE 2012 • TASTED IN AŸ

100% pinot noir; 100% 2009, but released too young to be labelled as such; saignée of 100% skin-contact pinot noir; 10g/L dosage

Renowned for his long-lived Cumières rouge Coteaux Champenois, it's no surprise that Geoffroy's Rosé de Saignée also improves with time post-disgorgement, and even two years after release it's showing compelling primary freshness of pomegranate, red cherry, pink pepper and mixed spice. The hue is still a full, vibrant pomegranate, the bead very fine, structure softly mineral and the finish persistent.

GEOFFROY BLANC DE ROSÉ EXTRA BRUT NV $$$$

89 points • 100% 2011 • DISGORGED SEPTEMBER 2013 • 3G/L DOSAGE
• TASTED IN AŸ
95 points • 100% 2009 • DISGORGED DECEMBER 2011 • 1G/L DOSAGE • TASTED IN AŸ

50% pinot noir, 50% chardonnay macerated in a saignée method

When Geoffroy first conceived this cuvée it was intended to be released as a vintage, but he was captured by its floral fruitiness after 16 months in the cellar, and hence released it as a non-vintage, which was a mistake. I have never understood it in this guise, with its high-strung malic tension, simple fruit profile, short, dry finish and angular mouthfeel. To its credit, the 2011 is clean in its subtle expression of redcurrants, watermelon and pepper and its vibrant crimson pink hue. No surprise that this cuvée blossoms with time, and Geoffroy has held back 800 bottles to release as a vintage wine. The secret to the NV cuvée is to leave it in your cellar for at least five years, which may seem counterintuitive for a rosé disgorged young, but such is the sustaining power of malic acidity that it will blossom gloriously. The 2009 vintage is proof, and three years after disgorgement it sings with vivacious poise and elegant purity of red cherry and strawberry fruit, riding a glorious wave of malic acidity.

GEOFFROY EXTRA BRUT MILLÉSIME 2005 $$$$

91 points • DISGORGED SEPTEMBER 2014 • TASTED IN AŸ

Geoffroy's vintage wine is a blend of the best barrels, hence a dramatically different blend every year – here 53% chardonnay, 30% pinot noir and 17% meunier; totally vinified in barrels; no chaptalisation, no added yeast, no malolactic fermentation, no fining or filtering; aged under cork; 4g/L dosage; 6095 bottles

This is a cuvée that appreciates a large glass to open up. Full oak fermentation dominates, contributing savoury and spicy characters of curry, turmeric and Tabasco, rounding crunchy malic acidity and soothing the firm phenolic grip inherent in the 2005 harvest. It finishes long and silky.

The Champagne Guide

GEOFFROY EXTRA BRUT MILLÉSIME 2004 $$$$

90 points • DISGORGED MAY 2014 • TASTED IN AŸ

71% chardonnay, 29% pinot noir; 2g/L dosage; 6096 bottles; otherwise as per 2005 vintage notes

The dominance of new oak in this vintage has always bothered me, with toasty, smoky barrel characters and firm structure quashing ripe fruit notes reminiscent of fruit cake. An additional two years on lees since its release has helped it to integrate, but it cries out for at least another few years for acidity to soften and oak to integrate. It remains to be seen whether it will ever emerge from the forest.

GEOFFROY EXTRA BRUT MILLÉSIME 2002 $$$$

95 points • DISGORGED JANUARY 2014 • TASTED IN AŸ

60% pinot noir, 35% chardonnay, 5% meunier; 4g/L dosage; 3810 bottles; otherwise as per 2005 vintage notes

A grand vintage for Geoffroy, basking in the glory of another few years on lees since I last tasted it, arriving in a happy place for re-release in 2015, with the malic drive to live more than a decade yet. This is a champagne of expansive presence and focused elegance, tapping deep into chalk minerality, while sustaining wonderfully youthful lemon and white peach fruit, evolving to great complexity of mocha, exotic spice, fig and vanilla.

GEOFFROY EXTRA BRUT MILLÉSIME 2000 $$$$

92 points • DISGORGED JANUARY 2014 • TASTED IN AŸ

70% chardonnay, 30% pinot noir; 4g/L dosage; 5565 bottles; otherwise as per 2005 vintage notes

Projecting the yellow-fruited richness of the season, this is a cuvée that basks in the glory of locuts, figs, golden delicious apples, pears and lemon zest, filled out with the mixed spice of bottle age and the biscuity complexity of barrel fermentation, controlled by strict malic acidity and nicely balanced phenolic mouthfeel. Even this generous vintage needs more time still for its malic acid to soften. This bottle was slightly let down by a faint dustiness, probably tainted by one of its two corks.

GEOFFROY EXTRA BRUT MILLÉSIME 1999 $$$$

94 points • DISGORGED JANUARY 2014 • TASTED IN AŸ

50% pinot noir, 50% chardonnay; 4g/L dosage; 4000 bottles; otherwise as per 2005 vintage notes

Grand testimony to the magical, sustaining endurance of malic acidity and the age worthiness of Geoffroy's champagnes, even the warm 1999 season screams for more time for its tense malic acidity to soften. There's an enticingly fresh raspberry fruit personality to this vintage, backed by intense fruit mince spice, plum pudding and honey, finishing with drive and persistence.

GEORGES LAVAL

(Zhor-zheh Lah-vahl)

6 RUELLE DU CARREFOUR F-51480 CUMIÈRES
www.georgeslaval.com

'*I have a Burgundy vision of champagne,' declares Vincent Laval. 'I want to taste grapes in the glass.
First I make wine, then I make champagne.' His business card simply says 'Vigneron', and here, as
in Burgundy, it's all about the vineyards. The tiny 2.5-hectare estate on the slopes of Cumières was one of the first
seven in Champagne to be tended organically in 1971, and is now fully certified. The pure expression of its fruit
is maintained by religious avoidance of chaptalisation (radical for Champagne), and grapes are harvested at full
maturity with a high 11 degrees potential alcohol. 'Even if the potential is not high, we don't add sugar to increase
the alcohol,' he says. 'We don't make wine to get drunk, but to enjoy as a drink.'*

There is no sign above the door to Laval's tiny premises on Ruelle du Carrefour in Cumières, a reflection of the minute scale of this grower, with a total production of less than 10,000 bottles annually.

This allows Vincent and his father Georges, who still helps out, to do everything by hand. A horse ploughs almost half the vineyard, with hopes to encompass the full estate. By reducing soil compaction, and by using natural composts and avoiding pesticides and herbicides for more than 30 years, they have established vineyards with very deep root systems, drawing on the salty minerality of the Cumières chalk.

A dramatic display on their cellar wall bears stark testimony to this: two vines, one with deep, strong roots plunging vertically downward; the other with just a thin web of surface roots. The first was planted by Vincent's grandfather in an organic vineyard, and the second at a similar time on the same soils in a neighbour's vineyard,

managed using traditional viticulture. When the family purchased the neighbour's vineyard, they ripped it up and replanted. 'We are lucky to be on chalk, and we must taste the chalk in our wines,' Laval declares.

His philosophy is to consider his wines in the same spirit as white Burgundy, an accurate comparison for his generous champagne style, and the same hands-on, low-intervention approach follows through every stage of production. No chaptalisation, natural fermentation and no fining or filtering mean the only addition is sulphur as a preservative, and this only in very small amounts at the press. In a troubling trend, he is progressively lowering sulphur, with just 10mg/L added (half the level of five years ago), no additions after the press, and sometimes none at the press, either. 'After the wine is finished, it is rich and can defend itself against oxidation, so it doesn't need more sulphur at bottling,' he believes. Unfortunately, a number of his current cuvées are evidence to the contrary, destroyed by premature oxidation, even in freshly disgorged bottles in his cellar.

There is no dosage in any cuvée, except the entry Premier Cru Brut, with a tiny 4g/L. Every wine is fermented slowly in barrels of three to 15 years of age, which he buys from Chassagne-Montrachet in Burgundy. Malolactic fermentation occurs naturally, and wines remain on lees in barrel, tasted regularly until he deems them ready to be bottled. Riddling is performed by hand.

Half the estate vines are now aged over 30 years, and some date from 1966, 1946 and 1931, planted to 40% chardonnay, 40% pinot noir and 20% meunier. These are very old vines for a region that typically replants every 30–35 years, and yield a minuscule 23–30 hL/hectare — less than one-third of Champagne's average. 'If a plot produces good fruit even with low yields, it is fine for me,' he says. 'Champagnes of low yield are completely different, giving more character, more concentration and more expression of the soil.'

The tiny scale of the vineyard means Laval needs to purchase from friends, keeping organic fruit and selling the rest. He currently cannot meet demand, selling out every year. He expects to have sufficient fruit to grow production by 8000 bottles, and is rapidly expanding his cramped premises to accommodate. The house and cellar next door were acquired in 2009, a cellar dug and another neighbouring property purchased in 2013, and in 2015 another house in the village was acquired for its cellar for ageing bottles. This expansion will facilitate longer ageing, by more than doubling the area of the cellar. 'Not difficult, because it's so small!' he grins.

Laval's Brut non-vintage is blended from three vintages of reserve wines kept in barrel on lees. Before the new vintage is fermented, parcels from the same vines are added to the reserves in barrel for fermentation, in something of a modified solera system. This unusual practice increases the complexity of the wine, while long barrel ageing on lees instils deep texture and wood spice notes. Laval favours younger vine fruit for reserves, for its higher acidity and greater ageing capacity.

When Laval's cuvées don't succumb to premature oxidation they can age long, and even his non-vintage benefits from some years in the cellar. Impressively informative back labels declare vintages, blends, disgorgement dates and dosage levels.

Sensibly, Laval's non-vintage philosophy is to make the best wine he can every year, rather than attempting to maintain a consistent style. For a producer as small as this, with a blending palette constrained to but one village, vintage fluctuations are invariably dramatic. His vintage philosophy is daring, perhaps too daring, in producing single-vineyard vintage cuvées of just one variety, which does not bode well in weaker seasons like '05, '06 and '07. But in great vintages, his wines shine.

With well-situated vineyards and painstaking attention to detail, this is an estate whose pedigree exceeds its minute size. 'I don't produce champagne to make money, but to make taste,' Laval sums up. 'It is my life.'

GEORGES LAVAL LES CHENES CUMIÈRES PREMIER CRU BRUT NATURE
2010 $$$$

93 points • DISGORGED JANUARY 2015 • TASTED IN CUMIÈRES

100% chardonnay, harvested at more than 11 degrees potential alcohol; 880 bottles

2010 was a harvest of good maturity for Laval, reflected in ripe honeydew notes in the wine. It upholds purity and freshness in clean, well-focused apple and pear fruit, propelled by finely textured, softly structured chalk minerality, well-defined acid line and impressive persistence. It will age.

GEORGES LAVAL LES CHENES CUMIÈRES PREMIER CRU BRUT NATURE
2009 $$$$

89 points • DISGORGED APRIL 2014 • TASTED IN CUMIÈRES

It leads out promisingly, with fine chalk minerality and fig, citrus and quince fruit, and maturity contributing toast, brioche, mixed spice and sugared almonds. It deteriorates into burnt-orange oxidative development, which renders the finish a little dry and tired.

GEORGES LAVAL CUMIÈRES PREMIER CRU BRUT NATURE NV $$

87 points • 2012 BASE VINTAGE • DISGORGED JANUARY 2015 • ONE-THIRD EACH
PINOT NOIR, MEUNIER & CHARDONNAY; 30% RESERVES OF PINOT NOIR
• TASTED IN CUMIÈRES
91 points • 100% 2009 • DISGORGED OCTOBER 2012 • 50% CHARDONNAY,
30% PINOT NOIR, 20% MEUNIER • TASTED IN CUMIÈRES
88 points • 100% 2006 • DISGORGED FEBRUARY 2015

The 2012 base is plagued by oxidative characters of vinegar, gherkins, curry powder and freshly tilled earth, dominating taut lemon freshness and fine chalk minerality. An unfortunate victim of a low sulphur regime. Laval used a little more sulphur in 2009, and it now shows the biscuity, honeyed, ginger notes of its warm season. The palate is dry, savoury and taut, with notes of bruised pear and chalk mineral texture lingering on a long finish. A little dosage would help this tense style. The 2006 vintage is smoky, dry and tense, with great persistence, though a coarse, dusty finish and notes of burnt orange point to premature oxidation.

GEORGES LAVAL LES HAUTES CHEVRES BRUT NATURE 2009 $$$$$

94 points • DISGORGED APRIL 2014 • TASTED IN CUMIÈRES
Old-vine pinot noir planted 1931 and harvested at 11.5 degrees potential alcohol

A beautifully elegant and chalk-textured blanc de noirs that captures the spirit of Cumières in impressive primary freshness of red apples, figs and grapefruit, accented with layers of mixed spice. Fine-ground chalk mineral texture meshes seamlessly with the soft, creamy texture of barrel fermentation, finishing long and refined. Laval added twice the sulphur dioxide in 2009 that he does today, and this wine is all the better for it.

GEORGES LAVAL LES HAUTES CHEVRES BRUT NATURE 2012 $$$$$

89 points • DISGORGED FEBRUARY 2015 • TASTED IN CUMIÈRES
100% pinot meunier planted between 1930 (mainly) and 1971, harvested at 11.5 degrees potential alcohol

This cuvée is not due for release until 2017, but on the day it was disgorged in Laval's cellar it already showed the telltale vinegar, gherkin and dust notes and dry, coarse mouthfeel of oxidation. The juice received just half the sulphur dioxide of 2009, clearly insufficient here. Some pretty strawberry and red cherry fruit has survived amidst levels of salt minerality impressive for meunier.

GEORGES LAVAL MEUNIER DE LA BUTTE BRUT NATURE 2006 $$$$$

93 points • DISGORGED MAY 2009 • TASTED IN CUMIÈRES
100% meunier from lieu-dit Les Chenes La Butte, planted in 1930 and 1946 in just 20cm of soil over chalk

Such is the intensity and complexity here that it holds a little oxidation confidently, rich with all manner of strawberries, baked peach, burnt toffee, crème caramel, coffee and chocolate mousse — an entire dessert buffet in a glass — yet, as always for Laval, finishing dry and focused with great length and fine chalk minerality.

GODMÉ PÈRE ET FILS

(Gurd-may Pear e Feess)

6/10

10 RUE DE VERZY 51350 VERZENAY

www.champagne-godme.fr

Pinot noir rules the northern slopes of the Montagne de Reims, and it's unusual for chardonnay to account for half a grower's plantings. The Godmé family has tended its vines in the majestic grand cru of Verzenay on the northern slopes of the Montagne de Reims for five generations, bottling estate champagnes since as early as 1930. Today, 100,000 bottles are produced each year from 12 hectares, widely spread across 84 parcels spanning five villages. An impressive four hectares of chardonnay in Villers-Marmery is responsible for blanc de blancs cuvées that outshine even Godmé's blanc de noirs.

Viticulture is the firm focus for Hugues Godmé, the fifth generation to tend his family's vines in Verzenay. When I visited, he was in the vineyards, where he spends much of his time.

'Organics takes time!' he grins, having maintained an organic approach since 2005, with full certification granted in 2013. His aspiration is to use organics to encourage deep roots that draw the minerality and salinity from the soil.

Insecticides and herbicides are avoided, organic treatments and composted manure are embraced, and mid-rows are ploughed and planted to cover crops, encouraging deeper roots. The result has been later ripening, producing wines that retain greater acidity at the same level of ripeness.

Parcels are kept separate and fermented by wild yeast largely in enamelled steel tanks, with an increasing proportion in oak barrels. Single vineyard cuvées are fermented and aged for one year in barrels.

As the climate continues to warm in Champagne, malolactic fermentation is blocked in an increasing number of parcels, including all reserve wines. Godmé's blends finish between zero and 60% malolactic fermentation, maintaining freshness and focus.

Godmé maintains 400,000 bottles in its cellar, an impressive four times its annual production, reflective of long lees ageing for all of its cuvées. Non-vintage blends also receive generous proportions of reserve wines of between 40% and 70%.

Concentrated grape must is used for dosage, retaining purity and clarity, the finishing touch to carefully balance cuvées that sensitively reflect the fine salt mineral texture of Verzenay, the greatest of all the terroirs of the northern Montagne de Reims.

GODMÉ PÈRE & FILS INTÉGRAL PREMIER CRU EXTRA BRUT NV $$

92 points • 2007 BASE VINTAGE • TASTED IN VERZENAY

50% chardonnay, 30% meunier, 20% pinot noir; 40% reserves from 2006, 2005 and 2004; 20% barrel fermented; 50% malolactic fermentation; zero dosage

The focused restraint of chardonnay and malic acidity are heightened by the absence of dosage, a difficult recipe in Champagne, yet Godmé pulls it off with beautiful balance, thanks to the generosity of Verzenay. Succulent peach and fig fruit lingers with purity and persistence.

GODMÉ PÈRE & FILS PREMIER CRU BRUT RESERVE NV $$

93 points • 2010 BASE VINTAGE • TASTED IN VERZENAY

60% chardonnay, 30% meunier, 10% pinot noir; 60% reserves, half from 2009, the remainder 2008 and 2007; 20% fermented in barrels; 55% malolactic fermentation; 7g/L dosage

Characterful and well crafted, this is a cuvée that finds a harmonious balance between the tension of chardonnay with malic acidity and the richness of deep and generous reserves. All the fanfare of figs, mixed spice, Christmas cake and citrus rind pull into a finish of well-focused acidity and finely textured salt minerality.

GODMÉ PÈRE & FILS BLANC DE BLANCS NV $$

92 points • 2010 BASE VINTAGE • 65% RESERVES OF 25% 2008, AND 40% 2007 & 2006
• TASTED IN VERZENAY
94 points • 2009 BASE • TASTED IN MELBOURNE

60% barrel fermented; 60% malolactic fermentation, 7g/L dosage

The 2010 base doesn't carry quite the crystalline grace of last year's blend, but it is a blanc de blancs of excellent integration and immediate appeal. A large proportion of Villers-Marmery makes for a style of ripe yellow summer fruit and fig generosity and subtle fruit sweetness. Generous reserves and barrel fermentation build layers of nutmeg and mixed spice.

GODMÉ PÈRE & FILS BLANC DE NOIRS GRAND CRU BRUT NV $$

91 points • 2008 BASE VINTAGE • TASTED IN VERZENAY, SYDNEY & MELBOURNE

100% pinot noir; 40% reserves from 2007, 2006, 2005 and 2004; 50% barrel fermented; 50% malolactic fermentation; 6g/L dosage

The power of Verzenay pinot noir is paraded in flamboyant, persistent red fruits and excellent anise flavours. It's a characterful and slightly rustic style of chewy, dry, fine-grained phenolic structure, underlined with salty minerality on a long finish. A bottle tasted in Australia was dried out and contracted.

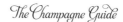
The Champagne Guide

GODMÉ PÈRE & FILS GRAND CRU EXTRA BRUT NV $$

91 points • 2009 BASE VINTAGE • TASTED IN VERZENAY

70% reserves of 20% 2008, 20% 2007 and 30% 2006, 2005 and 2004; 80% barrel fermented; 30% malolactic fermentation; 4g/L dosage

A blend of old vines between 60 and 80 years of age, this is a cuvée that resonates with the deep, salt-infused mineral texture of Verzenay. For such a strong predominance of reserves, it upholds surprising primary freshness of white peach and lemon zest purity. The palate is textural, with fine phenolic grip, good acid focus, a creamy bead and taut, bone-dry finish.

GODMÉ PÈRE & FILS LES ALOUETTES PREMIER CRU 2006 $$$$

95 points • 2006 VINTAGE • TASTED IN VERZENAY
92 points • 2005 VINTAGE • TASTED IN MELBOURNE

100% chardonnay; 100% barrel fermented, no malolactic fermentation; 3g/L dosage

From a single, tiny half-hectare plot in Villers-Marmery, the inaugural 2004 vintage was my favourite Godmé cuvée of its time, and the 2006 has staged a rousing repeat performance. It's a blanc de blancs of impressively controlled confidence, generous but not intense, full but not powerful. Juicy white peaches and succulent fresh figs are softened and caressed by barrel fermentation to build impressive presence of roast nuts, golden fruit cake and honey and a creamy generosity and silky, buttery mouthfeel that transcend the presence of malic acidity. A long finish simmers gently with the salty mineral depth of Villers-Marmery.

GODMÉ PÈRE & FILS ROMAINES PREMIER CRU 2006 $$$$

94 points • TASTED IN VERZENAY

100% meunier; 100% barrel fermented; no malolactic fermentation; 2g/L dosage

The second release from this single, tiny half-hectare plot in Ville-Dommange presents a wonderfully focused style of poised minerality, drawing tension and structure unusual for meunier. Even at this age, it maintains characterful fruit focus of crunchy red berry fruits, soft yellow mirabelle plums, taut lemon zest and mixed spice, finishing long, balanced and poised.

GODMÉ PÈRE & FILS ST MARTIN GRAND CRU 2006 $$$$

93 points • TASTED IN VERZENAY

100% pinot noir; 100% barrel fermented; no malolactic fermentation; 2g/L dosage

The second vintage release from this single-hectare plot in Ville-Dommange is loaded with all the generosity of white peach, fig, white Christmas cake and exotic spice, a merry parade pulled neatly into line by taut malic acidity and firm textural structure. It concludes just a touch dried out and oxidised, yet maintains good length and drive.

GOSSET

(Goh-say)

8/10

3 RUE DE MALAKOFF 51200 ÉPERNAY
www.champagne-gosset.com

stablished in 1584, centuries before the bubble was ever put into champagne, Gosset rightfully claims to be the oldest wine house in the region. Far from a staid, traditional establishment, Gosset is on the move, having relocated its production to the impressive Épernay cuverie and cellars of Château Malakoff, purchased from Laurent Perrier just in time for vintage 2009. In the midst of change, the house maintains an unwavering consistency, thanks largely to one man, Jean-Pierre Mareigner, its talented chef de cave of 32 years. Under his direction, the house style of no malolactic fermentation, clean-cut structure and enduring longevity remains as fine as ever, with the exception of its Brut Excellence NV entry wine, which seems a strange misfit, in both philosophy and quality.

Previously operating from five different locations, Gosset is now basking in the opportunity to grow into the huge cuverie of Château Malakoff, with a capacity of 2.6 million litres, far exceeding the requirement for an annual production of 1.1 million bottles.

The substantial premises, constructed in 1860 on two hectares of parkland next door to Pol Roger, came fully equipped with vinification facilities and disgorgement and labelling lines. Its 1.5 kilometres of deep cellars have a capacity for 2.5 million bottles, and house part of the stock of more than 4 million. The rest remain in Gosset's historic headquarters in Aÿ, where riddling and disgorgement are still conducted.

Gosset's roots in Mareigner's birth town of Aÿ remain strong in spite of the move and the company's tiny vineyard holdings. With just one hectare to

its name, Gosset purchases 99% of its fruit from 200 growers in 60 different villages, exclusively premier and grand cru in the Marne department.

The consistency of supply is a credit to Mareigner's long-term relationships with growers, some of whom have supplied Gosset for three generations. He knows them all so well that when they phone him they announce themselves by first name only. As evidence of its faith in these relationships, Gosset does not operate press houses in the villages, instead entrusting its growers to crush on its behalf.

Every village and grower is kept separate during vinification, which is performed in stainless steel tanks, temperature regulated to maintain ferments below 18°C. 'Our goal is to keep what nature has given us,' explains Mareigner. 'No centrifuge, no filtering until immediately before bottling, and no malolactic fermentation.'

The impressive freshness and remarkable ageing potential of malic acidity calls for long cellaring prior to release, and the great vintages of Gosset will live exceedingly long. Like Pol Roger next door, Gosset's deep cellars maintain a temperature below 11°C, drawing out the second ferment over six months to produce a very fine bead. A low dosage of 8g/L or less is used across the Grande range, and no more than 5g/L across the prestige Celebris trio, which accounts for a tiny 2% of the production of the house.

The beautifully poised Grande Réserve is on the rise, now representing more than 40% of production, pushing Brut Excellence down to just 30% (a tiny representation for an entry wine in the grand scale of champagne house production). This is just as well, because Brut Excellence is something of an ironic aberration in the excellence of the house, made using partial malolactic fermentation and a full dosage of 11g/L. Gosset would do well to drop this cuvée altogether and sell off the fruit, or at least downgrade it to a completely different brand, as Billecart does. For now, at least, there's quite a disparity between this bottle and and the rest of the portfolio, which is referred to by the house as the 'antique' range. It is here that Mareigner's masterful skill is showcased, evidenced perhaps most demonstrably in his exceptional ability to achieve texture, finesse and harmony without malolactic fermentation.

GOSSET BRUT EXCELLENCE NV $$

86 points • 2011 BASE VINTAGE • TASTED IN ÉPERNAY

45% pinot noir, 36% chardonnay, 19% meunier; 25% reserve wines; a blend of almost 50 villages; full malolactic fermentation; 10g/L dosage

The 2010 base made for a challenging Brut Excellence, but the difficult 2011 vintage has made for an even more disappointing rendition of this substandard cuvée, completely at odds with the rest of the Gosset range. It lacks precision, fruit expression and persistence, a dry, dusty, mushroomy style of tilled earth and potatoes.

GOSSET GRANDE RÉSERVE BRUT NV $$

94 points • 2010 BASE VINTAGE WITH RESERVES FROM 2009 AND 2008 • DISGORGED NOVEMBER 2014 • TASTED IN ÉPERNAY & MELBOURNE

Roughly 45% chardonnay, 40% pinot noir and 15% meunier; 15% reserves; no malolactic fermentation; 9g/L dosage; 40% of the production of the house

Grand Réserve is perpetually among the most reliable NVs on the shelves, and retains its full majesty even in the 2010 vintage. Mareigner admires the elegance and structure of this season and has captured both accurately in this blend. It's tightly coiled in its newly disgorged guise, with subtle reductive complexity of struck flint, toasted Parisian baguette and white pepper. Fresh lemon and pear fruit of elegant finesse meet subtle biscuity notes of bottle age, energised by long-lingering malic acidity and Gosset's signature of prominent, gently rolling, fine chalk mineral finesse. Impressive now, it will blossom in bottle as it builds flesh and secondary character.

GOSSET GRAND BLANC DE BLANCS BRUT NV $$$

95 points • 2010 BASE WITH 20% RESERVES FROM 2009 & 2008
• DISGORGED LATE 2013 • TASTED IN ÉPERNAY
96 points • 2008 BASE WITH 2007 RESERVES • TASTED IN ÉPERNAY

Two-thirds Côte des Blancs for freshness and finesse, one-third Montagne de Reims for body and structure; no malolactic fermentation; 9g/L dosage

Gosset's refined mineral style and thrilling malic acid vitality suit blanc de blancs precisely, and the new member of the Gosset family is only getting more refined. The 2010 base is an exactingly crafted apéritif style of refined pear and lemon zest, with layers of ground almond complexity. Lees age has been tactically deployed to create a lovely creamy texture without malolactic fermentation, while the generosity of the Montagne de Reims counters the need for high dosage. The tension of driving malic acidity and fine chalk minerality creates a seamless finish with the potential to hold its freshness for many years yet. The scintillating 2008 base exemplifies the capacity of this cuvée to elevate with time in bottle, attaining a lofty pinnacle of white citrus and white peach freshness, illuminated by crystal-clear minerality and brilliantly integrated malic acidity.

GOSSET GRAND ROSÉ BRUT NV $$$

96 points • 2010 BASE WITH 10% RESERVES FROM 2009 • DISGORGED SEPTEMBER 2013 • TASTED IN ÉPERNAY & MELBOURNE

60% chardonnay, 40% pinot noir; 8% pinot noir red wine from Ambonnay and Bouzy; no malolactic fermentation; 9g/L dosage; 130,000 bottles

With its confident chardonnay lead, low proportion of red wine and signature cut of malic acidity, the structure and elegant lightness of 2010 lends itself brilliantly to the delicate and graceful Gosset rosé style, transcending the woes of the season to produce one of the most ethereal Gosset rosés in recent memory. Airy rose petals, red cherries and pink grapefruit as light as the thinnest clouds glide over glittering crystals of chalk minerality, laced together with refined malic acidity and a superfine, creamy bead. Such is its exacting freshness that it looks freshly disgorged even at 18 months post-disgorgement, culminating in sublime elegance and haunting persistence.

GOSSET GRAND MILLÉSIME 2004 $$$

96 points • DISGORGED JANUARY 2014 • TASTED IN ÉPERNAY & MELBOURNE

55% chardonnay, 45% pinot noir; no malolactic fermentation; 8g/L dosage

Some champagnes keep returning year after year, like distant loved ones at rousing and treasured reunions. The large yields of 2004 have blessed Grand Millésime with an elongated release cycle. Gosset's splendid mandate of beautifully ripe fruit in tension with the electric zap of malic acidity is exemplified in this refined season, a wine of inherent internal harmony, grace, poise and superb balance. Ten years in bottle has heightened its creamy texture and its warm richness of plum liqueur, golden fruit cake, anise, ginger, nutmeg and roast nuts. It's at once exotically complex, yet taut and refined, clutching the elegant finesse of 2004 on a long, drawn-out finish of brilliant malic acidity, unswerving purity and the ever-present, ultra-fine texture of chalk minerality.

GOSSET CUVÉE CELEBRIS VINTAGE EXTRA BRUT 2002 $$$$

97 points • DISGORGED SEPTEMBER 2014 • TASTED IN ÉPERNAY

52% chardonnay, 48% pinot noir; from the grand crus of the Côte des Blancs and Aÿ, Bouzy, Ambonnay, Verzy and Verzenay; no malolactic fermentation; 5g/L dosage

Children of 2002, meet your 30th birthday present. As predicted before its release in September 2013, Celebris is evolving in slow motion, with the stamina to live for a lifetime. It takes the energy of 2002 and the depth of almost 12 years on lees and zaps it with a charge of malic acidity that jolts everything into a state of frenzy, slaying innocent, youthful white flowers, peaches, white cherries and golden delicious apples with an ice shard of acidity that screams out for years to soften. Pinot noir has arisen in bottle to a deep and beguiling stature of plum liqueur, black cherries, dark fruit cake and quince of grand concentration. A fine, chewy structure unites the texture of long lees age with the pronounced, mouth-filling salt minerality that bores to the core of Champagne's greatest grand crus.

GOSSET CUVÉE CELEBRIS ROSÉ EXTRA BRUT 2007 $$$$

97 points • DISGORGED SEPTEMBER 2013 • TASTED IN ÉPERNAY

59% chardonnay, 33.5% pinot noir, 7.5% pinot noir red wine from Ambonnay and Bouzy; no malolactic fermentation; 5g/L dosage

The most subtle rosés are the most enchanting, and Mareigner has conjured the epitome of elegance by seeking a small selection of what he calls the most 'shy' villages in the very fresh vintage of 2007. Even 18 months post-release, this is an introverted and structured wine that demanded an hour of focused observation for me to get my head around. And when it did finally unravel, a captivating spectacle appeared, at first a rosé more about structure, mouthfeel and restrained lightness, then wonderful depth of black cherries, strawberry hull, blood orange and mixed spice emerged, before finally hinting at its age in almonds and brioche. Its framework is a chewy structure and tannin presence so fine it's impossible to tell where tannins finish and pronounced grand cru salt minerality begins. Malic acidity sits surprisingly comfortably in the midst of this, drawing a tight finish out very long. Don't drink it now but if you must, give it plenty of time to wake up in the largest Burgundy glass you can conjure.

GOSSET CUVÉE CELEBRIS ROSÉ BRUT 1998 $$$$

98 points • TASTED IN ÉPERNAY

60-62% chardonnay, 38-40% pinot noir; 7.5% pinot noir red wine; no malolactic fermentation

The profound longevity of Gosset Rosé is epitomised in this grand expression of an outstanding season. At a glorious 17 years of age, the balance that it attains between breathtaking primary fruit, voluptuous secondary allure and ravishing tertiary character is flawless. A magnificent core of black cherry and blood orange fruit is orbited by dried fruits and strawberry jam in a cloud of the sweetest pipe smoke. Its years have only heightened its textural expression, amplifying its wonderfully creamy structure.

GUY CHARLEMAGNE

(Ghee Shar-le-mahn)

6/10

4 RUE DE LA BRÈCHE D'OGER 51190 LE MESNIL-SUR-OGER

www.champagne-guy-charlemagne.com

The Charlemagne family has made and sold its own champagnes since 1892, predating the house of Salon directly across the road in Le Mesnil-sur-Oger. The family is privileged to six glorious hectares of vines of average age 42 years in the village, one in neighbouring Oger and a little in Mancy and Cuis, yielding beautifully mineral chardonnay. This is a grower of two faces, with half its production of 130,000 bottles drawn from six hectares in the Sézanne and one in Glannes, producing more rustic blends of chardonnay and pinot noir. The purity of its terroirs is preserved through vinification in stainless steel tanks with full malolactic fermentation, with the exception of the cleverly named flagship of the house, Mesnillésime, of which 30% is vinified in 225-litre oak barrels without malolactic fermentation. Guy Charlemagne is astute in reserving Le Mesnil and Oger fruit for its refined and age-worthy blanc de blancs cuvées, and it is on these wines that this skilful and affordably priced grower rests its reputation.

GUY CHARLEMAGNE GRAND CRU RESERVE BLANC DE BLANCS BRUT NV $

94 points • 2010 BASE VINTAGE • TASTED IN LE MESNIL-SUR-OGER

100% chardonnay from Les Mesnil-sur-Oger and Oger; reserves from 2009 and 2008; aged on lees 2-3 years; 8g/L dosage

This is where the real business of Guy Charlemagne kicks off, a fantastically mineral-driven wine, quite a contrast to the Sézanne cuvées of the house, and very little more to pay, making this a fantastically affordable blanc de blancs. Impressive drive and focus of lemon zest, grapefruit, crunchy pear and fennel linger with considerable persistence, with notes of brioche providing dimension. With excellent, honed acid cut and impressive chalk mineral mouthfeel, this is a cuvée with the potential to live for a decade, and how often do you hear that at this price? I had no idea of the price when I tasted this cuvée for the first time — and I'm delighted!

GUY CHARLEMAGNE BRUT NATURE NV $

86 points • 2010 BASE VINTAGE • TASTED IN LE MESNIL-SUR-OGER

70% chardonnay, 30% pinot noir; reserves from 2009 and 2008; zero dosage

Layers of mixed spice, lemon zest and crunchy apple are interrupted by earthy, savoury notes and a firm texture reflective of the rustic nature of Sézanne.

GUY CHARLEMAGNE BRUT CLASSIC NV $

92 points • 2010 BASE VINTAGE • TASTED IN LE MESNIL-SUR-OGER

50/50 chardonnay and pinot noir from Sézanne; reserves from 2009 and 2008; aged 2 years on lees; 8g/L dosage

Apple, pear and lemon zest fruit lead out, with maturity bringing notes of honey, mixed spice, baked apple and fig. Nicely integrated acidity and energetic drive hold its precision on the finish, with the subtle phenolic grip of Sézanne, but ultimately defined by finely honed acidity and good persistence.

GUY CHARLEMAGNE CUVÉE CHARLEMAGNE GRAND CRU BLANC DE BLANCS BRUT 2009 $$

94 points • TASTED IN LE MESNIL-SUR-OGER

100% chardonnay from Le Mesnil-sur-Oger and Oger; first press juice only; aged 3-4 years on lees; 6g/L dosage

This was one of the first 2009s that I tasted as a finished champagne, and for a season that probably won't yield many vintage wines, this is a surprisingly confident start. It's predictably coiled at this precocious age, with a tension between fresh lemon and grapefruit, tense acid cut and the subtle brioche complexity of bottle age. It's set off with a fine, creamy bead, chalk mineral texture and good persistence. Give it a few more years to soften and develop, and it will effortlessly see out the end of the decade.

GUY CHARLEMAGNE MESNILLÉSIME EXTRA BRUT 2004 $$

95 points • TASTED IN LE MESNIL-SUR-OGER

100% Le Mesnil-sur-Oger chardonnay from old vines of average age 65 years; 70% vinified in stainless steel with malolactic fermentation, 30% in 225L oak barrels without malolactic; aged at least 6 years on lees; 3g/L dosage

There's beautiful craftsmanship on display here. It takes some tenacity to bottle Le Mesnil-sur-Oger with a dose of malic acidity, and even more to do so with some small oak fermentation. Guy Charlemagne has pulled off the challenge with impeccable sensitivity, creating a wine of volume and tension, at once rounded and rich, yet honed, refreshing, persistent and — crucially — celebrating the wonderful minerality of the village. Great complexity of brioche, biscuits and mixed spice hovers on a palate of tiny, creamy bead and finely structured texture.

H. BILLIOT FILS

(H. Beey-yoh Feess)

5/10

1 Place de la Fontaine 51190 Ambonnay

www.champagnebilliot.fr

Henri Billiot showcases the ripe intensity of one of Champagne's finest pinot noir villages. With fastidious attention to detail, he strives to capture the expression of his five hectares of old, low-yielding pinot noir (75%) and chardonnay vines exclusively in grand cru Ambonnay. All but one of his 18 parcels are enviably positioned on the mid-slopes of the village. Everything is done by hand in the cellar, an achievable feat for an annual production of just 45,000 bottles. To preserve freshness, fermentation takes place in enamelled steel tanks, malolactic fermentation is avoided and virtually no dosage is used. His wines carry a rounded ripeness and powerful fruit sweetness that will appeal to some. It's great to see disgorgement dates now declared on back labels.

H. Billiot Fils Cuvée Tradition Brut NV $$

92 points • Tasted in Melbourne

75% pinot noir, 25% chardonnay; no malolactic fermentation

Billiot captures the stature of Ambonnay pinot noir in a full straw hue and a spicy, complex and characterful style that contrasts the body and depth of the variety with a frame of textural, savoury structure. Lively malic acidity keeps the finish tight. It has a feeling of authenticity, albeit in a slightly unpolished demeanour, with a gently robust phenolic firmness that tussles with its raw acidity. This tension is well controlled, and not out of place for fruit of such magnitude.

HENRI GIRAUD

(On-ree Zhi-row)

(5/10)

71 BOULEVARD CHARLES DE GAULLE 51160 AŸ

www.champagne-giraud.com

CHAMPAGNE
HENRI GIRAUD

The Giraud-Hémart family has diligently tended vines on the south-facing slopes of Aÿ since 1625, making this the oldest champagne house still owned by its founding family. It was not until current head of house, 12th generation Claude Giraud, that champagnes were made under the family name. An annual production of about 250,000 bottles is sourced from the family's 10 hectares, spread across 35 small plots, supplemented with fruit purchased largely from family and friends, all of which is pressed by Giraud. Planted to 70% pinot noir and 30% chardonnay, the magnificence of Aÿ is captured, thanks to vines of a minimum 30 years of age, planted on thin topsoils and deep chalk, tended according to organic principles and harvested at full ripeness. Musts are cold settled at 10°C prior to fermentation, to enhance clarity and aroma, and all cuvées go through full malolactic fermentation. About one-third are vinified in 228-litre barrels from the Argonne forest south-east of Aÿ, an oak industry which Claude has been instrumental in reviving since 1989. He says his generous and silky Fût de Chêne and Code Noir cuvées are fresher and more lively as a result, though oxidation plagued my most recent tasting.

HENRI GIRAUD ESPRIT DE GIRAUD BRUT NV $$

93 points • TASTED IN SYDNEY & MELBOURNE

70% pinot noir, 30% chardonnay; fermented in stainless steel and aged in tank on lees for 1 year

This invitingly rich, fruitful expression of Aÿ is a cracking entry point for Giraud, epitomising the fresh red berry fruits of pinot noir, and the crunch of fresh lemon with clarity and clean definition. Its breadth is pulled into tight focus on the finish by a cut of citrus zest and soft mineral structure. A characterful, integrated and persistent expression of the glories of Aÿ.

Henri Giraud Esprit de Giraud Blanc de Blancs NV $$

95 points • Tasted in Sydney & Melbourne

Montagne de Reims chardonnay; fermented in stainless steel tanks and 10% in oak barrels

The slopes of the Montagne de Reims are home to chardonnay of affable character, and this blanc de blancs of intensity yet finesse offers an enticing counterpoint to the tension of the Côte des Blancs. It's more honed and focused than ever at the moment, with a tense line of ripe acidity drawing long and energetic over a fine backbone of pronounced, expressive chalk minerality.

Henri Giraud Hommage à François Hémart Grand Cru NV $$

87 points • Tasted in Sydney & Melbourne

70% pinot noir, 30% chardonnay from Aÿ; fermented in vats and matured for 6 months in small oak barrels

Destroyed by savoury, vinegary oxidation, rendering the finish developed and tart.

Henri Giraud Code Noir Brut NV $$$$

88 points • Tasted in Sydney & Melbourne

100% pinot noir vinified and aged in Argonne oak

In its sleek, modern, streamlined bottle, this deep golden yellow-tinted blanc de noirs is a celebration of the bountiful grandeur of Aÿ. Its grand dimensions embrace the far-flung realms of champagne, propagating with great persistence. At odds with the integrity that this cuvée has exhibited in the past, this is a wine in which toasty, woody character fights with oxidative development and firm, sour acidity.

The Champagne Guide

Henri Goutorbe

(On-ree Goo-tawb)

5/10

9 BIS RUE JEANSON 51160 AŸ

www.champagne-henri-goutorbe.com

The Goutorbe family ran a viticultural nursery before becoming winegrowers in their home town of Aÿ. The label, established in the late 1940s, has grown to encompass an impressive 25 hectares, including six in Aÿ, and good sites in Mareuil-sur-Aÿ, Mutigny, Bisseuil, Avenay-Val-d'Or and Hautvillers, providing for 200,000 bottles annually. Pinot noir makes up more than two-thirds of plantings, with the remainder largely chardonnay. Every cuvée is sourced exclusively from the estate, is fermented in stainless steel tanks, undergoes full malolactic fermentation and is aged at least three years on lees in Goutorbe's deep, cold cellar. Dosages are based on concentrated wine must rather than sugar. The result is a style that captures the rich expression of these privileged terroirs, while maintaining impressive control.

HENRI GOUTORBE BRUT TRADITION NV $

93 points • 2010 BASE VINTAGE • TASTED IN AŸ, SYDNEY & MELBOURNE

70% pinot noir, 25% chardonnay, 5% meunier; DIAM closure

This is a refreshing take on Aÿ pinot noir, with a lively pale straw hue and well-focused ripe lemon zest, red cherry and crunchy pear fruit of excellent line and length. It's underscored by soft chalk mineral texture and long, ripe, well-poised acid line. A half bottle tasted in Aÿ was slightly oxidised, rendering the finish a little vinegary.

HENRI GOUTORBE CUVÉE MILLESIME GRAND CRU BRUT 2005 $$

89 points • TASTED IN SYDNEY & MELBOURNE

75% pinot noir, 25% chardonnay from Aÿ; 8g/L dosage

The Millesime captures the authority of Aÿ with formidable presence and generous ripeness, regrettably stretched too far in the warm 2005 season, leading out exuberant, then collapsing into a dried-out, contracted finish.

HENRIOT

(On-ree-oh)

7/10

81 rue Coquebert 51100 Reims

www.champagne-henriot.com

CHAMPAGNE

HENRIOT

MAISON FONDÉE EN 1808

Behind the magnificent 'Les Aulnois' 18th century manor house, home of Thomas Henriot in Pierry on the outskirts of Épernay, lies an immaculately ordered and symmetrical French garden. It offers a window into the mind of the eighth-generation managing director of Henriot. 'This is exactly the image of what we want to do at Henriot,' he told me as he rearranged his croquet set into precise position. Balance, order and a classic approach are his philosophy for gardening, for life and for champagne. 'I do not like wines that go in strange directions. I like to know where we are and where we are going.' This mindset defines what he refers to as the 'DNA of the house': meticulously assembled and long-aged cuvées built on a core of Côte des Blancs chardonnay.

In 2008 Henriot celebrated its 200th year of in-dependent family ownership, one of the last remaining houses to be run continuously by the founding family from the outset. That same year, Thomas Henriot received an unexpected call from his father Joseph to join the company. He was appointed managing director in January 2014.

Family ownership has afforded the privilege of building a long-ageing house style that might otherwise be infeasible for a house producing 1.3 million bottles annually. This is achieved through a strong reliance on chardonnay and virtually no meunier. Long ageing on lees is reflected in a whopping 5–6 years of stock held continuously in the company's extensive cellars under Reims, as well as reserve wines back to 1990.

Thirty-three hectares of estate vineyards are located mainly in the great Côtes des Blancs villages, with smaller holdings in Avenay-Val-d'Or, Verzy and Verzenay. Vines averaging an impressive 25–30 years of age are tended respectfully, with grasses cultivated in mid-rows, and her-bicides and fertilisers avoided. The family sources from a further 100 hectares of vineyards under long-term con-tracts. Every parcel is kept separate and fermented in small stainless steel vats, which can lead some cuvées to tend towards a reductive savouriness, not unusual for chardonnay-led blends. Full malolactic fermentation pro-vides soft structures, with dosages between 8 and 11g/L.

Henriot's long-aged Cuvée des Enchanteleurs is a powerfully characterful flagship, this year accompanied by a new cuvée in secret production for 25 years.

Henriot Brut Souverain NV $$

92 points • 2009 base vintage • Disgorged October 2013 • Tasted in Reims, Brisbane, Sydney & Melbourne

50% chardonnay largely from the Côte des Blancs, 45% pinot noir largely from the Montagne de Reims, 5% meunier; a blend of 25 villages; 25% reserves; 9g/L dosage

A chardonnay lead infuses an impressive and surprisingly bright lemon, grapefruit and pear freshness for this long-aged entry cuvée. Maturity speaks, in tones of roast almonds, even suggestions of olives and coffee beans, of a complexity rarely found at this price. Integrity, line and persistence culminate in the creamy texture of lees age and the frothy, softly salty chalk minerality of the Côte des Blancs. It's recently contracted into a dry finish.

Henriot Blanc de Blancs Brut NV $$

93 points • 2009 base vintage • Disgorged December 2013 • Tasted in Brisbane, Sydney & Melbourne

Largely Côte des Blancs (Le Mesnil-sur-Oger, Avize, Chouilly, Vertus) and Montgueux, Trépail, Épernay and the Vitry region; 30% reserve wines; aged on lees 4–5 years; 10g/L dosage; DIAM

Understated elegance and backward purity make this the most refined Henriot Blanc de Blancs I can recall. A brilliant pale straw hue is testimony to the energy it retains even after more than five years. It's a gentle style of yellow citrus, white stone fruits and granny smith apple, celebrating lees age in a soft, creamy texture, and almond, nougat and toasted brioche characters. Soft, fine chalk minerality and a balanced acid line are well integrated. Any lack of distinction in persistence or character it more than makes up for in gentle, caressing appeal and graceful refinement.

Henriot Rosé Brut NV $$

92 points • 2008 base • Disgorged May 2013 • Tasted in Brisbane, Sydney & Melbourne

60% pinot noir, largely from the Montagne de Reims; 40% chardonnay, largely from the Côte des Blancs, a blend of 15 villages; 25% reserves; aged 4 years on lees; 10g/L dosage

With impressive intensity and poise, yet retaining elegance, this is a refined and restrained rosé that juxtaposes chalk mineral texture with soft, fine phenolic structure and pretty rose hip, red cherry and pink pepper character. This base has been in the market for two years and is now showing its sensitivity, recently evolving rapidly to a medium salmon copper hue, with youthful red fruits rusting into orange, tamarillo, oregano and toast.

Henriot Rosé Millésime 2008 $$

96 points • Tasted in Brisbane

Glorious restraint emanates in a pretty, glowing, pale salmon hue, an almost invisible bouquet, and a palate exalting in the wonderful texture of long lees age. Delicate red cherry and wild strawberry fruit dances with youthful verve, just beginning to relax into subtly toasty, creamy maturity, amid nuances of vanilla and almond meal. Silky, mouth-embracing texture harmonises the magical touch of bottle age with soft chalk-infused minerality, drawn out by the fine acid line of the exceptional 2008 vintage. This is a rare 2008 to drink now.

Henriot Brut Millésime 2006 $$

93 points • Tasted in Brisbane

An exuberant and full-flavoured vintage, projecting intense yellow citrus and stone fruits, fully evolved to a place of medium straw hue and toasty, spicy, bready maturity, accented with ginger and a hint of marmalade. It's bang on for drinking right away, fully integrated, textural and holding its acid line and persistence.

Henriot Cuvée des Enchanteleurs Brut 1998 $$$$$

96 points • Tasted in Brisbane

50% chardonnay and 50% pinot noir from Mailly-Champagne, Verzy, Verzenay, Le Mesnil-sur-Oger, Avize and Chouilly; aged on lees at least 12 years; 10g/L dosage

Full straw hue, with a gold tint. Throbbing with dark fruit cake, roast figs, grilled pineapple and dried nectarines, this is a rich, powerful Enchanteleurs, evolving incrementally and unhurriedly from its majestic position of two years ago. The greatest terroirs of the northern Montagne de Reims meet some of the strongest grand crus of the Côte des Blancs, seamlessly uniting in the intense 1998 season. It strikes an engaging juxtaposition between fruit presence and the burnt butter, roast cashew nut and prune development of 17 years of maturity, with tertiary complexity rising in notes of green olives, exotic pipe smoke and toffee. A vintage of considerable amplitude and breadth, retaining control and precision on a long finish of fine chalk minerality and immense presence. It's right at its peak drinking now, and will hold for a few more years yet.

Henriot Cuve 38 La Réserve Perpétuelle Blanc de Blancs NV $$$$$

97 points • 2007 base, bottled in 2009 • Tasted in Reims from magnum

In 2015, Henriot unveiled a remarkable new prestige cuvée, which it had secretly held in production for an incredible 25 years. In 1990, Joseph Henriot set aside a special vat of grand cru Côte des Blancs chardonnay. An addition has been made in each of the best vintages since, largely from Chouilly and Avize, with lesser contributions from Le Mesnil-sur-Oger and Cramant, in something of a solera system. The proportion of each vintage addition may be as little as 1% of the blend, or as much as 18%, according to taste. The blend has grown to fill a 467hL tank, held at 14°C to retain freshness, and, to make space for each addition, the same volume is removed, bottled exclusively in magnums with less than 5g/L dosage and aged for a further five years. Only 1000 magnums will be released each year.

I was privileged to be the first outside the house to see a sneak preview of this unprecedented new concept. This was not the first time I've witnessed the other-worldly freshness that can be sustained by annually refreshing a grand old solera in a big tank, but nothing prepared me for the unbridled joy of youth radiating from this glass. I was stunned that a blend whose youngest component was seven years old, and oldest no less than 24 years, could trap such a bright straw hue, breathtaking lemon blossom and lemon zest fragrance and vibrant focus. The wisdom of maturity is articulated in aged richness of nougat character, but still far from tertiary in its development. A taut, dry, saline finish and an appropriate reductive note rejoices in the texture of a quarter of a century on lees, amplifying the depth and definition of inimitable Côtes des Blancs grand cru minerality. It deserves a big glass and lots of air, but it will blossom with another five years of age, and will effortlessly take another 25 years in its stride.

The Champagne Guide

HURÉ FRÈRES

(Oo-ray Frair)

6/10

2 IMPASSE CARNOT 51500 LUDES

www.champagne-hure-freres.com

CHAMPAGNE

HURÉ FRÈRES

Brothers Pierre and François Huré are third-generation viticulturist and winemaker for their small family house in Ludes. A 10-hectare estate is located largely in their home town, and in Ville-Dommange near Reims, and as far-flung as Serzy-et-Prin and Brouillet in the Vallée de l'Ardre and Vavray-le-Grand in Vitry. Vines are managed sustainably, minimising herbicides and using organic composts and natural ground cover. Reserves are stored in oak vats and tanks, complementing the fruity appeal of meunier-led cuvées of admirable youthful freshness.

HURÉ FRÈRES INVITATION BRUT NV $

92 points • TASTED IN BRISBANE

50% meunier, 35% pinot noir, 15% chardonnay; 25-40% reserves; aged 30-36 months on lees; 8g/L dosage

A lively, vibrant, youthful and fruity apéritif capturing the elegant red fruits of northern Montagne meunier with vibrancy and verve, accenting fresh red cherry and strawberry fruit with nuances of nutmeg and anise. It's graceful and light on its feet, supported by a focused line of lively acidity and a gentle undercurrent of softly chalky minerality.

HURÉ FRÈRES MÉMOIRE EXTRA BRUT NV $$

93 points • TASTED IN BRISBANE

45% meunier, 45% pinot, 10% chardonnay; solera of 30 reserves since 1982; aged 1 year in a 45hL oak foudre; 3g/L dosage

A compelling and seamless union of the creamy texture of lees age, the elegant red fruits, citrus and gentle bath-salts chalk minerality of the northern Montagne, the tangy acid line of youth, and the soft, charcuterie complexity of oak barrels. The accord makes for an enticingly textured champagne, of character, persistence and potential.

J. LASSALLE

(J. Lah-sahl)

6/10

21 RUE CHÂTAIGNIER 51500 CHIGNY-LES-ROSES
www.champagne-jlassalle.com

CHAMPAGNE
J. LASSALLE
— PROPRIÉTAIRE DE VIGNOBLES —

It takes great sensitivity to create wines that communicate the subtleties not only of the place that has given them birth, but also the very personalities of those who have brought them to life. When I first tasted the enchanting champagnes of J. Lassalle, I knew nothing of the estate or the family behind them and was immediately captivated by their dainty restraint and feminine beauty, arousing my curiosity to discover how such delicate sophistication could be achieved. It all made sense when I met the three generations of delightful women who, for more than 30 years, have nurtured this immaculate estate in the charming village of Chigny-les-Roses.

Ever since Jules Lassalle passed away in 1982, his wife, Olga, daughter Chantal and grand-daughter Angéline Templier have worked closely together to treble the size of their family estate to 16 hectares and an annual production now approaching 150,000 bottles. Templier oversees winemaking, ably assisted by her mother. Olga, now 94, still helps with management and administration. 'We don't need any men to help!' Templier grins.

The meticulous attention to detail of these women shines in every stage of production. The winery at their home in the village is pristine, bathed in white light, one of the cleanest little facilities I've visited anywhere. 'We do everything as my grandfather did, but because we are girls we have a feminine touch, and you can feel it in the wines,' says Templier.

The Lassalles have been making champagnes exclusively from their premier cru vineyards since 1942. Their aspiration is to express the clay soil terroir of the northern slopes of the Montagne de Reims, so all vineyards are tightly located within 10 kilometres of the house. Meunier is king here, comprising 50% of plantings. Chardonnay (25%) takes a confident, if surprising, lead in Lassalle's most sublime cuvée, and pinot noir makes up the remaining 25% of the estate. The family is privileged to own a significant proportion of old parcels, upholding an average vine age of 40 years, and some up to 50. 'They make great wines, so we don't replant them!' Templier exclaims. Any fruit of insufficient quality is sold to large houses.

Blends comprise all three champagne varieties in proportions varied according to the season, bolstered by a generous stock of five years of reserve wines. Preserving freshness at every stage is a high priority. Grapes are pressed on the first floor and the juice is piped directly to settling tanks below to avoid oxidation. Every cuvée undergoes full malolactic fermentation. The philosophy in the winery is to maintain the tradition of Templier's grandfather, while growing progressively. 'I don't want to follow trends, I just want to be respectful of the traditional style of the product we make,' says Templier.

Much of the historical equipment of the estate is still in use, including enamelled tanks and the traditional press installed in 1965, and all cuvées are still riddled by hand.

Long ageing is inherent to the house style, and when rosé demand outstripped supply, the cuvée was put on allocation rather than releasing it earlier. 'The only thing we have to sell the house is our quality, and it is very important for us to respect this, so we told our clients to wait,' Templier explains.

Non-vintage cuvées are aged at least four years, and vintage cuvées 6–10 years, necessitating a large cellar stock of 400,000–450,000 bottles. The estate also holds back unusually large reserves, and currently holds as much reserve as new wine in storage. 'We're always full and running out of room!' says Templier.

To facilitate growth, the building next door was bought in 2007 and the winery expanded to a capacity of almost 100,000 litres. A new press was purchased, new cellars dug under the building, and temperature-controlled stainless steel tanks installed to allow separate vinification of the estate's many small parcels.

In late 2013, the Lassalles were presented with their biggest growth opportunity yet: an invitation to buy the neighbouring estate of a cousin in the village, providing much-needed production and cellar space and, most of all, 4.5 glorious hectares of vineyards in Chigny-les-Roses, Ludes and Rilly-la-Montagne, all conveniently neighbouring existing Lassalle plots. When I visited during vintage 2014, the first of the new fruit was arriving and I was privileged to the first tour of the new premises. The Lassalles are excited about the opportunity to expand production from 100,000 to 150,000 bottles, but are cautious about maintaining quality, so are slowly evolving production progressively over four years.

Refined new labels were introduced in 2015, with elegant white space reflecting the graceful appeal of the house and courtyard. The bottling code laser-etched on every cuvée is the disgorgement date.

Don't miss these impeccably crafted cuvées of generous fruit presence, purity, and the most intricately judged balance.

J. Lassalle Préférence Premier Cru Brut NV $

92 points • 2010 BASE VINTAGE WITH 2009 RESERVES • Disgorged November 2014 • Tasted in Chigny-les-Roses

60% meunier, 20% pinot noir, 20% chardonnay; 35-40% reserve wines; aged 4 years on lees; 8-9g/L dosage; 60,000-70,000 bottles

Templier likes emphasising the aromas of meunier, structured with chardonnay and pinot noir. There is a delicacy and purity to this lively, clean, fruit-focused style, with crisp lemon, apple and pear framed neatly in a fine, creamy bead and soft, subtle mineral structure true to the premier cru villages of the northern Montagne. Well-integrated acidity and dosage linger on a persistent finish. More recent tastings have revealed some dry extract character of the challenging 2010 season.

J. Lassalle Premier Cru Brut Rosé NV $$

89 points • 2011 BASE VINTAGE WITH 2010 RESERVES • Disgorged June 2014 • Tasted in Chigny-les-Roses

70% pinot noir, 15% meunier, 15% chardonnay; 7% red wine from a parcel of 50-year-old vines in Chigny-les-Roses; 9g/L dosage

Templier uses just a small addition of 7% red wine to create a delicate, salmon colour. 'We want something light and delicate — maybe this is our feminine side!' she says. The current disgorgement does not carry any of the dainty refinement and clean precision that I love about this cuvée, an unfortunate victim of two bad-tempered seasons. Dry almond skin, bitter hazelnut and green coffee bean notes detract, though it does uphold the elegant fruit profile and finely balanced acid line of the house.

J. Lassalle Blanc de Blancs Millésime 2006 $$

90 points • Disgorged June 2014 • Tasted in Chigny-les-Roses

From 30-35-year-old vines; aged 8 years on lees; 8-9g/L dosage

The mandate of this cuvée is to express the rounded, soft character of the clay soils of Villers-Allerand chardonnay that Templier describes as 'body built', very different in style to the Côte des Blancs. The 2006 meets the brief, a complex style of sweet and sour grapefruit and honeydew, subtly earthy, with soft lemon pith texture providing gentle grip to the back palate. Acidity is well balanced, supported by nicely integrated dosage that lingers long and gentle on the finish.

J. Lassalle Cuvée Angéline Premier Cru Brut Millésime 2008 $$

96 points • Disgorged May 2014 • Tasted in Chigny-les-Roses

60% pinot noir, 40% chardonnay from old parcels in Chigny-les-Roses and Rilly-la-Montagne; never more than 6000 bottles

The flagship of the house, created from the same parcels since 1973, epitomising the elegance of northern Montagne pinot noir and the exacting precision of Lassalle. The tension of the wonderful 2008 vintage plays to this style emphatically, making for an effortless, scintillating and captivating champagne that sings with soprano high notes of white and red cherry fruits, backed by tenor harmonies of brioche, toasted almonds and nougat. Fantastically refined acid structure and mineral texture make for a finish both vibrant and approachable.

J. Lassalle Special Club 2006 $$$

95 points • Disgorged September 2014 • Tasted in Chigny-les-Roses

60% chardonnay, 40% pinot noir; a selection in the winery of the very best parcels of elegance, finesse and balance; aged 8-10 years on lees

The philosophy here is of greater freshness and delicacy, hence a stronger representation of chardonnay. In 2006, this makes for a lively style of vibrant acid line and pretty, elegant clarity of lemon zest, pear and apple. It's impeccably pure, layering fragrant citrus over a tense core of focused acidity and fine chalk mineral texture. Long lees age has built subtle almond brioche complexity, a richly textured structure, creamy bead and great line and length. It's backward, refreshing and age-worthy, though one bottle tasted was more developed, a medium to full straw hue, with notes of orange rind, dried nectarine, marzipan, patisserie, even coffee bean, and a fine, chewy grip.

JACQUART

(Zhah-khah)

34 BOULEVARD LUNDY 51100 REIMS
www.champagne-jacquart.com

*J*acquart is the brand of the Alliance Champagne Group, a cooperative representing one of Champagne's largest sources of grapes. The group is owned by 1800 growers, holding over 2600 hectares (and counting), spanning more than 60 crus across the Côte des Blancs, Vallée de la Marne and Côte des Bar. Jacquart has grown dramatically since it was founded just over 50 years ago, now vinifying 1200 parcels separately from 350 hectares of its vineyard pool to create 3 million bottles of pleasant chardonnay-led blends of prominent dosage. Freshness, purity and elegance are the mandates of the house, upheld by 34-year-old chef de cave Florian Eznack, who left Veuve Clicquot to join the house in 2011. Its chardonnay-focused style calls for long ageing, and non-vintage cuvées are matured a minimum of four years, blanc de blancs at least six years and Cuvée Alpha seven or more. The house has a goal to become one of the top ten champagne houses by growing to 4 million bottles, which would seem a straightforward aspiration given its enormous grower base.

JACQUART BRUT MOSAÏQUE NV $$

90 points • 2009 BASE VINTAGE • TASTED IN BRISBANE & MELBOURNE
91 points • 2008 BASE VINTAGE • TASTED IN SYDNEY & MELBOURNE

45-50% chardonnay, 30% pinot noir, 20% meunier; focus of selection on the grand crus of the Côte des Blancs and Montagne de Reims; at least 30% reserve wines an average of 2 years old; a blend of 60 villages; 8g/L dosage

The 2009 base is a clean and accurate blend, with chardonnay clearly in the lead, speaking in articulate notes of lemon and pear, with the complexity of pinot's red apple, and mature cellar notes of honey, cinnamon and toasted brioche. A gentle, tangy acid line keeps things lively. The dosage of 10g/L could be lighter, leaving a sweet, candied suggestion to the finish. A crowd-pleasing blend, built on quality fruit. One bottle tasted was tired and developed, with bruised apple notes. The 2008 base vintage heightens its red berry presence, acid focus and chalk mineral mouthfeel.

JACQUART ROSÉ NV $$

90 points • 2009 BASE VINTAGE • TASTED IN BRISBANE
87 points • 2008 BASE VINTAGE • TASTED IN SYDNEY & MELBOURNE

Same base as Brut Mosaïque, with 20% pinot noir red wine from Aÿ and Les Riceys; 8g/L dosage; more than 300,000 bottles

Jacquart's rosé mandate is impact and attack, which it achieves with a solid dose of pinot noir red wine, contributing colour, body and grip. In the 2009 base vintage, a full salmon crimson hue evolved to copper tints with time in bottle, with soft and fruity red apple, cherry and strawberry flavours, honeyed dosage and a firm, fine tannin texture that makes for a chewy mouthfeel. A rosé of body, flesh and sinew, ready for main-course fare. The 2008 base has developed prematurely to oxidised burnt-orange notes.

JACQUART BLANC DE BLANCS 2006 $$

92 points • TASTED IN BRISBANE, SYDNEY & MELBOURNE

A blend of 10 grand crus and 4 premier crus on the Montagne de Reims and Côte des Blancs; aged 6 years on lees; 6.5g/L dosage; less than 100,000 bottles

Creaminess and silkiness are the aspiration for Jacquart's Blanc de Blancs, tactically employing long lees age to tone low-dosage grand cru chardonnay. The soft and immediate demeanour of the 2006 harvest meets this brief precisely, already at the peak of its maturity, with layers of toasted coconut, nougat, almond, vanilla custard, nutmeg and honey biscuits over a core of secondary lemon, white peach and hints of fig generosity. A fine acid line brings drive and freshness to this generous style, lingering long and silky amidst well-defined, finely salty chalk minerality, keeping things lively. It's engaging and well balanced, the dosage of the house apparent yet appropriate for the energy of chardonnay.

JACQUART CUVÉE ALPHA BRUT VINTAGE 2006 $$$$

91 points • TASTED IN BRISBANE

50% chardonnay from Chouilly and Sillery and 50% pinot noir from Trépail and Villers-Marmery; 7 years on lees; 6g/L dosage; just a few thousand bottles

An early-developing vintage, having already attained the peak of its maturity. This wine captures the soft, juicy, fruity mood of the season, overlaying it with the spice, toast and wild honey of lees age. It has more dosage than it calls for in a season so inherently rounded and approachable. A wine of persistence and crowd-pleasing appeal.

JACQUART CUVÉE ALPHA 2005 $$$$

91 points • TASTED IN BRISBANE, SYDNEY & MELBOURNE

A mandate of complexity and depth is delivered in layers of dried peach, ginger, mixed spice and honey. The stamp of the stress of the 2005 season is dramatic in a full yellow hue, and dried-out, slightly desiccated finish. Nonetheless it upholds admirable silky creaminess and soft persistence, true to the mood of the house.

Jacques Picard

(Zhak Pee-khah)

5/10

12 RUE DU LUXEMBOURG 51420 BERRU

www.champagnepicard.com

CHAMPAGNE
JACQUES PICARD

PROPRIÉTAIRE-RÉCOLTANT

From its home on the slopes of Mount Berru, seven kilometres north-east of Reims, the Picard family crafts champagnes with an insightful touch. Well-considered, strategic use of generous proportions of chardonnay, abundant reserve wines and selective employment of oak fermentation and maturation conspire to build fleshy, layered complexity, sensitively tweaked with low dosage and selective blocking of malolactic fermentation to preserve vivacity. With no other estate bottling champagnes in Berru, it is difficult to distinguish the skill of the maker from the potential of the place. Wherever the credit is directed, there is no denying that this beautifully complete set of champagnes transcend their terroirs.

The history of viticulture in Berru dates from at least the 12th century. On a gentle slope of easterly exposition 4 kilometres from Verzy and Verzenay, the geology is not dissimilar, with thin brown topsoil over deep chalk, producing chardonnay of body and roundness. On the strategic battlefront of World War I, the vineyards of the village were almost completely destroyed, to be replanted by Roger Picard, then mayor of the village, after World War II.

The estate has been run by the same family for three generations. Jacques Picard made his first sparkling wines in the early 1960s, and his daughters Sylvie and Corinne and their husbands took over in the 1990s. Corinne's husband, José Lieven, oversees the vineyards and winemaking.

The estate is privileged to own 17 hectares in Berru, meunier in Montbré and a small parcel of pinot noir in Avenay-Val-d'Or. Berru chardonnay is the focus, comprising 70% of holdings, supported by 20% meunier and 10% pinot noir.

The Picards believe in *lutte naturelle* (natural control) and practise *culture raisonnée* (reasoned culture), some time ago convincing the entire community of the village to use sexual confusion through the use of hormones as a method of insect control, in order to reduce use of pesticides. Sustainable viticulture is the focus, and grasses have been planted in mid-rows to control erosion.

'We refuse to be strictly organic, not organic, or bio-dynamic, as one system is not an integrated approach,' says Lieven. 'There are good ideas within all three and I like to pick and choose.' He runs one vineyard organically so as to observe the impact on the wine over many years.

A sparkling-clean, gravity-fed winery has been strategically engineered to minimise their carbon footprint. No air conditioning is installed, as air is able to pass by convection through a 150-metre underground pipe to cool. Lieven is more focused on the vineyards than on vinification. 'We aim to keep things clean and do as little as possible,' he says. Picard's wines are aged at least three years in cellars dug into chalk under the house.

Vinification is matched to the mood of the year, with selective use of barrel vinification, malolactic fermentation blocked or encouraged according to the parcel, and dosage tweaked to suit the disgorgement. Lieven visits Louis Latour in Burgundy every June, tastes from different barrels, cleverly marks those he likes, then returns in September to buy them.

The gentle eastern exposition of Berru retains freshness in chardonnay, making reserve wines important for balance; hence almost a full year of production is held in reserve. Freshness is retained by holding a solera of reserves of Berru chardonnay below 16°C. Commenced in 1998, this solera is impressively

characterful, tangy and taut, with a tight acid line. Such was its success that Lieven commenced a solera of Montbré meunier in 2008, which retains admirable fragrance and lively definition.

An early morning start to harvest on the slopes of Mareuil-sur-Aÿ.

Jacques Picard Brut NV $$

93 points • 2010 BASE VINTAGE WITH RESERVES FROM THE FIVE VINTAGES PRIOR
• Tasted in Berru

60% chardonnay, 35% meunier, 5% pinot noir; 9g/L dosage

Picard successfully tones the fleshiness of Berru chardonnay with malic acidity and low dosage, building complexity with large proportions of reserve wines and long ageing on lees. A strong chardonnay lead retains the precision and focus of lemon fruit amidst the rounded generosity of red apples. A taut line of fine acidity and softly gentle chalk mineral texture provides impressive energy and definition to this backward and lively style. It will benefit from time to build.

Jacques Picard Blanc de Blancs Brut NV $$

93 points • 100% 2009 • Tasted in Berru

100% Berru chardonnay from five parcels; aged 3 years on lees; 8-9g/L dosage

'Maybe I am too old to think that you can put a vintage on every bottle?' muses Lieven. Then he adds, with refreshing frankness, 'It's nice chardonnay, but it's not on a level synonymous with vintage champagne.' He's a harsh critic, because the wine has the propensity to age impressively. Youthful and lively, it brims with crunchy nashi pear, granny smith apple, grapefruit and lemon zest of good length and focus. A very fine, creamy bead juxtaposes a strong acid line and deep layers of firm minerality, more coarse than the Côte des Blancs and finer than Sézanne. It will appreciate time to soften and integrate.

The Champagne Guide

JACQUES PICARD BRUT NATURE NV $$

90 points • BASE VINTAGE 2009 • TASTED IN BERRU

75% chardonnay solera spanning 1998 through 2008; 25% meunier and a touch of pinot noir from 2009; zero dosage

Lieven crafts his Brut Nature from scratch, being 'disappointed with brut nature named simply because it has no dosage'. Smart philosophy, though difficult to execute in his terroirs. Notes of mushroom quickly blew off to reveal a note of grapefruit zest bitterness characteristic of Berru. This is a cuvée exclusively for diehard champagne lovers. It's high-strung, hard and aggressive, with firm acidity, well-defined salt minerality and a fine, creamy bead.

JACQUES PICARD ART DE VIGNE BRUT MILLÉSIME 2005 $$$

87 points • TASTED IN BERRU

60% single-vineyard Berru chardonnay from 30-year-old vines; 20% single-vineyard Montbré meunier from 22-year-old vines; 20% single-vineyard Avenay-Val-d'Or pinot noir from 50-year-old vines; fully fermented and matured in old barrels with bâtonnage (lees stirring) for 6 months; no malolactic fermentation; 5g/L dosage

Lieven released the 2005 before the longer-ageing 2004. True to a lesser season, this is a wine of firm, drying tension and taut acid structure accentuated by barrel work and malic acidity. It's dusty and dry with star anise and woodspice notes.

JACQUES PICARD ART DE VIGNE BRUT MILLÉSIME 2003 $$$

90 points • TASTED IN BERRU

Zero dosage

The generous 2003 season produced a good result in Picard's elegant terroirs. Lieven had hoped to block malolactic fermentation, but it started spontaneously. Nonetheless, the wine retains lively acidity to counter its firm, drying and slightly bitter style. It's long, finely textured and expressive in its spicy orange rind, lemon zest, marmalade and white Christmas cake personality.

JACQUES PICARD ART DE VIGNE BRUT MILLÉSIME 1999 $$$

89 points • TASTED IN BERRU

Zero dosage

Waves of lavish character of spicy yellow fruits, cloves, mirabelle, mixed spice, bees wax, brioche and wild honey clash with a finish defined by firm, high-strung malic acidity and impressive mineral definition. It's too aggressive for its age, and lacks the fruit depth on the finish to hold out in the cellar for this level of acidity to soften.

JACQUES SELOSSE

(Zhak Sur-loss)

7/10

59 RUE DE CRAMANT 51190 AVIZE

www.selosse-lesavises.com

JACQUES SELOSSE

VINS DE CHAMPAGNE AVIZE

The expression of terroir has been one of the great advances of Champagne of the past three decades, and no grower has been more influential in its progress than Anselme Selosse. 'We should take what nature has given us and not interfere' is a philosophy he pursues more obsessively than any other, making him a visionary mentor who has inspired a generation of growers in Champagne. Since taking over from his father in 1980, his example has been a revolution in the region, radically pioneering lower yields farmed according to biodynamic principles and a handmade, Burgundian approach quite unlike any other in Champagne. His wines are as strong as the convictions behind them, and rank among the ripest and most expressive in all of Champagne. Regrettably, his Burgundian approach too often pushes his wines beyond the realms of sound champagne and into the outer limits of oxidation. Yet the wines of Selosse rank high among the most prized sparkling wines of all, and each year his entire production of 57,000 bottles quickly vanishes into the cellars of collectors across the globe. These are rare champagnes, and priced accordingly.

There is no name in Champagne more talked about right now than Anselme Selosse, and no grower more controversial. He is one of the most profound thinkers in the modern wine world on the role of the soil as the interface between the terroir and the vine. 'The terroir expresses itself in the minerality, the flavour and the intensity of the wine,' he explains.

'The bedrock on which we plant our vines is rarely directly soluble, and it is only by the action of micro-organisms that it is able to be transformed to be absorbed by the roots and impart its mineral signature. The population of micro-organisms is specific to its location, and a short distance away, when the population changes, the terroir changes.'

For Selosse, terroir encompasses the entire eco-system, and anything that might disrupt the intricate balance of biodiversity is to be vigorously avoided. This

is intuitive winegrowing of the highest order, a rigorous biodynamic regime, yet vigorously non-prescriptive, encouraging balance through such techniques as soil respiration by planting grasses in the mid-rows, abandoning pesticides, and hard pruning to limit yields.

The result is fruit of full ripeness, capturing the detail and character of spectacular estate holdings spanning 47 parcels across 7.5 hectares, located primarily in the grand crus of the Côte des Blancs, including four hectares of chardonnay in his home village of Avize, one hectare in each of Oger and Cramant and smaller plots in Le Mesnil-sur-Oger, and pinot noir in Aÿ, Ambonnay and Mareuil-sur-Aÿ. Selosse produces fewer than 60,000 bottles each year.

A conspicuously Burgundian approach is pursued in the winery. 'A lot of people consider vintage to be finished when the grapes are picked, but for me it continues through the vinification and all the way to bottling,' he says.

In 2008 he purchased an old Avize château with 200-year-old cellars built on four levels. Each of 47 different plots is pressed separately in his press house at the level of the vines above the village, flowing by gravity into settling tanks below, then down to barrels on a third level. Every parcel is fermented using wild yeast in puncheons, foudres and Burgundy barrels of all sizes, purchased from some of Burgundy's finest estates.

Maintaining solids in the fermentation juices is an important element of the Selosse style. 'Solids in the juice provide nutrients and antioxidant protection for the wine,' he explains, 'adding texture, nutty flavours and deep colour.' These characters build as the wines are held in barrel over one year, enhanced with weekly bâtonnage (lees stirring).

Malolactic fermentation is free to occur (or not) as each parcel evolves. Minimal sulphur dioxide is used, and only ever prior to fermentation. This is fraught with danger in an oxidative, barrel-matured wine style, and every 2014 and 2013 barrel sample that I tasted was oxidised. Selosse has been at the forefront of low dosage in Champagne, using less than 7g/L, and usually less than 3g/L. Each cuvée is aged long on lees prior to release — up to eight years in the case of 'Substance', made using a true solera going back to 1986.

These radical methods make the wines of Selosse unique in flavour and stature in all of Champagne. These are inherently textural, vinous wines that have as much in common with white Burgundy as they do with champagne. Not to be hurried, they benefit tremendously from a decant and plenty of time to open up in a large glass to allow volatility to blow off. They evolve dramatically and polarise even the most seasoned champagne drinkers.

Such big, oxidative, unashamedly broad styles with all too often fino sherry-like development are more than confronting, yet there are bottles of some cuvées out there that are not oxidised, and these can be mesmerising. The trouble is, that's a very expensive chance to take. If you do choose to take the plunge, your best chances are with very large glasses and plenty of time to breathe.

Selosse's latest creations are three single-vineyard, single-varietal champagnes from Le Mesnil-sur-Oger, Aÿ and Mareuil-sur-Aÿ. Produced in tiny volumes, they will fascinate those who enjoy his oak-driven, oxidative style.

Selosse's champagnes are as distinctive and original as the man who masterminded them. Anselme regularly travels to Spain, where he focuses on sherry production, 'because he is a bit obsessed with oxidation!' as one of his close grower friends put it.

Anselme's young son Guillaume returned to the estate in June 2012 and is assuming increasing responsibility. Labels are impressively informative, detailing disgorgement dates, dosage, blends and often the base vintage.

Selosse's luxury hotel, Les Avisés, goes from strength to strength, and his brilliant chef Stéphane Rossillon continues to serve up one of the most memorable and hospitable dining experiences in all of Champagne.

The Selosse revolution continues.

JACQUES SELOSSE INITIALE BLANC DE BLANCS BRUT NV $$$$

96, 94 and 91 points • DISGORGED 8 OCTOBER 2014 • TASTED IN AVIZE (THREE TIMES)

A blend of three successive vintages from Avize, Cramant and Oger; 33,000 bottles

Initiale accounts for more than 50% of Selosse's production, and such is its variability that this and VO are the two cuvées in this guide for which I have decided to publish different scores for the same disgorgement tasted in the same place (though on three separate visits). When Initiale is on form (as it was on one occasion for me), it is a bright, full yellow hue and delivers great definition, linear focus and persistence of preserved lemon, fig and glacé peach amidst extravagant layers of marmalade, mixed spice and Christmas cake, underlined by fine chalk minerality. Lesser bottles show the degradation of oxidation in notes of burnt orange and toast, developing a bitter grapefruit pith texture.

Jacques Selosse VO Version Originale Blanc de Blancs Extra Brut NV $$$$

93 and 88 points • Disgorged December 2013 • Tasted in Avize (twice)

A blend of 3 successive vintages from Avize, Cramant and Oger; vinified in oak barrels; aged 3.5-4 years on lees; zero dosage; 3600 bottles

Signature Selosse, such is the bombastic complexity of VO that it resembles mature white Burgundy as much as it does champagne. Remarkable ripe intensity transcends Côte des Blancs chardonnay in its panoply of flavours of ripe yellow fruits, pineapple, fig, preserved lemon and mixed spice. The freshest bottles cling to primary grapefruit definition, while more developed examples have deteriorated into notes of bruised apple, marmalade and dry, vinegary astringency.

Jacques Selosse Le Mesnil-sur-Oger Les Carelles NV $$$$$

90 points • Disgorged February 2014 • Tasted in Sydney

Single-vineyard Le Mesnil-sur-Oger; solera blend; aged 5-6 years on lees; less than 4g/L dosage

Burnt orange and marmalade oxidation washes over layers of mixed spice and butterscotch, finishing with grip and assertiveness. In spite of its oxidative development, it carries impressive body and length. If oxidative styles are your vibe, this is worth a try.

Jacques Selosse Aÿ La Côte Faron NV $$$$$

92 points • 2007 base vintage • Disgorged April 2014 • Tasted in Avize & Sydney

100% pinot noir; single-vineyard Aÿ

Expressive chalk mineral texture declares the terroir of Aÿ, while impressive depth and length of cherry, fig, mixed spice and butterscotch tell the story of barrel and bottle development. In classic Selosse form, it's rich, ripe and full, with notes of cumquat marmalade and burnt orange pointing to oxidation — though, to its credit, it's not dried out on the finish.

Thin soils on the east-facing slopes of Avize grow mineral-infused chardonnay that ranks among the longest-lived in all of Champagne.

The Champagne Guide

Jacques Selosse Mareuil-sur-Aÿ Sous le Mont NV $$$$$

93 points • Disgorged February 2014 • 2007 base vintage • Tasted in Avize & Sydney

100% pinot noir; single-vineyard Mareuil-sur-Aÿ

A wine of character and great persistence, sustained by the focused acid line and fine salt mineral freshness of Mareuil-sur-Aÿ. It upholds lemon zest notes and even pepper, amidst the depth of fig and Old Spice. Some development is reflected in candied orange rind, marmalade and butterscotch characters.

Jacques Selosse Millésime Blanc de Blancs Brut 2002 $$$$$

97 points • Tasted in Avize

Two parcels of old vines in Avize

Towards the end of the biggest Selosse tasting I have ever been privileged to, Anselme scuttled off to his cellar and returned with a bottle that singly restored my faith, not just with the emphatic statement that a Selosse cuvée can utterly and comprehensively transcend oxidation, but that it is conceivable for it to age long and gracefully. The result is shadowy, enchanting and profoundly terroir-driven. Signature Selosse ripeness is trumpeted in voluptuous waves of grilled pineapple, lemon meringue, fig, dried pear, honey, ginger, brioche, golden fruit cake and haunting exotic spice. Avize declares itself in beautifully poised, frothy seasalt chalk minerality that lingers with terrific length and line. It's at once silky, creamy and magnificently poised. And did I say there's no oxidation? At all. There you have it, the finest Selosse cuvée I have ever tasted, though regrettably exceedingly rare.

Jacques Selosse Millésime Blanc de Blancs Brut 2003 $$$$$

92 points • Tasted in Avize

For this hot season at 12 years of age, this cuvée sustains impressively defined acidity. It's loaded with spicy complexity and notes of orange-cream dark chocolate. Oxidation plagues it with marmalade development and some dryness on the finish, though it does come through with impressive persistence.

Jacques Selosse Substance Blanc de Blancs Extra Brut NV $$$$$

96 points • 1998 base vintage • Tasted in Avize

100% Avize chardonnay; 1998 bottling of a solera of every vintage back to 1986; 3000 bottles

A mature bottling of Selosse's celebrated old solera, testimony to its ability to mature post-disgorgement, though the solera is a lot older and more developed now, so I'm not certain the same endurance can be extrapolated to more recent disgorgements. A full yellow gold hue, this is an enthralling assemblage of secondary and tertiary development reminiscent of exotic fig, Old Spice, blood orange, burnt butter and pipe smoke. Acidity is well poised, keeping its voluminous proportions and exuberant complexity well in check, culminating in a finish of exceptional persistence.

JACQUESSON

(Zhak-soh)

9/10

68 RUE DU COLONEL FABIEN 51530 DIZY
www.champagnejacquesson.com

CHAMPAGNE
JACQUESSON
— FAMILLE CHIQUET —

No champagne house today is on a trajectory of ascent as steep as Jacquesson. While many houses are on the prowl for more fruit to increase production, Jacquesson is drastically slashing its yields and its contracts to radically improve quality in spite of lowering quantity. When others set out to make a consistent blend every year, Jacquesson throws uniformity to the wind to draw the best blend out of every vintage. Each time I look, this little house in the village of Dizy appears more like a fanatical grower producer. Purely on the refinement of its current cuvées, Jacquesson has leapt from ranking among Champagne's top 20 houses to a lofty position among its top 10.

The concept of non-vintage champagne has never sat quite right with me. Blending multiple vintages to deal with the ups and downs of the seasons makes sense. But creating a consistent style that tastes the same every year has never seemed quite right.

When a particularly blessed season arrives, why must it always be dumbed down for the sake of uniformity? Or must it?

'We were making a regular non-vintage at Jacquesson until we became progressively frustrated with it,' Jean-Hervé Chiquet told me when we first tasted his oddly named Cuvée No 734 in the tasting room of the family estate in Dizy.

'We face such vintage variation at this extreme, with fantastic vintages followed by disasters, that our ancestors found that the only way to handle the seasons was to blend vintages to produce consistent wine. This is why 90% of Champagne's production does not carry a vintage. In spring 1998 we were working on our non-vintage from 1997 base and we found a blend that was

very nice, but not the same as the previous non-vintage and not able to be reproduced. At the time, we made an inferior wine to match the consistency of the house. We decided then that there should be a better rule. We thought, what happens if we don't try to imitate what we did last year, but start from a blank sheet of paper and make the best wine that we can every year?'

And so Cuvée 728 was born from 2000 vintage base. 'A vintage with reserve wine,' as Jean-Hervé calls it. A different blend every year is reflected by a consecutively rolling number (1272 less than the vintage year) — a 'stupid number', according to Jean-Hervé. 'But two things don't change: the fruit sources and the taste of the two guys who do the blend!'

RADICAL CHANGE

Those two guys are brothers Jean-Hervé and Laurent Chiquet, whose family purchased the company in 1978 and transferred its headquarters to their own family's historic estate. 'I spent 10 years campaigning to my father that we could do something differently,' Jean-Hervé says.

'Then in 1988 he allowed me and my brother to take over and we spent 12 years changing everything about the structures of the company and the vineyards. But in 2000 we realised that the changes were not reflected in the wines, so it was then that we changed the entire range. We took big risks in changing the style to introduce the 700 series. A risk of losing most of our customers and a risk of big investment with no return for some years. We had to be good friends with our bank manager!'

While 2002 marked the turning point of what Jean-Hervé describes as 'deconstructing Jacquesson', a champagne house is like an ocean liner and it takes a generation to turn around. 'Our last Late Disgorged 2002 will be sold between 2019 and 2021, from a regime we started talking about in 1978, so it takes 43 years for the change to fully take effect.' And the Jacquesson revolution is far from over yet.

The house has introduced a series of drastic changes to raise quality in recent vintages. At a time when many houses are seeking to extend their fruit sources, Jacquesson has radically initiated just the opposite. Yields were lowered in 2008 at the same time as fruit purchases were strategically slashed from 40 hectares to just eight, lowering annual production of 350,000 bottles by 23%, with estate vines now supplying almost 80% of needs. 'The quality of what we grow means we are less satisfied with the fruit we buy, so we dropped those vineyards that were not up to the standard of our rising expectations,' Jean-Hervé declares.

Further, the age of release of the 700 series has been progressively stepped up, from three years on lees for Cuvée 733 (2005 base) to four years for Cuvée 736 (2008), with the hope of stretching Cuvée 739 (2011) to 4.5 years. Meanwhile, allocations have been further lowered by holding back an average of 15,000 bottles from each release since Cuvée 733, to release as a Late Disgorged 700 series, with an additional 4–5 years of bottle age. 'We may be the only champagne producer to take the risk of releasing their entry wine at nine years of age!' Jean-Hervé suggests. These are radical measures for any wine region, unheard of for a champagne house, and reflect resoundingly in the calibre of the 700 series today.

FANATICAL GROWER

Jacquesson's cuvées are complex blends that age impressively and reflect the intricate attention to detail applied at every step of their creation. This begins in the vineyards. According to Jean-Hervé, there are five factors in wine: 'Terroir, viticulture, viticulture, viticulture and winemaking!' He describes Jacquesson as a grower more than a champagne house, and himself and his brother as 'frustrated growers'. It is this philosophy that underpins the recent transformation of the house. I visited Jacquesson's vineyards towards the end of harvest 2014 and was stunned at how immaculately they are kept.

Their goal in the vineyards is to grow less fruit, slightly riper, to draw out the mineral character of the terroir. Jacquesson directly controls 28 hectares of enviably located premier and grand cru vineyards, 17 in Dizy, Aÿ and Hautvillers, and 11 in Avize, with an additional eight hectares sourced from contract growers in the same villages, who Jean-Hervé describes as 'neighbours and friends'. Jacquesson harvests half the fruit it purchases, and now only buys from its neighbours, 'because we want to see every single berry with our own eyes'. The house today is 40% smaller than it was 25 years ago, now producing just 280,000 bottles. 'Of course, we aim to increase the price.' Expect a price rise with Cuvée 740.

The estate has experimented with organics, with 10 hectares now fully organic, and the remainder run under a minimal-sulphur regime. When I questioned why full organic certification was not the agenda, Jean-Hervé's sensible response was, 'We are here to make good wine as our primary priority.' And 2012 was a strong case in point, with his organic fruit lost to mildew. 'I have always been convinced that a 100% organic system is not reasonable in Champagne's climate,' he explains.

Traditional methods are used throughout: little or no soil improvers, no herbicides or pesticides, minimal spray regimes, use of ploughing, cover crops between rows, and pruning to control vigour, increase ripeness, and limit yields to an average of around 60hL/hectare — just two-thirds of Champagne's average. 'The problem with Champagne is that every grower considers the maximum yield permitted by the appellation to be an economic minimum,' he admits. He describes cover cropping as particularly effective in controlling yields, but acknowledges that until recent environmental priorities became prominent, this was practised by significantly fewer than 1% of Champagne growers. Selection is very important to Jacquesson, and all tailles is sold, as well as any declassified parcels.

Jacquesson's attention in the vineyard allows its cuvées to capture the expression of the soil, exemplified in its trilogy of single-vineyard, single-varietal, single-vintage wines produced in minuscule volumes (never more than 10% of production in total), from three special little plots in Aÿ, Dizy and Avize. 'Terroir is the most unfair part of the wine business — you either have the right place or you don't!' Jean-Hervé says. 'It is very important to talk about terroir in champagne.' And talk terroir these cuvées do, articulating chalk mineral textures of disarming clarity. Jacquesson's single-vineyards and late-disgorged 700 series cuvées are tiraged under cork.

HANDS-OFF WINEMAKING

Jacquesson's scrupulous practices in the vineyard are mirrored in its hands-off approach in the winery. All fruit used by the house is pressed in its own press houses. 'Pressing is very important in champagne because we have this stupid idea of making white wine from red grapes!' he exclaims. 'We must hand-pick and press close to the vineyard or we'll end up with jam.'

Gentle vertical presses are used, and the very first juice is removed 'because it has washed the outside of the grapes'. Each parcel is vinified separately in large 45hL oak foudres to allow the wine to breathe, after which it is left on lees and stirred for several months. This process produces creaminess and body, and has an antioxidant effect, reducing sulphur dioxide additions.

'Malolactic fermentation is the eternal debate in Champagne,' Jean-Hervé suggests. 'We favour malolactic fermentation as we don't want to use heavy sulphur dioxide additions or filtration.' Traditionally, Jacquesson has run malolactic fermentation to completion, but more recently has blocked it in less than 20% of ferments by using cooling. There is also no fining, 'to maintain the aromatic potential of the fruit'.

Reserves for the 700 series wines are the previous blends, kept separate in oak barrels and enamelled tanks, with reserves back to Cuvée 735 (2007) base currently in stock.

All Jacquesson cuvées have been extra brut (less than 6g/L dosage) since 2000, although only recently declared on labels. 'We never intended to make extra brut, but we just don't think our wines need more dosage,' says Jean-Hervé.

Dosages have become progressively lower, but this trend has never been a conscious decision. 'Some of our wines have no dosage, not because we wanted to make zero-dosage wine, but because they were better wines this way,' he says.

Back labels are among the most informative of any champagne house, shamelessly declaring disgorgement date, dosage, base vintage, blend and even precise production quantities. There are no secrets here, just great champagnes, and better than ever. As Jean-Hervé puts it, 'At Jacquesson, we just want to grow great fruit and make great wines.'

JACQUESSON CUVÉE NO 738 EXTRA BRUT NV $$

94 points • 2010 BASE VINTAGE • DISGORGED APRIL AND JUNE 2014
• TASTED IN DIZY & SYDNEY

61% chardonnay, 21% meunier, 18% pinot noir; 33% reserves; 2.5g/L dosage; 265,000 bottles

Jacquesson pulled out every stop for this cuvée in the challengingly warm and wet 2010 season, producing no single-vineyard wines and using a very high proportion of chardonnay to build finesse and elegance. 'The idea of this cuvée is to give the identity of the base vintage, but we had to put a lot of things in here to make it work!' exclaims Jean-Hervé. And work it does, an impressive result for the season, albeit, inevitably, a lesser example of 700 series. As ever, it's coiled and tense on release, will benefit from a few more years to flesh out, and will blossom magnificently over the coming decade. Chardonnay takes the lead in impressive focus of crunchy lemon and grapefruit, opening into crunchy red apple and the subtle spice of barrel fermentation. More recent tastings have shown generous suggestions of golden fruit cake and fruit mince spice. Skilfully managed barrel work spins beautifully woven texture without oxidation or oak character, building a fine, creamy mouthfeel that amplifies salty minerality. A well-crafted and characterful wine of driving structure, charged with excellent acid line, finishing even, dry and long.

JACQUESSON CUVÉE NO 737 EXTRA BRUT NV $$

95 points • 2009 BASE VINTAGE • DISGORGED JANUARY 2014 • TASTED IN DIZY, SYDNEY, MELBOURNE & BRISBANE

43% chardonnay, 30% meunier, 27% pinot noir; 30% reserves; 3.5g/L dosage; 250,000 bottles

To properly respect the 700 series, treat it like a vintage wine, and don't be alarmed when it's introverted and tightly restrained on release. It will open beautifully a year later, and truly blossom five or 10 years on. The 737 looks more comfortable every time I come back — on first showing, tightly clenching its grapefruit, apple and pear fruit; more recently shedding its crystalline brittleness to make way for silky finesse, buttery notes, and the subtle almond, biscuit and spice of barrel fermentation. A primary core of lemon and apple fruit remains the main act, propelled by superb, fine salt mineral presence, a creamy bead, seamless line and grand persistence.

JACQUESSON CUVÉE 734 DÉGORGEMENT TARDIF EXTRA BRUT NV $$$$

95 points • 2006 BASE VINTAGE • DISGORGED OCTOBER 2014 • TASTED IN DIZY

54% chardonnay, 26% meunier, 20% pinot noir; 27% reserves; aged on lees more than 7 years; 16,200 bottles

I was the first outside the house to taste Jacquesson's second DT, and it's even more refined than the first. The coiled focus and poise exhibited here transcend the generous immediacy of 2006, with lively lemon and white peach fruit, vibrant acidity and pronounced salt chalk minerality infusing a dynamic youthfulness and grand longevity, with a decade of potential before it yet, and likely much more. Secondary complexity is building slowly, with notes of marzipan, brioche and a hint of honey, finishing with the enticing texture and creamy mouthfeel of long lees age.

JACQUESSON CUVÉE NO 733 DÉGORGEMENT TARDIF EXTRA BRUT NV $$$$

93 points • 2005 BASE VINTAGE • DISGORGED SEPTEMBER 2013 • TASTED IN DIZY & SYDNEY

52% chardonnay, 24% meunier, 24% pinot noir; 22% reserves; 2.5g/L dosage; 16,000 bottles

Jacquesson presented a pre-release offer of its first DT before anyone had tasted it — and the entire 16,000 bottle production sold in one month. The phenolic texture and grip of 2005 make for a more firmly structured cuvée that is evolving more quickly than other 700 series releases. Crunchy grapefruit, lemon zest and pear definition is upheld amidst layers of brioche, butterscotch, mixed spice and subtle tertiary notes of wood smoke. A wine of vitality on release, it has quickly evolved into developed characters of burnt orange, bitter almonds, fruit mince spice and wood spice, with a long, dry finish of hazelnut skin bitterness.

JACQUESSON DIZY TERRES ROUGES ROSÉ RÉCOLTE EXTRA BRUT 2008 $$$

95 points • DISGORGED FEBRUARY 2014 • TASTED IN DIZY

Skin-contact rosé of pinot noir, half macerated for 28 hours, and half free-run for greater finesse this vintage; 1.35 hectare single vineyard on the boundary of Dizy and Hautvillers, planted 1993; vinified in oak foudres; 3.5g/L dosage; 9000 bottles

Terres Rouges has been an evolution of experimentation for Jacquesson, and this is the first time Jean-Hervé feels completely happy that he's achieved his aspiration of a pronounced expression of pinot noir, yet with finesse. It's a particularly full-bodied and firmly structured rosé of deep crimson hue — think halfway between champagne rosé and full-blown red Burgundy. It has the structure to match, with a firm, fine tannin backbone, structured and chewy, yet harmonious and confident, ready for protein such as pink meats. Gorgeous complexity of subtle rose petal and musk aromas glide over tangy pink grapefruit and fresh raspberries, cherries and strawberries, accented by the gentle, savoury spice of barrel fermentation. There's a contrast here between focused tension and savoury complexity that will benefit from time to soften and build.

JACQUESSON DIZY CORNE BAUTRAY RÉCOLTE EXTRA BRUT 2005 $$$$$

96 points • DISGORGED OCTOBER 2014 • TASTED IN DIZY & SYDNEY

South-west facing single-vineyard Dizy on the boundary with Aÿ, planted 1960 on millstone-grit gravel over clayey marl and Campanian chalk; 100% chardonnay; vinified and aged in oak casks on lees; unfiltered; 1.5g/L dosage; 5200 bottles

Jean-Hervé has no idea why his father planted chardonnay in Dizy, but a half-century later these old vines have tapped so deep into the terroir that the voice of the soil speaks above the tones of the fruit and the expression of the barrels. The chalk mineral impression of this cuvée is inexplicable, though irrefutable in all recent vintages, from a site with chalk no less than 2.5 metres under the surface, in a village unrecognised for chardonnay of structure. Grapefruit and lemon zest are backed by the subtle almond-meal notes of long lees age, finishing structured and scaffolded with impressive energy and drive, a standout wine from a difficult season. A bottle tasted in Sydney showed more development of coffee bean, cocoa and blood orange flavours, with some bitter orange-zest grip on the finish.

JACQUESSON AVIZE CHAMP CAÏN RÉCOLTE EXTRA BRUT 2005 $$$$$

97 points • DISGORGED OCTOBER 2014 • TASTED IN DIZY

Due south-facing single-vineyard Avize; 1.3 hectares; planted 1962 on surface chalk; 100% chardonnay; vinified and matured in oak casks on lees; unfiltered; 2.5g/L dosage; 10,000 bottles

The terroir of Avize is so all-consuming that you can literally smell the violent tidal wave of surging, heaving salt minerality coming. The bouquet is a salty sea breeze, a steamy whiff of bath salts that heralds an intricately crystalline salt structure. The frothing, energetic interplay between chalk minerality and beautiful acid line is captivating, amplified by subtle barrel texture and long lees age that gently massage the cut of Avize. Magnificent freshness and coiled potential, even at a decade of age, suggest that it calls for another decade yet to fully come into its own. There are few 2005 champagnes of which this can be said. Jacquesson has conjured one of the finest.

JACQUESSON AŸ VAUZELLE TERME RÉCOLTE EXTRA BRUT 2005 $$$$$

96 points • DISGORGED OCTOBER 2014 • TASTED IN DIZY

Tiny plot of just 0.3 hectare, due south-facing on the mid-slope of Aÿ, not far from the Dizy border; planted by Jean-Hervé Chiquet in 1980 on calcerous soil 60-70cm over chalk bedrock; 100% pinot noir; vinified and matured in oak casks on lees; unfiltered; 2.5g/L dosage; 2500 bottles

This tiny pocket is Jacquesson's finest terroir of all, giving birth to a champagne for long contemplation in large glasses, and preferably not for at least five years yet. The 2005 is the vintage to drink while 2004 and 2002 mellow long in the cellar. This is a vintage driven by the structure and dry, textural grip of the season, expressed in notes of wood spice and quince. In time, fruit rises to enchanting reflections of poached strawberries, red apples and cherries, laced with ginger and exotic spice. A finely structured texture unites creamy lees age with chalk mineral depth. A rousing celebration of Aÿ pinot noir.

JACQUESSON AVIZE DÉGORGEMENT TARDIF EXTRA BRUT 1997 $$$$$

96 points • DISGORGED SEPTEMBER 2013 • TASTED IN DIZY

100% chardonnay from three vineyards in Avize; full malolactic fermentation; zero dosage; 595 bottles

A vintage forever in the shadow of 1995 and 1996, but Jean-Hervé prefers 1997 to 1996 in Avize, and this wine is one of the highlights of the vintage. The exceptional expression of the fine, salt mineral signature of Avize energises great complexity of yellow mirabelle plum, fig, preserved lemon and glacé peach. Endearing brioche and bready notes celebrate the long lees ageing of barrel-fermented chardonnay. A delightfully tense and elongated palate reflects backward development and promising potential.

JACQUESSON DÉGORGEMENT TARDIF EXTRA BRUT MILLÉSIME 1995 $$$$$

97 points • DISGORGED SEPTEMBER 2013 • TASTED IN DIZY

55% chardonnay, 45% pinot noir; no malolactic fermentation; 390 bottles

At a full 20 years of age, the enduring longevity of Jacquesson is declared in a vintage that sings with the high notes of fresh, zesty grapefruit of great energy and tension. Layers of glorious secondary complexity of fig, patisserie, honey and mixed spice are only beginning to hint at the enticing pipe-smoke nuances of tertiary development. Age has layered lees-infused texture over a lingering chalk mineral mouthfeel. This release is infinitesimal, but the statement that it makes in declaring the tireless longevity of the current Jacquessons is monumental.

JACQUINOT & FILS

(Zha-key-noh e Feess)

5/10

34–36 RUE MAURICE CERVEAUX 51200 ÉPERNAY

www.champagne-jacquinot.com

CHAMPAGNE

JACQUINOT
&FILS

* J*ean-Manuel Jacquinot trained as an oenologist at Veuve Clicquot before taking over production at his small family-owned estate in Épernay in 1998. Now general manager, he oversees production from 17 hectares of vineyards. With the exception of a blanc de noirs, all cuvées are led by a strong majority of chardonnay, and no meunier is used. The results are harmonious, well-balanced cuvées, aged deep in chalk cellars 19 metres under Épernay.

JACQUINOT & FILS PRIVATE CUVÉE BRUT NV $$

92 points • TASTED IN BRISBANE

70% chardonnay, 30% pinot noir; 20-30% reserve wines

An attractive contrast between youthful lemon zest and the brioche complexity of bottle age, led by the elegance of chardonnay, with pretty red-fruit support from pinot noir. Dosage is apparent, yet well integrated. It's clean, vibrant, light and long, making for a balanced apéritif style.

JACQUINOT & FILS HARMONIE MILLÉSIMÉ 2000 $$$$

93 points • TASTED IN BRISBANE

80% chardonnay, 20% pinot noir; aged a decade on lees

Jacquinot's flagship is a rich and complex champagne of medium straw gold hue and fleshy, rounded and rich personality, true to the depth of character typical of 2000. Roast nut, dried pear, even white Christmas cake and cherry pie complexity make for a flavoursome and engaging style of persistent length and seamless balance. It's ready to go right away, without the zest and drive to last longer.

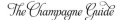

JÉRÔME PRÉVOST

(Zheh-rowm Preh-voh)

7/10

2 RUE DE LA PETITE MONTAGNE 51390 GUEUX

CHAMPAGNE

La Closerie

Les Béguines

Across every style and region of the wine world, the very greatest makers share an intuitive approach that transcends any prescriptive grapegrowing or winemaking regime. Besides Anselme Selosse (of Jacques Selosse) himself, no one in Champagne personifies this more dramatically than Jérôme Prévost. When others follow regimes of traditional viticulture, organics or biodynamics, Prévost adopts a natural approach, keeping his senses attuned to the vines and responding gently. In a region that strives to mould every vintage into a house style, Prévost makes only a vintage wine and sees it as his role to support the vines to maximise the expression of the season, though sadly releases it too early to label it as a vintage. He harvests not on sugar or acidity, but on the sensation of the skins of the grapes in his mouth. He can't tell you if his wines go through malolactic fermentation ('I don't do analysis — the wines do what they want'). And he doesn't add dosage, not because this is his philosophy, but because the wine doesn't need it. 'Wine is not about philosophy,' he declares. This is winemaking by emotion, a world away from the formal, clinical approach of Champagne. With a big smile and a genuine, warm and unflustered approach, Prévost makes wines much like himself. Fleshy, vinous and brimming with exotic spice, these are some of the finest expressions of pure, single-vineyard, single-vintage meunier in all of Champagne.

In 1987, at the age of 21, Prévost inherited the 2.2 hectare vineyard planted in the 1960s by his grandmother in Gueux on the Petite Montagne. There is only one vineyard and one variety and, until a recent foray into rosé, there was only one wine, too.

Prévost made his first wine in 1998, with the help of his friend, Anselme Selosse. It was a sign of the regard in which Anselme held the young Jérôme that he lent him space in his winery in Avize to make his first four vintages. There is a clear synergy of philosophy between the two.

Prévost treasures the 55-million-year-old soils of his village and proudly showed me a sample, teeming with fossils of ancient sea life like some geology museum artefact — the secret, he says, to the minerality of his wine. Here, the chalk is deep, starting 25 metres below the surface, and he has spent 12 years working the soil to encourage deeper roots to build minerality in his wines. This is very much a lesser terroir of Champagne. 'I cannot understand how Jérôme Prévost can make wines as good as he does where he is,' Jacquesson's Jean-Hervé Chiquet told me recently. 'He is very talented.'

And he pays close attention to his vineyard. 'The soil used to be very hard, but now it is very easy to work. I plough the mid-rows and avoid herbicides. It's all about building up the micro-organism population in the soil, and that takes time,' Prévost says.

He is emphatic that this is not biodynamics. 'Biodynamics is like a religion and I don't agree with that,' he explains. 'It's too much like a recipe, but every plot of land is different. You have to work with emotion and sensation and learn from nature, not from a book. You have to go out in the vines and feel the sun and the wind, with all of your senses attuned, to taste with your eyes and your ears.'

Grapes are harvested at a high level of maturity, achieved with tiny yields of 45hL/hectare, less than half Champagne's average. His role is to support his vines to draw out the expression of the year. 'I do not know which years are good years because for me every year is different,' he says. 'I have two girls, educated in the same way, but each is different and I love them both with the same love. My wines are the same. In the vineyard, every year is very different and this is what I enjoy about it.

'I do not understand the philosophy of making champagne taste the same every year. It is not my role to determine the style of the wine. The wine is the wine and it has its own way. In the winery, I do not want my stamp to show. I have to work very softly. To make a white wine I do nothing in the cellar — I work hard in the vineyard, press and put it in barrels,' he says.

Fermentation relies exclusively on natural yeasts from the vines. 'Different yeasts give different aromas, so you have to use natural yeast to make complex wines,' he explains. Since different yeasts have different tolerances to sulphur, he uses only very low levels of sulphur, so as not to inhibit weaker strains. Fermentation takes place entirely in barrels, both small and large, including a few Acacia barriques for the first time in 2012, and wines remain in barrel for 10 months, so as to breathe and not develop reductive characters. There is only one wine (the rosé is made from the same base as the white),

so the blend is made up of every barrel. Prévost prizes the complexity achieved by blending many small ferments of parcels from one vineyard. Every wine receives the same dosage of a minute 2g/L. 'I don't think about that, they all get the same!' he says.

It's a shame Prévost's wines are released so young, as it takes years for them to blossom. Bottles are not vintage dated, but the year of harvest is coded in the fine print of the front label, beginning 'LC'.

He was excited to make red wine for rosé from meunier for the first time in 2007. A tiny volume of a single barrel is worked by hand, even using a bucket to 'pump' over twice a day. 'It's a marvellous thing!' he exclaims. 'Working directly with the grapes to make red wine is like a gift for me. In Champagne traditionally we never put the skin in the wine, but I don't understand this because all the good things about the grape are just under the skin!' Harvesting at full ripeness is the key, because maturity of the skin is more important to him than sugar and acid levels. This is achieved by sourcing red wine from an old part of the vineyard affected by a virus which produces very small and very few berries, reducing yields and intensifying the fruit. He always adds 10% to the white of the vintage to produce a rosé of slightly different colour each year.

Prévost makes just 13,000 bottles every year in the outhouses of his charming 1924 cottage in Gueux and a little cellar on his street. It's a small space, containing his barrels, one small blending tank, one forklift and a cellar in an old World War I armaments store. He was riddling when I visited most recently, which he does by hand twice daily in the same little space. 'It is very small, but enough for my two hands,' he says. Such is his tiny scale that he refers to his friend Pierre Larmandier's small estate of Larmandier-Bernier as 'a factory'.

The scarcity of Prévost's wines makes them hard to find, but the hunt is richly rewarded. Don't look for a bottle with his name on it. The name of the vineyard is prominent and his name is lost in the fine print.

This is just as he would have it.

JÉRÔME PRÉVOST LA CLOSERIE LES BÉGUINES $$$

89 points • TASTED IN GUEUX

2013 base vintage ('LC13' on front label); 100% meunier; no dosage

Tasted almost a year before its release, this is a desperately youthful wine with tense, primary acidity only heightened by the 2°C air temperature in Jérôme's winery when we tasted in the depth of winter. In this state, it showed some notes of garlic and onion reduction, surprising for Prévost. They did not dissipate with air as the wine warmed up, though may with time in bottle. Crunchy bitter grapefruit rides over a finely chalky palate and creamy bead.

Jérôme Prévost La Closerie les Béguines $$$

95 points • Tasted in Gueux & Sydney

2012 base vintage ('LC12' on front label); 100% meunier; 2g/L dosage

The 2012 is Prévost's finest vintage since 2008, furnishing a dynamic, exuberant and exact manifestation of the inimitable personality of pinot noir. It oozes in red berry and red cherry fruits, with a vibrant core of lemon, grapefruit and crunchy pear, overlaid with exotic notes of golden delicious apple and mixed spice. Hints of patisserie and toasty complexity are just beginning to materialise. A well-composed meunier of complexity and allure, contrasting fleshy body with accurate acid line and finely poised structure, culminating in grand persistence.

Jérôme Prévost La Closerie les Béguines $$$

92 points • Tasted in Gueux

2009 base vintage ('LC09' on front label); 100% meunier; 2g/L dosage

Prévost's 2009 has lapped up its time in bottle, at last finding integration for toasty, biscuity oak. Its baked apple personality has evolved to a bruised apple character, sustaining crunchy pear flavours. It's buttery and secondary and at the same time textured and structured, with subtle, chewy red apple skin texture on a long finish.

Jérôme Prévost La Closerie Fac-simile Rosé NV $$$$

93 points • Tasted in Gueux

2013 base vintage ('LC13' on front label); 100% meunier; 10% red wine; no dosage

Tasted long before release, under the same early and challenging conditions as the white, Prévost's rosé shows all the hallmarks of greatness in a few years' time. A medium, vibrant salmon-pink hue introduces a lively style of enticing, tangy strawberry hull, pink grapefruit, pomegranate, pink pepper and a hint of charcuterie. It holds with impressive persistence and softly textured structure.

Jérôme Prévost La Closerie Fac-simile Rosé NV $$$$

95 points • Tasted in Gueux & Sydney

2012 base vintage ('LC12' on front label); 100% meunier; 10% red wine; 2g/L dosage

Prévost fuses dynamic freshness with body and dimension in this outstanding season of character and energy. It's a pretty medium-salmon hue, packed with pink pepper, wild strawberries, crunchy pink lady apples and pink grapefruit of primary purity and lively poise, all laced together on a long finish with a fine silver ribbon of graceful acidity, and soft, supple mineral texture. It's disarmingly enduring and beautifully enchanting.

Joseph Perrier

(Zhoh-sef Per-riay)

5/10

69 AVENUE DE PARIS 51016 CHÂLONS-EN-CHAMPAGNE

www.josephperrier.com

DEPUIS 1825

Joseph Perrier

CHAMPAGNE

Founded in 1825, this medium-sized house was family owned until its purchase by the Alain Thiénot Group in 1998. Holdings of 21 hectares in Cumières, Damery and Hautvillers satisfy nearly a third of its production of about 800,000 bottles annually, supplemented from growers, including a strong proportion of chardonnay from Vitry-le-François near the house's home of Châlons-en-Champagne. For reserve wines, 600-litre oak barrels are used. The house style is ripe and generous, often taking the apple-roundness of meunier and the sweetness of dosage a little too far.

JOSEPH PERRIER CUVÉE ROYALE BRUT VINTAGE 2002 $$$

92 points • TASTED IN BRISBANE, SYDNEY & MELBOURNE

50% chardonnay, 41% pinot noir, 9% meunier; a blend of 14 premier and grand cru villages; aged at least 6 years on lees

A celebration of maturity in a full straw hue and rich notes of fig, mixed spice, white Christmas cake, gingernut biscuits and generous secondary yellow stone fruits. The best bottles maintain a long and even palate, but it's right at the end of its life now, and two bottles I tasted had collapsed into bitter, vinegary, burnt-orange oxidation.

JOSEPH PERRIER CUVÉE JOSÉPHINE 2004 $$$$

93 points • TASTED IN BRISBANE

52% chardonnay, 48% pinot noir; a blend of premier and grand cru villages

Surprisingly youthful and precocious for its age, capturing the energy and elegance of 2004. Maturity has brought a medium straw hue and nuances of nougat, fresh almonds, vanilla and copha. Comfortably integrated acidity and soft, fine chalk mineral structure carry the finish with gentle flow, interrupted by prominent dosage. Will age yet.

KRUG

(Khroo-k)

5 RUE COQUEBERT 51100 REIMS

www.krug.com

To those of us gazing in from the outside in wide-eyed wonder, Krug is to Champagne as Domaine de la Romanée-Conti is to Burgundy and Pétrus is to Bordeaux. It possesses a grandeur, an other-worldliness, an amplitude that is as lofty as its mesospheric price. Krug's grand hierarchy of prestige begins at a higher price than any other in Champagne, and its single-vineyard wines rank among the most expensive in the world. Krug is the king of champagnes. And it has something mystical, too.

I've always wondered if the magic of Krug is real. If one worked here for long enough, would the sparkle evaporate, the cellar turn into just a dank, dark hole, the barrels become just dirty old kegs, the cracks in the walls reveal these old buildings for what they are, and the day-to-day reality expose the hyperbole of one of the most clever of all French marketing spiels?

I'm not the only one who has wondered. Julie Cavil, one of four in a talented young winemaking team headed by Eric Lebel, made a flippant passing comment when I first met her.

'When I joined here, I went behind the scenes because I suspected that not everything was done as it is said to be. But I found that it is,' she said. The sparkle in her eye and that glimmer of don't-pinch-me-in-case-I-wake-up wonder told me this was no marketing line. The magic, it seems, is real.

And it has to be, hasn't it? Some can fake wines of mediocre standards — but no one, anywhere, ever, can fake wines at this level. The wines of Krug are among the most revered in the world.

'I've been talking about Krug for over 20 years, but in 2011, I really discovered what it is about!' exclaims sixth-generation director, Olivier Krug. The revelation was the discovery of a book buried in the company archives for more than 160 years. The personal notebook of Olivier's great-great-great-grandfather was written to document the philosophy of Krug just five years after he founded the house in 1843. In it he expounded the principles of creating a champagne of great richness and yet great elegance, of selecting only the finest elements from the greatest terroirs, rejecting mediocre fruit and, revolutionary at the time, making both a non-vintage and a vintage cuvée. To this day, a resolute commitment to these very ideals has secured Krug's position as the most luxurious, most exclusive and most decadent of all champagnes. And, most extraordinary of all, its champagnes are only getting better.

PERFECTIONISM BEFORE TRADITION

From the outset, Krug has courageously pursued perfectionism ahead of traditionalism. 'Joseph was not a non-conformist, he was a very serious German guy, but he was ready to go beyond the rules to create something different,' Olivier reflects. 'He left the stability of the largest house in Champagne in 1842, with a vision to create a champagne that didn't exist.'

That same daring spirit flows in Olivier's blood, relentlessly pursuing the very finest grapes, regardless of variety, vineyard classification or village reputation, and fanatical vinification, regardless of cost.

Meunier is prized, even in these wines of untiring longevity. Classification tastings are conducted blind, with no regard for a vineyard's cru. Krug purposely does not constrain itself to grand cru, nor even to premier cru, and its reach has extended as far even as the village of Les Riceys at the most southerly extreme of the Côte des Bar, on the border of Burgundy.

In a region not traditionally associated with longevity, its winegrowers were amazed when Krug invited them to taste their reserve wines at two, three, five and even 15 years of age. 'They were astounded that their wines could be kept all that time, and were extremely moved and very emotional,' Julie recalls.

Krug owns just 21 hectares, less than 35% of the vineyards required to meet an annual production of an undisclosed figure somewhere in the vicinity of 650,000 bottles. Olivier says that Krug is not selling any more bottles today than it was 15 years ago, though production has increased by an undisclosed amount to facilitate slow future growth in sales.

Estate vineyards are supplemented with fruit from some 70–100 loyal growers, some of whom have supplied the house since its foundation. Olivier explains that they have recently formalised contracts based on individual plots, but with the flexibility to maintain quality in difficult vintages.

'One grower called us in 2010 and said, "I have a different plot for you because yours was done by rot",' he says. Few champagne houses can claim such loyalty. Olivier personally visits the vineyards every day during harvest.

I was privileged to tag along for a day during vintage 2014 and witness the calibre of his plots and pristine condition of their fruit. Olivier is very friendly with his growers and workers in the press houses, showing them photos on his phone when he visits.

Krug pays a premium for higher quality grapes, and pays its picking teams mostly by the hour rather than the usual rate by the kilogram, an important distinction in ensuring stringent selection in the vineyards. Pickers are instructed to drop anything with rot, burnt or weak berries. I was surprised by just how much fruit was dropped in the mid-rows of Clos d'Ambonnay.

OBSESSED WITH DETAIL

Krug's long-ageing style begins with fruit harvested with more acidity and less sugar, so pHs are usually lower than the rest of the region.

'In 2010 we started in Clos du Mesnil two days before the official regulated start of harvest,' Olivier explains. 'Everyone in the village said we were mad, but they were all watching for when we started because they know we are obsessed with detail!'

The secret at Krug lies in the detail. 'Joseph set some rules for an absolute detail for everything,' Olivier says. 'And we focus even more intently on the details today.' Grapes are selected plot by plot and pressed individually by their growers. 'Even if a grower chooses grapes from the same part of the village, we ask him to press as many parcels as he can.'

Olivier's late father, Henri Krug, told him, 'If you have a chance to vinify a wine on its own, you will express more of its personality. The more individuality you get, the more precise you can be with your selection.'

'It is as if I have a friend who paints the most beautiful panorama covering a wall, so lifelike and so detailed that it is as if the wall is not there,' says Olivier. 'And he paints the sky using 200 different shades of blue. Pale for the horizon, grey-blue for the east and deep blue for the west. But if he mixed all 200 shades of blue together and used the same proportions to paint the sky, it would have nothing of the same detail. So it is with blending champagne. We make 240 separate vinifications of parcels that could all be blended into just three vats.'

To facilitate this, 36 stainless steel double vats of small capacity were installed in 2007, increasing the small-batch storage capacity of the winery. In keeping each plot separate, reserve wines can be kept fresher. 'Some plots have more potential to age than others, and if they were all vinified together, the blend would lose the freshness of the freshest parcels,' he explains.

Last year one of Krug's largest growers in Avize came to taste his six reserve wines back to 1998. 'He knows which plots are in each sample and we don't,' Oliver recounts. 'He went white when he tasted them. Out of 20 plots that he has supplied us over 13 years — more than 250 wines in all — five of those six reserves were from the same plot. None of us had any idea, because what we do is by taste, not by recipe. Such is our attention to detail in the tasting room.'

Krug's winemaking team admits to an obsession with numbers. Krug works with 200–250 very small parcels of fruit every vintage, all of which are tasted after vintage and again the following year. Any not up to Krug's exacting standards go somewhere else in the

Louis Vuitton-Moët Hennessy (LVMH) group. In the past 15 years, Krug has grown its reserves from 60 to 150 different wines, dubbed 'treasures' by Olivier.

At any time, all of these are under consideration for Grande Cuvée, and all are also tasted annually. Olivier and his uncle Rémi join the winemaking team for the tastings. The final blend comprises more than 100 parcels, spanning eight to 10 vintages, reflecting a different recipe every year. 'Our job every year is to recreate the most generous character of champagne,' says Olivier. A particular 1995 reserve wine from Bouzy has been tasted every year for 16 years and is yet to be allocated to the blend. There are still two 2001 reserve wines in Krug's cellar. As always, taste before reputation. 'Even in a crap vintage there are still great wines,' grins Olivier. Reserves are kept fresh in 150 small tanks, deep in the cellar at a stable 11–13°C. At any given time there are 5 million bottles in the cellar, 10 times the annual production, a massive ratio that reflects this long-ageing style.

Wetting the barrels at Krug Clos d'Ambonnay in anticipation of the 2014 harvest.

MAGNIFICENT LONGEVITY

Krug attributes its longevity to the primary fermentation of all of its wines in more than 4000 small, 205-litre oak barrels. When I arrived in July 2011, I was confronted by a sea of barrels in preparation for vintage in Krug's large courtyard, packed in so tight that there were but narrow access ways to each of the buildings. And Krug has more barrels on site at its Clos du Mesnil and Clos d'Ambonnay vineyards. It uses these not for oak flavour or aroma, but to build richness, complexity, balance and a 'high fidelity' that is not possible in stainless steel.

This is achieved by using only old casks, of average age 20 years, currently dating back to 1964. They are decommissioned after about 50 years, when they become too difficult to repair. Seguin Moreau barrels were used exclusively in the past, but Taransaud have been introduced recently. 'It took six years of tasting trials to establish the best coopers for Krug,' Julie tells me. Such is the attention to detail here. All barrels are purchased new and are seasoned for a few years by fermenting the second and third press before it is sold for distillation. A waste of a new barrel, but that's Krug! Olivier is adamant that Krug is not special just because it is fermented in oak. 'When we started, every champagne was fermented in oak, and it still was 50 years ago!' he points out. When I asked to take his photo in front of the barrels, he politely proposed a different backdrop, eager to downplay the focus on oak.

To uphold freshness, Krug's wines spend just a few weeks in cask and are transferred to tanks following fermentation. Contact with oxygen during ferment-

ation furnishes Krug with a resilience when it contacts oxygen as it ages, infusing its wines with rock-solid consistency. I have not seen the degradation of freshness in Krug bottles that plagues many other champagnes as they travel around the world. These are wines capable of ageing magnificently for decades.

When a bottle in Krug's museum cellar popped as its cage was replaced recently, the board and winemakers were immediately assembled to taste the wine blind. Vigorous debate ensued as to whether it was from the 1950s or the 1960s, but it was decided it was too fresh for the 1960s. It turned out to be 1915 — all the more remarkable because the Côte des Blancs was under occupation during World War I and the wine was made exclusively from pinot noir, without the structural longevity of chardonnay.

Olivier doesn't like talking about malolactic fermentation, but lab analysis reveals the presence of malic acid as a key agent in Krug's longevity. 'Eric Lebel says he doesn't care about malolactic, but of course he cares,' reveals Olivier. 'Nothing is done to start it and nothing is done to stop it.' In 2013, just two or three of Krug's 240 fermentations went through malolactic fermentation. Even some parcels of the searingly high-acid 1996 vintage retained full malic acidity.

Although Grande Cuvée is released when it is ready to drink, after a long ageing process, Olivier has been intrigued by the number of collectors who age it further. 'Visitors now talk about Grand Cuvées from the '40s, '50s, '60s and '70s,' he reports. 'Many of our customers now put it down for five years or more.' He enjoys hosting dinners around the world for Krug lovers to bring their oldest Grand Cuvée.

It is now finally possible to ascertain the age of Krug's cuvées, thanks to an ingenious ID code printed above the barcode of every bottle, the first three digits of which indicate the trimester (first digit) and year (second and third digits) in which it was disgorged. Using this code, Krug.com and the new Krug app will reveal the season and year in which the bottle was shipped, the number of years over which it has aged, the blend and the vintage story for vintage wines. For non-vintage blends, it will reveal the number of wines and each of the vintages.

RELENTLESS PURSUIT OF QUALITY

Krug's quest for quality in spite of the cost knows no limits. Krug Clos du Mesnil 1999 was to be released in 2010, but the final tasting pre-labelling was a disappointment. 'It did not have extravagant purity, it was shy and boring, you don't want to sit next to this wine!' Olivier explains.

So the decision was made to cancel its release, in spite of an offer from China to purchase the entire production of more than 10,000 bottles at full price. Olivier opened a bottle for me this year, 'to show that there is no compromise at Krug'. It was tense, introverted, deeply mineral and magnificent, though not as coherent as the 1998 or 2000. A secure 96 points. 'We will destroy the bottles and blend it away,' Olivier declared.

'The first thing you learn here is patience,' admits Julie. 'There is a different time here. The clock in the courtyard is a symbol of the house. Time is very important in this place.'

Long ageing prior to release makes it impossible for Krug to follow trends, even if it wanted to. It takes 20 years to make a bottle of Grand Cuvée, since reserve wines are built up over 10 years, and seven or eight years of stock is perpetually ageing on lees.

Ownership of Krug rests with LVMH, which has remained sufficiently detached to leave most of the decisions in the hands of the family. Since he joined the company in 1989, Olivier has built the Japanese market into the most important for Krug. 'Everyone in Champagne was laughing when we went to Japan,' he said. 'And that's the reason they are still not there today!'

Krug's respect for a timeless tradition of rigorous selection, genius winemaking and masterful blending secures its inimitable position at the pinnacle of sparkling wine in the world today.

KRUG ROSÉ BRUT NV $$$$$

98 points • 2006 BASE VINTAGE WITH RESERVES BACK TO 2000 • DISGORGED WINTER 2012/2013 • TASTED IN YARRA VALLEY

59% pinot noir, 33% chardonnay, 8% meunier; partial malolactic fermentation on approximately two-thirds of parcels; 7g/L total sugar

Like Grande Cuvée, Krug Rosé is a multi-vintage blend, but the association strictly ends here. This is a much smaller volume, representing roughly just 10% of the production of the house, assembled from the ground up. Pinot noirs from the best vines in Aÿ are treated to a short fermentation on skins and then blended with pinot noir, meunier and chardonnay fermented in small oak casks as white wine, before ageing for a minimum of five years in bottle. Rosé is a relative newcomer at Krug, first released in the 1980s. Such was the visionary daring of Olivier's late father Henri Krug, and his brother Rémi, that when their father opposed the creation of a pink wine, they secretly produced a trial rosé. On pouring it blind for their father in 1976, he exclaimed, 'It is finished for us because someone in Champagne has copied Krug!'

Its ethereal restraint and delicate air seems a paradox in the grand decadence of Krug, but such is the detailed intricacy of this medium salmon-tinted cuvée that it dances with light-footed grace on a stage of epic complexity. Absolute restraint and taut freshness of red fruits and lemon zest slowly unravel to a world of spicy complexity of truffles and game. An impeccable acid profile and pinpoint bead define a remarkable finish of mind-blowing seamlessness, impeccable line and unrelenting persistence. Most thrilling of all, its minerality is all-encompassing, mouth-embracing and emphatically chalk-infused.

The Champagne Guide

KRUG GRANDE CUVÉE NV $$$$

97 points • 2006 BASE VINTAGE WITH 11 VINTAGES BACK TO 1990 • DISGORGED
SUMMER 2013 • TASTED IN REIMS

44% pinot noir, 35% chardonnay, 21% meunier; a blend of 142 wines; ID 213035

97 points • 2005 BASE VINTAGE WITH 12 VINTAGES BACK TO 1990 • DISGORGED
SUMMER 2012 • TASTED IN REIMS, PERTH, SYDNEY & MELBOURNE

44% pinot noir, 37% chardonnay, 19% meunier; a blend of 134 wines; ID 312036

97 points • 2003 BASE VINTAGE WITH 10 VINTAGES BACK TO 1988 • DISGORGED
SPRING 2011 • TASTED IN REIMS

51% pinot noir, 30% chardonnay, 19% meunier; a blend of 120 wines; ID 211021

Krug leads off where most other champagne houses end, and this is every bit a prestige cuvée.
Krug is adamant that it has no hierarchy in its cuvées, but price and style dictate that Grande
Cuvée is always the starting point. Interestingly, the house pours in reverse order, tasting Grand
Cuvée last. 'My father said, "Red carpet for every Krug!"' explains Olivier. 'There is no special
treatment here, and every grape at Krug is given the same respect.'

Krug's winemaking team describes Grande Cuvée as its most exciting and most challenging
wine to produce each year. It is a blend of the three champagne varieties, but there is no formula
or recipe except to maintain not so much the consistency of the style (as the house has claimed
in the past), but the best that can be produced each year. Krug Grande Cuvée and Rosé are built
on a high proportion (30–50%) and wide spectrum (6–10 vintages) of reserve wines. Reserves
are kept in tank for five, 10 and even 20 years. After blending, Grande Cuvée spends at least a
further six years on lees in bottle to build its characteristic golden amplitude. An additional year
of ageing was added thanks to slow sales during the financial crisis of 2008 and 2009. Grande
Cuvée accounts for 85% of the production of the house.

Grande Cuvée is a paradox of tense freshness, profound maturity and inimitable complexity.
In its current summer 2013 disgorgement it sings with a youthful definition of breathtaking
lemon and lemon zest, with marvellous layers of strawberries, figs and tangelos. It opens with
a fanfare into a maelstrom of molten wax, wisps of smouldering truffle, Christmas spice and
kirsch. Decadently rich, extravagantly complex and thunderingly expansive, Grande Cuvée is a
vinous champagne of multifaceted personality, yet ever-heightened tension and unerring focus,
tapping into deep wells of scintillating, swirling minerality. For Krug to capture more vitality
and freshness than ever from base vintages as rounded and immediate as 2006, and as firm and
rich as 2005, is testimony to the unparalleled skill of this house. Every bit as enchanting as its
legendary reputation promises, this is a champagne to drink slowly from large glasses, to witness
an entire universe of captivating theatrics unfold as it warms.

Older disgorgements served at the house and around the world demonstrate the enduring
consistency of this cuvée and its profound propensity to retain its vitality. The 2005 base
contrasts beguiling freshness with transcendental pipe-smoke complexity. The house has
re-released the 2003 base to coincide with the launch of its vintage wine from the same season,
to make the resounding point that this controversial season has the capacity to age marvellously.
It unites remarkable freshness of just-picked citrus with the depth of juicy stone fruits and
grand complexity of bees wax and leather. Definitive and immovable, apart from one tired bottle
in Australia, every one of the more than half-a-dozen bottles of different ages that I've tasted
recently has upheld a stability unmatched by any other house. The precision of recent releases
is unprecedented, and just how many decades they might hold in the cellar is anyone's guess.

Krug Vintage 2003 $$$$$

96 points • Disgorged summer 2013 and winter 2013/2014 • Tasted in Reims

46% pinot noir, 29% chardonnay, 25% meunier; ID 114001 and 313044

No one expected Krug to release a vintage from this record hot, tiny-yielding season, and certainly not with an unusually high proportion of meunier. 'If you look at this blend on paper, it looks like the opposite of what you'd expect in a prestige cuvée!' Olivier admits. 'Our impressions of the wines were the opposite of what we were hearing from others in Champagne. And the more we tasted the wines, the more we fell in love with some, though not all. So we decided to express the character of the year and make one of the smallest vintages at Krug in 60 years. The trick with 2003 is that we chose parcels on the aromatics of the grapes, not on the acidity, and we found some truly great wines with surprising balance, freshness, aromatic expression and vivacious fruit.' With Avize and Le Mesnil-sur-Oger largely wiped out by spring frost, the blend is built on chardonnay from Villers-Marmery and Trépail, the elegance of pinot noir from the northern Montagne de Reims and the depth of Clos d'Ambonnay (with no Clos d'Ambonnay released this vintage), and the vivacity and expression of meunier from Sainte-Gemme, Villevenard and Courmas. In memory of its intense sun, Krug dubbed the vintage 'vivacious radiance'.

In a vintage when most houses didn't release a prestige cuvée, or shouldn't have, I was apprehensive when Olivier introduced this cuvée. At this age, the wines of 2003 are characterised by dry extract and firm phenolic structure, but Krug takes this mood and presents it gracefully rather than aggressively. A lemon zest and grapefruit purity and a wonderfully tense, energetic vitality completely transcend a season that has generally not held its freshness. It delivers signature Krug impact with clarity seen nowhere else in 2003, layered with fig, dried peach, bees wax, butterscotch, nougat, exotic spice, wood smoke and incense. It really comes into its own on the finish, holding its integrity, precise line, profound persistence and exact, salty, super-fine chalk mineral definition like no other. How has Krug pulled off such a feat? Stringent selection and tiny production enlivened by malic acidity. The toughest seasons define the greatest estates. This was my top wine of the vintage. And then along came Clos du Mesnil …

Krug Vintage 2000 $$$$$

98 points • Disgorged autumn 2012 • Tasted in Reims & Perth

43% chardonnay from Trépail, Villers-Marmery, Avize and Le Mesnil-sur-Oger; 42% pinot noir from Ambonnay, Bouzy and Aÿ; 15% meunier from Sainte-Gemme and Villevenard; ID 412048

The potential for a Krug vintage wine is only identified after the blend of Grande Cuvée has been secured, and all the reserves earmarked. 'Our challenge with Grand Cuvée is to make a consistent wine that erases all the character of the vintage,' Olivier explains. The most extreme and spectacular wines are kept aside as reserve wines; those with the most pronounced character of the vintage become the vintage wine. Krug's vintage comprises just 4–5% of production, making a statement to reflect the story of the year, rather than a creative expression.

Krug dubs Vintage 2000 *gourmandise orageuse* — stormy indulgence — after its chaotic season, among its most intense and warmest declared vintages, alongside 1947, 1959, 1976, 1982 and 1989. It carries a gentle and calm demeanour that belies its tumultuous season. In spite of glowing generosity, it's somehow transfixed in time, held in suspended animation and astonishingly barely evolved from its release four years ago, yet somehow even more expressive. The sheer endurance of even a warm vintage is a marvel, finding a new lease on life in Krug's capable hands, with remarkable freshness and vitality infused by a taut yet silky line of malic acidity, drawing its multifaceted complexity into tight control. Aglow with yellow summer fruits becoming orange zest, the great intensity of Krug resonates in rumbling depth of butterscotch, honey, molten wax, toast and hints of smouldering hearth. All the silky lusciousness of 2000 is on parade, amidst deep-set mineral expression and silky texture on a finish of sheer concentration and wonderful poise. A brilliant Krug, right at its prime, with no sign of waning anytime soon.

The Champagne Guide

Krug Clos du Mesnil 2003 $$$$$

97 points • Disgorged autumn 2013 • Tasted in Reims

8671 bottles and 679 magnums, less than the usual 11,000-12,000 bottles; ID 413064

Clos du Mesnil is the most famous vineyard in all of Champagne, and one of the world's finest chardonnay sites outside the grand crus of Burgundy. An inscription in the vineyard states that vines were planted and the wall built in 1698. On the day of my most recent visit, Olivier discovered that Krug had bought grapes from Clos du Mesnil since 1864. The 1.85 hectare clos is divided into five or six plots and 19 separate vinifications. On pure chalk in the heart of the finest and most age-worthy of Champagne's chardonnay villages, this east-facing slope achieves less ripeness than some of Le Mesnil-sur-Oger's due south-facing slopes, all the more suited to Krug's long-ageing style.

'My father purchased the plot in 1971 to secure a supply of chardonnay,' Olivier explains. 'They didn't expect this plot to produce amazing wines, but when they tasted all the still wines that year, they realised this little clos behind the big rusty gate in the middle of the village did not taste the same as the other wines from Le Mesnil. It was used in the blend at the time, but the same story repeated until the outstanding 1979 harvest, when my father suggested they should make a single wine. My grandfather said, "Never! You will ruin the philosophy of Krug! This is only one grape and one year and one little garden!" But my father made a test and they fell in love with it.'

There's something remarkable about Clos du Mesnil that is infused in its fruits from the outset. The powerful, intoxicating aroma of the cask hall at the vineyard mid-vintage is enthralling. A taste of the 2014 vintage from barrel mid-ferment, just eight days old, revealed the most concentrated and structured champagne of the season.

If Krug Vintage 2003 was unexpected, Clos du Mesnil 2003 was downright preposterous, if not for the record heat of the season, then for the devastating spring frosts that wiped out 90% of the village, though the clos itself fared better. There is no fingerprint of place more pronounced than the mineral voice of the soil that resonates in the most distinctive champagnes. Even this bad-tempered season could not dampen the earth-shaking minerality of Clos du Mesnil. It rumbles to the very core of the earth deep below this mesmerising site, then rises on the finish, like a shard of pure chalk erupting from the surface of the clos itself. It utterly trumps the phenolic grip of the season, which fades into complete oblivion. It is instead seamlessly composed, even silky, yet wielding a shining sabre of lemon and grapefruit that slices through its core with razor precision, charged with high-voltage malic acidity. This vector of pristine purity unravels a universe of complexity of bees wax, almond, nougat, toast, vanilla, fig, honey, mixed spice and, in time, hints of truffles. Even at 12 years of age, its focus and tension are captivating, its reverberating volume and depth awe-inspiring. This is not just the wine of the vintage, it is an entrancing champagne by any standards, vintage aside. The throne remains secure for the queen of blanc de blancs.

Krug Collection 1982 $$$$$

100 points • Tasted in Brisbane

54% pinot noir, 30% chardonnay, 16% meunier; original disgorgement

Krug releases minute volumes of its greatest vintages at the prime of their maturity as Krug Collection. After two tiny seasons, 1982 delivered Champagne's most abundant harvest ever, a generous season of heat right through summer and into September, punctuated by well-timed rain. Of two bottles opened by Olivier last year, I lucked upon the one in the most impeccable condition, testimony to Krug's incredible endurance, even in a powerful vintage.

Only the very greatest champagnes attain a grand maturity so seamless it is as if their light dims to a soft-focus twilight of dark mystery that stirs the depths of your soul. To stand in this place and behold a bottle that has reached this point with flawless precision is perhaps the greatest privilege afforded by champagne. A firmament of complexity stretches from horizon to horizon, spanning diverse and obscure constellations of burnt grapefruit, preserved orange, baked fig, pipe smoke, exotic spice, ginger, even iodine and seaweed, yet all somehow intricately and harmoniously connected. In time, decades-old pinot noir awakens in a great, dark expanse of plum depth that subsumes a palate of remarkable persistence, and mineral texture of pinpoint starlight brilliance. This is one of the most profoundly complex champagnes I have ever had the privilege of experiencing. Behold.

LAHERTE FRÈRES

(La-airt Frair)

3 RUE DES JARDINS 51530 CHAVOT-COURCOURT

www.champagne-laherte.com

champagne-laherte.blogspot.com

CHAMPAGNE

DEPUIS   1889

'More than anything, my father and I are trying to respect the soil, expressing the style of the clay and limestone,' says the young Aurélien Laherte. This is the soil of the historic little village of Chavot-Courcourt, on the border of the Côte des Blancs and the Vallée de la Marne. 'The clay gives us chardonnay that is fruitier than the Côte des Blancs, and the limestone meunier that is finer than the Vallée de la Marne,' he says. For a production of now 120,000 bottles, Laherte Frères boasts a very large portfolio of 11 cuvées that preserve the detail of its terroirs in wines of taut, linear persistence, and at times assertive structure.

With a history of grape-growing in the village spanning seven generations, the extended Laherte family accounts for almost one-third of Chavot's population of 350. The 10 hectares from which the estate sources across 75 parcels in 10 nearby villages have been passed down through the generations, and all are still owned and tended by members of the immediate family. French law dictates registration of the domaine as a négociant-manipulant, but for all practical purposes it should be considered as a grower producer, with the exception of its entry Brut Ultradition NV, for which supply is supplemented with two hectares of purchased fruit.

A complex array of vineyard parcels span the Coteaux Sud d'Épernay (Chavot, Moussy, Épernay, Vaudancourt and Mancy, with chardonnay, pinot noir and meunier), Côte des Blancs (Vertus and Voipreux, with chardonnay) and Vallée de la Marne (Le Breuil and Boursault, with meunier). In 2014, four hectares of Montagne de Reims vineyards were added to the sourcing pool.

'We would like our wines to express that they are not from the Côte des Blancs or the Montagne de Reims, but to be expressive of our village,' Aurélien says. In tasting young vins clairs, the distinctive saltiness of the chalk minerality of Chavot is unique compared with his parcels from other villages. The oldest vines have been cultivated here by different generations of the family for more than 68 years.

An ecological approach is taken, with half the vineyard holdings managed biodynamically, and the rest essentially organically, 'to facilitate the natural expression of the vine and increase its aromatic potential,' Aurélien explains. He reports seeing increased mineral character in biodynamic plots as vines push deeper into the chalk, encouraged by ploughing by horse in spring and autumn to break up the surface. Natural pesticides and herbicides are used, and yields are limited.

'When we started with biodynamics in 2005, we found the fruit was cleaner and more consistent during vinification,' he says. 'The wines were fruity, held good acidities, and the bottles maintained their freshness for longer after they were opened.'

A vintage wine is made every year, even in the challenging 2010 season. 'If you work diligently, you don't need to be afraid of the quality of the vintage,' he suggests. 'In Champagne, many people just add more sugar or leave a wine on lees for longer if it's not right, but for us we simply make the wine.'

Villages, crus and varieties are separated, and matched to the age and style of one of 280 barrels as the musts leave one of two traditional presses. 'We have lots of complexity in the vineyard, so we try to obtain the same complexity in the winery using different fermentation vessels,' explains Aurélien. He considers the matching of parcels to the right vessels to be his most important task in the winery. 'The work we are doing in the vineyards has increased the potential of our fruit, so we have increased the quantity of oak in the last five years.' More than 80% of parcels are now fermented and aged in oak, as has been the tradition here for more than 25 years. Barrels vary from four to 40 years of age, and include several large 100-year-old foudres from Alsace for reserve wines. Five small barrels are purchased each year from Domaine de la Romanée-Conti, where they have aged Le Montrachet, no less. Since 2011, pinot noir and meunier have been selectively vinified in barrels used for red Burgundy in the hope of increasing red fruit character and tannins. Two new foudres were acquired in 2014, and cellaring space was extended by 60,000 bottles to facilitate longer ageing. An increase in production of 10,000 bottles in 2014 equates to an increase of four months of ageing in the cellar.

Some lees stirring is performed to build richness. Malolactic fermentation is blocked in most cuvées, but may proceed spontaneously or by design for particular years and varieties. In Laherte's structured and savoury terroirs, malic acidity makes for a tricky balance in young cuvées with increasing use of small-format oak, all too often resulting in assertive and drying structures. Laherte has trialled some barrels without sulphur, but is not yet convinced. 'Good acidity and low pH mean we don't need to use much sulphur, but without any we lose something of the soil and the precision of the fruit,' he says.

A unique 'Le Clos' vineyard of just 0.3 hectares in Chavot has been planted to seven varieties to preserve the heritage of the estate. 'We found the lost varieties of our ancestors in our old plots, and we have embarked on a project to recreate champagne with the same taste as 250 years ago,' Aurélien explained as he showed me through the prized site at the top of the village. Chardonnay, meunier, pinot noir, fromenteau, petit meslier, pinot blanc and arbane are harvested and pressed together, wild yeast fermented in barrel without malolactic fermentation, and blended with a reserve solera of every vintage since 2005 and bottled as 'Les 7'.

Attention to every detail is the key at Laherte, right down to the cork. Every wine has been sealed with DIAM for more than six years. 'I don't want to lose all our work to the cork!' Aurélien exclaims. 'Our goal is to preserve freshness, fruit and minerality in our wines, and our tests indicate that DIAM is most effective, providing protection against changes in temperature and humidity as our wines travel around the world.'

Aurélien has worked hard to slowly evolve the estate since he began working alongside his father, uncle and grandparents in 2005, and his spirit of experimentation and evolution continues. They now produce 11 cuvées each year, all but two of which are made in tiny volumes of just a few thousand bottles. Each boasts a refreshingly informative back label, detailing villages, assemblage, vinification, dosage and disgorgement date.

LAHERTE FRÈRES EXTRA BRUT ULTRADITION NV $

88 points • 2012 BASE VINTAGE • DISGORGED JULY 2014 • TASTED IN CHAVOT

60% meunier, 30% chardonnay, 10% pinot noir from 10 villages in the Coteaux Sud d'Épernay and Vallée de la Marne; 40% reserves; fermented in barrels (80%), tanks and foudres; around 50% malolactic fermentation; 4.5g/L dosage

Cleverly named Ultradition, 'because our work in the vines and the winery now is not traditional,' Aurélien explains. 'We are trying to do something different.' This is certainly a characterful expression of an entry cuvée, with plenty of complexity of apple, fig, lemon butter and the mixed spice, anise and ginger of barrel maturation. Some dry extract on the finish is heightened by toasty barrels and low dosage, conspiring to create dry, textural grip, typical of this cuvée. Malic acidity keeps things tense and tight.

LAHERTE FRÈRES GRAND BRUT ULTRADITION NV $

89 points • 2012 BASE VINTAGE • DISGORGED FEBRUARY AND JULY 2014 • TASTED IN CHAVOT, SYDNEY & MELBOURNE

As per Extra Brut Ultradition, with a touch more dosage (7g/L), which draws out characters of lemon butter and red apple, as well as helping to soften dry aldehydic grip on the finish. Bright malic acidity draws everything out long and fresh.

LAHERTE FRÈRES BLANC DE BLANCS BRUT NATURE NV $$

91 points • 2012 BASE VINTAGE • DISGORGED MARCH AND JULY 2014
• TASTED IN CHAVOT, SYDNEY & MELBOURNE

50% reserves from 2011; a blend of four villages, particularly Chavot and Épernay; vinified in foudres and 228L barrels; zero dosage

The aspiration here is to draw out the salinity of young chardonnay through vinification in barrels and lees contact. Aurélien concedes that it's very young and hopes to work towards releasing it later. Vibrant malic acidity and salty chalk minerality define a tight, young, mineral-accented style, backed with good depth of lemon, grapefruit and white stone fruits. Patisserie and almond nuances are probably as much an artefact of barrel work as maturity. It concludes with finely textured, chewy grip and good persistence. Will benefit from a few years for its acidity to soften.

LAHERTE FRÈRES ROSÉ ULTRADITION BRUT NV $

85 points • 2012 BASE VINTAGE • DISGORGED JANUARY 2014 • TASTED IN CHAVOT

45% meunier, 30% pinot noir, 10% chardonnay, 15% red wine; 40% reserves from 2011; partial malolactic fermentation; 7g/L dosage

Aurélien finds his blended rosé his most challenging wine to make, with the tannins of red wine clashing with the citrus of chardonnay, hence the blend is predominantly black grapes, including some from his wife's family in Bouzy. In future it will include a portion macerated on skins. For now, it's a pretty medium salmon-pink hue, with soft, gentle fruit profile and creamy bead. A savoury mouthfeel of dry extract grip leaves the finish firm and bitter.

LAHERTE FRÈRES LES VIGNES D'AUTREFOIS DEUX MILLE DIX EXTRA BRUT 2010 $$

85 points • DISGORGED MAY 2014 • TASTED IN CHAVOT

100% meunier from Chavot and Mancy vines planted between 1947 and 1964; fermented in 228L barrels; no malolactic fermentation; 2.5g/L dosage

Laherte produces Les Vignes d'Autrefois and Les Empreintes every year regardless of the season, a daring philosophy in a vintage like 2010, where he admits the fruit was overripe and botrytis set in. The full straw yellow hue and grilled pineapple of overripe fruit meet the prominent botrytis characters of apricot, mushroom and firm, coarse, dry extract. Ripeness and botrytis conspire to leave the finish coarse and unfocused.

The Champagne Guide

Laherte Frères Les Empreintes 2009 $$

93 points • Disgorged January 2013 • Tasted in Chavot

50% Chavot pinot noir planted 1983, 50% Épernay chardonnay and chardonnay muscate (an aromatic chardonnay clone) planted 1957; wild fermented in barriques of at least 2 years of age; no malolactic fermentation; aged 3 years on lees; 3g/L dosage; 3000 bottles

There is complexity and character here, with lemon citrus and apple definition supported by lovely layers of almond meal and patisserie. Age has integrated its malic acidity well, building impressive texture and creamy, leesy mouthfeel, though retaining vibrant, lively, salty minerality. A long, confident finish promises medium-term potential.

Laherte Frères Les 7 Extra Brut 05-11

89 points • 2011 base vintage • Disgorged December 2013 • Tasted in Chavot

Single-vineyard Chavot; previously labelled Les Clos; 18% chardonnay, 18% meunier, 17% pinot blanc, 15% petit meslier, 14% pinot noir, 10% fromenteau, 8% arbane; planted 2003; 60% 2011; 40% perpetual reserve blend of 2005 through 2010; co-fermented with wild yeast in Burgundy barrels of at least 10 years of age; matured in barrel for 6 months with regular lees stirring; no malolactic fermentation; 4g/L dosage

An opulent and multidimensional fruit salad anticipated by its recipe, spanning the contrasting expressions of citrus and stone fruits of all kinds, starfruit and unripe honeydew. It's exotic and complex, with a tight malic acid line and coarse phenolic bite characteristic of the challenging 2011 season. A young, firm and slightly awkward style, reflecting inconsistency of ripeness. It finishes with good length and will benefit from time to mellow. Great to see an NV cuvée sensibly named with a declaration of its vintages.

Laherte Frères Deux Mille Six Extra Brut 2006 $$

92 points • Disgorged December 2013 • Tasted in Chavot

85% Épernay chardonnay, 15% Mancy and Chavot pinot noir; average vine age 35 years; vinified in 30% new oak; aged 7 years on lees; 4.5g/L dosage

This label has been superseded by Les Empreintes, as Aurélien finds the new oak influence too pronounced here. This is nonetheless testimony to the ageing potential of the estate, with oak and long lees maturity uniting in a creamy and alluring style of full straw hue and layered, spicy, rich patisserie, butter, custard, vanilla and brioche complexity. It's held in stead thanks to well-integrated acidity and fine salt mineral texture.

Laherte Frères Rosé de Saignée Les Beaudiers Extra Brut 2012 $$

92 points • Disgorged November 2014 • Tasted in Chavot

100% meunier from old Chavot vines planted in 1953, 1958 and 1965; macerated for 12 hours; wild fermented and aged for 6 months in barrels of at least 6 years of age; no malolactic fermentation; 3.5g/L dosage

A deep, vibrant crimson pink hue anticipates a unique rosé style of pretty pink pepper, wild strawberry and exact rhubarb flavours, supported by a fine, creamy bead and a firm, fine tannin backbone. There is solid mouthfeel here, and tannin grip closer to red wine than champagne, but it retains its poise and appeal, finishing long and distinctive with fresh rhubarb and pink pepper. Drink with main-course duck.

LALLIER

(Lah-liay)

4 PLACE DE LA LIBÉRATION 51160 AŸ

www.champagne-lallier.fr

*T*he young house of Lallier was established in 1996, purchased by winemaker Francis Tribaut in 2004, and in 2011 moved operations from its 18th century vaulted cellars in Aÿ to a new facility in Oger. The estate is privileged to eight hectares in Aÿ and four in Cramant, Chouilly and Vertus, providing for one-quarter of its annual production of 450,000 bottles, the remainder sourced from across the Montagne de Reims and Côtes des Blancs. Fermentation takes place in stainless steel tanks using only natural yeasts, and partial malolactic fermentation maintains freshness. These are clean, well-balanced and fruit-focused champagnes, though entry cuvées can lack character and presence.

LALLIER GRANDE RÉSERVE GRAND CRU BRUT NV $$

85 points • DISGORGED MID-2014 • TASTED IN SYDNEY & MELBOURNE

65% Aÿ pinot noir, 35% Côte des Blancs chardonnay; 8g/L dosage

Dusty, dried-out and aldehydic, with a hard and contracted finish, destroyed by oxidation.

....

LALLIER GRAND CRU BLANC DE BLANCS NV $$$

91 points • DISGORGED MID-2014 • TASTED IN SYDNEY & MELBOURNE

70% Aÿ, with 30% Côte des Blancs; aged 4 years on lees

Always a highlight of Lallier's portfolio, this is a cuvée that balances the expressive depth and intensity of Aÿ with the freshness of Côte des Blancs. Lemon drops and lemon zest of lively focus are balanced by candied dosage and salty chalk mineral texture on a long finish.

The Champagne Guide

LANSON

(Lohn-soh)

6/10

66 RUE DE COURLANCY 51100 REIMS

www.lanson.com

*T*here *is something about Lanson that has always struck me as quite extraordinary. For the ninth-largest Champagne house, with a 4 million bottle annual production (the majority of which is Black Label Brut NV, frequently discounted to one of the lowest prices of any champagne on the shelves), this is a house that has maintained remarkable consistency. All the more astonishing considering that it was purchased by Moët in 1991 and cunningly on-sold less than six months later, with just two of its 208 hectares of magnificent vineyards. It should take 15 years for a house of this magnitude to recover from such a blow, but I have enjoyed Black Label as my house champagne many times over the past decade, and in recent tastings of vintage wines spanning 30 years, that ominous dip that everyone anticipated simply never came. How is this possible?*

One man. Jean-Paul Gandon commenced here in 1972, making his tenure of more than 40 years extraordinary, even in a region as historic as Champagne. More than this, he spent his first 15 years overseeing the sourcing of the grapes and must in the vineyards, a role which he retained when he was promoted to chef de cave in 1986.

His new owners astutely left him free rein to source, make and blend the wines as he saw best. He was a talented winemaker, certainly, but more than this, he was connected, and his relationships with the growers spanning 500 hectares of Lanson sourcing across Champagne have infused this house with a startling resilience in the midst of its tumultuous corporate ride of recent decades.

In 2013, Hervé Dantan joined Lanson as assistant chef de cave in anticipation of Jean-Paul Gandon's pending retirement.

Dantan comes with an impressive track record of 22 years of innovation, transforming Mailly Grand Cru into one of Champagne's top cooperatives. And he has immediately ushered in an exciting new era at Lanson. Dantan's first priorities have been to facilitate small-parcel vinification and to increase texture in the wines. To this end, 55 new small tanks of 50–100hL capacity, a new reserve wine cellar and 23 new foudres were installed just in time for the 2014 vintage.

'Without malolactic fermentation, we need to add creamy texture, and we hope that the use of oak and micro-oxygenation can help with this,' he says.

'We want to keep the style fresh and crisp, while adding creamy complexity.' His foudres are thus for complexity and not for wood character, through ageing (not fermenting) chardonnay and pinot noir. 'I don't envisage making a special oak-matured cuvée, but expect that a very small contribution of just 5–10% will add complexity to our blends.'

Lanson's distinctive house style of blocking malolactic fermentation makes for an excitingly high-strung, age-worthy champagne, true to Gandon's aspiration of 'maintaining freshness, power and fruit character'. The non-vintage receives complexity from a minimum of three years' ageing on lees, power and structure from a 50% dose of pinot noir from the Montagne de Reims and Côte des Bar, minerality from chardonnay on the southern slopes of the Montagne de Reims, and a balancing touch of just 15% Vallée de la Marne meunier. Lanson uses meunier only in its entry non-vintage cuvées.

Thanks to Gandon, Lanson has been able to maintain grand cru fruit sources for all of its vintage wines, which are generally a 50/50 blend of pinot noir and chardonnay, aged a minimum of five years on lees prior to release, and usually considerably longer — remarkable for one of the lowest-priced vintage wines on the shelves.

Such maturation calls for a total cellar stock of 20 million bottles in Lanson's six kilometres of drives under Reims.

These are wines that age effortlessly, building slowly and purposefully in bottle, and I have recently been stunned by the stamina of late-disgorged 1979, 1983, 1988, 1990 and regular-disgorged 1996 and 1998.

Lanson is impressive in printing disgorgement dates on the back of every cuvée and its new website is refreshingly informative, with technical sheets detailing blends and villages for every cuvée.

To commemorate its 250th anniversary in 2010, Lanson launched a series of 'Extra Age' cuvées. The concept was unusual but inspired, a trilogy of three non-vintage cuvées, each from three mature vintages chosen to complement each other. These were not simply late-disgorged versions of its non-vintage cuvées, but purpose-assembled to age gracefully.

Lanson is the primary brand of the Lanson-BCC group, champagne's second-largest after LVMH.

LANSON BLACK LABEL BRUT NV $

91 points • 2011 BASE, WITH RESERVES FROM 10 VINTAGES BETWEEN 2010 & 2000 • DISGORGED JULY 2014 • TASTED IN REIMS

93 points • 2010 BASE VINTAGE • DISGORGED JANUARY AND FEBRUARY 2014 • TASTED IN VERZENAY & BRISBANE

92 points • 2009 BASE VINTAGE • DISGORGED APRIL 2013 • TASTED IN SYDNEY & MELBOURNE

92 points • 2008 BASE VINTAGE • DISGORGED OCTOBER 2012 • TASTED IN SYDNEY & MELBOURNE

50% pinot noir from the Montagne de Reims and Côte des Bar; 35% chardonnay from the Côte des Blancs, Montagne de Reims and a little from Sézanne and Vitry; 15% meunier from the Vallée de la Marne; a blend of 50-60 villages; 20% reserve wines, including part of the previous blend; no malolactic fermentation; 8g/L dosage; more than 3 million bottles

Lanson tactically doubled the dose of reserve wines to boost the tricky 2011 vintage. This cuvée accurately contrasts a profound statement of freshness of apple, pear and lemon zest fruit with the toastiness of bottle age and depth of reserves, the honeyed sweetness of well-balanced dosage, and the classic, tense malic acid signature of the house. The balance is refined and the line and length are accurate, making Black Label one of the best of the readily available bargain champagnes. The 2010 base is particularly distinguished, currently in a wonderful place, and well poised to hold itself for some years to come. Two bottles of this base that I tasted at the house were exceptional, and two were just a little flat in their fruit expression. The 2009 and 2008 base blends show even less development, particularly zesty and energetic.

LANSON ROSE LABEL BRUT ROSÉ NV $

88 points • 2011 BASE VINTAGE • DISGORGED JULY 2014 • TASTED IN REIMS
89 points • 2010 BASE VINTAGE • DISGORGED JUNE 2014 • TASTED IN BRISBANE
93 points • 2009 BASE • DISGORGED JUNE 2013 • TASTED IN SYDNEY & MELBOURNE
94 points • 2008 BASE VINTAGE • DISGORGED APRIL 2012 • TASTED IN VERZENAY

50% pinot noir, 35% chardonnay, 15% meunier; a unique base to the Black Label; a blend of
50-60 villages; 7% red wine reserves equally from Les Riceys, Bouzy and Cumières; 25% reserve
of last year's blend; no malolactic fermentation; aged 3 years on lees; 8g/L dosage; 320,000 bottles

There is a dazzling elegance and an understated delicacy to this gorgeous rosé that its blatant
strawberry mousse-coloured livery belies. Don't be put off by this or its teeny price, because this
is a beautifully crafted rosé of purity and subtlety, one of the real bargains of rosé champagne.
Pinot noir and chardonnay are blended from the most elegant premier and grand crus with
a judicious dose of red wine of pretty aromatics and soft tannins to create a medium salmon
hue and a delicate freshness. The 2011 base presents a lively and elegant fruit profile of red
apple and strawberry fruit, with well-defined malic acidity, though the tough season lacks the
finesse, precision and graceful mouthfeel characteristic of this label, finishing with a dusty, dry
almond-skin texture. My tasting of the 2010 base revealed one bottle with a subtly dusty, musty
backdrop and the hardness of firm, dry extract, and another faintly oxidised, stale and stripped
of fruit expression. The 2009 and 2008 bases are pristine in their elegant strawberry, raspberry,
pink grapefruit and lemon mood, with fresh malic drive and fine, mineral mouthfeel.

LANSON GOLD LABEL BRUT VINTAGE 2005 $$

92 points • DISGORGED MARCH AND SEPTEMBER 2014 • TASTED IN REIMS, SYDNEY,
MELBOURNE & BRISBANE

53% pinot noir from Verzenay, Verzy, Aÿ and Bouzy, 46% chardonnay from Avize, Le Mesnil-
sur-Oger, Oger and Trépail; no malolactic fermentation; 6g/L dosage

Hervé Dantan is frank about 2005: 'ripe and generous, not a great vintage'. He's spot on, though
the Lanson style of malic acidity and long lees age goes some way towards flattering this season.
The richness of the vintage leaps out in bountiful yellow summer fruits and grilled pineapple,
set confidently against a complex, secondary backdrop of crème brûlée, brioche, vanilla, quince,
wood spice and even a suggestion of mint. As it builds maturity, the coarse dry extract and
phenolic grip that characterise the vintage are increasingly subsumed by its warm generosity.
Well-focused malic acidity enlivens the finish, energising the lemon zest core of this richly
flavoured style. The result is a lesser Gold Label but a good result for the season, making for
a vintage to drink over the next few years, while the 2004 and 2002 soften in the cellar.

LANSON GOLD LABEL VINTAGE BRUT 2004 $$

94 points • DISGORGED SEPTEMBER 2013 • TASTED IN SYDNEY & MELBOURNE

52% pinot noir, 48% chardonnay; no malolactic fermentation; 8-9g/L dosage

I love the energy of malic acidity in charging Lanson Vintage with tremendous potential to improve in the cellar.
In the two years since its release, the youthful purity of 2004 has rounded into white peach, butter and roasted
almonds. It's in an impressive place of great line and length, with the stamina to age another decade yet.

LANSON EXTRA AGE BRUT NV $$$

95 points • DISGORGED JULY 2013 AND JUNE 2014 • TASTED IN REIMS

A blend of 2004, 2000 and especially 2002; 60% pinot noir from Verzenay, Mareuil-sur-Aÿ and Bouzy; 40% chardonnay from Avize, Chouilly, Cramant, Oger, Le Mesnil-sur-Oger, Vertus and Cuis; no malolactic fermentation; aged 10 years on lees

The leader of Lanson's senior citizens owes its superiority to a predominance of the majestic 2002 vintage, boring deep into the chalk bedrock of (particularly) Verzenay and Cuis to draw out intricate definition of mineral texture. It has hardly moved in the two years since its release, with the whip-crack of malic acidity keeping things energetic, refreshing and enduring. At the same time, a calm sense of completeness comes in the seamless harmony of brioche and nougat, layered with captivating multidimensional complexity, blessed with the fine-grained, silky, creamy texture of long lees age.

LANSON NOBLE CUVÉE BRUT MILLÉSIMÉ 2000 $$$$

96 points • DISGORGED NOVEMBER 2012 • TASTED IN REIMS

70.5% Avize and Oger chardonnay; 29.5% Verzenay pinot noir; no malolactic fermentation

One of the finest Lanson cuvées I have ever tasted, and undoubtedly the greatest of the modern era. Such was its searing acidity on our first encounter four years ago that I wrote, 'Don't chill it too much, for risk of being impaled by an ice shard of malic acidity!' It has since toned magically, evolving to a happy place of marzipan, nougat, vanilla and anise, with that acid-cut serving to tone the expressive fruit generosity of yellow summer fruits that define this sun-drenched season. The elegance of chardonnay takes the lead, holding hands seamlessly with malic acidity and uniting to produce a style of breathtaking freshness and endurance. Its mineral definition has erupted with the pure chalk of Avize and Oger, speaking confidently and articulately, lingering with great determination and seamless poise, the epitome of persistence and of sheer longevity that transcends its vintage. It still has another 15 years of life in it yet. Children of 2000, this is your wine.

LANSON VINTAGE COLLECTION 1976 $$$$

93 points • DISGORGED MID-2014 • TASTED IN REIMS FROM MAGNUM

53% chardonnay, particularly from Le Mesnil-sur-Oger and Trépail; 47% pinot noir; 3g/L dosage

A very hot, low-acid vintage that hasn't lived as confidently as the great seasons of Lanson, now beginning to tire. Exuberant, exotic richness of glacé apricot, locut, toffee, pipe smoke and spice dips into burnt-orange oxidation and a drying finish of phenolic grip. Long lees age has created a lovely creamy texture, which lingers on a very long finish. More than admirable for the season.

LARMANDIER-BERNIER

(Lah-mohn-diay-Bear-niay)

8/10

19 AVENUE DU GÉNÉRAL DE GAULLE 51130 VERTUS

www.larmandier.fr

CHAMPAGNE
LARMANDIER-BERNIER

'*To create a wine that deeply expresses its terroir*' *is Pierre Larmandier's aim, stated on the back of every one of the 140,000-odd bottles that leave his little cellar in Vertus each year. But to this fastidious grower, terroir in itself is not enough. 'Terroir is to wine what the score is to music,' he suggests. 'What's the point if the grape variety, the vine plant (the instrument) and the winegrower (the performer) are not up to standard?' Some growers are known for their focus on the vines, others for their attention in the winery, but few find a balance in every detail like Pierre Larmandier.*

Larmandier has grown holdings from 10 to 15 hectares since he came back to the family estate in 1988, blessed with impressive terroirs in the Côte des Blancs, spread across a total of 80 plots in the premier cru village of Vertus — including substantial holdings on the mid-slopes close to Le Mesnil-sur-Oger, supplemented with an impressive 2.5 hectares in the grand cru of Cramant, nearly 1 hectare in each of Avize and Chouilly, 0.2 in Oger, and 0.5 in the little villages of Bergères-lès-Vertus, Voipreux and Villeneuve-Renneville-Chevigny surrounding Vertus. Chardonnay is king here, and Larmandier tends just two hectares of pinot noir in Vertus for rosé and red wine.

'Chardonnay is very adaptable, and if you cultivate it carefully it will take its expression from the soil,' he explains, likening the diversity of his various plots to that of Puligny-Montrachet and Chablis.

'It would be a shame if we didn't bring our vineyards to your glass!' he says. And bring them he has, through one of the most sensible and diligent regimes anywhere in Champagne.

ORGANO-REALIST

Biodynamically certified since 2004, Larmandier describes himself as an 'organo-realist'. Every time I visit, he whisks me off in his four-wheel drive to one of his key plots in Vertus. One year, he'd heard rumours of an oïdium breakout around the village and wanted to get onto it right away.

As we approached one of his plots, we passed other growers out treating for oïdium. 'That man,' he said, pointing out one, 'is the worst in the village for always treating.' We found a little oïdium in Larmandier's plot, 'but it is not so bad so we will not treat yet. We're not too concerned about a little disease in the vineyards. Some people say grass is a disease, too!'

Larmandier cultivates grasses in the mid-rows during winter and ploughs until close to harvest. He considers

Early morning mist graces the majestic grand cru slopes of Cramant towards the end of harvest 2014.

an absence of herbicides to be the key in the vineyard. 'Organic or not is less important than abandoning herbicides,' he suggests. 'Everyone says they control weeds by ploughing, but I see them spraying with herbicide!' With neighbouring vines in such close proximity, it's impossible to conduct a biodynamic regime without some influence from those who do not farm naturally. Larmandier is matter-of-fact: 'We try to do the best we can, but it is not ideal. We still manage to be different to the others, even though we are among them.' Biodynamics is difficult to manage across so many plots, some just 200 square metres, spanning 15 kilometres north to south. 'We spend more time on the road than in the field with the tractor!' he says. And he calls his cousins in each village to check how much it has rained. 'We need to time our copper applications very carefully to combat disease.'

Since beginning conversion to biodynamic viticulture in 2000, Larmandier has noted a drop in yields, regulated by grasses in the mid-rows. He currently produces just 60–70hL/hectare. 'In the village, you are considered a bad grower if you do not produce 100hL/hectare,' he says. 'People produce too much in the Côte des Blancs, and the big houses just buy everything. They say I'm crazy to produce less than 100hL.'

He says 2012 was one of the toughest seasons he can recall in 25 years of managing his vines, yielding just two-thirds of his usual small harvest. Incessant rain made it difficult for him to get into the vineyards to cultivate the soil. 'We do our best with biodynamics, but when it's crazy, it's crazy!' he exclaims.

Larmandier likes old vines and tries to keep them as long as he can; some are as old as 80 years. 'My ideal is to never replace them, which is all very well, but then you don't have any grapes!' he says. In order to create more competition and push the roots deeper, he is slowly replanting at 10,000 vines per hectare, more

than the regional average of 7500. 'This is contrary to the way of thinking in Champagne, but if I want to improve concentration without increasing my harvest, I think this is the way,' he explains.

'You can only extract so much minerality per square foot before it is diluted, but with more vines you can extract more.' While others focus on grapes per square metre of leaves to produce more aromatic wines, for Larmandier the key is the more Burgundian focus on grapes per square metre of soil.

'The soil is the most important thing,' he emphasises. 'With deep roots in good soils, 80% of the work is done.' Here, on the lower slopes below the village of Vertus, the chalk lies 80 centimetres below the surface. He considers his average vine age of 35 years to be very important. 'The roots have a better depth and are better able to extract the minerality from the chalk. We are very lucky to have the place we do, and we work very hard in the vineyard to make the most of it,' he says.

Along with an expression of minerality, his priorities are the roundness and linearity achieved by harvesting grapes at optimal ripeness. 'It is important for us to work the soil to achieve a lower pH in the wine, allowing us to wait longer to harvest, to achieve ripeness without lacking freshness.'

Even in the record heatwave of 2003 he was able to achieve freshness. 'Attention to the soil is increasingly important in these warmer vintages, so as to achieve phenolic maturity and not just sugar ripeness.' Larmandier harvests on taste rather than sugar levels.

NON-INTERVENTIONIST WINEMAKING

His sensitive and non-interventionist approach informs all he does. 'My philosophy used to be that terroir was everything and the hand of man was nothing, that our work in the vineyard was all that mattered,' Larmandier clarifies. 'But now we understand that the work we do and the choices we make in the winery are important, too.' Larmandier did not study oenology and says it's impossible to simplify winemaking to a recipe. 'If you work in the vineyards, your mind is not only on acid and alcohol numbers but on expression,' he says. 'Every year I have an oenology student come to work with me and they want to measure everything but I say, "First, you must taste!"'

To draw out the character of each site, wild yeast is used for primary and malolactic fermentations, with every ferment relying exclusively on its own natural yeasts. There is no filtration, 'because every time you filter or fine you lose a part of what you have worked hard to achieve in the vineyard'. Very low levels of preservative (sulphur dioxide), and ever lower dosages of around 4g/L are used. 'After all the care lavished on our wines, we are not going to add anything which might go against them!' Larmandier exclaims. Low sulphurs dictate that every wine is free to proceed through malolactic fermentation, and reserve wines are kept in tank under temperature control to maintain freshness.

Larmandier doesn't like the 'austerity' of stainless steel fermentation, and has increased the proportion of oak vinification from 40% to 70%, for controlled oxidation and complexity. He appreciates the expression achieved in oak, and has experimented with egg fermenters for rosé for the past four years (though finds the result too rounded); recently, a new amphora arrived for rosé. 'Perhaps it can give us a little bit more complexity for the blend?' he suggests. He confesses he likes to follow fashions 'a little bit', but won't go too far as he doesn't like oxidation.

'In Champagne we are blenders, and different fermentation vessels give us more components for the blends. With more concentration in our fruit, stainless steel is too closed and there's more risk of reduction,' he explains. He maintains a delicate balance to keep his wines fresh, admitting that he's afraid of oxidation.

When I first visited in 2011, he was putting the finishing touches on a new building to provide space to work with more barrels. He still uses the first barrels he purchased in 1988, and has bought new barrels every year since 1999, 'because a used barrel has a personality of the wine, but we only want to express the personality of our vineyards'.

He doesn't want new oak characters to interfere, so new barrels comprise just 3% of his larger non-vintage blends for their first two years. Even tastings of his young vins clairs from second-use barrels display very subtle oak influence. He has purchased large foudres of the more subtle Austrian oak since 2001, and three more arrived in 2013.

Extra space also provides opportunity to hold stock in bottle for longer, and his cellar now houses 500,000 bottles, sufficient for an average of 3.5 years on lees across his cuvées, with the aim of increasing his non-vintages from two years to three.

Larmandier's non-vintage philosophy is to let every vintage express its character. 'We are not blessed with making our non-vintage wines taste the same every year,' he says. Bottling codes are easy to decode, with the last four digits denoting the month and year of disgorgement. The other digits in the code are the base year.

Larmandier-Bernier exemplifies the levels of purity and mineral focus that can be drawn out of primarily premier cru terroirs with sufficient care and attention. These exceedingly fine wines rightfully rank high among the finest of Champagne's grower producers.

LARMANDIER-BERNIER LATITUDE BLANC DE BLANCS À VERTUS EXTRA BRUT NV $$

93 points • 2012 BASE VINTAGE • DISGORGED NOVEMBER 2014 • TASTED IN VERTUS, SYDNEY & MELBOURNE

35% reserves; vinified and aged in casks, wooden vats and stainless tanks on lees for almost 1 year with bâtonnage; unfined and unfiltered; aged in bottle at least 2 years; 4g/L dosage

Sourced exclusively from the same 'Latitude' of the generous terroir of southern Vertus, this is intentionally a less mineral, easy to drink blanc de blancs. The first disgorgement of the excellent 2012 base vintage is very tight, focused and textural at this young age. It encapsulates the freshness of youthful Vertus chardonnay in its grapefruit, apple and pear characters, while building great textural presence of chalk minerality and lees-derived mouthfeel, culminating in a long finish of biscuity complexity and beautiful acid line.

Larmandier-Bernier Longitude Blanc de Blancs Premier Cru Extra Brut NV $$

94 points • 2011 BASE • DISGORGED MAY 2014 • TASTED IN VERTUS, SYDNEY & MELBOURNE

40% reserves; two-thirds Vertus, one-third Avize, Cramant and a little Oger; vinified and aged in casks, wooden vats and stainless tanks on lees for almost 1 year with bâtonnage; unfined and unfiltered; aged in bottle at least 2 years; 4g/L dosage

A captivating wine, blended from four of chardonnay's most beguiling villages, sharing roughly the same 'Longitude'. As always, it's the tremendous chalk minerality of these terroirs that is most engaging, gliding long and seamless from start to finish, utterly defying the lesser 2011 base vintage in a manner that very few other growers and houses have pulled off. Stunning purity of lemon and apple is backed by the complexity and appeal of bottle age in notes of brioche, biscuits and toast, seamlessly connected by a focused, tense acid line. In recent tastings, notes of red apple and starfruit have begun to materialise, accurately encapsulating the subtle exoticism of Vertus.

Larmandier-Bernier Rosé de Saignée Premier Cru Extra Brut NV $$$

95 points • 100% 2011 • TASTED IN VERTUS, SYDNEY & MELBOURNE

Vertus single-vineyard pinot noir; too young to be labelled as a vintage; old vines harvested ripe at very low yields; cold macerated 2-3 days for colour without tannin; fermented and aged 1 year in enamel-lined steel vat; aged 2 years in bottle; full malolactic fermentation; 3g/L dosage

This wine is a paradox of the highest order, a salute to the genius of its maker and the depth of its old-vine sources. How a 100% Côte des Blancs rosé from an elegant east-facing Vertus site can land midway between a graceful champagne rosé and an expressive red cherry pinot noir is truly astounding. Larmandier set out to make 'a rosé, not a white champagne with colour', marrying the power of pinot noir with the elegance of the village and, goodness, has he done it! A profoundly vinous champagne of full crimson hue, with a characterful and enticing display of pure red cherries, watermelon, guava and spicy redcurrants. It's more savoury this year, led by pink pepper, even beetroot. Minerality of mouth-filling dimensions surges and froths, charged with acidity both tense and refined. Impeccably managed structure offers grip, body and texture without bitterness or hardness. Drink it young and fresh. It's as special as it is inimitable. Most profoundly, Larmandier has achieved this resounding success in the tough 2011 season. Kudos.

The high village of Mutigny peers over a sea of dawn fog enveloping the Marne, signalling the change of seasons at the end of vintage 2014.

The Champagne Guide

Larmandier-Bernier Terre de Vertus Premier Cru Blanc de Blancs Brut Nature 2009 $$$

94 points • Tasted in Vertus & Sydney

Several parcels on similar terroirs spanning 2.5 hectares of Vertus mid-slopes; vinified and aged in casks, wooden vats and stainless steel tanks on lees for almost 1 year with bâtonnage; unfined and unfiltered; aged in bottle for at least 4 years; zero dosage

The intense mineral texture and layers of mouth-filling chalk of the northern slopes of Vertus learn much from the neighbouring grand cru of Le Mesnil-sur-Oger, and Larmandier is astute in separating these from the more rounded character of southern Vertus (in his 'Latitude' cuvée). Terre de Vertus is all about preserving this salt mineral fingerprint, which it does with laudable prowess even in the ripe, 'solar' 2009 vintage. The precision of Vertus chalk provides definition to the flamboyant ripeness of Vertus, manifested as golden delicious apple, cumquat, honey and ginger exoticism over a core of grapefruit and pear purity. A wine of poise and balance, finishing very long and taut with a touch of dry extract texture. Signature Vertus.

Larmandier-Bernier Vieille Vigne de Cramant Grand Cru Extra Brut 2007 $$$$

94 points • Tasted in Vertus & Sydney

Two nearby vineyards in the heart of Cramant; vines aged between 50 and 77 years; vinified and aged on lees in casks and wooden vats with bâtonnage for almost 1 year; unfined and unfiltered; aged in bottle at least 5 years; 2g/L dosage

To Larmandier, Cramant is a different world that deserves to be showcased solo. Like the Terre de Vertus, he prints the vintage only on the back label, 'because the place is more important than the vintage'. He says that in this special part of Cramant, his carefully cultivated old vines are less sensitive to seasonal fluctuations, and he could make a vintage every year. There's inherent power here, indicative of the intensity of one of the Côte des Blancs' strongest villages, tamed with the classic finesse of Larmandier's sensitive touch. It celebrates the sunny, succulent generosity of Cramant in layers of white stone fruits, well disciplined by lemon, grapefruit, a long acid line and pronounced texture, embedded with deep layers of salt-infused chalk minerality. Age has blessed it with depth of brioche and gingernut biscuits, yet it remains lively and focused. One bottle in Australia was slightly more developed, with subtle blood orange character.

Larmandier-Bernier Les Chemins d'Avize Grand Cru Blanc de Blancs Extra Brut 2010 $$$$

92 points • Tasted in Vertus

Single-vineyard Avize; vinified in casks and wooden vats and aged on lees with bâtonnage for almost 1 year; unfined and unfiltered; 2g/L dosage

The second release of Larmandier's fourth single-vineyard cuvée, a more elegant style from the flat of Avize. With botrytis stress after heavy August rain, 2010 was a tricky season, resulting in less acidity than usual, making for a soft style that lacks the precision and drive of great seasons. Nonetheless, it's nicely balanced, capturing the salt mineral presence of Avize with apple and pear fruit definition and notes of almond development. Still desperately young, it will benefit from short-term ageing to build complexity, though doesn't possess the inherent drive to live long.

LARMANDIER-BERNIER LES CHEMINS D'AVIZE GRAND CRU BLANC DE BLANCS EXTRA BRUT 2009 $$$$

95 points • TASTED IN YARRA VALLEY

My first encounter with this new cuvée pre-release left a lasting impression, and two years on it has blossomed precisely as anticipated. A beach-fresh and youthful blanc de blancs, loaded with lemon zest, crunchy apple and beurre bosc pear purity, it captures a picture-perfect snapshot of the refined, soft, salty texture of Avize chalk, harmonious yet firm, with well-balanced oak providing structural definition and great sustaining power in the cellar. The small blend necessitated use of small barrels, and Larmandier thought the oak was a bit strong on release, but it's now found its happy place in subtle almond complexity. Very classy.

LARMANDIER-BERNIER VERTUS ROUGE COTEAUX CHAMPENOIS PREMIER CRU MILLÉSIME 2012 $$

94 points • TASTED IN VERTUS

Old-vine Vertus pinot noir; 10% whole bunches; macerated for 12 days; matured in barrels for nearly 2 years; bottled mid-2014; a little more than 2000 bottles

Larmandier's family has a long tradition of still red wine, producing one of the great Coteaux Champenois, naturally more tense and mineral-focused in Vertus than the deeper style of the warmer slopes of the Montagne de Reims. It's now only made in exceptional years, and the excellent, very ripe, small grapes of 2012 beckoned a red wine instead of a rosé. A gorgeous fragrance of precise rose petals, red cherries and strawberries is more reminiscent of the ethereal perfume of Chambolle-Musigny than it is of Vertus. The palate follows true, delicate and fragrant, with pretty red cherry fruits and beautifully fine tannins. Acidity is bright yet impeccably well integrated. A stunningly fragrant, elegant and graceful Coteaux Champenois that will live long. Just to prove it, Larmandier produced a very old Larmandier-Bernier Vertus Rouge Coteaux Champenois from his mother's cellar, with no indication of its age, but he suspects 1975 or 1976. It was in impeccable condition, alluring and wonderful, still possessing freshness of fruit mince spice and prunes, layered with leather and game, propelled by soft, silky tannins and nicely integrated yet well-defined tannins (95 points).

LARMANDIER-BERNIER SPECIAL CLUB 1996

98 points • TASTED IN VERTUS

The inimitable minerality of the soft chalk expression of Cramant is timeless, and almost 20 years on, this cuvée declares its origins with remarkable precision. A blend of 75% Cramant with Vertus, the Special Club was ceased in 2000, as Larmandier-Bernier preferred not to blend Cramant. Larmandier served me this wine blind and I was captivated by its wonderfully elegant poise and remarkable freshness. With no overbearing concentration or assertiveness of acidity, I did not guess 1996. It dances with lemon freshness amidst fantastic complexity of mixed spice and golden fruit cake, becoming quince and butter in time. A deep well of Cramant salt chalk minerality brims from its core, a grand testimony to the astonishing longevity of Larmandier-Bernier, with decades of potential yet.

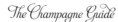

LAURENT-PERRIER

(Lohr-rohn-Peh-riay)

6/10

51150 TOURS-SUR-MARNE
www.laurent-perrier.com

CHAMPAGNE

MAISON FONDÉE
1812

Laurent-Perrier is on a steep growth curve. Substantial expansion in recent years has seen the house climb to number five in Champagne by volume. A new cuverie, constructed in time for the 2009 harvest, added capacity for another 150 vins clairs and now handles production for the group, including de Castellane, Delamotte and Salon. With an annual production of 7 million bottles (almost two-thirds of which are L-P Brut), Laurent-Perrier is unusual in having found a reasonably comfortable equilibrium in that precarious balance between volume and finely tuned quality. These are champagnes with a flattering demeanour of precision, delicacy, elegance and tension, though some inconsistency has recently begun to creep into some cuvées.

Laurent-Perrier's success is less by virtue of its domain vineyard holdings (which supply just 11% of its total needs of 150 hectares) than by the skill and vision of its people. The talented Alain Terrier was its longstanding chef de cave from 1975 to 2005, and was succeeded by Michel Fauconnet, his offsider for more than 20 years. I have requested an audience with Michel each time I have visited Champagne, and I very much look forward to meeting him. Hopefully next time.

The secret to Laurent-Perrier's wines today delves deep into the history of a house that recently celebrated its 200th birthday. The late Bernard de Nonancourt, founding president of the Laurent-Perrier Group, was a visionary who spent half of the last century transforming and expanding the company. His innovations changed the face of modern champagne. Under his leadership, the house boldly launched its non-vintage prestige cuvée, Grand Siècle, in 1957, a rosé well ahead of its time in 1968 (then considered a joke by the Champenois, now the best-selling champagne rosé in the world) — and, perhaps most influential of all, inspired by brewers of beer, Laurent-Perrier was the first house in Champagne to use stainless steel tanks in the 1960s.

De Nonancourt's vision was one of freshness, finesse and elegance based on chardonnay, which to this day maintains the majority stake in every cuvée (representing double Champagne's average) except rosé. No meunier is used, apart from a 15% touch in L-P Brut. This creates a house style of precision and tension, unusual among houses of this scale.

To celebrate its bicentenary in 2012, the house commissioned a major addition and renovation to its cuverie. In the same location as Champagne's first stainless steel tanks, the Grand Siècle winery is an atmospheric display of stainless steel reserve tanks custom-built with graceful curves, no seams, and narrow spouts to reduce oxidation.

Laurent-Perrier has a very real commitment to sustainability: vineyard manager Christelle Rinville refuses to fly in aeroplanes, encourages workers to use bicycles, plants grasses in the mid-rows and uses only non-invasive chemicals in all estate vineyards. The winery is almost self-sufficient in its use of water.

The tight, chardonnay-driven house style is softened through malolactic fermentation in all cuvées, and long lees ageing of at least four years at 11°C in 10 kilometres of cellars under the house in Tours-sur-Marne.

Regrettably, consumers remain oblivious to Laurent-Perrier's long ageing. The house fails to disclose disgorgement dates and base vintages on labels, and also refuses to provide this information when requested, for reasons I fail to understand. I was declined this information again this year, despite repeated requests.

These are long-ageing wines of a clean sophistication that transcend the scale of this operation.

Laurent-Perrier L-P Brut NV $$

91 points • Tasted in Brisbane, Sydney & Melbourne

50% chardonnay, 35% pinot noir, 15% meunier; aged 4 years on lees; 10g/L dosage

At 62% of Laurent-Perrier's production, this cuvée alone accounts for around 5 million bottles annually, which makes its high proportion of chardonnay and long ageing all the more impressive. It's a happy party quaffer in a fresh and fruity style, with lemon zest, red apple and white peach fruit. Tangy acidity is comfortably balanced by well-integrated dosage and a creamy bead. It finishes subtly firm and earthy, with a touch of phenolic grip.

Laurent-Perrier L-P Ultra Brut NV $$$

91 points • Tasted in Brisbane, Sydney & Melbourne

55% chardonnay, 45% pinot noir; bunch selection of grapes with high sugar and low acidity from 15 villages in ripe vintages; aged 4 years on lees; zero dosage

Laurent-Perrier has a very long history with zero dosage, having first launched its 'Grand Vins Sans Sucre' in the 1800s, relaunched by Bernard de Nonancourt in 1981. Today, this cuvée is champagne's best-selling brut nature, in a well-balanced and high-strung apéritif style. This disgorgement presents clean nashi pear and grapefruit, with subtle flinty reductive notes and the almond complexity of bottle age. It's razor tight in its lemon-juice acid line, finishing bracingly dry, yet upholding freshness, purity and salt mineral definition. This is a zero dosage for champagne diehards to drink with oysters.

Laurent-Perrier Millésimé 2006 $$$

92 points • Tasted in Brisbane

The warm and immediate 2006 vintage makes for a soft and creamy Laurent-Perrier, with notes of zesty, spicy grapefruit contrasting golden delicious apple. Its structure relies equally on acid drive as subtle phenolic grip, having built softly textural, creamy, nutty character during time on lees. It shows relaxed balance and appeal, without persistence or endurance for further ageing.

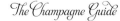

LAURENT-PERRIER CUVÉE ROSÉ BRUT NV $$$

94 points • TASTED IN BRISBANE, SYDNEY & MELBOURNE

100% pinot noir from 10 different crus, predominantly in the Montagne de Reims, including Ambonnay, Bouzy, Louvois and Tours-sur-Marne; hand sorted

Laurent-Perrier macerates its rosé for 12–72 hours, depending on fruit ripeness, until the colour is fixed and the aroma resembles freshly picked raspberries. So crucial is timing, legend has it that the first chef de cave, Edouard Leclerc, slept by the tank to stop it just in time! This wine has achieved that elusive ideal of volume and finesse; the world's best-selling rosé champagne epitomises the ultra-restraint of rosé's finest expressions. All the more remarkable for the challenging saignée method. Its latest incarnation of medium salmon hue is a beautifully elegant expression of strawberry hull, red cherry and pink pepper, with an enticing waft of flinty reductive aroma, opening in time to the glorious depth of black cherries. A delightfully composed rosé of excellent line, energetic acid backbone and softly mineral mouthfeel, confidently upholding the long and great legacy of this label.

LAURENT-PERRIER GRANDE SIÈCLE NV $$$$$

97 points • TASTED IN BRISBANE, SYDNEY & MELBOURNE

De Nonancourt's vision was to produce a multi-vintage prestige cuvée able to maintain consistent quality. This is achieved by blending only grand cru fruit from the best crus in the finest years declared by Laurent-Perrier. The blend places it among the oldest champagnes on the shelves. Sadly, the consumer is oblivious to this, as the bottle gives no clue to either its disgorgement date or its splendid maturity. Despite a huge internal debate, the house refuses to budge on this, and declines to disclose base vintages even on my request. This makes managing collections a challenge, which is a shame, as Grand Siècle ages magnificently, long beyond its release.

Even in its grand maturity, this wine is staggeringly youthful, somehow mustering pristine freshness of crunchy grapefruit, lemon zest, pear, fig and an enticing reductive note of gunflint. It simultaneously celebrates long lees age in glorious notes of toasted brioche and butter, and a creamy, silky mouthfeel. There's a vibrancy to its tangy and enduring acid line, accented by gently expressive chalk minerality, beckoning for more time in the cellar. It will be a decade before it attains the full heights of its towering magnificence, and much longer before it begins to fade.

LAURENT-PERRIER ALEXANDRA GRANDE CUVÉE ROSÉ 2004 $$$$$

94 points • TASTED IN BRISBANE

80% grand cru pinot noir, 20% grand cru chardonnay, macerated together; 7–8g/L dosage

From its disposition of calm maturity on release two years ago, I'm surprised and impressed with how evenly it has evolved, upholding its medium salmon hue and copper tints and its elegant and balanced complexity. Red fruits are beginning to fade as glimpses of secondary, savoury complexity rise. A long finish is carried by a textural mouthfeel and soft tannin structure, with dry extract lending subtle firmness. I'm in two minds as to whether it's at the end of its life, set to slowly begin to fade into callow dryness, or perhaps have a second wind and build depth and flesh on the finish as tertiary character rises.

LE BRUN-SERVENAY

(Ler Bru-Sair-veh-nay)

7/10

14 PLACE LÉON BOURGEOIS 51190 AVIZE

www.champagnelebrun.com

When Patrick Le Brun's parents were married in 1955, they brought together the house of Le Brun in Avize, and the estate of Servenay in Mancy in the Coteaux Sud d'Épernay. His estate remains a seamless, if somewhat unusual, union of the two families, maintaining the Le Brun cellars directly next door to Erick de Sousa in Avize, and the Servenay press house and cuverie, six kilometres over the hill in Mancy, rebuilt in 2013. Le Brun's almost six hectares of enviably positioned chardonnay in Cramant, Oger and (especially) Avize provide 80% of the estate's needs, supplemented by about 1.5 hectares of pinot noir and meunier from Mancy and its surrounding villages. These are distinctive champagnes in their remarkable freshness, pristine purity and staggering longevity, particularly expressive of the salty chalk mineral signature of Avize, heightened through the blocking of malolactic fermentation across all cuvées.

It wasn't many generations ago that malolactic fermentation became commonplace in Champagne, before which every wine of the region was blessed with the sustaining endurance, if at times disarming austerity, of malic acidity.

Those houses and growers who have conscientiously retained malic acidity while upholding carefully balanced appeal are due high admiration.

Patrick Le Brun struggled to convince his father to block malolactic fermentation, maintaining that malic acidity is crucial for preserving the freshness and smoothness in his grapes' aromas. It also charges his cuvées with tremendous sustaining power. I have tasted Patrick's cuvées back to the 1970s on more than one occasion with him, and it is breathtakingly apparent

that these champagnes mature at but half the pace that one might expect. Even pre-1982 cuvées with full malolactic fermentation still look backward in their evolution.

Built on majestic grand cru chardonnay and finished with low dosages of typically 5–7g/L, with most cuvées also available as extra brut of typically 3.5g/L dosage, these could be challenging champagnes were it not for Le Brun's meticulous attention to picking at perfect ripeness, his exacting precision in vinification, and his patience in long ageing in the cellar. Freshness is preserved through vinification in tank, with just a small amount of red wine in barrel for rosé.

'Our purpose is to translate in the glass the elegance and minerality of the terroir of our vineyards,' declares

Le Brun, the fifth generation of the Servenay family, and the fourth on the Le Brun side to tend grapes in these sites. His vines are old by Champagne standards, some older than 80 years, with roots that plunge 10–12 metres into the chalk. 'We plough and plant grass in the mid-rows to encourage competition and force the roots deeper,' he explains. Yields of 60–80hL/hectare (60–80% of Champagne's average) are important for achieving full ripeness.

The champagnes of Le Brun-Servenay live up to their brief with exacting clarity, and represent outstanding value for money. Recent tastings of the 1976 and, particularly, 1981 vintages have evidenced the sheer stamina and longevity of this house.

LE BRUN-SERVENAY BRUT RÉSERVE NV $$

90 points • 2011 BASE VINTAGE • TASTED IN AVIZE

50% chardonnay, 25% pinot, 25% meunier; chardonnay reserves from 2010, 2009 and 2008; made in small stainless steel vats; no malolactic fermentation; aged at least 3 years on lees; 7g/L dosage

A core of Avize chardonnay, with Mancy pinot noir and meunier, this is a blend of fine structure and backbone, scaffolded with gentle chalk mineral texture. It's earthy and suppressed, with understated apple and citrus fruit, though lacking in freshness and aromatic lift, the child of a tough season.

LE BRUN-SERVENAY BRUT SÉLECTION BLANC DE BLANCS GRAND CRU NV $$

94 points • 2011 BASE VINTAGE • TASTED IN AVIZE

90% Avize and Cramant, 10% Oger; vines of average age 25 years; reserves from 2010, 2009 and 2008; no malolactic fermentation; 7g/L dosage

The pristine delights of Le Brun-Servenay are proclaimed for all to relish even in this entry cuvée. A beautifully pale, fresh and pure expression of perfectly ripe chardonnay, with aromas of lemon and granny smith apple, and the subtle complexity of almond nougat. Charged with the coiled potential of electric malic acidity, this is an exceptionally affordable and accurate expression of the fine, chalky minerality of the Côte des Blancs, making for a refreshing apéritif of creamy bead and subtle dosage.

LE BRUN-SERVENAY CUVÉE BRUT ROSÉ NV $$

95 points • 2010 BASE VINTAGE • TASTED IN AVIZE

Same chardonnay base as Brut Séléction; 10% red wine from 2009 from old-vine Mancy pinot noir and a touch of meunier; red wine half aged in oak barrels for 18 months; no malolactic fermentation; aged at least 3 years on lees; 7g/L dosage

Rosé was the first cuvée I ever tasted from Le Brun-Servenay and it singly inspired me to visit the house, now a regular stop on all of my Champagne sojourns. Built on the fresh purity and electric structure of Brut Séléction, the achingly pristine elegance of Le Brun-Servenay's rosé comes as no surprise. A touch of red wine creates a pretty, pale salmon hue, and an elegant and reserved mood of subtle rose petal, pomegranate, strawberry and red cherry fruit. It's ultra-refreshing and taut, with fine chalk mineral mouthfeel and delicate, lingering persistence. It takes real craftsmanship to create such a graceful rosé without malolactic fermentation.

LE BRUN-SERVENAY CUVÉE CHARDONNAY BRUT MILLÉSIME VIEILLES VIGNES 2005 $$

95 points • TASTED IN AVIZE

Blanc de blancs from Avize for elegance, Oger for minerality and Cramant for presence and freshness; old vines aged 45-80 years; no malolactic fermentation; aged 9 years on lees; 5g/L dosage

The precision of Le Brun-Servenay trumps the firmness of the warm 2005 season with the fine, mineral precision of the great grand crus of the Côte des Blancs. It strikes a graceful harmony between the lemon fruits of chardonnay, the generosity of yellow stone fruits of 2005, and the gentle, soft, toasty, spicy complexity and creamy texture of maturity. It's neatly supported by a fine, creamy bead and well-integrated dosage. Impressive for 2005.

LE BRUN-SERVENAY EXHILARANTE VIEILLES VIGNES MILLÉSIME 2006 $$$

96 points • TASTED IN AVIZE

80% chardonnay from Avize, Cramant and Oger; 10% pinot noir for structure; 10% meunier for fruitiness; Le Brun's oldest vines 60-80 years old on soil 15cm above chalk; no malolactic fermentation; aged 8 years on lees; 5g/L dosage

Le Brun-Servenay's malic freshness and exceptionally mineral grand crus unite to energise even the otherwise rounded and early-drinking 2006 season with a definition and stamina that lifts it not only above most from this vintage but, remarkably, even high above the 2004 of the same cuvée. The exacting precision and fine mineral backbone of grand cru chardonnay strikes a compelling accord with Le Brun's finely structured malic acidity and the creamy, textural suppleness of long lees age. Gentle notes of anise and honey biscuits rise gloriously amidst lemon and apple precision. It promises a grand future, set to outlive most from this vintage.

LE BRUN-SERVENAY BLANC DE BLANCS X.B. EXTRA BRUT 2.5 NV $$$

95 points • 2011 BASE VINTAGE • RESERVES FROM 2010, 2009, 2008 AND 2007 • TASTED IN AVIZE

Avize, Cramant and Oger; no malolactic fermentation; aged at least 3 years on lees; 2.5g/L dosage

Patrick Le Brun teamed up with Les Crayères sommelier Philippe Jamesse to create his new X.B. (Extra Brut) cuvées. In the hands of mere mortals, the chalk mineral texture of the great Côte des Blancs grand crus in concert with the vivacity of chardonnay's malic acidity screams out for the calming presence of dosage. But this talented duo has infused this dashing new cuvée with an outstanding acid line and precise chalk mineral spine, with just an invisible dash of sweetness, without any hint of hardness or austerity. Enticing, exact lemon fruit has slowly begun its gentle evolution into brioche and gingernut biscuits.

LE BRUN-SERVENAY ROSÉ ULTIME X.B. EXTRA BRUT 3.2 NV $$$

94 points • 100% 2010 VINTAGE • TASTED IN AVIZE

90% chardonnay, predominantly from Cramant and Avize, aged 1 year in tank; 10% red wine of 80% pinot noir and 20% meunier from Mancy, aged 1 year in barrel; no malolactic fermentation; 3.2g/L dosage

A pale, bright salmon hue is merely window dressing here, for in crystalline structure, glittering energy, scintillating malic acidity and a touch of gunflint reduction, this wine is all about unadulterated, majestic grand cru chardonnay. Fine chalk mineral texture and coiled energy infuse grand potential for a long life.

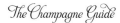

The Champagne Guide

Le Mesnil

(Ler Meh-neel)

5/10

19–32 RUE CHARPENTIER LAURAIN 51190 LE MESNIL-SUR-OGER

www.champagnelemesnil.com

Le Mesnil competes only with Mailly Grand Cru as Champagne's greatest cooperative, and in value for money it has no rivals. This large establishment has 553 member growers who tend a good 305 hectares, spanning some of the best sites in the most age-worthy grand cru of the Côte des Blancs. It presses grapes for many of the big names of Champagne, and bottles just 8% of production under its own label. Vinification is performed in stainless steel at a controlled temperature of 18°C to preserve the fresh expression of the village. Its finest cuvées proclaim the racy tension and commanding presence of Le Mesnil-sur-Oger, at enticing prices.

LE MESNIL BLANC DE BLANCS GRAND CRU BRUT NV $$

91 points • TASTED IN SYDNEY & MELBOURNE

Full malolactic fermentation; 12.5g/L dosage

One of the more affordable experiences of the elegance and power of Le Mesnil, with the inimitable chalk mineral texture of the village forming an undercurrent to racy, taut lemon and grapefruit zest, underscored by almond complexity. Dry extract is a little more prominent than usual in this release, and the finish is slightly contracted.

LE MESNIL BLANC DE BLANCS GRAND CRU SUBLIME BRUT VINTAGE 2006 $$

94 points • TASTED IN SYDNEY & MELBOURNE

A world away from the coarse 2005, the generous complexity of 2006 has found its happy place in the structured village of Le Mesnil-sur-Oger. Complexity of ginger, brioche and mixed spice provide flesh to an energetic spine of focused lemon juice acidity. Fine Le Mesnil chalk mineral structure provides focus and endurance to the finish.

LOMBARD & CIE

(Lom-bar e See)

---

1 RUE DES CÔTELLES BP118 51024 ÉPERNAY

www.champagne-lombard.com

Thierry Lombard is the third generation of his family to run the medium-sized Épernay house of Lombard & Cie. About 8% of an annual production of 1.5 million bottles is produced from 10 hectares of largely premier cru estate vines in the western Montagne de Reims and Épernay, planted to all three champagne varieties. The remainder is sourced from long-term growers managing 150 hectares. The house harvested the first organic fruit from its own vineyards in 2015, and hopes to obtain certification within three years.

When I visited Lombard's premises in Épernay for the first time in 2015, I was impressed by the number of shiny little temperature-controlled stainless steel tanks of 500–2500 litres, permitting fermentation to be conducted parcel by parcel, producing a house style of freshness and vitality. Malolactic fermentation is usually allowed to proceed to completion, but is blocked in low-acid harvests. The house keeps a stock of 3 million bottles in its cellars, which dictates a relatively early release. A blanket 7g/L of dosage across the house (except rosé, which can be a touch higher) is a refreshingly low level of sweetness, though the acidity can look a little firm in these young blends. They appreciate a little bottle age to show their full potential.

South of the Côte des Blancs, Sézanne is planted largely to chardonnay, producing more rustic wines from heavier soils.

Lombard & Cie Brut Référence NV $$

87 points • 2012 base vintage • Tasted in Épernay

40% meunier, 40% pinot noir, 20% chardonnay; full malolactic fermentation; aged 2 years on lees; 7g/L dosage

Intentionally an apéritif style, this is a young, primary and zesty cuvée defined by grapefruit and crunchy pear fruit and well-balanced dosage. Dusty mushroom notes and precocious, young acidity conspire to leave the finish a little coarse, simple and short.

Lombard & Cie Brut Premier Cru NV $$

89 points • 2011 base vintage • Tasted in Épernay
89 points • 2008 base vintage • Tasted in Melbourne

50% chardonnay, 50% pinot noir; 7g/L dosage; DIAM closure

A light, refreshing, simple, primary apéritif style of red apple and lemon fruit and well-defined acidity on a persistent finish. Some dustiness on the end distracts from an otherwise pure style.

Lombard & Cie Brut Rosé Premier Cru NV $$

90 points • 2011 base vintage • Tasted in Épernay & Melbourne

60% chardonnay, 40% pinot noir, including 10% pinot noir red wine from Verzenay; 9g/L dosage; DIAM closure

Much more refined than its bold pink label suggests, this is an elegant, refreshing rosé of medium, vibrant salmon hue, and fresh rosewater, strawberry hull and pink grapefruit character. Led confidently by chardonnay, it's young and lively, with taut acidity and clean, elegant fruit purity.

Lombard & Cie Brut Grand Cru Blanc de Blancs NV $$

88 points • 2010 base vintage • Tasted in Épernay

50% Le Mesnil-sur-Oger, 25% Chouilly, 15% Avize, 10% Cramant; no malolactic fermentation on the Le Mesnil component; 7g/L dosage

A young, refreshing, slightly austere blanc de blancs, accented by the tension of Le Mesnil-sur-Oger malic acidity. A fine, creamy bead and pure lemon and grapefruit are interrupted by a cabbage note of reductive complexity.

LOMBARD & CIE BRUT GRAND CRU NV $$

92 points • 2010 BASE VINTAGE • TASTED IN ÉPERNAY

50% Montagne de Reims pinot noir, 50% Côte des Blancs chardonnay; 7g/L dosage

Equal proportions of chardonnay and pinot noir support each other confidently, providing depth and drive, with lemon zest freshness and strawberry hull liveliness. Impressive fruit drive and definition reflect grand cru sourcing, well supported by soft mineral texture and excellent acid line, offering energetic appeal.

LOMBARD & CIE BRUT GRAND CRU MILLÉSIME 2008 $$

94 points • LATE 2014 DISGORGEMENT • TASTED IN ÉPERNAY & MELBOURNE

60% chardonnay, 40% pinot noir; 7g/L dosage

Barely moved since its release two years ago, the great 2008 vintage energises a captivating wine of well-articulated structure and deep, ultra-fine mouthfeel of chalky minerality. It sings with primary freshness of lemon, grapefruit, white nectarine and strawberry hull, with only very subtle almond meal complexity beginning to rise. Backward and pure, it captures the spirit of an enduring season, with a long future before it. Great value in age-worthy champagne.

LOMBARD & CIE TANAGRA BRUT GRAND CRU NV $$$$

91 points • 2008 BASE • TASTED IN ÉPERNAY

50% Le Mesnil-sur-Oger chardonnay, 30% Chouilly chardonnay, 20% Verzenay pinot noir; reserves from 2007 and 2006; fermented in stainless steel vats; around one-third matured in 600L oak demi-muid barrels; 7g/L dosage.

In its distinctive trademarked, bottle, this is a structured cuvée that reflects the angles of its bottle, built more around sinew and scaffolding than it is around flesh. Subtle crunchy pear and grapefruit are visible within its high-tensile frame. Firm, taut 2008 acidity conspires with the grip and texture of barrel age to create a style that demands time in the cellar to build flesh. A distinctive champagne for well-seasoned palates looking for something different.

LOMBARD & CIE TANAGRA BRUT ROSÉ GRAND CRU NV $$$$

89 points • 100% 2012 • TASTED IN ÉPERNAY

Rosé de saignée entirely from Verzenay; only partially destemmed for a maturation of 2-3 days in barrel; 5g/L dosage

This is a raw and edgy rosé of structure and dry mouthfeel, with a full, vibrant, crimson-red hue, and flavours of pomegranate, musk, blood orange and tamarillo uniting in a structured style of firm tannin grip and grapefruit-pith bitterness.

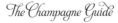

LOUIS ROEDERER

(Loo-ii Roh-dehr-air)

9/10

21 BOULEVARD LUNDY BP66 51053 REIMS

www.champagne-roederer.com

MAISON FONDÉE EN 1776

LOUIS ROEDERER
CHAMPAGNE

Louis Roederer is unlike any other champagne house of its magnitude. The largest independent, family-owned and -managed champagne maker of all is privileged to 235 hectares of superbly located vineyards, supplying a grand 70% of its needs for an annual production of 3 million bottles. With 410 blocks and 450 tanks and casks at his disposal, chef de cave Jean-Baptiste Lécaillon describes his role as 'à la carte winemaking'. He hates the word 'blend'. 'We don't blend, we combine,' he says. 'I love art, and like a great painter we add colour rather than blending.' There are few in Champagne today with an intellect as sharp, an attention to detail as acute and a nerve as strong as Lécaillon. For 15 years, he has championed extraordinary initiatives in Roederer's vineyards unparalleled in the region, and a regime in the winery to match. Never have his wines looked more characterful, or more precise.

There was once a time when Louis Roederer was purely a négociant house, but over the years it has strategically acquired vineyards to amass one of the largest proportions of estate vines among the big champagne houses. These are well situated across some 16 villages, spanning the Montagne de Reims, Vallée de la Marne and Côte des Blancs. More than two-thirds are grand cru level.

All of Louis Roederer's vintage wines are assembled exclusively from estate properties, and even its entry Brut Premier NV now boasts 55% estate fruit, and rising.

'I do not say that Roederer is a champagne house for the vintage wines,' says Lécaillon. 'We are three growers, one in Montagne de Reims, one in Vallée de la Marne and one in Côte des Blancs.'

Roederer is continuing to expand its estate and has averaged an additional two hectares every year for the past decade, all on chalk soils. 'Chalk is the style of Roederer,' Lécaillon declares. 'It produces more focused wines, while clay produces more round and soft styles.'

The vast majority of estate vines are on chalk, with a particular focus on the chalk-rich Côte des Blancs, home to 80 hectares of Roederer vines. The company owns no vineyards beyond Cumières in the Vallée de la Marne because of the higher clay content here.

'We have wonderful terroirs and our goal is to express each of them,' Lécaillon says. For an operation of this scale, the attention to detail in the vineyards is unprecedented. Old vines are used to limit yields, as is green harvesting, in what Lécaillon dubs 'haute couture viticulture'. Over the past 15 years, he has customised the pruning, budding, trellising, ploughing and harvesting of each vineyard to suit the cuvée to which it is destined.

A team of 800 pickers sorts fruit in the vineyard, and it is sorted again before it is pressed. 'The only way

I can get quality is by paying pickers by the hour, not by the kilogram,' he emphasises. This is rare in Champagne.

BIODYNAMICS ON A GRAND SCALE

Most remarkably, Roederer now tends 65 hectares of vineyards biodynamically, including more than half of those that contribute to Cristal. An incredible 25 hectares are ploughed by horse. Biodynamics on such a scale is unheard of in Champagne, and Roederer's operation is the biggest in the region by an order of magnitude.

In the village of Cumières, where Roederer has a strong presence, the tiny, fanatical biodynamic grower Vincent Laval recently mentioned that he prefers Roederer's attention to viticulture to that of small growers using industrial methods. High endorsement.

Lécaillon has set aside plots for experimentation in each of the three regions of Champagne, and fruit from biodynamic vines is compared with traditional viticulture from the same village. I was surprised at just how much more salty minerality and texture was evident in 2012 vins clairs from biodynamic sources.

'When the soil looks better, the vines look better, the fruit looks better, and we get more ripeness, more acidity and more iodine salinity to the minerality,' explains Lécaillon, for whom ripeness is 'the game'. He attributes greater precision in biodynamic fruit to decreased vigour in the vines, and greater mineral expression to deeper roots. 'We cannot explain this with measurements, but this is the way with biodynamics — we can only see it by tasting.'

Roederer began experimenting with biodynamics in 2003, after a false start in 2000. Fifteen years on, Lécaillon says it will take 40 years to draw any solid conclusions. But he has discovered that a different approach is necessary in each region, easier on well-draining chalk in the Côte des Blancs and Montagne de Reims, and harder on clay in the Vallée de la Marne. 'There are some years in which biodynamics is much better and some years in which it is not so effective,' Lécaillon explains. 'It performs well in vintages in which the vines struggle under particularly wet or dry conditions.' In the wet 2011 and 2014 seasons, he harvested his best fruit in biodynamic vineyards. He suspects this may be a result of thicker skins providing greater resilience in biodynamic fruit. While he is convinced of the philosophy of biodynamics, certification is not the goal. 'We see it as just one means of achieving terroir expression,' he says. 'We are constantly learning.'

This learning curve was particularly steep in 2012, and Roederer reported losses of 30–50% in some plots, and greater under biodynamics. 'It involves so much risk,' Lécaillon explains. 'Biodynamics removes all the safety of chemicals, and if it's not done properly you can really get caught quickly.' He accepts the loss of 2012 and suggests that the experience was helpful for his team to really get on top of biodynamics.

At the end of vintage 2014, I shadowed Lécaillon for a day in his vineyards and was stunned by a stark difference between healthy biodynamic vines and struggling organic plots on neighbouring sites. I took 7500 words of notes and learnt more about viticulture in Champagne that day than ever before. 'In order to survive we must decrease the chemicals that we use,' he told me. 'By removing the comfort of chemicals, my team has to work like vignerons, to really understand the terroir, not like robots. It really is a culture of coming back to the terroir.'

À LA CARTE WINEMAKING

Lécaillon's aim is to emphasise terroir and downplay house style and varietal character, which he achieves by pushing for ripeness, encouraging a little oxidation at harvest, and blocking malolactic fermentation. Roederer's focus on its vineyards opens up opportunities for greater refinement in the winery. Regulated yields allow harvesting at full ripeness, rendering chaptalisation unnecessary, unless the season is very difficult — an impressive mandate, and I believe unprecedented at this scale in Champagne. In recent years, wild yeast ferments have been introduced. Biodynamic plots are harvested early, fermented wild, and used to seed other ferments.

Malolactic fermentation is generally avoided, except in some higher-acid parcels destined for the non-vintage Brut Premier, generally just 20–25% of the blend. 'The only way to avoid malo is to produce fruit in the vineyard that doesn't require it — ripe fruit with soft malic acid,' notes Lécaillon, who prefers to obtain the right acid balance in the vineyard than the winery.

'Malolactic fermentation was first conducted in Champagne in 1965,' he points out. 'It can be useful in a difficult year, but it must be a safety tool, not a systematic procedure, and this is especially true with global warming.' The house completely blocked malolactic fermentation on all estate and contract fruit in 2012, 2006, 2003, 2002 and 1999.

Basket presses run 24/7 throughout vintage, as it takes three hours to press the first cuvée. Unusually, the solids are retained, producing a cloudy juice. 'We feel this expresses terroir better and gives greater protection against oxidation,' Lécaillon explains.

A new cuverie was built in 2007 to enable every block to be vinified separately in a custom-made tank or large oak vat, according to the power of the fruit tasted in the vineyard. 'Each tank and vat is a vineyard with a roof!' Lécaillon suggests. 'My workers must think of each parcel in the winery as a site, not as a lot.' Oak fermentation was reintroduced in 1999, and today about 20% of the vintage is fermented in oak, and aged on lees with bâtonnage for texture, phenolics and roundness. Lécaillon does not consider phenolics to be a dirty word in Champagne. 'Oak phenolics and the right fruit phenolics draw out salinity on the sides of the tongue and bring out another dimension to the flavour.'

'We hate oxidation — it is a betrayal of terroir,' adds Lécaillon. 'Lees contact and bâtonnage protect from oxidation.' This creates a reductive style, which has at times produced savoury overtones that distract from fruit purity in Roederer's vintage wines, though this has been better controlled in recent years. 'I make wines reductively because I want them to age.' Vins clairs fermented in oak show richer texture, without taking on oak flavour. Reserve wines are aged in 150 large old oak foudres (15–50 years of age), and *liqueur d'expédition* is kept in casks for as long as a decade. Four vintages of *liqueur d'expédition* are kept in vat at all times to allow the dosage for each blend to be tweaked. Dosages of typically 8–11g/L sometimes appear a little high for the natural ripeness of Roederer's fruit.

Non-vintage wines are aged on lees in bottle for three years, vintage wines for four years, and Cristal for six or seven (with 2007 and 2009 Cristal due to land in 2015 and 2016 respectively, and the enduring 2008 in 2017, the first ever non-sequential release). This requires a large stock of 18 million bottles squirrelled away in Roederer's cellars, with 3 million leaving every year.

Roederer's attention to detail in its vineyards and winery shine even in its non-vintage Brut Premier. In 2007, Lécaillon constructed a gleaming, state-of-the-art, all-new facility devoted exclusively to this cuvée (and a dedicated rosé facility in the same year). This facilitated its own dedicated team, earlier classification of fruit, fewer blendings (just four each year) and less pumping, all of which he credits for the rise in Brut Premier. Representing 80% of the production of the house, this is a masterfully assembled cuvée. Lécaillon describes Champagne as a 'permanent innovation'. Such is his attention to tuning the finest details that he tweaks the pressure to suit each cuvée, bottling riper vintages at five atmospheres, and more classic, lean seasons at six.

He emphasises that age in bottle on cork is crucial for his cuvées, and after three years he prefers the effect of natural cork to DIAM. His batch testing of corks is the most rigorous I have seen anywhere. Of every batch of 100,000 corks, 460 are agitated in water for 45 minutes and the water then tasted. This is repeated for 200 batches every year, and sometimes a batch is tested twice, and if a single tainted cork is found, the entire batch is rejected. His team rejects one batch in three. No doubt this is why, in all my years of tasting, I've only ever found one cork-tainted bottle of Roederer. If only every house were so stringent in its cork testing.

In a fantastic development in disclosure, Louis Roederer has followed Krug's lead, and its website and app now reveal the base vintage, year of bottling and year of disgorgement from the bottling code of any cuvée. May more houses do likewise!

The rise of Roederer's Brut Premier is thanks in part to its gleaming new state-of-the-art facility, dedicated exclusively to this cuvée.

LOUIS ROEDERER BRUT PREMIER NV $$

94 points • 2010 BASE VINTAGE • DISGORGED MARCH 2014 • TASTED IN BRISBANE
95 points • 2009 BASE VINTAGE • TASTED IN REIMS, PERTH & BRISBANE
94 points • 2007 BASE VINTAGE • TASTED IN MELBOURNE

40% pinot noir, 40% chardonnay, 20% meunier; one-third reserves sourced from young-vine Cristal sites; a blend of 40 villages; 55% estate vineyards; base wines from estate vines fermented in oak casks with bâtonnage (lees stirring); reserves fermented in tanks and matured in large oak casks for up to 8 years; 20-25% malolactic fermentation; aged 3 years on lees; 9.5g/L dosage; 2.4 million bottles

I've long adored Brut Premier, a masterful presentation of impeccably ripe fruit of intricate balance and abundant appeal: a dependable bargain in the non-vintage champagne stakes. It's on the rise in its new, dedicated facility. Until the 2009 base, Brut Premier reserves came from a solera, in Lécaillon's view, lacking focus and 'showing too much character of having been made in the cellar'. The solera is now no more, bringing greater focus, more precise mineral articulation and greater emphasis on ripe fruit. Dosage was sensibly dropped from 10–11g/L to 9.5g/L. The result in 2010 is a wonderful accord between pretty lemon blossom, apple and pear fruit, the spicy, toasty, nutmeg allure of barrel fermentation and bottle age, and the racy freshness of malic acidity. It's at once impeccably fresh and enticingly complex, with a long finish of soft chalk minerality. The 2009 is even more precise in its floral lift, red cherry definition and mineral detail. A triumph.

LOUIS ROEDERER BRUT VINTAGE 2008 $$$

96 points • DISGORGED MAY 2014 • TASTED IN REIMS & BRISBANE

80% pinot noir from Verzy and Verzenay for strength, softened with 20% chardonnay from east-facing Chouilly near Cramant; almost 50% fermented in large oak casks; 25% malolactic fermentation to balance high malic acid of 2008

The planets aligned as the vivacious 2008 season collided with the full impact of Lécaillon's innovation in the vines and the wines. The fallout just might be the greatest Roederer vintage in recent history. The ethereal perfume that runs through the palate is enthralling, lending a fragrant rose petal air to spectacular pinot noir expression, purity and drive of fresh lemon, white cherry, red apple and grapefruit. A magnificent confluence of electric energy and resonating depth, as the racy, streamlined tension of 2008 malic acidity traces out a high-tensile cage that will support decades of evolution in the cellar. All manner of barrel- and bottle-derived personality infuses flesh, body and nuances of fig, nutmeg, even mocha. Wonderfully pronounced minerality is drawn out by roots thrust deep into chalk, thanks to 40–50% of sourcing from biodynamically farmed sites. Fairly light delicacy, breathtakingly primary definition and impeccably ripe fullness make for a captivating display right away, but the full pyrotechnics display is yet to come.

LOUIS ROEDERER BRUT VINTAGE 2007 $$$

95 points • TASTED IN BRISBANE

70% Verzenay pinot noir, 30% Avize chardonnay; half oak fermented; no malolactic fermentation

Lécaillon chooses his strongest pinot noir vineyards on clay soils for this blend, building a multi-layered, complex and gastronomic wine. This philosophy sits well in the elegant aura that defines 2007, producing a young, precocious, zesty blend, with primary candied lemon and lemon sherbet enveloping an intense core of lemon butter fullness. Layers of chalk mineral texture meld seamlessly with fine phenolic mouthfeel, gathering momentum on a long, seamless finish.

Louis Roederer Blanc de Blancs 2009 $$$

95 points • Tasted in Reims

Blend of Avize, Le Mesnil-sur-Oger and Cramant; no malolactic fermentation; 20-25% oak fermented; 8-10g/L dosage

Lécaillon's philosophy for blanc de blancs is to push ripeness very hard, keeping yields 30% down and picking in Avize as high as 11.8 degrees potential. This is exemplified in a vintage that he describes as 'rich, round and exuberant', producing a blanc de blancs of power, flesh, sinew and mid-palate strength that draws long through the finish. Even in the midst of such ripeness, the chalk mineral signature of these villages shines brilliantly. A whiff of struck-flint reduction accents captivating hints of fresh white pepper, washing over a rich core of preserved lemon and ripe fig, with toasty, spicy, brioche notes emphasised by a touch of barrel fermentation. The tension of malic acidity brings everything into line, drawing the finish out honed and energetic.

Louis Roederer Blanc de Blancs 2008 $$$

96 points • Tasted in Reims & Brisbane

50% Avize, 25% Le Mesnil-sur-Oger and 25% Cramant; six ripe plots in the middle of the villages on pure chalk; 30% oak fermented; no malolactic fermentation; no chaptalisation; low mousse of 4 atmospheres of pressure

To Lécaillon, masterminding champagne is 'always a blend of paradoxes', exemplified in a vintage he describes as 'razor blade', in which he pushed ripeness to the extreme to emphasise creaminess, upheld full malic acid cut, built depth with oak fermentation, and then softened the impression of malic acidity with low pressure. The final result is a rousing celebration of the thrilling energy and precision of 2008, with breathtaking elegance and effortless poise. It dances on a stage of impeccable, salty, deeply mineral chalk, juxtaposed with impressive Roederer body, flesh and ripeness of grapefruit, beurre bosc pear, apple, lemon and even fig. It's at once powerful and characterful, and simultaneously taut and enduring. In time, subtle spicy, toasty, biscuity complexity begins to materialise. A thrilling wine that will live for decades, singing with the exuberance of 2008.

Louis Roederer Rosé 2009 $$$

95 points • Disgorged January 2014 • Tasted in Reims & Brisbane

70% ripe, south-facing Cumières pinot noir for energy and freshness; 30% north-facing Chouilly chardonnay for minerality and acidity; saignée method, blended after cold maceration according to colour; 20% matured in oak tuns

Lécaillon says north-facing Chouilly chardonnay is the New World equivalent of adding acid. The result unites the body and flesh of Cumières pinot noir with the tension of Chouilly chardonnay in this medium salmon-tinted rosé. Multidimensional complexity is inherent to the Roederer style, here delivered with elegance and restraint. Raspberries, red apples, quince and cherry kernels unite with subtle suggestions of struck flint and white pepper reduction, coffee beans and mocha, on a beautifully creamy palate, textured with a touch of large-format oak fermentation. Malic acidity sits comfortably in the warm 2009 season, supported by soft, rounded, salty minerality, offering tension without brittleness. More advanced than the 2008 already, with hints of toastiness beginning to develop, it upholds liveliness and energy, promising medium-term potential.

LOUIS ROEDERER ROSÉ 2008 $$$

96 points • TASTED IN REIMS, BRISBANE, YARRA VALLEY & MELBOURNE

60% ripe, south-facing Cumières pinot noir, cold soaked for 7-10 days (saignée method), blended with 40% north-facing Chouilly chardonnay for acidity; 20% matured in oak, weekly bâtonnage; 10% malolactic fermentation; aged 4 years in bottle; 12.7g/L total sugars

Lécaillon believes his rosé recipe to be unique in Champagne, producing a very different result every year. It hit new heights in 2008, perfectly coinciding with the opening of his new, state-of-the-art facility dedicated to rosé, with its own sorting table, cooling room and plunging equipment, all gravity fed and covered with carbon dioxide to avoid oxidation. This classic vintage snaps high-tensile acidity and chalk mineral texture from black-and-white into vivid high-definition 3D. Every element delicately placed, seamlessly connected and supporting the greater whole, like a masterpiece of cinematography in the hands of the most fastidious director. Prepare for a breathtaking flight over fields of red roses, orchards of tangy white cherries, endless plains of anise and perfect rows of strawberries. It pulls into a white-knuckle vertical ascent of intricately silky malic acidity and textured mineral chalk of lively poise and elegant focus. Two years after release, its graceful allure is undimmed, more silky than ever, upholding pinpoint purity amidst captivating struck-flint reduction. Roederer's most riveting rosé episode, certain to keep you on the edge of your seat.

LOUIS ROEDERER ET PHILIPPE STARCK BRUT NATURE MILLESIMÉ 2006 $$$

94 points • DISGORGED MARCH 2014 • TASTED IN REIMS

Cumières with a little Vertus chardonnay; two-thirds pinot noir, one-third chardonnay and a touch of meunier, all picked and pressed together; 100% wild fermented in oak tuns; half aged in 9000L foudres; no malolactic fermentation; reductive winemaking; half the usual sulphur dioxide; zero dosage; low pressure of 4.5 atmospheres; 60,000 bottles

Lécaillon introduced me to Roederer's first new cuvée since 1974 as we stood in the heart of his remarkable 10-hectare biodynamic vineyard in Cumières that conceived it. 'The terroir had to be the key,' he said. 'This was the secret to making this wine. I didn't set out to make a zero-dosage wine, I just found that the terroir didn't need it. The paradox of this cuvée is that the marketing is about Philippe Starck, but the cuvée is all about the terroir.' After trialling extra brut blends from Cumières, Vertus and Hautvillers in 2003, 2004 and 2005, it was the ripeness achieved on the sunny, south-facing slope of Cumières in the warm 2006 vintage that brought this cuvée to life, in all of its generosity and purity of yellow summer fruits, pear, apple and mixed spice. The minerality of Cumières glistens brilliantly, impeccably framed by malic acidity. It takes a masterful touch to achieve harmony with malic acidity without dosage, and Lécaillon has pulled off the tight-rope act with such precision that it doesn't look like zero dosage. More than that, it's still definitively Roederer and characteristically Cumières. There may be a 2009 release, or this may a one-off. I don't mind the uncharacteristic informality of its love-or-hate label, but I wish it declared its Cumières origins. The marketing campaign to go with it missed the ultimate opportunity to tell the remarkable story of the most incredible biodynamic vineyard in all of Champagne. That's what this cuvée is really all about.

LOUIS ROEDERER CRISTAL BRUT 2006 $$$$$

96 points • DISGORGED IN 2013 • TASTED IN BRISBANE & PERTH

60% pinot noir from Verzenay, Verzy, Beaumont-sur-Vesle, Aÿ and Mareuil-sur-Aÿ; 40% chardonnay from Avize, Le Mesnil-sur-Oger and Cramant; a pool of 50 hectares of vines more than 30 years of age on the most chalky mid-slopes, yielding 50% less than the appellation; 60% biodynamic vineyards, with a goal of 100% by 2020; 20% matured in oak barrels with weekly bâtonnage; no malolactic fermentation; matured 7 years on lees; 9g/L dosage; typically 150,000–300,000 bottles

The secret of Cristal is that it's built to age, and its reductive style screams out for some years of post-disgorgement to truly blossom. For its price and reputation, Cristal is a relatively early release in the world of prestige cuvées, though Lécaillon points out that 30 years ago it enjoyed only three years on lees, when he joined the company 20 years ago it only had four, and now it has six or seven.

2006 Cristal is the finest since 2002, and this generous and warm season is already in a happy place a year after release, though it's only going to elevate over the next decade. Lécaillon has achieved restraint and subtlety even in this vintage, thanks to a stringent selection regime of the most 'elegant, lean, pure and precise' parcels for Cristal. It takes some time in the glass for its personality of citrus zest crunch, stone fruit succulence and red cherry vivacity to rise, underlined by the subtle roast nut and biscuit characters of barrel fermentation, and the honey nougat, preserved citrus and glacé nectarine influence of bottle age. Struck flint and fennel add to the multidimensional complexity, hallmarks of Cristal's reductive style. The 2006 is a vintage of body and fullness, carrying with even line and grand persistence, enlivened by impeccably focused malic acidity. An undercurrent of soft, fine, mouth-filling chalk minerality is profound and captivating.

LOUIS ROEDERER CRISTAL BRUT 2005 $$$$$

93 points • DISGORGED IN 2012 • TASTED IN BRISBANE

As for the 2006, except: 55% pinot noir from Verzenay, Verzy, Beaumont, Vesle and Aÿ; 45% chardonnay from Avize, Cramant and Le Mesnil-sur-Oger; 8–10g/L dosage

The child of a challenging season, 2005 is the least Cristal of the modern era, though upholding an impressive standard for this warm vintage. The original disgorgement of this voluptuous season fleshed out neatly two years ago, elevating its fleshy yellow stone fruit and fig flavours, but has now contracted to a dry and chewy style with a note reminiscent of rusty railroad tracks. Fruit has begun to subside, making its toasty, reductive spectrum more prominent. Drink up.

LOUIS ROEDERER CRISTAL 2002

97 points • DISGORGED IN 2008 • TASTED IN BRISBANE

Testimony to the magical transformation of Cristal with bottle age, this epic vintage has now reached an enchanting place, and it doesn't look like it will leave for decades yet. The grand paradox of the greatest champagnes: seamless, silky, generous, focused, elegant and rich, all at the same time. It upholds pure, clean youthfulness of fresh pear, stone fruits, dried peach and preserved lemon, propelled by an undercurrent of finely structured mineral texture and silky malic acid line.

Louis Roederer Cristal 1999

95 points • Tasted in Brisbane

7-8 g/L dosage

After the hottest summer in Champagne since 1959 (though 2003 trumped it) this is a rich Cristal that has hit its peak. Candied citrus rind and fig fruit is upheld amidst the secondary development of rich, spicy, biscuity complexity and the beginnings of smoky tertiary maturity. Phenolic texture works surprisingly well in this generous style, with a subtly chewy mouthfeel. Be sure to catch it before it begins to dry out.

Louis Roederer Cristal 1995 $$$$$

98 points • Tasted in Brisbane

15-20% malolactic fermentation; 7-8g/L dosage

Announcing the first ever re-release of Cristal. In 2016, the house will launch this late-disgorged, lower-dosage release of just a few hundred bottles. Few will have the chance to partake, but we can all be inspired to have the stamina to leave the great vintages of Cristal in our cellars for 20 years, the age at which Lécaillon finds a good balance of youth and evolution, after 10 years on lees and 10 years on cork. A classic Champagne vintage, 1995 produced a benchmark Cristal. After two decades it has attained a magical place of ravishingly silky refinement, perfectly seamless, yet with the purity and tension of lemony acidity to age for decades yet. Profound length and line ripple with precise detail of preserved citrus, dried stone fruits, baked apple, layer upon layer of spice, and the gently rising smoky complexity of grand old age.

Louis Roederer Cristal 1993

98 points • Disgorged in 2004 • Tasted in Reims
95 points • Disgorged in 2005 • Tasted in Brisbane

58% chardonnay, 42% pinot noir; 7-8 g/L dosage

A difficult and wet season in which pinot noir suffered, hence an unusually high proportion of chardonnay for Cristal. Nonetheless, the best bottles uphold remarkably graceful, seductive presence amidst calm confidence. Creamy complexity of layers of nougat and vanilla wash over a core of gorgeous fig and glacé peach of impeccable line, length and silky completeness. Lesser bottles show more developed, biscuity, caramel notes and chewy, grippy phenolics, yet uphold the acidity to keep the finish focused, clean and long.

A sunny early morning start to harvest 2014 on the grand cru slopes of Bouzy. Pickers come from all over Europe, as well as nearby villages.

MAILLY GRAND CRU

(My-ii Groh Khrew)

5/10

28 Rue de la Libération 51500 Mailly-Champagne

www.champagne-mailly.com

Of Champagne's 137 cooperatives, only Le Mesnil rivals Mailly Grand Cru as the fairest of them all. Mailly's 75 owners supply fruit for 500,000 bottles each year, from some 730 parcels on 73 hectares, exclusively in one village, representing one-third of the glorious Mailly-Champagne grand cru on the northern slopes of the Montagne de Reims. Mailly is unusual in dedicating 90% of its fruit to its own label, selling just 10% to négociants and none back to its own growers. Mailly's non-vintage cuvées showcase the deep colour and up-front fruit character of the area, while its finest prestige cuvées capture the elegant mineral precision of the northern Montagne.

In the erratic climate of Champagne, the inability to blend with other villages makes a single-cru estate particularly challenging.

Wine critic Michel Bettane upholds Mailly-Champagne and Aÿ as the two villages in Champagne with sufficiently varying exposition and soils to confidently produce a monocru. Half of Mailly's slopes are north-facing, and the remainder have easterly and even southerly aspects, since the hill slopes gently back up below the village. Soils likewise vary dramatically from the top of the village to the bottom, in some places with chalk very close to the surface, and in other areas two metres below.

Mailly has taken strategic advantage of this diversity and Hervé Dantan, its talented and longstanding chef de cave from 1991 to 2013, set up the cooperative with some 150 tanks, an incredible number for its size, to facilitate individual vinification of small parcels. In 2012, a new area of the winery was dug to provide space for more small tanks, providing for a blending palette of

more than 60 wines, including reserves back to 2002, stored in small stainless steel and enamelled tanks and oak foudres. A solera system for reserves has been in operation for 20 years. The house sources two-year-old barrels from Bordeaux and Burgundy.

The cooperative describes its approach as 'Burgundian', with so many plots in the same village, all within two kilometres and all pressed at the cooperative. Its vineyards are managed by 25 families, with whom it works closely. It has divided the village into 30 areas and has established a test plot in each, which it has analysed since 1998. The results have enabled it to better support its growers, setting the start of harvest for each part of the village, and decreasing use of chemicals in the vineyards by 75% over 15 years.

Mailly's north-facing slopes on chalk subsoils draw out the mineral freshness of pinot noir, which comprises 75% of plantings, with chardonnay making up the remainder. The cooperative is proud to uphold an average vine age of 25 years, though has been asking its growers to plant more chardonnay. The old growers in the village say that their pinot noir has the elegance and minerality of chardonnay, and their chardonnay has the weight of pinot noir.

The cooperative's glass building stands proudly in the village, above seven levels of cellars and a kilometre of chalk crayères, dug by hand 20 metres below the surface by the founders of the cooperative every winter from 1929 to 1965. This is now the home of two million bottles, representing an impressive four years of stock.

Hervé Dantan accepted a position at Lanson in February 2013, replaced at Mailly by Sébastien Moncuit, from a family of growers in the Côte des Blancs, with a decade of experience at Château Malakoff and three years consulting for growers, including Pascal Agrapart, Francis Egly and Anselme Selosse.

MAILLY GRAND CRU BRUT RÉSERVE NV $$

89 points • 2011 BASE VINTAGE • TASTED IN MAILLY-CHAMPAGNE, BRISBANE, SYDNEY & MELBOURNE

75% pinot noir, 25% chardonnay; 35% reserves from 10 vintages; 5% barrel fermented; aged 3 years on lees; 9g/L dosage

With a deep, full straw yellow hue, the stone fruits' generosity of Mailly pinot noir and the cut of grapefruit zest lead out, but are interrupted by an earthy and drying finish of ground coffee and mocha notes, showing the dusty coarseness of the tough 2011 vintage. It's biscuity and secondary, with a rich pinot noir mid-palate and spicy finish.

MAILLY GRAND CRU EXTRA BRUT NV $$

90 points • 2008 BASE VINTAGE • DISGORGED MID-2013 • TASTED IN MAILLY-CHAMPAGNE

75% pinot noir, 25% chardonnay; aged 4-5 years on lees; zero dosage and 2g/L natural residual sweetness; 30,000 bottles

Far ahead of the trend, Mailly has been making Extra Brut since 1955 and it now accounts for 6–7% of production. The philosophy is a blend of plots of high maturity, reflected in a deep, full yellow gold hue. The dominance of pinot noir, the richness of the village and the ripeness of the fruit make the zero dosage style sit comfortably, emphasising the fine, soft, salty mineral texture of the village. It carries with good length and well-focused acid line, amidst layers of secondary complexity of butterscotch, and a surprising and unmistakable note of peppermint.

MAILLY GRAND CRU DÉLICE NV $$

87 points • 2010 BASE VINTAGE • TASTED IN MAILLY-CHAMPAGNE

75% pinot noir, 25% chardonnay; same blend as Brut Réserve, with one more year on lees; 35g/L dosage

Brut Réserve doesn't need any more sweetness. This version takes on a medium to full straw yellow hue and flavours of candied yellow fruits, with a note of mushroom on a sweet palate of reasonable persistence.

The Champagne Guide

Mailly Grand Cru Brut Rosé NV $$$

92 points • 100% 2009 • Tasted in Mailly-Champagne

Saignée style from 90% old-vine pinot noir on sunny south-facing slopes, with 10% chardonnay for lightness, brightness and balance; full malolactic fermentation; 8g/L dosage; 45,000-50,000 bottles

At more than five years of age, this could well be labelled as a vintage, but the house does not want to confuse it with L'Intemporelle Rosé. The trouble is, it is emphatically a child of its season, the pronounced exuberance of 2009 vastly at odds with the refreshing energy of the 2008 last year, both equally valid in their own idiosyncratic ways. With a medium copper crimson hue, the warm 2009 season captures great red fruits complexity with freshness and character, packed with raspberry, tomato and pink pepper. Tannins are fine and well balanced, melding seamlessly with the chalk mineral structure of the village. It leads out confidently, flows into a well-composed mid-palate, but the finish is just a touch weak in persistence and confidence.

Mailly Grand Cru Blanc de Noirs NV $$$

95 points • 2009 base vintage • Tasted in Mailly-Champagne & Melbourne

100% pinot noir, selected from plots known for their finesse; full malolactic fermentation; 15% reserves; vinified in tanks; 8g/L dosage

For some inexplicable reason the base 2008 vintage of this cuvée has been totally, utterly and gloriously trumped by the 2009, a classic and magnificent expression of northern Montagne pinot noir. It's at once rich, fleshy, voluminous, powerful and full-bodied in its full yellow gold hue and its plum fruit, mixed spice and honey flavours, yet at once beautifully vibrant in its acid line and expressive chalk mineral texture. For its depth of colour, it retains surprising freshness, impressive seamlessness and great persistence.

Mailly Grand Cru Brut Millésimé 2007 $$$

91 points • Disgorged mid-2013 • Tasted in Mailly-Champagne

75% pinot noir, 25% chardonnay; aged 5 years on lees; 6g/L dosage

For a vintage of finesse and delicacy, this is a cuvée of surprisingly full yellow gold hue and fleshy, rich, full-bodied style of expansive butterscotch, grilled pineapple, yellow mirabelle plum and grapefruit. This maelstrom pulls into a long and characterful finish of firm, fine, grippy mouthfeel and lively acidity, ultimately a little firm and disjointed.

Mailly Grand Cru Millésimé 2006 $$$

90 points • Tasted in Brisbane, Sydney & Melbourne

75% pinot noir, 25% chardonnay; 6g/L dosage

I adored this glorious depiction of Mailly pinot noir on release two years ago, and this voluptuous, fleshy and full-bodied style still oozes the intensity of a rich vintage in a powerful village. It's layered with mixed spice, bruised red apple fruit, plum, peach and golden fruit cake. There is some oxidative development at play here, though the best two bottles that I tasted had the fruit intensity and persistence to cope — just. The third was oxidised.

MAILLY GRAND CRU L'INTEMPORELLE MILLÉSIMÉ BRUT 2008 $$$$

96 points • TASTED IN MAILLY-CHAMPAGNE

60% pinot noir, 40% chardonnay; a blend of just four or five plots; vinified in tanks; 8g/L dosage; 15,000 bottles

Crafted as an apéritif style of freshness, finesse and elegance, a brief that the high-tensile 2008 vintage plays to with exacting precision in this generous village. A full yellow gold hue, true to the deep tone of the house, it mounts fresh waves of grapefruit and lemon zest with all the depth of fruit mince spice and anise, a captivating assemblage of the personality of pinot noir with the definition of chardonnay and the magnificent cut of the vintage. The acid line is very long and focused, energising the fine chalk minerality of Mailly with fastidious focus.

MAILLY GRAND CRU L'INTEMPORELLE ROSÉ BRUT 2008 $$$$

96 points • TASTED IN MAILLY-CHAMPAGNE

60% pinot noir, 40% chardonnay; the base of L'Intemporelle with a minuscule 2.5-3% red wine of Coteaux Champenois rouge; 8g/L dosage; just 5000 bottles

It is a profound lesson in the intricacies of champagne blending to see the tremendous impact that less than 3% of red wine can make in transforming a cuvée. The colour is shifted to a pale copper hue, and pretty, subtle strawberry and red cherry fruits overlay a core of fruit mince spice. Soft, subtle tannin texture meshes harmoniously with chalk mineral texture that wells up from its core and lingers on a very long finish of richness, structure and poise.

MAILLY GRAND CRU LES ÉCHANSONS MILLÉSIMÉ BRUT 2004 $$$$

93 points • TASTED IN MAILLY-CHAMPAGNE

75% pinot noir, 25% chardonnay, mostly from 80-year-old vines; 6g/L dosage; just 6400 bottles

Les Échansons is intentionally a contrast to the elegance of L'Intemporelle — and a powerful village, large majority of pinot noir, old-vine concentration and 11 years of bottle age make for a foreboding foursome, conspiring in a full yellow gold hue and grand intensity of butter, grilled pineapple, fleshy peach, fig, spice and wild honey. Rich body and presence close with good line and length on a dry finish of grippy, chewy mouthfeel and slightly coarse, drying texture.

MAILLY GRAND CRU MAGNUM COLLECTION MILLÉSIMÉ 1996 $$$$$

93 points • DISGORGED JANUARY 2014 • TASTED IN MAILLY-CHAMPAGNE FROM MAGNUM

3g/L dosage; 1000-1800 magnums

An old Mailly of full golden yellow hue, great length and character. Layered tertiary complexity of quince, butterscotch, toast, coffee bean, burnt orange and ash reflects some oxidation, amidst quince-like gritty textural grip, though the lively acidity of 1996 holds strong.

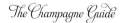

The Champagne Guide

MARC HÉBRART

(Mark E-brah)

18 RUE DU PONT 51160 MAREUIL-SUR-AŸ

*M*arc Hébrart has been making his own champagnes in Mareuil-sur-Aÿ since 1964, and his son Jean-
Paul from the age of 19 in 1983. The estate is privileged to 15 hectares of vines of average age 28 years,
spread across 65 plots of 75% pinot noir in Mareuil-sur-Aÿ, Avenay, Bisseuil, Mutigny and Aÿ, and 25% chardonnay
in Chouilly and Oiry. Jean-Paul Hébrart is married to Isabelle Diebolt of Diebolt-Vallois, though the businesses
function autonomously. His wines contrast elegant fruit expression with the mineral signature of great terroirs.

MARC HÉBRART PREMIER CRU BRUT ROSE NV

92 points • 2010 BASE VINTAGE • TASTED IN MELBOURNE

2009 reserve; 50% Mareuil-sur-Aÿ chardonnay; 2009 red wine from Mareuil-sur-Aÿ aged in small oak barriques;
7.5g/L dosage

An elegant and fragrant blend of bright, pale salmon hue and pretty red cherry and strawberry fruits, backed with
savoury notes of cherry kernel and brambles, and a subtle tannin firmness on the finish.

MARC HÉBRART SPECIAL CLUB 2008

94 points • TASTED IN MELBOURNE

55% pinot noir, 45% chardonnay; a blend of Mareuil-sur-Aÿ, Oiry and Chouilly; 6.5g/L dosage

A wonderful juxtaposition of generous, concentrated, ripe Mareuil-sur-Aÿ pinot noir, the balanced restraint of
chardonnay, and the fine structure of excellent, lingering chalk minerality. Balanced, tightly poised and persistent,
it's an admirable showcase of good terroirs in a classic season.

Marguet Père & Fils

(Mah-gair Pear e Feess)

---

1 PLACE BARANCOURT 51150 AMBONNAY
www.champagne-marguet.fr

'Making champagne has become too much of a recipe,' proclaims the young Benoît Marguet. 'It has to come from a vineyard, not from winemaking or marketing. Some growers today have the energy to pull champagne back to its roots and to focus on the vineyards. You have to be good in the vineyard and you cannot cheat.'

It was Olivier Krug who introduced me to Benoît, whose family is one of Krug's most historic growers in the grand cru of Ambonnay, and still sells fruit to the house from two of its 10 hectares. Its grand old vines, of average age 38 years, are superbly located on 7.3 hectares in Ambonnay, two hectares in Mailly-Champagne and 0.7 hectares in Bouzy, planted to pinot noir, meunier and 40% chardonnay, significant for these parts of Champagne.

Marguet's ancestors have made and sold champagne here since 1870. In that year, Benoît's great-great-great-uncle famously grafted his 100-hectare estate in anticipation of phylloxera. The practice was outlawed at the time, and he was shut down and the estate sold. Clearly he was ahead of his time: 30 years later grafting was the only solution to phylloxera.

This spirit of daring innovation lives on in Benoît, a champion of a new generation of Champenois with a mandate to do everything as naturally as possible. 'We need to pull back to natural techniques,' he says. 'When I started to plough the vines and plant grasses in the mid-rows in 2003, I was seen as crazy.' His father didn't accept his radical practices, so he travelled the world, and was accepted back in 2005 to make the wines. 'In 2008 they allowed me to farm the vineyards and in 2009 I converted the estate to biodynamics.

'My aim is to connect more intimately with the plant and with the wine,' Benoît explains. Though not yet certified, he is moving towards full biodynamic production. 'Biodynamics is one way, but there are many others, and I want to go further than biodynamics,' he says. Since 2010, the vineyards have been ploughed with his two horses, to enhance the ecological harmony.

Benoît is fanatical in analysing the soils of his plots. After discovering that biodynamics was enhancing the character of each site, he began producing cuvées of individual lieux-dits, 'because I am a Burgundy fan!' In vintages not of the potential to stand alone as a lieu-dit, he declassifies into a blend of a single cru. He also buys up to 15% of old-vine fruit from organic and biodynamic friends in other villages. The result is one of the largest portfolios of any Champagne grower: 16 cuvées, no less.

Benoît continues his natural approach in the press house and winery. 'Rather than using classic oenology, we have adopted natural techniques based on homeopathy and naturopathy,' he explains, suggesting he's perhaps 10 years ahead of his time.

Everything is now fermented with wild yeast in oak vats and barrels of between two and nine years of age (and a few new each year). He designed and had made egg-shaped oak vats 'in the divine proportions'. For the past three years he has used no sulphur dioxide preservative at all, though none of these cuvées are yet disgorged. Zero sulphur necessitates full malolactic fermentation. I am more than a little nervous about any strict zero-sulphur regime, as I've seen many more disasters than successes in Champagne, though Benoît says he is attuned to the need to acclimatise his wines to oxygen, and to techniques such as jetting to protect them during disgorgement. Time will tell. He is still experimenting and yet to fully settle on his style.

Benoît has printed disgorgement dates on back labels since 2009, among the first in Champagne to do so. His cuvées present the generous character and mineral definition of his terroirs, though the rustic, funky characters of barrel fermentation and oxidation can at times distract.

MARGUET PÈRE & FILS ELEMENTS GRAND CRU EXTRA BRUT NV $

90 points • 2010 BASE VINTAGE • DISGORGED MARCH 2014 • TASTED IN BRISBANE
A blend of Ambonnay and Bouzy; 65% pinot noir, 35% chardonnay; 33% reserves from 2009 and 2004; 3.2g/L dosage

93 points • 2009 BASE VINTAGE • DISGORGED OCTOBER 2013 • TASTED IN AMBONNAY
63% pinot noir, 37% chardonnay; 30% reserves from 2008 and 2004; 4g/L dosage

The 2010 base holds a full straw hue with a copper tint, leading out with the generosity of Ambonnay and Bouzy pinot noir in grand complexity of plums and black cherries, set against toasty oak and a hint of charcuterie. It quickly falls into a dry, constrained, savoury finish, structured with fine phenolic grip and dry extract, though nonetheless upholds good red fruit line. The 2009 represents a stronger base of tense grapefruit and lemon zest, with some sappy barrel fermentation notes and an intense finish, underlined by salty chalk mineral texture.

MARGUET PÈRE & FILS SAPIENCE PREMIER CRU EXTRA BRUT 2006 $$$$

91 points • TASTED IN BRISBANE
66% biodynamic Trépail chardonnay from David Léclapart, 33% organic Cumières pinot noir and meunier from Vincent Laval; fermented and aged for two years in used white Bordeaux barrels; 3g/L dosage

Marguet's new luxury cuvée is a fascinating and innovative concept, not so much because it may be the first prestige cuvée to be certified organic, but because of the collaboration that it represents. It is made with Hervé Jestin, former chef de cave of Duval-Leroy, who sells the same wine under his own label as 'Jestin Extra Brut'. Sapience is a collaboration between Benoît Marguet, Benoît Lahaye in Bouzy, Vincent Laval in Cumières, and David Léclapart in Trépail, with an aspiration to craft a champagne using extreme biodynamic methods. Made in Marguet's cellars, this first release comprises chardonnay from Léclapart and pinot noir and meunier from Laval, with pinot noir from Lahaye cued for the next release. With a full straw yellow hue, this is a wine that reverberates with deep complexity of ripe fruit and firm oak, uniting to give impressions of golden syrup, burnt marmalade, tree sap and glacé peach. The power of fruit and oak make for a thundering bouquet and an impactful entry, but lose steam quickly on the palate, finishing short, with dominant oak making the finish dry, callow and hard, tussling with oxidative development — a shame after promising so much.

MOËT & CHANDON

(Mo-wet e Shon-don)

20 AVENUE DE CHAMPAGNE 51200 ÉPERNAY

www.moet.com

FONDÉ EN 1743

MOËT & CHANDON

CHAMPAGNE

I thought I had Moët & Chandon figured out. We all know the wines, we've witnessed the PR machine in full grind, and I've visited command central in Épernay countless times over almost 15 years. But when chef de cave Benoît Gouez granted my request to shadow him for a day at the height of harvest 2014, I witnessed sparkling wine production like I had never conceived. The sheer magnitude of this operation is mind-boggling, but we all knew that. What astounded me most was the groundbreaking technology in play and an attention to detail no one thought possible on this scale. This is one of the most exciting wine outfits on earth. And it's downright terrifying.

THE GIANT OF CHAMPAGNE IS ON THE MOVE

In just 12 days, 15,000 pickers harvest an incredible 5000 hectares of vines spanning 230 villages for Moët & Chandon, Dom Pérignon and Mercier. Of these, 1180 hectares are estate vineyards, half of which are grand crus and one-quarter premier crus, making Moët not only the largest vineyard holder, but privileged to more of the best sites than any other.

No human hand touches the picking crates after they leave the vineyards, arriving at Moët's headquarters in Épernay or its grand new Mont Aigu winery in Oiry, to be unloaded by robotic arms and carried up to the presses on an airport luggage system. A computerised sorting system to classify each picking box on visual quality is currently being trialled. When I visited Mont Aigu, an ocean of 6000 picking crates was queued ready to be pressed.

Meanwhile, a fleet of 80 tankers delivers juice from press houses in the villages, each equipped with nitrogen to inhibit oxidation. When they back up at

Mont Aigu, a computer automatically directs juice to one of 250 sparkling new fermentation tanks, without a human hand touching a hose or a tap. In a world first, every ferment is computer monitored every five seconds, allowing Gouez's team to manage each ferment precisely, anticipating when they will peak, and speeding up or slowing down their pace to avoid reductive or oxidative characters. On the day I visited, 80,000 litres of juice arrived at this facility. Such is its efficiency that the place felt quiet and calm.

On grand display to the stream of traffic on the main road from Épernay to the Côte des Blancs, behind floor-to-ceiling glass on every side, Moët's Mont Aigu winery must be the most sophisticated sparkling facility in the world, boasting Death Star-like automation on every front, dedicated exclusively to Moët Brut Impérial NV. To extend the capacity of Moët's 28 kilometres of historic cellars under Épernay, its new 50 million bottle cellar at Mont Aigu is also the world's first in which bottles are transported to disgorgement by unmanned laser-guided vehicles.

After recent expansions, the total storage capacity of this facility reached 14.5 million litres in time for vintage 2014, bringing the total capacity across the two sites to a whopping 60 million litres, the equivalent of 80 million bottles of Moët, Dom Pérignon and Mercier. Precisely how many they sell today is a closely guarded secret, but my estimate is at least 38 million across the three brands annually, with production somewhere in the order of 50 million. To put this in perspective, the other 5000 houses, cooperatives and growers in Champagne between them produce about 250 million bottles. All the brands of Moët's owner, luxury giant Louis Vuitton-Moët Hennessy (or LVMH, including Veuve Clicquot, Ruinart and Krug) between them account for a whopping 60 million bottles, 20% of all champagne sales. Rumours in the region point to a target of 100 million within a decade, in strategic anticipation of rising global demand for champagne. The group is already so far ahead in both value and volume that it more than exceeds its two nearest rivals, Lanson-BCC and Vranken-Pommery, put together.

Unprecedented antics

Mont Aigu is a striking monument to Moët's growth, and the company is working overtime to secure supply to fill it, even door-knocking growers with enticing incentive offers. In June 2012, LVMH made a tactical and unprecedented play. An advertisement placed in local newspapers announced that it would pay 4% more for its grapes in the 2012 vintage.

An aggressive buyer in the champagne market for some years, this was the first public announcement of its intentions. There are loud grumblings in Champagne about this brazen wielding of power. As the largest purchaser in the region, when Moët sets a price, everyone follows. Some perceive the move as a strategic attempt to put pressure on grape supply and push smaller players out of the market. It's not as simple as this. Champagne has long paid its growers like no other appellation in France, and higher grape prices are ultimately to their benefit, shoring up the foundation of the region. Moët's commitment to purchasing fruit rather than vins clairs made by other producers can only be a good thing, both for the growers and for quality. And the rise of Moët to date has been for the greater good of Champagne in another way, too.

In conversations across the region, from the largest houses and cooperatives to the smallest growers, I am continually impressed by the high regard in which Moët & Chandon is held. 'I cannot think of another producer in the world who has produced wine as well as

Moët on such a scale,' Jacquesson's Jean-Hervé Chiquet remarked recently.

The Champenois salute Moët as an ambassador for their region, for its groundbreaking and ongoing work in breaking into emerging markets such as China and India. There is genuine gratitude that this trail-blazing paves the way for other champagne brands to follow.

And growing markets demand growing supplies. This is nothing new for Moët. Founded in 1743, the company claims to be the first house of champagne. It came into international prominence under Jean-Remy Moët, who inherited the house from its founder, his grandfather, Claude Moët, in 1789. It is said Jean-Remy was already dreaming about Asian markets before the end of that century.

Since this time, Moët has mushroomed like no other champagne house, and the real danger today is that its explosive growth may topple the balance in Champagne. The biggest question of all is how Moët can sustain quality in the wake of such unprecedented growth.

Perpetual evolution

'For me it is not a matter of size, but a matter of paying attention to the details,' Gouez says. 'To be able to adapt and to fight every year, to get the best out of what nature gives you.'

The precision of the technology at his disposal to analyse this detail is groundbreaking in sparkling wine production. He now has hand-held analysers to instantly measure the sugar, acid and pH of a bunch of grapes without picking a single berry, tools to measure the pressure in a bottle without opening it, even a centrifuge that might replace his presses. Vineyards are analysed by satellite to pinpoint which areas to fertilise. With 12 full-time staff, his Épernay R&D lab was the only one of its kind in Champagne, until he replicated it at Mont Aigu. 'Some people will see all this and think it's all very industrial, but it's all for the sake of maintaining the character of the grapes,' Gouez explains.

Technology and resources aside, by far the most important initiative that he has introduced since he commenced at Moët in 1998 has been in tasting and testing every press sample that arrives during vintage. This may seem trivial, but such is the scale of this operation that no one believed he could pull it off. I witnessed the long lines of samples assembled in the vintage lab and could hardly believe it myself. Gouez works 14-hour days during harvest (16 hours or more on bad days) and during that time he and his team of four taste and test every one of up to 800 press samples that arrive. He personally tastes half of them. 'This is so important,' he tells me. 'It's impossible to assess the

An ocean of some 6000 picking crates cued to be pressed in Moët's state-of-the-art Mont Aigu facility at the height of vintage 2014.

quality of a parcel by simply looking at the analysis.' Across vintage, his team tastes and allocates some 7500 batches to 800 tanks, filling every tank within 24 hours, and adapting their classification according to the vintage. Notes on each batch are beamed to the iPads of workers in the winery.

'I believe bigger is better,' Gouez says. 'I don't consider quality and quantity to be mutually exclusive in Champagne. A small grower in one village has nothing to compensate for difficult weather. Grower wines are very good, and I have friends among many of them, but by nature the quality of champagne is uneven. The more grapes you can access, the more you can be consistent.'

It's a principle that appears to have worked for Moët in recent years. At more than 20 million bottles every year, its Brut Impérial is the biggest blend in Champagne, and currently as fresh as I've seen it. 'This is a wine that is always evolving, because the climate, the technology, the market, the consumers and the world have changed,' Gouez explains.

Of course, quality does not automatically come with quantity, and his team has embraced innovation and worked hard to refine the style.

'We have worked on the preparation of our ferments to provide the right level of oxygenation so they don't get too stressed,' Gouez says. 'This reduces the reductive flavours, allowing room for the expression of the precision and cleanliness of the fruit.' Lower dosage has also been a refreshing trend in recent years, and more refined than ever in his current cuvées. 'In the past, we were known for higher dosage, but today Brut Impérial is 9g/L, one of the lowest among the grande marques,' he points out. This comes in response to both riper fruit and a changing consumer palate, seeking elegance and purity. 'We will continue to evolve,' he says. 'It's perpetual, and we need to continually revisit our style and our values.'

The Moët ambition is a fruit-driven style of freshness, brightness and purity. He prizes the ripeness and phenolic maturity of warmer vintages over acid definition, not a philosophy I subscribe to, but nonetheless a valid house style.

'We want our champagnes to taste of the grapes they're made of,' says Gouez, who points out that 90% of the wine is made simply in getting the grapes and the pressing right. He tries not to do too much in the winery. To this end, winemaking is purposely reductive, vigorously minimising oxidation and religiously avoiding oak. 'The size and diversity of our vineyard sources is the key to consistency,' he says.

Richard Geoffroy, who oversees Moët's production, names tightening up consistency and improving viticulture as the two key focus areas for the future of the house. Complexity is built through fermentation using yeasts produced in its own lab. All Moët & Chandon cuvées are blends of the three champagne varieties, and all undergo malolactic fermentation.

Moët has introduced DIAM closures and two other brands of micro-agglomerate corks, first with its vintage wines, so as to send the message that this is a quality initiative. All corks are batch tested 200 at a time, and rejected if more than 2.5% defects or 1% critical defects are detected. Gouez maintains that it's impossible to ask for zero defects for fear of rejecting everything (though Louis Roederer successfully maintains zero tolerance).

These are rounded, commercial champagnes, but recent efforts have certainly refined the style in spite of the monumental scale of production. The phenolic maturity of the Moët house style is not my favourite in Champagne, but the more I get to know Gouez and Geoffroy and their philosophies, and the more I see behind the curtain of this incredible operation, the more profound respect I have for their attention to detail while producing tens of millions of bottles. The philosophy, the technology and the execution are, quite simply, unprecedented on this scale, anywhere on earth.

'Whatever we do at Moët, we like to do it big and bold, to share Moët with the world!' Gouez rejoices. That they do.

MOËT & CHANDON BRUT IMPÉRIAL NV $$

87 points • 2011 BASE VINTAGE • DISGORGED AUGUST 2014 • TASTED IN BRISBANE, MELBOURNE, PERTH, SINGAPORE & DUBAI
89 points • 2011 OR 2010 BASE VINTAGE (GOUEZ WASN'T CERTAIN) • TASTED IN BRISBANE FROM MAGNUM

39% pinot noir, 33% meunier, 28% chardonnay; first blend of the year 35% reserves, second 30%, third 20-25%, mostly from the previous year; a blend of more than 100 different wines; aged 24 months on lees; 9g/L dosage

At well over 20 million bottles, and rising steeply, this one wine accounts for more than 7% of Champagne's production. To put this in perspective, the vines that supply this label alone would cover an area close to 4000 rugby fields! This is a blend of everything from everywhere, on an oceanic scale that makes a single blend impossible, dictating three quite different blends every year. The aim is to use young and fruity reserves of two vintages to build consistency by contributing any elements missing from the latest harvest. There is thus no recipe, with a different dosage and different liqueur for every batch. 'I call this tailor-made winemaking,' says Gouez. 'We have to adapt and be flexible.'

The mind-boggling scale of Brut Impérial makes its improvement in recent years all the more impressive, presenting pretty freshness of lemon zest, pear and apple. Reductive notes of grilled toast are a hallmark of the house. The difficult 2011 season leaves its mark in a dry, biscuity palate and notes of tilled earth on the finish. Nonetheless, it upholds good length, fresh acidity and fine-tuned dosage, concluding as dry and refreshing as I've seen it. From magnum it predictably carries more precision and purity.

MOËT & CHANDON ROSÉ IMPÉRIAL NV $$

87 points • 2011 BASE VINTAGE • DISGORGED DECEMBER 2013 • TASTED IN BRISBANE

47% pinot noir, 37% meunier, 16% chardonnay; 10-15% red wine; 20-30% reserve wines; 9g/L dosage; around 3 million bottles

Moët has a very long history with champagne rosé, evidenced by a letter of order from Napoleon dated 1801. Today, rosé represents an impressive 17% of total sales, prompting the opening of a new facility to double red wine production capacity next year. It's intentionally in the same style as its Brut Impérial, though crafted from a unique blend. To create intensity of colour and lightness on the palate, Moët is unique in Champagne in employing a Beaujolais technique of heating and macerating meunier at 70°C for a couple of hours to extract colour and flavour without tannins. Short macerations produce red wines of lighter colour, which explains a large dose of 20–25% red wine in the blend. Gouez focuses a lot of attention on rosé production and is currently trialling a centrifuge to replace the press.

A full, bright crimson hue, this is a generous rosé of red apple and strawberry fruit, with a note of tomato. A dry, savoury, earthy grip leaves the finish short and simple, likely a remnant of the challenging 2011 season. Like the white, dosage is well tuned, the best balance I've seen in Moët & Chandon.

Moët & Chandon Grand Vintage 2006 $$$

89 points • Disgorged March 2013 • Tasted in Brisbane, Sydney, Melbourne & Perth

42% chardonnay, 39% pinot noir, 19% meunier; aged 7 years on lees; 5g/L dosage; DIAM closure

Vintage production is just 1% of the house, making this cuvée significantly less than 300,000 bottles. Gouez has replaced 'Moët & Chandon Vintage' with 'Vintage by Moët & Chandon', with labels of bold vintage declaration, to focus more on the style of the season than the house. He is looking for four things in a vintage: sufficient maturity of at least 9.5 degrees potential, no rot, ageing potential from either acidity or phenolic structure, and finally character — something special, not simply the stamp of the season. 'The idea is not to follow a recipe, but to listen to the wines and create a vintage with uniqueness and charisma,' he says. The blend and the selection of parcels change to reflect the character of the season, looking for those that are most interesting and original. 'We start from scratch. I choose the grapes from anywhere I want, and I don't care if it's meunier or if it isn't grand cru.' The maturation has also evolved, previously released after five years on lees and now after seven, allowing the dosage to be lowered to just 5g/L. Disgorgement date, dosage and blend are clearly displayed on the back label — impressive detail for a house of this magnitude.

For Gouez, 2006 is about amplitude, volume and expansive mouthfeel, built on a ripe phenolic structure. This makes for an early-drinking style, with orange and lemon zest on release, now fully secondary in its creamy finesse and buttered toast and biscuity complexity, set in the Moët style of subtle reductive tension. Gentle phenolic grip defines its structure more than acidity. It finishes dry, with notes of boiled sweets on release, now showing well-integrated dosage.

Moët & Chandon Grand Vintage Rosé 2006 $$$

89 points • Disgorged July 2013 • Tasted in Épernay & Brisbane

47% pinot noir, 33% chardonnay, 20% meunier; 23% red wine of pinot noir; the first vintage made in Moët's new red winemaking facility; DIAM closure

Moët harvests red wine for its vintage rosé from its best estate pinot noir plots of low-yielding old vines, green harvested to reduce yields when necessary. Twice the necessary vineyard area is prepared, to permit choice of the grapes with the best phenolic maturity to provide structure. Red wine is macerated for 5–7 days to draw out ripe, soft character, without hard tannins.

With dusty, tilled earth and a dry phenolic palate of chewy tannin grip and subtle almond-skin bitterness on release, it's appreciated a year in bottle for its red apple and pear fruit, layers of spice, freshly baked gingernut biscuits and hint of roast tomato to emerge. A full crimson hue in a savoury and secondary style, it's already at its peak, true to the early-developing nature of 2006. It upholds its persistence amidst soft phenolic presence and well-integrated dosage.

Moët & Chandon Grand Vintage 1999

91 points • Disgorged in 2008 • Tasted in Brisbane

Gouez compares the warm 2006 vintage with the ampleness and integration of 1999. It's now biscuity, honeyed, toasty, rounded and soft, with notes of cappuccino and crème brûlée, finishing with gentle, ripe phenolic grip. A 1985 magnum to follow was corked.

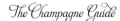

The Champagne Guide

MOËT & CHANDON ROSÉ VINTAGE COLLECTION 1999

91 points • DISGORGED SEPTEMBER 2012 • TASTED IN ÉPERNAY

48% pinot noir, 26% chardonnay, 26% meunier; 22% red wine; 7g/L dosage; DIAM closure

Medium copper crimson in hue, this warm season rosé is now savoury, complex and toasty, with roast hazelnut notes and a dry finish of phenolic grip. It finishes short and robust with firm tannin grip, but in time opens up to black fruit presence, the finish drawing out into reasonable persistence.

MOËT & CHANDON VINTAGE COLLECTION ROSÉ 1985

95 points • DISGORGED MAY 2006 • TASTED IN ÉPERNAY

60% pinot noir, 40% chardonnay

Gouez finds it difficult to liken any vintage of the 1980s to 2006, but puts 1985 closest, albeit with more acidity. At 30 years of age, it's this acid poise that impresses me most about this season, blessing it with a long, refined, silky finish absent from warmer, phenolic-driven seasons. Its golden copper hue upholds crimson notes, and its palate presents distinctive characters of blackcurrant, ginger cake, butterscotch and long-lingering spicy, biscuity complexity, encased in finely structured tannin grip of well-integrated balance.

MOËT & CHANDON GRAND VINTAGE COLLECTION 1911

94 points • DISGORGED JANUARY 2011 • TASTED IN BRISBANE

7g/L dosage

After more than a century, there's no apparent effervescence left, evolving to a yellow hue with a copper tint. An exceptionally intense and voluptuously complex old wine reminiscent of panettone, with all of its crystallised fruits, butter, burnt orange, vanilla and butterscotch. Some volatile acidity (vinegar) is apparent, which Gouez suggests was probably developed both before and after bottling. Its grand maturity is declared in savoury notes of green olive complexity. An interesting curio, of great length and integrity, though it would have been a better drink long ago.

Moët & Chandon MCIII Brut 001.14 $$$$$

95 points • Base vintage 2003 • Disgorged July 2014 • Tasted in Brisbane

37.5% 2003 (50% chardonnay and 50% pinot noir); 37.5% three vintages, 2002, 2000 and 1999, vinified in tanks and aged for 5-7 months in 50hL oak foudres; 25% three vintages of Moët Grand Vintage Collection disgorged from the cellar, 1999, 1998 and 1993; '001.14' on the front label denotes the first batch, disgorged in 2014; 5g/L dosage; just a few thousand bottles in the first release; expect a lofty price point in the vicinity of Dom Pérignon P2

Moët's new prestige cuvée has been in creation for 15 years, first trialled in 2000, a blend of wines spanning 10 years, aged in three different 'universes', then matured on lees for a further 10 years. The focus is on 'ripe, rich, solid vintage years' (hence a choice of 2003 for the first release, with 2006 coming next), and base wines of 'richness, intensity and weight'. Gouez says he doesn't understand the idea that acidity is a key in the ageing of champagne. 'The warmer vintages age well as the wines are based more on phenolic structure than on acidity. We need the warm-vintage phenolic bitterness of pinot noir to sustain this blend.'

The result is a palate shape consistent with the house style of Moët, a wine of textural grip and structure, with the phenolic firmness of 2003 polished by the creamy effect of long lees age. Flavour profile is a celebration of lees maturity, too, in notes of brioche, toast, honey and ginger cake. This is a cuvée that blossoms with plenty of time in a large glass, with notes of grilled toast reduction blowing off to reveal primary, succulent ripe peach, fig and all the tertiary allure of coffee bean and dark chocolate. Phenolic grip softens and integrates into a finish of integrity and outstanding persistence. It's as distinctive as it is unique, and I have every suspicion that it will only get better with another five years post-disgorgement.

The philosophy of this cuvée bores to the very core of the fundamental question of what makes great, age-worthy champagne: acid structure or phenolic texture; classic seasons or warmer vintages? It's a dilemma increasingly relevant to the Champenois as global warming continues to intensify the already erratic weather patterns of this marginal region, and yet there is nothing new about this discussion. There have always been some vintages in Champagne that are warm, even hot; it's just that there are more of them now. As the Champenois continue to hone their craft in the vines and the cellars, house styles are becoming ever more distinctly defined. This and the rising grower movement serve to increase the diversity of champagne styles on offer, and this can only be a good thing for those of us enthralled with the detail of this great region. This affords plenty of space for subjective stylistic preference. There are great palates in the sparkling world that adore the intensity and grip inherent in warm seasons like 2003. I respect this, and I make no apology that, for me, classic vintages like 2008 are the ultimate expression of champagne. Personal taste aside, the highest aspiration of any wine must be its ability to articulately communicate its terroir, and in Champagne this has no more noble expression than in carrying the chalk mineral texture of the ancient geology of the land. Phenolic grip and dry extract are, to me, the textural equivalent of background white noise. No matter how pure the high notes of minerality that fingerprint the greatest terroirs, the phenolic coarseness of warm vintages will always distract, like the static on an AM radio. I wrote 3000 words of notes when Gouez unveiled MCIII. Minerality was not one of them.

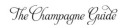

NICOLAS FEUILLATTE

(Ni-khoh-lah Fer-yat)

CD 40A PLUMECOQ 51530 CHOUILLY

www.feuillatte.com

CHAMPAGNE

Nicolas Feuillatte

Centre Vinicole–Champagne Nicolas Feuillatte' is Champagne's oldest and largest cooperative, and Nicolas Feuillatte is its key brand. The gargantuan operation comprises a collective of 82 cooperatives, with more than 5000 growers tending 2250 hectares of vines across more than 300 villages, covering 7% of Champagne's surface. Production facilities span a full 12 hectares of high-tech buildings, with a capacity of 30 million litres — so large that they act as a second production and storage site for Moët & Chandon. At any time 65 million bottles of Nicolas Feuillatte are ageing here, with a capacity of 100 million, and more than 9 million are sold each year, making the brand Champagne's third largest. All cuvées are produced from premier and grand cru vineyards, in stainless steel tanks. The cooperative relies on a high proportion of meunier (50%), and lesser amounts of pinot noir (25%) and chardonnay (25%). It's a primary, fruity style, with dosage now evenly balanced for the first time.

NICOLAS FEUILLATTE BRUT RÉSERVE PARTICULÉRE NV $$

89 points • TASTED IN BRISBANE, SYDNEY & MELBOURNE

40% pinot noir, 40% meunier, 20% chardonnay; a blend of 150 crus; aged 3 years on lees; 10g/L dosage

A medium straw hue and very slight bouquet introduce a palate of primary, lively lemon, pear and apple, as clean, fresh and youthful as I have ever seen this cuvée. Acidity and dosage are more finely balanced than ever, too. Other bottles show more development in toasted brioche and preserved lemon character. All finish short and simple.

NICOLAS FEUILLATTE BRUT ROSÉ NV $$

86 points • TASTED IN BRISBANE, SYDNEY & MELBOURNE

60% pinot noir, 30% meunier, 10% chardonnay; 18% red wine from pinot noir and meunier; 25% reserves; aged 3 years on lees; 10.5g/L dosage

A rosé of medium crimson hue, with a fruity mood of rose hip, musk stick, red berries and black cherries interrupted by savoury, brambly notes and firm tannin/phenolic grip that renders the finish robust and rustic. A short, simple rosé that lacks grace.

NICOLAS FEUILLATTE PALMES D'OR VINTAGE BRUT 2004 $$$$

93 points • TASTED IN BRISBANE, SYDNEY & MELBOURNE

60% chardonnay from Chouilly, Cramant, Oger, Le Mesnil-sur-Oger, Avize and Montgueux near Troyes; 40% pinot noir from Bouzy, Verzy, Verzenay, Aÿ and Ambonnay; aged 9 years on lees; 7.5g/L dosage

A 2004 at the height of its maturity, brimming with all the intensity of plum liqueur, honey, gingernut biscuits, toasted brioche and butterscotch over a core of red cherry and preserved lemon intensity. It's creamy and succulent, with soft acidity supported by fine, grippy phenolic structure on a finish of average persistence. A reliable Palmes d'Or of balanced poise.

NICOLAS FEUILLATTE PALMES D'OR BRUT ROSÉ 2005 $$$$

89 points • TASTED IN BRISBANE, SYDNEY & MELBOURNE

Rosé de saignée of 100% pinot noir; 50% Bouzy and 50% Les Riceys; aged at least 5 years on lees; 7g/L dosage

The saignée process has produced a deeply coloured rosé of full crimson hue with an orange sunburst rim. This is a powerfully fruity and exotic champagne of musk stick, red liquorice, tamarillo and a hint of Campari spice. Bitter phenolic grip balances its intensity, though leaves the finish a little callow and firm. For all its extroverted flamboyancy, it loses gusto and fades quickly.

PALMER & CO

(Pal-mair e Co)

67 RUE JACQUART 51100 REIMS

www.champagne-palmer.fr

CHAMPAGNE

Palmer & Co

*P*almer is a Reims-based cooperative with more than 200 members spread across some 40 villages and 365 hectares of vineyards, almost half of which are classified as grand or premier crus. Chardonnay comprises a high 50% of sourcing, hailing from the Montagne de Reims premier crus of Trépail and Villers-Marmery, and it is the generous concentration and bright structure of these villages that define the house style (supplemented with a little chardonnay from Barbonne in the Sézanne), bolstered with 40% pinot noir and 10% meunier, sourced mostly from the villages of the northern Montagne de Reims (and a little from Les Riceys in the Aube). Liqueurs are made from reserve wines aged in oak barrels. About 70% of production is sold to négociant houses, and the standard of the current releases suggests that the cooperative is diligent in reserving the finest for its own cuvées, the best of which represent great value for money.

PALMER & CO BRUT RÉSERVE NV $

93 points • DISGORGED MARCH 2014 • TASTED IN BRISBANE

50% chardonnay from Villers-Marmery, Trépail and Barbonne; 40% pinot noir from Mailly-Champagne, Verzenay, Rilly-la-Montagne, Ludes and Les Riceys; 10% meunier from Rilly-la-Montagne and Ludes; 30% reserves including some from a 20-year-old solera; aged 4 years on lees; 8–9g/L dosage

A distinctive and compelling style that well articulates the depth, concentration and vibrancy of the northern Montagne de Reims. Chardonnay asserts its lead in a pale to medium straw hue, bright for its age, and fresh, zesty, fruit focus of lemon and pear. The toasted brioche and honey notes of four years of bottle age provide a gentle backdrop of complexity, finishing with impressive line, length and dosage that pokes out just a little on the end. Great value nonetheless.

PALMER & CO ROSÉ RÉSERVE NV $$

89 points • DISGORGED APRIL 2014 • TASTED IN BRISBANE

Brut Réserve with 15% red wine from ripe fruit of Montagne de Reims and Les Riceys; 30% reserves including some from a 20-year-old solera; aged 2.5 years on lees; 8–9g/L dosage

Red apple fruit and savoury tomato nuances define a bright, medium salmon-pink rosé. Dosage and acidity find an even balance, though the grip of dusty, dry extract renders the finish a little firm and coarse.

PALMER & CO BLANC DE BLANCS 2008 $$

94 points • DISGORGED OCTOBER 2014 • TASTED IN BRISBANE

85% Trépail and Villers-Marmery, 15% Barbonne; aged 5 years on lees; 8–9g/L dosage

The depth and body of northern Montagne chardonnay, with a touch of textural grip from Sézanne, looks flattering in the tense and energetic 2008 season, upholding a bright, pale straw hue and an intense, primary core of white peach and lemon zest. Subtle almond-meal complexity is the only clue to its age, promising years of potential yet, thanks to a pronounced, well-focused, yet softly integrated acid line, creamy bead and excellent persistence.

Autumn colours highlight the vines under a dawn mist, veiling the grand cru slopes of Aÿ at the close of vintage 2014.

The Champagne Guide

PASCAL DOQUET

(Pas-khal Doh-khay)

7/10

44 Chemin du Moulin de la Censé Bizet 51130 Vertus

www.champagne-doquet.com

*T*he annual release letter Pascal Doquet sends to his customers from his cellar on the edge of Vertus reads more like that of a tiny boutique in Burgundy than a champagne producer. In it he recounts the stories of recent vintages, the tribulations of a rigorous organic regime in far-flung vineyards and the intricacies of 10 different cuvées, in their limited availability. Every detail of the philosophy and practice of this tiny estate translates into wines of effortless form and beguiling beauty, making this a mailing list that every lover of blanc de blancs should subscribe to.

Third-generation winemaker Pascal Doquet has been making champagne under his parents' label of Doquet Jeanmaire since 1982, and has led the estate since 1995. It was not until 2004 that he gained independent control and began marketing the brand under his own name, following acquisition of shares held by his sisters. This opened up the opportunity for Doquet to embark upon a daring organic regime to more accurately draw out the terroirs of each plot.

While he abandoned the use of herbicides as early as 2001, it was not until 2004 that he fully tuned in to sustainable viticulture, resolutely pursuing practices in harmony with nature and the planet, as he puts it. Full organic certification was granted in 2007. 'Respect of the soil is important,' he explains as he proudly shows photos of the health of his vines compared with neighbouring plots.

His is an intuitive approach, constantly experimenting and adapting his techniques and treatments to suit the site and the season. All plots are ploughed, and spontaneous flora is maintained in the mid-rows for a rich and complex biodiversity.

Doquet prepares his own organic composts and applies hardwood bark, grape marc and shredded branches to encourage biological activity. He is exploring new alternatives to copper and sulphur sprays for protection against disease.

He admits that a meticulous organic approach is a constant challenge in Champagne's climate, and particularly tricky to manage in vineyards separated by 75 kilometres. His 8.66-hectare estate is solidly rooted in the Côte des Blancs, with 3.5 hectares in Vertus, Bergères-lès-Vertus and Le Mont Aimé just south of Bergères, and a magnificent 1.7 hectares in Le Mesnil-sur-Oger. A further 3.5 hectares are located in the communes of Bassuet and Bassu in the region of Perthois in the Vitry to the east. Vines boast a maturity of up to 77 years, with a weighted average of 37 years, very high for Champagne. Chardonnay rules across the estate, with just 5% pinot noir, and no meunier.

PASCAL DOQUET   269

Doquet's goal is to harvest at full maturity to avoid chaptalisation. 'Chaptalisation should be the exception in Champagne,' is his radical suggestion. To this end, he green harvests to bring yields down to around 65hL/hectare, just two-thirds of the permitted appellation volume. This provides an annual production of 70,000 bottles, exclusively from estate vines.

Pascal Doquet makes wine by the philosophy of letting the vines and the wine tell him what to do, while forever experimenting and striving to improve. There are no strict rules and he varies his techniques in the cellar from year to year. Some wines go through malolactic fermentation, others do not. About one-third are fermented in oak and two-thirds in enamelled stainless steel, which he says is less prone to developing reductive characters. The natural yeasts of each vineyard are used for fermentation, and wines spend 4–5 months on lees in vats, and 11 months in barrels with bâtonnage. Dosage is low — always under 7g/L, and usually around 4.5g/L. Concentrated grape must is used instead of sugar because it tastes closer to the natural sweetness of the grapes.

A massive stock of 350,000–450,000 bottles is held in large cellars cut into chalk to permit long ageing of typically 4–5 years, crucial for blanc de blancs that hold their youthful vigour with pristine clarity. Vintages are released only when they're ready. DIAM closures have been used for exports since 2007. Doquet likes the closure, but admits that it's not so popular in France. Back labels are informative, declaring disgorgement date, dosage, base vintage and percentages of reserves.

The intuitive and sensitive approach of Pascal Doquet creates beautifully expressive and deeply terroir-driven wines. All but three non-vintage blends showcase individual villages, of which Le Mesnil-sur-Oger and Vertus are his jewels.

Pascal Doquet Horizon Blanc de Blancs Brut NV $$

89 points • 2011 base vintage • Disgorged March 2014 • Tasted in Vertus

Chardonnay from Bassuet and Bassu in Perthois in the Vitry; organically certified; 33% 2010 reserves; 12% vinified in barrels; no chaptalisation; full malolactic ferment; aged 3 years on lees; 7g/L dosage

Structure leads before fruit in the third release of Doquet's Horizon, resonating with the chalk and grey clay of Perthois, 50 kilometres east of his home in Vertus. Pear and apple fruit present a subtle note of pepper, while biscuity dryness and some phenolic grip on the finish reflect the difficult 2011 season. It lacks fruit precision and freshness, but upholds good acid line and well-balanced dosage.

Pascal Doquet Arpege Premier Cru Blanc de Blancs Extra Brut NV $$

92 points • 2009 base vintage • Disgorged February 2014 • Tasted in Vertus

A blend of Vertus, Villeneuve and Le Mont Aimé; reserves from 2010 (19%) and 2008 (31%); 20% vinified and aged for 6 months in small old barrels; aged in bottle on lees 3 years; full malolactic fermentation; 4.5 g/L dosage

An impressively assembled expression of the freshness of the southern Côte des Blancs, capturing well-structured chalk minerality, amplified ingeniously by the texture of barrel fermentation. This is a long-aged non-vintage blend, with apple and pear fruit beginning to become secondary in notes of almond meal. Low dosage accents its tight acid line and dry, textural mouthfeel, though it upholds persistence and integrity through the finish.

PASCAL DOQUET VERTUS PREMIER CRU COEUR DE TERROIR 2004 $$

96 points • TASTED IN VERTUS

Blend of vineyards mid-slope in the north of Vertus; 50% vinified and aged 6 months in oak; full malolactic fermentation

Vertus is the biggest and one of the most diverse villages in the Marne, and Doquet is astute in presenting his northern vineyards separately to those of the south. This cuvée rejoices in the strength, longevity and mineral structure of terroirs that clearly have more in common with nearby Le Mesnil-sur-Oger than they do with southern Vertus. It captures a splendid interplay between primary poise of lemon and grapefruit, rising complexity of buttered toast and crème brûlée, and the pronounced, fine mineral texture of pure chalk. This grand spectacle holds with fantastic line and length, making for a definitive and benchmark expression of Vertus.

PASCAL DOQUET PREMIER CRU LE MONT AIMÉ BLANC DE BLANCS 2005 $$

93 points • TASTED IN VERTUS

40% vinified in oak barrels, 60% in enamelled stainless steel tanks; aged on lees in tank and barrel for 6 months; full malolactic fermentation; 3.5g/L dosage

Pascal Doquet has bottled the precise lemon zest, red apple and grapefruit of Mont Aimé in the commune of Coligny at the extreme south of the Côte des Blancs, accurately preserving the chalky minerality of its sandy and stony soils. This well-crafted cuvée has come out of its shell in the two years since its release, blossoming into focused lemon zest and grapefruit freshness, accented with notes of nutmeg and vanilla bean. For such a warm vintage at a decade of age, its lively acid line is a refreshing surprise, and the dry extract grip of its textural finish aligns comfortably with well-poised salt minerality.

PASCAL DOQUET GRAND CRU BLANC DE BLANCS DIAPASON BRUT NV $$

94 points • 2006 BASE VINTAGE • DISGORGED JANUARY 2015 • TASTED IN VERTUS

100% Le Mesnil-sur-Oger; 16% 2005 reserves; 25% vinified and aged in old barrels; full malolactic fermentation; 5g/L dosage

For all intents and purposes, this is a vintage champagne, and a very pretty expression of the warm 2006 season. Few in this season have harnessed such exacting freshness, energy and endurance, testimony to the calibre of Doquet's terroirs, in what is arguably Champagne's most confident Grand Cru. It ripples with yellow citrus fruits and just-ripe pear, slowly forming the complexity of butter and patisserie. Minerality is silky and harmonious, yet exudes all the youthful confidence of the village, drawing out a smooth, long finish of exacting line.

Pascal Doquet Le Mesnil-sur-Oger Grand Cru Coeur de Terroir Blanc de Blancs Brut 2004 $$$

96 points • TASTED IN VERTUS

50% vinified and aged in oak barrels for 6 months; full malolactic fermentation; 4.5g/L dosage

Doquet preserves the heart of the character of Le Mesnil-sur-Oger with thrilling poise and freshness, even at 11 years of age. Retaining a medium straw hue, it's backward and enduring, yet creamy and enticing, with crystalline minerality that froths with sea salt texture on a very long tail. Superb presence of lemon blossom, crunchy apple and beurre bosc pear are tickled with just the slightest suggestions of nougat and anise. Brilliant.

Pascal Doquet Le Mesnil-sur-Oger Grand Cru Coeur de Terroir Blanc de Blancs Brut 2002 $$$

97 points • TASTED IN VERTUS

30% vinified in oak; no malolactic fermentation; 4.5g/L dosage

Assembled in tiny volumes from four different lieux-dits in Le Mesnil-sur-Oger — the thundering Chétillons, Champ d'Alouette, Finciart and Coullemets du Midi — this is a dazzling take on a high-strung and enduring season. I loved it when it was first unleashed two years ago, but never did I anticipate that it would retain such ravishing poise and freshness in the wake of such splendid concentration. It glitters in the radiance of deep, creamy, salty chalk minerality, energising preserved lemon and dried pear fruit. More than 12 years in the cellar has infused an internal harmony, beginning to gather momentum of almond and liquorice complexity. Breathtakingly seamless, it carries with unerring line and captivating persistence. One of the most enthralling monocru champagnes of the year.

Pascal Doquet Vertus Coeur de Terroir 2002 $$

95 points • TASTED IN VERTUS

70% chardonnay, 30% pinot noir; full malolactic fermentation

This is classic Vertus in a great season, preserving the definition of lemon rind in a persistent and focused style of fine, dry chalk mineral texture. Long lees age has infused a medium straw hue and developed captivating complexity of butterscotch, butter, anise, ginger and preserved lemon.

Pascal Doquet Vertus Premier Cru 1996

96 points • DISGORGED MAY 2012 TASTED IN VERTUS

DIAM closure

A warm greeting of all the tertiary character of pipe smoke, warm hearth and toast flows into a captivating spectacle of secondary baked fig, dried peach, marmalade and mixed spice. Brilliant, expressive chalk minerality defines a finish of outstanding persistence. The riveting drive and immortal freshness of 1996 acidity promise another entrancing decade of life yet.

PAUL BARA

(Pawl Bah-rah)

8/10

4 RUE YVONNET 51150 BOUZY
www.champagnepaulbara.com

*P*aul Bara knows Bouzy history so well he wrote the book on it. Celebrating its 180th anniversary recently, his family estate boasts 11 hectares of low-yielding grand cru vineyards on 33 parcels in the village. An annual production of 120,000 bottles embodies the characterful intensity of Bouzy pinot noir, comprising nine hectares of the estate, the remainder chardonnay. Impressive vine age averaging 35–40 years keeps yields in check and ripeness in balance. Exuberance is well toned, with freshness and vibrancy preserved by fermenting in small enamelled and stainless steel tanks, low dosages and blocking of malolactic fermentation. Malic acidity is given long periods to soften, with NV cuvées relying on generous proportions of reserve wines and bottle ageing of almost three years; vintage wines at least five years. Long one of the village's great estates, the legacy lives on in the hands of Paul's daughter, Chantale.

PAUL BARA COMTESSE MARIE DE FRANCE BLANC DE NOIRS
2002 $$$$

96 points • TASTED IN YARRA VALLEY

100% Bouzy pinot noir from 40–50-year-old vines; fermented in small enamelled and stainless steel tanks; no malolactic fermentation; 10g/L dosage; 6000 bottles

Unashamedly blanc de noirs, celebrating vast, expansive fruit presence of old-vine Bouzy magnitude, this is purposely a more voluminous style to Bara's Special Clubs. It ripples with the full grandeur of voluptuous plum liqueur, cherry slice, pineapple and dark fruit cake. Quite some wizardry is called for to draw impeccable control and refinement from such extravagant fervour, and Bara masters this with poised malic acidity, creamy texture and soft, chalk-laden minerality, propelled by the definition of 2002. A remarkable wine, soaked in feisty intensity, bathed in velvety warmth, all the while upholding sure-footed balance and graceful strength.

PAUL CLOUET

(Pawl Cloo-ay)

10 RUE JEANNE D'ARC 51150 BOUZY
www.champagne-paul-clouet.com

CHAMPAGNE
PAUL CLOUET

Marie-Therese Bonnaire sells 50,000—60,000 bottles of her affordable cuvées from her family vineyards in Bouzy and Chouilly. She is married to Jean-Louis Bonnaire, who makes her wines in his modern facility in Cramant, though they somehow never attain quite the same purity or character as his own Bonnaire cuvées.

PAUL CLOUET GRAND CRU BRUT NV $

90 points • 2010 BASE VINTAGE • TASTED IN BOUZY

80% pinot noir, 20% chardonnay; 2009 reserves; 8g/L dosage

A spicy cuvée, already well developed into the secondary spectrum of mixed spice, gingernut biscuits and brioche, with a short, dry finish. It's a little contracted in fruit presence, yet retains good acid length and soft texture.

PAUL CLOUET BRUT MILLÉSIME 2007 $$

93 points • TASTED IN BOUZY

80% pinot noir, 20% chardonnay; 8g/L dosage

A compelling contrast of the generosity of Bouzy with the wonderful tension of the elegant 2007 season. Taut acidity and finely focused chalk minerality draw out a long finish, while plenty of back palate presence of brioche and roast nut complexity make it ready to enjoy right away.

PAUL DÉTHUNE

(Pawl Deh-tune)

7/10

2 RUE DU MOULIN 51150 AMBONNAY

www.champagne-dethune.com

The Déthune family has tended its vines on the privileged slopes of Ambonnay since 1610. Today, the young Pierre Déthune and wife Sophie sensitively manage seven hectares of 70% pinot noir and 30% chardonnay entirely within the village. Seven cuvées draw complexity and diversity from 34 different Ambonnay parcels vinified separately, some in large oak foudres and small oak 'pièces' from the forests of Champagne. 'We want to show that the same grapes from the same village can produce seven different styles by varying the blends, the ageing and the use of oak,' Sophie explains. Their 50,000 bottles confidently express the luscious power and characterful poise of Ambonnay and quickly sell out every year.

The Déthunes effectively tend their vines organically, having employed organic composts and avoided insecticides and herbicides for 20 years, though they have purposely shunned organic certification over concerns surrounding copper sulphate fungicide.

'Pierre's grandfather was organic without knowing it, and 100 years later we still have copper in the vineyard from his treatments. This is not good for the vines,' Sophie explains. 'Champagne's difficult climate calls for liberal use of fungicides, particularly in wet vintages like 2012, but we do not want to use massive amounts of copper sulphate.' Pierre is instead trialling essential oils in the vineyards. 'I need every grape I can harvest, so I cannot take risks that might jeopardise any of our crop.' The Déthunes harvest 11 tonnes per hectare, quite a contrast to the 28 tonnes of one of their neighbours.

Pierre's father, Paul, introduced mechanisation in 1960. 'They had an easier job — and we are going backwards!' he exclaims, detailing the time and attention required to control grasses planted in the mid-rows since 2001. 'We intend to leave the vineyards for the next generation, so it is important for us to preserve the environment.' Fifty-four square metres of solar panels on the roof of the 17th century buildings provide one-fifth of the winery's electricity, and rainwater services a similar proportion of water requirements.

The Déthunes are careful not to harvest too late, to hold freshness and check the exuberance of Ambonnay pinot noir. Sophie works with the picking teams to inspect the fruit and ensure a stringent selection.

They aim to complete harvest of all 34 parcels within eight days. All are vinified separately, those destined for Brut NV in stainless steel, and reserves and other cuvées in large vats and small barrels of up to 20 years of age. Vats work harmoniously with the Déthune's fruit, though small oak barrels tend to assert themselves prominently. They buy a few new 205-litre champagne oak barrels each year. 'We have 42 in all, and that's all we have room for!' says Sophie.

Space constraints have necessitated storage of their longest-aged cuvées off-site. They recently purchased the house next door and dug a new cellar, to double their storage capacity. This will permit a small increase in production, enabling them to keep the 15% of their fruit that they currently sell to Veuve Clicquot for La Grande Dame.

Disgorgement dates are printed on the back of every bottle. A dosage of 10g/L is used across all cuvées, suiting the strength and vitality of the house style.

PAUL DÉTHUNE GRAND CRU BRUT NV $$

93 points • 2011 BASE VINTAGE • DISGORGED JULY 2014 • TASTED IN BRISBANE

70% pinot noir, 30% chardonnay

A medium straw hue with a subtle blush tint, this is a wonderfully succulent, juicy celebration of Ambonnay pinot noir, in all of its wild strawberry and red cherry glory, underlined by creamy, crème brûlée development and an appropriate touch of bitter tannin grip, which unites with salty minerality to tone its exuberant fruit ripeness. Excellent length and flamboyant fruit appeal are controlled by well-defined structure.

PAUL DÉTHUNE CUVÉE PRESTIGE PRINCESSE DES THUNES BRUT NV $$$

95 points • 2005 BASE VINTAGE • DISGORGED JULY 2013 • TASTED IN AMBONNAY

70% 2005, 30% reserve from a perpetual solera of 40 vintages made and aged in oak vats; 50% pinot, 50% chardonnay; vinified entirely in 3200-3400L oak vats of at least 5 years of age; aged 7 years on lees; 9g/L dosage; 2500 bottles

More than 40 years ago, Pierre's father Paul commenced a solera to which every vintage since has contributed. The complexity that such depth of maturity contributes to a blend is mesmerising, evoking memories of black fruit cake, liquorice and plum liqueur. One might expect a dissonance between such far-fetched exoticism and the primary fruit depth of yellow mirabelle plums of the 2005 vintage, and the vanilla, buttered toast and marzipan of oak. The true skill of this cuvée comes first in harmonising this maelstrom seamlessly, and second in bringing poise to the ripe and too often rather clumsy 2005 vintage. It has now evolved to a point of silky, polished finesse and enchanting appeal unexpected in Ambonnay — every bit as magnificent as it was two years ago, and then some.

PAUL DÉTHUNE CUVÉE A L'ANCIENNE BRUT 2007 $$$$

93 points • DISGORGED SEPTEMBER 2014 • TASTED IN AMBONNAY

50% chardonnay, 50% pinot noir from a single parcel of 40-year-old vines; vinified and aged in 205L oak barrels; aged under cork for 6 years; just 1000 bottles

A complex and multi-layered champagne of inimitable character, colliding the depth and impact of Ambonnay with the assertive personality of small oak barrels. There's more than a little tension in this accord, small oak barrels emphasising the edgy nature of this cuvée, perhaps more than they need to, accenting fine tannin texture, yet at the same time creamy and silky. Cork age helps with this, but it screams for more time for oak to soften and integrate. A panoply of exoticism rolls in waves of bees wax, after-dinner mints, grilled pineapple, green coffee beans and glacé orange, exploding in a crescendo of outstanding persistence.

The Champagne Guide

PAUL GOERG

(Pawl Gerg)

30 RUE DU GÉNÉRAL LECLERC 51130 VERTUS

www.champagne-goerg.com

aul Goerg is the sister brand of Napoléon under the cooperative of Vertus. Together, the two labels comprise two-thirds of the production of the group, with the remainder sold. Vertus chardonnay is the theme of Paul Goerg, supplemented with a little fruit from neighbouring villages, particularly Le Mesnil-sur-Oger. While richer and more rounded parcels are destined for Napoléon, chef de cave Jean-Philippe Moulin sets aside those of pure, elegant delicacy for Paul Goerg, aspiring to a long-aged style of clean, mineral precision. In his seven years, Moulin has lowered dosage from 9g/L to 7g/L. These are simple, tightly structured cuvées that appreciate bottle age.

PAUL GOERG TRADITION BRUT NV $

91 points • 2008 BASE VINTAGE • TASTED IN HAUTVILLERS

60% chardonnay, 40% pinot noir; 85–90% Vertus, with a little chardonnay from the villages behind Vertus; 7g/L dosage

A clean, balanced and simple style of red apple and lemon fruit with brioche and honey complexity, supported by soft chalk minerality, a fine, creamy bead and a touch of honeyed dosage.

....

PAUL GOERG BLANC DE BLANCS NV $$

90 points • 2007 BASE VINTAGE • DISGORGED SEPTEMBER 2014 • TASTED IN HAUTVILLERS

Vertus chardonnay; 7–8g/L dosage

A tense and tight style of medium straw hue, presenting good persistence of apple and pear fruit, with bottle age contributing almond notes. It culminates in a fine bead, soft, salty minerality and a touch of bitter almond texture.

PAUL GOERG BRUT 2005 $$

91 points • DISGORGED JULY 2014 • TASTED IN HAUTVILLERS
Chardonnay from Vertus and a little from Le Mesnil-sur-Oger; 6g/L dosage

With a medium straw hue, this is a biscuity and secondary style reminiscent of hazelnut cream, expressing the ripeness and grip of 2005, yet admirably retaining the refreshing acidity of Vertus and Le Mesnil. It finishes with good length, a creamy bead and a touch of nutty grip.

PAUL GOERG BRUT 2004 $$

93 points • DISGORGED EARLY 2014 • TASTED IN HAUTVILLERS
Chardonnay from Vertus and a little from Le Mesnil-sur-Oger; 6g/L dosage

Testimony to the drive and endurance of 2004, this cuvée still holds a medium straw hue and impressive poise of red apple and lemon fruit. It's maturing slowly and confidently into brioche and honey notes, sustained by fine chalk minerality and well-integrated acid line, which linger through a long finish.

PAUL GOERG CUVÉE LADY 2004 $$$

94 points • DISGORGED EARLY 2014 • TASTED IN HAUTVILLERS
85% chardonnay, 15% pinot noir; 90-95% Vertus with a little Le Mesnil-sur-Oger; 6g/L dosage

Elegance, balance and longevity are the mantra here, with a drop of pinot noir for body. The result instead showcases the exotic personality of Vertus in grand fruit richness of glacé peach, orange, red apple and boiled sweets. It holds its freshness amidst a long and well-balanced finish of focused acidity, soft minerality and creamy mouthfeel.

PAUL GOERG CUVÉE LADY 2002 $$$

95 points • DISGORGED EARLY 2013 • TASTED IN HAUTVILLERS

Paul Goerg's flagship holds impressive poise and medium straw hue in the outstanding 2002 season, and a decade on lees has built wonderful layers of crème caramel, gingernut biscuits and burnt butter. A finish of great persistence and appeal sings with well-integrated acidity and the expressive salt chalk minerality of Vertus.

PERRIER-JOUËT

(Per-riay Zhoo-ay)

5/10

28 AVENUE DE CHAMPAGNE 51201 ÉPERNAY

www.perrier-jouet.com

The past 20 years have been turbulent for Perrier-Jouët, changing hands three times before it was taken over by current owners, Pernod Ricard, in 2005. In the midst of this rollercoaster, the house has been fortunate to retain most of its vineyards, with 65 hectares now providing for one-quarter of its annual production of 3 million bottles, ranking it as Champagne's 10th-largest house. From its founding just over 200 years ago, the vision of the house has focused on the floral elegance of chardonnay, and today more than half of the estate's holdings lie in the Côte des Blancs, particularly in the grand crus of Cramant, Avize and, to a lesser extent, Chouilly. The jewel of the house is the glorious Cramant, where it is privileged to the very finest sites in the village. For chef de cave Hervé Deschamps, 'Perrier-Jouët is about the elegance, freshness, fruitiness and roundness of chardonnay, with power and biscuity complexity.' His is a house style of soft, rounded, creamy generosity.

For Deschamps, the origin of the fruit is of utmost importance, and he sources from no less than 70 villages across Champagne. 'The best chardonnay comes from the Côte des Blancs, Trépail, Villers-Marmery, the Sézanne and the Vitry, and for Perrier-Jouët, it's all about the Côte des Blancs,' he says, adding that Villers-Marmery is also an important source. He uses pinot noir for perfume rather than strength, favouring Mailly-Champagne, Verzy, Verzenay, Aÿ, Avenay-Val-d'Or and Les Riceys, and meunier from Dizy, Damery, Venteuil and Vincelles. Maintaining acidity and avoiding high ripeness is his priority in the vineyards, which he admits is a challenge in the wake of global warming.

A total of 300 tanks permit the flexibility to keep not only each village separate, but the early, middle and late picks also. Everything is vinified in stainless steel, with full malolactic fermentation. Symbolic of its focus on chardonnay's floral elegance, the Belle Epoque flagships are presented in a distinctive, enamelled bottle of Art Nouveau Japanese anemones. The luscious branding of the house is likewise a tribute to the Art Nouveau era.

I met Hervé for the first time this year and was immediately drawn to his warm smile, humility and candour. 'When I joined Perrier-Jouët 32 years ago, I knew about winegrowing, as my grandfather grew grapes, but I'd never blended a wine before!' he revealed. He learnt his art over a decade under his predecessor, André Bavaret.

Hervé's openness is rare and refreshing in the big-brand champagne world, and as he methodically presented each of the cuvées of the house, no topic was off limits, even production volumes of each cuvée.

Perrier-Jouët Grand Brut NV $$

85 points • 2011 base vintage • Tasted in Épernay & Brisbane
90 points • 2009 base vintage • Tasted in Sydney & Melbourne

40% pinot noir, 40% meunier, 20% chardonnay; 12-20% reserves; aged at least 2.5 years
on lees; 9g/L dosage; 2 million bottles; DIAM closure

Base vintage makes a profound statement here, the bad-tempered 2011 making for a dusty, mushroomy style of dry extract, quashing its elegant lemon and white peach fruit. By contrast, the smiling generosity of 2009 makes for a smooth, buttery, fruit-focused and powerful style of succulent white peach, fig and candied mouthfeel, with a little more dosage than it needs.

Perrier-Jouët Blason Rosé NV $$

88 points • 2012 base vintage • Tasted in Épernay
89 points • 2010 base vintage • Tasted in Sydney & Melbourne
91 points • 2009 base vintage • Disgorged January 2012 • Tasted in
    Brisbane

50% pinot noir, 25% meunier, 25% chardonnay; Grand Brut base with 15% red wine purchased from
Bouzy, Ambonnay, Vertus, Cumières and Les Riceys, among others; DIAM closure; 200,000 bottles

The aspiration for Blason Rosé is an elegant colour and fruity style, created with red wine of strong colour and soft tannin. Perrier-Jouët has been making rosé since 1959 and is currently increasing its production, though only makes it in vintages in which the red wine is of sufficient quality. It's a pretty, primary, fruit-focused style of medium salmon hue that delivers raspberry and strawberry fruits and pink pepper, supported by candied dosage and balanced acid line. Fine tannins are gentle and well handled, supporting a finish of persistent, even appeal. The 2009 base is a particularly good release for Blason Rosé, still young and fresh even three years after disgorgement. The 2010 is now more succulent, with dosage more prominent. The 2012 finishes with some dusty dryness, though holds good acid line and persistence.

Perrier-Jouët Belle Epoque Vintage 2006 $$$$

93 points • Tasted in Épernay & Brisbane

50% chardonnay from Cramant, Avize, Le Mesnil-sur-Oger and a little Vertus; 45% pinot noir
from Mailly-Champagne, Verzy, Verzenay and Aÿ; 5% meunier from estate vines in Dizy to bridge
chardonnay and pinot noir; 9g/L dosage; DIAM closure; 1 million bottles

True to the mood of 2006, this is a buttery, toasty, honeyed wine that has quickly evolved to a place of secondary character of preserved lemon and candied orange rind, capturing the appealingly silky succulence of Perrier-Jouët. Lees age has enhanced its textural mouthfeel, while balanced acidity and dosage sit comfortably on the finish. It looks a fraction fresher in Épernay than it does around the world, with the chalk mineral emphasis of Cramant and Avize more prominent. For the price, there's not a lot of character or distinction here, but there's no shortage of comfortable appeal.

PERRIER-JOUËT BELLE EPOQUE ROSÉ 2006 $$$$$

94 points • TASTED IN ÉPERNAY

50% pinot noir from Mailly-Champagne, Aÿ, Ambonnay, Mareuil-sur-Aÿ and Verzy; 45% chardonnay from Cramant, Avize and Le Mesnil-sur-Oger; 5% meunier from Dizy and Venteuil; same base as Belle Epoque with 10% red wine, particularly from Aÿ and sometimes Vertus; 8g/L dosage; DIAM closure

A floral style is the aspiration for Belle Epoque Rosé, but at a decade of age, the generous 2006 season delivers much more. Medium salmon copper in hue, it's alive with wild strawberries, strawberry shortcake, secondary complexity of burnt butter and brioche, becoming subtle tertiary intrigue of warm hearth. Gentle chalk mineral structure and a fine bead sparkle through a finish elongated by an elegant acid line.

PERRIER JOUËT BELLE EPOQUE ROSÉ 2004 $$$$$

93 points • TASTED IN SYDNEY, MELBOURNE & BRISBANE

This is a style of supple, easy-drinking appeal, now fully evolved into a secondary sphere of ginger, anise, toast, boiled orange and the last flickers of primary red berry fruits. Its acidity now fully integrated, it upholds good persistence and a soft, creamy mouthfeel. It's at the end of its life now, and was more confident in its refreshing focus a year ago.

PERRIER-JOUËT BELLE EPOQUE BLANC DE BLANCS 2002 $$$$$

95 points • TASTED IN ÉPERNAY

7g/L dosage; 12,000 bottles

It was celebrated grower Pierre Larmandier who once told me that Perrier-Jouët owns the finest terroir in Cramant. I suspect the two neighbouring plots that contribute to this cuvée were part of what he was talking about. 'Bourons Leroy' and 'Bourons du Midi' enjoy a perfect south-easterly exposure in the glorious mid-slope of the village. This is the first release of this label, and from the outset it steps up as the glittering triumph of the house. Cramant sings with full operatic gusto in pretty lemon-blossom high notes, reverberating with magnificent depth and succulent breadth, enlivened with beautifully structured, impeccably fresh and definitively pronounced salty chalk minerality. The energy of the great 2002 season sustains it, while long bottle age piles on layers of honey, butter, brioche and ginger. A classic.

Alongside Perrier-Jouët's two million bottles of Grand Brut NV and one million of Belle Epoque, its 12,000 bottle production of this cuvée is minuscule. No surprise it's the most sublime creation of the house.

PHILIPPONNAT

(Fi-li-poh-nah)

6/10

13 RUE DU PONT 51160 MAREUIL-SUR-AŸ

www.philipponnat.com

1522

PHILIPPONNAT

CHAMPAGNE

*I*f the finest vineyard sites are the most important asset of any Champagne house, Philipponnat is particularly privileged. Its 17 hectares of mostly pinot noir span Mareuil-sur-Aÿ, and its neighbours Aÿ, Mutigny and Avenay-Val-d'Or, but its most prized is the splendid, sun-drenched Clos des Goisses, one of the most powerful and distinctive sites in all of Champagne. The walled vineyard of 5.5 hectares lies on the east of Mareuil-sur-Aÿ at the very heart of Champagne, the juncture at which the Côte des Blancs, the Vallée de la Marne and the Montagne de Reims meet. With perfect south-facing aspect, a dramatic slope of 30–45 degrees towards the Marne ('Gois' means 'very steep' in the local dialect!), catching the sun in its full perpendicular strength, and shielded from the westerly winds, this is one of the warmest micro-climates in Champagne, boasting temperatures to equal those of Burgundy. The subsoil is pure chalk, following the gradient of the hill under a thin layer of poor topsoil, so roots quickly strike chalk, pervading the wines with minerality. Mareuil-sur-Aÿ is a mere premier cru, and Clos des Goisses is perhaps the most striking case of all for a much more detailed classification of Champagne vineyards.

Philipponnat's house style is particularly intense, relying primarily on the power of Montagne de Reims pinot noir from south-facing estate vineyards. Additional supplies are sourced from a further 60 hectares of vineyards, particularly from the Côte des Blancs and Vallée de la Marne, and excess is purchased each vintage to permit lesser parcels to be declassified.

Yields are restricted and optimal physiological maturity is sought through slightly delayed harvests. Clos des Goisses is 1–1.5°C warmer than other nearby vineyards, and is harvested at 13 degrees potential, the maximum permitted in the appellation.

The opulence of Philipponnat's ripeness can be disarming, and the phenolic coarseness that this creates can be disconcerting.

Fruit of high sugar ripeness calls for winemaking processes that preserve freshness in every detail. This begins with vinification close to the vineyards in Mareuil-sur-Aÿ. When Philipponnat owners Lanson-BCC invited Charles Philipponnat to return and manage the family business in 2000, his first initiative was to construct a new winery in Mareuil-sur-Aÿ and discontinue processing in Reims. He has since worked on improving viticulture through natural fertilisation and decreased use of chemicals, which made for riper grapes, allowing for lower dosage, so every cuvée above the entry NVs is extra brut. Charles Philipponnat has also focused on longer oak ageing, cleaner blends, increasing pinot noir and decreasing meunier in the top cuvées, and finally, recently introducing new smart, minimalist, modern labels across the range. He remains personally very involved in the tastings and blending of the house.

Freshness is preserved through use of only the first pressings, cool fermentation in temperature-controlled stainless steel, blocking of malolactic fermentation in the most powerful parcels according to the vintage, use of a minimum of 30% chardonnay, and moderate dosage.

The strongest parcels of pinot noir and chardonnay (about 20% in all, representing 40–60% of vintage wines) are fermented in barrels, which vary between new and 5–6 years old, for complexity and oxidation. At least 50% of each cuvée is aged in barrels. Walking into the barrel hall, the aroma of oak is intoxicating, like nowhere else in Champagne. Such is the strength of Philipponnat's bold fruit that oak flavour does not tend to dominate, though its structure can disrupt already heightened phenolics.

The barrel hall is climate controlled to block malolactic fermentation in every barrel. All reserve wines are matured for six months in small- and large-format oak. Reserve wines for Brut Royale are kept in a solera system of fractional blending in foudres for six months, then into small barrels, re-blended every year to incorporate mature wines without losing freshness. Non-vintage cuvées receive 20–30% reserve wines and are aged 3–4 years in bottle. The house doubles the minimum ageing times across its cuvées, necessitating a stock of 2.5 million bottles in its 1.5 kilometres of 17th-century cellars. It maintains some 250 barrels, purchased after two or three vintages in Burgundy, and upheld for about 10 seasons at Philipponnat.

Grand cru Avize chardonnay arriving at the press in vintage 2014.

Philipponnat sells 500,000 bottles annually, all of which boast some of the most informative back labels of any house, declaring the date of disgorgement, the blend, barrel maturation and dosage; the house claims to be the first in Champagne to also indicate the base year of its blends. An excellent new website adds more informative detail on every cuvée.

The 17 Clos de Goisses parcels are vinified separately, half in tank and half in barrel, as has been tradition since 1935. The vineyard comprises about two-thirds pinot noir and one-third chardonnay, from vines aged 8–45 years, with an average of 30.

While 5.5 hectares has the capacity to produce 55,000 bottles, on average just 17,000 bottles are made annually — sometimes as few as 5000 or as many as 20,000 — with the remainder declassified into other Philipponnat cuvées.

Clos des Goisses is produced every vintage, but not always released. The house believes that it represents the first single bottling in Champagne, and it is testimony to the site that almost every year since 1956 has been released.

Philipponnat Royale Réserve Non Dosé NV $$

91 points • 2010 base vintage • Disgorged June 2014 • Tasted in Mareuil-sur-Aÿ

Brut Royale without dosage; 65% pinot noir, 30% chardonnay, 5% meunier; 20–30% reserves from solera; 37% barrel matured; partial malolactic fermentation; aged 3 years on lees; zero dosage

This same base vintage with 8g/L dosage always looks stronger, making the Non Dosé version a strong case for the importance of dosage and the inherent danger of making a zero-dosage champagne without designing it purposely from the ground up. This is only exemplified in the presence of high-strung malic acidity and the toasty, spicy, vanilla influence of oak. The result is tense and firm, though its fine salt chalk mineral expression is exact.

Philipponnat Royale Réserve Brut NV $

90 points • 2011 BASE VINTAGE WITH 30% RESERVES • DISGORGED NOVEMBER 2014 • TASTED IN MAREUIL-SUR-AŸ

92 points • 2010 BASE VINTAGE WITH 37% RESERVES • DISGORGED SEPTEMBER 2014 • TASTED IN MAREUIL-SUR-AŸ & MELBOURNE

65% pinot noir, 30% chardonnay, 5% meunier; 37% reserves from solera; a blend of 20 villages; partial malolactic fermentation; aged 3 years on lees; 8g/L dosage

In its medium straw guise, the 2010 base is a characterful, spicy, fleshy and complex style that resonates with the full depth of Mareuil pinot and all the theatrics of 50% barrel maturation. Layers of coffee, dark chocolate, coffee bean and spice wash over a core of crunchy grapefruit and dried pear, energised with the zap of 50% malic acidity that brings freshness and focus to a long finish of well-integrated dosage. Tasted just a few months post-disgorgement, the 2011 represents a more restrained blend that will benefit from time in bottle to flesh out, though is let down by the savoury mushroom notes of 2011 that disrupt its precision and focus.

Philipponnat Royale Réserve Rosé Brut NV $$

94 points • 2008 BASE VINTAGE • DISGORGED MARCH 2014 • TASTED IN MAREUIL-SUR-AŸ

75% pinot noir, 20% chardonnay, 5% meunier; 7% pinot noir red wine; 25-30% reserves from solera; 18% barrel matured; partial malolactic fermentation; 9g/L dosage

A tiny dose of red wine is sufficient to produce a medium salmon hue in this pretty and creamy style. It rejoices in the energy and lively malic acidity of 2008, well toned by the creamy texture of partial barrel maturation and five years of lees age. The gentle precision and lingering persistence of strawberry and red cherry fruits are blessed by brioche complexity. The best Philipponnat Rosé I've tasted. All hail the great 2008 vintage!

Philipponnat Blanc de Noirs Brut 2008 $$

95 points • DISGORGED JANUARY 2014 • TASTED IN MAREUIL-SUR-AŸ

100% pinot noir from 5-6 Montagne de Reims premier and grand crus; partial malolactic fermentation; aged 5 years on lees; extra brut dosage of 4.3g/L, though labelled brut

'Noir is the new black!' the house announced when this new label recently replaced its Réserve Millésime. It's a captivating union of the focus, tension and bright, lively red fruits of 2008 pinot noir, with the silky, creamy texture of barrel fermentation. The generosity of the house style lends itself well to the energetic tone of 2008, heightening fine chalk mineral texture without diminishing the full fanfare of complexity of fig, mixed spice, gingernut biscuits and coffee beans.

The Champagne Guide

Philipponnat Grand Blanc Brut 2006 $$

93 points • Disgorged April 2014 • Tasted in Mareuil-sur-Aÿ

70% Côte des Blancs premier cru and grand cru chardonnay; 30% Clos des Goisses chardonnay; half stainless steel, half barrel vinification; malolactic fermentation in tanks only; extra brut dosage of 4.3g/L, though labelled brut

The ripe 2006 vintage in concert with a strong dose of the all-conquering Clos de Goisses creates a generous and fleshy style, tactically pulled into line by lively malic acidity and the chalk mineral presence of the Côte des Blancs. A core of lemon zest and white peach is enlivened with all the spectacle of ginger cake, toast, biscuits and vanilla, lingering long and full, yet well focused. True to 2006, this is a rich blanc de blancs, yet retains articulate definition.

Philipponnat Grand Cru 1522 Brut 2005 $$$

93 points • Disgorged December 2013 • Tasted in Mareuil-sur-Aÿ

65% pinot noir, 35% chardonnay from grand cru vineyards; partial barrel vinification; partial malolactic fermentation; aged more than 7 years on lees; extra brut dosage of 4.3g/L, though labelled brut

This label is a commemoration of the first proof of the Philipponnats growing pinot noir in Aÿ in 1522. The voluptuous curves of pinot noir are amplified three-fold, in the stature of grand cru Montagne de Reims sites, the luscious warmth of 2005 and the voluminous character of barrel fermentation, flinging it to the outer realms of champagne concentration. All the ripeness of grilled pineapple and white peach collides with the spicy, nutty, coffee bean presence of oak. It's pulled into line by malic acidity, which brings definition and grapefruit liveliness to a long, rich finish. Extended lees age has heightened its creamy texture, and phenolics bring some softly bitter grip, which helps to pull this solid and powerful style into line. It's characterful, engaging and in a happy place right now at the end of its release.

Philipponnat Clos des Goisses Brut 2005 $$$$$

95 points • Disgorged November 2013 • Tasted in Mareuil-sur-Aÿ

65% pinot noir, 35% chardonnay; 50% vinified in barrels; no malolactic fermentation; aged 7.5 years on lees; extra brut of 4.3g/L dosage, though labelled brut

For its lofty credentials (and price to match), Clos des Goisses should consistently rank in the highest echelons of Champagne. If sheer, booming power were the only criterion it would have no equal. The house describes it as a 'big, Burgundian style of champagne!' But to me its thumping ripeness can be alarming, creating disconcerting phenolic coarseness, though I respect that some other commentators are somewhat more forgiving of this than I. But here comes the surprise, because the characteristically ripe, exuberant and coarse 2005 vintage has yielded a Clos des Goisses that ranks among my favourites of recent times, and I can't think of any other champagne of which I could say the same. Perhaps it's that the expansive volume of the season has accentuated its well-defined core of grapefruit, lemon and roast fig, rising to meet looming intensity of oak-derived coffee beans, fruit cake, dark chocolate, hazelnuts and butterscotch? In the midst of this swirling vortex, chalk mineral structure confidently raises its head, infusing a tension and freshness to a creamy mouthfeel, somehow bolstered by subtle bitter grapefruit texture. The freshness it upholds is astonishing for the site, the season and the recipe, and it may even go down among the better ageing wines of the vintage.

PIERRE GIMONNET & FILS

(Pee-yair Zhi-moh-neh e Feess)

8/10

1 RUE DE LA RÉPUBLIQUE 51530 CUIS

www.champagne-gimonnet.com

'The difference between a good wine and an exceptional wine is only a question of very, very small details, but we must focus on every detail all of the time,' declares Didier Gimonnet, who oversees his family's estate with his brother, Olivier. The champagnes of Pierre Gimonnet & Fils are intricately assembled by masterful hands exclusively from enviably positioned and painstakingly tended old vines. Every cuvée sings its aspiration of 'precision, purity and minerality', each speaking articulately of its place in the northern Côte des Blancs through expressive, chalky minerality, without one molecule of detail out of place. With high-strung tension, crystalline structure and rapier-sharp precision, these are blanc de blancs champagnes charged with an energy that will sustain them long indeed. They represent some of the best-value apéritif champagnes of all.

'My father always told me the most important thing is to make wine, and after that to sell it at a reasonable price,' Didier explains. From one of Champagne's most intelligent growers, wines of such purity and fine-spun, mineral-laden precision should sell for much higher prices. Little wonder Gimonnet has experienced strong global demand in recent years, fully allocating its production of 250,000 bottles. There is not a champagne in this collection unworthy of your table this year.

GRAND VINEYARDS

'Our champagnes have a personality because of the vineyards they come from,' Didier says. 'In Champagne, as everywhere, the most important thing is the origin of the grapes.' The family owns a substantial estate of 28 hectares, most proudly located in the heart of each of their village's terroirs, almost exclusively in the Côte des Blancs.

In a region afflicted with generally young vines, more than two-thirds of Gimonnet's are now over 40 years old, close to half are more than 50, and one hectare more than a century — incredible numbers for a region that typically replants every 35 years. Every bottle of Gimonnet comes exclusively from these vineyards; not a single grape is purchased from growers.

'When you have great terroir, it is a child's game to create a great blend,' Didier says. Half of Gimonnet's vineyards are located in its premier cru home village of Cuis, which he is frank in admitting is not a great terroir. 'With less body and structure, Cuis does not have the character, body or structure of a grand cru, but it has higher acidity, giving us very fresh wines,' Didier explains. 'Without doubt, the best of our domains are in Cramant. I compare Cramant with lace — it is precise and delicate, with an interesting, chalky minerality, and it has a concentration but is not heavy.' He holds 5.5 glorious hectares in the village.

One hectare in the more stony soils of Oger contributes concentrated, spicy, smoky power and graphite minerality; two hectares in Vertus have less power, but more exotic tropical fruit character; while a substantial 5.5 hectares in Chouilly add a fruity elegance. A little pinot noir is derived from just half a hectare, shared between Aÿ and Mareuil-sur-Aÿ.

'Fruitiness, elegance, power and minerality can therefore be determined according to the villages that we use in each blend,' Didier clarifies. 'Our objective is to make wines of minerality, not of explosive fruit.'

UNCOMPROMISING MIXOLOGISTS

Of Gimonnet's considerable 12 hectares of grand cru holdings, three-quarters are located in the prized heart of the mid-slopes of their villages. Some in Champagne suggest Didier's blends do not do justice to the greatness of his terroirs. In the hands of others, these holdings could yield thundering single-cru old-vine cuvées from the grand crus of Cramant, Chouilly and Oger, but to do so would deprive Gimonnet of the powerful blending material that so eloquently lifts the mood of Cuis in all but the very first of his nine blends. He singles out the strength of Oger as an exception, making it tricky to blend without dominating.

'I created a single Oger cuvée last year, as I'm not clever enough to know how to blend all of it!' He defines the best terroirs as those that respect others in a blend. 'Champagne is a blend, and a grand terroir is one that can be blended without dominating,' says Didier, who has been dubbed a 'mixologist'. This blending is the key to the philosophy of the house. 'I am against mono-terroir,' he says, 'but I am adept at very polished blends that combine the qualities of different terroirs to produce complexities. When I present the house I always say I'm not a winemaker, just an interpreter of terroir.'

Gimonnet owns 12 grand cru vineyards, but does not produce a single wine that can be labelled grand cru, 'because they're better balanced when blended with premier cru parcels to confer freshness of acidity and balance between concentration, finesse and elegance,' Didier explains. 'The blend is the highest ideal here, more than the sum of the parts.'

His mantra is to produce the most balanced wines, not those that can be labelled to command the highest prices. A noble pursuit, rare in Champagne, and it begins in the vineyards.

METICULOUS ATTENTION TO PURITY

When I visited at the height of harvest 2014 I found Olivier in the vineyards and Didier on the forklift unloading grapes in the winery. They are both very hands-on, and have the help of only two others in the winery. 'It is very important for the quality for me to be here,' Didier says.

'The date of harvest is very, very important,' he maintains. 'Just four days too early or too late and it will disrupt concentration, structure and elegance.'

He prizes minerality and freshness above concentration, so does not harvest at the maximum maturity, but at the optimum level of ripeness to give a good balance of alcohol potential and high acidity. To achieve this, yields are moderated to around 11–12 tonnes/hectare (equating to about 75hL/hectare), compared with a potential of 18–20 tonnes.

The goal of every stage of vinification is to preserve purity, freshness and minerality with the utmost precision. Gimonnet's winery is a pristine declaration of this mandate, a bathroom-fresh environment of floor-to-ceiling tiles and gleaming stainless steel. 'It is like cooking,' Didier suggests. 'To create purity you must have the freshest ingredients.'

Vinification is as simple as possible, 'so the expression is due only to the terroir and the maturity of the fruit'. With 90% of vineyards within four kilometres of the house, all grapes are pressed within six hours of harvest. Gimonnet presses more lightly than most, so of the little he harvests he extracts even less juice, but juice of finer quality. As at Billecart-Salmon and Pol Roger, the juice is clarified at 10°C for 24 hours prior to fermentation, a crucial procedure for the refined elegance of the style. Selected yeast is then added to achieve a rapid start to fermentation.

'My goal is to have the juice in fermentation less than two days after picking; this is very important for maintaining purity and freshness.' Fermentation and maturation take place only in temperature-controlled stainless steel tanks. 'Our grapes come from good terroirs, and we want no other taste than that of the fruit in our wine.' Every plot is vinified separately. There are 40 parcels in the estate, and hence 40 tanks. The tendency of Cuis chardonnay to oxidise quickly in tank dictates that reserve wines are instead kept on fine lees in magnums under crown seal, allowing them to mature and develop body, while retaining purity and freshness, without evolving too rapidly. An unusual and painstaking process, it takes six people to open 10,000 bottles a day.

Malolactic fermentation is employed in all wines to soften the high acidity of Cuis. A light dosage of 8g/L of sugar is used, as little as 5g/L in the vintage cuvées, and there is no impression of sweetness. 'Dosage is very important to avoid angular wines without introducing the taste of sugar,' Didier explains. He considers it crucial to oxidise the liquor before adding it to the bottle. 'It seems like nothing, but it makes a subtle difference to the taste.' He uses only a small amount of sulphur as a preservative, but sufficient to uphold freshness.

Timing of disgorgement is likewise given careful consideration, with every bottle freshly disgorged to order. Disgorgement dates are printed on bottles sent to countries that request them, including the US and Italy. 'The date of disgorgement is very important in champagne,' Didier points out. 'A cuvée is very different six months after disgorgement than it is two years after disgorgement.' More than half of Gimonnet's non-vintage cuvées are sealed with reliable Mytik DIAM closures, as his trials have found these to preserve freshness more reliably than natural cork.

Enviable vineyards and meticulous practices stir strong demand, and Gimonnet has been working to increase production to keep up. Not as easy as it sounds, according to Gimonnet. 'We don't want to be wine merchants by buying grapes to increase production,' he emphasises. 'We don't want to make volume, we want to make the quality that we like and then offer

The grand cru hillside of Cramant, where Gimonnet holds its finest terroirs, bringing concentration and plumpness to its blends.

it on allocation. We therefore need to buy vineyards with the potential of our style. But there are not many vineyards on the market, and when they are they are too expensive.' Over the past decade, five hectares have been purchased in the Côte des Blancs to increase production by about 50,000 bottles.

Gimonnet's cuvées represent some of the Côte des Blancs' best buys this year, and one represents the best value I've seen in five years.

PIERRE GIMONNET & FILS CUIS PREMIER CRU BRUT BLANC DE BLANCS NV $

93 points • 2011 BASE VINTAGE (73%) WITH 6% 2010, 16% 2009, 4% 2007, 1% 2006
• DISGORGED OCTOBER 2014 • TASTED IN CUIS & BRISBANE
93 points • 2010 BASE VINTAGE (80%) WITH 9.8% 2009, 4.2% 2008, 5% 2007, 1% 2002
• TASTED IN SYDNEY & MELBOURNE

100% Cuis chardonnay; reserve wines are the previous year's blend, stored in magnums; full malolactic fermentation; aged 2 years 8 months on lees; 6.5g/L dosage; DIAM closure; 95,000 bottles

Only the toughest seasons truly define the greatest estates. After a hot summer and wet harvest, Didier Gimonnet is understated in describing 2011 as 'not a simple vintage to make this wine', but the result is a resounding testimony to his terroirs and his exacting attention to detail. With no vintage wines made, this blend is the best of the village. Tense, edgy and savoury on release, it's blossomed with a further six months in bottle into a merry celebration of the freshness of Cuis, the quintessential apéritif and one of the most pristine champagnes for its price. Freshness and purity of lemon and crunchy nashi pear are well toned by the texture and complexity of bottle maturity, lending bready, biscuity nuances and drawing out notes of white pepper and anise. The fine salt chalk minerality of the village is energised by crystalline acidity. It's quintessential Cuis, classic Gimonnet and fantastic value champagne. This was the single white champagne that I chose to serve at my 40th birthday party in 2015 (2008 base, from magnum).

PIERRE GIMONNET & FILS ROSÉ DE BLANCS 1ᴱᴿ CRU BRUT NV $$

94 points • 2012 BASE VINTAGE • DISGORGED SEPTEMBER 2014 • TASTED IN CUIS & BRISBANE

94% chardonnay; 48% Chouilly for fruitiness and elegance, 15% Cramant for plumpness, 10% Oger for masculine strength and spicy minerality, 22% Cuis for vivacity and freshness; Gastronome 2012 with 6% Bouzy pinot noir; aged 2 years on lees; 6.5g/L dosage; DIAM closure; 15,000 bottles

Gimonnet has toned his cracking and cleverly named rosé with an even smaller dose of pinot noir this year, not least because it costs him almost €15 a litre to buy red wine. This is blended with his vintage Gastronome cuvée — his blanc de blancs with the most body. Charged with 80% grand cru chardonnay, the result upholds its mantra of sustaining the mouthfeel, persistence and surging bath-salts chalk minerality of the Côte des Blancs with great accomplishment, touched with the palest salmon pink hue and the lightest reflections of white cherries and strawberry hull, lifted with pretty rose petal notes. Delightfully restrained and refreshingly tense, it's more about crystalline precision than flavour. One of the most refreshing apéritif rosés this year, serve it like a delicate blanc de blancs, not like a rosé.

OGER GRAND CRU PAR PIERRE GIMONNET & FILS BRUT NV $$

91 points • 2011 BASE VINTAGE • TASTED IN CUIS

Blend of three Oger chardonnay parcels; aged on lees 2-2.5 years; 6.5g/L dosage; 9000 bottles

Labelled 'Oger Grand Cru' (in large letters) 'by Pierre Gimonnet & Fils' (in fine print) because 'this is not the style of Gimonnet', Didier has found the southern Côte des Blancs character, smoky strength, graphite minerality and forward development of Oger difficult to reconcile with his northern blends. Hence a monocru cuvée by default. It's powerful, bold, spicy and intense, propelled by a grapefruit core, developing into patisserie and almond, with the subtle smokiness of the village. Its acidity is quite austere, heightened by a tight cage of earthy, chalky minerality, in spite of the evolution in its flavour profile, culminating in a long, dry finish. A characterful cuvée to soften for one more year in the cellar, then drink right away.

PIERRE GIMONNET & FILS CUVÉE GASTRONOME 1ᴱᴿ CRU BLANC DE BLANCS CUVÉE BRUT 2010 $$

92 points • DISGORGED JANUARY 2015 • TASTED IN CUIS

The aspiration of Gastronome is to present the spirit, elegance and freshness of a non-vintage, with structure and body. The fruity depth and approachability of Chouilly Mont Aigu provides the core, balanced with the power of Cramant and Oger, the freshness of Cuis and a 'petite mousse' of 4.5 atmospheres for creaminess. Tasted just two weeks after disgorgement, the 2010 meets the brief already, presenting an expressive and primary demeanour of peach, grapefruit, red cherry kernel and anise. Great acid line and lingering chalk mineral structure reinforce its primary poise.

Pierre Gimonnet & Fils Cuvée Gastronome 1ᴱᴿ Cru Blanc de Blancs Cuvée Brut 2009 $$

93 points • Disgorged September 2014 • Tasted in Cuis & Brisbane

39% Chouilly for fruit and elegance, 26% Cuis for vivacity and freshness, 20% Cramant for plumpness, 15% Oger for masculine strength and spicy minerality; 'petite mousse' of 4.5 atmospheres; 6.5g/L dosage; 22,000 bottles

Gimonnet admires the gentle, rich and approachable 2009 vintage as one of the best of the decade after 2002 and 2008. He's captured its spirit in generosity of golden delicious apple, yellow mirabelle plum and pear fruit that provide dimension and depth to the signature white citrus of the Côte des Blancs. Five years of ageing has brought considerable complexity of biscuity, honeyed maturity, accented with notes of ginger, nougat, anise and mixed spice. The finish draws out long, with signature salt-rich chalk mineral texture and the creamy mouthfeel of lees age. It's ready to drink now.

Pierre Gimonnet & Fils Cuvée Gastronome 1ᴱᴿ Cru Blanc de Blancs Cuvée Brut 2008 $$

95 points • Tasted in Sydney & Melbourne

43% Chouilly, 29% Cuis, 16% Oger, 7.5% Cramant, 4% Vertus; full malolactic fermentation; 'petite mousse' of 4.5 atmospheres; 7g/L dosage; 33,000 bottles

Gastronome 2008 is like stepping outside and inhaling a breath of brisk winter morning air, such is its youthful freshness and breathtaking delicacy. It's retained every nuance of its delightfully coiled focus in the two years since its release, with airy high notes of lemon blossom, white peach, white pepper and a rising note of almond nougat. A mouthful of shattering chalk minerality and unnerving texture articulates the voice of the northern Côtes des Blancs. Alongside 2002, 2008 is Gimonnet's standout vintage of the past decade, honing elegant refinement of the highest order. I've sealed it up in my cellar for another five years yet.

Pierre Gimonnet & Fils Cuvée Fleuron Brut 1ᴱᴿ Cru Blanc de Blancs 2009 $$

93 points • Tasted in Cuis

'Fleuron' means 'best of', created when there was only one non-vintage and one vintage wine in the house. Today it's Gimonnet's signature vintage cuvée, a blend of the best parcels from each village, boasting more than four-fifths grand cru Côte des Blancs, a preposterous proportion for a wine of this price. Gimonnet's goal here is to capture the taste of the domaine in a single blend, more about structure and focus than the immediacy of Gastronome. The 2009 meets the mandate in a very precise guise just before release, launched before the 'more strict' 2008. Lingering apple and pear fruit is backed by a creamy bead and fine chalk texture of mineral grip and character, providing structural precision.

PIERRE GIMONNET & FILS CUVÉE FLEURON BRUT 1ᴱᴿ CRU BLANC DE BLANCS 2006 $$

94 points • DISGORGED SEPTEMBER 2014 • TASTED IN CUIS & BRISBANE

39% Cramant, 36% Chouilly, 17% Cuis, 8% Oger; 6g/L dosage; 41,000 bottles

Gimonnet describes the 2006 season as uniting the minerality of 2004 with the clumsy richness and structure of 2005. It furnished a very complete Fleuron, permitting a higher proportion of Cramant. The result is an engaging assemblage that contrasts the juicy stone fruits of Cramant and the ginger and orange rind of Oger with the vivacity of white citrus and the spicy, toasty, biscuity complexity of bottle age. The accord is enthralling, with silky creamy, leesy texture, commanded by the elegant yet deep-set chalk minerality of Gimonnet, swooping into a finish of impressive line and length. It's evolved with exacting precision since its release two years ago, and is now ripe for drinking.

PIERRE GIMONNET & FILS EXTRA BRUT CUVÉE OENOPHILE 1ᴱᴿ CRU BLANC DE BLANCS NON DOSÉ 2008 $$

95 points • DISGORGED OCTOBER 2014 • TASTED IN CUIS & BRISBANE

Fleuron 2008 without dosage; 33.5% Cramant, 32.5% Chouilly, 22% Cuis, 10% Oger, 2% Vertus; aged 5 years on lees; zero dosage; 5000-10,000 bottles of the 50,000 of Fleuron 2008

Didier Gimonnet's sincerity is refreshing. 'I am not a lover of champagne without dosage, as dosage is part of the tradition of our region, and even 4–5g/L rounds out the wine. Wine without dosage is interesting when it's recently disgorged, but when I pull them out of the cellar 18 months later I always prefer the same wine with a little dosage to add complexity and balance.' Nonetheless, sales of his zero-dosage Oenophile are on the rise. This is not a dedicated blend, but chosen from the cellar each year according to which cuvée has the natural balance to stand best without dosage. Olivier Gimonnet considers this cuvée too young for zero dosage. I tasted it three times over six months and it got better every time. High-tensile definition contrasts depth of character in this exactingly crafted expression of an incredible vintage. Distinct oyster shell and sea breeze characters are present on the palate and — unusually for champagne — on the nose, its pronounced Côte des Blancs terroirs burst from the glass. There's all the unashamed grip and tension of grapefruit, lemon and distinctive ginger, too, defined by an incisive, steely acid line, contrasted cunningly with fine, creamy lees texture and a very fine bead. The result is a chiselled and highly sophisticated champagne, not for the uninitiated, but it will enthral oyster fanatics, and is certain to improve for a decade and beyond.

PIERRE GIMONNET & FILS SPECIAL CLUB BLANC DE BLANCS 2009 $$$

95 points • TASTED IN CUIS

Gimonnet's Special Club is a blend of the best of each vintage with the aspiration of creating an elegant style that's greater than the sum of its parts. It's built on old vines of 40–100 years of age, relying on Cramant for structure, balanced with the silkiness of Chouilly Mont Aigu and the definition of Cuis. The 2009 presents a grand contrast between the concentration and intensity of grapefruit, lemon, crunchy pear, anise and ginger, and the all-pervading chalk mineral presence and pose of the northern Côte des Blancs. It's gradually amassing biscuity lees complexity and textural mouthfeel. It will benefit from plenty more years to continue to build.

PIERRE GIMONNET & FILS SPECIAL CLUB GRANDS TERROIRS DE CHARDONNAY 2006 $$$

96 points • DISGORGED AUGUST 2014 • TASTED IN CUIS AND BRISBANE

65% Cramant for structure and minerality (almost half from vines over a century of age), 22.5% Chouilly for elegance (more than half from vines over 50 years); 12.5% Cuis for freshness; old vines of 40-90 years of age; aged on lees more than 7 years; 4.5g/L dosage; 15,000 bottles

Dynamic purity, bright youthfulness and focused definition belie its age. A masterfully crafted, seamless assemblage of apple and fig depth, undercut by the lemon and grapefruit definition of northern Côte des Blancs chardonnay, and gently brushed with nuances of maturity in roast almond, brioche, butterscotch and anise complexity. The finish follows a delightfully persistent acid line, with a creamy bead and frothing bath salts minerality that is at once prominent and at the same time gentle and silky. Wonderfully polished and harmonious now, this is an earlier maturing Special Club that will evolve beautifully over the next five years.

PIERRE GIMONNET & FILS SPECIAL CLUB MILLÉSIME DE COLLECTION BLANC DE BLANCS 2008 $$$

97 points • TASTED IN CUIS

57% Cramant, 29% Chouilly, 14% Cuis and a little Vertus

There is an inherent subjectivity in the pricing of wine that rarely, oh so rarely, sees a prestige cuvée of the utmost finesse and the most enduring stamina hit the ground at a jaw-droppingly affordable price. This is the best value sparkling wine I have tasted in the past five years. There you have it. The only thing with any hope of rivalling it is the 2002 vintage of the same cuvée. In a back-to-back shootout, my money is on the 2008. If you're after one wine to discover the marvels of old champagne, buy a case now, promise you won't touch a bottle for 10 years and keep one for at least 30. In its raw, youthful innocence, it's the epitome of introverted, tightly coiled restraint. Beguiling transparency of pure acid drive propels an incredible finish that splashes long and strong with frothy, salty chalk minerality. Brilliant white cherries and citrus ring out in clear peals like church bells to an undercurrent of the most subtle nuances of nougat and anise. A cuvée of effortless poise, unmitigated drive and breathtaking, scintillating, crystalline purity.

A 13th century church stands sentinel over the vines of Chavot-Courcourt, between the Côte des Blancs and the Vallée de la Marne.

The Champagne Guide

PIERRE PÉTERS

(Pee-yair Peh-tair)

8/10

26 RUE DES LOMBARDS 51190 LE MESNIL-SUR-OGER

www.champagne-peters.com

PROPRIÉTAIRE-RÉCOLTANT

Very few champagnes more eloquently articulate their terroirs than those of Pierre Péters. Many encounters with the young Rodolphe Péters, exploring the fruits of three decades, have left me mesmerised by the remarkable capacity of the chardonnay vine to extract the salty minerality of the Côte des Blancs' finest grand crus and preserve it in its wines for time eternal. This little estate, more than any other, has given me the realisation of another dimension to champagne, one in which minerality assumes a personality all of its own. And I have discovered Les Chétillons, the Le Montrachet of Le Mesnil-sur-Oger.

The Péters family has tended its vines in Le Mesnil-sur-Oger for six generations, and made its own champagne since 1919. Today, the estate is the custodian of just over 19 hectares of well-placed vineyards spanning more than 60 plots in nothing but the finest grand crus of the Côte des Blancs: Oger, Cramant, Avize and, especially, Le Mesnil-sur-Oger.

ATTENTIVE VINEYARD CARE

Rodolphe Péters took control in 2008, but has been helping his father with the blending since 1994, and knows his vines as well as anyone in Champagne. I quickly discovered just how well when I first met him in late July 2011, four weeks before harvest, when he was about to depart for holidays.

'Everyone says I am a crazy man taking holidays until August 19, but I wrote in my book in May that we would begin harvest on August 23, 24 or 25 and I have not revised this since.' A remarkable insight in one of Champagne's most erratic years, in which others extended their projections by as much as four weeks. 'That's crazy,' he says, 'but I spend more time than any of them in my land.'

Péters' vines are lavished some of the most attentive care in all of Champagne. 'I am reluctant to walk in the vines for fear of crushing the chalk,' he says. I have never heard this from any other grower, but there are few other places that enjoy such ready access to chalk, just 10–30 centimetres below the surface in Le Mesnil-sur-Oger. For this reason, deep roots to access the minerality of the chalk are not the priority for Péters.

'Minerality deep in the chalk is not accessible to the plants, but the interface between the topsoil and the deep soil is where the roots are able to find it,' he explains. The role of micro-organisms and worms in mixing the deeper soils and making this minerality available to the roots is crucial, and he works hard to keep the soil alive with organic material. Grass is

Chardonnay grapes ripe for harvest during vintage 2014.

INNOVATIVE VINIFICATION

To preserve character and maintain freshness, Péters has recently commissioned a new cuverie, to allow him to focus more attention on the finer details of vinification. 'You cannot keep your two feet still on the ground!' he grins. New computer-controlled presses provide more precise control and allow him to keep smaller blocks separate. He personally tastes the juice as it comes off the press, and makes the press cuts by taste, not by the authorised volumes.

Péters stringently protects the juice from oxygen at all times, and ferments in small stainless steel tanks under temperature control. His recent passion has been experimentation with different vessels for storing reserves. A new room with natural temperature control is dedicated to concrete tanks, which he describes as the 'opposite concept to eggs', designed to decrease movement inside and produce fresher, more earthy and less fruity wines. He has also introduced a large Croatian oak foudre, not for oak flavour, but for increasing the texture and creaminess of reserves. With two additional foudres commissioned in early 2015, he now maintains a balance of 50% reserves in stainless steel, 30% in concrete and 20% in foudres.

He considers structure and freshness to be derived from a combination of minerality, acidity and 'pleasant bitterness' from lees contact, and hence keeps wines on gross lees for long periods after alcoholic fermentation. The presence of gross lees keeps the wines fresh, permitting a low level of sulphur dioxide as a preservative.

FORGOTTEN RESERVE

Péters was concerned about the tendency of reserve wines to lose their freshness over time, necessitating use of the best wines as reserves, rather than in vintage and prestige cuvées. This led to a radical reinvention of the non-vintage blend in 1997. Every reserve wine, spanning 1988 to 1996, was blended into a modified solera which became the ongoing reserve, topped up every year, except in 1999 and 2003, which were kept separate to preserve the purity of the reserve. Kept on fine lees in a stainless steel tank at 13–14°C, the process of refreshing each year keeps the reserve lively. In 2011, a sample up to and including the 2010 vintage amazed me that a wine of such complexity could still retain such purity of grapefruit and preserved lemon.

This reserve solera embodies Péters' philosophy of keeping the memory of the estate alive in his Cuvée de Réserve Blanc de Blancs Brut NV, which claims a generous 40% reserve wine. His aim is to showcase the terroir of grand cru blanc de blancs, achieved with

planted in the mid-rows to provide competition for surface roots, forcing them down to the interface with the chalk.

He is adamant that he cannot keep his soils alive using certified organics. 'My philosophy is to follow the best procedures of the best of all philosophies,' he says, comparing the health of his vines with his own health, treating his allergies with a mixture of conventional medicine, vitamins and homeopathy. 'My first responsibility is to take care of my workers, the first people in contact with the chemicals I use — and by protecting them, I naturally take care of my customers, the vines and the environment.' His soil analyses have revealed high levels of copper sulphate from years of treatment by previous generations, detrimental to the soil, but permitted under biodynamics. He instead relies mainly on conventional treatments to protect his vineyards.

A natural balance is achieved in the vineyards, thanks to the regulating effect of old vines (averaging more than 30 years of age) and competition from grasses in the mid-rows. 'The fashion now is to say low yields and high maturity, but Champagne was not built on this — it was built on a comfortable balance of production to achieve the correct level of ripeness and acidity.' He considers pH, rather than acidity, to be the best indicator of balance, always aiming for low pH as a sign that he has captured the minerality of the soil.

The racy acidity of Péters' cuvées has traditionally been softened by full malolactic fermentation, but since Rodolphe has been in command, he has selectively blocked malolactic in some tanks.

60% of the current vintage from 50 plots spanning all of his Côte des Blancs estate vineyards, including Les Chétillons.

'The reserve is the key to the quality, making it easy to maintain consistency,' he says. It's a genius concept, and such is the class of the reserve that he has released it as its own cuvée, aptly named La Réserve Oubliée — 'the forgotten reserve'.

Cuvée de Réserve and Péters' vintage blend L'Esprit draw estate chardonnay from across the Côte des Blancs' grand crus. 'I like to think of each of the villages as a season, according to how they make me feel when I taste the vins clairs,' Péters explains.

'Le Mesnil-sur-Oger is the grey of winter for its sharp, stony minerality — austere and cold in character, with a cold sea breeze that gives the feeling of being in Normandy in winter.

'Oger is spring, for its elegant white flowers and white fruits, the first white sunlight and the first blossoms of the fruit trees. Its amphitheatre concentrates the sunlight and provides warmth. It is very soft and feminine, giving you the feeling of spring after a long winter.

'Avize is all about the character of summer, more orange than yellow in its full-bodied, showy and developed chardonnay of rich, ripe grapefruit, orange and mandarin. Its terroir is less chalky and more graphite in its structure.

'The south-east facing slope of Cramant is like the brown of fall, the perfect chardonnay, of similar profile to Le Mesnil, yet less cold. More lemony, with a creamy chalkiness and nuances reminiscent of vanilla, sweet spices, dried fruits and something dry, like dried flowers or cinnamon, that evokes autumn leaves falling before winter.

'I have parcels that really express each of these characters and I focus on these for my vintage blend. If a vintage expresses more summer and autumn, it is released as a vintage wine, but if it is more winter and spring I blend it as a non-vintage extra brut,' says Péters.

THE LE MONTRACHET OF LE MESNIL

Not far from the village itself, Les Chétillons is one of the finest sites for sparkling winegrowing in Le Mesnil-sur-Oger or, indeed, anywhere on earth. Here the chalk is never more than 10 centimetres from the surface, so the vines are effectively rooted in pure chalk. In slope and exposition, Péters describes it as perfect — not too much and not too little.

The family has nurtured three plots in these calcareous soils since 1930, with vines now an impressive 50 and 71 years old. Each has been vinified separately and blended to produce a single-vintage wine since 1971.

Péters speaks of the minerality of Les Chétillons as crushed oyster shells, sea salt, and flavours of the ocean that laid down the chalk millennia ago. 'If you taste a stone in the vineyard, it is salty,' he explains, and it is this that infuses the mineral texture in his wines.

The mesmerising minerality of this extraordinary site remains steadfast in every old vintage I have tasted, right back to 1985. Through changes of season and winemaker, flavours evolve, intensity builds and bubbles fade, but the minerality remains transfixed. 'It is a stake, it stays for a very long time,' he declares.

Such is the demand for Péters' wines that he is not able to offer every cuvée in every market. He is very concerned that his annual production of 160,000 bottles is no longer able to meet the demand of his loyal customers.

'I try my best to purchase more vineyards, but another two hectares is nothing in terms of increasing production. And it will cost €3 million.'

Le Mesnil-sur-Oger, the Côte des Blancs' most confident grand cru, and the source of some of Champagne's longest-lived chardonnay.

PIERRE PÉTERS CUVÉE DE RESERVE BLANC DE BLANCS BRUT NV $$

93 points • 2012 BASE VINTAGE • TASTED IN LE MESNIL-SUR-OGER
92 points • 2009 BASE VINTAGE • TASTED IN SYDNEY & MELBOURNE

60% current vintage, 40% reserve solera dating from 1988; grand cru Côte des Blancs; 7.5g/L dosage; DIAM closure

With all the theatrics of Péters' masterful reserve solera, this is a deeply layered cuvée with notes of mixed spice, mandarin and orange. The 2012 base captures the focus, energy and stature of grand cru Côte des Blancs in a riper and more approachable style. Chalk-focused minerality makes for a finely poised and long finish. The 2009 base has shed the ravishing, crystalline freshness of two years ago, softening into red apple and pear accents, with fine mineral texture.

PIERRE PÉTERS CUVÉE LA RÉSERVE OUBLIÉE BLANC DE BLANCS BRUT NV $$

96 points • 2008 BASE VINTAGE • DISGORGED JUNE 2014 • TASTED IN LE MESNIL-SUR-OGER

Perpetual reserve solera of 19 vintages spanning 1988 through 2008, missing only the inferior 1999 and 2003; stored 18 months on lees in tank before blending; 4g/L dosage from grape juice aged in a small barrel; DIAM closure

Few reserves can boast such ravishing integration, seamless internal harmony and sheer completeness, a credit to both the genius of this modified solera and the painstakingly tended vines that feed it. The contrast of eminent refinement and bewildering complexity is other-worldly, broadcasting lively freshness of lemon and grapefruit, set against a deeply layered backdrop of brioche and crème brûlée. Its richness is profound, held in focus by the formidable presence of salt chalk mineral structure. The brilliant crystalline purity of the exquisitely refreshing 2008 vintage makes for the best blend of this cuvée yet.

PIERRE PÉTERS CUVÉE MILLÉSIME L'ESPRIT BLANC DE BLANCS 2009 $$$

93 points • TASTED IN LE MESNIL-SUR-OGER

A blend of four vineyards, one each in Le Mesnil-sur-Oger, Oger, Avize and Cramant; 3.5g/L dosage

Rodolphe was concerned by the overripeness, low acidity and dried extract of 2009, yet he has controlled it well here. There's volume and richness, certainly, but its structure is not hard or bitter, leaving space for its chalk minerality to express itself confidently and gracefully, which keeps the finish fresh and lively. Ripe nectarine flavours and mixed spice define a creamy style.

Pierre Péters Cuvée Spéciale Blanc de Blancs Les Chétillons 2009 $$$

96 points • Tasted in Le Mesnil-sur-Oger

4.5g/L dosage; 7000 bottles

Rodolphe was worried by the ripe profile of the 2009 vins clairs, but they have since tightened into a pure and precise style. Pure lemon and white peach fruit are accented with the subtle warm-season notes of mandarin, making for a beautiful expression of a riper year. It's creamy and silky, yet focused, confident and fresh. Even a warmer vintage does little to perturb the bracing mineral fingerprint of this inimitable site, drawing unrelenting chalk minerality all the way to the horizon.

Pierre Péters Cuvée Spéciale Blanc de Blancs Les Chétillons 2008 $$$

99 points • Tasted in Le Mesnil-sur-Oger

6g/L dosage; 11,000 bottles

Les Chétillons articulates its mineral birthplace with greater precision than I have tasted anywhere in Champagne outside the thundering single vineyards of Krug itself, and no vintage expresses this more exhilaratingly than 2008. It is desperately youthful in its stark, pre-release state, transfixed in time like an ice man, yet every element is perfectly integrated, like a choral effect in which individual voices are lost. Concentrate hard and you'll hear soprano top notes of pure lemon blossom and glorious white fruits over alto whispers of the most elegant almond nougat. The mineral signature of Les Chétillons is crystalline, like ground glass, yet impeccably creamy and enticing, permeating the wine with chalky sea salt and oyster-shell notes that heave and froth with the waves of the ocean that created this remarkable place 55 million years ago. Its length is in another league, navigating undeterred for minutes, propelled by an acid line that shimmers like jet exhaust. Patience is in order, as Rodolphe may release the 2010 vintage first. The 2008 won't be ready to drink for at least 20 years, anyway. Whenever he chooses to release it, be sure to be first in line. I'll see you there.

Pierre Péters Cuvée Spéciale Blanc de Blancs Les Chétillons 2007 $$$

97 points • Tasted in Le Mesnil-sur-Oger

The 2007 was the first vintage in which Rodolphe was granted full control, and his first challenge came in holding back on harvesting after a cool summer. It proved to be the right decision, articulated most brilliantly in Les Chétillons. The result is a restrained, focused and introverted release, projecting an aura of gleaming white peach, grapefruit, fig and lemon zest presence. Minerality rises above its fruit, with its cool season infusing a silky chalk presence that hovers like a still morning mist over deep-set salty texture. It's magnificently coiled, with an outstanding line, gripping persistence and a surprising approachability from the outset, yet holds a seemingly limitless reserve of energy to thrust it upward for many years yet.

PIPER-HEIDSIECK

(Pee-per E-dseek)

6/10

12 ALLÉE DU VIGNOBLE 51000 REIMS

www.piper-heidsieck.com

I first visited Piper-Heidsieck 15 years ago, and left more than a little bemused by its Disney-like automated tour. Thank goodness it is no more. Piper-Heidsieck has come a long way since then, transformed by champagne genius Daniel Thibault from an austere non-malolactic to a more appealing malolactic style, relying on meunier to bring roundness to the blend, and now ascending again in both quality and price under Thibault's friend and offsider, talented chef de cave Régis Camus.

Piper-Heidsieck is made alongside the smaller Charles Heidsieck (page 91) in an impressive cuverie at Bezannes on the southern outskirts of Reims, using the same production methods, from essentially the same pool of vineyards and reserve wines.

Camus' efforts begin in the vineyards, in liaising with vignerons, some of whom have been supplying Piper for five generations. It is a sign of his close relationships with some of his growers that he is godfather to their children and invited to their weddings.

Camus was nervous to fill Thibault's big shoes after his untimely death in 2002, but determined to maintain his legacy in Charles Heidsieck and to take it further in revitalising Piper-Heidsieck. Since the mid-2000s, Charles and Piper have found their own separate lives in the selection of crus, styles and ages.

'It is all about the magic of the blend!' Camus explains. 'It is very important for me that the nuances of the wines speak so as to express the styles of the two different houses.' His goal for Piper is elegance, brightness and fruitiness, which he speaks of in terms of a floral register, a fruity register and a toasty register in each of the wines. 'I aim to evoke the first days of spring in Piper, with springtime flowers, sun, vegetal nuances, chlorophyll, fog and smoke.' The fruity register follows the floral register.

'Piper is all about apples, pears and citrus, like biting into a crunchy granny smith apple, with a nervousness, minerality and tension.' The vivacious, dynamic Piper style, with its lighter colour, is designed for warmer weather, to be poured at 6–8°C.

For Camus, the true measure of a house is the quality of its brut NV and he has worked hard to elevate Piper's Brut NV. In his frank and unpretentious manner he shares how much he had enjoyed Taittinger NV with friends recently.

'The NV wines are the real business for me,' he says. 'After that it's all about having fun! The vintage wines are the vacation photos of the season, signed by Piper or by Charles!'

Non-vintage wines are blends of all three champagne varieties. He uses pinot noir as the core of the blend, the 'vertebra' or 'DNA molecule'; chardonnay for its dynamic liveliness ('It's me on Saturday night!'); and meunier for its fruitiness and freshness, and because 'we particularly like its crunchiness'.

Reserve wines represent about half of the harvest, comprising a strong percentage of Charles, and Piper as little as 6% and as much as 18%. 'I want to see just how far certain wines will go,' Camus explains. Most of his reserves are chardonnay and pinot noir, but he is proud to show off a tank of 2004 meunier from Verneuil of stunning freshness and vivacity. 'This breaks the absurd impression that meunier can't age!' Reserve wines are stored in 300–500hL stainless steel tanks to guard their freshness, 'so we can use them whenever they're needed, frozen in time like an ice man!'

Fermentation and maturation are performed exclusively in stainless steel. 'The only wood here is the boardwalk above the tanks!' he quips. The wines are finished with a broad sweep of full dosage of 11g/L to balance the vivacity, though this can look a little obvious. These are generous levels of dosage for modern Champagne, but they do tend to integrate neatly into the wines.

Sales of 4.4 million bottles make Piper Champagne's eighth-largest house, and third-largest exporter. Vivacity and tenacity are the goals for its bright, fruity style.

PIPER-HEIDSIECK CUVÉE BRUT NV $

91 points • 2010 BASE VINTAGE • TASTED IN BEZANNES, BRISBANE, SYDNEY, MELBOURNE & PERTH

55% pinot noir, 25% meunier, 20% chardonnay; 10-15% reserves; 100 villages; matured 2-3 years on lees; 11g/L dosage

Fresh, lively, fruity and precise, Piper is reliable champagne at a great price, making it perfect for weddings, parties, anything. Such is its consistency that there is no dip for the 2010 base, which Camus describes as 'not a great vintage'. It's laced with fresh, fruity red apple and lemon zest, becoming patisserie, fig, mixed spice and roast nuts. A very subtle touch of dry, dusty extract is well countered by honeyed dosage, making this a style to tuck into in its youthful fruitiness. Piper has fulfilled its mandate to grow this cuvée into a more serious, textural and complex offering, representing great value for money.

PIPER-HEIDSIECK ESSENTIEL CUVÉE BRUT NV $$

94 points • 2008 BASE VINTAGE • DISGORGED MARCH 2013 • TASTED IN BEZANNES & BRISBANE

11% reserve; aged 4 years on lees; 7g/L dosage

Some years ago, while tasting different lots of the Brut NV blend, one lot stood out as particularly special. Based on the splendid 2008 vintage, it was left in the cellar for an additional year and bottled as a new, more serious extension of the label. The back label refreshingly features back vintage, reserves, dosage and bottling and disgorgement dates. This cuvée commands a whole new level of respect, because never has Piper-Heidsieck Brut seen such heights. It's a very different shape to the Brut NV, charged with the energy, vivacity and pristine acid line of 2008, well framed in the toasty, honeyed, caramelised intrigue of bottle age. It's creamy and textured and tangy all at the same time, with a long finish and magnificent acid spine. It's bang on for drinking right away, but won't fade anytime soon.

PIPER-HEIDSIECK ROSÉ SAUVAGE NV $$

92 points • TASTED IN BEZANNES & BRISBANE

Piper-Heidsieck Cuvée Brut with 20% pinot noir red wine; 55% pinot noir, 25% meunier, 20% chardonnay; 15% reserve wines; 11g/L dosage

The house goes a little far in describing this as 'the most extravagant and audacious rosé in the world' but, in its full, unabashed crimson red hue, it is certainly at the deep end of the champagne rosé pool. In colour, palate grip, concentration and food-matching versatility, it's best considered part-way between champagne rosé and red Burgundy, and should be served from big red wine glasses, as they do at the house. Distinctive, inimitable, potent and rustic, this is a champagne rosé with a personality all of its own. There's creaming soda here, sarsaparilla, too, blood orange, Redskins and tangelos and tamarillos. True to its fluoro-pink label, it's ready for loud parties. For all its flamboyance, it's got length, tight acid line, well-integrated dosage and finely textured tannin grip, just to prove it has a serious side, too.

PIPER-HEIDSIECK CUVÉE SUBLIME DEMI-SEC NV $$

90 points • TASTED IN BRISBANE

This cuvée is clean and pristine, which may sound trite, but this in itself immediately places it among the best demi-secs in Champagne. Succulent white stone fruits are evolving into a place of butter and roast nut character, defined by honey both in sweetness and in flavour. For a sweet champagne, this is a top choice, and the best I have seen this cuvée.

PIPER-HEIDSIECK VINTAGE BRUT 2006 $$

92 points • TASTED IN BEZANNES, SYDNEY, MELBOURNE & BRISBANE

51% chardonnay, 49% pinot noir from 17 premier and grand crus; aged more than 6 years on lees; 11g/L dosage

The hot summer of 2006 yielded muscular pinot noir ('too strong' for Camus) and fruity chardonnay, producing a luscious, rounded, simple and fruity Piper that I tipped two years ago as a vintage to drink young and fresh. I've tasted it on four or five occasions since and it peaked in early 2014, showcasing its veritable fruit cart of red apple, pear and lemon zest. The cart has since predictably toppled into a place of toasted brioche, butterscotch, roast almonds and caramel, but it holds poise and definition in its acid line, making for a zesty finish that upholds finely balanced mineral texture. The party isn't over yet.

The Champagne Guide

PIPER-HEIDSIECK RARE MILLESIME 2002 $$$$

96 points • TASTED IN BEZANNES, MELBOURNE & BRISBANE

70% chardonnay from Avize, Vertus and the Montagne de Reims; 30% pinot noir from Aÿ; 11g/L dosage

This is indeed rare, the eighth vintage since 1976, and it keeps on coming, still current in the market four years after release. And, my goodness, it looks more and more remarkable with each passing year. It still glows in elegantly medium straw hues, impressively bright in hue for 13 years of age. An enticing note of gunflint reduction leads out, drawing with it a wonderfully complex yet compact and elegant array of succulent yellow stone fruit characters. The seamless, creamy, silky integration that it has attained in the years since its release is captivating, seamlessly melding a rising complexity of wood smoke and buttered toast. Its chalk minerality is fine, salty and pronounced, uniting the finesse of the Côte des Blancs with the firmer definition of the Montagne. It epitomises the gentle, textural minerality, harmonious personality and magnificent persistence of chardonnay in this epic vintage. I have long admired Rare 2002, but never have I been more captivated by the place of calm satisfaction to which it has evolved today. There is harmony here, and peace, like the gentle misty haze before dawn. A place that makes you slow down, and begs you to stay.

PIPER-HEIDSIECK RARE MILLESIME 1998 $$$$$

97 points • TASTED IN BRISBANE FROM MAGNUM

60% chardonnay, 40% pinot noir; bottled only in magnums

The endurance of the great 1998 season is proclaimed in large format. In its glowing straw radiance, this vintage has evolved significantly from its outlook of two years ago, to a calmer and more contemplative place of tertiary maturity, settling into all the inviting, cosy comfort of wood smouldering in a warm hearth, of toffee simmering on the stove, of the spiciest and most flavoursome dried pears conceivable, and of succulent yellow stone fruits lavished with vanilla custard. It's creamy and deeply textured, infused with magnificent strokes of large-format lees age, sustained by a wonderful line of acidity that holds its poise and freshness, even at 17 years of age. It has attained its ravishing best and will hold it for some years yet.

A panorama towards Avenay-Val-d'Or, from the high village of Mutigny behind Aÿ, at the change of seasons near the close of vintage 2014.

POL ROGER

(Pol Roh-zheh)

9/10

1 RUE WINSTON CHURCHILL 51200 ÉPERNAY

www.polroger.com

CHAMPAGNE

POL ROGER

Stepping into Pol Roger's production facility in Épernay is like entering a different world. 'We call this the kitchen,' introduced managing director Laurent d'Harcourt. This was not like any kitchen I'd ever seen. Immaculately polished stainless steel tanks perfectly reflected shiny white tiles and snow-white surfaces. It was as if we were entering a brain surgery unit or a NASA assembly room, and I had an uneasy feeling that I might be asked to don a body suit, lest I contaminate this precision machine with a single molecule of foreign material. I have been buying Pol Roger for decades, but it was not until that moment that everything about this celestial estate suddenly snapped into perfect focus. The champagnes that emerge from this extraterrestrial building are as desperately precise, intricately delicate and flawlessly pristine as its polished interior, revealing the manifesto that defines all that lies within. And Pol Roger is on the rise.

It hasn't always been this way. The disorganised regime of the 1990s was 'a mess', according to d'Harcourt. The pace of transformation amazes me every time I visit Pol Roger. Since chef de cave Dominique Petit joined the company in 1999, after 24 years at Krug, more than €15 million has been invested in upgrading the winemaking facilities alone.

And it never seems to stop. The stainless steel fermentation space was updated in 2001, 2004, 2008, 2010 and 2011, and now provides full capacity to vinify every parcel separately. New cold-settling and fermentation halls were installed in 2011, alongside six new tiny 2200-litre tanks. The cellar was extended, and the cellar floors concreted to reduce vibrations from electric vehicles. More consistent and more precise disgorgement and dosage machines were also installed. In 2013, the old concrete tanks were refreshed, in 2014 a new cuverie for reserve wines was constructed, and in early 2015 a grand new reception room completed. Even the address has changed, after the street was renamed. Pol Roger now proudly stands at 1 Rue Winston Churchill.

Pol Roger's investment is not to increase production, but to improve quality and consistency. Having already grown from 1.5 million to 1.8 million bottles annually, there is no immediate plan to increase further.

'Every year for the past 14 years we have seen results in the consistency of the wines from the work we are doing in the winery,' d'Harcourt explains. 'We have made a solid investment to ensure the family house remains secure in the family's hands into the 21st century.'

GRASS ROOTS RELATIONSHIPS

In 2014, I was privileged to an even deeper insight into the internal workings of this incredible company. Laurent d'Harcourt granted my request to shadow him for a full day mid-harvest, and the moment I sat down in his car as we set off in the morning, I was surprised by what I discovered. There on his passenger seat was the full harvest data of the company, which he was personally tracking and updating daily. 'I have more than 70 presses where our growers and our own vineyards press, and I spend all of harvest doing miles and miles visiting them,' he revealed. And these are not just flippant visits. 'Half of my visits are a breakfast, lunch or dinner. And sometimes two breakfasts a day!' Now *there's* a managing director who's engaged with the grass roots of his company. 'We have partnerships,' he explains, 'and we work with families for generation after generation.' It's dedication like this that sets Pol Roger apart.

Our first stop was Diebolt-Vallois (see page 114), one of the finest growers in Cramant, where I witnessed some of the cleanest fruit I saw going into any press that vintage. Such is the demand for this famous grower that it sells its own wines on allocation, and yet it proudly supplies Pol Roger (as does Pierre Gimonnet in the next village, who is in the same situation). More than this, such is the pride of the Diebolt family in the partnership that many of its workers were proudly wearing Pol Roger t-shirts.

Pol Roger provides for an impressive 51% of its production from 90 hectares of estate vines. 'These holdings allow us to be more consistent over the long term,' clarifies d'Harcourt. The remainder is sourced exclusively from the Marne, and most importantly from Épernay and Chouilly, from long-term contracts under an arrangement that pays bonuses for quality. 'We are Pol Roger, we are not really growers,' d'Harcourt admits. 'Many of the growers from whom we source also care for vineyards that we own ourselves. They cultivate our vineyards, we press all the fruit and then give a portion back to them as payment.'

Last year, Pol Roger renewed its grower contracts to strengthen its sourcing in some grand crus, to enhance its capacity to make its Blanc de Blancs, Vintage and Sir Winston Churchill cuvées. The house already produces a higher proportion of vintage wines than virtually any other, and this only bolsters its position.

EXACTING PRECISION

The rise of Pol Roger is very much a credit to the exacting precision of Dominique Petit, who transformed a disorganised regime with an attention to detail learnt at Krug. The house preference for stainless steel over concrete and oak barrels rests on judicious temperature control of its musts during clarification and vinification. Musts undergo a double cold-settling process at just 5°C, producing the most pristine juice — a process that Petit's predecessor, James Coffinet, brought to Pol Roger from Billecart-Salmon. Held below 18°C, a cool primary fermentation is drawn out over 15 days, maintaining fruit freshness and aromatic definition.

Secondary fermentation is likewise cool, thanks to Pol Roger's 7.5 kilometres of cellars, which are among the coolest (9–11°C) and deepest (up to 33 metres) in Épernay. Most of the bottles rest in the deepest parts of the cellar. This slow fermentation produces wines of great finesse, fine effervescence and enduring longevity. 'Greater precision in the first and second fermentations have enabled a trend towards lower dosage,' explains d'Harcourt. The house tests dosages between 6g/L and 9g/L, and has currently settled around 8g/L.

Everything in the cellar is done by hand by a team of no more than 10. Pol Roger boasts four of the remaining 15 riddlers still working in Champagne. Each turning 50,000–60,000 bottles a day, it takes 4–5 weeks to riddle each bottle. Every bottle is stacked in the cellar by hand, including every non-vintage wine — a painstaking process for a company with an incredible 9.5 million bottles in its care. 'Our neighbours think we are strange with such a huge inventory!' d'Harcourt exclaims.

With such a regime of excellence in the vineyard and winery, under the ownership of the same family since the house was founded in 1849, Pol Roger's success is no surprise. 'We have been selling champagne in all of our markets under allocation in recent years,' d'Harcourt reveals. 'We could sell two or three times the volume in the UK, but we don't want to be too dependent on one market. We've been telling some markets to stop selling, particularly Blanc de Blancs and Sir Winston Churchill, because we don't have enough to send! We could increase our size, but we would lose our soul.'

That's a line you don't often hear from any medium-sized wine company in the current climate. And with ever-improving facilities every time I visit, this company is poised for even greater things to come.

It certainly is a different world at Pol Roger.

Pol Roger Brut Réserve NV $$

94 points • 2009 base vintage • Mid-2014 disgorgement • Tasted in Épernay, Sydney, Melbourne, Perth & Brisbane
93 points • 2008 base vintage • Tasted in Sydney & Melbourne

A blend of the three champagne varieties in roughly equal proportions; 25% reserve wines; 150 parcels from 30 crus; 42-54 months on lees in bottle (previously 36-48); 9-10g/L dosage; 1.3-1.4 million bottles; bottle code indicates packaging date, with the first digit denoting the year, and next three digits the day of that year

Pol Roger's infamous 'White Foil' is an attractive and refreshing apéritif, and the 2009 base has transcended its season and delivered the freshest, purest expression of this cuvée I can remember — the ultimate validation of 15 years of winery upgrades. On first release, it sang with all the youthful jubilation of lemon zest, crunchy apple and pear, harmonising with finely honed chalk minerality. Now, towards the end of its release, it is still every bit as impressive, showing its maturity in toasted marshmallow, wild honey and nutmeg flavours and a creamy mouthfeel. The new-found palate line and persistence in this cuvée is singly the most laudable achievement of the new Pol Roger.

Pol Roger Pure Extra Brut NV $$

94 points • 2010 base vintage • Tasted in Épernay, Brisbane, Sydney, Melbourne & Perth

The 3 varieties in roughly equal balance; a different blend to Brut Réserve; more floral and less acidic; zero dosage

This is as fine as I have ever seen Pure, a masterfully crafted and spotlessly pristine zero-dosage. It's the quintessential apéritif, as crystal clear as a mountain stream, darting with lemon blossom, lemon zest and granny smith apples, beautifully contrasting the allure of toasted brioche, anise, honey and gingernut biscuits. A shard of taut acidity meets expressive fine, salt-rich chalk minerality, holding the finish in bone-dry tension and razor-aligned precision.

Pol Roger Blanc de Blancs Brut 2008 $$$

96 points • Disgorged December 2014 • Tasted in Épernay

100% Côte des Blancs grand crus: Oiry, Chouilly, Cramant, Avize and Oger; full malolactic fermentation; 9g/L dosage

Pol Roger's success with Blanc de Blancs has overtaken it: the cuvée has been over-allocated and the house has made the call to release this vintage after less than six years on lees (the 2006 had eight years and the 2002 had nine). This is a shame for a vintage as long-lived as 2008, but don't let this slow you down — only you must promise that under no circumstances will you pop a bottle before 2018. It will not be until at least 2028 that it finally unravels to reveal its full glory. Right now, it's the epitome of coiled tension, delicately setting lemon zest, white pepper, marzipan and wonderful struck-flint reduction against a dizzying shard of pure acidity. An undercurrent of frothing, salty minerality glistens brilliantly as the most striking high note of this incredible season. It's scintillating, crystalline and thrilling.

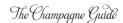

Pol Roger Blanc de Blancs Brut 2006 $$$

95 points • DISGORGED DECEMBER 2014 • TASTED IN ÉPERNAY

Aged 8 years on lees; 8g/L dosage

The approachable and round 2006 season has yielded just a small production of this cuvée, the vintage to drink while the 2008 rests in the cellar. It unites succulent white peach and honeyed richness, in a soft and immediate style, yet contrasting beautifully with classic Pol lemon blossom freshness. Ginger and honey-biscuit maturity is emerging, kept well under control by a very linear acid line, classic Côte des Blancs salt minerality and grand persistence.

Pol Roger Blanc de Blancs Brut 2004 $$$

96 points • DISGORGED EARLY 2014 • TASTED IN ÉPERNAY, BRISBANE, SYDNEY, MELBOURNE & PERTH

For a house once led by pinot noir, Pol Roger is increasingly focusing on chardonnay in its vintage wines, and recent vintages of its Blanc de Blancs demonstrate why. Testimony to the molecular precision of Pol Roger's exacting regime, the propensity of this cuvée to age is astonishing, and the past few vintages seem to escalate every time I come back to them. The 2004 is a vintage that oozes character and intensity, yet upholds the laudable vivacity and impeccable poise of the house. At 11 years of age it's building in layers of bottle-aged complexity and growing in fruit stature, evolving to an engaging and attention-grabbing place of grilled pineapple, poached pear, nutmeg, burnt butter and nougat. It washes with the softly frothy salt minerality of grand cru Côte des Blancs, carrying dynamic energy and freshness through a long, creamy finish. It's magnificent now, and will power on for some years yet.

Pol Roger Brut Vintage 2006 $$$

94 points • DISGORGED DECEMBER 2014 • TASTED IN ÉPERNAY

60% pinot, 40% chard; from 20 grand & premier crus in the Montagne de Reims & Côte des Blancs; full malolactic

The sublime 2002 and 2004 were tough acts to follow, and here comes the vintage to drink while they both wait in the wings. The warm-season 2006 is already deeper in hue, loaded with a fanfare unexpected for Pol Roger: tropical fruits, passionfruit, red apples and succulent nectarines, becoming vanilla cream and almond brioche. The precision of the house comes to the rescue in prominent chalk mineral structure and persistent lemony acidity.

Pol Roger Brut Vintage 2004 $$$

96 points • TASTED IN ÉPERNAY, BRISBANE, SYDNEY, MELBOURNE & PERTH

60% pinot noir, 40% chardonnay; aged at least 8 years on lees

A classic Pol vintage, without quite the theatrics of 2002, yet with an effortless purity, inherent energy and drive all its own. There's a calm refinement to 2004, expressed impeccably in an even accord between pinot's lively red cherry and wild strawberry fruits, and chardonnay's zest and lemon sherbet. The slow-motion ageing of Pol Roger's cold cellars is evident in this youthful vintage, and only recently has it begun to gently declare secondary complexity of honey and butter on toast and vanilla nougat. Magnificent poise of scintillating, crystalline minerality is seamlessly entwined with the creamy silkiness of long lees age. Another great vintage in the distinguished lineage of Pol Roger, with the tension and conviction to live for years yet.

Pol Roger Brut Rosé 2006 $$$

95 points • Tasted in Épernay, Sydney, Melbourne & Brisbane

The same base as Brut Vintage, with around 15% Montagne de Reims pinot noir red wine, purchased by the company 'because we are not good at vinifying red wine ourselves'; 60% pinot noir, 40% chardonnay; from 20 grand cru and premier cru villages in the Montagne de Reims and Côte des Blancs; full malolactic fermentation

Another beautifully graceful Pol Roger Rosé of medium salmon hue, this is a vintage that projects elegant focus of pretty wild strawberry and red cherry fruit and an impression of tamarillo, backed with toasty, savoury, roast nut complexity. With tannins so fine they're virtually invisible, it's softly mineral and coasts with excellent line, length and body. Vibrant acid poise is perfectly integrated with subtle dosage.

Pol Roger Brut Rosé 2004 $$$

95 points • Tasted in Sydney & Melbourne

65% pinot noir, 35% chardonnay from grand cru and premier cru vineyards of the Montagne de Reims and Côte des Blancs; 15% pinot noir red wine; aged 7 years on lees; 9g/L dosage

The most exuberant and vinous Pol Rosé of recent times, this is a change of pace after the slender catwalk curves of 2002 and the elegant finesse of 2000. For all its enthusiasm of redcurrants, blood orange and pink pepper, it has remained exactingly true to the purity, finesse and elegance of Pol Roger. Its full crimson hue has developed a copper tint since its release two years ago, but it has lost nothing of its intrigue of long-lingering plum pudding, mulled-wine spice and smouldering embers. Fine, well-controlled phenolics mesh seamlessly with fine chalk mineral structure.

Pol Roger Cuvée Sir Winston Churchill 2004 $$$$$

98 points • Disgorged November 2014 • Tasted in Épernay

Predominantly pinot noir, with some chardonnay, all from grand cru vineyards under vine at the time of Churchill; cold settled at 6°C; fermented below 18°C; full malolactic fermentation; secondary fermentation in the lowest part of the cellars (9°C); aged almost 10 years on lees

The blend of Sir Winston Churchill is a closely guarded secret. I ask d'Harcourt every time we taste a new vintage. 'I have not been drunk enough yet to tell you!' he replies. I'll keep working on it. Elusive details aside, Sir Winston is looking particularly dignified and refined in 2004, with a surprisingly primary, youthful air, yet all the understated poise of classic Sir Winston demeanour. It leads with the rhythm of pinot noir in red cherry and strawberry fruit, even a hint of musk, backed by the citrus fruits of chardonnay. Entrancing freshness is reinforced in subtle wafts of struck flint and grilled toast reduction, cascading into a torrent of impeccably refined acidity, swirling into a river of minerality that flows deep and swift all the way to the distant horizon. Effortless grace and youthful vigour lurk under that distinguished exterior.

The Champagne Guide

Pol Roger Cuvée Sir Winston Churchill 2002 $$$$$

99 points • Tasted in Épernay, Brisbane, Sydney & Melbourne
As for the 2004

The 2002 is the most ethereal Sir Winston since 1996, epitomising that elusive paradox of mesmerising persistence, spiralling minerality and dizzying longevity while upholding understated elegance at every moment. At 13 years of age its refinement and coiled purity are something to behold, gracefully volunteering pristine, gentle white citrus, yellow stone fruits, anise and struck flint, ever so slightly suggesting the brioche, butter and honey of bottle maturity. Chalky minerality rises like a tidal wave above it all, ultra-fine, chalk-exact and seamlessly integrated. There's a peacefulness, a contentedness and an inviting harmony to this wine, like the silence of a cosmic skyscape late on a mid-summer's night. To encounter it is to experience the soul-stirring and disarmingly unsettling sensation of confronting a thing of profound beauty.

Pol Roger Cuvée Sir Winston Churchill 2000 $$$$$

97 points • Tasted in Sydney & Melbourne

Sir Winston transcends the soft immediacy of 2000 in an elegant and understated demeanour of honed focus, silky refinement and delicate reductive character. Magnificent complexity is rising as the yellow-fruited lusciousness of the season begins to uncurl, ever so slowly gaining nutty, buttery complexity to the rhythm of 15 years of age. Propelled by attentive acid control and an undercurrent of soft, lingering chalk mineral texture, this is a vintage that has retained remarkable poise and freshness, with all the integrity to hold for many years yet.

Pol Roger Cuvée Sir Winston Churchill 1999 $$$$$

96 points • Tasted in Sydney & Melbourne

The 1999 has been a Sir Winston of awesome power from the outset, and it's predictable that this warm vintage would be one of the earlier-developing seasons of the modern era. It's ripe to drink right away, a creamy and luscious style of white Christmas cake, honey and mixed spice. It's generous, silky and creamy, yet retains balanced poise on a never-ending-story finish.

Pol Roger Cuvée Sir Winston Churchill 1996 $$$$$

99 points • Tasted in Sydney & Melbourne

A towering monument to the greatest and most enduring vintage of the 1990s, Sir Winston is a grand juxtaposition of cavernous complexity and authoritative acidity. Reverberating presence, looming intensity and the resonating tertiary complexity of green olives and smoky hearth are intricately juxtaposed with a heightened acid line that lingers and splashes long and strong. It's attained an enchanting pinnacle in its journey, but such is its startling core of energy, who can say what surprises may yet be in store?

ROGER COULON

(Roh-zheh Coo-loh)

5/10

12 RUE DE LA VIGNE DU ROY 51390 VRIGNY

www.champagne-coulon.com

Terroir is not only about the earth, but about the people who manage it,' upholds Eric Coulon, whose highest ideal is to communicate the expression of his terroir, with an intuitive approach according to the season. 'I don't manage the year, the year manages the champagne!' Eric and his wife Isabelle are the eighth generation of winemakers in their family, and practise an almost biodynamic approach — no small feat across more than 80 plots, spanning five villages of the Petit Montagne, Chouilly and Villers-Allerand. Planted to 40% meunier, 30% pinot noir and 30% chardonnay, vines date from 1924, with an impressive average of 38 years of age. Finesse and elegance are the aspiration, chaptalisation is only practised when necessary, and a low pressure of 4.5 atmospheres is used instead of the usual six. Parcels are increasingly fermented in oak when the season is up to it. These are gentle and approachable cuvées of character.

ROGER COULON LES CÔTEAUX DE VALLIER CUVÉE HÉRITAGE NV $$$

94 points • 2003 BASE VINTAGE • TASTED IN MELBOURNE

Single-plot Vrigny; 80% chardonnay, 20% pinot noir; chardonnay aged in barrels on lees for 18 months; 2002 reserves; aged 10 years on lees; 3g/L dosage

Roger Coulon lost his father when he was 14, and so learnt his craft from his grandfather; the century-old heritage of that craft is upheld in this cuvée. It captures the ripeness and concentration of 2003, and counters it confidently with the energy and dynamism of 2002, producing a powerfully exotic wine of grilled pineapple, fig, star fruit, spice and preserved lemon. It finishes with admirable definition of taut lime and lemon, fennel, a creamy bead, and long, lingering salt minerality. Drink now.

Ruinart

(Roo-ee-nar)

7/10

4 Rue des Crayères 51100 Reims

www.ruinart.com

THE FIRST ESTABLISHED
CHAMPAGNE HOUSE

réderic Panaïotis grew up between his grandparents' chardonnay vines in Champagne, and the variety remains close to his heart, making him very much at home as chef de cave at Ruinart since 2007. The longest-established champagne house of all has an affinity with chardonnay's freshness, finesse and elegance, and all of its finest cuvées lead with this variety, even its prestige rosé. Without the might of Moët & Chandon, the brand impact of Veuve Clicquot or the cachet of Krug, Ruinart lurks as the low-profile member of the Louis Vuitton–Moët Hennessy family. On Reim's famed Rue de Crayères, its premises hide behind the grand street presence of Pommery and Veuve Clicquot. This is just as Panaïotis would have it. 'In France we have a saying, if you live underground, you live happy!' he says. But on its performance, Ruinart has no need to lie low. Its cuvées are most pure and pitch-perfect, with NV cuvées dipping just a little this year in the wake of the ill-tempered 2011 vintage.

Champagne is planted to just 28% chardonnay, making this the rarest of the region's three key varieties, and the hardest to source. Ruinart owns just 10% of its vineyards, including longstanding resources of 15 hectares of chardonnay in the grand crus of Sillery and Puisieulx on the eastern slopes of the Montagne de Reims, providing a richer and rounder style than the Côte des Blancs.

Long-term contracts with growers form the vast bulk of Ruinart's supplies, supplemented in recent times through vineyards acquired from Lanson and Joseph Perrier. This has enabled the house to increase its annual production from 1.4 million to 2.5–3 million bottles over the past two decades. 'Ruinart is in demand, so I'm getting all the chardonnay I can find!' Panaïotis exclaims. Annual growth today is under 5%.

To maintain the aromatic freshness and elegance of its fruit, the Ruinart house style is decisively reductive. 'We hate oxygen!' he declares, describing his approach as the antithesis of Bollinger and Krug. A pneumatic press is used instead of a traditional champagne press, to guard the juice against oxidation, and inert nitrogen gas protects the wine at every stage of production. Vinification takes place only in stainless steel. 'We have absolutely no need of oak in any of our wines,' Panaïotis states.

Ruinart's cuvées often carry flattering hints of struck flint or gunpowder, remnants of reductive winemaking. 'My goal is to take reduction even further!' proclaims Panaïotis. 'The stinky white Burgundy thing, I just love it! Like Domaine Roulot, but they use oak. The question is how to do it without oak!'

To soften the austerity of young chardonnay, all cuvées undergo full malolactic fermentation, and non-vintage wines are balanced using respectable quantities of reserve wines. This makes for a style that permits refreshingly low dosages, declining admirably over recent years. The dosage is tweaked for successive disgorgements of Ruinart's prestige Dom Ruinart cuvée, typically lowering as the wine ages.

'For me, it's not a matter of numbers, but of balance,' Panaïotis explains.

Ruinart's distinctive rounded bottles make riddling challenging, and the house relies exclusively on gyropalettes, which Panaïotis claims give a far better result. The clear glass of these bottles renders the wine susceptible to lightstruck degradation, making it vital to store them in the dark.

Ruinart has occupied its premises in Reims since 1768, and was the first in Champagne to use the 3rd-century Roman crayères (chalk mines) under the city to age its champagnes.

Its location on top of the hill makes its eight kilometres of cellars some of the deepest and most spectacular in the region, plunging to depths of up to 38 metres. These are the only cellars in Champagne classified as a national monument — a distinguished home for such graceful champagnes.

Chardonnay, the rarest of Champagne's three key varieties, and the mainstay of Ruinart.

Ruinart Blanc de Blancs Brut NV $$$

94 points • 2011 base vintage with 2010 and 2009 reserves • Disgorged May 2014 • Tasted in Brisbane

93 points • 2009 base vintage • Tasted in Sydney, Melbourne, Perth & Yarra Valley

A blend of 20-25 crus, mostly premier crus from Côte des Blancs and Montagne de Reims, with parcels from Sézanne, Vitry and the Massif de Saint-Thierry for approachability and maturity; 25% reserves; full malolactic fermentation; aged 24-28 months on lees; 9/L dosage

Panaïotis has been very clever in the 2011 vintage. There's power and intensity here that tactically furnishes a silky mouthfeel, serving to smooth out the structural firmness of this difficult vintage. He has constructed it around a core of Montagne de Reims chardonnay of rich, succulent yellow summer fruits and — unexpectedly but flatteringly — an intense spicy personality of distinct fresh liquorice and gingernut biscuits, meshing seamlessly with the grip of preserved lemon. A Ruinart of body and flesh, strategically deploying Montagne de Reims chardonnay to give a mid-palate fleshiness reminiscent of the body of pinot noir, which creates a more extroverted Ruinart of earlier-drinking appeal, endearing in its own characterful way. The 2009 has dipped a little from the vivid electricity of its release two years ago.

R DE RUINART BRUT NV $$

91 points • BASE VINTAGE 2011 • DISGORGED JULY 2014 • TASTED IN BRISBANE

51% pinot noir, 9% meunier, 40% chardonnay; a blend of around 50 different crus across Champagne, though little Aube; reserves from 2010 and 2009; full malolactic fermentation; 9g/L dosage; 60% of the production of the house, hence more than 1.5 million bottles

After Panaïotis joined Ruinart, he recalls that 'it took a couple of years to figure out what was going on, and 2009 was the first year when I said, "Right, we can now start to do things! I don't think there's much I can do with the blanc de blancs or the rosé, but I can do things with R de Ruinart!"' His energy continues, pulling a noble result out of the early, wet and rot-plagued 2011 season. Pinot noir declares its lead in generous red apple, red cherry and bitter grapefruit, lingering with spicy anise, ginger and a hint of gun-flint reduction. This is a characterful R de Ruinart that unites fruit integrity with the biscuity complexity of bottle age. The 2011 season leaves its mark in a subtle, dusty, astringent grip on the finish, but the fruit has the intensity and perseverance to handle it.

RUINART BRUT ROSÉ NV $$$

91 points • 2011 BASE VINTAGE • DISGORGED APRIL 2014 • TASTED IN BRISBANE

20-25% reserves from 2010 and 2009; 45% chardonnay from the Côte des Blancs and Montagne de Reims, 36% pinot noir from the Montagne de Reims and Vallée de la Marne; 19% pinot noir red wine, with a short maceration of 5 days to extract colour but not tannin structure; 9g/L dosage

Ruinart's rosé is intentionally fresh, fruity, aromatic and approachable, full in colour but light in structure. A large dose of chardonnay defines the house style of restraint and soft, chalky mineral mouthfeel, while a strong inclusion of red wine infuses a full crimson hue and aromas and flavours of all shades of red: wild strawberries, raspberries, cherries, red apples and rose hip. It fades a little in the savoury, tilled earth-like grip of 2011, lending a little dryness to the finish, though retains admirable, vibrant fruit persistence and lively acid line. A vintage to enjoy young and fresh, before it collapses into dry astringency.

DOM RUINART BLANC DE BLANCS BRUT 2004 $$$$$

96 points • DISGORGED JUNE 2013 • TASTED IN BRISBANE

100% grand cru chardonnay; 69% Côte des Blancs (Chouilly, Avize and Le Mesnil-sur-Oger), 31% Montagne de Reims (Sillery, Puisieulx, Mailly-Champagne and Verzenay); aged 8 years on lees; 5.5g/L dosage

Ruinart's flagship blanc de blancs plays the high strings of the Côte des Blancs to the thick orchestral scoring of Montagne de Reims, filling out chardonnay's pitch-perfect freshness with layers of creamy generosity. The 2004 delivers vitality and an edginess emphasised by prominent, diamond-cut acidity, underscored by the nostalgic timbre of inimitable Côte des Blancs chalk minerality. A distinctive air of reductive character blows through in gunpowder and fennel notes, the signature of Ruinart and of chardonnay, while a decade in Ruinart's ancient chalk mines has deepened its voice with tones of nougat, toasty complexity and a hint of smoked bacon. Its euphoric vigour and sheer stamina surpass even the masterpiece of 2002, promising two decades of potential in the cellar. Large glasses will be your best ally when it is finally time to awaken this sleeping beauty.

SALON

(Sah-loh)

10/10

5–7 RUE DE LA BRÈCHE D'OGER 51190 LE MESNIL-SUR-OGER
www.salondelamotte.com

CHAMPAGNE

SALON
Le Mesnil

There is only one Salon, and there has only ever been one. One wine of one variety from one vintage, sourced from one region (Côte de Blancs) and one village (Le Mesnil-sur-Oger). The romantic ideal ends abruptly here, however, because this is not a single-vineyard wine, nor even an estate wine. The fruit of the single-hectare estate vineyard of Jardin de Salon is currently declassified to its lower-tier sister house, Delamotte, because the vines are just 14 years old. Salon is sourced from 15 hectares owned by 19 longstanding growers, all of whom sell their fruit only to Salon. Winemaking is handled by the owner of both houses, Laurent-Perrier.

The minute scale of this operation sank in as I absorbed it from the homely tasting room in the house in Le Mesnil-sur-Oger. The windows framed the Jardin vineyard stretching up the gentle slope just outside. Directly below, a decade of future releases lay waiting in the small cellar. There are only 10 employees here: six in the cellar and four in the office. Production is typically about 50,000 bottles, and only in worthy vintages. There is no non-vintage wine, so production is limited to the finest years, of which the current release, 2002, is just the 38th since 1905.

It was in that year that Eugène-Aimé Salon created Champagne's first blanc de blancs, originally only for personal consumption. To this day it remains among the most celebrated and most expensive. Of the original vineyards from which Eugène-Aimé Salon purchased, all but two are still part of Salon's sourcing. The philosophy from the beginning was to build a champagne that could age, and every element of its production is honed towards this goal. The first pressing is used exclusively, fermented in stainless steel under temperature control. Its natural acidity is upheld by blocking malolactic fermentation, distinguishing it from Delamotte. Aged for an average of 10 years before release, the timing for each vintage is determined according to when it is ready. Riddling is performed by hand, and bottles are disgorged according to when they are released. This usually equates to four to six disgorgements across two years of release. Dosage is tweaked for each disgorgement, typically 5–6g/L.

Salon is usually among the last houses to release its vintage wine; even at this age, it is far from its peak. 'Whenever I produce a vintage I say, "This is not for me or for my children, but for my grandchildren",' declares

Salon Delamotte president Didier Depond, who considers the perfect time to drink Salon to be after 20 years.

'It takes 20 years to truly define a great wine,' he suggests. 'We are always very surprised by the potential of Salons opened from the '70s, '60s and even '50s.'

Laurent-Perrier's vineyard manager Christelle Rinville follows each vineyard throughout the year, and monitors all cultures and treatments that are applied. Depond is afforded the freedom to manage the house independently, and feels no pressure to increase volumes, in spite of limited supply and high demand.

'It's difficult to increase the volume because the vineyards are limited,' he points out. 'And it would be a disaster to increase the number of vintages we release.' A noble stance at a time when some houses appear set on churning out flagship champagnes in lesser seasons.

There will be no 2000 Salon, after mid-August hail devastated the Le Mesnil harvest. The 2002 will be followed by 2004, 2006, 2007 and 2008 (in magnum only), bettering Salon's longstanding average of fewer than four vintages each decade. The 1996, 2002 and 2008 are upheld by the house to be the finest vintages for long ageing.

Chardonnay, the key to Champagne's first blanc de blancs, Salon.

Salon Cuvée S Blanc de Blancs 2002 $$$$$

97 points • Disgorged early 2014 • Tasted in Le Mesnil-sur-Oger & Sydney
60,000 bottles

Didier Depond considers 2002 the perfect image of Salon, of blanc de blancs and of Le Mesnil. The long wait is over and it's finally here — but the caveat is that it still needs at least 10 years to uncurl, and will effortlessly live for 50. There's an inherent contradiction here that embodies the ripeness and the stamina of 2002: on release it is one of the most coiled Salons, desperately clinging to incisive youthfulness, exceedingly backward for its age, yet at the same time intense, driven and emphatically concentrated. It has followed a gentle curve of evolution at the pace of a giant sea turtle, charged with a flash of pure lemon blossom, grapefruit, pear and fennel of brilliant precision and refined elegance. With time in a large glass it stirs and rises slowly and assuredly in a towering display of ginger, fig, even tangelo and white cherries. Glimmers of anise, brioche and almond tell the story of 11 years in the cellar, accented with a wisp of grilled-bread reduction. Its structure is a revelation, with very fine, salty chalk minerality integrating softly, then rising on the finish to mouth-embracing mineral texture that personifies Le Mesnil. The characteristic poise of Salon triumphs, somehow, surprisingly yet marvellously, delivering authoritative control with light-footed restraint and delicacy.

Salon Cuvée S Blanc de Blancs 1997 $$$$$

97 points • Tasted in Sydney

The rounded integration of the warm 1997 season produced a maturity of fruit that made for a more accessible Salon from the outset, yet acidity on par with 1996 has had it confidently in the cellar, and it has not waned one iota in the five years since its release. It now beckons with enticing allure, its primary fruit presence having mellowed to a place of transcendental complexity of brioche, butter, honey and long-lingering spice, caressed by a silky, creamy mouthfeel and permeated by omnipresent Le Mesnil chalk minerality.

TAITTINGER

(Tet-ahn-zhay)

8/10

9 PLACE SAINT-NICAISE 51100 REIMS

www.taittinger.com

CHAMPAGNE
TAITTINGER

Reims

'*My grandfather gave me a book when I was five years old,' Pierre-Emmanuel Taittinger recalls. 'In the dedication he wrote, "To my grandson, who will one day be an entrepreneur and be the guardian of the family tradition."' Little did he know how true his prophecy would prove to be, and just what it would take to achieve. In these days of corporate takeovers, it's a gutsy commitment to buy back the family business. When most of the heirs voted to cash in and Taittinger was sold in 2005, Pierre-Emmanuel launched a fierce, year-long buy-back for his branch of the family, to the tune of €550 million, with the help of family friends and French bank Crédit Agricole. The family has since built up its stake in the company to almost half, with the remainder mostly in the hands of its friends. Annual sales of 5.6 million bottles rank Taittinger as Champagne's sixth-largest house.*

The fulfilment of his grandfather's prediction returned Taittinger to its place among the last big independent, family-owned houses that uphold the family name not only on the label, but in their management. Pierre-Emmanuel remains president of the company, his dynamic son, Clovis, is export director, and his delightful daughter, Vitalie, handles the company's artistic vision. The board and family are involved in each cuvée's tastings. 'My father leads the tasting, but it is a collective decision,' says Clovis.

It's a compelling story of fighting for the family business in the middle of one of the biggest corporate jungles anywhere in the wine world. It took Pierre-Emmanuel years to bring his buy-back to fruition, and it was not until 2008 that it was complete. The vintage wines from this new regime are yet to emerge from the hallowed caverns of Taittinger, but its non-vintage wines have never looked more refined.

NATURAL VITICULTURE

Taittinger's 288 hectares of vineyard holdings, predominantly in the Montagne de Reims and Côte des Blancs, provide for half of the company's annual production, with recent growth of around 7% each year. Half of its own vines are pinot noir, 35% chardonnay and 15% meunier. Chardonnay plays a significant role in the house style, sourced predominantly from the Côte des Blancs.

The Champagne Guide

An increasingly eco-friendly approach is taken in the vines, with a reduction in the use of pesticides and elimination of herbicides. 'We are aiming to use half the usual dose of chemicals,' outlines Taittinger's young and talented deputy general manager, Damien Le Sueur, 'and in 2010 we used less than six treatments across all our vineyards.'

The house is not seeking organic certification, to retain the flexibility to use full doses when difficult seasons dictate. Nonetheless, natural treatments remain the preference, and attention has been given to trellising to provide ventilation to balanced canopies. Grasses are planted in the mid-rows of 80% of estate vineyards, believed to be an unprecedented proportion for an estate of this size, and ploughing is used for weed control, sometimes by horse. Green harvesting to limit yields is only used when necessary, such as in the high-yielding year of 2004, when as much as 40% of fruit was dropped in some vineyards.

Taittinger employs 700–800 pickers and is purposeful in paying them by their time, not by volume, which is rare in Champagne. 'It is more difficult to demand quality if we pay by volume, so we never do that,' explains Le Sueur. 'We explain to them what we want in terms of quality and tell them to be selective.'

Taittinger prizes its growers and takes an approach of building good relationships rather than supervising quality. 'To us, they are not just a number; a personal relationship is important,' says Le Sueur. 'It's about long-term relationships, of remaining loyal and maintaining confidence.' Pierre-Emmanuel Taittinger is actively involved during the harvests and visits all of Taittinger's press houses. 'They are proud to see him, as they appreciate the image of Taittinger and the family involvement.'

ATTENTIVE VINIFICATION

At the time of the family buy-back, the decision was made to work only with the finest juices, using around 10% of the tailles of chardonnay only in the Brut Réserve NV and Brut Prestige Rosé NV, and only the first pressing in the other cuvées. 'We only use the tailles from chardonnay because the tailles of the black grapes are too heavy,' Le Sueur explains. 'Too much of the tailles in the blend makes them too strong and mature, but we want to produce very fine and accurate wines.' Excess tailles are exchanged for the cuvées of other houses.

In the winery, fermentation is conducted in tanks below 18°C to preserve freshness. Malolactic fermentation is allowed to complete on all cuvées, crucial for softening these chardonnay-led styles. 'I say we work

with four varieties: chardonnay, pinot noir, meunier and time!' says Le Sueur, emphasising the importance of maturity in allowing these nervy styles to develop. Non-vintage wines are aged on lees for at least three years, Prélude Grand Crus Brut NV for a minimum of five years, vintage wines for longer again, and the flagship Comtes de Champagne eight years or more (the current vintage is 2006).

Such long ageing necessitates large cellar stocks. Taittinger ages 3 million bottles of Comtes de Champagne at 9–10°C in its breathtaking four kilometres of galleries under its headquarters in Reims, including a section of 4th-century Roman crayères. Its remaining stores of some 23 million bottles are kept in a facility in town. This tremendous stock facilitates an average of more than 4.5 years on lees, a massive duration for any house.

Taittinger bottles under natural cork, since it hasn't found its cuvées to evolve in the same way under DIAM. Since mid-2014, all cuvées except Comtes de Champagne have boasted a QR code that reveals the bottling and disgorgement dates. I'm told there's also a way to locate this information on the website, but I couldn't find it.

COMTES DE CHAMPAGNE

Taittinger's flagship Comtes de Champagne holds an enviable position among the very finest blanc de blancs. It is sourced principally from Avize and Le Mesnil-sur-Oger, and to a lesser extent from Oger, Chouilly, Cramant, Vertus and Bergères-lès-Vertus.

'We are lucky to work with a huge quantity of wines from the Côte des Blancs, allowing us to choose the best samples for Comtes de Champagne each year,' explains cellar master Loïc Dupont. 'We look for the vats that represent the typicity of each cru, to build the expression of the vintage. Avize brings elegance, finesse and balance, Le Mesnil-sur-Oger contributes body and a subtle reduction akin to grilled bread, Chouilly delivers roundness, Cramant grilled almonds, and Oger elegant citrus.' Just 5% is aged for four months in oak barrels, one-third new, and up to four years old — not for strength, but to bring subtle notes of toast and brioche to the delicacy of chardonnay.

Taittinger's depth of reach into the Côte des Blancs grand crus has made Comtes de Champagne one of Champagne's most consistent blanc de blancs, and every even-numbered vintage since 1996 has been nothing short of transcendental.

The Taittinger family tradition remains as alive and well as ever, in the capable hands of Pierre-Emmanuel, his children, and their loyal and talented team.

Taittinger Cuvée Brut Réserve NV $$

93 points • 2011 BASE VINTAGE WITH 38% RESERVES • TASTED IN REIMS & BRISBANE
92 points • 2009 BASE VINTAGE WITH 30% RESERVES FROM 2008, 2007 AND 2006
• DISGORGED EARLY 2014 • TASTED IN PIERRY

40% chardonnay, 35% pinot noir, 25% meunier from crus in the Montagne de Reims, the Côte des Blancs, the beginning of the Vallée de la Marne, chardonnay from Sézanne and pinot noir from estate vineyards in the Côte des Bar

Taittinger always prepares its Brut Réserve blend first, and only if the vintage is deemed of sufficient quality are its other cuvées assembled. This philosophy, together with a generous inclusion of reserves, has produced an impressive result from the tricky 2011 base, a wine that upholds pretty white-peach fruit and lemon zest vivacity with the almond, brioche and toast notes of bottle age. A touch of struck-flint reduction reflects its chardonnay lead. It's a refreshing apéritif of persistence, poise and fine mineral structure. One bottle I tasted showed some dry extract bitterness on the finish. The 2009 base upholds its core of lemon zest sparkle, while evolving to a more secondary mood of honey and ginger, with a suggestion of firm dryness to the mouthfeel.

Taittinger Les Folies de la Marquetterie NV $$

92 points • TASTED IN SYDNEY & MELBOURNE

Taittinger's first single-estate wine is blended from parcels surrounding its Château de la Marquetterie in Pierry, just south of Épernay. The typicity of the site is emphasised using viticulture to drop yields to around half of Champagne's average, through green harvest and elimination of soil supplements. The objective is to use no chaptalisation. Some parcels are vinified in large, 10-year-old, 4000-litre foudres to provide subtle oxygenation without oak character. The result is rounded, rich and generous, relying heavily on crop reduction to build depth and character of ripe peach fruit, with bottle age reflected in brioche and mixed spice. It culminates in well-balanced acidity and good persistence.

Taittinger Cuvée Nocturne NV $$

90 points • 2010 BASE VINTAGE • TASTED IN REIMS, SYDNEY & MELBOURNE

Exactly the same blend as Brut Réserve, aged another year (4-4.5 years on lees), with 17.5g/L dosage

Taittinger has pimped Nocturne into what it calls a 'disco version', doubling production and decorating it in a shiny iridescent purple disco ball, to great success. It's a much more serious offering than its livery suggests, because this is simply a more mature and slightly sweeter version of Brut Réserve (not too cloying, and not a 'leftovers' cuvée of rotten fruit and too much tailles, as sweet champagnes too often tend to be). By comparison, this is well made, fresh, clean and fruity, with peach, apricot and pineapple fruit, boiled sweets and the honey and roast nuts of maturity. It's not too sweet, particularly when served well chilled. Turn down the lights, crank up the volume and give it a swing.

The Champagne Guide

Taittinger Nocturne Rosé NV $$$

93 points • 2011 BASE VINTAGE • TASTED IN REIMS

Exactly the same blend as Prestige Rosé, aged another year (3-3.5 years on lees), with 17.5g/L dosage

This is far more sophisticated than its shimmering night-club sleeve suggests: Taittinger has transcended the tribulations of 2011 to create one of the best sweeter champagnes I've tasted in years. As per the white Nocturne, the secret is firstly that it's a more mature version of the dry cuvée, and secondly that it's not too sweet. It's a pretty, clean, fresh and characterful style of medium crimson hue, and flavours and aromas spanning pomegranate, pink pepper, red cherries, poached strawberries and red liquorice, becoming toasty, with complexity of patisserie, anise and cherry kernel. Its fine minerality stands up to slightly candied dosage, but give it a chill and it's ready to party.

Taittinger Cuvée Brut Prestige Rosé NV $$$

94 points • 2010 BASE VINTAGE • DISGORGED DECEMBER 2014 • TASTED IN SYDNEY, MELBOURNE & BRISBANE

15% pinot noir red wine from Ambonnay, Bouzy and Les Riceys

This young disgorgement is a fresh, lively and elegant Taittinger Rosé of medium crimson salmon hue, presenting a delightfully delicate air of rose petal, pink pepper, red cherry and wild strawberry. Transcending the challenges of the 2010 season, pitch-perfect fruit integrity, purity and freshness are evenly supported by focused acid line, all coasting in unison on a smooth, well-defined chalk mineral surface. A captivating rosé of fine-strung harmony.

Taittinger Cuvée Prélude Grand Crus Brut NV $$$

96 points • 2008 BASE VINTAGE • DISGORGED DECEMBER 2014 • TASTED IN REIMS & BRISBANE

100% 2008, though not declared as a vintage; 50% Côte des Blancs chardonnay, 50% northern Montagne de Reims pinot noir for freshness; a large proportion of Mailly-Champagne; grand cru parcels selected to show the characters of their crus, rather than the mood of the vintage; 9g/L dosage

Taittinger selects its grand cru parcels of elegance, finesse, delicacy and structure for its Prélude, reserving those with more power for the Comtes de Champagne Rosé. Prélude exudes a tightrope tension between power and precision, and never has this been more pronounced, nor more enthralling, than in the dazzling 2008 vintage. It's a refreshingly bright medium straw hue, anticipating the vivacious freshness that is to come. Lively, focused purity of lemon and white peach fruit expands generously into a palate of grand cru proportions, underscored by the background track of bottle maturity in tunes of almond, roast nuts and biscuits. Wonderfully fine, grand cru mineral texture pulls through an immensely chalky finish. This is one of the greatest Préludes, epitomising the mantra of this cuvée.

TAITTINGER CUVÉE BRUT MILLÉSIMÉ 2006 $$$

93 points • Tasted in Pierry, Brisbane, Sydney & Melbourne

50% chardonnay, largely from Avize, Le Mesnil-sur-Oger, Oger, Chouilly, Vertus, Villers-Marmery and Trépail; 50% pinot noir, largely from Ambonnay, Aÿ, Verzenay, Bouzy, Écueil, Sacy, Rilly-la-Montagne, Hautvillers and Pierry; 70% grand cru and 30% premier cru parcels selected for their vintage typicity; 9g/L dosage

The lower acidity of the warm, mature 2006 vintage has made for a rounded and approachable style that peaked in 2014, and has since softened into deep-set baked apple and peach fruit, becoming increasingly toasty, honeyed and spicy. It upholds its core of grapefruit and white peach focus, softly supported by understated chalk minerality, integrated acidity and dosage, with the phenolic grip of a warmer season beginning to take hold.

TAITTINGER COMTES DE CHAMPAGNE BLANC DE BLANCS 2006 $$$$$

97 points • Tasted in Reims & Pierry

Avize and Le Mesnil-sur-Oger, the pillars of Comtes, supported by Oger, Chouilly and Cramant; 5-6% aged in barrels for 4-5 months, to add body and subtle burnt vanilla and coconut character; 9g/L dosage

On the eve of its release, the 2006 brings back all the wonder of classic Comtes, the innocence of a joyful childhood, a free-as-air dash through endless blue daylight and a breathless plunge into an icy mountain rock pool. A wine of coiled energy, focus and precision, it leads with lemon, lime, grapefruit, crunchy apple and pear. Then it drops back a gear, with a fleeting suggestion of pineapple that hints at the volume of the ripe 2006 season, yet not for a moment volunteering any secondary development yet. Magnificent tones of gun flint and grilled toast reduction linger through a finish of great focus and stamina. Its textural presence is mouth-embracing, permeating every crevice, masterfully uniting very fine phenolic grip with delightfully fine, frothing salt minerality that bores to the very core of the finest chalkfields of the Côte des Blancs.

TAITTINGER COMTES DE CHAMPAGNE BLANC DE BLANCS 2005 $$$$$

94 points • Tasted in Reims, Pierry, Brisbane & Yarra Valley

'It was harder to make Comtes de Champagne in 2005, as the still wines were more mature and more dried-out right from the start, and these are the same characters we see in the wine now,' responded Damien Le Sueur, when I queried the decision to release Comtes in this challenging season. At a decade of age, its pale to medium straw hue is impressively subtle and bright for this warm vintage. Flamboyant intensity of citrus, apple and pear fruit is becoming secondary and spicy, with pronounced, biscuity, toasty, hazelnut maturity setting in. This is a Comtes of masculine strength, with considerable intensity and presence lingering long amidst a palate rejoicing in the texture of lees age, at once soft and creamy, chewy and full. The dry extract, dusty, bitter almond character and grip of 2005 are pronounced, interrupting the otherwise seamless flow of the finish, but the wine has grown into itself admirably since its release.

Taittinger Comtes de Champagne Rosé 2006 $$$$$

96 points • Tasted in Reims & Pierry

70% pinot noir from Ambonnay, Mailly-Champagne, Verzy and Verzenay, including 12% red wine from Bouzy; 30% chardonnay from Avize, Le Mesnil-sur-Oger, Oger and Chouilly; no oak; just 5–10% of the production of Comtes de Champagne

If the philosophy of Comtes de Champagne is that of restraint, the aim of its extroverted Rosé sister is of aromatic explosiveness and energy. Previously released younger than the blanc, the house has discovered how magnificently the Rosé ages, and this is the first time the releases have coincided, with the aim of releasing the Rosé even later in future. The finesse and grace of this release seem at odds with its brief and its full crimson copper hue, particularly in the warmth of the 2006 vintage, possessing a latent power that will take some years yet to fully unravel, making this a rare champagne rosé for the cellar. There is primary freshness here of picture-perfect red cherries, strawberries, raspberries, guavas, pomegranates, even pink lady apples and musk. Age has ushered in a subtle suggestion of smoked charcuterie. A rosé wine of excellent length and drive, powered by considerable structure of firm, fine tannins, masterfully crafted to effortlessly support a long and harmonious finish, without in any way disrupting beautifully defined bath-salts minerality.

Taittinger Comtes de Champagne Rosé 2005 $$$$$

94 points • Tasted in Reims & Pierry

58% pinot noir from Verzenay and Mailly-Champagne; 30% grand cru Côte des Blancs chardonnay; 12% Bouzy pinot noir red wine; no oak

Taittinger has responded to the ripe 2005 season with an intentionally rich and vinous rosé, textural and complex from the outset, with a body that cleverly juxtaposes the dry savouriness of the season. I predicted two years ago that this was a rosé to catch young, and its light has now just begun to dim. Luscious, ripe, primary red berries and cherries have started to evolve into quince and pink pepper. A vintage of considerable concentration, age has heightened its muscular power, sinewy tannins and dry, dusty grip, though it has admirably retained balance and composure.

Taittinger Comtes de Champagne Rosé 1996

98 points • Tasted in Reims

The arresting stamina of 1996 emphatically confirms the mesmeric endurance of the Comtes Rosé. It's a sunburst of full crimson copper radiance, illuminating a dashing core of blackcurrant, black cherry and raspberry fruit, overflowing in a dreamy cascade of truffles, wood spice, coffee and dark chocolate, with a puff of sweet, exotic pipe smoke. Minerality, tannins and phenolics unite to produce a mouthfeel that is at once softly structured and as smooth as still water, fed from a deep well of 1996 concentration and acid drive.

TARLANT

(Tahr-lohn)

6/10

Rue de la Cooperative, Oeuilly 51480

www.tarlant.com

'Our goal is to express the personality of our unique place,' declares young Benoît Tarlant, and there are few in Champagne who have gone to greater lengths to do so. Within six years of taking the lead at his family estate in 1999, he had eliminated dosage in 80% of his annual production of 120,000–130,000 bottles, no mean feat in a house that preserves tension with malic acidity. 'I am not a cane sugar or beet sugar maker, I produce grapes!' he declares. His is an intuitive and sensitive approach that dares to ride the cutting edge of practice in the vineyard and the winery. 'There are no rules — it depends on the grapes!' he exclaims. A unique display of dried herbs in a corner of the winery celebrates a regime of cover crops and treatments that he dubs 'herbal therapy'. Fermentation is conducted mostly in barrels, some tanks and even small clay amphorae. 'The goal is not the method, the goal is to make great wine,' he sums up, exemplified in a large range of champagnes energised by malic acidity and characterised by the creamy generosity of ripe fruit, barrel fermentation, liberal use of reserve wines and long ageing. Tarlant's Zero is one of champagne's best brut natures.

Benoît Tarlant's family has tended its vines in the Vallée de la Marne since 1687, and made its own wine since the 1870s, and champagne since 1929. Today, the family is one of the most distinguished growers in its village of Oeuilly.

'Our priority is to take care of the vines and make our wines,' says Benoît, who has relished the opportunity to mark his own print on the estate while working alongside his grandfather Georges, his parents Jean-Mary and Micheline, and his sister Mélanie.

HERBAL THERAPY

Mostly on the southern side of the river, Tarlant's north-facing sites require meticulous attention, and even the use of a tractor winch to haul equipment up the rows of the steepest vineyards in the village. North- and east-facing slopes are prized for retention of acidity, particularly in meunier.

Benoît took me to the edge of the vines on the eastern side of the village. 'The Marne Valley is defined by the river, cutting like a knife and making many soil types,' he explained, pointing out six different soil varieties between us and the river, less than 800 metres away. 'Our job is to keep the character of each vineyard.' Tarlant's 14 hectares are spread across 57 plots, each of which are vinified separately. An extensive range of 2012 vins clairs exemplifies the distinctiveness of mineral expression and flavour profile of each plot.

Most of these vineyards were planted by his family and boast an average age of 34 years. The estate has had opportunity to increase slightly as the contracts on his grandfather's vineyards end, though only one hectare has been gained in this way in recent years. Benoît credits chalk in the soil for a diversity of grape selection.

'This area is best suited to black grapes, as chardonnay is quite rustic,' he points out, explaining his breakdown of 50% pinot noir, 30% chardonnay, 18% meunier and 2% petit meslier, arbane and pinot blanc.

Benoît prizes the diversity of his many plots, but admits it's a challenge to manage so many distinct sites using techniques sympathetic to organic practices. Three hectares are managed biodynamically, some organically, neither certified, and the remainder rely on his ingenious regime of 'herbal therapy'. A wide range of herbs are planted in the vineyards, including oregano, which he harvests for pizzas and salads. Small concoctions are made from the plants and sprayed on the vines to protect against fungus attacks. He says 2012 was a good year to practise. 'We only lost 30% of fruit in our vineyards with herbal therapy, but 40% with organics and 50% with biodynamics.'

INTUITIVE WINEMAKING

The goal is to harvest ripe, tasty grapes with balanced acidity. To this end, malolactic fermentation is completely blocked. 'I think malolactic is an industry mistake from the 1960s and 1970s,' Benoît suggests. 'Traditionally, the majority of champagne was without malolactic fermentation. It makes sense to me to show the wine naturally, with its natural acidity.'

Intensity, precision and presence of texture are Benoît's priorities. Every transfer in the winery is performed by gravity. The traditional champagne pressing regime is taken one step further, by carefully splitting the juice from the first pressing into two separate components, and the tailles into two components. 'I hate pre-blending, so we vinify every parcel separately,' he explains. 'We should respect the origin of the place here in Champagne as much as they do in Burgundy.'

Two-thirds of the harvest is barrel fermented using wild yeast, without additions of enzymes or bentonite for clarification or stabilisation. The remainder is tank fermented in temperature-controlled stainless steel to preserve vitality. Inspired by friends in Italy, Benoît experimented with ageing in four 200-litre clay amphorae in 2012, for greater oxygen exchange than in barrels, though he's quick to point out he doesn't want to make orange wines.

Barrels are always purchased new and maintained until they are up to 30 years of age. 'I'm not a big fan of new barrels, but as a non-malolactic cellar, I don't want to bring the wolf into the sheep pen!' Benoît exclaims, in reference to the risk of introducing bugs from used barrels. Parcels fermented in new barrels are always blended. 'I prefer older barrels, but after long ageing of 7–10 years, the impact of a well-managed new barrel is not so scary!'

Bâtonnage is used to help finish fermentation and to build texture. 'I love working with barrels, so the wines can breathe and not look so monolithic,' he says. Reserve wines are aged in oak casks, and he incorporates at least three vintages in his Zero Brut, which he considers crucial for this style. Long bottle ageing is also critical in this process. Non-vintage wines are typically matured at least 3.5 years in bottle, and vintage wines typically 10 years.

'When I was young, I wanted to hurry the disgorgement, but my grandfather taught me to wait six years by showing me the profound texture and character that developed as the wine breathed over time. I don't want to show a wine until it reveals its personality.'

ZERO DOSAGE

Benoît's ultimate goal is to make zero-dosage champagne. 'We don't need to add sugar to Chablis, so why do we need to do it with champagne?' He aims to pick grapes ripe when he can. 'We must always reach the prettiest maturity, not the highest maturity, so adding sugar should not be a question.' The point is not zero dosage, but to create wine of flavour and atmosphere. He chaptalises when he has to and uses low dosages of less than 6g/L in cuvées that require it, though he doesn't enjoy adding dosage.

Benoît's father has been making Zero Brut since the early 1980s, long before zero dosage was the rage in Champagne. 'Back then you could count on one hand all the people making this style in Champagne,' Benoît points out. 'I'm scared that it's becoming trendy now.'

It took him six years to build Tarlant Zero to the major cuvée of the estate, now representing around 100,000 bottles annually — a monumental feat for one of Champagne's better composed examples of this challenging style. He has also elevated Rosé Zero to the main rosé of the house.

'There are perhaps four or five zero-dosage rosés

now, but when I began in 2000 it was a no-man's land, and I had no one else's wines to look at,' he says. He made six trials of pinot noir and meunier, each with skin contact, blended from red and white wines and blended with chardonnay. 'The question with zero-dosage rosé was how to get acid and tannin to live together. I found the skin-contact wines too angular in their tannin expression, so I prefer to blend.' Benoît chose chardonnay blended with pinot noir red wine, but the evolution continues. The current dilemma is an attempt to build greater persistence using white wine from black grapes — a challenge because even white pinot noir contributes tannins.

Benoît has recently released his first series of single-vineyard wines. 'I'm not here to make single vineyards, but sometimes the taste of the samples makes it irresistible!' he exclaims. 'The first year I experienced real taste, explosiveness and length in single parcels was 2003.'

He recently added a new building to extend the winery, not to increase production but to provide space to work with his 57 plots and a portfolio now spanning 13 cuvées. All have boasted informative back labels since 2000, detailing terroirs, cépages, vintages, disgorgement and bottling dates and dosage. Most of his cuvées in the market today are the same vintages he showed me as sneak previews two years ago, and I'm impressed at how slowly and confidently they have evolved.

TARLANT ZERO BRUT NATURE NV $

94 points • 2007 BASE VINTAGE • DISGORGED SEPTEMBER 2014 • TASTED IN BRISBANE

One-third of each of the champagne varieties from the Vallée de la Marne; vines more than 25 years of age; fermented in stainless steel; reserve wines aged in oak barrels; no malolactic fermentation; zero dosage; ~100,000 bottles

Benoît Tarlant has sensitively honed every stage of viticulture and production to foster balance in his Zero Brut, aiming for an accuracy, purity and directness that he likens to playing darts. Flavour, not austerity, is a priority here, with ripe fruit, three reserve vintages and long bottle ageing creating balance and presence. The high-acid 2007 season was not an easy base on which to build this style, calling for some chaptalisation, though the result is impressive and has demonstrated exceptional stamina since I first tasted it two years ago. There is grand depth and richness here, exalting in the fleshy body of the Vallée de la Marne in gloriously ripe yellow mirabelle plum, white peach and grapefruit, and the layered, toasty richness of honey, orange cream and fruit-mince spice of 6.5 years of lees age. In the midst of such marvellous complexity, it upholds its freshness thanks to an electric zap of malic acidity, culminating in a crescendo of fine chalk mineral texture and grand persistence.

TARLANT BRUT RESERVE NV $

93 points • 2007 BASE VINTAGE • DISGORGED JULY 2014 • TASTED IN BRISBANE

Zero Brut with dosage; one-third of each of the Champagne varieties from the Vallée de la Marne; fermented in stainless steel; reserve wines aged in oak barrels; no malolactic fermentation; 6g/L dosage

Tarlant once created Zero Brut by omitting dosage from Brut Reserve, in the pattern of most houses, but Benoît turned the tables and now creates a little Brut Reserve from Zero Brut. It's quite remarkable just how much impact 6g/L dosage has in a wine engineered from the ground up to cope without dosage. It lifts glacé pear notes and adds a honeyed sweetness to the finish, diminishing the tension of acid structure and the impression of chalk minerality. The full fanfare of complexity still parades itself confidently. As always, the no-added-sugar version has the edge.

The Champagne Guide

Tarlant Rosé Zero Brut Nature NV $

93 points • 2008 BASE VINTAGE • DISGORGED JULY 2014 • TASTED IN BRISBANE

85% chardonnay, 15% pinot noir red wine from the Vallée de la Marne; fermented in stainless steel; 2007 reserve wines aged in oak barrels; no malolactic fermentation; zero dosage

A very pretty rosé of medium to full salmon crimson colour, with elegant crispness that unites the primary freshness of strawberry hull and pomegranate with the building presence of red cherries and red apples. Soft, fine tannins meld comfortably with fine-spun, salty chalk minerality, while malic acid cut keeps the finish tense and lively, energised by the velocity of 2008.

....

Tarlant La Matinale Prestige Millésime Brut Nature 2003 $$

93 points • DISGORGED JANUARY 2014 • TASTED IN BRISBANE

45% pinot noir, 28% chardonnay, 27% meunier; blended from five vineyards; fermented in stainless steel vats and oak barrels; no malolactic fermentation; zero dosage

All the warm, luscious volume of 2003 is presented in a full straw hue and ripe mirabelle plums and apricots, bolstered with the biscuity, ginger and golden fruit cake allure of barrel fermentation and a decade on lees. The whole grand affair is pulled into consummately well-contained focus with the tension of malic acidity and subtle, bitter grip of well-handled dry extract. It stands tall, at the extreme end of champagne magnitude, and ready to drink right away.

....

Tarlant BAM! Blanc Arbane Meslier NV $$$$

92 points • 2009 BASE VINTAGE • DISGORGED JANUARY 2015 • TASTED IN BRISBANE

50% petit meslier, 27% pinot blanc, 23% arbane; single-vineyard Oeuilly; 2008 and 2007 reserves; fermented and aged for 9 months in fourth-use oak barrels with regular lees stirring; no malolactic fermentation; zero dosage

Of all the Champagne varieties that fall outside the safe ground of the three usual suspects, this release of BAM! — in complete contrast to its name — is one of the most graceful and precise. This hasn't always been the case, and the progress of rapid evolution in this cuvée is a resounding credit to Benoît's dextrous flexibility to learn fast. Presenting a much more composed and settled demeanour than the searing 2008 base, this is a blend that captures the subtly exotic nuances of its three varieties in glimmers of star fruit, honeydew and nashi pear, set against a backdrop of pure white citrus. For young vines, its seamlessness, integration and lingering poise are more than impressive, thanks in no small part to clever use of barrel fermentation and lees stirring to create texture and harmony. Kudos, Benoît.

....

Tarlant La Vigne d'Or Blanc de Meuniers Brut Nature 2004 $$

90 points • DISGORGED JANUARY 2015 • TASTED IN BRISBANE

100% meunier from a single vineyard in Oeuilly of vine age 65 years; fermented and aged for 9 months in fourth-use oak barrels with regular lees stirring; no malolactic fermentation; zero dosage

The malic acidity of the 2004 vintage brings a tension to the volume of old-vine Oeuilly meunier, contrasting ripe peach and yellow mirabelle plums with a firm, high-tensile acid line, exacerbated by zero dosage. It leads out confidently, but concludes with some balsamic notes, oxidative and a little tired.

Tarlant La Vigne Royale Principauté de Condé Blanc de Noirs 2003 $$$$

92 points • Disgorged October 2014 • Tasted in Brisbane

100% pinot noir from a single vineyard in Celles-lès-Condé of vines of 30 years of age; fermented and aged for 9 months in fourth-use oak barrels with regular lees stirring; no malolactic fermentation; 2g/L dosage

Powerful, rich and bombastic, from the outset this is a juicy, rounded and bouncy pinot noir, crammed with succulent, cooked yellow summer fruits, baked apples, cinnamon and nutmeg. In the two years since it was lobbed into the world, it has evolved to a full straw yellow hue and a tertiary temperament of dark fruit cake, coffee and even dark chocolate. This serves to round out its muscular, phenolic texture, leaving just a touch of bitterness and edgy grip not out of place in such a voluminous style. Malic acidity holds the composure of the finish. A friendly giant, ready for main-course action.

Tarlant La Vigne d'Antan Non Greffée Chardonnay Brut Nature 2002 $$$

95 points • Disgorged May 2014 • Tasted in Brisbane

100% chardonnay from a single ungrafted vineyard in Oeuilly; fermented and aged for 9 months in fourth-use oak barrels with regular lees stirring; no malolactic fermentation; zero dosage

Tarlant's 'Vines of Yesteryear' showcases ungrafted chardonnay on an ancient terroir. The juncture at which a wine attains a three-way balance of primary, secondary and tertiary allure is a captivating moment. After 13 years, malic drive upholds chardonnay's youthful lemon and apple fruit, layered with all the enchanting honey, brioche and fruit-mince spice of maturity, culminating in a rumbling upsurging of coffee bean, mocha and green olive. It has the edgy tension and grip to live confidently for at least as long again, and it's only going to get better.

Tarlant Cuvée Louis Hommage à Louis Tarlant Vin de Rivière Extra Brut NV $$

95 points • 1999 base vintage • Disgorged October 2014 • Tasted in Brisbane

50% chardonnay and 50% pinot noir from a single Oeuilly vineyard on the Marne river with vines of average age 65 years; reserves from 1998, 1997 and 1996; fermented and aged for 9 months in fourth-use oak barrels with regular lees stirring; no malolactic fermentation; 1.7g/L dosage

Tarlant's original and chalkiest vineyard, 'Les Crayons', is closest to the cooling influence of the Marne, the quintessential expression of Oeuilly. The wine rises to its grand credentials, a radiant and monumental expression of the generosity of 1999 and the grand depth of decades of maturity. The presence of pineapple, golden delicious apple and locut is suspended in the gaping cavern between the dynamic cut of malic acidity and the deep, reverberating complexity of grand old age, whispered in tones of green olives, sizzling tinder and exotic spice. It's attained the glorious twilight of maturity, with grand, distinguished perseverance. For all it represents, it's surprisingly affordable.

ULYSSE COLLIN

(Oo-lees Kohl-la)

6/10

21 RUE DES VIGNERONS 51270 CONGY

CHAMPAGNE
Ulysse Collin

Olivier Collin is a young face on the rise among Champagne's growers, inspired after working with Anselme Selosse to reclaim a portion of his family's vines in Congy in the Sézannais to produce his first vintage in 2004. He has since re-established the family winery and cellar and reclaimed 8.7 hectares in the village, neighbouring Vert-la-Gravelle and nearby Barbonne-Fayel, planted to chardonnay and pinot noir. His vines are largely aged 30–60 years, tended using a combination of organic and conventional practices, applying organic compost, ploughing and avoiding pesticides. He is experimenting with biodynamics and aims to convert to organics in the coming years. Winemaking is likewise natural, relying on wild yeasts to complete very long fermentations in predominantly five-year-old and 15% new barriques. All cuvées to date have been single-vineyard blanc de blancs or blanc de noirs, showcasing the grainy minerality and power of the Sézannais. Back labels declare base vintages and disgorgement dates.

ULYSSE COLLIN LES ROISES BLANC DE BLANCS EXTRA BRUT NV $$

93 points • 2009 BASE VINTAGE • DISGORGED MARCH 2013 • TASTED IN MELBOURNE
100% chardonnay; fermented and aged for 13 months in barriques; aged on lees 2-3 years; zero dosage

A spicy single-vineyard blanc de blancs, the essence of the Sézanne. A firm and textural chalk mineral undercurrent propels intense white grapefruit and pink lady apple of considerable presence, into a trailing finish of exotic spice.

ULYSSE COLLIN LES MAILLONS BLANC DE NOIR EXTRA BRUT NV $$$

92 points • 2009 BASE VINTAGE • DISGORGED MARCH 2013 • TASTED IN MELBOURNE
100% pinot noir; fermented and aged for 13 months in barriques; aged on lees 2-3 years; zero dosage

With a slight copper tint to its hue, this is a cuvée that proclaims its pinot noir personality in a powder puff of spicy, up-front floral fragrance. It leads out flamboyant and precocious, and closes serious and structured, encapsulating the textural, mineral structure of the Sézanne.

VAZART-COQUART ET FILS

(Vah-zah Kho-khar e Feess)

6/10

6 RUE DES PARTELAINES 51530 CHOUILLY
www.champagnevazartcoquart.com

The Vazart family has sold champagne from its 11 hectares of estate vineyards exclusively in the Côte des Blancs grand cru of Chouilly for more than 60 years. Tall in stature and in warmth, Jean-Pierre Vazart is a gentleman with a broad smile and a very precise approach in the vineyards and the winery. Since he took charge of the estate 20 years ago, he has meticulously crafted a ripe fruit style in every cuvée that articulates the quintessential expression of Chouilly terroir. 'With soils like these, how could I do anything less?' he says graciously.

The story of Chouilly is all about the robust character and mineral expression of chardonnay, which makes up 95% of Vazart-Coquart's 30 plots of vines, averaging 30 years of age. 'My father has the récoltant-manipulant's mind, wanting to make everything himself, so after a few years of buying red wine, he hid some plantings of pinot noir in a lesser-known part of Chouilly,' reveals Jean-Pierre. Chouilly pinot noir was approved as grand cru in 2009. 'Next time I plant it, it will be on the road so everyone can see it!' he grins.

Perfectly ripe fruit is Jean-Pierre's goal, with a target of 10.5–11 degrees of potential, as he finds 11.5 too rich. 'I do all I can to avoid chaptalisation!' he declares. Fruit maturity is achieved through limiting yields by green harvesting and cultivating grasses between the rows. His 11 hectares yield more than he can make in his small winery and cellars, so he sells everything surplus to his 70,000-bottle requirements to Veuve Clicquot. 'Of course, the best parcels are for me, but they know what they buy!' he smiles. Veuve Clicquot chef de cave Dominique Demarville is a friend of Jean-Pierre's from school, and he enjoys a very flexible contract. 'If I have a small harvest, I can sell them less, and if I have a big

harvest, they buy everything I don't need.' It doesn't get any better than that.

Jean-Pierre's aspiration in the winery is to preserve the character of his grapes, so he uses stainless steel vats 'for their neutrality' rather than oak barrels, and cultured yeasts rather than wild. Malolactic fermentation is carried to completion, and deep reserve stocks are employed to soften the robust character of Chouilly.

Reserve wines are stored as a perpetual blend in a 20,000-litre tank. Dating back to 1982, it's one of the oldest soleras in Champagne, held fresh at 12°C. Each year, 50% is taken for Brut Réserve NV, Extra Brut NV, Rosé and for dosage liqueurs, and replenished with the current harvest. The solera is given priority over vintage cuvées and receives the estate's highest-potential fruit.

Jean-Pierre's production is currently spread across two premises in the village, and he has plans for a new building to integrate the two sites, with the hope of making the 2016 harvest in the new facility.

Jean-Pierre Vazart knows his craft intimately, and his sensible and sensitive approach makes him one of the most attentive growers in Chouilly. His terroir-driven cuvées are set off with stylish new labels.

Vazart-Coquart & Fils Réserve Blanc de Blancs NV $$

93 points • 2011 base vintage • Tasted in Chouilly

25% reserve solera dating back to 1982; 8.5g/L dosage; 40,000 bottles

Impeccably crafted and uncomplicated, this is a quintessential apéritif champagne that declares the signature of Chouilly and the precision of blanc de blancs. Pretty and refreshing lemon blossom, lemon zest and crunchy red apple flow into classic Chouilly richness of white peach and grapefruit, supported by subtle, well-integrated dosage and soft, characterful, finely poised chalk minerality.

Vazart-Coquart & Fils Grand Cru Blanc de Blancs Extra Brut NV $$

91 points • 2009 base vintage • Tasted in Chouilly

3000-4000 bottles

In its pale straw guise, this is a racy, clean and refreshing blanc de blancs of taut lemon and lime zest and a searing acid finish. Zero dosage makes for a tense, dry and firm finish, redeemed in part by a fine, creamy bead.

Vazart-Coquart & Fils Rosé NV $$

90 points • 2011 base vintage • Tasted in Chouilly

15% red wine; 20% reserve solera back to 1982; 9g/L dosage; 5000 bottles

A fresh, pretty and lively rosé of medium crimson watermelon luminescence, brimming with strawberries, raspberries and red cherries. It's spicy and textural, flailing on a short, firm finish of dry extract, a victim of the 2011 season.

Vazart-Coquart & Fils Special Foie Gras Blanc de Blancs Sec NV $$

91 points • Tasted in Chouilly

30g/L dosage; no more than 1000 bottles per year

Jean-Pierre's father, Jacques, loved foie gras, but not Monbazillac or Sauternes, so he created a sweet wine of his own. The base vintage is a secret, and at an average of more than 10 years of age, it's loaded with endearing secondary complexity of toffee, honey, toast and brioche, overlaying its ripe stone fruit core. A little burnt-orange maderisation suggests it's seen better days.

VAZART-COQUART & FILS BRUT GRAND BOUQUET BLANC DE BLANCS 2008 $$

96 points • 9G/L DOSAGE • TASTED IN CHOUILLY

Jean-Pierre Vazart describes the 2008 harvest as the 1996 vintage with balance. I'll be quoting him for years to come! His Grand Bouquet personifies the season, gracefully refined, and at the same time a laser-precise, glow-in-the-dark yellow green vector of pure citrus and frozen apple with remarkable thrust, energy and determination. It completely dissolves its dosage in a vast ocean of fine chalk minerality. Patience is called for — it won't blossom until it hits its teen years, and it will live confidently to 25 and beyond.

VAZART-COQUART & FILS SPECIAL CLUB 2006 $$$

95 points • DISGORGED EARLY 2014 • 7G/L DOSAGE • TASTED IN CHOUILLY

Grand Bouquet is tiraged on crown cap, and the same wine tiraged on cork is Special Club, because 'after ageing they are completely different, of course!' That they are. It takes Vazart half a day to disgorge 500 bottles (tasting every one for cork taint), the same time it takes to disgorge 3000 in crown cap. The vivacity, precision and fine chalk minerality of Chouilly chardonnay infuses 20 years of potential into even the warm and typically early-maturing 2006 harvest. It's a tense expression of lemon zest, crunchy nashi pear and lingering grapefruit spice, slowly building notes of brioche amidst a fine, creamy bead.

Sunset marks the close of vintage 2014 over Moët's Mont Aigu lodge, perched amidst the grand cru hillsides of Chouilly.

VEUVE CLICQUOT

(Verv Khlee-kho)

7/10

1 PLACE DES DROITS DE L'HOMME 51100 REIMS

www.veuve-clicquot.com

Veuve Clicquot

■ REIMS FRANCE ■

Dramatic developments are underway in the bellows of Veuve Clicquot that are only just beginning to bubble to the surface. Its characterful, full-bodied, pinot-focused wines are more refined every time I look, an astounding feat for a house with a dizzying annual production of 18 million bottles, ranking a confident number two by volume behind Moët & Chandon in Louis Vuitton–Moët Hennessy's (LVMH's) champagne kingdom. Even Clicquot's conspicuous 'Yellow Label' non-vintage, in its inimitable, trademark, mango-orange livery, is looking trim and fit today, having lost its curvaceous sweetness — quite a workout for a cuvée that alone accounts for a whopping 15 million bottles every year. Its vintage wines are where Veuve Clicquot really steps up, and La Grande Dame has entered a new age of dashing, mineral-infused refinement. For an operation of such a grand scale, the consistency of Veuve Clicquot is unrivalled in all of Champagne.

'Veuve Clicquot is a big house where we have a big responsibility to maintain the style, but every day we work to improve the quality,' chef de cave Dominique Demarville explains as he shows me through one of his two expansive wineries in Reims. With a glimmer in his eye he announces, 'The winery is like a kitchen where we can experiment!'

Then he thrusts open a gigantic door to reveal a grand spectacle of proportions I have never witnessed anywhere in Champagne. Oak barrels. Huge oak barrels. New foudres of 5000 litres and 7500 litres. Lots of them. I know of winemakers proud to show off just one of these beauties. And here, hidden in an enormous warehouse somewhere in the depths of Veuve Clicquot, are 30 of them, lined up in all of their towering magnificence of intricately crafted French oak, perfectly interconnected with arteries of polished stainless steel.

These 200,000 litres of oak-fermented wine — a tiny drop in the ocean of Clicquot — will become just 5–10% of its vintage wines, and a smaller proportion of non-vintage reserves. Leading me around the room to sample from his battalion of barrels, Demarville is as excited as a kid with a room full of new toys. 'Sometimes my team tells me I'm too involved in what I'm doing, but I work with my heart and not my head,' he confesses as he pours me an Oger chardonnay of which he's particularly proud. 'Barrel fermentation offers the chance to improve without changing the Clicquot style,' he explains. 'To add some spice!'

PROGRESSIVE TRANSFORMATION

It's a subtle twist, but it typifies the evolution that is slowly transforming one of Champagne's biggest players, leaving no stage of production untouched, revolutionising vineyards, vinification, and most notably its regimes of malolactic fermentation, reserves and dosage. 'The Veuve Clicquot style is about richness, but also about brightness: strong and full-bodied and at the same time fresh,' Demarville clarifies. It's in brightness and freshness that he has most demonstrably refined these wines since taking the helm in 2006, at just 39 years of age.

This has not been an easy time to drive such evolution. 'With climate change, we are seeing vintages which are more and more diverse,' he reveals. Since 2000, the house has declared just five vintages: 2002, 2004, 2006, 2008 and 2012 (and no Vintage Brut in 2006 or La Grande Dame in 2002).

Demarville remains confident about the future. 'So many things have happened in Champagne over the past century, and we will adapt again. We will adjust our winegrowing and winemaking to ensure we can continue to make champagnes of elegance and minerality.'

PRIVILEGED VINEYARD RESOURCES

'Everything starts in the vineyard!' Demarville declares, and for Clicquot, this represents a substantial and enviably positioned resource of 382 hectares of estate vines, including a wealth of grand crus, providing for just 20% of its needs, with a further 125 hectares supplied by LVMH vineyards, boosting the total to 30%. The remainder is sourced from 1200 growers with an average of less than one hectare each. Many have supplied fruit to no other company for some generations. Top price is paid when the quality warrants it.

One famous grower–producer in Ambonnay, who has trouble supplying demand for their own cuvées, and hence wants to keep as much of their fruit as they can, still sells to Veuve Clicquot because the company provides great support and expertise for managing their vineyards. 'Not every house is like this, but Clicquot is very good,' they revealed. Last year, the company created a new association to encourage its young growers.

Clicquot's own vineyards are planted to almost 50% chardonnay — a high proportion in Champagne, particularly for a house in which every cuvée is led by pinot noir. The Montagne de Reims has been the focus for Clicquot historically, and it is the proud custodian of some of the finest sites for pinot noir in Verzy, Verzenay and Bouzy. These form the core of La Grande Dame. 'Our goal is to showcase what we can do in the vineyards,' Demarville reveals. The 2008 La Grande Dame will be 95% pinot noir and 2012 will be 90%.

I was privileged to an inside perspective at Clicquot, shadowing Demarville on four separate occasions during harvest 2014, visiting growers and experiencing his press centre in Verzy and red winemaking facility in Bouzy. I was confronted by his dedication: over the three weeks of harvest, he visits every press centre and 15–20% of his vineyards to engage with his growers. 'Motivation, motivation, motivation!' He works long days from 6am each day and spends 80% of his time in the vineyards, including in the Côte des Bar, where the house sources 15% of its needs. 'I have a dream,' Demarville announces. 'I hope that one day in Champagne we will pay for grapes according to quality, not according to volume and vineyard designation.'

Clicquot is working to enhance quality by reducing use of herbicides, and planting grasses in the mid-rows of its vineyards to encourage deeper roots. 'We are changing our view about grape-growing and what we're doing with the growers,' Demarville says. 'We are more aware of what happens in the soil, of how to follow the ripening of the grapes, and we are tasting the grapes more and more during the ripening season. This all helps to increase the quality of our wines.' Outside of harvest, Demarville spends more than one-third of his year in the vineyards, the part of his job he loves the most. 'Champagne is a wine, and you can't make a good wine without understanding what happens in the vineyards.'

EVOLUTIONARY WINEMAKING

Veuve Clicquot has trialled earlier harvesting and other means of retaining acidity. 'In the wake of climate change we must manage not only what happens in the vineyards, but also the winery,' Demarville clarifies. He has traditionally allowed every parcel to complete malolactic fermentation, but since 2007 has experimented with blocking malolactic in some parcels destined for its reserves and vintage cuvées. 'About 10–15% without malolactic fermentation will likely help our wines, without changing the style,' he suggests. This has created a dilemma in maintaining consistency, since malolactic fermentation also contributes texture.

The introduction of Demarville's prized foudres in 2007 may prove to be the answer, providing barrel fermentation texture without oak flavour to a house style that has traditionally relied on stainless steel tanks. He stepped up the regime in 2012 — a vintage of 'amazing acidity' — by blocking malolactic fermentation in half the foudres. These vins clairs looked incredible at just a few months of age, but the real proof came in the launch of the spellbinding 2008 vintage this year. He plans to introduce more foudres in the future.

The threat of more extreme vintages in the wake of climate change has also bolstered Demarville's resolve to increase his stocks of reserve wines. 'Look at the last four harvests — 2008 was exceptional, with high acidity and lots of structure; 2009 was ripe, with low acidity; 2010 was dilute, and 2011 was very inconsistent. If you don't have sufficient stocks of reserve wines, you can't make great non-vintage champagne,' he points out. On average, Yellow Label Brut Non-Vintage receives 35% reserve wines, increasing every year, with 42% in 2011.

'Our style of lots of body, complexity and richness needs a lot of reserve wines,' he explains. Clicquot holds the biggest collection of reserve wines in Champagne besides Krug. These are amazing wines, and at a full quarter-century of maturity, a 1988 Cramant was ravishingly concentrated and complex, with allusions of chocolate. Clicquot holds the equivalent of an entire year of production in more than 400 different reserve wines, each of which is tasted twice every year, allocated before they begin to decline. All are held fresh on lees without filtration in tanks cooled to below 14°C.

Demarville points out that it's easier to control and refine wine in stainless steel tanks with temperature control, than under oak without temperature control. 'We are able to be more precise with our blending now, which has enabled us to reduce levels of dosage,' he says. 'We are not reducing dosage due to climate change, but because we have better control in the winery. Over the past 40 years we have been able to build greater purity and precision and so reduce dosage gradually.'

It's a flattering trend for Clicquot, embodied most emphatically in Yellow Label Brut Non-Vintage, which was candied and sweet with 12g/L dosage five years ago, now much more refreshing at 9g/L. Demarville has resisted the 'low-dosage lobby', as he calls it. 'We have a different vision in that the final sensation of sugar is affected not only by quantity, but by time in the cellar after dosage. Our vintage wine is released a year after disgorgement, so the impact of the sugar is diminished.'

Rosé is an increasingly important style for Clicquot, representing 5–6% of sales, with forecasts that this will double. 'Our demand for rosé has been amazing!' he exclaims. 'It's growing as a category so much faster than white champagne, fuelled by incredible improvements in the style over the past five or six years.'

Ten hectares of estate pinot noir vines are allocated to red wine production for rosé in Bouzy alone, green harvested to reduce yields to 30–40% less than normal, and picked at high maturity. Clicquot also sources from 'top' growers in Bouzy and Ambonnay, and in 2012, for the first time, signed a contract with direct suppliers dedicated to red wines, to grow production. The house operates a state-of-the-art winery dedicated to red wine production in Bouzy, Demarville has created a new room for red wine storage in Reims, and a red wine facility is currently being built in the Aube. When he showed me through his Bouzy facility I was stunned at its pristine cleanliness mid-vintage. Samples of red wine ferments displayed breathtaking violet and rose petal aromatics, culminating in the most profound Champagne red wine I've ever tasted. From the earth-shaking Clos Colin parcel on the mid-slope of Bouzy, there is complexity and depth that I have only ever seen in grand cru red Burgundy. It's fittingly reserved for La Grande Dame Rosé.

After much anticipation, I'm delighted Clicquot has introduced QR codes on its Cave Privées and La Grande Dame, hoping to roll these out across its full range, to reveal disgorgement dates, blends and dosages.

Veuve Clicquot has plans to grow slowly, expecting to outgrow its facilities on Rue des Crayères in Reims within five or six years, and has intentions to create a new winery close to Reims. 'We are trialling many things in winemaking today, so we have the answers to design our new facility,' explains Demarville.

The lack of pretence and big-company 'spin' of Dominique Demarville is refreshing in the world of corporate champagne. I have come to a high respect for what this man has achieved in his short time. There are few in Champagne who could seamlessly refine a house as large as this. The 2008 base Yellow Label was his first blend, and the finest I have seen.

'It is because 2008 is an amazing year!' Demarville responds. 'And I am very fortunate to have a talented and passionate team.'

Chardonnay harvest 2014 in a Veuve Clicquot vineyard in Trépail on the eastern slopes of the Montagne de Reims.

Veuve Clicquot Yellow Label Brut NV $$

91 points • 2010 BASE VINTAGE • DISGORGED AUGUST 2013 • TASTED IN BRISBANE
92 points • 2008 BASE VINTAGE • TASTED IN MELBOURNE

50-55% pinot noir, 28-33% chardonnay, 15-20% meunier; from 50-60 villages; 25-40% reserves;
15 million bottles

It takes Demarville and his team four months of daily tastings to make Yellow Label, tasting
2000 different wines and selecting 400–500 to make up the final blend. Their expertise is
reflected in a gentle trajectory of refinement over recent years. Pinot noir leads out confidently
with red apple, red cherry and mixed spice, over a toasty and bready backdrop of bottle-derived
complexity, finishing with subtle phenolic grip and good persistence. Lively acid line and well-
integrated dosage make for a well-assembled, accurate and appealing apéritif. The 2008 base
is still the best ever, but for a difficult season, the 2010 is a more than laudable achievement
at this volume.

Veuve Clicquot Rosé Brut NV $$

92 points • 2010 BASE VINTAGE • DISGORGED LATE JULY 2013 • TASTED IN
BRISBANE, SYDNEY & MELBOURNE

50-55% pinot noir, 28-33% chardonnay, 15-20% meunier; 25-40% reserve wines; Brut Yellow Label
with 12% red wines from the villages that Demarville upholds as Champagne's best for red wine
production: Bouzy, Ambonnay, Verzy, Verzenay, Dizy, Aÿ, Cumières and Les Riceys; 10g/L dosage;
1.4 million bottles annually

This is a lesson in what a difference 12% red wine can make in a blend, particularly in the hands
of one of the finest red wine outfits in all of Champagne. In its medium salmon guise, this is
an elegant, refined and pretty rosé, in an appealingly fruit-focused style of vibrant red berries,
red apple, lemon zest and pink pepper. Tannins are impeccably handled, leaving lively acidity to
define the structure completely uninterrupted by well-integrated dosage. A long finish confirms
a particularly distinguished Clicquot Rosé.

Veuve Clicquot Vintage Brut 2008 $$$

96 points • DISGORGED MID-2014 • TASTED IN REIMS

61% pinot noir from Ambonnay, Bouzy, Ay, Tauxières-Mutry, Avenay-Val-d'Or, Verzy and Verzenay; 34% chardonnay
from Avize, Cramant, Le Mesnil-sur-Oger, Oger and Vertus; 5% meunier, mostly from Ludes and Dizy; 5% aged in large
oak foudres; 8g/L dosage

Demarville lists 2008 in the top 10 vintages for Clicquot, a season of 'wonderful depth, minerality and a fine and
delicate spirit'. The wine he has drawn from this is as great as any Clicquot vintage I have tasted. A year before
its release, it's wound up tight, with coiled tension and tightly clenched acidity, yet at once light-footed in its airy
delicacy. Beach-fresh lemon of high-noon brightness is the theme, touched with suggestions of blood orange rind
and the beginnings of nougat and brioche. A glimpse of oak lends just a subtle, well-integrated toasty note, but the
real highlight is its breathtakingly fine, expansive chalk mineral landscape. The secret with this vintage is to keep
your hands off it for as many decades as you possibly can. It has the euphoric freshness to outlive even the most
disciplined willpower.

The Champagne Guide

VEUVE CLICQUOT VINTAGE BRUT 2004 $$$

95 points • DISGORGED OCTOBER 2012 • TASTED IN BRISBANE, SYDNEY & MELBOURNE

62% pinot noir, 30% chardonnay, 8% meunier; around 20 grand cru and premier cru Marne villages; 7g/L dosage

Clicquot's noble commitment to releasing fewer vintages offers us the wonderful opportunity to spectate as its cuvées evolve gracefully through release cycles that linger for year after year. I loved 2004 Clicquot on first sight in 2011, and now it's in an even happier place. For the pinot-led, full-bodied style of Clicquot, it was tightly wound on release, and has evolved a wonderful layer of secondary complexity of brioche, ginger cake, roast nuts, honey and vanilla, upholding delightful red berry, fleshy white peach, white currant and citrus zest of awesome poise. It's supported all the way by that refined acid line that has always defined this vintage, and soft chalk minerality that unites seamlessly with the texture of long lees age, set off by one of the lowest dosages ever for a Clicquot vintage. It's evolving majestically, with no sign of fading anytime soon.

VEUVE CLICQUOT VINTAGE ROSÉ 2008 $$$

96 points • DISGORGED MID-2014 • TASTED IN REIMS

Veuve Clicquot Vintage Brut 2008, with 14% red wine from Bouzy; 7g/L dosage

It's in Clicquot's red wine facilities that I've encountered some of the most transcendental red wines in all of Champagne, but as they're reserved exclusively as rosé blending components, I've wished there were some way for the world to experience these enthralling wines. It took a vintage of the beguiling transparency of 2008 to provide the window. It's not just about the colour, though it could be: so radiant is its full salmon hue, it's almost luminescent. Nor is it just about the fragrance, enchantingly delicate in its rose petals, wild strawberries and musk, which permeate, ethereal and unrelenting, all the way through the palate. No, the true mastery of red winemaking in Champagne is tannin texture, and this wine is a case study in how it's done: so subtle that it does nothing to interrupt the profound chalk minerality of an elegant season, yet at the same time furnishing the understated grip that promises enduring potential. This is one of the most sublime Clicquot rosés of all, with a freshness hard to fathom at seven years of age, charged by a lightning bolt of brilliant acidity, the signature of this classic season.

VEUVE CLICQUOT VINTAGE ROSÉ 2004 $$$

95 points • DISGORGED MARCH 2013 • TASTED IN BOUZY & BRISBANE

Vintage Brut 2004 with red wine; 62% pinot noir, 30% chardonnay, 8% meunier; 15% red wine from Bouzy; a blend of about 20 Montagne de Reims grand and premier crus; 9g/L dosage

Clicquot's Vintage Rosé philosophy is to blend its Vintage Brut with red wines of structure and tannin to create more character. Already in the market for 3.5 years, the bottle I tasted in Bouzy took me by complete surprise, showing even less development than this cuvée exhibited two years ago, endowed in magnificent elegance and grace, with a freshness of red berry, apple and pear that belied its medium crimson copper hue. A wine of very fine chalk minerality, subtle tannins and outstanding persistence, promising a very long future. A bottle tasted in Australia was much truer to the evolution I anticipated, notably toasty and savoury, with nuances of flinty reduction. Its fleshiness had dimmed, making space for tannin structure to step forward, asserting itself with structural drive yet, to its credit, in no way dried out or bitter. Its depth of tertiary complexity is yet to build, placing it in something of an in-between phase. It's progressing to a happy place, and needs another five years to get there.

Veuve Clicquot La Grande Dame Brut 2006 $$$$

96 points • Disgorged early 2014 • Tasted in Reims

53% pinot noir, largely from Verzy and Verzenay, with a touch of Bouzy, Ambonnay and Aÿ; 47% chardonnay, predominantly from Avize, Oger and Le Mesnil-sur-Oger; 8g/L dosage

In response to the generous, rounded, supple 2006 season, Demarville's predecessor, Jacques Péters, increased the share of chardonnay in his final La Grande Dame. Demarville confessed to some nervousness at launching the 2006 after the calibre of the linear and refined 2004. The two seasons certainly stand in contrast, with the 2006 already much more approachable and immediate. It launches confidently into generous, rich ginger, honey, toast, roast nuts and brioche, well into its phase of secondary evolution, yet in no way broad or developed. Citrus-zest liveliness defines a honed focus, while a fine chalk mineral structure keeps the finish lively and energetic.

Veuve Clicquot La Grande Dame Brut 2004 $$$$

98 points • Disgorged June 2013 • Tasted in Brisbane, Perth & Yarra Valley

61% pinot noir from Verzenay, Verzy, Bouzy, Ambonnay and Aÿ; 39% chardonnay from Avize, Oger and Le Mesnil-sur-Oger; 70-75% estate vines; 100% malolactic fermentation; 8g/L dosage

I've been besotted with the disarmingly youthful LGD 2004 from my very first taste in early 2012. I have always upheld that it needs more time, yet nothing prepared me for just how much this cuvée has ascended in the past 18 months. I've lined it up at least five times against the other top prestige cuvées, most of which boast significantly higher prices, and it has ranked among the best every single time. The 2004 ushers in a new age of LGD, dramatically high-pitched and as glittering as fresh powder snow in full sun. Its minerality shimmers with ethereal chalk dust and sea-salt texture, penetrating deep into the mouth, illuminated by dazzling acidity. It launches with euphoric white citrus, yellow stone fruits and white cherries, increasingly morphing into nougat, vanilla, anise and toasted brioche, tightly contained within a delicate shell. Softly salty chalk minerality glimmers and dances long and enduring on an awe-inspiring finish. This is a breathtaking La Grande Dame, slowly accumulating warm generosity without shedding coiled tension, still hiding decades of potential in its folds. Enjoy the spectacle right away, and come back in a decade for a mesmerising encore.

Veuve Clicquot La Grande Dame Rosé 2006 $$$$$

96 points • Disgorged mid-2014 • Tasted in Reims

La Grande Dame 2006, with 15% red wine from Veuve Clicquot's Clos Colin vineyard in Bouzy

Clicquot's Vintage Rosé's ideal is for the grapes to speak, and La Grande Dame Rosé's ideal is for the soil to speak. And speak it does, with an avalanche of tumbling fury of chalk minerality that melds so seamlessly with very fine, impeccably managed tannins that it's impossible to detect where one finishes and the other starts. Clos Colin delivers a red wine of folkloric magnificence, building a medium copper salmon hue. It swoops and dives with white cherry and candied cherry character, and a hint of flinty reductiveness not unusual for LGD Rosé on release. This is a rosé of finely poised acid line and a structure to sustain it longer in the cellar than one might expect for this warm season. Patience.

The Champagne Guide

VEUVE CLICQUOT LA GRANDE DAME ROSÉ 1989

98 points • ORIGINAL DISGORGEMENT, PROBABLY 1997 • TASTED IN BOUZY

A case study in graceful strength, and quintessential evidence of the ability of rosé to blossom decades after disgorgement, even in a year of considerable heat. With the medium crimson copper hue of middle age, it's now enchantingly silky, with a graceful finesse, effortless presence and layers of butterscotch, golden fruit cake, ginger, dried nectarine and fig, culminating in the fragrance of tilled earth warmed by the first golden sunlight of dawn. It lingers with pinpoint accurate line, outstanding persistence and a very fine bead.

VEUVE CLICQUOT CAVE PRIVÉE BRUT 1989 $$$$$

95 points • TASTED IN REIMS

67% pinot noir, 33% chardonnay; 4g/L dosage

Veuve Clicquot has the resourcefulness to set aside a respectable allocation of every vintage release for its late-disgorged Cave Privée, a remarkable collection of 700,000 bottles of a depth and magnitude that must be unmatched in all of Champagne. A bold venture, not least because vintages that don't age well will never surface. Demarville considers 1989 one of the best vintages of the last 30 years, with a ripe concentration that sustains it in spite of lower acidity. It's now attained its glorious peak, a handsome expression of the secondary development of champagne, full of roast almonds, brioche, ginger cake and honey, finishing with a flourish of pine sap and a wisp of warm hearth. It's creamy and caressing, contrasting soft, dry, mineral structure with a silky, buttery flow, upholding accurate acid line, fine mineral integrity, and the chewy structure of a warm season. If 1989 was your year, open it for your next birthday.

VEUVE CLICQUOT CAVE PRIVÉE BRUT 1982 $$$$$

94 points • DISGORGED IN 2010 • TASTED IN REIMS

66% pinot noir, 34% chardonnay; 4g/L dosage

Here's evidence that high-yielding Champagne vintages are capable of soaring beyond 30 years with effortless grace. Attaining a calm confidence in its old age, it's now deep and tertiary, with notes of chocolate, burnt orange, roast nuts, butterscotch and even pink grapefruit. It lingers with perseverance and fine chalk minerality, sustained by focused and lively acidity. This bottle showed more oxidative development than a far superior bottle I tasted two years ago. The best bottles will live happily for a few years yet.

Veuve Clicquot Cave Privée Rosé Brut 1990 $$$$$

98 points • Disgorged March 2011 • Tasted in Reims

56% pinot noir, 33% chardonnay, 11% meunier; 17% Bouzy red wine; 4g/L dosage

At this age, every bottle is its own universe, and at a full, majestic 25 years of age, this one happens to be breathtakingly fresh, a world away from the bottle I tasted two years ago. It's still a lively medium salmon hue with a subtle copper tint, a stunning and seamless accord between the primary pink pepper, pomegranate, strawberry and red cherry fruit and lively acid of youth, and deep tertiary complexity, conjuring memories of pine nettles, sweet pipe smoke and the warm glow of smouldering embers. Brilliant acid line and determined focus promise decades of life yet. Delivering such formidable power while sustaining arresting finesse is one of Champagne's highest arts, captured here in a melodramatic juxtaposition of reverberating complexity and ageless freshness.

Veuve Clicquot Cave Privée Rosé Brut 1989 $$$$$

97 points • Tasted in Reims from magnum

Two-thirds pinot noir and one-third chardonnay, blended with pinot noir red wine; 4g/L dosage; 24,825 bottles

The evolution of champagne in magnums is always much slower and more assured than in standard bottles, exemplified at this grand age. There is a freshness here of pink pepper, red cherry and strawberry fruit, enlivened by pronounced, wonderful chalk mineral definition and focused acid line, steadily evolving to the colour of the warm glow of early morning sunrise. Inhale, and you step out of a cool, damp morning in a towering pine forest, into an old hunting lodge, with pine sap sizzling from logs in a dusty stone fireplace. Sip, and you meet the most enchanting air of leathery old grand cru red Burgundy, with all of its truffles, 'sous bois' (forest undergrowth) and mushrooms. Reserve this enchanting old rosé for long, melancholy nights before glowing embers in faraway places.

Veuve Clicquot Cave Privée Rosé Brut 1979 $$$$$

98 points • Disgorged 2011 • Tasted in Reims

61% pinot noir, 33% chardonnay, 6% meunier; 4g/L dosage

The 1979 has proven to be the most enduring vintage of the '70s, and happened to be privileged to the highest proportion of red wine of any Clicquot vintage (19%). This serves to draw out its Burgundian-like pinot noir personality, even at a dignified 36 years of age. If its salmon copper hue is a testimony to the mesmeric longevity of 1979, then its primary aromas and flavours are nothing short of spellbinding. Wild strawberries and fresh cherries still abound, underpinned by a lifetime of gathered complexity akin to old red Burgundy, expressed in white truffles, venison, charcuterie, balsamic vinegar, kirsch, pepper, and it goes on. Mineral definition remains impeccably pronounced, acidity lingers long and true, and the bead is fine and creamy. A towering monument to magnificent old rosé, with no hint of crumbling on any side.

The Champagne Guide

VEUVE FOURNY & FILS

(Verv Fawny e Feess)

7/10

5 RUE DU MESNIL 51130 VERTUS

www.champagne-veuve-fourny.com

CHAMPAGNE

Vᵉ **FOURNY & FILS**

une Famille, un Clos, un Premier Cru

*W*hen a tiny plot on pure chalk in the coveted 'Le Mont Ferré' hillsides of the northern end of Vertus towards Le Mesnil-sur-Oger came up for sale in the summer of 2011, offers poured in from big houses, but the grower chose the brothers Emmanuel and Charles-Henry Fourny as its new custodians. The offer was indicative of the respect with which the young fifth-generation growers manage some of the finest terroirs in Vertus. Their location on Rue du Mesnil on the northern edge of Vertus is a clue to their success, with vineyards capturing the more mineral side of the premier cru village neighbouring the grand cru of Le Mesnil-sur-Oger itself.

When I first visited just four weeks before the scheduled start of vintage 2011, Rue du Mesnil was completely closed off. Veuve Fourny's winery was totally gutted and swarming with construction workers. Emmanuel Fourny emerged from an early-morning meeting with his builders.

'We are grateful for the cooler weather,' he said, 'because there's no chance our new winery would be ready for an early vintage!'

It was the beginning of a grand new era for a family who has tended vineyards at the southern end of the Côte des Blancs since 1856 and made its own champagne since 1931. Theirs is one of the most expressive champagnes of the character of their beloved village of Vertus.

VINEYARD FOCUS

Veuve Fourny's focus remains resolutely and exclusively on Vertus, apart from a small parcel in Cramant. 'I like to express the terroir of Vertus and show that you can have a lot of expression with just one village,' says Emmanuel, who has a self-confessed obsession with purity and precision.

The sunny, south-east-oriented slopes of Vertus are a great part of the Côte des Blancs for him to bottle his vision. 'Vertus gives us better expression of fruit than the neighbouring grand crus of Le Mesnil-sur-Oger and Oger,' he explains. 'The chardonnay here has more of a pinot noir richness to it, which enables us to create blends exclusively from chardonnay that can be complete.'

The brothers are now harvesting riper than in the past, aiming for 10.4–10.5 degrees potential, diminishing the need for chaptalisation. 'I am convinced that the riper you pick the grapes, the more pronounced the minerality,' says Emmanuel. This is evolving the house style towards the riper, more exotic fruit spectrum of Vertus, resembling notes of ripe oranges. It is yet to be seen how this bodes for longevity.

The east-facing slopes of the village nurture chardonnay of fresh definition, while its warmer south-facing aspects are among the only vineyards of the Côte des Blancs planted to pinot noir. The brothers own 8.7 hectares, predominantly on the mineral hillside of 'Le Mont Ferré' on the border of Le Mesnil-sur-Oger, where thin soils bless vines with easy access to chalk, and a south-east aspect imparts greater fruit expression than the more rounded style of south-facing slopes.

They manage a further 3.6 hectares of family vines now owned by their cousins, supplemented with almost eight hectares managed according to an organic philosophy, most of which were originally part of the family estate. The Fournys work closely with their growers, whom they describe as 'small, serious and interested in separation of plots for precision winemaking'. These are mostly young growers and friends, who are invited back to taste their plots after vinification. In all, the brothers manage the vineyards and harvests for a sizeable 60% of the grapes they purchase. A total of 20 hectares provides for an annual production of 200,000 bottles.

Estate vines now average a hefty 45 years of age. 'Vines over 30 years transform the minerality of the chalk into the salty minerality of the wine, which we feel is very important,' Emmanuel explains. Such old vines ensure that yields are very low for Champagne, averaging below 60hL/hectare, less than two-thirds of Champagne's average, 'to produce a balance in our wines'. Green harvests are conducted in high-yielding years like 2004, when 30% of the crop was dropped.

Veuve Fourny balances a resolute commitment to the environment with a realistic awareness of the limitations of viticulture in a climate as marginal as this. Vineyard practice is essentially organic, with the exception of sprays, which are used when necessary. Grasses are cultivated in the mid-rows of one-third of vineyards, another third is cultivated to bare soil, and herbicide has now been eliminated across all vineyards. Insect breeding is controlled using pheromones, canopy management is used instead of chemicals to control botrytis, and composting is used in place of fertiliser.

A normal spray regime is used to manage mildew, particularly in years like 2012, when it saved the crop.

Vertus chardonnay has the richness to confidently stand alone.

'We like the organic philosophy, but we don't want to sacrifice our grapes to mildew,' Emmanuel says, referring to a trial the brothers conducted shortly after returning to the family estate in the mid-1990s. Synthetic chemicals were forsaken in two parcels, but the wild spread of mildew necessitated weekly sprayings with copper sulphate — permitted under biodynamics, despite its toxicity and detrimental effect on the soil and vine growth. Much of the crop was lost and they returned to non-toxic synthetic products.

On the same site as the house on Rue du Mesnil, Clos Faubourg Notre-Dame is a tiny plot of less than one-third of one hectare, purchased by the brothers' grandfather in 1920, but it was only in 1990 that Emmanuel and Charles-Henry proposed to their mother that the vineyard be bottled separately.

With just 40 centimetres of soil before the chalk, they consider it a good plot, 'not better, but different, holding its freshness as a long-ageing style'. Its micro-climate is protected by the enclosure. This plot is the source of their flagship cuvée. The brothers' grandmother built a house on part of the clos in 1965, which they removed in 2012 after she passed away. They have replanted this part of the vineyard to chardonnay, though won't use the fruit in this wine until the vines have reached 12 years of age.

MINIMAL-INTERVENTION WINEMAKING

The brothers are excited about the potential of their new winemaking facility to capture greater detail from every parcel. Previously, the press house was in a different location to the winery. Tanks and winemaking equipment that had gradually amassed over the years were not well suited to small-batch winemaking, so they boldly sold it all and created the new winery from scratch. A huge investment for a small company, and all the more impressive with no imperative to increase production.

Charles-Henry was initially sceptical about the outlay, preferring to see the investment poured into more vineyards, but he was impressed with the outcome, enabling them to separate every single parcel for the first time. 'The new winery is completely adaptive to the size of the plots, giving us greater precision in the details,' he said. 'It will help us make a more precise expression of each place, so you can expect our wines to be finer.'

The 60 plots from which the brothers source are quite distinct, and they showed me 2012 vins clairs that revealed that even parcels just 150 metres apart can show significant diversity. These can now be kept separate for the first time, thanks to a small press that runs 24 hours a day during vintage, and tanks to keep 20 blends, compared with just 12 previously.

Fourny's philosophy of respect and minimal intervention in the vineyards applies equally in the winery, an insulated building built from stone from northern Burgundy and wood from the nearby Vosges. Glass is utilised to capture natural light, all waste water is recycled on the gardens, and a natural cooling system pulls air in when it's cooler outside.

To preserve purity, only the first pressings are used, and the tailles are sold. Vintage wines are unfiltered, and non-vintage wines will follow from the 2012 base. They now use half the sulphur dioxide preservative of the past, but never so low that wines are at risk from oxidation, with wines held on lees for protection. To further inhibit oxidation, barrels are topped weekly rather than monthly. Malolactic fermentation is used selectively, so as to maintain tension in each cuvée, with an average of about three-quarters of parcels completing malolactic. Wines are aged on lees with bâtonnage for 6–8 months after primary fermentation, and aged in bottle between 2.5 and 9 years. The purity of the house style permits refreshingly low dosages, never more than 6g/L, from grape liqueur rather than sugar.

Emmanuel learnt the craft of barrel fermentation with bâtonnage in Burgundy, and this has been a key element of the house style since he commenced in 1990. 'I don't like oxidative champagne, so I don't want to be extremist with wood,' he says. The goal is not to impart the taste of wood, but rather to create fresh, focused and textured wines. 'Micro-oxygenation in barrels enhances the minerality of the soil.'

New barrels are purchased from Burgundy and used for ageing a rich resource of some 200 reserve wines. A preference is given to small, 208-litre barrels to keep small plots separate and provide a balance of surface area and volume. Across the estate, 25% of parcels are fermented in old barrels of 5–15 years of age, and most cuvées are blended with more citrus-accented parcels from tanks.

In 2014 a new 4000-litre foudre was purchased for fermenting and storing reserve wines for Grande Reserve NV and Blanc de Blancs NV, with an aim to avoid oxidation and maintain freshness better than small barrels. The plan is to purchase another foudre every year for the next five years.

This thoughtful approach produces wines that display sensitive oak influence, imparting great resilience and long-ageing potential.

Since 2006, all Veuve Fourny wines have been sealed with Mytik DIAM closures. A five-year trial of DIAM and natural cork revealed DIAM-sealed bottles to be consistent and fresh, with pure fruit, while those under natural cork were more evolved, and 'each bottle had its own personality'. The letter of reply when a corked bottle is returned has not been sent out once since the change was made. Emmanuel refers to natural cork as 'Russian roulette' and regards DIAM as a revolution, crucial for upholding the freshness and purity of the house.

Back labels have been updated to feature impressive detail, including disgorgement date, terroirs, cépage, vinification, assemblage, dosage and even the type of cork. 'More and more people consider champagne like they do table wine,' Charles-Henry explains. 'Our customers keep champagne in their cellars and need to keep track of it.'

Demand for Veuve Fourny has put supply on allocation in every market. The hope is to increase the bottle age of Grande Réserve and Blanc de Blancs from 2.5 years to 3–4 years, but this will take time to achieve, as these cuvées comprise 60% of production.

There is no goal to increase production, even with increased vineyard resources from the 2011 acquisition. 'Our goal is to grow the quality, not the volume, continuing to focus on the vineyards and the winery,' says Emmanuel. 'It depends on whether your goal in life is money or pleasure. My goal is to be able to host tastings and dinners in Japan and Australia and for people to say, "Your wines are wonderful!" That's the goal for me.'

It's a goal the brothers are capably translating into the bottle. The pristine champagnes of Veuve Fourny encapsulate their aspiration of purity, precision and freshness.

Veuve Fourny & Fils Cuvée Grande Réserve Premier Cru Vertus Brut NV $$

89 points • 2011 BASE VINTAGE WITH 50% RESERVES FROM 2010, 2009 & 2008
• DISGORGED SEPTEMBER 2014 • TASTED IN VERTUS
90 points • 2010 BASE VINTAGE WITH 40% RESERVES FROM 2009, 2008 & 2007
• DISGORGED DECEMBER 2013 • TASTED IN BRISBANE, SYDNEY & MELBOURNE

80% chardonnay, 20% pinot noir; 90% Vertus, 10% Cramant and Oger; 20% aged in small oak barrels; 6g/L dosage; DIAM closure

Picking a few weeks after everyone else, the Fourny brothers were happy with the standard of 2011, though both 2011 and 2010 carry a dry extract grip that I've not seen in Fourny before. The high proportion of reserves in this cuvée helps to lift its fruit presence of crunchy grapefruit zest, beurre bosc pear, apple and subtle complexity of almond spice and honey puffs. A firmly textured finish is accented by tangy, primary acidity in the 2011 base, while the 2010 unites rounded balance with fine mineral texture.

Veuve Fourny & Fils Cuvée Blanc de Blancs Vertus Premier Cru NV $$

91 points • 2011 BASE VINTAGE WITH RESERVES FROM 2010, 2009 & 2008
• TASTED IN VERTUS
93 points • 2010 BASE VINTAGE WITH 20% RESERVES FROM 2009, 2008 & 2007
• DISGORGED DECEMBER 2013 • TASTED IN BRISBANE

Low-yielding vines of 50-56hL/hectare, about half of Champagne's average; predominantly from 1950s vines in Fourny's best terroir of Le Mont Ferré; harvested later and with higher concentration; 20% aged in oak barrels on lees; 6g/L dosage; DIAM closure

The 2011 base is expressive of the exotic personality of Vertus, filled with grand complexity of boiled orange and fig, contrasting accurate, salt chalk mineral definition with well-defined acid tension. In the 2010 base, Fourny's mandate of purity and precision shimmers in purity and focus of lemon blossom, lemon zest and lemon juice of soap-powder brightness, while a touch of barrel influence draws out biscuity, brioche depth.

Veuve Fourny & Fils Cuvée Blanc de Blancs Vertus Premier Cru Brut Nature NV $$

90 points • 2011 BASE VINTAGE • TASTED IN VERTUS

Reserves from 2010, 2009 and 2008; low-yielding vines of 50-56hL/hectare, about half of Champagne's average; predominantly from 1950s vines in Le Mont Ferré; harvested later and with higher concentration; 20% aged oak barrels on lees; zero dosage; DIAM closure

Under the command of old vines, the chalk soils of Le Mont Ferré hark more to the mineral structure of the thundering grand crus to their north than to the more fruity premier crus around them, and without the interruption of dosage, the strength of strong, salt-infused mineral texture is pronounced. Fourny's fanatical attention to ripe fruit from low-yielding old vines is declared in boiled orange exotics, finishing with good persistence, though marked by the dry tension of 2011.

The Champagne Guide

Veuve Fourny & Fils Cuvée Monts de Vertus Blanc de Blancs Extra Brut 2009 $$

94 points • Disgorged October 2014 • Tasted in Vertus

This is the new name for the vintage cuvée, always the same single-plot Les Barilliers, in the heart of Vertus near Le Mesnil-sur-Oger; vinified in tanks; 75% malolactic fermentation; aged 6 years in bottle; 3–4g/L dosage; DIAM closure

An exuberant wine from a warm vintage that captures the exoticism of Vertus in boiled orange, glacé fig, mixed spice and grapefruit pith. Resonating with great soils tapped by deep roots, the minerality is very well defined and salty, supported by nicely balanced acidity which draws out a long finish.

Veuve Fourny & Fils Cuvée Blanc de Blancs Vertus Premier Cru Vintage Extra Brut 2008 $$

95 points • Disgorged April 2014 • Tasted in Vertus

As per 2009

A great expression of a fantastic vintage in a mineral-rich site, this is a cuvée of striking complexity, brimming with spice, toast, even blood orange, coffee and dark chocolate. True to the precision of 2008, its core is resolute, a focused expression of lemon vivacity and crunchy red apple. A vintage of great longevity.

Veuve Fourny & Fils Cuvée Blanc de Blancs Vertus Premier Cru Vintage Extra Brut 2007 $$

94 points • Disgorged December 2014 • Tasted in Vertus

As per 2009

The Fournys describe 2007 as a charming vintage, and have captured the elegance and confidence of Vertus in a fresh acid line and soft voice of wonderfully textured, frothy, salty minerality. They've layered this backdrop with the lingering complexity of brioche, coffee and dark chocolate, providing immediate appeal, without interfering with a structure that will hold it for a few years yet.

Veuve Fourny & Fils Cuvée Blanc de Blancs Vertus Premier Cru Vintage Extra Brut 2006 $$

95 points • Tasted in Sydney & Melbourne

As per 2009

An invigorating vintage Fourny that holds its head as high as ever, brilliantly contrasting zesty tension, generous expression and awe-inspiring persistence. Purity is retained in lemon zest freshness, crunchy pear and apple fruit, while age has drawn out subtle almond development. At its core it remains backward and lively, with fruit propelled upwards by all-pervading chalk mineral texture that propagates pristine line and length. Great potential to accelerate for some years yet.

Veuve Fourny & Fils Cuvée R de Vve Fourny & Fils Vertus Extra Brut NV $$

93 points • 2009 BASE VINTAGE • DISGORGED JANUARY 2014 • TASTED IN VERTUS, SYDNEY & MELBOURNE

2009 (aged 1 year in old oak) and 2008 (aged 2 years in old oak); 90% chardonnay, 10% pinot noir; predominantly from Les Barilliers, in the heart of Vertus; average vine age 42 years; fully fermented and aged with bâtonnage in small oak barrels of 4-15 years of age; aged 4 years in bottle; 3g/L dosage; DIAM closure

The honed restraint of Fourny's pristine fruit, meeting the ravishing complexity of old oak and swirling, tossing minerality, makes for quite a display. Fermentation in old oak barrels amplifies bath-salts minerality drawn from the thin soils of the north of Vertus near Le Mesnil-sur-Oger by grand old vines. Carefully crafted old oak cranks things up a notch from Fourny's other non-vintage cuvées, making for a taut and dry blend of R, with a mouthfeel of grapefruit pith texture. High-tensile acidity contrasts low dosage, calling for another few years for oak and acid to relax.

Veuve Fourny & Fils Cuvée du Clos Fg Notre Dame Premier Cru Vertus Extra Brut 2005 $$$$

93 points • DISGORGED DECEMBER 2014 • TASTED IN VERTUS

100% chardonnay; 100% vinified and aged for 9 months on lees in oak barrels of 5-6 years of age; full malolactic fermentation; 3-4g/L dosage; DIAM closure

The Fourny brothers describe their flagship wine as 'eternal' and so, it seems, it is, even in the generous 2005 season. Its acidity is unnerving, its salty chalk mineral structure well scaffolded and its oak support confident, with a structure heightened by the hazelnut bitterness and dry texture of the vintage. The exoticism of Vertus shines in glacé orange and exotic spice, with a rumbling undercurrent of butterscotch, toast and roast nuts. Tight acidity and firm, dry extract make for an assertive finish that demands a decade or more for its oak to soften and mellow.

Veuve Fourny & Fils Cuvée du Clos Fg Notre Dame Premier Cru Vertus Extra Brut 2004 $$$$

93 points • DISGORGED DECEMBER 2014 • TASTED IN VERTUS

As per 2005

Lock up the cellar and throw away the key: Clos Faubourg Notre Dame always needs a very long time to come together. The 2004 projects the lemon and orange citrus freshness of Vertus, softened and rounded thanks to barrel fermentation and almost a decade of bottle age. The grapefruit-pith bitterness characteristic of this cuvée brings grip and definition to a finish of soft, creamy chalk minerality. It needs years to uncoil, and when it does finally emerge, drink it slowly from large glasses at white wine temperature.

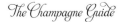

VILMART & CIE

(Viil-mar e See)

5 RUE DES GRAVIÉRES 51500 RILLY-LA-MONTAGNE
www.champagnevilmart.com

CHAMPAGNE

In the heart of the village of Rilly-la-Montagne, a stained-glass window handcrafted by René Champs hangs proud in the reception room of Vilmart & Cie. In five scenes of vivid colour and geometric intricacy, the hands-on attention to detail of Vilmart is depicted in hand pruning, tilling the soil with a hoe, hand picking, pressing, and vinification in large and small oak barrels. It's a fitting tribute to the champagnes of this lauded grower, which faithfully reflect every element of their painstaking production in seamlessly interlocking detail and slightly larger-than-life colour.

'My philosophy is to make wine first and bubbles and effervescence second,' fifth-generation grower Laurent Champs explains.

On the northern slopes of the Montagne de Reims, the leading grower of Rilly-la-Montagne has set a pace since followed by eco-friendly growers everywhere. Painstakingly tended family vineyards, confident but masterful use of oak and an absence of malolactic fermentation make for full and vinous wines that uphold great purity and fine-drawn detail.

The Vilmarts have tended vines in the premier cru village of Rilly-la-Montagne since 1890, and their wines today are sourced exclusively from 11 hectares of family-owned vines in the village and nearby Villers-Allerand. A majority of vines 40–45 years of age provide low yields, planted almost exclusively to chardonnay (60%) and pinot noir (37%), with just 3%

meunier. 'Vilmart is a paradox with so much chardonnay in a village planted to 80% pinot noir and meunier!' Champs points out. In a village long famous for its pinot noir, it's Vilmart's chardonnay-led cuvées that shine brightest, thanks to chalk just 40 centimetres below the surface. 'Chardonnay in Rilly-la-Montagne has a good balance between fruitiness, roundness and a minerality more open and less direct than the Côte des Blancs,' he explains.

A pioneer of eco-friendly viticulture, Vilmart's 12 plots have been organic since 1968, with grasses cultivated in mid-rows. 'I try to respect the soil, the environment and the people as much as I can,' he says. Such is the attention to detail here that soils between the rows of vines have been tilled with a hand hoe for five generations, and no chemical fertilisers, herbicides or pesticides are used. 'My father was organic since

1970, but it was too complex, so I try to balance the philosophies of different methods. I am not convinced that one regime is the answer, so I try to adapt to the seasons, which change dramatically here!'

Since his arrival in 1990, Laurent Champs — great-great-grandson of the founder of the estate, Désiré Vilmart — has carefully refined vinification. 'My wines have something to say to you, and hence the winemaking is different to classic winemaking,' he says. Everything is fed by gravity, and after traditional Coquart pressing and 24 hours settling, all juices are sent straight to oak for fermentation and ageing for 10 months, non-vintage wines in 35–40-year-old foudres of 2200–5000 litres (for micro-oxygenation without oak flavour), and vintage wines in 225-litre Burgundy barrels and 600-litre demi-muids.

Barrels are purchased from Meursault after just one use, and recycled until they are six years old. 'Fifteen years ago we were treated like dinosaurs for using barrels, but now it is very trendy in Champagne!' says Champs. Malolactic fermentation is completely blocked in all cuvées.

Of champagne's practitioners who make full use of oak without malolactic fermentation, the wines of Laurent Champs are among the most seamless and well integrated. 'Wood is a good servant, but a bad master!' he points out. 'It is only there to draw out the flavours of the vintage. I like wines of creamy softness, silky, yet still fresh.' His wines meet the aspiration with resounding precision. These are cuvées of freshness, elegance and richness, articulating the salty minerality of the northern Montagne with unusual clarity, while utilising the creamy texture of oak fermentation to integrate malic acidity, blessing young cuvées with a harmonious approachability while upholding age-worthy endurance.

A new labelling system prints the cépage and disgorgement date on the back of every bottle.

VILMART & CIE GRANDE RÉSERVE BRUT PREMIER CRU NV $$

92 points • 2012 BASE VINTAGE • DISGORGED JUNE 2014 • TASTED IN RILLY-LA-MONTAGNE

70% pinot noir, 30% chardonnay; 2011 reserves; fermented and matured for 10 months in large oak foudres; no malolactic fermentation; 10g/L dosage

Grand Réserve and Rubis are Vilmart's only cuvées led by pinot noir, and they never hit the high notes of his other cuvées. That said, this is a well-crafted, harmonious and seamless rendition of Grande Réserve. Large oak fermentation integrates lemon, grapefruit and dried pear fruit with well-defined malic acidity, drawing out notes of roast hazelnut and subtle spice. The accord produces a soft mouthfeel and creamy bead, while upholding freshness and definition.

VILMART & CIE GRAND CELLIER BRUT PREMIER CRU NV $$

93 points • 2011 BASE VINTAGE • DISGORGED FEBRUARY 2014 • TASTED IN RILLY-LA-MONTAGNE

70% chardonnay, 30% pinot noir; reserves from 2010 and 2009; fermented and matured for 10 months in large oak foudres; no malolactic fermentation; 8-9g/L dosage

Laurent describes Grand Cellier as 'audacious and elegant', expressive of the fresh citrus notes and saltiness of Rilly chardonnay. It rises to the expectation, confidently chardonnay-led in its grapefruit and lemon character, capturing a salty mineral mouthfeel more pronounced than others on the northern slopes of the Montagne. Vibrant, enduring malic-acid drive promises to sustain it long in the cellar, yet even at this young age it is not hard or austere, massaged graciously by barrel fermentation and bottle age, which add their own nuances of coffee bean and hazelnut.

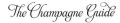

VILMART & CIE GRAND CELLIER D'OR BRUT PREMIER CRU 2010 $$$

94 points • DISGORGED MAY 2014 • TASTED IN RILLY-LA-MONTAGNE

80% chardonnay, 20% pinot noir; from vines over 45 years of age; fermented and matured for 10 months in 220L oak barrels; no malolactic fermentation; 8-9g/L dosage

Young chardonnay with full malic acidity, vinified entirely in oak, can be a formidable combination, and the seamless harmony in this wine is testimony to Laurent Champs' sensitivity and skill. This was one of the first finished 2010 vintage wines I tasted, and even in its infantile, pre-release state it portrays a calm integration between fruit, oak and malic acidity. Champs' vintage philosophy is to draw out the natural expression of the year, which he describes in 2010 as 'delicate, creamy and feminine'. It's currently quite precocious in its generous exotic fruit exuberance of grilled pineapple and star fruit, over a core of focused grapefruit and lemon, underscored by brioche and toasted marshmallow. An impressive result for the season, with long lingering malic acidity and salty chalk mineral texture hovering on a harmonious and seamless finish.

VILMART & CIE GRAND CELLIER D'OR BRUT PREMIER CRU 2009 $$$

95 points • DISGORGED JUNE 2013 • TASTED IN RILLY-LA-MONTAGNE

80% chardonnay, 20% pinot noir; from vines over 45 years of age; fermented and matured for 10 months in 220L oak barrels; no malolactic fermentation; 8-9g/L dosage

To Champs, 2009 was a season of excellent balance between sugar and acidity, already open and creamy on release. It rolls through an enticingly complex array of fig, white peach, golden fruit cake, pepper and exotic spice, seamlessly laced together by Champs' magical touch in small oak barrels. The buttered-toast notes of maturity are beginning to emerge. It's at once silky, textural and long, and at the same time bright in its malic acid structure.

VILMART & CIE COEUR DE CUVÉE PREMIER CRU 2007 $$$$

95 points • DISGORGED MAY 2014 • TASTED IN RILLY-LA-MONTAGNE

80% chardonnay, 20% pinot noir; from Vilmart's oldest vines of 55 years of age yielding under 45hL/hectare, less than half of Champagne's average; only the heart of the pressing; fermented and matured for 10 months in small oak barrels of 1-3 years of age; no malolactic fermentation; 8-9g/L dosage

Such is the prominence of aromas of hazelnuts, vanilla and coffee from very classy barrels that one braces for a thud of oak stave impact on the palate. Thankfully, no such blow is delivered, its oak instead furnishing surprisingly supple, creamy, silky smoothness, without a hint of interruption to the refreshing flow of grapefruit and lemon, characteristic of the flavoursome and fresh 2007 vintage. Its crafted integration and seamless longevity are a credit to Champs' skill in the cellar. Don't drink it too soon, too cold or from narrow flutes.

VILMART & CIE COEUR DE CUVÉE PREMIER CRU 2006 $$$$

96 points • DISGORGED JUNE AND SEPTEMBER 2013 • TASTED IN RILLY-LA-MONTAGNE

As per 2007

Vilmart's top cuvée in a vintage that Champs describes as 'solar, rich, complex, mature and open' is an unexpectedly exhilarating display of silky, seamless texture. Grand complexity is on parade, with fruit and oak cartwheeling in perfect unison in a fanfare of peach, fig, grapefruit, preserved lemon, nougat, sugared almonds and vanilla. Persistence and line are outstanding, charged with well-integrated malic acidity, finishing with energetic drive, untiring persistence and pinpoint control.

VILMART & CIE GRAND CELLIER RUBIS PREMIER CRU BRUT NV $$$$

92 points • 2011 BASE VINTAGE • DISGORGED NOVEMBER 2013 • TASTED IN RILLY-LA-MONTAGNE

90% pinot noir, 10% chardonnay; around 15% red wine; 2010 reserves; base wines fermented and aged for 10 months in large oak foudres; red wines aged in 600L demi-muids; no malolactic fermentation

Rubis is classically deep and savoury, and the 2011 season serves to heighten its personality. A full salmon hue, it's a style of prominent structure, entwined with pink pepper, tangerine and pomegranate. Red wine tannins contribute savoury grip, chewy mouthfeel and the suggestion of tilled earth. Wood work brings a creaminess to the bead, drawing out great persistence of the finish.

Pinot noir grapes ready to be pressed in vintage 2014. Many houses still employ the traditional champagne press for gentle extraction of juice.

The Champagne Guide

EPILOGUE
Connection

The greatest honour of my life in champagne is to share my discoveries with friends old and new around the world. Every year I am greatly blessed to pour champagne in countless forums, from an intimate circle of friends to lavish corporate events in high places, all the way to my huge public Taste Champagne events, showcasing hundreds of cuvées. Assembling the greatest champagnes on earth and worthy food to match is a tremendous thrill, but there is always a higher purpose.

'Champagne is a link,' Richard Geoffroy told me recently as he reflected on 25 years as chef de cave of Dom Pérignon, while negotiating the busy streets of Épernay at the end of a long day at the height of harvest 2014. 'My greatest privilege in life with Dom Pérignon has been about the people. It is such an honour to access people's minds and hearts, even after knowing them for just an hour or two.'

I think about this link myself every time I open a bottle of champagne. My aspiration is to facilitate a connection, to draw out expressions of how this cuvée smells, tastes and feels to each person. No two impressions are exactly alike, and there are never any wrong answers in this game. My privilege is to affirm each person's reaction, to draw a tangible link between the intimacy of personal taste and the grand tale of the creation of each champagne, and to provide an insight into the places, procedures and people who have brought it to life and left their stamp on its personality.

In the midst of this conversation, we discover and celebrate the remarkable uniqueness of personal taste. A special and intimate connection is established between individuals. Champagne transcends culture, politics and experience.

'My privilege has been to experience a synthesis of here and there, of the east and the west,' reflects Geoffroy. 'And in recent years I've started to realise that all humans on this planet aspire to the same things. Cultural and political barriers may be there, but above all of that we're ultimately on about the same things. And wine lovers need to be reminded of these fundamentals, because sometimes we get lost in egos and image.' Taste possesses an inherent innocence and elemental authenticity that connects us all.

One's personal taste is a window into a lifetime of experiences, born of the aromas of childhood, fashioned by the flavours of youth, forever moulded by the idiosyncratic characters of sojourns to places near and far, always touched, in small ways and large, by the tastes of every person around us.

Aroma and flavour are the keys to our deepest memories, the doorways to our most treasured places, and the connections to our most intimate relationships. Even the most fleeting wisp of scent can instantly ignite an explosion of memories. Or, in the words of perfume mastermind Luca Turin, 'to briefly turn the most arid mind into a fairy garden, to make us lament the passing of loves and losses we know full well we never had'.

'Champagne really allows you to reach,' says Geoffroy. 'It's incredible. It's so powerful. It is because there is a ritual to wine. It is intimate. You share the injection of something. And when you share a ritual, it is like ...' And he raises his hand like a knife, gestures a cut on his wrist, and rubs his wrists together to intimate blood brothers.

The goal of this book is to facilitate connections. To link your own taste with the unique story of the creation of each champagne. It is my wish that it will guide you to make opportunities to build deeper connections with the people in your life.

INDEX
Rise to the Top

Champagnes without page numbers are featured at www.champagneHQ.com

100 POINTS

Bollinger Extra 1914, 80
Bollinger R.D. Extra Brut 1996, 80
Dom Pérignon Oenotheque 1990, 123
Dom Pérignon Oenotheque 1996, $$$$$, 123
Krug Collection 1982, $$$$$, 217

99 POINTS

Billecart-Salmon Cuvée Nicolas François Billecart 2002, $$$$, 70
Bollinger R.D. Extra Brut 1988, 80
Pierre Péters Cuvée Spéciale Blanc de Blancs Les Chétillons 2008, $$$, 297
Pol Roger Cuvée Sir Winston Churchill 1996, $$$$$, 307
Pol Roger Cuvée Sir Winston Churchill 2002, $$$$$, 307

98 POINTS

Billecart-Salmon Cuvée Nicolas François Billecart 1988, 70
Billecart-Salmon Cuvée Nicolas François Billecart 2000, $$$$, 71
Charles Heidsieck Blanc de Millénaires 1995, $$$$$, 94
Charles Heidsieck Champagne Charlie 1985, 94
Dom Pérignon 2002, 121
Dom Pérignon P2 1998, $$$$$, 123
Dom Pérignon P2 Rosé 1995, $$$$$, 122
Gosset Cuvée Celebris Rosé Brut 1998, $$$$, 177
Krug Rosé Brut NV, $$$$$, 214
Krug Vintage 2000, $$$$$, 216
Larmandier-Bernier Special Club 1996, 232
Louis Roederer Cristal 1993, 250
Louis Roederer Cristal 1995, $$$$$, 250
Pol Roger Cuvée Sir Winston Churchill 2004, $$$$$, 306

Taittinger Comtes de Champagne Blanc de Blancs 2004, $$$$$
Taittinger Comtes de Champagne Rosé 1996, 319
Veuve Clicquot Cave Privée Rosé Brut 1979, $$$$$, 336
Veuve Clicquot Cave Privée Rosé Brut 1990, $$$$$, 336
Veuve Clicquot La Grande Dame Brut 2004, $$$$, 334
Veuve Clicquot La Grande Dame Rosé 1989, 335

97 POINTS

Agrapart & Fils Minéral Blanc De Blancs Grand Cru Extra Brut 1984
Billecart-Salmon Blanc de Blancs Brut 2004, $$$$, 70
Bollinger R.D. Extra Brut 2002, $$$$$, 79
Deutz Amour de Deutz Rosé Brut 2006, $$$$$, 110
Deutz Cuvée William Deutz Brut Millésimé 2002, $$$$, 109
Dom Pérignon 2004, $$$$$, 120
Duval-Leroy Femme de Champagne 2000, $$$$, 133
Egly-Ouriet Grand Cru Blanc De Noirs Vieilles Vignes NV, $$$$, 136
Gosset Cuvée Celebris Rosé Extra Brut 2007, $$$$, 177
Gosset Cuvée Celebris Vintage Extra Brut 2002, $$$$, 177
Henriot Cuve 38 La Réserve Perpétuelle Blanc de Blancs NV, $$$$$, 186
Jacques Selosse Millésime Blanc de Blancs Brut 2002, $$$$$, 199
Jacquesson Avize Champ Caïn Récolte Extra Brut 2005, $$$$$, 204
Jacquesson Dégorgement Tardif Extra Brut Millésimé 1995, $$$$$, 205
Krug Clos du Mesnil 2003, $$$$$, 217
Krug Grande Cuvée NV, $$$$, 215
Laurent-Perrier Grande Siècle NV, $$$$$, 235
Louis Roederer Cristal 2002, 249
Pascal Doquet Le Mesnil-sur-Oger Grand Cru Coeur de Terroir Blanc de Blancs Brut 2002, $$$, 272

Pierre Gimonnet & Fils Special Club Millésime de Collection Blanc de Blancs 2008, $$$, 292
Pierre Péters Cuvée Spéciale Blanc de Blancs Les Chétillons 2007, $$$, 297
Piper-Heidsieck Rare Millesime 1998, $$$$$, 301
Pol Roger Cuvée Sir Winston Churchill 2000, $$$$$, 307
Salon Cuvée S Blanc de Blancs 1997, $$$$$, 313
Salon Cuvée S Blanc de Blancs 2002, $$$$$, 313
Taittinger Comtes de Champagne Blanc de Blancs 2006, $$$$$, 318
Veuve Clicquot Cave Privée Rosé Brut 1989, $$$$$, 336

96 POINTS

Agrapart & Fils Minéral Blanc De Blancs Grand Cru Extra Brut 2008, $$$, 36
Agrapart & Fils Venus Blanc de Blancs Grand Cru Brut Nature 2008, $$$$, 37
André Clouet 1911 NV, $$, 44
André Clouet Brut Millésime 2002, $$, 43
André Clouet Brut Millésime 2008, $$, 43
Benoît Lahaye Extra Brut 2008, $$, 59
Billecart-Salmon Le Clos Sainte-Hilaire 1999, $$$$$, 71
Bollinger La Grande Année Brut 2004, $$$$
Bollinger La Grande Année Rosé 2004, $$$$$
Bollinger Rosé Brut NV, $$, 78
Camille Savès Cuvée Anais Jolicoeur 2008, $$, 87
Camille Savès Cuvée Prestige Brut NV, $$, 87
Charles Heidsieck Rose Millésime 2006, $$$, 93
De Sousa & Fils Cuvée des Caudalies Blanc de Blancs Grand Cru Brut NV, $$$, 103
De Sousa & Fils Cuvée des Caudalies Brut Rosé NV, $$$, 103

Deutz Blanc de Blancs Brut 2008, $$$, 108

Deutz Brut Millésimé 2008, $$$, 107

Deutz Brut Rosé 2009, $$$, 109

Dom Pérignon Rosé 2002, 122

Dom Pérignon Rosé 2004, $$$$$, 122

Dom Ruinart Blanc de Blancs Brut 2004, $$$$$, 311

Duval-Leroy Femme de Champagne 2004, $$$$, 133

Egly-Ouriet Grand Cru Brut Rosé NV, $$$, 136

Egly-Ouriet Grand Cru Brut Tradition NV, $$$, 135

Eric Rodez Cuvée Zéro Dosage NV, $$, 143

Eric Rodez Emprinte de Terroir Chardonnay Grand Cru 1998, 144

Eric Rodez Emprinte de Terroir Pinot Noir 2002, $$$$, 142

Gatinois Aÿ Grand Cru Brut Millésime 2008, $$, 162

Gosset Grand Millésime 2004, $$$, 176

Gosset Grand Rosé Brut NV, $$$, 176

Henriot Cuvée des Enchanteleurs Brut 1998, $$$$$, 186

Henriot Rosé Millésime 2008, $$, 185

J. Lassalle Cuvee Angéline Premier Cru Brut Millésime 2008, $$, 190

Jacques Selosse Initiale Blanc de Blancs Brut NV, $$$$, 197

Jacques Selosse Substance Blanc de Blancs Extra Brut NV, $$$$$, 199

Jacquesson Avize Dégorgement Tardif Extra Brut 1997, $$$$$, 205

Jacquesson Aÿ Vauzelle Terme Récolte Extra Brut 2005, $$$$$, 205

Jacquesson Dizy Corne Bautray Récolte Extra Brut 2002

Jacquesson Dizy Corne Bautray Récolte Extra Brut 2005, $$$$$, 204

Jacquesson Millésime 2000, $$$$

Krug Vintage 2003, $$$$$, 216

Lanson Noble Cuvée Brut Millésimé 2000, $$$$, 226

Le Brun-Servenay Avize 1981

Le Brun-Servenay Exhilarante Vieilles Vignes Millésime 2006, $$$, 238

Louis Roederer Blanc de Blancs 2008, $$$, 247

Louis Roederer Brut Vintage 2008, $$$, 246

Louis Roederer Cristal Brut 2006, $$$$$, 249

Louis Roederer Rosé 2008, $$$, 248

Mailly Grand Cru L'Intemporelle Millésimé Brut 2008, $$$$, 254

Mailly Grand Cru L'Intemporelle Rosé Brut 2008, $$$$, 254

Pascal Doquet Le Mesnil-sur-Oger Grand Cru Coeur de Terroir Blanc de Blancs Brut 2004, $$$, 272

Pascal Doquet Vertus Premier Cru 1996, 272

Pascal Doquet Vertus Premier Cru Coeur de Terroir 2004, $$, 271

Paul Bara Comtesse Marie de France Blanc de Noirs 2002, $$$$, 273

Pierre Gimonnet & Fils Special Club Grands Terroirs de Chardonnay 2006, $$$, 292

Pierre Péters Cuvée La Réserve Oubliée Blanc de Blancs Brut NV, $$, 296

Pierre Péters Cuvée Spéciale Blanc de Blancs Les Chétillons 2009, $$$, 297

Piper-Heidsieck Rare Millesime 2002, $$$$, 301

Pol Roger Blanc de Blancs Brut 2002, $$$

Pol Roger Blanc de Blancs Brut 2004, $$$, 305

Pol Roger Blanc de Blancs Brut 2008, $$$, 304

Pol Roger Brut Vintage 2004, $$$, 305

Pol Roger Cuvée Sir Winston Churchill 1999, $$$$$, 307

Taittinger Comtes de Champagne Rosé 2006, $$$$, 319

Taittinger Cuvée Prélude Grand Crus Brut NV, $$$, 317

Vazart-Coquart & Fils Brut Grand Bouquet Blanc de Blancs 2008, $$, 328

Veuve Clicquot La Grande Dame Brut 2006, $$$$, 334

Veuve Clicquot La Grande Dame Rosé 2006, $$$$$, 334

Veuve Clicquot Vintage Brut 2008, $$$, 332

Veuve Clicquot Vintage Rosé 2008, $$$, 333

Vilmart & Cie Coeur de Cuvée Premier Cru 2006, $$$$, 346

95 POINTS

Agrapart & Fils Minéral Blanc De Blancs Grand Cru Extra Brut 2007, $$$, 36

Agrapart & Fils Terroirs Blanc de Blancs Grand Cru Extra Brut NV, $, 35

Alfred Gratien Cuvée Brut Classique Rosé NV, $$, 39

Alfred Gratien Cuvée Paradis Rosé NV, $$$$, 40

André Clouet Grande Réserve Blanc de Noirs Brut NV, $$, 42

André Clouet Le Clos 2008, $$$$$, 44

André Jacquart Experience Millésimé Le Mesnil-sur-Oger Blanc de Blancs Grand Cru 2006, $$$, 46

AR Lenoble Collection Rare Grand Cru Blanc de Blancs 2002, $$$, 50

AR Lenoble Cuvée Gentilhomme Grand Cru Blanc de Blancs Millésime Brut 2006, $$$, 50

AR Lenoble Grand Cru Blanc de Blancs Chouilly Brut 2008, $$, 49

Benoît Lahaye Blanc de Noirs Extra Brut NV, $$, 58

Benoît Lahaye Rosé de Macération Extra Brut NV, $$, 59

Bérêche & Fils Le Cran Ludes Premier Cru 2007, $$$$, 63

Billecart-Salmon Blanc de Blancs Grand Cru Brut NV, $$$, 68

Billecart-Salmon Brut Rosé NV, $$$, 69

Bollinger La Grande Année 2005, $$$$, 79

Bollinger La Grande Année Rosé 2005, $$$$$, 79

Bollinger Special Cuvee Brut NV, $$, 78

Bruno Paillard Blanc de Blancs 2004, $$$, 84

Bruno Paillard Blanc de Blancs Reserve Privée Brut NV, $$$, 84

Camille Savès Carte d'Or NV, $$, 86

Camille Savès Millésime 2008, $$, 86

Cattier Clos du Moulin Rosé NV, $$$$, 90

Charles Heidsieck Millesime Brut 2000, $$$

Charpentier Terre d'Emotion Rosé NV, $$, 96

De Sousa & Fils Brut Rosé NV, $$, 102

De Sousa & Fils Grand Cru Réserve Blanc de Blancs Brut NV, $$, 102

Delamotte Blanc de Blancs 2007, $$$, 104

Delamotte Blanc de Blancs NV, $$, 105

Deutz Blanc de Blancs 2007, $$$, 109

Deutz Brut Millésimé 2007, 107

Diebolt-Vallois Blanc de Blancs NV, $, 115

Diebolt-Vallois Cramant Blanc de Blancs 1989, 116

Diebolt-Vallois Fleur de Passion Blanc de Blancs 2006, $$$$, 116

Dom Pérignon Rosé 2000, 121

Duval-Leroy Blanc de Blancs Brut Nature Millésime 2002, $$$, 132

Duval-Leroy Femme de Champagne Rosé de Saignée 2007, $$$$$, 133

Emmanuel Brochet Les Hauts Meuniers Extra Brut 2008, $$$, 139

Franck Bonville Grand Cru Avize Blanc de Blancs Brut Millesime 2008, $, 152

Geoffroy Extra Brut Millésime 2002, $$$$, 167

Godmé Père & Fils Les Alouettes Premier Cru 2006, $$$$, 173

Gosset Grand Blanc de Blancs Brut NV, $$$, 176

Guy Charlemagne Mesnillésime Extra Brut 2004, $$, 179

Henri Giraud Esprit de Giraud Blanc de Blancs NV, $$, 182

J. Lassalle Special Club 2006, $$$, 190

Jacquesson Cuvee 734 Dégorgement Tardif Extra Brut NV, $$$$, 203

Jacquesson Cuvée No 737 Extra Brut NV, $$, 203

Jacquesson Dizy Terres Rouges Rosé Récolte Extra Brut 2008, $$$, 204

Jérôme Prévost La Closerie Fac-simile Rosé NV, $$$$, 209

Jérôme Prévost La Closerie les Béguines, $$$, 209

Lanson Extra Age Brut NV, $$$, 226

Lanson Gold Label Brut Vintage 2002, $$

Larmandier-Bernier Les Chemins D'Avize Grand Cru Blanc de Blancs Extra Brut 2009, $$$$, 232

Larmandier-Bernier Rosé de Saignée Premier Cru Extra Brut NV, $$$, 230

Le Brun-Servenay Blanc de Blancs X.B. Extra Brut 2.5 NV, $$$, 238

Le Brun-Servenay Cuvée Brut Rosé NV, $$, 237

Le Brun-Servenay Cuvée Chardonnay Brut Millésime Vieilles Vignes 2005, $$, 238

Louis Roederer Blanc de Blancs 2009, $$$, 247

Louis Roederer Brut Vintage 2007, $$$, 246

Louis Roederer Cristal 1999, 250

Louis Roederer Rosé 2009, $$$, 247

Mailly Grand Cru Blanc de Noirs NV, $$$, 253

Moët & Chandon MCIII Brut 001.14, $$$$$, 264

Moët & Chandon Vintage Collection Rosé 1985, 263

Moussé Fils Special Club Brut 2008, $$$$

Pascal Doquet Vertus Coeur de Terroir 2002, $$, 272

Paul Déthune Cuvée Prestige Princesse des Thunes Brut NV, $$$, 276

Paul Goerg Cuvée Lady 2002, $$$, 278

Perrier-Jouët Belle Epoque Blanc de Blancs 2002, $$$$$, 281

Philipponnat Blanc de Noirs Brut 2008, $$, 284

Philipponnat Clos des Goisses Brut 2005, $$$$$, 285

Pierre Gimonnet & Fils Cuvée Gastronome 1er Cru Blanc de Blancs Cuvée Brut 2008, $$, 290

Pierre Gimonnet & Fils Extra Brut Cuvée Oenophile 1er Cru Blanc de Blancs Non Dosé 2008, $$, 291

Pierre Gimonnet & Fils Special Club Blanc de Blancs 2009, $$$, 291

Pol Roger Blanc de Blancs Brut 2006, $$$, 305

Pol Roger Brut Rosé 2004, $$$, 306

Pol Roger Brut Rosé 2006, $$$, 306

Pol Roger Brut Vintage 2002, $$$

Tarlant Cuvée Louis Hommage à Louis Tarlant Vin de Rivière Extra Brut NV, $$, 324

Tarlant La Vigne d'Antan Non Greffée Chardonnay Brut Nature 2002, $$$, 324

Vazart-Coquart & Fils Special Club 2006, $$$, 328

Veuve Clicquot Cave Privée Brut 1989, $$$$$, 335

Veuve Clicquot Vintage Brut 2004, $$$, 333

Veuve Clicquot Vintage Rosé 2004, $$$, 333

Veuve Fourny & Fils Cuvée Blanc de Blancs Vertus Premier Cru Vintage Extra Brut 2006, $$, 341

Veuve Fourny & Fils Cuvée Blanc de Blancs Vertus Premier Cru Vintage Extra Brut 2008, $$, 341

Vilmart & Cie Coeur de Cuvée Premier Cru 2007, $$$$, 345

Vilmart & Cie Grand Cellier d'Or Brut Premier Cru 2009, $$$, 345

Zoémie De Sousa Cuvée Umami Grand Cru Extra Brut Vintage 2009, $$$$$, 102

94 POINTS

Agrapart & Fils Expérience Blanc de Blancs Grand Cru Brut Nature NV, $$$$, 37

Agrapart & Fils l'Avizoise Blanc de Blancs Grand Cru Extra Brut 2008, $$$$, 37

Alfred Gratien Brut Millésime 2000, $$$, 40

Alfred Gratien Cuvée Paradis Brut 2006, $$$$, 40

André Clouet Brut Millésime 2009, $$, 43

André Clouet Rosé No 3 Brut NV, $$, 43

André Clouet Silver Brut Nature NV, $$, 42

A picker carries the harvest to the end of the row during vintage 2014 in Bouzy.

The Champagne Guide

AR Lenoble Grand Cru Blanc de Blancs Chouilly Brut 2006, $$

AR Lenoble Grand Cru Blanc de Blancs Chouilly Brut NV, $$, 48

Ayala Blanc de Blancs Brut 2007, $$$, 54

Ayala Blanc de Blancs Grand Cru 2004, $$$, 54

Ayala Cuvée Perle d'Ayala Millésimé Brut 2005, $$$$, 54

Barons de Rothschild Blanc de Blancs Brut NV, $$$, 56

Benoît Lahaye Brut Nature NV, $$, 58

Benoît Lahaye Violaine NV, $$$$, 58

Bérêche & Fils Campania Remensis Extra Brut Rosé 2010, $$$, 62

Billecart-Salmon Extra Brut NV, $$, 68

Bonnaire Blanc de Blancs Grand Cru NV, $, 81

Bruno Paillard Premiere Cuvée Brut NV, $$, 84

Camille Savès Cuvée Rosé NV, $$, 87

Charles Heidsieck Brut Réserve NV, $$, 92

Charles Heidsieck Rosé Millésime 1999, $$$, 94

Claude Carré et Fils Cuvée Passion Brut Millésime 2002, $$, 97

Couche Père et Fils Perle de Nacre Blanc de Blancs Extra Brut NV, $$, 98

Delamotte Blanc de Blancs 2004, 105

Deutz Brut Classic NV, $$, 108

Deutz Brut Vintage 2006, 109

Deutz Cuvée William Deutz 1999, 110

Diebolt-Vallois Prestige Brut Blanc de Blancs NV, $$, 115

Dom Pérignon 2005, $$$$$, 121

Dumangin J. Fils Le Rosé Brut NV, $, 128

Dumangin J. Fils Le Vintage Extra Brut Premier Cru 2004, $$, 128

Eric Rodez Cuvée Blanc de Noirs NV, $$, 142

Eric Rodez Cuvée des Grands Vintages Brut NV, $$$, 144

Eric Rodez Cuvée Les Genettes Pinot Noir 2010, $$$$, 143

Fleury Père & Fils Blanc de Noirs Brut NV, $$, 147

Fleury Père & Fils Rosé de Saignée Brut NV, $$, 148

Francis Boulard Les Murgiers Blanc de Noirs Extra Brut NV, $$, 151

G.H. Mumm Brut Selection Grand Cru NV, $$, 155

G.H. Mumm Cuvée R. Lalou Brut 2002, $$$$$, 156

Gaston Chiquet Blanc de Blancs d'Aÿ Grand Cru NV, $$, 158

Gaston Chiquet Special Club Brut Millésime 2007, $$, 159

Gatinois Aÿ Grand Cru Brut Rosé NV, $$, 162

Geoffroy Empreinte Brut Premier Cru 2008, $$, 165

Geoffroy Extra Brut Millésime 1999, $$$$, 167

Geoffroy Rosé de Saignée Premier Cru Brut NV, $$, 166

Georges Laval Les Hautes Chevres Brut Nature 2009, $$$$$, 170

Godmé Père & Fils Romaines Premier Cru 2006, $$$$, 173

Gosset Grande Réserve Brut NV, $$, 175

Guy Charlemagne Cuvée Charlemagne Grand Cru Blanc de Blancs Brut 2009, $$, 179

Guy Charlemagne Grand Cru Reserve Blanc de Blancs Brut NV, $, 178

Jacquesson Cuvée No 738 Extra Brut NV, $$, 202

Lanson Gold Label Vintage Brut 2004, $$, 225

Larmandier-Bernier Longitude Blanc de Blancs Premier Cru Extra Brut NV, $$, 230

Larmandier-Bernier Terre de Vertus Premier Cru Blanc de Blancs Brut Nature 2009, $$$, 231

Larmandier-Bernier Vertus Rouge Coteaux Champenois Premier Cru Millésime 2012, $$, 232

Larmandier-Bernier Vieille Vigne de Cramant Grand Cru Extra Brut 2007, $$$$, 231

Laurent-Perrier Alexandra Grande Cuvée Rosé 2004, $$$$$, 235

Laurent-Perrier Cuvée Rosé Brut NV, $$$, 235

Le Brun-Servenay Brut Sélection Blanc de Blancs Grand Cru NV, $$, 237

Le Brun-Servenay Rosé Ultime X.B. Extra Brut 3.2 NV, $$$, 238

Le Mesnil Blanc de Blancs Grand Cru Sublime Brut Vintage 2006, $$, 239

Lombard & Cie Brut Grand Cru Millésime 2008, $$, 242

Louis Roederer Brut Premier NV, $$, 246

Louis Roederer Brut Vintage 2006, $$$

Louis Roederer et Philippe Starck Brut Nature Millesimé 2006, $$$, 248

Marc Hébrart Special Club 2008, 255

Moët & Chandon Grand Vintage Collection 1911, 263

Palmer & Co Blanc de Blancs 2008, $$, 268

Pascal Doquet Grand Cru Blanc de Blancs Diapason Brut NV, $$, 271

Paul Goerg Cuvée Lady 2004, $$$, 278

Perrier-Jouët Belle Epoque Rosé 2006, $$$$$, 281

Philipponnat Réserve Millésimée 2000, $$$

Philipponnat Royale Réserve Rosé Brut NV, $$, 284

Pierre Gimonnet & Fils Cuvée Fleuron Brut 1er Cru Blanc de Blancs 2006, $$, 291

Pierre Gimonnet & Fils Rosé de Blancs Premier Cru Brut NV, $$, 289

Piper-Heidsieck Essentiel Cuvée Brut NV, $$, 299

Pol Roger Brut Réserve NV, $$, 304

Pol Roger Brut Vintage 2006, $$$, 305

Pol Roger Pure Extra Brut NV, $$, 304

Raphaël et Vincent Bérêche Vallée de la Marne Grand Cru Extra Brut 2002, $$$$, 64

Roger Coulon Les Côteaux de Vallier Cuvée Héritage NV, $$$, 308

Ruinart Blanc de Blancs Brut NV, $$$, 310

Sélèque Cuvée Spéciale Premier Cru Extra Brut NV, $

Taittinger Comtes de Champagne Blanc de Blancs 2005, $$$$$, 318

Taittinger Comtes de Champagne Rosé 2005, $$$$$, 319

Taittinger Cuvée Brut Prestige Rosé NV, $$$, 317

Tarlant Zero Brut Nature NV, $, 322

Veuve Clicquot Cave Privée Brut 1982, $$$$$, 335

Veuve Fourny & Fils Cuvée Blanc de Blancs Vertus Premier Cru Vintage Extra Brut 2007, $$, 341

Veuve Fourny & Fils Cuvée Monts de Vertus Blanc de Blancs Extra Brut 2009, $$, 341

Vilmart & Cie Grand Cellier d'Or Brut Premier Cru 2010, $$$, 345

Vincent Charlot Le Fruit de ma Passion Extra Brut 1998, $

93 POINTS

Agrapart & Fils 7 Crus Brut NV, $, 35

Alfred Gratien Cuvée Brut Classique NV, $$, 39

André Jacquart Brut Expérience Blanc de Blancs Premier Cru NV, $$, 46

AR Lenoble Blanc de Noirs Bisseuil Premier Cru 2009, $$, 49

AR Lenoble Cuvée Intense Brut NV, $, 48

AR Lenoble Cuvée Les Aventures Grand Cru Blanc de Blancs Brut NV, $$$, 50

Armand de Brignac Brut Gold NV, $$$$$, 51

Benoît Lahaye Le Jardin de la Grosse Pierre 2010, $$$$, 59

Bérêche & Fils Campania Remensis NV, $$$, 62

Bérêche & Fils Les Beaux Regards Chardonnay Brut Nature 2010, $$$, 62

Bérêche & Fils Reflet d'Antan Brut NV, $$$, 64

Billecart-Salmon Brut Réserve NV, $$, 68

Billecart-Salmon Cuvée Sous Bois Brut NV, $$$, 69

Boizel Joyau de France Brut Millésime 2000, $$$$, 74

Bonnaire Grand Cru Blanc de Blancs Millésime 2005, $, 82

Bruno Paillard Premiere Cuvee Brut Rosé NV, $$$, 84

Camille Savès Extra Brut NV, $$, 86

Camille Savès Millésime 2000, $$, 87

Cattier Clos du Moulin Brut Premier Cru NV, $$$, 90

Cattier Cuvée Renaissance 2006, $$, 90

Charles Heidsieck Rosé Réserve NV, $$$, 93

Charpentier Rosé Brut NV, $, 96

Charpentier Terre d'Emotion Blanc de Noirs Brut NV, $$, 96

Claude Carré et Fils Blanc de Blancs Premier Cru Brut NV, $$, 97

Delamotte Rosé NV, $$$, 105

Deutz Amour de Deutz Blanc de Blanc Brut Millésimé 2005, 110

Diebolt-Vallois Blanc de Blancs Vintage 2007, $$, 116

Diebolt-Vallois Brut Rosé NV, $$, 115

Dosnon & Lepage Recolte Rosé NV, $$, 125

Dumangin J. Fils L'Extra-Brut Premier Cru NV, $, 129

Duval-Leroy Fleur de Champagne Premier Cru Brut NV, $$, 131

Egly-Ouriet Les Vignes de Vrigny Premier Cru Brut NV, $$$, 135

Emmanuel Brochet Le Mont Benoit Extra Brut NV, $$, 139

Eric Rodez Cuvée des Crayères NV, $$, 142

Fleury Père & Fils Sonate No 9 Opus 10 Extra Brut NV, $$$, 148

Francis Boulard Blanc de Blancs Brut Nature NV, $$, 150

G.H. Mumm de Cramant Blanc de Blancs Brut, $$$$, 156

Gatinois Aÿ Grand Cru Brut Millésime 2006, $$, 162

Gatinois Aÿ Grand Cru Brut Réserve NV, $$, 162

Geoffroy Expression Brut Premier Cru NV, $$, 165

Georges Laval Les Chenes Cumières Premier Cru Brut Nature 2010, $$$$, 169

Georges Laval Meunier de La Butte Brut Nature 2006, $$$$$, 170

Godmé Père & Fils Brut Rosé NV, $$

Godmé Père & Fils Premier Cru Brut Reserve NV, $$, 172

Godmé Père & Fils St Martin Grand Cru 2006, $$$$, 173

Henri Giraud Esprit de Giraud Brut NV, $$, 181

Henri Goutorbe Brut Tradition NV, $, 183

Henriot Blanc de Blancs Brut NV, $$, 185

Henriot Brut Millésime 2006, $$, 186

Huré Frères Mémoire Extra Brut NV, $$, 187

Jacques Picard Blanc de Blancs Brut NV, $$, 194

Jacques Picard Brut NV, $$, 194

Jacques Selosse Mareuil-sur-Aÿ Sous le Mont NV, $$$$$, 199

Jacques Selosse VO Version Originale Blanc de Blancs Extra Brut NV, $$$$, 198

Jacquesson Cuvée No 733 Dégorgement Tardif Extra Brut NV, $$$$, 203

Jacquinot & Fils Harmonie Millésimé 2000, $$$$, 206

Jacquinot & Fils Symphonie Rosé Millesime 2007, $$$

Jérôme Prévost La Closerie Fac-simile Rosé NV, $$$$, 209

Joseph Perrier Cuvée Joséphine 2004, $$$$$, 210

Laherte Frères Les Empreintes 2009, $$, 221

Lanson Vintage Collection 1976, $$$$, 226

Larmandier-Bernier Latitude Blanc de Blancs à Vertus Extra Brut NV, $$, 229

Le Brun-Servenay Avize 1976

Louis Roederer Cristal Brut 2005, $$$$$, 249

Mailly Grand Cru Les Échansons Millésimé Brut 2004, $$$$, 254

Mailly Grand Cru Magnum Collection Millésimé 1996, $$$$$, 254

Marguet Père & Fils Ambonaicus Grand Cru Rosé 2009, $

Nicolas Feuillatte Palmes d'Or Vintage Brut 1999, $$$$

Nicolas Feuillatte Palmes d'Or Vintage Brut 2004, $$$$, 266

Palmer & Co Brut Réserve NV, $, 267

Pascal Doquet Premier Cru Le Mont Aimé Blanc de Blancs 2005, $$, 271

Paul Clouet Brut Millésime 2007, $$, 274

Paul Déthune Cuvée a l'Ancienne Brut 2007, $$$$, 276

Paul Déthune Grand Cru Brut NV, $$, 276

Paul Goerg Brut 2004, $$, 278

Perrier-Jouët Belle Epoque Rosé 2004, $$$$$, 281

Perrier-Jouët Belle Epoque Vintage 2004, $$$$

Perrier-Jouët Belle Epoque Vintage 2006, $$$$, 280

Philipponnat Grand Blanc Brut 2006, $$, 285

Philipponnat Grand Cru 1522 Brut 2005, $$$, 285

Pierre Gimonnet & Fils Cuis Premier Cru Brut Blanc de Blancs NV, $, 288

Pierre Gimonnet & Fils Cuvée Fleuron Brut 1er Cru Blanc de Blancs 2009, $$, 290

Pierre Gimonnet & Fils Cuvee Gastronome 1er Cru Blanc de Blancs Cuvée Brut 2009, $$, 290

Pierre Péters Cuvée de Reserve Blanc de Blancs Brut NV, $$, 296

Pierre Péters Cuvée Millésime L'Esprit Blanc de Blancs 2009, $$$, 296

Ployez-Jacquemart Extra Quality Brut NV, $$

Pol Roger Cuvée Riche NV, $$

Roger Coulon Blancs de Noirs Millesime 2006, $$

Taittinger Cuvée Brut Millésimé 2006, $$$, 318

Taittinger Cuvée Brut Réserve NV, $$, 316

Taittinger Nocturne Rosé NV, $$$, 317

Tarlant Brut Reserve NV, $, 322

Tarlant La Matinale Prestige Millésime Brut Nature 2003, $$, 323

Tarlant Rosé Zero Brut Nature NV, $, 323

Ulysse Collin Les Roises Blanc de Blancs Extra Brut NV, $$, 325

Vazart-Coquart & Fils Réserve Blanc de Blancs NV, $$, 327

Veuve Fourny & Fils Cuvée du Clos Fg Notre Dame Premier Cru Vertus Extra Brut 2004, $$$$, 342

Veuve Fourny & Fils Cuvée du Clos Fg Notre Dame Premier Cru Vertus Extra Brut 2005, $$$$, 342

Veuve Fourny & Fils Cuvée R de Vve Fourny & Fils Vertus Extra Brut NV, $$, 342

Vilmart & Cie Grand Cellier Brut Premier Cru NV, $$, 344

The Champagne Guide

92 POINTS

Alfred Gratien Grand Cru Blanc de Blancs Brut 2007, $$, 40

AR Lenoble Rosé Terroirs Brut NV, $$, 49

Ayala Brut Nature NV, $$, 53

Barons de Rothschild Brut NV, $$, 56

Barons de Rothschild Rosé NV, $$$, 56

Bérêche & Fils Coteaux Champenois Ormes Rouge 2012, $$, 64

Bérêche & Fils Vallée de la Marne Rive Gauche Meunier Extra Brut 2010, $$$, 63

Billecart-Salmon Extra Brut Vintage 2006, $$$, 69

Boizel Cuvée Sous Bois Brut 2000, $$$$$, 74

Bollinger La Côte aux Enfants 2002, $$

Bonnaire Ver Sacrum Blanc de Blancs Brut NV, $, 82

Camille Savès Carte Blanche NV, $, 86

Charles Heidsieck Millésime Brut 2005, $$$, 93

Charpentier Brut Millésime 2008, $, 96

Cuvée Carbon Vintage 2006, $$$$$, 99

Devaux Blanc de Noirs NV, $$, 113

Devaux Grande Réserve Brut NV, $$, 112

Diebolt-Vallois Fleur de Passion Blanc de Blancs 2005, $$$$, 116

Dom Pérignon 2003, 121

Dom Pérignon Rosé 2003, $$$$$, 122

Dosnon & Lepage Recolte Blanc de Noire NV, $$, 125

Dumangin J. Fils Premium Single Vineyard Blanc de Blancs Extra Brut 2000, $$$$, 129

Emmanuel Brochet Les Hauts Chardonnay Extra Brut 2009, $$$, 139

Eric Rodez Cuvée Les Beurys Pinot Noir 2010, $$$$, 143

Fleury Père & Fils Fleur de l'Europe Brut Nature NV, $$, 147

Francis Boulard Les Murgiers Blanc de Noirs Brut Nature NV, $$, 150

Francis Boulard Millésime Extra Brut 2006, $$, 150

Gatinois Aÿ Grand Cru Brut Tradition NV, $$, 161

Geoffroy Brut Premier Cru Volupté 2007, $$$, 165

Geoffroy Extra Brut Millésime 2000, $$$$, 167

Godmé Père & Fils Blanc de Blancs NV, $$, 172

Godmé Père & Fils Intégral Premier Cru Extra Brut NV, $$, 172

Godmé Père & Fils Les Alouettes Premier Cru 2005, $$$$

Guy Charlemagne Brut Classic NV, $, 179

H. Billiot Fils Cuvée Tradition Brut NV, $$, 180

Henriot Brut Souverain NV, $$, 185

Henriot Rosé Brut NV, $$, 185

Huré Frères Invitation Brut NV, $, 187

J. Lassalle Préférence Premier Cru Brut NV, $, 189

Jacquart Blanc de Blancs 2006, $$, 192

Jacques Selosse Aÿ La Côte Faron NV, $$$$$, 198

Jacques Selosse Millésime Blanc de Blancs Brut 2003, $$$$$, 199

Jacquinot & Fils Private Cuvée Brut NV, $$, 206

Jérôme Prévost La Closerie les Béguines, $$$, 209

Joseph Perrier Cuvée Royale Brut Vintage 2002, $$$, 210

Laherte Frères Deux Mille Six Extra Brut 2006, $$, 221

Laherte Frères Rosé de Saignée Les Beaudiers Extra Brut 2012, $$, 221

Lanson Gold Label Brut Vintage 2005, $$, 225

Larmandier-Bernier Les Chemins d'Avize Grand Cru Blanc de Blancs Extra Brut 2010, $$$$, 231

Laurent-Perrier Millésimé 2006, $$$, 234

Lilbert Fils Blanc de Blancs Grand Cru Brut NV, $

Lombard & Cie Brut Grand Cru NV, $$, 242

Mailly Grand Cru Brut Rosé NV, $$$, 253

Marc Hébrart Premier Cru Brut Rose NV, 255

Marguet Père & Fils Extra Brut 2008, $$

Pascal Doquet Arpege Premier Cru Blanc de Blancs Extra Brut NV, $$, 270

Pierre Gimonnet & Fils Cuvee Gastronome 1er Cru Blanc de Blancs Cuvée Brut 2010, $$, 289

Piper-Heidsieck Rosé Sauvage NV, $$, 300

Piper-Heidsieck Vintage Brut 2006, $$, 300

Serge Mathieu Tradition Pur Pinot Blanc de Noirs Brut NV, $

Taittinger Les Folies de la Marquetterie NV, $$, 316

Tarlant BAM! Blanc Arbane Meslier NV, $$$$, 323

Tarlant La Vigne Royale Principauté de Condé Blanc de Noirs 2003, $$$$, 324

Ulysse Collin Les Maillons Blanc de Noir Extra Brut NV, $$$, 325

Veuve Clicquot Rosé Brut NV, $$, 332

Vilmart & Cie Grand Cellier Rubis Premier Cru Brut NV, $$$$, 346

Vilmart & Cie Grande Réserve Brut Premier Cru NV, $$, 344

91 POINTS

Agrapart & Fils Complantée Grand Cru Extra Brut NV, $$, 36

Alain Thiénot Brut Rosé NV, $$

Alfred Gratien Brut Nature NV, $$, 39

André Clouet Le Clos 2006, $$$$$, 44

André Jacquart Mesnil Experience Blanc de Blancs Grand Cru NV, $$$

Ayala Perle d'Ayala Millésimé Brut Nature 2002, $$$$, 54

Barons de Rothschild Extra Brut NV, $$, 56

Benoît Lahaye Naturescence Extra Brut NV, $$

Boizel Ultime Extra-Brut NV, $$$, 73

Camille Savès Bouzy Rouge Coteaux Champenois 2004, $

Canard-Duchêne Charles VII Grande Cuvée des Lys Blanc de Blancs Brut NV, $$

D de Devaux La Cuvée Brut NV, $$, 113

D de Devaux Ultra Extra Brut NV, $$, 113

Delamotte Brut NV, $$, 105

Diebolt-Vallois Brut Tradition NV, $, 115

Dumangin J. Fils Premium Single Vineyard Blanc de Blancs Dessus le Mont Brut 2005, $$, 129

Dumangin J. Fils Premium Single Vineyard Blanc de Blancs Dessus le Mont Extra Brut 2006, $$, 129

Duval-Leroy Cuvée des Meilleurs Ouvriers de France Sommeliers Brut NV, 131

Fleury Père & Fils Notes Blanches Brut Nature NV, $$, 147

Francis Boulard Blanc de Blancs Les Vieilles Vignes Extra Brut NV, $$, 151

Franck Bonville Cuvée Les Belles Voyes Blanc de Blancs Brut NV, $$

G.H. Mumm Brut Millésimé 2004, $$

G.H. Mumm Brut Millésimé 2009, $$, 155

G.H. Mumm Cuvée R. Lalou Brut 1999, $$$$$

Gaston Chiquet Cuvée de Réserve Premier Cru Brut NV, $$, 159

Gaston Chiquet Cuvée Or Brut Millésimé 2005, $$, 159

Geoffroy Extra Brut Millésime 2005, $$$$, 166

Geoffroy Pureté Brut Nature NV, $$, 165

Godmé Père & Fils Blanc de Noirs Grand Cru Brut NV, $$, 172

Godmé Père & Fils Grand Cru Extra Brut NV, $$, 173

H. Blin Champagne Brut NV, $

Jacquart Cuvée Alpha 2005, $$$$, 192

Jacquart Cuvée Alpha Brut Vintage 2006, $$$$, 192

Joseph Loriot-Pagel Blanc de Blancs 2007, $

Joseph Perrier Cuvée Royale Brut NV, $$

Laherte Frères Blanc de Blancs Brut Nature NV, $$, 220

Lallier Grand Cru Blanc de Blancs NV, $$$, 222

Lallier Premier Cru Rosé Brut NV, $$$

Lanson Black Label Brut NV, $, 224

Laurent-Perrier L-P Brut NV, $$, 234

Laurent-Perrier L-P Ultra Brut NV, $$$, 234

Le Mesnil Blanc de Blancs Grand Cru Brut NV, $$, 239

Lombard & Cie Tanagra Brut Grand Cru NV, $$$$, 242

Mailly Grand Cru Brut Millésimé 2007, $$$, 253

Marguet Père & Fils Sapience Premier Cru Extra Brut 2006, $$$$, 257

Moët & Chandon Grand Vintage 1999, 262

Moët & Chandon Rosé Vintage Collection 1999, 263

Napoléon Rosé Brut NV, $$

Oger Grand Cru par Pierre Gimonnet & Fils Brut NV, $$, 289

Pascal Doquet Anthocyanes Rosé Premier Cru NV, $$

Paul Goerg Brut 2005, $$, 278

Paul Goerg Tradition Brut NV, $, 277

Perrier-Jouët Blason Rosé NV, $$, 280

Philipponnat Clos des Goisses Brut 2000, $$$$$

Philipponnat Royale Réserve Non Dosé NV, $$, 283

Pierre Fedyk Brut NV, $

Piper-Heidsieck Cuvée Brut NV, $, 299

Pommery Cuvée Louise 1999, $$$$

R de Ruinart Brut NV, $$, 311

Ruinart Brut Rosé NV, $$$, 311

Vazart-Coquart & Fils Grand Cru Blanc de Blancs Extra Brut NV, $$, 327

Vazart-Coquart & Fils Special Foie Gras Blanc de Blancs Sec NV, $$, 327

Veuve Clicquot Yellow Label Brut NV, $$, 332

Veuve Fourny & Fils Cuvée Blanc de Blancs Vertus Premier Cru NV, $$, 340

90 POINTS

Boizel Blanc de Noirs NV, $, 73

Bollinger La Côte aux Enfants 2012, $$

Charpentier Réserve Brut NV, $, 95

Deutz Rosé Brut NV, $$, 108

Devaux Cuvée Rosée Brut NV, $$, 113

Dosnon & Lepage Recolte Blanche Blanc de Blancs NV, $$, 125

Duval-Leroy Blanc de Blancs Grand Cru Millésime 2006, 132

Eric Rodez Cuvée Blanc de Blancs NV, $$, 144

Francis Boulard Les Rachais Blanc de Blancs Brut Nature Millesime 2007, $$$, 151

G.H. Mumm Brut Millésimé 2006, $$, 155

Gaston Chiquet Rosé Brut Premier Cru NV, $$, 159

Geoffroy Extra Brut Millésime 2004, $$$$, 167

J. Lassalle Blanc de Blancs Millésime 2006, $$, 190

Jacquart Brut Mosaïque NV, $$, 191

Jacquart Rosé NV, $$, 192

Jacques Picard Art de Vigne Brut Millésime 2003, $$$, 195

Jacques Picard Brut Nature NV, $$, 195

Jacques Selosse Le Mesnil-sur-Oger Les Carelles NV, $$$$$, 198

Lanson Vintage Collection 1990, $$$$

Laurent-Perrier Millesime 2004, $$$

Le Brun-Servenay Brut Réserve NV, $$, 237

Lombard & Cie Brut Rosé Premier Cru NV, $$, 241

Mailly Grand Cru Extra Brut NV, $$, 252

Mailly Grand Cru Millésimé 2006, $$$, 253

Marguet Père & Fils Reserve Grand Cru Extra Brut NV, $, 257

Michel Loriot Monodie ou Meunier Majour Extra Brut 2007, $$

Paul Clouet Grand Cru Brut NV, $, 274

Paul Goerg Blanc de Blancs NV, $$, 277

Philipponnat Royale Réserve Brut NV, $, 284

Piper-Heidsieck Cuvée Sublime Demi-Sec NV, $$, 300

Pommery Grand Cru Vintage Brut 2004, $$

Raphaël et Vincent Bérêche Cote Premier Cru Extra Brut NV, $$, 64

Taittinger Cuvée Nocturne NV, $$, 316

Tarlant La Vigne d'Or Blanc de Meuniers Brut Nature 2004, $$, 323

Vazart-Coquart & Fils Rosé NV, $$, 327

Veuve Fourny & Fils Cuvée Blanc de Blancs Vertus Premier Cru Brut Nature NV, $$, 340

89 POINTS

Bérêche & Fils Brut Réserve NV, $$, 63

Boizel Brut Réserve NV, $$, 72

Boizel Joyau de France Brut Rosé 2004, $$$$, 74

Cattier Blanc de Blancs Brut NV, $, 89

Cattier Brut Absolu NV, $, 89

Cattier Brut Rosé NV, $$, 90

De Sousa & Fils Cuvée 3A Extra Brut NV, $$, 103

Dumangin J. Fils La Cuvée 17 Brut NV, $, 128

Duval-Leroy Clos Des Bouveries Brut 2005, $$$$, 132

Franck Bonville Grand Cru Blanc de Blancs NV, $, 152

G.H. Mumm Blanc de Noirs de Verzenay NV, $$$, 156

Gaston Chiquet Brut Tradition Premier Cru NV, $$, 158

Geoffroy Blanc de Rosé Extra Brut NV, $$$$, 166

Georges Laval Les Chenes Cumières Premier Cru Brut Nature 2009, $$$$, 169

Georges Laval Les Hautes Chevres Brut Nature 2012, $$$$$, 170

Godmé Père & Fils Millésime Grand Cru 2004, $$

H. Blin Champagne Brut Millésime 2004, $

Henri Goutorbe Cuvée Millesime Grand Cru Brut 2005, $$, 183

Henriot Brut Millésime 2005, $$

J. Lassalle Premier Cru Brut Rosé NV, $$, 189

Jacques Picard Art de Vigne Brut Millésime 1999, $$$, 195

Jérôme Prévost La Closerie les Béguines, $$$, 208

Joseph Loriot-Pagel Cuvée de Reserve 2006, $

Joseph Loriot-Pagel Cuvée de Réserve 2006, $$

Laherte Frères Grand Brut Ultradition NV, $, 220

Laherte Frères Les 7 Extra Brut 05-11, 221

Lombard & Cie Brut Premier Cru NV, $$, 241
Lombard & Cie Tanagra Brut Rosé Grand Cru NV, $$$$, 242
Mailly Grand Cru Brut Réserve NV, $$, 252
Moët & Chandon Grand Vintage 2006, $$$, 262
Moët & Chandon Grand Vintage Rosé 2006, $$$, 262
Napoléon Brut Vintage 2000, $$
Napoléon Tradition Brut NV, $$
Nicolas Feuillatte Brut Réserve Particulére NV, $$, 265
Nicolas Feuillatte Palmes d'Or Brut Rosé 2005, $$$$, 266
Palmer & Co Rosé Réserve NV, $$, 268
Pascal Doquet Horizon Blanc de Blancs Brut NV, $$, 270
Paul Clouet Cuvee Prestige Brut NV, $$
Paul Déthune Blanc de Noirs Grand Cru Brut NV, $$$
Prieur Grand Prieur Brut NV, $$
Prieur Grand Prieur Millésime Brut 2000, $$
Veuve Fourny & Fils Cuvée Grande Réserve Premier Cru Vertus Brut NV, $$, 340

88 POINTS

Boizel Grand Vintage 2007, $$$, 73
Boizel Joyau de France Millésime 1996, $$$$, 74
Cattier Brut Vinothèque 2007, $$, 89
Duperrey Vintage Brut 2006, $$
Duval-Leroy Brut NV, $$, 131
Duval-Leroy Rosé Prestige Brut NV, $$, 131
Fleury Père & Fils Extra Brut 2002, $$$, 148
Henri Giraud Code Noir Brut NV, $$$$, 182
Henri Laurent NV, $
Jacquart Extra Brut NV, $$
Laherte Frères Extra Brut Ultradition NV, $, 219
Lanson Rose Label Brut Rosé NV, $, 225
Lombard & Cie Brut Grand Cru Blanc de Blancs NV, $$, 241
Paul Goerg Absolut Extra Brut NV, $$
Paul Goerg Rosé NV, $$
Paul Louis Martin Bouzy Grand Cru Brut 2007, $$
Roger Coulon Réserve de L'Hommée NV, $

87 POINTS

Boizel Blanc de Blancs NV, $, 73
Bonnaire Variance Blanc de Blancs Brut NV, $$, 82

Cattier Blanc de Noirs Brut NV, $$, 89
Cattier Brut Premier Cru NV, $, 88
Charles Orban Blanc de Blancs NV, $
Duperrey Brut Rosé NV, $
Gaston Chiquet Insolent Brut NV, $, 158
Georges Laval Cumières Premier Cru Brut Nature NV, $$, 170
Henri Giraud Hommage à François Hémart Grand Cru NV, $$, 182
Jacques Picard Art de Vigne Brut Millesime 2005, $$$, 195
Joseph Loriot-Pagel Carte d'Or NV, $
Lombard & Cie Brut Référence NV, $$, 241
Mailly Grand Cru Délice NV, $$, 252
Michel Loriot Authentic Meunier Blanc de Noirs Brut NV, $
Moët & Chandon Brut Impérial NV, $$, 261
Moët & Chandon Grand Vintage 2004, $$$
Moët & Chandon Rosé Impérial NV, $$, 261
Napoléon Blanc de Blancs Brut NV, $$
Pommery Brut Apanage NV, $$
Prieur Grand Prieur Blanc de Blancs Brut NV, $$

86 POINTS

Ayala Brut Majeur NV, $$, 53
Ayala Rosé Majeur NV, $$, 53
Canard-Duchêne Cuvée Léonie Brut NV, $$
Cattier Glamour Sec NV, $$
Cattier Rosé Glamour NV, $$
Château de Bligny Grand Réserve NV, $
Francis Boulard Grand Cru Grande Montagne Extra Brut NV, $$, 151

Gosset Brut Excellence NV, $$, 175
Guy Charlemagne Brut Nature NV, $, 179
Joseph Loriot-Pagel Carte d'Or NV, $
Michel Loriot Palmyre Brut Nature NV, $
Moutard Grande Cuvée Brut NV, $
Nicolas Feuillatte Brut Rosé NV, $$, 266
Paul Louis Martin Bouzy Grand Cru Brut NV, $$
Vincent Testulat Carte d'Or Brut NV, $

85 POINTS

Alain Thiénot Brut NV, $$
Boizel Brut Rosé NV, $$, 72
Duperrey Premier Cru Brut NV, $
G.H. Mumm Cordon Rouge Brut NV, $$, 154
Joseph Loriot-Pagel Cuvee de Reserve 2005, $
Laherte Frères Les Vignes d'Autrefois Deux Mille Dix Extra Brut 2010, $$, 220
Laherte Frères Rosé Ultradition Brut NV, $, 220
Lallier Grande Réserve Grand Cru Brut NV, $$, 222
Perrier-Jouët Grand Brut NV, $$, 280
Vieille France Brut NV, $$

84 POINTS

Alain Thiénot Brut Millésime 2005, $$$
Canard-Duchêne Authentic Green Brut NV, $$
G.H. Mumm Le Rosé Brut NV, $$, 155
Jean-Pierre Marniquet Brut Réserve NV, $$

Benoît Lahaye and his Burgundy horse, named Tamise, who works his vineyards in Bouzy.

GLOSSARY

ACIDITY A crucial element that gives champagne its tangy freshness, vitality and life, and a sharp, clean taste on the finish.

AGRAFE A large metal 'staple' to secure the cork during second fermentation and bottle ageing. Historically, used prior to the invention of capsules, and retained today by some houses and growers.

APÉRITIF A drink used to get the tastebuds humming before a meal (champagne, naturally!).

ASSEMBLAGE The process of blending a wine (see page 25).

AUTOLYSIS The breakdown of dead yeast cells during ageing on lees, improving mouthfeel and contributing biscuity, bready characters (see page 26).

BALTHAZAR 12-litre bottle (usually filled with champagne fermented in standard bottles or magnums). Be sure to have help on hand to pour it (and drink it!).

BARRIQUE Small oak barrel of 225-litre capacity.

BÂTONNAGE Stirring of the lees in barrel or tank.

BEAD Bubbles. The best champagne always has tiny bubbles, the product of the finest juice fermented in cold cellars.

BIODYNAMICS An intensive viticultural regime of extreme organics, eschewing chemical treatments and seeking a harmonious ecosystem.

BLANC DE BLANCS Literally translates as 'white from white'. White champagne made exclusively from white grapes, usually chardonnay, but may also include arbane, petit meslier, pinot blanc and/or pinot gris.

BLANC DE NOIRS Literally 'white from black'. White champagne made exclusively from the dark-skinned grapes pinot noir and/or meunier. This is achieved by gentle pressing removing the juice from the skins before any colour leaches out.

BRETTANOMYCES 'Brett' is a barrel yeast infection, considered a spoilage character in champagne. It may develop further in bottle, manifesting itself as characters of boiled hot dog, antiseptic, horse stable, barnyard, animal or sweaty saddle, adding a metallic bite to the palate and contracting the finish.

BRUT Raw/dry, containing less than 12g/L sugar (formerly less than 15g/L sugar).

BRUT NATURE OR BRUT ZÉRO No added sugar (less than 3g/L sugar).

CAPSULE Crown cap.

CARBON DIOXIDE The gaseous by-product of fermentation that is responsible for the bubbles in sparkling wine.

CAVE Cellar.

CÉPAGE Grape variety or blend of varieties.

CHAMPAGNE Wine from the region of the same name in north-east France. Champagne with a capital 'C' refers to the region; with a lower-case 'c' to the wine. French law prohibits the name for sparkling wines grown elsewhere.

CHAPTALISATION The addition of sugar (yes, this is legal in France) or concentrated grape juice to increase the alcohol strength of the wine (see page 25).

CHEF DE CAVE The 'chief' or 'chef' in the cellar (champagne winemaker).

CIVC The 'Comité Interprofessionnel du vin de Champagne', a semi-public agency of the French government to represent the growers and houses in overseeing the production, distribution, promotion and research of the wines of Champagne.

CLOS Historically a walled vineyard, though the walls may no longer exist.

COEUR DE LA CUVÉE 'Heart of the cuvée', the middle of the pressing, yielding the best juice.

COOPÉRATIVE DE MANIPULATION (CM) A co-op of growers who produce champagne under their own brand.

CORKED Cork taint is an all too common wine fault resulting from the presence of 2,4,6 trichloroanisole (TCA) in natural cork. It imparts an off-putting, mouldy, 'wet cardboard' or 'wet dog' character, suppressing fruit and shortening the length of finish (see page 28).

CORK TAINT See 'corked'.

COTEAUX CHAMPENOIS Champagne released as still wine, mostly red; typically made in tiny quantities, and mostly by smaller producers.

CRAYÈRES Roman chalk pits, now gloriously atmospheric cellars under Reims.

CRÉMANT Formerly used to describe slightly less fizzy champagnes (2–3 atmospheres of pressure), but no longer permitted on champagne, and instead often used for French sparkling wines produced outside of Champagne. Not to be confused with the village of Cramant in the Côte des Blancs. Mumm's de Cramant cuvée is both crémant (in the traditional sense) and exclusively sourced from Cramant.

CROWN CAP A metal seal like a beer cap, used to seal a champagne bottle during second fermentation and lees ageing.

CRU A commune, village, vineyard or officially classified 'growth'.

CUVÉE The first pressing of the grapes (2050 litres from 4000 kilograms of grapes), yielding the best juice. Also refers to an individual blend or style.

CUVERIE Tank room.

DÉBOURBAGE Settling of the solids from the must prior to fermentation (see page 25).

DÉBOURBAGE À FROID Cold settling to clarify the juice, as practised by Billecart-Salmon, Pol Roger and others.

DÉGORGEMENT Disgorgement.

DEGREES POTENTIAL The ripeness at which grapes are picked, which determines the alcohol content of the finished wine.

DEMI-MUID Large oak barrel of 500–600-litre capacity.

DEMI-SEC Half-dry or medium-dry (32–50g/L sugar).

DIAM Mytik DIAM is a brand of champagne closure made by Oeneo, moulded from fragments of cork which have been treated to extract cork taint. Its reliable performance has made it an increasingly popular choice for champagne in recent years (see page 28).

DISGORGEMENT Removal of a frozen plug of sediment from the neck of the bottle (see page 26).

DOSAGE The final addition to top up the bottle, usually a mixture of wine and sugar syrup called *liqueur d'expédition* or *liqueur de dosage*. A dosage of 10–12g/L of sugar is typical in champagne (see pages 26 and 31).

DOUX SWEET 50+ g/L sugar (Coca-Cola is 150g/L).

ÉCHELLE DES CRUS 'Ladder of growths', Champagne's crude classification of vineyards by village, expressed as a percentage.

ÉLEVAGE The process of 'bringing up' a wine, encompassing all cellar operations between fermentation and bottling.

EXTRA BRUT Extra raw/dry (less than 6g/L sugar).

EXTRA DRY OR EXTRA SEC Off dry (12–17g/L sugar).

FERMENTATION The conversion of sugar to alcohol by the action of yeasts. Carbonic gas is produced as a by-product.

FLUTE Narrow champagne glass.

FOUDRE Very large oak cask, typically with a capacity between 2000 litres and 12,000 litres.

GRAND CRU The highest vineyard classification. In Champagne, a classification is crudely applied to a village and all the vineyards within its bounds acquire the same classification. Seventeen villages are classified as grand cru.

GRANDES MARQUES An obsolete, self-imposed term for the big champagne brands. Still used informally.

GREY IMPORTS See 'Parallel imports'.

GROWER PRODUCER A champagne producer who makes wines from fruit grown only on his or her own vineyards; 5% of fruit is permitted to be purchased. Olivier Krug defines a grower

champagne as one made from your garden.

GYROPALETTE A large mechanised crate to automatically riddle champagne bottles.

INOCULATE To seed a ferment with yeast.

JEROBOAM A 3-litre bottle, previously typically filled with champagne fermented in standard bottles or magnums. However, it is now a legal requirement that it must be made in its own bottle from first bottling.

LATE DISGORGEMENT A champagne that has been matured on its lees for an extended period.

LEES Sediment that settles in the bottom of a tank, barrel or bottle, primarily dead yeast cells.

LIEU-DIT Individually named plot or vineyard site.

LIGHTSTRUCK The degradation of wine exposed to ultraviolet light. Sparkling wines in clear bottles are most susceptible (see page 29).

LIQUEUR DE DOSAGE See 'Liqueur d'expédition'.

LIQUEUR D'EXPÉDITION The final addition to top up the bottle, usually a mixture of wine and sugar syrup.

LIQUEUR DE TIRAGE A mixture of sugar and wine or concentrated grape juice added immediately prior to bottling, to produce the secondary fermentation in bottle (see page 26).

LUTTE RAISONNÉE Literally 'reasoned struggle', a middle ground between conventional viticulture and organic farming, reducing the use of herbicides and pesticides while retaining the right to employ them in times of need. Often a sensible approach in Champagne's erratic climate.

MACERATION Soaking of red grape skins in their juice in the production of red or rosé wine (see page 14).

MAGNUM A 1.5-litre bottle. According to the Champenois, the perfect size for two, when one is not drinking.

MAISON House.

MALIC ACID A naturally occurring acid in grapes and other fruits, particularly green apples. It is most pronounced in grapes in cold climates and is responsible for champagne's searing acidity, which is usually softened through malolactic fermentation.

MALOLACTIC FERMENTATION 'Malo' is the conversion of stronger malic (green apple) acid to softer lactic (dairy) acid (see page 25).

MARQUE D'ACHETEUR (MA) Buyer's own brand. An 'own label' owned by a supermarket or merchant.

MÉTHODE CHAMPENOISE An obsolete term for the traditional method of sparkling winemaking, now 'Méthode Traditionnelle' or 'Méthode Classique'.

MÉTHODE TRADITIONNELLE The official name for the traditional method of sparkling winemaking, in which the second fermentation occurs in the bottle in which the wine is sold.

METHUSELAH A 6-litre bottle, usually filled with champagne fermented in standard bottles or magnums.

MILLÉSIME Vintage.

MINERALITY The texture and mouthfeel of a wine derived from its soil (see page 27).

MOUSSE See 'Bead'.

MUSELET Wire cage to hold a champagne cork in the bottle.

NEBUCHADNEZZAR A 15-litre bottle, usually filled with champagne fermented in standard bottles or magnums. Do not attempt while home alone!

NÉGOCIANT-MANIPULANT (NM) Champagne producer who purchases grapes and/or unfinished wines. A négociant may also include up to 95% estate grown fruit.

NON-VINTAGE (NV) A champagne containing wine from more than one vintage.

OENOTHÈQUE Literally a wine library or shop. Sometimes used to refer to bottles held back for extended ageing.

OÏDIUM Powdery mildew, a fungal disease that can have a devastating effect on grape crops.

ORGANICS A viticultural regime that avoids the use of any synthetic pesticides, herbicides, fungicides or other treatments. Copper is permitted, though criticised in some circles for a toxicity higher than that of some synthetic products.

OXIDISED A wine that has reacted with oxygen. At its most extreme, oxidation can produce browning in colour, loss of primary fruit, a general flattening of flavours, a shortening of the length of finish, or even a vinegar or bitter taste (see page 28).

PARALLEL IMPORTS Champagne brought into a country by parties other than the usual agent, typically via a third-party country. Good for keeping pricing competitive, but can become problematic if transportation or storage are compromised.

pH The level of acid strength of a wine expressed as a number. Low pH equates to high acidity; 7 is neutral.

PHENOLICS A grape compound responsible for astringency and

The abbey stands sentinel over harvest 2014 on the slopes of Hautvillers.

bitterness in the back palate. It is particularly rich in stems, seeds and skins, and especially prevalent in champagnes from warm vintages such as 2003 and 2005.

PIÈCE Small oak barrel of 205-litre capacity in Champagne (228 litres in Burgundy).

POIGNETTAGE The vigorous shaking of the bottle after corking to mix the wine and liquor. It can also refer to the old practice of shaking the bottle by hand to stir up the lees and enhance autolytic flavours, rarely used today, though still upheld by De Sousa and Dumangin J. Fils.

PREMIER CRU The second highest vineyard classification, awarded to 41 villages. In Champagne, a classification is crudely applied to a village, and all the vineyards within its bounds acquire the same classification.

PRESTIGE CUVÉE The flagship champagne or champagnes of a brand, typically the most expensive. Olivier Krug says it should be defined as one that can age.

PRISE DE MOUSSE The second fermentation that creates the bubbles (see page 26).

PUPITRE Hand riddling rack.

RÉCOLTANT-COOPÉRATEUR (RC) Champagne grower selling wine under his/her own brand, made by his/her cooperative.

RÉCOLTANT-MANIPULANT (RM) Champagne grower who makes wine from estate fruit; 5% of grapes may also be purchased to supplement production.

REDUCTIVE A wine made or aged with limited contact with oxygen may develop reductive characters, hydrogen sulphide notes akin to struck flint, burnt match and gunpowder. At their extreme, these can manifest themselves as objectionable notes of rubber, rotten eggs, garlic, onion or cooked cabbage.

REHOBOAM A 4.5-litre bottle, usually filled with champagne fermented in standard bottles or magnums.

REMUAGE The riddling process (see page 26).

RESERVE WINES Wines held in the cellar for future blending in a non-vintage cuvée (see page 26). Usually aged in tanks, although sometimes kept in barrels or bottles.

RIDDLING The process of moving the lees sediment into the neck of the bottle prior to disgorgement, either by hand or by gyropalette (see page 26).

SABRAGE A technique for opening a champagne bottle with a sabre. Practice is recommended prior to attempting this in public. I tried it once with vague success, but was picking up splinters of glass for days.

SAIGNÉE A technique in which rosé is made by 'bleeding' off juice from just-crushed pinot noir or meunier grapes after a short maceration (soaking) on skins prior to fermentation (see page 26).

SALMANAZAR A 9-litre bottle, usually filled with champagne fermented in standard bottles or magnums.

SEC Dryish (17–32 g/L sugar).

SOLERA A system of fractional blending through a system of wines of different ages, with the bottled wine drawn from the last stage. Also used in Champagne to refer to a simplified system of perpetual blending, in which successive vintages are added to a single tank.

STALE Lacking in fruit freshness.

SUR LATTES See 'vins sur lattes'.

SUR POINTE The storing of bottles neck down, between riddling and disgorgement. Sometimes also used for long-term storage of undisgorged bottles. With the lees settled in the neck, it is believed the wine stays fresher for longer.

TAILLES Coarser, inferior juice that flows last from the press.

TCA See 'Corked'.

TERROIR A catch-all term for anything that defines the character of a vineyard — soil, micro-climate, altitude, aspect, exposure, slope, drainage, and even the hands that tend it.

TIRAGE Bottling of the blended wine with an addition of sugar and yeast, so as to provoke the second fermentation in bottle (see page 26).

TUN Large oak barrel, typically around 1000 litres in volume.

VENDANGE Vintage or harvest.

VIEILLES VIGNES Old vines.

VIGNERON Vine grower.

VIN CLAIR Still base wine that has undergone its primary fermentation and (potentially) malolactic fermentation, but not its secondary fermentation.

VINS SUR LATTES Champagne bottles laid on their side, having undergone second fermentation, but yet to be riddled. Also refers to the legal but shady practice by which champagne houses purchase finished but yet to be disgorged champagne made by another producer, to then market under their own label.

VINTAGE Wine from a single year.

ZERO DOSAGE No sweetness is added during the final addition to top up the bottle (see page 26).

Author thanks

I owe a great debt of gratitude to hundreds of champagne producers and their agents for their hospitality and generosity in inviting me into their homes, cellars, tasting rooms and vineyards, and offering the privilege of discovering their stories and their wines. A project of this magnitude is only possible with a cast of thousands. Here are some of the many to whom I owe a special thanks.

Pascal Agrapart, Renaud Bancilhon, Thomas Begault, Laurent Bénard, Raphaël Bérêche, Fran Berry, Philippe Bienvenu, Marie Thérèse Bonnaire, Paul Boothby, Nick Bowring, David Boyce, Tim Boydell, Jeanine Bribosia, Michel Brismontier, Emmanuel Brochet, Cyril Brun, Denis Bunner, Nat Burch, David Burkitt, François Caille, Andrew Cameron, Audrey Campos, Régis Camus, Elodie Caraskakis, Lorraine Carrigan, Michelle Catanzariti, Jean-Jacques Cattier, Laurent Champs, Alexandre Chartogne, Louis Cheval-Gatinois, Jean-Hervé Chiquet, Nicolas Chiquet, Jean-François Clouet, Greg Corra, Roger Coulon, Sophie Couvreur, Nicholas Crampton, Mark Cunliffe, Catherine Curie, Anthony D'Anna, Hervé Dantan, Michel Davesne, Rachel Day, Mel De Barra, Antoine de Boysson, Isabelle de Latour, Nicoletta de Nicolo, Hervé Deschamps, Charlotte De Sousa, Erick De Sousa, Dominique Demarville, Didier Depond, Guy de Rivoire, Gilles Descôtes, Pierre Déthune, Sophie Déthune, Laurent d'Harcourt, Isabelle Diebolt, Anne-Laure Domenichini, Pascal Doquet, Marie Doyard, Elisabeth Drysdale, Peter Dubourdieu, Nathalie Dufour, Ross Duke, Sarah Duke, Gilles Dumangin, Stuart Dunn, Olivier Dupré, Benoît Duval, Veronica Egan, Francis Egly, Adam Emirali, Peter Endry, Tim Evans, Jean-Sebastien Fleury, Ben Hasko, Peter Hasko, Charles-Henry Fourny, Emmanuel Fourny, Inge Fransen, Vanessa Frey, Jean-Paul Gandon, Dominique Garreta, Eric Geniaux, Jean-Baptiste Geoffroy, Richard Geoffroy, Susanne Geppert, Axel Gillery, Didier Gimonnet, Jean-Noël Girard, Hughes Godmé, Benoît Gouez, Sandy Grant, Tim Hampton, Tony Hancy, Neil Haywood, Thomas Henriot, Caroline Henry, Katri Hilden, Anton Hobbs, Rachel Hofman, Linda Holmes, Christian Holthausen, Antoine Huray, Samantha Isherwood, Darren Jahn, James Johnston, Olivier Krug, Benoît Lahaye, Aurélien Laherte, Pierre Larmandier, Sophie Larmandier, Vincent Laval, Bianca Lazzaro, Patrick Le Brun, Ian Leamon, Jean-Baptiste LeCailllon, Sylviane Lemaire, Stephen Leroux, Thierry Lombard, Katie MacAulay, Fiona MacDonald, Antoine Malassagne, Anne Malassagne, Kellie Mar, Magalie Marechale, Jean-Pierre Mareigner, Benoit Marguet,

Didier Mariotti, Kirsty Marshall, Anthony McConnel, Craig McDonald, Sally McGill, Euan McKay, Julie-Amandine Michel, Xavier Millard, Stéphanie Mingam, Emma Morris, Hadrien Mouflard, Jean-Philippe Moulin, Phoebe Murray, Bruce Nancarrow, Steven Naughton, Stephanie Noël, Cam O'Keefe, Alice Paillard, Bruno Paillard, Kaaren Palmer, Fréderic Panaïotis, Michel Parisot, Rodolphe Péters, Pascale Petry, Jérôme Philipon, Charles-Antoine Picart, Vince Pignatelli, Randall Pollard, Jérôme Prévost, Jody Rolfe, Brenton Quirini, Matthew Quirk, Grant Ramage, Philippe Reboul, Robert Remnant, Alex Retief, Philip Rich, Raymond Ringeval, Philippe Rivet, Braden Robb, Sandra Robbertse, Eric Rodez, Antoine Roland-Billecart, Florent Roques-Boizel, Thierry Roset, Fabrice Rosset, Hervé Savès, Anselme Selosse, Chris Sheehy, Nesh Simic, Gary Steel, Melinda Steel, Huon Stelzer, Linden Stelzer, Rachael Stelzer, Tim Stock, Clovis Taittinger, Angéline Templier, Marie-Agnès Thomas, Jean-Pierre Vazart, Chloé Verrat, Patrick Walsh, Rob Walters, Andy Warren, Steve Webber, Matthew Withers, Neville Yates.

Research for this book is entirely self-funded, including all travel and accommodation in Champagne.

TYSON STELZER was named The International Wine & Spirit Competition Communicator of the Year 2015, The Wine Communicators of Australia Australian Wine Communicator of the Year 2013, and The International Champagne Writer of the Year 2011 in The Louis Roederer International Wine Writers' Awards.

He is the author of 15 wine books and a regular contributor to 15 magazines including *Wine Spectator, Decanter, Qantas The Australian Way, Australian Gourmet Traveller Wine Magazine* and *Wine Companion Magazine*. He contributes sparkling wine reviews to the *James Halliday Australian Wine Companion* and is a contributor to Jancis Robinson's *The Oxford Companion to Wine*, 3rd edition. Tyson is a consultant to Qantas Airways First Class and Business Class champagne selection. He is the host of the television series *People of the Vines* and the founder of the Teen Rescue Foundation to address teen alcohol abuse.

As an international speaker, he has presented at wine conferences in the UK, Italy, Japan, South Africa, New Zealand and Australia. Tyson is a regular judge and chairman at Australian wine shows. He publishes regular updates on all things champagne at ChampagneHQ.com.

Tyson is 39 years of age and lives in Brisbane with his wife Rachael and sons Linden and Huon.